Cities in American History

Cities in
American History

Edited, with Introductions, by

Kenneth T. Jackson and Stanley K. Schultz
Columbia University   The University of Wisconsin

Alfred A. Knopf   New York

THIS IS A BORZOI BOOK
PUBLISHED BY ALFRED A. KNOPF, INC.

Copyright © 1972 by Alfred A. Knopf, Inc.
All rights reserved under International and Pan-American Copyright Conventions. Published in the United States by Alfred A. Knopf, Inc., New York, and simultaneously in Canada by Random House of Canada Limited, Toronto. Distributed by Random House, Inc., New York.

Trade Edition: ISBN 0-394-47558-5
Text Edition: ISBN: 0-394-31147-7

Library of Congress Catalog Card Number: 72-160265

Design by Jack Ribik

First Edition

987654321

TO ELIZABETH WILLINS JACKSON
AND CHRISTOPHER AND BENJAMIN SCHULTZ

PREFACE

This book is designed primarily for use in courses in urban history or urban studies or as supplementary reading in an American history survey. Because much of the work being accomplished in this field is interdisciplinary and is by young scholars, the editors have sought to acquaint students with the most recent interpretations available and with a large sampling of the exciting questions now being studied. Eleven of the essays that follow were written especially for this book by some of the most talented young scholars now studying the city in American history. The reprinted selections, chosen on the basis of their significance, readability, and general interest, are also recent; only one was published before 1962, and all but four are dated 1965 or later.

In a single volume of readings covering a broadly defined subject, the problem of proportionment is especially difficult. The editors have tried to provide a broad geographical coverage of American cities, giving special attention to the "inarticulate" elements of those cities—the common man, the ethnic minorities, the blacks—and to the historical dimension of problems now disturbing the urban populace—mass transit, public education, vice, racial violence, metropolitan government, and city planning. In several of the essays, concepts and techniques of social science are used to test hypotheses relating to the city; most of the other selections are analytical as well as descriptive. The editors have contributed interpretive commentaries and have concluded the book with their suggestions for further readings.

The editors wish to acknowledge their gratitude for the cooperative spirit of the individual authors who contributed essays specifically for this volume. Professor Zane L. Miller of the University of Cincinnati offered a number of ideas which the editors found exceedingly helpful. Our thanks are also due Estelle Freedman of Columbia University, Paul Berkowitz of the University of Wisconsin, Arthur Strimling, Judith Rosenberg, and James Wittenmyer of Alfred A. Knopf, and especially our wives, Barbara and Dorothea.

KENNETH T. JACKSON *New York City*

STANLEY K. SCHULTZ *Madison, Wisconsin*

CONTENTS

*Original essays written for this volume

*Original essays written for this volume

*Original essay written for this volume

PART ONE

THE CITY IN AMERICAN HISTORY

"The United States," according to historian Richard Hofstadter, "was born in the country and has moved to the city." Demographically, few trends could be more obvious. In 1790 fewer than 5 percent of all Americans lived in places with 8,000 or more inhabitants and the typical citizen was a small farmer. In 1970, when superhighways and super jetliners crisscrossed the land, about 80 percent of the population lived in major metropolitan areas and the typical citizen was reported to be a suburban housewife in Dayton, Ohio. Urbanization has become a central fact of modern American life.

Urban growth is not a recent phenomenon, however. Nor did the urban crisis begin with riots in the Watts section of Los Angeles in 1965. Frederick Jackson Turner, who in his essay "The Significance of the Frontier in American History" viewed the city as the logical result of the closing of the frontier and the ending of the nation-building process, and Charles A. Beard, who regarded the city as the handmaiden of industrialization, have cast such long shadows over American scholarship that the role of the city in the United States remains little understood. Actually, the concentration of population in tight little communities was important to American development even in the colonial period, when Philadelphia and Boston ranked among the half-dozen leading cities of the British Empire. Moreover, in terms of percentage growth, American cities advanced more rapidly between 1820 and 1860, when the frontier was still open and industrialization was still in its early stages, than in any comparable period in American history. On the world stage, urban growth in the young republic was equally dramatic; in the first half of the nineteenth century only Great Britain, then at the height of its power and influence, urbanized more rapidly than the United States. By 1890, a century after the first national census, the number of city dwellers was 139 times larger than the 1790 figure, although the American population as a whole had multiplied only sixteenfold.

Statistics for individual communities often were even more startling. The nation seemed to be alive with city boosters, each of whom could point to sharp increases in population and deliver excited speeches about the limitless possibilities of his particular town. In Minneapolis, as in countless other communities, enthusiasts claimed that their site "was fated to be a city in the very nature of things, long before the river, or the island had their names, or the white man had started his original westward trek." Pride in growth, in itself, was a break with traditions in Europe, where for centuries city-builders had devoted their best energies to raising sturdy walls to keep invaders out. In the United States, "upstart communities" were apt to judge themselves by their ability to attract rather than keep out migrants. In Europe, and especially in England, the word "city" had a very precise meaning; in America, as Daniel J. Boorstin has noted, any place could be referred to as a "city," and many promoters incorporated the word in the very name they chose for a place (Virginia City, Dodge City, Carson City), in the hope that the wish might father the fact. The Earl of Derby noted humorously in 1826 that "In the course of the last two days we passed several cities—some of them however almost invisible and one or two literally in the condition of Old Sarum." And another observer noted dryly in 1834: "It is strange that the name of city should be given to an unfinished log house, but such is the case in Texas."

Even with all the propaganda and excitement of land speculators eager to grow rich, not every potential or promising urban site could become a city or even a town. The rapidity and degree of urbanization were closely tied to agricultural technology, for the very existence of cities depended upon the ability of the farm population to produce a surplus beyond its immediate needs. As the productivity of the agricultural sector increased, the proportion of the population free to engage in nonfarm activities grew proportionately. But even if it were theoretically possible for everyone to live in cities, not every place could be a city. For every Chicago or San Francisco or Atlanta there were dozens of places whose founders had similar aspirations but whose names today are familiar only to those who live near them.

Whether a given city grew and prospered or stagnated and perhaps died depended on its locational advantages and on the aggressiveness and foresight of its civic and business leaders. The advantage of abundant water power led to the initial textile boom at Fall River, Massachusetts, and to the great success of the flour milling industry at Minneapolis; nearby extractive industries provided the major growth impetus of Tulsa, Oklahoma City, and Butte; and special recreational advantages benefitted Bar Harbor, Miami, and Hot Springs. Most large

American cities received their initial impetus from commerce and were therefore placed at a natural "transportation break"—that is, a point where it was feasible for travelers to change their method of conveyance (and possibly the ownership of various commodities). In the prerailroad era, navigable water provided the usual transportation break, and the biggest cities were those with the best ocean harbors or river sites. New York City, Philadelphia, Boston, Charleston, Norfolk, and Newport were essentially ocean ports whose fortunes were wedded to their piers and wharves. As the population moved westward, large-scale urban growth occurred at strategic Pittsburgh, where the Allegheny and Monongahela rivers converge to form the Ohio River. Similarly, Louisville grew up several hundred miles downstream where irregular shoals forced an interruption of river travel. St. Paul was laid out at the head of navigation on the Mississippi River; San Francisco, on the finest harbor on the West Coast; Detroit, on the narrow waters between Lake Erie and Lake Huron; St. Louis, near the confluence of the Missouri and Mississippi rivers; and Buffalo, at the entrance to the Erie Canal. In the Great Plains and Rocky Mountain regions, where navigable waterways were few, Santa Fe, Topeka, and Denver grew up at the intersection of great land routes. There, as elsewhere, the transportation break accounted for the development of banks, warehouses, exchanges, and wholesale emporiums.

The development of central place theory has underscored the importance of a strategic location in explaining urban growth, but a geographical site favorable to trade rarely sufficed to guarantee success. The experience of Cairo, Illinois, or the Town of America, as it was initially dubbed, illustrates how local aspirations often outran achievement. A glance at the map reveals the basis of the hopes for Cairo. Located at the confluence of the Mississippi and Ohio rivers, the frontier town seemed to possess matchless potential. Charles Dickens, on an American tour in 1842, was appalled by the half-built houses there. He described the community as a "place without one single quality, in earth, or air, or water, to commend it." But the people of Cairo thought big. They threw up high levees against both rivers and made their city a stop on the main line of the Illinois Central Railroad. A French traveler at mid-century revealed that Cairo "aspires to become some day a colossal center of progress, the key of all the commerce of the South, West and Northwest." And General Clark Carr was even more optimistic. "The time is sure to come when Cairo will be the largest city in the world," he said. Yet the river town did not long remain even the largest city in southern Illinois. Soon after the Civil War, as flood waters periodically destroyed its hinterland, Cairo began to decline. For more than a century it has remained stagnant, seedy, and dissolute. Its population, which reached a peak of 15,000 in 1920, had declined to less than 6,200 by 1970. Recently, Cairo has ranked first in unemployment and poverty in Illinois and has been the scene of violent racial antagonisms.

The general pattern of the failure of Cairo's early settlers to fulfill their aspirations for the town was typical of hundreds of small communities and of some larger cities. Sandusky, Ohio, and Galveston, Texas, seemed to offer more promise than Cleveland and Houston, yet each became a mere tributary of its larger neighbor. Similarly, Norfolk, Virginia, had a fine harbor, a central location for coastal trade, and a good river route to the interior, but it never lived up to its early promise. Wichita and Atlanta, on the other hand, possessed no distinctive geographical advantages and yet achieved dominance over a wide hinterland.

The difference between prosperity and stagnation for a city frequently lay in the quality of its leaders and the degree to which they were willing to risk their resources in the struggle for economic empire. The competition between the leaders of Chicago and the leaders of St. Louis for control of the nation's heartland illustrates how important the quality of city leadership could be. Both cities had excellent locations and ample resources to assure substantial growth. But in 1845 St. Louis was older, larger, more prosperous, and more promising than Chicago. The fur trade, the Mexican War, the settlement of the upriver country, and the gold rush all indicated that St. Louis was the strategic gateway to the West. During the age of steamboating before the Civil War, a million passengers a year traveled to and from St. Louis, and the volume of goods passing through the city far exceeded the combined volumes for Cincinnati and Louisville. The future seemed equally assured because St. Louis leaders were comforted by a spurious economic theory which held that commerce would inevitably move north and south along the meridians, and thus along the Mississippi River, rather than east and west via railroads and man-made canals; that tropical and temperate zones had complementary economies; and that water was the essential route of commerce. Thus assured by God and nature that their city would be *the* great metropolis of mid-America and perhaps the world, St. Louis leaders became overconfident and overconservative. They thought no special efforts were necessary to ensure future dominance, and they invested available capital in river shipping instead of facing realistically the transportation challenge posed by the railroads. The leaders of Chicago entertained no such illusions. While their rivals in St.

Louis clung to the old method of river transportation, they sent railroad after railroad—the Burlington, the Rock Island, the Illinois Central, the Santa Fe, the Chicago and North Western, to name but a few—into the economic hinterland of St. Louis. Through imagination and risk, they made Chicago the nation's most important railroad center by 1860 and in the process reoriented the trade of the Middle West. The corn, wheat, and beef that had been flowing south to New Orleans found a new course toward Chicago and the East, from which it was never diverted. By 1890 Chicago had become the nation's second largest city and had far surpassed St. Louis in almost every measure of size and influence. In fact, the Windy City, dynamic, powerful, and sprawling, became the symbol of the young and ambitious nation—in the words of Carl Sandburg, a "tall bold slugger set vivid against the little soft cities."

More was at stake in the competition among cities than local vanity. Richard C. Wade has suggested that the domination of Northwest trade by Chicago instead of St. Louis altered the course of the Civil War by helping to ensure that the Northwestern states would enter on the side of the Union. Had St. Louis remained the dominant trade center and the Mississippi the dominant trade route, Illinois, Iowa, Wisconsin, and other Middle Western states would have been tied economically to the Confederacy through their dependence upon New Orleans.

Another important result of urban imperialism was the leadership that cities provided for the transportation revolution. New York City entrepreneurs introduced the world's first regularly scheduled shipping, or packet, service in 1817, and legislators from that city were instrumental in helping Governor DeWitt Clinton secure legislative approval for the staggering bond program that made possible the completion of the Erie Canal in 1825. The phenomenal success of that man-made water connection between the Hudson River and the Great Lakes transformed little Manhattan Island into one of the world's greatest cities and prompted canal-building schemes across the land. It was in the cities that road, canal, and railroad projects were instigated and fought for, and in city after city it was local as well as class interest that seemed to determine the direction and scope of transportation innovations. Because cities act somewhat like nations and seek to gain economic control of competing centers, transportation became a weapon in the urban warfare. For example, the rivalry between Philadelphia and Baltimore interests for economic control of the rich farming and coal resources of Pennsylvania, Maryland, and the Ohio Valley led directly to the Lancaster Turnpike, the Baltimore Canal, the "Golden Chain" to Pittsburgh, the Baltimore and

Ohio Railroad, and the Pennsylvania Railroad. Each innovation upset
established commercial relationships and spurred economic development
through the encouragement of new methods.

Economic health called for the expansion of a city's hinterland to prevent
infringement on its territory by competing cities. Charleston and Savannah,
Cincinnati and Louisville, Mobile and New Orleans, Seattle and Tacoma,
and Minneapolis and St. Paul were among the pairs of cities in
competition—usually quite bitter—for the same hinterland. In 1848, when
the Massachusetts legislature was considering financial support for the
Hoosac Tunnel, which was intended to eliminate a mountainous barrier
between Boston and Albany, an enthusiastic Bostonian reminded his
listeners:

Boston has remained comparatively stationary; for the last four years, we have not
built more than 300 houses in a year. How is it with New York? Miles of stately
edifices, of the most costly description, have been erected. It is absorbing the
commerce of the country, and why? Are the New Yorkers nearer Europe than we are?
On the contrary, we are 200 miles nearer England than they are. . . . What we want
then, are facilities for communication with the West.

Smaller communities fought one another for survival too. As Daniel J.
Boorstin notes in the following selection on "competitive communities,"
the county-seat wars in the West were characterized by both fraud and
violence. The decision to locate the state prison or state university or
state capital in a particular town often meant the difference between
wealth and poverty for the landowners and between steady employment
and the dole for the common workers. Thus the residents of many a
cow town on the Kansas frontier fought bitterly to attract the railroad and
then to make their town the favorite terminus for various cattle drives.
The promise of a better future depended upon promotion, aggressiveness,
locational advantages, and luck. In no case could a community forget
the competition. As a cattle-town newspaper proclaimed in the 1870s,
"No city can rest easy, content with what she has; some new Chicago
would spring up and steal all her trade."

Not everyone, of course, rejoiced in the growth of towns and cities and
in the increasing propensity of Americans to crowd onto a small fraction of
the landscape. Like the many southern planters who went so far as to
applaud the destructive yellow fever epidemics of the 1790s because
the pestilence warned people to avoid populous centers, Thomas Jefferson
placed his faith in the one-family farm and denounced the city as
incapable of passing along the rich American heritage. Alexis de Tocqueville,

a famed visitor to this country in the 1830s, viewed the growth of great cities as "a real danger which threatens the future security of the democratic republics of the New World." Later in the century, Minnesota Populist Ignatius Donnelly looked with sorrow toward a future when the sturdy yeoman would no longer control the nation he fed and the bright lights of the wicked city would blur the distinctions between night and day. And Joseph H. Ingraham, a popular novelist, wrote: "Adam and Eve were created and placed in a garden. Cities are the result of the fall." But the fear, anger, resentment, and frustration with which rural Americans regarded the rise of the city were best expressed by William Jennings Bryan at the 1896 Democratic National Convention in Chicago. Before a wildly enthusiastic throng, the young Nebraska legislator shouted, "Burn down your cities and leave our farms, and your cities will spring up again as if by magic; but destroy our farms, and the grass will grow in the streets of every city in the country." Bryan spoke for a farm population that seemed every year to produce more and earn less. The farmers' problems were acute and their complaints were justified, but they assumed incorrectly that the city was a parasite sucking their life's blood. Actually, city and farm both suffered from enormous problems; neither was the cause of the other's.

Defenders of urbanization could have pointed in 1896 to an impressive range of contributions to the national life made possible by city dwellers working in crowded surroundings rather than in the bracing atmosphere of the Great Plains or the mountains. These included the first struggle for inoculation, the first public schools, the first public health services, the first public libraries, the first victory for freedom of the press, the first fire protection systems and building codes, the best hospitals, and the finest cultural achievements. Technology was itself largely a product of the city, both in its relation to ease of communication and in its dependence upon an intellectual creativity that found its most congenial environment in areas of dense settlement. A nineteenth-century statistical study indicated that communities of 8,000 and more gave birth to almost twice as many men of note as their proportionate share, and that in fields such as science, engineering, and literature the ratio was far higher. And as Robert Higgs notes in his brief article, "Urbanization and Inventiveness in the United States," the cities produced new patents at a much higher rate than the nation as a whole. And the innovations in agriculture and industry made possible larger cities and reduced further the proportion of farmers to the total population.

Those who lived through the rapid urbanization of the United States in the nineteenth century were not sure that population concentration was the wisest or most moral course for their native land. But they did know that progress and urbanization seemed to go hand in hand. As Hinton Rowan Helper, a Southern critic of slavery and advocate of urbanization in the South, wrote in 1857: "Almost invariably do we find the bulk of the floating funds, the best talent, and the most vigorous energies of a nation concentrated in its chief cities; and does not this concentration of wealth, energy, and talent, conduce, in an extraordinary degree, to the growth and prosperity of the nation?" Helper, like others of his generation, gave only one answer— "Unquestionably."

1. COMPETITIVE COMMUNITIES ON THE WESTERN FRONTIER

Daniel J. Boorstin

In the winter of 1858, the young members of the Nininger Boys Lyceum in the Minnesota boom town, which had been first settled only eighteen months before (and was destined to disappear within five years), debated the question, "Has Hastings grown more than Nininger during the past year?" Another question that season was, "Does Washington deserve more praise than Bonaparte?" The answer to one was no more doubtful than to the other.

Citizens young and old of each upstart town saw themselves racing against all others, and their competitive spirit left its mark on American life. "On paper, all these towns were magnificent," Albert D. Richardson reported from Kansas in 1857. "Their superbly lithographed maps adorned the walls of every place of resort. The stranger studying one of these, fancied the New Babylon surpassed only by its namesake of old. Its great parks, opera-houses, churches, universities, railway depots and steamboat landings made New York and St. Louis insignificant in comparison. . . . It was not a swindle but a mania. The speculators were quite as insane as the rest."

Everything that fed the booster spirit intensified competition among communities; this competition in turn prevented or discouraged the centralizing of activities. We have already seen how such competition led to the shifting of state capitals. Sometimes a consequence of legislative efforts to compromise was purposely to separate a state's commercial from its political headquarters. Thus the contest between Lexington and Louisville led to the naming of Frankfort as the capital of Kentucky in 1792; from the struggle among Steubenville and Cincinnati and others, came the creation of Columbus as capital of Ohio in 1812. In the new states of a growing new country, the landscape showed neither a lordly castle nor an imposing ancient cathedral to proclaim historic rights to the seat of government. The competition was open.

The creation of large new political units—territories and states—provided many new opportunities for ambitious communities. The state capital was always, of course, the biggest prize, but there were others. In the sparsely settled West, there ought to have been enough political plums to go around: county seats, state universities, agricultural colleges, prisons, land offices, institutions for the poor, the insane, the blind, and the deaf. But it was not only existing communities that had to be satisfied. The cities of the future were numberless, and each demanded its share.

The lore of the West is full of the bitter rivalries of enterprising early settlers for a government handout to their community. Contests were none the less bitter because the competing towns were often figments of imagination. Booster optimists were ready to believe that the government prize itself would give reality and prosperity to their illusions; every such state institution meant buildings to be built, people to be employed, food, clothing, and services to be bought. It meant clients for the lawyers, patients for the doctors, customers for the shops, guests for the taverns and hotels. Above all, it meant increased population with the increased land values that always came along.

Some of the better-documented stories involved the railroads, for they had big money to spark a lively contest. The scramble for the location of the University of Illinois is a good example. Under the Morrill Act of 1862, the new university would receive a large grant of federal land; it would also be permanently supported by the state. Intense rivalry finally led the state legislature in January 1867 to pass an act permitting interested communities to submit bids. The promoters of four towns—Jacksonville, Bloomington, Lincoln, and Champaign—offered money, land, commodities, and then used every other kind of influence. Champaign had the advantage of the leadership of C. R. Griggs, a seasoned lobbyist and member of the state legislature. He was shrewd enough to raise a large sum, not for the official bid, but to finance the goodwill of the politicians who would award the prize. Then he toured the state to see that the money was effectively distributed, and, despite the threat of an investigation, he continued his activities after the legislature went into session.

The Illinois Central Railroad, which already ran through Champaign, was naturally interested in seeing the university there. It had there a large grant of land, much of it still unsold, it owned many town lots, and it would obviously profit from increased freight and passenger traffic. Therefore, it offered $50,000 in freight transportation as part of Champaign's bid, which altogether came to about $285,000. This bid was exceeded by those of the three other leading contenders: Lincoln offered $385,000; Bloomington, $470,000 (including $50,000 from the Chicago and Alton Railroad, which was competing with the Illinois Central); and Jacksonville, $491,000. But Griggs had put his money in the right places, preferring to line the pockets of legislators and political bosses instead of needlessly inflating the public bid. His shrewdness was rewarded on February 28, 1867, when, after much slander and contention, an act located the university at Champaign. The investment by the Illinois Central Railroad and by local boosters was speedily repaid with dividends. By 1870 Champaign–Urbana had already become the most populous town south of Chicago on the branch line, and real estate there was booming.

Since a state generally could support not more than one prison, one insane asylum, or one university, it became usual to disperse these institutions to spread the benefits. The institutions themselves often suffered, for they were not necessarily located in the most suitable places. There had to be prizes for everybody.

Happily, or unhappily, there were to be such prizes almost without number. The sparse population and the politically unorganized condition of the West actually helped make them possible. The largest political and legal subdivisions of the West were, of course, the "territory" or the "state," created and bounded by acts of the federal Congress, but the next smaller units were left to definition by the states themselves. There was no clear, simple, or general rule and, most important, there were no automatic answers supplied by history. In England, by contrast, the smaller unit of government, the "county," had been the product of centuries; it was originally the domain of a "count." The colonies too had generally been divided into counties. In the thirteen original states, counties had already acquired a historical, even patriotic, aura by the early nineteenth century. But what would happen in the unsettled new territories and states of the Southwest and the West? There, too, the subdivision (except in Louisiana) was to be called a "county."

The "county seat" (an Americanism, first recorded in 1803), the headquarters of each county, was where the administrative offices, the county court, the county jail, and the county records would all be located. If a town could not be a state capital, the next best thing was to be a county seat. The county's political, judicial, and administrative activities would build buildings, would attract people with money to spend, would boost town growth and insure against decay. Which town (or, which hope-for-a-town) should be named the county seat? How many counties should there be? The answers to these questions were anybody's guess. In unsettled states, one unbuilt place had no better historical claim than another. Since the boundaries of counties were also unsettled, even geographical considerations were hard to measure. A town could hardly claim that its "central" location in a county entitled it to be the headquarters, when the extent and boundaries of the county were still undecided.

The upshot was the "county-seat wars." Such wars might be struggles among several places to possess the headquarters of a particular county. In that case, one or another would prevail. Or, on the other hand, they might be struggles for the creation of more counties, in order to provide several towns with something to be the headquarters of. Thus the object might be either to take a prize away from a rival, or to persuade the legislature (when there was no theoretical limit to the number of counties) to create enough prizes to go around.

Counties were absolute creatures of state legislatures. Restricted only by the state constitution, a legislature could establish, abolish, enlarge, or diminish any county. In the new states, the county usually started as a geographic rather than a population unit. An act of the state legislature or an executive proclamation would define the boundaries of a county, leaving its detailed organization to the people who happened to reside there. Of course, in describing the boundaries of counties, as in locating the state capital and other state agencies, legislators were subjected to all kinds of pressures: blackmail, bribes, threats, and even physical violence. Land speculators with a fortune to gain (and their allies the town-boosters) were not easily discouraged nor were they pedantic in their arguments.

Commonly the war for the county seat took place in the newly delineated counties themselves, to whose voters state laws generally left the selection of the lucky place. Often land speculators took the lead, but town loyalty and the booster spirit made struggles passionate and even bloody.

Rarely did a new county contain a single preeminent town plainly meriting the seat. Usually the contest involved two or more contenders. Sometimes a proposed county contained no towns at all. In such cases, the competitive spirit had the widest possible field, since any group of speculators could enter their property in the race. Often these county-seat wars technically took place at the ballot box, but in scores of cases they were actually settled with payoffs, brickbats, and even with bullets. It was in the early decades, the organizing decades, of the new Western states, that contests were most common and most bitter. And they occurred not only when a county was first created. Where historical roots were shallow, where people and towns were accustomed to transplanting, urban leadership never seemed finally settled. The loser of this year's contest might hope to win back the prize the year after next; but by then it might have to contend against a brand new town that had only just sprung into prominence.

In Iowa, for example, about two-thirds of its ninety-nine county seats were located only after a contest with neighboring towns. Thirty-nine of Indiana's ninety-two counties have had more than one county seat during their history; some have had as many as seven different seats. Most of the counties in Kansas, Nebraska, and the Dakotas were scenes of such contests. All over the Southwest and West, again and again in the nineteenth century, Americans at the ballot box defended their investments, their personal hopes, and their civic pride.

When the earliest counties were being organized, there were few inhabitants. "The conditions were ideal for the organization of a county," one old settler remarked, "inasmuch as there was an office for every man." At a county-seat election in 1858 in Cuming County, Nebraska, the town of Dewitt, which received only seven votes, was defeated by West Point, which received all of twelve votes. When Nebraska Center was named county seat of Buffalo County, it consisted of one dwelling, one store building, and one warehouse. In Harlan County, Nebraska, where three "towns" competed for the county seat, both Republican City and Melrose comprised only a store, a hitching-post, and a clothesline, while their competitor, Alma, was said to be marked only by a buffalo skull.

Sometimes the proposed county-seat town was a purely speculative real-estate venture. When there was no town in a proposed county, it was tempting for speculators to offer the state a tract of land on condition that the county seat be located there. In Fillmore County, Nebraska, one man personally offered to build a courthouse at a cost of $2,500, and such offers were not uncommon. Speculators could buy a section of land (one mile square: 640 acres) at the total government price of $800, hoping, after it had been elevated into a county seat, to break it up into town lots. Figuring eight lots to the acre, there would be altogether 5,120 lots in the town section. If these could be sold at $100 apiece, which was not an extravagant price in the East, the total return (after spending, at most, three or four thousand dollars for surveying and other expenses) would be a tidy half-million dollars.

Some speculators bought tracts in rival towns. The businesslike explanation of C. J. ("Buffalo") Jones's heavy investments in six or eight county-seat contests in southwestern Kansas was that, if even only one of the towns he backed became a county seat, he would recoup all his losses and be financially independent for life.

If contests between nonexistent towns were often unscrupulous, in real towns contestants were hardly more willing to submit to an unpredictable, if fair, election. The small number of voters in many counties made attempts at a secret ballot futile. Lack of clear or strict voting qualifications added to the confusion; minors were usually allowed to vote. In a largely transient population, who could distinguish those who had come for the sole purpose of voting?

Kansas, a mid-nineteenth-century national battleground of slavery and of other issues large and small, continued to be the scene of some of the most ingenious, as well as some of the most colorful and most corrupt, county-seat battles. In Ford precinct of Gray County in the southwestern part of the state, in the 1870s a secret organization euphemistically called the "Equalization Society" was formed of seventy-two members. Their sole object (spelled out in a constitution and bylaws!) was to sell their votes as a block to whatever county-seat aspirant bid highest. The members attested their democratic faith by agreeing that the money received was to be divided among members equally. All were bound by oath to vote for the town to whom the sale was made, and violation of the oath was punishable by death. T. H. Reeves, a manager of Cimarron's campaign, offered the society for its votes the sum of $10,000, guaranteed by a bond supposedly signed by fifteen leading citizens of Cimarron. The society duly cast its seventy-two votes for Cimarron, which was named the county seat. When the society went to Cimarron for their payoff, they were told they could not be paid because the signatures on the bond were forged.

In Grant County, also in southwestern Kansas, the two contending towns were Ulysses and Appomattox. When, just before the election, it looked likely that Ulysses would win, two of the Appomattox managers entered into a secret pact with their opposite numbers from Ulysses to cover their losses. The pact provided that neither side would resort to bribery or other wrongful methods, and that the successful town company, whichever it might be, would reimburse its defeated rival for their expenses in attempting to build up their town. The defeated town would then be abandoned and all interests united in building up the town chosen as the county seat. Shortly before the polls closed, word of the pact leaked out at Appomattox. The rank and file of Appomattox boosters, thinking they had been sold out, took into custody the signers of the pact, threatened to lynch them, and finally let them go only after they promised to reimburse the campaign expenses of the populace. The people of Ulysses themselves had acquired a reputation for businesslike methods, for voters there were paid off at the rate of ten dollars apiece as they cast their ballots. While this system seemed fair enough to land speculators and town boosters, it failed to meet the approval of the Kansas Supreme Court, which set aside at least one such election. In the long run, however, cash-and-carry democracy prevailed, for Ulysses remained the seat of Gray County.

The cost of county-seat wars was high, not only in money but in violence, in blood, and even in lives. At Dodge City, Kansas, crews known as "killers" were brought into town for the county-seat contests. Although it is not definitely recorded that they killed anyone, their presence seems to have influenced the result. As late as 1885 in Stevens County, Kansas, a county-seat war between Hugoton and Woodsdale involved kidnapping, assassination, bribery, the use of militia, and several criminal trials which reverberated for over a quarter of a century.

Many individual promoters, and some whole towns, were deluded or disappointed. Even if the magical mushroom growth supposed to follow the declaration of a county seat did not always appear, some inevitable advantages seemed to come with the distinction. A town that still remained small after designation as a county seat might otherwise have disappeared altogether. A growing town was likely to grow still more. These optimisms were enough to spawn counties by the hundreds. Old counties never died! But new counties were continually being born: by the fission of old counties, by the subdivision of newly settled and newly organized territories and states. These multiplied and dispersed the agencies of government, giving more and more Americans a personal interest in the diffuseness of American politics and, incidentally, of American culture. In many states of the vast unpopulous West, counties were just as small geographically as those of Massachusetts; in Indiana, for example, a county averaged only half the size of those originally formed in Connecticut. By the time of the census of 1960, the United States was subdivided into

3,072 counties. Each had its own county seat, including a courthouse, a jail, and numerous administrative offices.

The counties remained an important and expensive feature of American life into the twentieth century. It was often said, in justifying them, that any farmer ought to be able to drive to his county courthouse and back in his horse and buggy between sunrise and sunset. Governor "Alfalfa Bill" Murray of Oklahoma, in the early twentieth century, actually argued that it was important to keep counties numerous and small in order to continue to encourage farmers to travel by horse and buggy rather than by automobile.

But by the twentieth century many of the myriad counties had become a burden on state finances. Few could afford the paved highways required by motor vehicles. Shifting centers of agriculture and industry had left many county governments without sources of tax support. The rise and expansion of cities with all their own political machinery now created new problems of competition for the once dominant county governments. But who would champion county consolidation? One could not combine several small counties into a single large one without abolishing their county seats, each with its complement of courthouses, poorhouses, and jails, and all their officials. This form of political suicide has not been popular. And thousands of American counties remain: a vivid vestige of the upstart age, of extravagant hopes and driving competitive ambitions, in a word, of the booster spirit.

In scores of other ways, too numerous to mention, the booster spirit of the upstart West fostered cultural diffuseness. What Richard C. Wade has called "urban imperialism"—the competition of numerous, fast-growing urban centers, each seeking to explore and exploit and attach itself to an undeveloped hinterland—played much the same role in the spread of civilization and commerce over this continent, that the competitive imperialisms of European nations played in developing and industrializing remote parts of Asia, Africa, and Oceania. The desire of each town to become the terminus of a canal or a railroad often produced canals and railroads, which became life-promoting arteries all along their way. This competition bred a fantastic transportation network which, by comparison with Western Europe, gave the United States a railroad mileage far out of proportion to her population.

2. CITIES AND YANKEE INGENUITY, 1870–1920[1]

Robert Higgs

The rise of the city has been the historic sign of a society on the march; it stimulated further adventure by bringing people together, pooling their efforts, promoting change by exchange, enlarging the world through contact with other peoples and cities. The great city became the center of unrest and disorder because it remained the center of creative activity.

—Herbert J. Muller, *The Uses of the Past,* 1952

In recent years economists have attempted to explain invention by reviving and elaborating upon the idea that inventive activity is essentially an *economic* endeavor which varies directly with its expected rate of return. In this essay I have used a broader context to analyze inventiveness in the United States during the half century after 1870 by taking into account the costs of information and by relating those costs to the locational distribution of the population between the countryside and the cities. The major empirical finding is that urbanization and inventiveness (that is, inventions per capita) were closely associated during the 1870–1920 period. This finding may well be significant for the explanation of economic growth as a self-sustaining process.

In the following discussion we shall take these crucial background conditions for granted: The American people during the 1870–1920 period were highly literate and highly motivated by economic incentives; and American inventors benefited from the existence of a patent system and from laws that provided strong protection for private property in any form. Such conditions, obviously, do not always prevail.

Our fundamental assumption is that inventive activity is an *economic* endeavor: the quantity of resources devoted to inventive activity varies directly with the expected rate of return on that activity. This assumption has been the foundation of much fruitful investigation in recent years,[2] but it is hardly a new approach. The writers of the United States Constitution subscribed to it when they gave Congress the power to establish a patent system "to promote the Progress of Science and useful Arts, by securing for limited Times to Authors and Inventors the exclusive Right to their respective Writings and Discoveries." In fact, it is difficult to find anyone who is really informed about the process of invention denying that inventors are economic men. Patent Commissioner W. E. Simonds remarked in 1891 that "perhaps no idea was ever so much opposed to reason and to evidence as the notion that inventors are not actuated by the motives common to the human race, and that if the incentive to invention be destroyed inventors will continue to invent from motives of pure benevolence."[3] And four years later Commissioner J. S. Seymour, anticipating Jacob Schmookler's model by more than a half century, said: "The relation which exists between industrial demand and inventive activity is very close. Each may be said to be dependent upon the other. In any line in which there is little or no call there will be but little inventive effort. On the other hand, should any change or advance in industrial conditions cause a sudden increased demand for some article, means for producing that article or its equivalent will be created very rapidly in the brains of ambitious inventors."[4]

There exists, we assume, a production function relating inputs of resources to outputs of inventions. This production function is not completely deterministic, since creative efforts are always surrounded by a good deal of uncertainty. Still, other things being equal, a hundred men working to develop an idea have a higher probability of succeeding than fifty men so occupied. We might say that the production function relates quantities of inputs to *expected values* (that is, mathematical expectations) of outputs, but this is merely an analytical flourish. An invention is usefully defined as a new combination of previously existing knowledge that satisfies some want. Inventive activity, then, is nothing more than the process of creating new useful information. From this way of conceptualizing inventive activity, it is only a short step to postulating that just two inputs enter the process: inventive talent and prior information.

If we suppose that inventive talent (native creativity) is randomly distributed throughout the population, then differences in inventive activity among regions or places must depend upon variations in the expected costs of acquiring information. Since rates of return depend upon both revenues and costs, two kinds of information are relevant. The first is information about opportunities for profitable invention, that is, about the extent of the market for invention; the second is information that can serve as inputs into the production of inventions. The former determines the potential inventor's expectation of the revenue stream his invention will generate; the latter, his expectation of the initial cost of producing the invention. Together these imply an expected rate of return, a signal encouraging him either to devote his energies to inventive activity or to use his talents and time in an alternative manner. To link inventiveness to urbanization within this analytical framework, we must show that information costs differed systematically between rural and urban areas. Such differences are in fact quite plausible for the 1870–1920 period in the United States.

The expected rate of return depends in part upon the expected stream of revenue from invention. Before mass communication, when most reliable information was acquired by direct observation or by word of mouth, the average search cost of information about potential markets for inventions was an increasing function of market distance. Therefore, the market *as perceived by the average potential inventor* was largely restricted to nearby locations. Assuming that the locational distribution of actual inventive opportunities coincided with that of the population, the probability that an opportunity would be perceived was then much higher for urban than for rural persons. Given the assumed relation between market distance and the average search cost of information, this proposition follows from the common definition of a city as an area of spatially agglomerated population and economic activity. Moreover, if the reasonable assumption be made that, in relation to population, actual inventive opportunities were disproportionately concentrated in the cities, there are even stronger grounds for postulating that the expected stream of revenue from invention was larger for urban than for rural persons.

The expected rate of return depends also upon the expected costs of inventing; here we can propose an inverse relation with urbanization. "In a pre-mass-communications context, such as the relatively compact cities of the late nineteenth century, where diffusion of technical knowledge [was] highly reliant upon personal interaction, the possibilities for invention ought to [have been] enhanced by the . . . network of interpersonal communications and confrontations."[5] In the absence of well-developed means of mass communication, the costs of acquiring information depended heavily upon *spatial proximity*. The expected costs of acquiring informational inputs were lower for the potential urban inventor than for his rural counterpart simply because of the enormously greater proximity of urban information carriers to one another. Spatial isolation was the greatest handicap for rural persons. To the extent that urban people were better educated, their advantages were compounded.

Combining the propositions about the expected revenue stream and the expected total costs of inventing, it follows that the expected rate of return on inventive activity was higher in the city than in the countryside. And this statement, together with our fundamental assumption, implies the testable hypothesis that the number of inventions per capita was greater among urban than among rural people in the United States during the half century before 1920.

A substantial body of evidence is consistent with this view of inventiveness. One recent study found that among American states in the 1870–1920 period, a difference of 10 percentage points in the proportion of the population living in cities was positively associated with a difference of 6 to 9 patents per 100,000 population, even when the influences of manufacturing and regional differences were held constant.[6] In the following paragraphs we shall further test the hypothesis by examining data for Connecticut, the nation's most inventive state throughout the 1870–1920 period. We shall seek to determine whether the relation between urbanization and inventiveness, already confirmed for the cross section of American states, also existed within Connecticut.

We have obtained the data examined here as a random sample from the *Annual Report of the Commissioner of Patents* for the years indicated. A sample of 200 inventions issued to Connecticut residents at quinquennial intervals was drawn for the period 1870–1915. Altogether, these ten samples contain 2,000 inventions, which would appear to be a sufficient number to support some generalizations in view of their being randomly selected. The sampling design called for collecting the name and residence of the inventor and a brief description of the invention. This procedure permitted a distinction to be drawn between the number of inventions and the number of inventors, but generally the correspondence between the two sets of data is so close that any statement about the one applies as well to the other.

To test the hypothesis that inventiveness and urbanization were directly related, we first classified the data according to the residence of the inventor. It is apparent that the data fall into three groups: Group I cities (Bridgeport, Hartford, New Haven, Waterbury, Meriden, and New Britain); Group II cities (New London, Stamford, Middletown, Norwich, Danbury, and Norwalk); and Group III, which includes all other residences, whether urban or rural. Except for 1870, every sample shows the six Group I cities accounting for well over half the inventions. The six Group II cities provided 9 to 18 percent, and Group III residences (again excluding 1870) were the source of 17 to 31 percent. The leading 12 residences (Groups I and II) generally provided about three-fourths of all the sampled inventions (see Table I).

To obtain an estimate of the *total* number of patented inventions in each location, we proceeded as follows: First, we determined the proportion that the sample size (which is always 200) constitutes in the total for the state at the particular date. Then we multiplied the reciprocal of this proportion by the number of sampled inventions for a particular place; the product is the estimated total number of patented inventions for that place. For example, in 1910 the state had 990 patents. The sample of 200 therefore constitutes approximately one-fifth of the total. In that year Waterbury inventors contributed 10 inventions to the sample. The estimated total number of Waterbury inventions is therefore $10 \times 5 = 50$.

Having obtained estimates of the total number of patented inventions in various locations, we divided them by the population figures for each place to obtain estimates of inventiveness (that is, inventions per capita), as shown in Table 2. (Those who are uncomfortable with small samples but believe in the Central Limit Theorem may wish to focus on the figures for the group aggregates and ignore the estimates for individual cities.) As Table 2 shows, Group I cities were the most inventive, though their advantage over Group II cities was on two occasions negligible. The inventiveness of Group III places, which include some small cities as well as all rural locations, was much lower; for 1890 to 1910 the level of Group III inventiveness was approximately equal to the United States average. Manifesting a great urban-rural inventiveness differential, these data are strikingly consistent with our hypothesis.

Cross-sectional evidence for American states and for Connecticut locations strongly supports a hypothesis that links inventiveness to urbanization. If one is willing to accept a time-series interpretation of this finding, it may well be significant for the explanation of economic growth as a *self-sustaining* process in the period before research and development had become institutionalized. To vastly oversimplify, urbanization was a response to changes in the relative profitability of agricultural and non-agricultural activities which in turn were the result of changes in expenditure patterns as per capita incomes rose. Therefore, in a setting in which peculiarities of comparative advantage in international trade or of sectoral increases in productivity did not strongly intervene, economic growth gave rise to urbanization.[7] But because urbanization encouraged greater inventiveness, it produced a *feedback effect* on growth by promoting more rapid technological progress. In this way urbanization was a cause as well as a consequence of economic growth, and the circle of a self-sustaining process was closed. Though the existence of this feedback

Table 1. Distribution by Locational Origin of Randomly Sampled Patented Inventions, Connecticut, 1870–1915

	1870	1875	1880	1885	1890	1895	1900	1905	1910	1915
Group I										
Bridgeport	11	30	24	42	21	32	35	28	24	29
Hartford	12	18	10	24	28	23	40	38	39	35
New Haven	33	29	55	26	22	19	31	21	27	20
Waterbury	7	11	15	12	25	15	5	8	10	25
Meriden	11	15	11	8	14	7	6	9	6	5
New Britain	3	6	9	4	24	11	5	11	27	12
Aggregate	77	109	124	116	134	107	122	115	133	126
Group II										
New London	2	5	2	9	2	8	1	2	2	5
Stamford	2	4	5	5	4	7	17	10	9	2
Middletown	4	7	5	3	6	2	3	13	5	2
Norwich	10	6	5	6	6	6	1	1	0	3
Danbury	3	2	1	8	7	6	2	5	4	0
Norwalk	3	4	0	1	6	4	6	4	2	5
Aggregate	24	28	18	32	31	33	30	35	22	17
Aggregate, I, II	101	137	142	148	165	140	152	150	155	143
Group III	99	63	58	52	35	60	48	50	45	57

Source: Randomly drawn from the *Annual Report of the Commissioner of Patents* for the years indicated.

mechanism be granted, however, the magnitude of its influence remains open to conjecture.

Table 2. Estimated Levels of Patented Inventions Per 10,000 Population, Connecticut Locations, 1870–1910

	1870	1880	1890	1900	1910
Group I					
Bridgeport	21.6	26.1	20.2	18.7	11.8
Hartford	11.8	7.1	24.8	19.0	19.7
New Haven	24.0	18.3	12.7	10.9	10.1
Waterbury	24.1	25.3	40.9	4.1	6.8
Meriden	39.0	21.3	30.4	9.5	11.0
New Britain	11.6	22.9	68.5	7.3	30.8
Aggregate	17.7	18.1	25.2	13.1	13.9
Group II					
New London	7.3	5.7	6.5	2.3	5.1
Stamford	70.0	60.0	30.2	40.6	17.9
Middletown	21.7	22.1	31.1	11.5	21.0
Norwich	22.2	9.9	17.3	2.3	0.0
Danbury	12.5	2.6	19.9	4.8	9.9
Norwalk	13.9	0.0	27.7	18.1	6.3
Aggregate	17.3	9.7	20.1	12.8	9.7
Aggregate, I, II	17.6	16.1	24.1	13.0	13.1
Group III	11.7	6.0	3.8	3.8	4.1

Source: Estimated by a procedure described in the text.

NOTES

1. This essay draws heavily upon two earlier papers by the author: "American Inventiveness, 1870–1920," *Journal of Political Economy,* LXXIX (May–June 1971), and "Urbanization and Inventiveness in the United States, 1870–1920," presented to a conference on "The New Urban History: Quantitative Explorations," Madison, Wisc., June 18, 1970.

2. R. R. Nelson, "The Economics of Invention: A Survey of the Literature," *Journal of Business,* XXXII (April 1959); R. R. Nelson, ed., *The Rate and Direction of Inventive Activity* (Princeton, N.J.: Princeton University Press, 1962); I. Feller, "Inventive Activity in Agriculture, 1837–1890," *Journal of Economic History,* XXII (December 1962); J. Schmookler, *Invention and Economic Growth* (Cambridge, Mass.: Harvard University Press, 1966); and G. H. Daniels, "The Big Questions in the History of American Technology," *Technology and Culture,* XI (January 1970).

3. *Annual Report of the Commissioner of Patents for 1891* (Washington: Government Printing Office, 1892), p. vi.

4. *Annual Report of the Commissioner of Patents for 1895* (Washington: Government Printing Office, 1896), p. xiii.

5. A. R. Pred, *The Spatial Dynamics of·U.S. Urban-Industrial Growth, 1800–1914* (Cambridge, Mass.: M.I.T. Press, 1966), p. 96.

6. Robert Higgs, "American Inventiveness, 1870–1920," *op. cit.*

7. H. A. Simon, "Effects of Increased Productivity upon the Ratio of Urban to Rural Population," *Econometrica*, XV (January 1947).

3. VARIETIES OF AMERICAN URBAN SYMBOLISM

Anselm L. Strauss

A host of American cities, despite all differences in size, location, or composition, continually try to validate the claims that they are typical, authentic American communities. They balance what they are and what they feel they stand for against a tacitly accepted formula of American values and national purposes. But the facts and symbols of urban life become interchangeable in the course of argument, become confused in meeting the difficulties of expressing a city's hopes and achievements in a straightforward definitive fashion. They become confused, too, because of certain ambiguities in what may be assumed to be *the* American way of life.

This ambiguity of American urbanity and American values is significantly reflected in a lively contention over which city best deserves the title of "most American." The admirers of Chicago, New York, Kansas City, and Detroit, at least, claim honors for the city of their choice. Such claims are not new. As far back at least as 1851, a Baltimorian reassured a local audience that Baltimore "may be said to be an epitome of the nation itself";[i] and upon occasion critics of certain American values may point to one of these cities as a repulsive exemplar of those values. But a uniform, homogeneous American culture spread evenly throughout the nation would allow no city to claim more Americanness than was possessed by other cities; nor could any then base its claim upon a different set of values.

As long ago as 1891, de Rousiers described Chicago as the most American city, remarking that, "It is here, indeed, that the American 'go ahead,' the idea of always going forward . . . attains its maximum intensity."[2] Some fifty-five years later, John Gunther writes that Chicago's "impact is overwhelmingly that of the United States, and it gives above all the sense that America and the Middle West are beating upon it from all sides."[3] In other words, he is stressing less its "striving" than its central position. A thousand miles away, the admirers of New York City stress rather different values. They assert that New York represents the nation at its most civilized and most creative; that it dominates the nation in every

Reprinted with permission of The Macmillan Company from *Images of the American City* by Anselm L. Strauss. © The Free Press, A Corporation, 1961.

way; and that more different kinds of Americans, drawn from more regions, live in New York than in any other metropolis.[4] The proponents of Kansas City dwell upon still different aspects of American culture; George S. Perry who described that city for *The Saturday Evening Post's* readers, saw it this way:

Kansas City is a kind of interior American crossroads and melting pot where the Southerner, the Northerner, the Easterner and the Westerner meet and become plain John American, with America unfolding . . . "in oceans of glory" in every direction. It got its start on the riches of Boston banks and Western lands and Northern furs. It is not only America's approximate geographical heart, but the center of gravity for her taste and emotion. The soap opera, movie or national magazine that doesn't "take" in Kansas City won't live long in the nation.[5]

Those who would give Detroit the honor of "most American," ignore the virtues of being of pioneer and dead-center America, and claim that Detroit best represents the spirit of modern twentieth-century America, exemplified in the city's superb system of mass production, in its drive, energy, purpose, and fusion of men and machines.[6] Pittsburgh's admirers claim similar industrial virtues for their city.[7] Indeed, a city need not even be among the largest to claim for itself, or to be proclaimed, the most typical of America. For instance:

It is a truism to say that Tulsa is the most American of American cities. All the forces that have gone into the making of a Republic have been intensified there. The successive stages through which the country as a whole has passed during three hundred years—Indian occupation, ranching, pioneering, industrial development . . . have been telescoped within the single lifetime of some of the older Tulsans. The result has been the quintessence of Americanism—its violence and strength, its buoyant optimism, its uncalculating generosity, its bumptious independence.[8]

The argument that one city best typifies America is couched in a standardized "logical" form: from a number of desirable attributes, certain ones are selected for emphasis while the remainder are ignored; and it is assumed or asserted that these selected attributes are possessed more abundantly by the admired city. In this way, many facets of American life are overlooked or given secondary status. The argument does not turn upon fact but upon value. Thus, if one values sheer quantity, then New York has most of everything; if one extolls the Midwest as the geographic heart of America and as the possesser of the most widespread and average national values, then he will deny priority to New York. In making such evaluations of their cities, Americans assess the nation's cultural assets and identify themselves with its history and destiny. When they represent a city as most American, they are conceiving it not only as unique and matchless but as the symbolic representative of esteemed national values.

Such great distinction can be claimed for few American cities; hence the citizens of the remaining urban centers must be content with a lesser assertion; namely, that their particular city represents at least one—and probably more—important aspect of American life. Thus, Iowa cities are conceived of as good places to live in because they appear to be friendly, peaceful, prosperous agricultural towns; and Fort Worth, Texas, surrounded by cattlemen's country, epitomizes the culture of that region. Such cities are parts of many Americas. The country is vast, its aspects staggeringly varied. Cities need not compete to share the nation's glory, they have only to point to those of their features wherein they typify some aspect, or aspects, of the entire American way of life.

Yet these aspects are not entirely congruent, in fact or in value. One of the most persistent clashes of value on the American scene has long been embodied in the sentimental preference of a rural existence to a thoroughly urban one. When Jefferson spoke of the danger of an American metropolitanism fated perhaps to destroy the sturdy virtues of a predominantly agricultural society, he was but expressing a dichotomy in American thought that persists to this day. Despite the continuous trend toward urbanization, our rural heritage remains potent, entering into American thought and action in increasingly subtle ways.

Eighteenth-century seaboard agriculture was not what farming became on the prairie a century later, nor what it is today in an era of large-scale mechanization. The men who worked the American soil and the lifestyles that they evolved have varied greatly in place and time. Yet an American mythology grew up by which it was maintained that agricultural pursuits necessarily bred a certain kind of man. This agrarian mythology is and was a complex set of beliefs consisting of many elements, some of which developed from the several kinds of frontier conditions and others of which evolved after the Civil War in opposition to the dreadful urban conditions. The spirit of this agrarian ideology can be suggested by the following few sentences.

Rural life is slow and unhurried. Men lead natural, rich lives. People are friendly and their relationships are informal, yet orderly. The agricultural population is homogeneous in custom and culture, if not in racial stock. The round of existence is stable and the community is religious, moral, honest. Men are, thus, not motivated by purely individualistic impulses. If all farmers do not love one another, at least they understand each other and do not manipulate and exploit each other as do city dwellers. The very physical surroundings are healthy, homelike, restful, not dense with population. Not the least: the rural man is a sturdy democrat, his convictions nourished by his contact with nature itself and with the equalitarian discussion held around the crackerbarrel and in the meeting house.[9]

These conceptions are linked by affect rather than by logic. They evolved under considerably different historical circumstances, some during the development of the New England township, some when the prairie was settled, others while western farmers were castigating the railroad kings, and yet others at a time when rural migrants to cities became demoralized by conditions there. Although the country–city dichotomy has been with us for many generations, the content of the argument on either side has varied from decade to decade—as both cities and countrysides became transformed. Ideas die hard: in the formation of our rural mythology, old ideas accrued to new ones instead of disappearing entirely, despite their incongruence with fact and with each other. Probably no single rural community has ever stressed equally all elements of the entire ideological complex, for its very ambiguity allows its use as an effective resource. The town can use it as well as the village; and the small city can boast of homelike surroundings and friendly atmosphere, in an invidious contrast with the larger urban centers.

Sizeable cities can also be designated as outright embodiments of rural values—as when the citizens of Des Moines aver direct kinship with soil and farm; and in so doing, they may symbolically act in ways more farm-like than the equally business oriented farmer. The residents of most cities, perhaps, signify their association with sentimental rurality more obliquely, not always recognizing the nature of that feeling of kinship. Cities are referred to by their residents as "The City of Flowers," "The City of Trees," "The City of Homes." They draw upon the rich stock of rural imagery without directly stating their debt. Large cities as they grow to great size abandon such nicknames, which no longer seem to represent what the city has become, but may emphasize in curiously subtle ways that their styles of urban life also partake of America's revered earlier heritage. Chicago—once called "The City of Gardens"—still boasts that it is the city of the prairie, and lays claim to a characteristic friendliness and informality that mark it off from, say, New York or Boston. (As George Perry says, "Chicago is a thousand times more relaxed, less 'mannered' than New York.")[10]

Like the smaller towns, the larger cities may stress one or more of the varied rural themes, thereby cashing in on a much wider ideological complex. The very statement that one's city is a "city of gardens" (albeit gardening is a far cry from farming), arouses connotations smacking of outdoor life, suggestions of qualities bred in close contact with the soil, of urbanites living a life of relaxation rather than of frantic pursuit of excessive monetary gain. The visitor to a city sometimes remarks, also, upon certain paradoxes because, while he notices that the place is marked only by a limited number of rural characteristics, he feels that these are among its important features. What he is really puzzling over is that all rural qualities are supposed to hang together; whereas in this particular city, surprisingly enough, they do not. The perception of such paradoxes is furthered by any obvious juxtaposition of rural and urban characteristics: a city nestled among beautiful mountains but marked by a high rate of crime and by horrendous slums, or a large urban center characterized by a noticeably leisured pace of life. Thus about Portland, Oregon, Richard Neuberger remarks: "Torn between her peaceful past and a brawling future as the Pittsburgh of the West, Portland just can't make up her mind. . . . As a result of this strange ambivalence, Portland is a combination of the rustic and the metropolitan."[11] Similarly, Elsie Morrow writes of Springfield, Illinois, that, "At best, Springfield is a very typical American city, with a special flavor and pleasantness. At worst it is a town which has grown old without ever having grown up. It is something between a backward country settlement and a cosmopolis."[12]

The obverse of such pleasantly toned rural mythology, of course, is an affectively linked set of vices: cities are locales of demoralization, discomfort, standardization, artificiality, vulgar materialism, dishonesty, and so on through a richly invidious lexicon. But the rural–urban dichotomy allows black to be called white, and white, black. City dwellers have long characterized their cities as places of progress, opportunity, and excitement, the very image of civilization in contrast to countryside, small town, small city, in contrast, even, to those larger cities which appear provincial. Small cities and even villages have, in turn, affirmed that they participate in an urbane and urban civilization. Anyone who peruses popular urban histories will notice how very sensitive are their authors about the artistic, musical, and literary "culture" of their towns; they carefully list all "cultural" accomplishments and proclaim the progressiveness of their towns by example and assertion. A town which is not civilized, not progressive, not exciting would seem to have a narrow range of options; its citizens must balance its slight amount of urbanity with presumed rural virtues, or must assert disinterest in (un-American) urban characteristics; or, more subtly, must ignore their place in the backwash of American urbanization and remain content to be where they are.

Whatever else may be true of American cities, they are certainly a most varied lot, being neither all cosmopolitan nor all homespun. Nonetheless, particular cities become symbolized as embodiments of different facets of a cheerfully ambiguous rural–urban dichotomy. Thus, emerging styles of urban life receive relatively easy explanation or rationalization. It is as if people were to say: "We are a city like this because we grew upon the prairie, or because we are surrounded by farms, or because our main businesses were founded by farm boys, or because we have no great influx of alien peoples." Likewise, each different population within a single city can rationalize its differential mode of living by appealing to one mythology or another—or to elements of both. Moreover, a city seemingly fated by geographical position and history to be of a certain kind can be envisioned as another kind, and can be directed toward that image by strong interest groups which draw upon different sets of sustaining beliefs. Any city which unquestionably is undergoing change from a commercial to a manufacturing center, or from an agricultural town to a distributing mart, can likewise find ready interpretations to account for otherwise baffling changes in its social characteristics. All such explanations, whether vigorously contested or merely assumed, are answers to that important query: what is the meaning of this city, what kind of a place is it?

The rural-versus-urban conflict that marks American life is crosscut by another ambiguity which turns on a contrast between tradition and modernity. City adherents sometimes stress a lengthy history or a blessedly short one. Votaries of a city with a long history will tend to link its origins with those of the nation itself. Being old—the ideology runs—a long-established city is less likely to be crude, vulgar, rough and ready; hence it will be more civilized, more civic-minded, more settled; its citizens will be more stable, have deeper personal and familial roots in the community; its population will be mostly native to it and its immigrants well assimilated; hence, fewer men will have been attracted there merely for opportunistic reasons. The older cities will have more cultivation of leisure, greater delicacy of human relations, and will pay more attention to matters which make for "taste" and "civilization."[13]

But the citizens of other American cities extoll the contrary virtues of youth and scant tradition. They regard their cities as relatively untrammeled by custom and convention. Just because their cities have not had time to settle down, they are supposed not to have developed rigid stances toward handling problems; they are therefore progressive and profoundly democratic, since men have fought their way to success there by their own honest efforts, benefiting neither from hereditary position nor from an elite upbringing. In these younger cities, it is believed that the lines between social classes have not yet grown into impermeable barriers; indeed, they may be denied to exist at all. A young city is conceived of as a place of freedom in still another sense. Its citizens have immigrated there of their own free will because they imagined it to be a place of considerable opportunity. Because the young community permits experimentation and the pursuit of opportunity, it is seen as an exciting place, at least more interesting than the stodgier older cities. Although the latter, by reason of their earlier origins, may perhaps rightfully claim superiority in the arts of civilization—so the argument runs—the more recently founded communities will soon overtake or surpass them; indeed the cosmopolitanism of the older cities may only, in some instances, be a form of decadence.

Ardent speakers for both younger and older cities stress only certain elements in the total available vocabularies; they glory now in a town's experimental attitude, now in its famous traditional styles of cooking; they even combine the attributes of age and youth. Such symbolization occurs without strict regard for fact, since cities, as we have seen, may be represented as rather old when they are actually quite young, and cities of similar age may be conceived of in very different temporal terms.

Tradition and history are often given a peculiar reverse twist, so that certain eastern coastal cities are considered not to have important American qualities, while certain western centers are assigned crucial roles in the making of the nation. It is asserted or implied that there are histories and histories; but the basic history of the country concerns the clearing of the forests and settling of the frontier. The pioneer romance thus crowds out the colonial. Any city whose citizens did not participate in the pushing back of the frontier cannot, therefore, possibly possess the mystical qualities stemming from that glorious enterprise.

But the frontier is a series of conceptions, not merely a set of facts. These conceptions are linked with various rural and urban virtues, with different periods of our history, and with particular American regions as well. In those sections of the country where the frontier as a geographic reality has but recently disappeared, the frontier as a concept refers more to the mining camp and the railroad center than to pioneer agricultural settlements. The frontier was a rough and tough place, where men were men and the hardiest won out. Some of the same associations remain coupled in Midwestern remembrances because of the region's boom-town tradition and because of the predominant romance of life on the open prairie. The Midwest is more than the geographic heart of the continent; many believe it to be at the core of what *is* America. Back East, the concept of the frontier has been sufficiently misted over by time so that it is referred to more obliquely ("the founders," "the settlers"), but these terms also carry a considerable charge of regional passion.

The frontier, as an idea, has also broken loose from any regional anchoring; it can be applied to endeavors in industrial, artistic, intellectual, and other nongeographic fields. Consequently, cities building upon the cumulative connotations of the frontier image can be thought of as commercial and industrial pioneers. A great metropolis like New York can strike its admirers as *the* "moving frontier" of the entire American economy and of the nation's civilization. The frontier concept allows some cities to be called currently progressive and others to be linked with the nation's slightly older history; while it may be used with relation to some cities so that it cuts both ways. An example is John Bowman's address to his fellow citizens of the Pittsburgh Chamber of Commerce, in which he reminded them of the city's great pioneer tradition:

But these qualities in men and women, you say, flared up generally among the pioneers of the time. . . . These qualities, however, did not flare up and stay flared up in any other community for so long a period nor did they reach so intense a glow as they did in Pittsburgh.

He goes on to claim that, "The significant fact now is that Pittsburgh through nearly a hundred years developed a new way of thinking, a new way of acting. These new ways became first nature in the people." And then, by simple transmutation, he views these ways as creative acts, and Pittsburgh's creativeness "was the application of creative ability to industry." This was its great contribution to Pittsburgh. And of course, "the old creativeness developed here through a long period, is still in Pittsburgh."[14]

But when a city settles down, this turn of events is likely to be greeted by criticism—criticism mixed, however, with expressions of nostalgia and joy over the community's improvements. The citizens may perceive that certain civic characteristics derive from the original pioneer spirit which founded and built the town, however astonished the original settlers might be if they could witness the town's transformation.[15]

When residents identify a city with different rural or urban conceptions and with different kinds of romantic histories, they may also identify it with reference to another persistent American dichotomy: regionalism versus national integration. Since our cities are so widely scattered on such different landscapes, it is difficult not to associate a city with its region. Its domestic architecture, the clothing, speech, and action of some of its residents all proclaim it—and the people themselves sometimes proclaim it with belligerence. As is usual with cultural antinomies, men find ample room for ambiguity and for subtle argument. Two cities of the same region may vie for regional supremacy on symbolic as well as economic grounds. Each will claim to represent the region better; each will stress somewhat different areal attributes. Since no region is entirely homogeneous—if only because of its competing urban centers—there is plenty of room for dispute. In a rapidly changing region, such as the "New South," there may be even less agreement unless the resources of ambiguity are utilized in a way such that one city claims to represent the Old South, while the other is quite content to represent the New South (although a city like Charleston can claim to represent both[16]). A region is usually not exactly coterminous with a state; therefore, a city such as Biloxi, Mississippi, can affirm kinship with New Orleans and with bayou culture rather than with the rest of Mississippi.

Some cities, by virtue of the populations which founded them or immigrated to them later, are considered to be less typical of their regions than are their neighbors; these may compensate by claiming other important American values. Conversely, however, a city may receive great waves of foreign immigrants without serious impairment to its position as a regional standard bearer. A few cities are so new that they and their residents share little in common with the rest of the region, in history or in taste, and so are constrained to build some sort of urban history, however flimsy, or to engage in other ceremonial gestures to reaffirm their association with their region. An interesting case is Kingsport, Tennessee, a small city planned and founded by Eastern bankers who were attracted to the site by abundant, cheap white labor. Kingsport's historian, writing when the city was only eleven years old, nevertheless argues that had the village but known it, it "was sleeping only that it might awake into a beautiful prosperous city" for "the moral and mental fibre of the sturdy, resourceful people of the Kingsport community required two centuries in the making." While it "is true that the new city was incorporated and began its municipal life only eleven years ago . . . back of all this, unknown to many of the citizens themselves perhaps, is a setting which would be a pride to any of the oldest cities in the country."[17]

A few urban centers gladly spurn extensive regional affiliation. Their residents prefer to think of them as supranational, even as "world cities," underline the city's role in the national economy, and flaunt its traits of national leadership, sophistication, cosmopolitanism, size, and other symbols of national and international placement. Some sense of the overwhelming impact of a world city is suggested by the breathless and inadequate ways its admirers attempt to sum it up. Thus, John Gunther, who first compares Chicago (the typical American city) with New York (the world city), writes that Chicago is "the greatest and most typically American of all cities. New York is bigger and more spectacular and can outmatch it in other superlatives, but it is a 'world' city, more European in some respects than American." Some pages later he writes that

now we come to New York City, the incomparable, the brilliant star city of cities, the forty-ninth state, a law unto itself, the Cyclopean paradox, the inferno with no out-of-bounds, the supreme expression of both the miseries and the splendors of contemporary civilization. . . . New York is at once the climactic synthesis of America, and yet the negation of America in that it has so many characteristics called un-American.[18]

Paul Crowell and A. H. Raskin merely say: "New York is not a city. It is a thousand cities, each with its own ninety-nine square miles."[19]

Many citizens of "world cities" make denigrating gestures toward more regionally inclined centers. They refer to those centers as less important, small-townish, hick towns, cow towns, and use other similar epithets. Consequently, these latter places may regard the more worldly centers with a suspicion that gains strength from the historic antagonism between countryside and city as well as from a regional passion against national centralization. However, no single city claims to be a national, or world, city in exactly the same way as any other does; and always regional traits are coupled with nonregional ones (ever by residents of New York City).

Sectionalism is closely allied with economic specialization inasmuch as the various continental areas function differently in our national economy. Cities tend to become known for the industries, commercial enterprises, and services that are typical of the surrounding area. National cities, of course, have more varied functions; hence when New York City residents insist that it has "everything," this means more than that it performs all the important economic functions. The full significance of the claim is that all (the best—and possibly the worst) styles of life can be found in New York. But the Florida resort city, the Illinois farm city, or the New England manufacturing town can all be conceived of by their residents as simultaneously truly regional and truly American because what they manufacture or trade or service is necessary to the nation.

Some products or services which are limited to certain cities are of sufficient national importance that those cities come to represent some particular facet of America: Pittsburgh and Detroit come readily to mind.

Although not all specializations are equally praiseworthy, or even savory, nevertheless observers of such cities as Reno and Calumet City can find ample justification for believing that sex, sin, and gambling are as much a part of American life as are automobiles or opera; and Pittsburgh residents could, until recently, declare that smoke-filled air and labor troubles were the inevitable accompaniment of heavy industrialization. As George S. Perry has phrased it:

Certainly Reno is an actual and highly special aspect of American life, as much as Monte Carlo is a part of European life. . . . Many Nevadans . . . referring both to the tourist business brought in and the large amount of tax load that gambling pays . . . remark simply: "You don't shoot Santa Claus." . . . For in the American mind, Reno remains to gambling and divorces what Pittsburgh means to steel and Hollywood to movies.[20]

Cities whose range of economic function is exceedingly narrow seem frequently to lack variety of social style and suffer from deficiencies in "culture" and other civic virtues esteemed in most towns. Hence residents from other cities may make them the butts of jibes and the objects of social criticism. In the main, the outsider misses the mark for, like physicians whose identities have grown up around the practice of specific medical skills or about the "ownership" of specific bodily areas, the specialized city tends to glorify its command over special skills and resources. Two spokesmen for a pair of our most specialized cities link special skills with the spirit of America. The first is Malcolm Bingay, writing in *Detroit is My Home Town.*

This fluidity of life, this refusal to "jell" or ever to grow old helps to explain why everything that is right or wrong which happens to our nation seems to break here first. It is that very spirit which first conceived the idea of throwing away millions upon millions of dollars of machinery as obsolete to make way for better machinery and greater speed to meet competition. This horror of obsolescence is the "Americanism" which permitted us to triumph in two great wars. . . . Other countries remained static in the sense that while they understood our standardization of parts—to a degree—they never did catch the imponderable elements of mass production in which there is nothing permanent but change.[21]

The second spokesman is Carl Crow, who, in *The City of Flint,* writes:

The history of the interesting and dynamic city of Flint has been worth recording because it is more than the chronical of an individual city. It epitomizes the history of America . . . America is a story of the industrial development which has brought us such a high standard of living.[22]

Citizens who are intensely interested in the futherance of the arts con-gregate in groups and associations that many other citizens believe are less central to the life of the community than other more vigorous business, social, and cultural institutions representing the interests of the town's more typical citizens. Sometimes cultural barrenness is excused in terms of the city's symbolic age. Given sufficient time, some say, the city will grow up, develop a rich cultural life, and take its place among the civilized cities of its size—and, one might add, among some cities a tithe of its size. The residents of Chicago sometimes use this strategy to console themselves or to ward off attack, and it is probably commonly used in other cities. Here is an instance from Birmingham, Alabama:

Birmingham somehow, for all her pride in the great labors which converted a cornfield into a great metropolis in little more than the span of one man's life, Birmingham is haunted by a sense of promise unfulfilled. Her more philosophic citizens are obsessed with this thought. They brood and ponder over it, and, searching their souls and the city's history, constantly seek the reason why. They come up with many answers. One is the obvious one of her youth. . . . Another answer is . . . Birmingham is a working town. . . . Painting pictures and composing music and writing books—even the widespread appreciation of those things—all rather come with time.[23]

When a specialized city becomes economically diversified, and creates or draws to it new populations with new tastes, the imagery associated with it changes radically. It remains no longer merely a steel city, a rubber town, or an agricultural community, but is represented widely as a more cosmopolitan center.

Although every city within the United States is American in a factual sense, some cities are in some other sense denied that status from time to time. Many visitors to the Southwest would agree with John Gunther that there one may feel almost as if he is leaving the United States. ("The first thing I thought was, 'Can this possibly be North America?' ")[24] But that reaction is not aroused solely by regional geography or by ethnic culture, for cities may be symbolically driven off the American landscape when they offend deeply felt standards of propriety. One critic of Pittsburgh some years ago bitterly characterized it as "A city inherited from the Middle Ages," and only partly admitted that it was one of us.[25] Reno is frequently a target for obloquy: a Reader's Digest article titled "Reno. Parasite on Human Weakness" is representative; its author, true to his title, could not admit that Reno is genuinely American.[26] Even Los Angeles, although it shares national characteristics conspicuously enough, seems to strike many people as odd or crazy; and, "according to its most severe critics, it is New York in purple shorts with its brains knocked out." The phrase is George S. Perry's; in less fanciful prose he sums up very well the partial denial of status to that large city when he adds that its "civilization has been declared to caricature, in one way or another, that of the entire nation."[27]

The residents of certain other cities sometimes display sensitivity to the ways in which their cities deviate from what they or outside critics conceive to be the normal national or regional urban patterns. Cincinnati has never quite recovered from Mrs. Trollope's visit nor from its reputation as a tradition-bound town located within a progressive, dynamic region.[28] When a city begins its history with a great promise but then suffers relative oblivion, it departs sufficiently from the usual regional expectations to require a set of supporting rationalizations. Thus a loyal resident of Marietta, Ohio, in 1903 mournfully took stock of a century that had passed without much progress for his town. He remarked that

a city may open the way for progress, and still not progress itself. . . . Evidently others cities . . . have excelled her [Marietta] in so many ways. . . . But at the beginning of the new century she stands young, strong, and vigorous, no longer old, except in name, with an ambition of youth and wealth of resource. . . . While it has thus taken a century of experience during which time she seems to move forward so slowly, it is well to consider that these years were spent in laying a firm and substantial foundation whereon to build the New Marietta.[29]

In another passage, we can watch a citizen of Vincennes, Indiana, trying to puzzle out why prophesies about cities sometimes fail to materialize. Commenting on Vincennes' bustling future after "a sort of Rip Van Winkle sleep," he wrote:

This bright prospect although long delayed might have been expected from the opinions of the place and its natural advantages expressed by the missionary fathers who first visited it. . . . These men were far seeing and almost with prophetic vision foretold the future of various places they visited. . . . In no instance have their prophetic utterances failed of fruition unless it shall be in the solitary instance of Vincennes.[30]

In urging his contemporaries on to greater civic harmony and energy, he added, "They made the same prophetic utterances with reference to Pittsburgh, Cincinnati, Louisville, Detroit, Chicago, St. Paul, St. Louis, San Francisco and many other cities. . . . And why should not their opinions with regard to Vincennes not be realized?"

The residents of most cities can escape feelings of non-typicality simply by stressing other sets of American traits, but when cities develop in astonishingly new ways, their citizens must claim, as I have already suggested, that clearly sanctioned American qualities (rurality, urbanity, sectionality) are actually present or exist in new, somewhat disguised forms.

Most curious of all is the case of New York, a city which has been passionately and repeatedly denied essential American status while its admirers have proclaimed it the greatest city in America. It is one thing to feel that this great metropolis is not the most typical of our cities, that from it foreigners receive a skewed and partial picture of the nation; but it is another matter to believe that New York is partly or wholly not American, or even "un-American." The grounds of attack and defense bring to sharp focus the ambiguity and clash of American values.[31]

In 1894 Theodore Roosevelt published an article titled, "What 'Americanism' Means" in which he argued:

There are two or three sides to the question of Americanism, and two or three senses in which the word "Americanism" can be used to express the antithesis of what is unwholesome and undesirable. In the first place we wish to be broadly American and national, as opposed to being local or sectional.[32]

In the second place, he reports, it is unwholesome for an American to become Europeanized, thus too cosmopolitan; and in the third place, the meaning pertains to those foreign immigrants who do not become quickly Americanized. These antitheses, which run through the arguments for and against New York City, can be found in another article titled "Is New York More Civilized Than Kansas?" which follows almost immediately after Roosevelt's in the same journal.[33] Kansas is defined as the more civilized (that is, as the more American) on a score of grounds, which include its homogeneity of ideal and tradition, its native population, its home life, its lack of class distinction, its religious and moral tone, and its optimal conditions for rearing children. New York is declared not to possess most of these qualities. The author even argues that Kansas is less isolated, in the civilizational as well as the geographic sense, because its greater number of railroads keep it in more intimate contact with all sections of the nation.

Through the years, New York has been accused of being too European, too suspiciously cosmopolitan, too aggressive and materialistic, too hurried and hectic, a city where family life and home life do not flourish but where —it is asserted or suspected—iniquity does. New York seems to sum up all the negative balances in the rural animus against cities, in the sectional argument against centralization and cosmopolitanism, and in the frontier bias against cities which do not share the mystic pioneer experience. No other American city is the target of such great or complete antagonism.

New York's admirers, whether they are native to the city or not, counter these arguments in two ways. They can maintain that the city is not actually deficient in these various regards. For instance, the New York Times Magazine makes its business the occasional publication of articles about the city which tacitly or explicitly set out to prove that New York really is a friendly place having unsuspected village-like qualities, a quiet home life, plus bits of rurality and even farming tucked away here and there. They also try to show that the large numbers of immigrants and their children are at least as American as citizens with longer native genealogies. When New Yorkers write about themselves or about their city, their affirmation of urban identity often takes that form. (Al Smith once wrote an article titled "I Have Seven Million Neighbors.")[34]

Side by side with the outright accusation that New York fails to participate in our wholesome, rural, or village heritage runs the assertion that
New York is actually our most representative city because it is our greatest.
"Greatness" can be attributed on quite different grounds, for each assertion
rests upon certain features of American culture judged to be of the highest
importance. New York is our last frontier, the place where persons of spirit
are drawn as by a magnet. It is the "moving frontier" of American culture,
the most important site of progress and innovation. It is the image of
America, for here the melting pot is at its most intense and here the New
America—racially or culturally—is being forged rather than in the most
homogeneous native American centers. Although the same theme of the
urban melting pot as the epitome of American civilization is applied to
other ethnically diverse cities,[35] New York is a place where all narrow local
sectionalism has disappeared: because it is a great world city, as is
twentieth-century America—is not this the American century! Even those
who hate New York may have to admit New York's typicality on the grounds
that if this is the America of today, then New York certainly best represents
it. Here, for instance, is Earl Sparling's anguished summation, complete with
reference to the pioneer past:

I find it an appalling place, rich for making money, poor for living. . . . But all of
that is one thing. It is a different thing to shrug the whole spectacle away as
something completely alien and not American. America cannot be absolved that
easily. Not only is New York American, but it is the mirror in which America, after
half a century of confusion, suddenly sees herself for what she is. . . . New York is
the soul of America. And Americans . . . see it . . . and wonder how all this
happened in a free, pioneer land.[36]

Is it any wonder that there is so much ambiguity in the symbolization of
this metropolis, this New York which "is at once the climactic synthesis of
America, and yet the negation of America in that it has so many characteristics called un-American?"[37] The attitude—and the bewilderment—of
many Americans can be summed up in the reactions of a girl from the
Midwest who, visiting New York for the first time, exclaimed that it was
"just a wonderfully exciting place but so unreal; it doesn't even have trees."
It is summed up also in a magnificently paradoxical set of sentences written
by the editors of Fortune magazine, as they struggled to relate New York
City to the national culture:

New York may be taken as a symbol, or it may be taken as a fact. As a symbol it is
a symbol of America; its noisy, exuberant, incalculable towers rise out of the water
like a man's aspirations to freedom. As a symbol it is the Gateway, the promise, the
materialization of New World. . . . But taken as a fact, New York is less Dantesque.
To most Americans the fact is that "New York is not America." It is un-American in
lots of ways. The concentration of power that exists among those spires is itself
un-American; so are the tumultuous, vowel-twisting inhabitants who throng the
sidewalks.[38]

The confusion continues. Two pages later, when the editors eloquently discuss the city's role as a great melting pot, they write, "In that sense New York *is* America," only to blunt the force of that assertion with "more than symbolically."

The strain between ideal and reality, or ideal and presumed fact, runs like a brilliant thread through all our antithetical thinking about America and about our cities. With a fine flair for significant ambiguities, *The Saturday Evening Post* included among more than 145 cities which it surveyed after World War II an article about "a little cow town." Its author asserted that "*The Saturday Evening Post* is running a notable series of articles about American cities. All this is well enough, but . . . if we have any truly national culture, it stems from the small town and near-by farm."[39] George S. Perry, in his book, *Cities of America*, could not avoid including, either, a chapter about a town of two thousand people; and, like the editors of *Fortune*, he uses those interesting terms "fact" and "symbol"—except that he applies them to a small city. "Madison, Wisconsin," he sentimentalizes,

is both a fact and a symbol that stands for many of the finest traits in the American character. It is a place where independent people get up on their hind legs and have their say. Again, it is a seat of serious learning. Moreover, it is surrounded by that basic harmony that derives from good land that has been treated intelligently and with respect. Finally, Madison's people are almost spectacularly unapathetic. They are concerned, interested, and willing to do something about almost any public question. In many ways Madison and its environs are a miniature model of the ideal America of which many of us dream.[40]

Fact and symbol, symbol and fact: it is as if the United States had developed an urbanized economy without developing a thoroughly urbanized citizen. Americans entered a great period of city building during the nineteenth century protestingly, metaphorically walking backward; and to some extent they still do, but in exceedingly subtle ways. In the various sections of the next chapter [of *Images of the American City*], I shall deal both with this protest against cities, and with the regional differences between American urban cultures. In the foregoing pages, we have merely scratched the surface of American urban symbolism.

NOTES

1. John P. Kennedy, "Address. Delivered before the Maryland Institute for the Promotion of the Mechanical Arts, 21st October, 1851," *Occasional Addresses* (New York: Putnam, 1872), p. 244.

2. Paul de Rousiers, *American Life* (New York and Paris: Firming-Didot), p. 73.

3. John Gunther, *Inside U. S. A.* (New York: Harper, 1946), p. 369.

4. Cf. The collection of articles edited by Alexander Klein, *The Empire City, A Treasury of New York* (New York: Rinehart, 1955); or Paul Crowell and A. H. Raskin, "New York, 'Greatest City in the World,' " in Robert S. Allen, ed., *Our Fair City* (New York: Vanguard Press, 1947), esp. pp. 37–129.

5. This article was reprinted in the collection titled *Cities of America* (New York: Whittlesey House, McGraw-Hill, 1947), p. 244; see also Henry Haskell and Richard Fowler, *City of the Future. A Narrative History of Kansas City* (Kansas City: F. Glenn, 1950), pp. 16–17; and Darrel Garwood, *Crossroads of America. The Story of Kansas City* (New York: Norton, 1948), p. 327. The latter volume especially exemplifies the conception of "crossroads" as the basis for attributing more Americanism to Kansas City than to any other city.

6. Cf. "Midwestern Birthday," *Time,* LVIII (July 30, 1951), 14.

7. Frank C. Harper, *Pittsburgh: Forge of the Universe* (New York: Comet Press, 1957), p. 10; and *Pittsburgh and the Pittsburgh Spirit* (Pittsburgh: Chamber of Commerce, 1928), but especially the address by John Bowman, "Pittsburgh's Contribution to Civilization," pp. 1–10.

8. Angie Debo, *Tulsa: From Creek Town to Oil Capital* (Norman, Okla.: University of Oklahoma Press, 1945), p. vii.

9. For two excellent discussions of the agrarian myth see Richard Hofstadter, *The Age of Reform* (New York: Knopf, 1955), esp. Part I, "The Agrarian Myth and Commercial Realities," and Part II, "The Folklore of Populism"; and Henry Nash Smith, *Virgin Land. The American West as Symbol and Myth* (New York: Vintage Books, 1955, and Cambridge: Harvard University Press, 1950), esp. Book III, "The Garden of the World," pp. 138–305.

10. Cf. G. S. Perry, "Philadelphia," *The Saturday Evening Post,* CCXVIII (September 14, 1946), esp. p. 82.

11. "Portland, Oregon," *The Saturday Evening Post,* CCXIX (March 1, 1947), 23.

12. "Springfield, Illinois," *ibid.* (September 27, 1947), 28.

13. This theme can be readily recognized in such books on older Eastern cities as Struthers Burt, *Philadelphia* (Garden City: Doubleday, Doran, 1945), and Cleveland Amory, *The Proper Bostonians* (New York: Dutton, 1947).

14. John Bowman, in Harper, *Pittsburgh and the Pittsburgh Spirit,* pp. 5–9.

15. Dorsha Hayes, *Chicago, Crossroads of American Enterprise* (New York: Julian Messner, 1944), p. 300; and Clara de Chambrun, *Cincinnati* (New York: Scribner, 1939), p. 319.

16. Cf. Robert G. Rhett, *Charleston. An Epic of Carolina* (Richmond, Va.: Garrett and Massie, 1940).

17. Howard Long, *Kingsport, A Romance of Industry* (Kingsport, Tenn.: The Sevier Press, 1928), pp. 76, 3–4.

18. *Op. cit.,* pp. 369–70, 549.

19. *Op. cit.,* p. 37.

20. "Reno," *The Saturday Evening Post,* CCXXV (July 5, 1952), 70, 72.

21. (Indianapolis: Bobbs-Merrill, 1946), p. 19.

22. (New York: Harper, 1945), p. 205.

23. "Birmingham, Alabama," *The Saturday Evening Post,* CCXX (September 6, 1947), 22.

24. *Op. cit.,* pp. 886–906, esp. p. 895.

25. F. Stother, "What Kind of Pittsburgh Is Detroit?" *World's Work,* LII (October 1926), 633–9.

26. Anthony Abbott in *Reader's Digest,* LX (February 1952), 119–22.

27. *Op. cit.,* pp. 232, 233.

28. Alvin Harlow refers to Mrs. Trollope in *The Serene Cincinnatians* (New York: Dutton, 1950).

29. Thomas J. Summers, *History of Marietta* (Marietta, Ohio: Leader Publishing Co., 1903), pp. 319–20.

30. Henry Cauthorn, *A History of the City of Vincennes, Indiana* (Cleveland: Arthur H. Clark Co., 1901), p. 220.

31. For some representative statements, pro and con, see: Mark Sullivan, "Why the West Dislikes New York. The Eternal Conflict Between City and Country," *World's Work,* LXI (1926), 406–11; "New York City," *Fortune,* XX (1939), 73–5, 83–5; Charles Merz, "The Attack on New York," *Harper's,* CLXIII (1926), 81–7; Earl Sparling, "Is New York American?" *Scribner's,* LXXX (1931), 165–73; Paul Crowell and A. H. Raskin, in Allen, *op. cit.,* pp. 38–9; Anonymous, "What is America?" *Nation,* CXXVIII (1921), 755; and Robert Benchley, "The Typical New Yorker," in Alexander Klein, *op. cit.,* pp. 338–42.

32. *Forum,* XVII (1894), 196–200.

33. J. W. Gleed in *ibid.,* pp. 217–34.

34. *American Magazine,* CXVI (August 1933), 36–8.

35. Elsie Morrow, "South Bend," *The Saturday Evening Post,* CCXXIV (June 14, 1942), 87; and "Brooklyn," *ibid.,* CCXIX (December 26, 1946), 14.

36. *Op. cit.,* pp. 165–73.

37. Gunther, *op. cit.,* p. 549.

38. *Op. cit.,* p. 73.

39. E. R. Jackman, "Burns, Oregon," *The Saturday Evening Post,* CCXX (January 31, 1948), 2.

40. *Op. cit.,* p. 221.

PART TWO

CITIES IN THE NEW WORLD, 1607-1800

America, according to traditional historians, began with an anachronism—society in the wilderness. Until recently scholars have emphasized the wilderness rather than society as the marrow of colonial America. Presumably, lonely men—and later, women and children—landed on rock-strewn coasts, hewed out rude encampments, and only gradually fought back the forests and fought off hostile Indians. In a wilderness setting the drama unfolded: the pioneers slowly gathered together into settled colonies; the colonies melded into political and economic units; and the units, in response to British imperial pressure, evolved into a nation. In 1790 the first federal census revealed the character of this nation: 95 percent of the population lived in rural areas or on one of several frontiers. America, according to the celebrated thesis of Frederick Jackson Turner, continually began anew on the frontier, "the meeting place between savagery and civilization." So generations of historians have narrated the plot of the nation's birth.

But the wilderness setting is misleading, if not completely illusionary. Society, not the wilderness, was the point of departure for colonial America. It was in early towns and cities that colony-wide and then national unity had its origins. From the beginning, America was an exercise in community settlement, an experiment in social order.

The very wildness of the New World demanded the creation of ordered communities. For protection against hostile Indians and the rigors of an unfamiliar environment, the colonists built fortress-like settlements. For a just and profitable distribution of agricultural lands, they gathered together in a handful of central locations instead of scattering over the countryside. To preserve and promote their religious institutions and to ward off the temptations of pride and profit that might lure them from old ways in a new land, they joined with one another in community settlement. To meet their colonial obligations as pawns in a European struggle for new markets and expanded trade routes, they banded together to found successful commercial centers, for in the wilderness anything less than success meant an end to survival. Thus, north and south along the Atlantic coastline, migrants planted colonies that were examples of communal order.

Whether in Virginia or Massachusetts, Georgia or Pennsylvania, the Carolinas or New York, the town was the characteristic mode of settlement. Towns evidenced a sense of community recently described by historian Kenneth A. Lockridge as "conservative corporatism"—a kind of enduring organization protecting the internal harmony of a stable membership, a single coalition ordering "land, taxation, regulation, morality." Although political, religious, and cultural differences distinguished towns from each other, the township system as an expression of unity, peace, and order suffused the landscape of colonial America. Two examples will illustrate this point.

In 1604 an English joint-stock company (a forerunner of the modern business corporation) formed, received a charter from the Crown, and planned a voyage to the New World. In 1607 the stockholders sent colonists to America. Landing in the vicinity of Chesapeake Bay, the settlers laid out the makings of a town. They built a fortified trading post, erected thatched houses, raised a central warehouse for economic supplies, and constructed a church. Although they immediately encountered unfriendly Indians and the specter of starvation, their discovery of the economic possibilities inherent in the tobacco weed promised to assure them of survival. Captain John Smith, an original settler and the town's first historian, described (with typical booster enthusiasm) the location for settlement as "a verie fit place for the erecting of a great cittie." By 1619 Jamestown, if not yet a "great cittie," was a thriving enterprise. Jamestowners had spread settlements out along three different rivers in the Virginia colony and had created some eleven other towns, or "plantations," as they called them.

To the north, other trading companies sent expeditions, hoping to found profit-making settlements to tap the presumably unbounded wealth of the New World. In 1620 the Plymouth Company, heeding the proposals of a group of English religious dissenters living in Holland who wished to emigrate, underwrote the expenses of transporting the Pilgrims to America. On the voyage the settlers drew up the famed Mayflower Compact, justly labeled the first "squatters' agreement" in American history. That document served as the first municipal charter in America. Its signers set the tone for future urban settlements by agreeing that for the purposes of preservation and order they would unite in a "civil Body Politick," a community of men under widely accepted laws and constitutions. Those who signed the Mayflower Compact and who survived the initial harsh winter of settlement became the "freemen"— those entitled to vote, to hold office, and to oversee the community's functioning. In essence, they were the original aldermen in the New World. Their kind of community organization, in slightly altered local forms, typified the subsequent founding of New England towns like Dedham, Sudbury, and Andover.

Later colonists repeated the Jamestown and Plymouth experiments. Both American necessity and European experience demanded fledgling urban settlements. The Englishmen who flocked to America during the seventeenth century left behind a nation whose prosperity and international prominence rested upon close connections among London and England's provincial cities. The Dutchmen who planted New Amsterdam on foreign shores (when it fell under English control in 1664 it was renamed New York) came from one of the most urbanized of European countries. The Quakers who settled Philadelphia in the 1680s, the London philanthropists in the early eighteenth century who dreamed of a Georgia colony dotted with checkerboard villages—these and other promoters of the New World were Old World men who associated economic, cultural, political, and intellectual life with an urban existence. They knew that the very word "civilization" meant an area characterized by cities as opposed to unpopulated or wilderness regions. Consequently, the patterns of town settlement in America unfolded along lines of European sentiment and practice. Although colonial urbanites rarely numbered over some 8 percent of the total population, they comprised a vitally important minority. Both as the outposts of empire and as expressions of the ordered hopes of men in the wilderness, towns and cities became the influential centers of colonial settlement in America.

By 1690 the five significant colonial cities were thriving. New York dated from 1625; Boston, from 1630; Newport, Rhode Island, from 1639; Charleston ("Charles Town," South Carolina), from 1680; and Philadelphia, from 1682. Smaller cities like Savannah, Norfolk, and Baltimore followed soon after. As described by historian Carl Bridenbaugh, the five major cities shared certain important and revealing similarities.

First, each of the major cities had arisen on a site geographically favorable for the ocean trade that had justified its initial founding. New York enjoyed the finest natural harbor on the Atlantic seaboard, but even a city like Philadelphia, planted 100 miles inland at the juncture of the navigable Delaware and Schuylkill rivers, had ready access to the water highways of the world. The second similarity derived from the first: all were commercial cities. Throughout the seventeenth century and well into the

eighteenth, Boston remained the dominant port, but each of the
others grew on a base of expanding commercial activity.

Third, each city bordered on a promising backcountry or hinterland—
promising in the context of the seventeenth and early eighteenth centuries.
There was little doubt that economically (and otherwise) the colonial
cities faced eastward, across 3,000 miles of ocean, toward the Old World.
But by the end of the seventeenth century the cities had begun to glance
westward as well, into the interior of the continent. The urban colonists
were themselves colonialists, men who recognized and wanted to grasp
economic opportunities for exploiting their own hinterlands. Already, as
geographer Jean Gottmann has observed, the colonial cities had
become the economic hinges of the continent, a string of eastern ports
that linked together the marketplaces of Europe and the interior of
America. Indeed, the colonialist ambitions of early urban Americans one
day would contribute to the disruption of British imperial rule. The
port cities would remain hinges, but hinges swung increasingly in the
interests of American profit.

All of the cities were fundamentally British in origin and development. By the
turn of the eighteenth century, to be sure, Puritan New England contained
French Huguenots in its larger towns and Scotch-Irish on its frontiers;
Philadelphia contained German, Danish, Swedish, Scottish, Irish, Dutch,
and French immigrants; and Charleston held a number of French
Huguenots. Nevertheless, for most of the seventeenth century the Dutch
of New Amsterdam had constituted the only major non-British group
of political importance in any of the cities. Once England had taken
over, that last vestige of non-British population had begun to wane. By
1700 New York City probably was more cosmopolitan in its population than
most European cities, yet its ruling groups were Anglo-Saxons. As the
eighteenth century wore on, the diversity of the urban population
increased. Europeans and African slaves entered the cities in ever-larger
numbers. A population mixture became one of the clearest indicators of
a growing division between city and country in the colonies. The
"Americans of 1776" included a motley assortment of nationalities. Still, by
the eve of the revolution, the dominant groups in each of the major cities
were of British lineage. Anglo-conformity—the principle that newcomers
had to adopt English customs and behavioral patterns—reigned in the
colonial cities. And, because the leadership groups shared a common
British background, urban dwellers tended to share similar political
institutions, emphasizing the "rights" of Englishmen.

Once founded, the cities experienced fairly rapid rises in population. As early as the 1650s, for example, Boston could claim over 2,000 citizens and a visitor could report in awe that it was a "sumptuous city," the "Center Towne and Metropolis of this Wildernesse," a "City-like Towne crowded on the Sea-bankes and wharfed out with great industry and cost," its streets lined with a "continued concourse of people." By the close of the seventeenth century the largest colonial cities were not small in relation to cities elsewhere in the world. In 1690 Boston contained 7,000 people; Philadelphia, 4,000; New York, 3,900; Newport, 2,600; and Charleston, 1,100. Despite the incidence of disease and the high mortality rates in the cities, populations increased in size and density throughout the eighteenth century. On the eve of the revolution Philadelphia with its 40,000 citizens was the largest of the colonial cities. New York held 25,000 people; Boston, 16,000; Charleston, 12,000; Newport, 11,000; and such secondary cities as Baltimore, Norfolk, and Providence housed, respectively, 6,000, 6,000, and 4,400 residents. Since, as a seaport, each city at any one time hosted a large transient population of seamen, buyers and sellers of goods, dockworkers, and others engaged in commercial activity, these figures probably represent a lower population size than the cities actually enjoyed.

Looking at the figures from a modern perspective, the temptation is to reject the phrase "colonial urbanization" as a misnomer. But urban size was historically and geographically relative. Within their own geographical regions, the colonial cities exercised an impact far out of proportion to their actual populations. In the New World, with its dispersed, agrarian population, a city of 5,000 or 10,000 inhabitants was a metropolis. Throughout the British Empire during the eighteenth century only London and one or two provincial English cities were any larger than Boston, Philadelphia, or New York. As the centers of an expanding and increasingly prosperous citizenry, colonial American cities deserved to be called "urban."

Population size alone, however, was not the crucial reason that such communities served as urban centers. Economically the cities functioned as centers for distributing the raw goods of the colonies to Europe and the finished goods of England throughout the colonies. The cities anchored a beginning network of communications that bound the colonists more closely together. They operated as listening posts for the intellectual soundings being taken in eighteenth-century Europe. With their bookstores, libraries, museums, and scientific associations, the cities also dominated colonial culture. Finally, as historian Carl Bridenbaugh and others have noted, the cities were "urban" in their collective response to social problems. A sense of community responsibility and power differentiated town from country society during the colonial period. City residents confronted some of the basic problems that have continued to plague urban dwellers down to the present. Congested housing, the dangers of fire, the ravages of disease, pollution in the streets and in the air, crime and inadequate police forces—such social problems are as old as our cities themselves. Only the nature of the collective urban response has changed over time.

The extent of response in colonial times depended largely upon the reactions of the economically and politically influential citizens. And in colonial cities a rising merchant class formed the most powerful of pressure groups. From the close of the seventeenth century until the revolution, commercial expansion in each of the seaport cities contributed to the creation of a merchant elite. As early as the 1720s, groups of successful traders, often acting together in loose concert, were beginning to exercise leadership. Because they were the wealthiest individuals in the cities, the merchants dominated the urban social and cultural life. They owned the largest homes, partied at the fanciest balls, most heavily supported the local arts, and occasionally contributed huge sums of money to philanthropic agencies. Because they comprised the one coherent economic interest group in the cities, the merchants usually carried the day on questions of local financial practices, new building construction, town safety (the protection of private property), and even street patterns in physically growing communities. Because their own livelihoods were intertwined so intimately with the maturing of the cities and the urban colonial status within the empire, they entered the political arena at home and abroad in increasing numbers. Throughout the first half of the eighteenth century merchants in all of the cities experienced a deepening sense of their own group interests as distinct from those of others. By mid-century they were merging into a separate and identifiable urban social class. In each city, as well as in each colony, the merchants were the only group sharing a generally common outlook on the economic and political problems of the day.

Chief among the external problems was the relationship of the colonies to England. From the 1670s to the turn of the century England had attempted to enforce existing laws and had passed new laws governing the commercial and internal relationships of the American colonies. In practice this meant that England had tried to exert stronger control over the merchant classes of the major cities. As early as 1673, when the empire sent its first customs commissioners to Boston and other ports, the merchants had protested that the sudden enforcement of the navigation acts violated the rights of Englishmen in the colonies, a charge others would repeat and back with force a century later. However, the flurry of British legislation and enforcement soon subsided. From the early eighteenth century until the 1760s the British again relaxed their grip on the colonies; a period of "salutary neglect" ensued, interrupted only briefly by the passage of the Molasses Act in 1733. That act, levied upon a major item of trade along the Atlantic seaboard and a New England staple in international commerce, could have aroused the ire of colonial merchants and led to hostilities. But it never was enforced rigidly. Even in Boston, where customs officials did attempt a crackdown, the merchants found that collectors would accept coins instead of certification. Where bribery failed, enterprising merchants like John Hancock turned to smuggling and quickly amassed fortunes.

Beginning in 1763 salutary neglect gave way to imperial reorganization. Under George Grenville, the new Chancellor of the Exchequer, the empire tightened the reins of colonial administration. First the Sugar Act (1764) and then the Stamp Act (1765) demonstrated British determination to profit from and closely control the colonial economy. The New World cities, experiencing an economic recession in the wake of the French and Indian War, were hardest hit by the reorganization scheme. The urban merchant class suffered the heaviest losses. A Philadelphia writer asked, "What is your City without Trade, and what the Country without a market to vend their commodities?" The Boston town meeting was more explicit, noting that "our Trade has for a long time labored under great discouragements, and it is with the deepest concern that we see such further Difficulties coming upon it, as will reduce it to the lowest Ebb, if not totally obstruct and ruin it." To make up their losses, merchants in Boston and elsewhere tried to expand their commercial areas. But legitimate trade and smuggling became ever more difficult. They then turned to the urban hinterlands to increase their spheres of influence. In this endeavor Philadelphia and New York merchants enjoyed more success than those of Boston. Indeed, of all the merchant classes in the cities, Boston traders had shared the least in the general prosperity of the 1740s and 1750s and saw their economic possibilities most crimped by British activities during the 1760s.

For all of their economic problems Boston merchants blamed the British. To better their opportunities, they organized as a pressure group, hoping to gain relief from the General Court of Massachusetts, to communicate with their counterparts in other cities, and to correspond with influential members of Parliament. Merchants in New York and Philadelphia soon followed suit. These merchants' associations provided much of the early resistance against Great Britain. Resistance to the empire came first in the colonial cities. There organization was easiest and grievances were strongest. Although the merchants were first to organize and resist, other urban groups quickly joined the struggle.

The general social structure in the cities had begun to change by the mid-eighteenth century. A prosperous and growing "middle class" was emerging. By 1760 perhaps two-thirds of all urban inhabitants, as defined occupationally, could be called middle-class: the artisans, shopkeepers, clerical workers, and a variety of skilled tradesmen constituted this new and increasingly important element in the population. Feeling the weight of recession and imperial reorganization nearly as heavily as were the merchants, and demanding a greater voice in local affairs, middle-class tradesmen and artisans started forming their own organizations. Further down the social ladder were those whom contemporaries called the "inferior sort." This class included free and slave blacks, indentured servants, Indians, mulattoes, unskilled laborers, and, as the largest group, the seamen, who provided the underpinnings of the cities' commercial activities. Next to black slaves, probably no more shabbily treated, socially depressed group than the seamen lived in the cities. British actions —chiefly impressment into the Royal Navy—and ill treatment from local city leaders made the seamen potentially the most explosive and violent group in the colonial cities. To protect themselves, and to protest the effects of imperial reorganization on their own employment, the urban lower classes organized. It was no accident that the Boston Massacre in 1770 involved a pitched battle between British soldiers and those whom John Adams described as "a motley rabble of saucy boys, negroes and molattoes, Irish teagues and out landish jack tarrs" (sailors). By the early 1770s, then, shifts in the internal social composition of colonial cities coalesced with economic recession and British intransigence to create a catalyst for revolt.

To argue that without urban discontent there would have been no American Revolution would be to exaggerate. For any explosion many elements have to come together. No flight of imagination is necessary, however, to see that the earliest sparks of rebellion flashed in the colonial cities. As the subsequent events of the revolution occurred, the cities remained in the front lines of action. First Boston, then other cities felt the impact of British occupation, suffered heavy population losses and widespread damage to commercial activities, and underwent a gradual attempt to recoup life and fortune after the final cessation of hostilities. Certainly the role played by the cities in shaping the forces leading to revolution must not be underestimated.

Nor should the importance of cities in the emergence of the new nation be undervalued. Major and secondary cities—Boston, New York, Philadelphia, Charleston, Baltimore, Albany, and Pittsburgh, among others—provided crucial leadership in building the United States. Urban commerce linked together the newly independent states; urban leaders successfully rallied their forces in the ratifying conventions for the Constitution; city newspapers advertised the concept of "union" and proved influential in promoting the Federalist cause.

From the earliest days of settlement in the New World until the settled world of a new nation, towns and cities occupied stage center in the drama of American development. From the outposts of empire, towns and cities evolved into communities in the wilderness. From the tinderboxes of revolution, cities developed into the foundries of a nation. By the end of the eighteenth century the cities had demonstrated their vitality in the American experience. Like their counterparts in other times and other places, American cities had emerged as the crucibles of civilization.

4. THE ABSENCE OF TOWNS IN SEVENTEENTH-CENTURY VIRGINIA

John C. Rainbolt

The Reverend Mr. John Clayton failed to provide the members of the Royal Society of London with the new and curious information they so relished when he reported in 1688 that the Virginia "Plantations run over vast Tracts of Ground . . . whereby the Country is thinly inhabited, their liveing is solitary & unsociable; tradeing confused, & dispersed; besides other inconviencys . . . ."[1] By the end of the seventeenth century the Virginians' failure to develop compact settlements was notorious.[2] What every knowledgeable Englishman knew in 1700, every attentive schoolboy knows today, for no textbook on early American history is complete without reference to the absence of towns in Virginia during the Tidewater period of its history. Historians attribute many of the peculiarities of the Old Dominion to this demographic pattern. The paucity of schools in comparison to colonial New England; the diffusion of power in a society lacking a center comparable to Philadelphia, Boston, New York, or Charleston; the weakness of institutional religion; the decay of the traditional militia system; the absence of a merchant class—these were all consequences, in part, of Virginia's failure to develop any significant ports or towns.

To explain the absence of towns in Virginia historians have stressed geographic influences and have implied that the basic social values and mental outlook of the colonists reinforced the environmental influences. The numerous navigable rivers and tributaries reaching inland from Chesapeake Bay permitted direct access to ocean-going vessels and reduced the need for commercial centers. The soil and climate facilitated the growth of tobacco which, owing to its tendency to deplete the soil, encouraged land engrossment and further discouraged compact settlement. Allegedly, these physical conditions were strengthened by the nascent agrarian values of seventeenth-century Virginians, whose attitudes anticipated the more sophisticated agrarian philosophy of Jeffersonian Virginia with its scorn for city life.[3] Finally, the colonial Virginians are said to have been skeptical towards efforts to shape the social and economic order to accord with

Reprinted from the *Journal of Southern History*, XXXV (August 1969), 343–60. Copyright 1969 by the Southern Historical Association. Reprinted by permission of the Managing Editor.

preconceived and unrealistic notions of what ought to emerge in the New World. Much of the writing on colonial America emphasizes that the environment rapidly produced practical habits of mind which led the settlers to become contemptuous of the efforts of armchair theorists in England to impose visionary schemes on America. In line with this general approach, scholars have implied that Virginians were skeptical of schemes to create towns artificially in the colony.[4]

These three themes offer a logical explanation for the evolution of the pattern of settlement in Virginia, yet there is ample evidence that Virginians did seek to overcome the geographic environment, and this evidence compels a rephrasing of the question. The proper formulation of the problem is not what forces prevented the emergence of towns but why Virginia leaders failed to overcome the geographic barriers to the creation of the centralized economic and social activity they so desired.

Articulate Englishmen both at home and in Virginia during the first century of the colony's history did not adhere to any incipient agrarian philosophy. The early promoters of colonial expansion assumed that the settlers in England's plantations would erect towns, and concern developed early in Virginia's history over the absence of compact settlements.[5]

The desire for towns increased when the price of Virginia's staple fell from the high rates which prevailed initially. At the end of the 1620s the price of tobacco collapsed, and for the remainder of the century prices fluctuated but remained low.[6] Throughout the last half of the seventeenth century, when the economic crisis in the tobacco market was most acute, analysts of Virginia were especially quick to suggest that the lack of towns lay at the heart of the province's economic difficulties. One theme appeared again and again: Virginia was the oldest colony and had more natural advantages than other provinces on the mainland but had failed to prosper owing to the lack of urban stimulus to economic activity.[7]

Increasingly, too, as the seventeenth century progressed, writers on Virginia, both in England and in the colony, emphasized that settlement in towns was necessary for an adequate social order. From the beginning of the colony its leaders had unconsciously associated compact settlement with social control, especially of the common people. Edwin Sandys, for example, wrote of the need for "orderly villages" in Virginia.[8] The early implicit association of towns and order became explicit in the second half of the seventeenth century. Concern for preserving authority increased because of periodic outbreaks of revolts by slave and indentured servants in the third quarter of the century and because of the general rise in social and political tension in the decades preceding and following Bacon's Rebellion.[9] Virginia's emerging planter elite came to appreciate the argument that towns might facilitate "good Discipline and careful tending . . . under faithful Teachers and Magistrates . . . ."[10]

Bacon's Rebellion especially fostered the belief that the colony needed towns for social and political as well as economic considerations. The dispersed mode of settlement on isolated plantations was cited as one of the fundamental causes of the revolt. The author of "Virginias Deploured Condition" explained that the lack of compact settlement in towns and the engrossing of large areas of land for plantations had forced the poorer planters to seek land in areas where they came into conflict with the Indians.[11] Philip Ludwell after the revolt urged the crown to encourage more compact settlements, and a proposal probably written immediately after the upheaval advocated the establishment of a port town in conjunction with a fort on each of the major rivers for protection both in time of war and in any future rebellion.[12] Nicholas Spencer reflected the impact of continued economic difficulties and political rebellion when he noted in 1680 that Virginians "are now growne sensible that our present necessityes, & too much to be doubted future miseryes are much heightened by our wild & Rambleing way of Liveing . . . ."[13] In contrast to the intellectual leaders of Jeffersonian Virginia, who extolled an agrarian life which facilitated greater individualism and mitigated against excessive control by political and religious institutions, articulate Virginians of the first century of the colony's history believed that authority was essential for social stability. They came to fear the wholly agrarian society for the same reasons that led later Virginians to praise it.

Indeed, the absence of towns seemed to seventeenth-century Englishmen at home and in the colony to produce an existence out of harmony with nature and with man's best inclinations. Shortly after the Restoration a Virginia clergyman argued that except for *"Hermites,"* the isolated way of living of Virginians differed from that of all other Christians, who settled in compact ways to facilitate regular public worship.[14] At the end of the century Francis Makemie charged that his fellow Virginians set themselves apart from all other creatures in God's universe. ". . . I must send them for a pattern to the whole World," he wrote; "yea, and to be upbraided by the Heathen Nations, who generally do cohabit. Let the Brute Beasts Check them, who generally resort together in Droves; I'll send them to the Fishes of the Sea, who swim together in shoals; The very fouls of the Air do flock together."[15] The wholly agrarian society thus appeared as an economic liability, a threat to social stability, and a violation of nature's decree.

Virginia's leaders rarely considered the possibility that the absence of towns might be an inevitable, irreversible consequence of the geography of the Chesapeake Bay area. Throughout the century the colony's rulers shared the assumption revealed by the anonymous poet who wrote in 1612 to promote the Virginia lottery:

Who knowes not *England* once was like
  a Wildernesse and savage place,
Till government and use of men,
  that wildnesse did deface:
And so *Virginia* may in time,

be made like *England* now;
Where long-lovd peace and plenty both,
    sits smiling on her brow.[16]

Like this poet, Virginia's leaders had unbounded confidence in the ability
of man, working through government, to "deface" nature as he desired.
However much Virginians in the last half of the century might have condemned such specific manifestations of British mercantilism as the Navigation Acts, they did not question the basic premises of the mercantilistic
economic-political mind. Like most Englishmen, Virginia's elite throughout
the century believed that government regulations and encouragement
could in large measure determine the nature of a society and its economy.

This assumption took concrete form in legislative schemes designed to
promote "cohabitation" in towns, especially port cities. In the first half of
the century sporadic efforts were made to make Jamestown the focus for
much of the colony's trade. After mid-century many legislative sessions
considered comprehensive schemes to transform the basic economic and
social structure of the province by creating port towns. On six occasions—
1655, 1662, 1680, 1685, 1691, and 1705—legislation to achieve this goal
passed the Assembly. The last three were suspended by the crown after
partial implementation.[17] In framing the laws the legislators relied heavily
upon restrictive provisions and coercion. Every statute forbade the lading
of tobacco or the sale of imports except at designated locations. The act of
1655, for example, decreed that traders could sell merchandise outside
the proposed centers of trade only after goods had remained unsold for
eight months. Each statute required counties to finance the construction of
public warehouses to accommodate trade. However, the Assembly increasingly tended to supplement coercion with persuasion by offering positive
inducements. The law passed in 1680 exempted from many taxes the
planters who settled in the proposed port towns and also stayed the collection of the debts of town residents for five years.[18]

These port acts were not thrust upon skeptical colonials. The first major
effort to develop towns in Virginia occurred during the Interregnum when
the influence of the home government on the affairs of the province was
minimal. During much of the 1650s Virginia was an autonomous colony.
In that decade, moreover, the lower house of the Assembly garnered
virtually all power and political initiative into its hands. The town measure
passed in 1662, although initiated by Governor William Berkeley, commanded the eager support of the colonial burgesses. Sir William reported
that the representatives supported the bill "w[i]th all chearfullnesse . . .
[and] with this unanimous Confession, that w[i]thout one, wee could
not long be civil, rich, or happy, that it was the first step to our security
from our Indian Enemies, and the onely meanes to bring in those Commodities all wise men had so long expected from us."[19] In 1680 the
burgesses were so eager to secure Governor Thomas Lord Culpeper's
consent to the "cohabitation" act that they agreed in return to establish a

permanent revenue fund for the provincial government. In 1691 the lower house endorsed the port act by an overwhelming margin of 38 to 1.[20]

Despite the desire and the numerous efforts to promote "cohabitation," port towns had not developed when the Tidewater period of Virginia history drew to a close in the early decades of the eighteenth century. As late as 1716 Hampton was described as the "place of the greatest trade in all Virginia." It consisted of but "one hundred houses . . . few of them of any note . . . ."[21] The paper port of Marlborough symbolized the failure of Virginians to achieve their goals. Marlborough had been designated by cohabitation acts as a suitable location for a thriving commercial center. After each act passed the Assembly, but before word of the crown's disapproval arrived, a flurry of activity occurred as lots in the area were purchased and construction of houses and warehouses was begun. But in 1726 there was only one small building twenty feet square to recall the hope that Marlborough would emerge a great port.[22]

The failure of Virginians to score even modest successes in the struggle against geography is explained, in part, by the unrealistic and impatient attitude with which they approached the task. In turning to government action to promote commercial centralization and social stability the burgesses in particular exhibited little of the skepticism supposedly characteristic of colonial attitudes toward the modification of their environment. Indeed the representatives in the lower house were invariably less realistic in their expectations and methods than were the English merchants, the home government, or the members of the provincial Council. The burgesses desired legislation which would simply declare that all trade would be confined to designated locations after a specified date regardless of the commercial facilities available. The major tobacco merchants, the crown, and the Council objected to this approach. They continually but unsuccessfully pointed out that trade could not be thus restricted until adequate storage facilities were constructed at the sites. The lower house, however, would not accept the argument that trade patterns should be "courted" rather than "forced."[23]

Equally unrealistic was the tendency of the representatives to demand the promotion of an excessive number of towns. Each burgess desired to have his own county blessed with a thriving port city, and the burgesses as a group "always appointed too many Towns . . . for every Man desiring the Town to be as near as is possible to his own Door . . . they have commonly contriv'd a Town for Every County . . . ."[24] One critic asserted that "every one being more sollicitous for a private Interest and Conveniency, than for a publick," demanded "Forty Towns at once, that is, two in every County, or none at all, which is the Countries Ruine."[25] These indictments were only slight exaggerations. In formulating a port act in 1685 the lower house initially demanded the creation of forty-five towns and only reluctantly compromised on a bill to create one port for each county.[26]

The unrealistic approach of the burgesses not only demonstrated their narrow concern for the local interests of their counties, but it reflected as well their faith in the unlimited ability of government to engage in social and economic engineering. The confidence of the burgesses may well have been an accurate representation of the sentiments of the common planters. To be sure, the numerous small farmers left few indications of their views, and the meager hints which survive do not all point in the same direction. Yet, on balance, the data indicate that the common planters did not so much resent the government's effort to force the growth of towns as they condemned the absence of immediate results.

Nathaniel Bacon in his efforts to appeal to the masses in 1676 did not repudiate the idea that the provincial government should act to shape the economy and the social order; rather, he apparently believed that he could best attract support by charging that the corruption of Berkeley and his clique had prevented adequate and effective action. The first accusation in Bacon's "Declaration of the People" condemned Sir William's government "For having upon specious pretences of Publick works raised unjust Taxes upon the Commonalty for the advancement of private Favourits and other sinnister ends but noe visible effects in any measure adequate."[27] The second charge pointed out that Berkeley in spite of his long tenure in office had not "in any measure advanced this hopefull Colony either by Fortifications, Townes or Trade."[28]

The grievances of the people as reported by the special commissioners dispatched to Virginia by Charles II to investigate the causes of Bacon's Rebellion also indicate that the common planters did not oppose government intervention in the economy but that they wanted immediate fruits from such efforts. The people of Isle of Wight County, for example, complained of "The great Quantityes of Tobacco levyed for Building Houses of publick use and reception at James Town, which were not habitable, but fell downe before the Finishing them."[29] Surry County echoed these sentiments, complaining "That great quantityes of tobacco were levied upon the poore inhabitants of this Collony for the building of houses att James Citty, which were not inhabitable by reason they were not finished."[30]

The suggestion then that towns did not develop because Virginia's burgesses or the planters for whom they spoke reflected a skeptical attitude toward economic planning could not be further amiss. Both representatives and planters expected government action to remold economy and society immediately. This resulted in the grandiose and impractical town acts and subsequently in resentment and a disinclination on the part of the planters to sustain such acts when the initial results proved disappointing. Had the burgesses had less confidence in the possibility of translating abstract visions into social and economic realities they might have formulated more modest but more effective policies.

A second impediment to effective town promotion lay in the conflicting views on the objectives of the cohabitation schemes. The crown, the English merchants, and the councilors on the one hand and the burgesses on the other gradually developed differing rationales for port legislation. In 1660 the leadership of the colony and the crown had been in substantial agreement that towns would somehow spur the diversification of Virginia's economy along the traditional lines envisioned by the old Virginia Company.[31] The forwarding of town growth became the explicit expression of a view, common to crown and colony as late as the Restoration, that Virginia's proper place in the emerging empire was to fulfill the Elizabethan vision of a province supplying the mother country with a variety of staples. The effort to create towns for this purpose evidenced a belief in the compatible interests of province and mother country.

Gradually this affinity of purpose broke down. By the last quarter of the century the burgesses in particular regarded commercial centralization as a means of fostering manufactures and of decreasing Virginia's economic and, to some extent, cultural dependence upon England. Edward Randolph warned in 1692 that the General Assembly was again drawing up a law to promote towns and that "one maine end of towns is to settle Manufactures & to live without any dependence upon Eng[lan]d . . . ."[32] Randolph, as was his habit, doubtless exaggerated the extent to which the burgesses desired economic autonomy. Yet he did recognize an important change in the motive behind the lower house's demand for cohabitation laws. The burgesses candidly admitted their expectation that a consequence of town growth would be an increase in local manufacture of goods previously imported from England.[33]

Robert Beverley reflected the attitude of the burgesses when he published *The History and Present State of Virginia* in 1705. A leading advocate of town promotion and diversification, he called upon Virginians to increase their economic self-sufficiency and lamented that they derived "no Benefit nor Refreshment from the Sweets, and precious things they have growing amongst them, but make use of the Industry of *England* for all such things."[34] Beverley thought Virginians should export more and different raw materials to England, but he hoped that the settlers would send to the mother country only the excess remaining after domestic manufacturers had satisfied the needs of the colony. Beverley no longer accepted as adequate the role in the empire assigned to Virginia by traditional mercantile concepts. Instead his writings imply an empire characterized by conflict of interests. He and the burgesses for whom he spoke had little sympathy for the notion that a common interest pervaded the relationship between mother country and colony. To him Virginia's role in the empire was to struggle for all the advantage it could get. The altered rationale for promoting towns was a reflection of this different concept of the colony's place in the empire.

This change in outlook reflected five decades of depressed tobacco prices and severe competition with English merchants for profit from the tobacco trade. It mirrored the colonists' hostility toward the Navigation Acts. It arose out of resentment against the crown's grants of Virginia land to courtiers. It derived from the presence after 1676 of governors indifferent to the colony's welfare. It resulted from the emergence of native-born Virginians to positions of political leadership. And it represented as well a reaction to the tendency of Englishmen to express with increasing candor the views that colonies existed for the benefit of the mother country and that colonials were different and inferior beings.

There was a parallel change in the attitude of the crown. Charles II's initial enthusiasm for diversification of Virginia's economy and for towns as a means to achieve that goal abated quickly. His interest could not survive his recognition after 1660 that the crown faced financial problems which demanded that all policy decisions be subordinated to the need for immediate revenue. To be sure, the traditional vision of a diversified economy in the Old Dominion included the idea that such an economy would eventually swell the royal revenues as the volume and value of trade increased. But in the short run diversification schemes threatened to divert the planters from tobacco, and the duties from the tobacco trade accounted for an important part of the government's revenues. With the outbreak of the Second Dutch War in 1664 the crown abandoned its support of the idea of diversification.[35]

The crown did not forsake its interest in towns, but it did alter its conception of their nature and purpose. Ironically, the crown grew more eager to promote ports as its support of diversification declined. It came to accept the view of the customs commissioners and colonial officials with special responsibilities for enforcing the Navigation Acts that port towns in Virginia would greatly facilitate the enforcement of those statutes. The dispersed trading pattern then existing permitted most lading to occur without the supervision or even the knowledge of colonial customs officials. Under these circumstances the planters allegedly avoided payment of more than half the duties on tobacco levied by the Plantation Duty Act of 1673 as well as provincial taxes used for the support of the Virginia government. Edward Randolph believed that the best method of enforcing the Navigation Acts in the Chesapeake Bay area was to allow only two ports of entry for Virginia and Maryland.[36] Revenue for the crown and the royal colonial government might be increased if trade were centralized. The home government, in short, hoped to centralize trade without fostering any significant growth of towns. The unfavorable report of the customs commissioners on the town act of 1680 summed up the crown's altered ideas. The commission pointed out that the instructions to Virginia governors to promote town acts was designed to secure "Wharfes and Keys" and not to promote compact settlement or economic diversification.[37]

The crown's position attracted support from the large English merchants trading in Virginia tobacco, if indeed the policy was not in large measure shaped by them. Throughout the last half of the seventeenth century these merchants, centered in London, fought to eliminate the smaller traders, most of whom operated from the outports. The London merchants for the most part conducted their tobacco trade to the Chesapeake within legal channels. The nature of their ventures made smuggling financially hazardous. They sent large ships into the Virginia rivers, and the value of the tobacco carried by their vessels was too great to risk forfeiture. Their ships returned to London where enforcement of the acts of trade was most effective. Compelled by interest and circumstance to forego smuggling, these large merchants naturally thought their competitors should also be forced to trade legally. They believed their rivals used their smaller ships "to run from one port & Creek to another" and engage in smuggling. The London merchants also deplored the importation by the smaller merchants of trash and bulk tobacco, which glutted the market with tobacco which could be sold at cut rates.[38]

The large merchants therefore backed the crown's efforts to improve enforcement of the acts of trade and accepted the idea that the creation of port towns would serve that end. Like the government, they were also concerned that the towns remain, as they put it, "modest." They wanted ports for the clearing and control of shipping and not as nuclei for an economic diversification which would lessen the Virginia market for English goods.[39]

By the end of the century the Virginia councilors supported the position of crown and merchants, but they acted from different motives, and they envisioned different long-range results from promoting the ports. Councilors were expected to back crown policy, and as large planters with close ties to the London traders their immediate interests dictated the same stance.[40] Furthermore, they controlled offices with emoluments which depended upon the collection of duties and the enforcement of the acts of trade.[41] At the same time the councilors were native Virginians who could not wholeheartedly subscribe to the crown's hostility toward diversification. William Byrd, a leading spokesman for the point of view of the Council, thus argued that the diversification which must inevitably result from even the modest program to encourage towns would not in the long run retard the production of tobacco or reduce the crown and provincial revenues.[42]

Despite the divergent attitudes of crown and merchants and councilors, the three allied themselves against the extravagant town schemes of the burgesses. The king and traders promoted modest port acts, hoping to focus and control trade without stimulating compact settlement and economic innovations inconsistent with the proper dependence of colonies; the Council supported such measures, believing that gradual and limited encouragement of ports was a surer road to diversification than the chimerical schemes of the lower house.

The interplay of conflicting approaches, motives, and interests behind the efforts to establish ports may be seen most clearly at work in the struggle over the port act of 1691. Efforts to work out a town act satisfactory to all interests had failed repeatedly during the administrations of

Thomas Lord Culpeper and Francis Lord Howard of Effingham prior to the Glorious Revolution. The state of the tobacco market after 1688 provided an incentive to renew these efforts. The political turmoil caused by the overthrow of James II and the disruption in trade occasioned by the outbreak of war with France reduced the number of tobacco ships coming to the Chesapeake Bay area. Many of the ships which did arrive bypassed Virginia in order to trade in Maryland, where the "Loose Government" run by the rebels who had overthrown proprietary rule winked at the Navigation Acts. Even the large planters in Virginia, who enjoyed excellent trade contacts with English tobacco merchants, had difficulty securing freight. The poorer planters received so little for their tobacco in 1691 that they were "hardly able to finde ... Ordinary Cloathing ..."[43]

The Glorious Revolution also stimulated in Virginia renewed concern for the social stability of the colony. News of the overthrow of James precipitated much talk against the legitimacy of the Virginia government and sparked small uprisings in the Northern Neck. Virginia's political leaders believed themselves fortunate to have escaped the more serious upheavals directed at their counterparts in New York and Maryland.[44] Confronted with economic crisis and reminded again of the tenuous authority exercised over the unruly and dispersed planters, the members of the first Assembly to meet after the Glorious Revolution turned inevitably to the task of promoting towns.

The new executive, Lieutenant Governor Francis Nicholson, arrived in Virginia in 1691 convinced that he should ensure tranquility by acquiescing in the demands of the Assembly. Nicholson at that time advised the Lords of Trade to delay action on the legislation he approved in order to pacify Virginians until legitimate authority had been reestablished in the provinces which had experienced revolts.[45] The port act of 1691 was one such measure accepted by Nicholson and his Council. Both protested the burgesses' demand for twenty ports and for prohibitions on the lading of tobacco and sale of goods outside the entrepôts, but they acquiesced rather than provoke a confrontation with the lower house in such seemingly perilous times.[46]

In agreeing that the port act should go into effect in October 1692 Nicholson doubtless expected to receive news of a royal disallowance or suspension before that date. Many planters, however, were confident that the new monarchs would confirm the measure, and preparations for the implementation of the port act began. The counties surveyed and laid out the port cities. Many of the locations were the same as those designated by earlier port bills. At these locations there had been some earlier construction of warehouses and houses, and efforts to develop these paper ports further now increased. By the spring of 1692 "considerable progress" had been made in the sale of town lots, and the larger planters were reported ready to invest large amounts of capital to promote the towns.[47]

Not everyone was pleased by the prospect of severe restrictions upon trading activity. Unnamed "evill minded persons" in some of the counties sought to obstruct the survey of the port sites.[48] Nicholson apparently encouraged opposition to the port act he had earlier signed. By the spring of 1692 the possibility that Virginia would catch the contagion of rebelliousness had passed, and Nicholson, freed from his earlier apprehensions, "tack'd about, and was quite the Reverse of what he was in the first [Assembly]." He privately boasted to the government in England that he was working to undo many of the measures he had sanctioned in his first Assembly.[49]

In England the port act occasioned "great debate and examinations" among Virginia's agents, the merchants, and the crown.[50] The contest was heated. The Virginia agents, James Blair, William Sherwood, and Patrick Smith, accused the tobacco merchants of ruining the colony by opposing all measures of economic reform. The merchants in turn condemned the Assembly's measure as totally unrealistic. If "Virginia [had] a million of people [more] than they have," they argued, "it might with some Color be alledged, it were possible or reasonable to make 20 Towns, & enjoin all buyers & Sellers to buy and sell in them." The merchants criticized the arbitrary confinement of trade to specific areas before adequate commercial facilities had been developed and urged that there be "a gradual drawing of People" into towns. They advocated persuasion rather than coercion.[51]

Predictably, the Commissioners of the Customs in their report to the Lords of Trade in March 1692 endorsed the merchants' arguments and recommended that no port law be accepted unless it provided for fewer ports and omitted restrictions on the right of the merchants and planters to buy and sell where it was most convenient. The Lords of Trade did not consider the matter until late June, at which time they incorporated the commissioners' report in a recommendation to the crown that the port act be suspended until the Virginia Assembly acceded to the changes demanded by the merchants and revenue officials. The queen in council accepted the recommendation on June 30, 1692, but the crown's decision came too late to be communicated to Sir Edmund Andros, who left England in early June to assume the governorship of Virginia.[52]

Andros arrived in Virginia in September 1692. By October he still had not received word of crown action on the port act. Since the measure did not have a suspending clause, several of the counties placed the act in operation. This partial implementation disrupted the tobacco trade. Some ship captains avoided Virginia and sought tobacco in Maryland. Virginia's commerce slumped, and hostility to the unevenly enforced act multiplied. Andros seems to have exerted no leadership in this confused period. During the fall and winter of 1692 he wrote letters pleading for specific orders.[53] Since there was no reply by March 1693, the Assembly was forced to end the confusion and allay growing opposition by suspending the law until the crown decision arrived.[54] The home government's orders came shortly before September 1, 1693, more than a year after the order-in-council. On that date Andros and the Virginia Council proclaimed the royal suspension of the port act already set aside by the Assembly.[55]

The lower house deeply resented the crown's action. The burgesses had expected better of William and Mary and were displeased to discover that the Glorious Revolution had not altered the home government's views on Virginia's role in the empire and the purpose of ports. Their disenchantment was reflected in a belligerent stance toward Andros' suggestion that the port act be amended. They rejected his proposals along with other recommendations. Randolph reported that "if they may not do as they please in Everything they will do just nothing."[56] The efforts to obtain a port act acceptable to the conflicting interests of the crown, the merchants, and the colony failed in 1693 as it had failed before and as it was to fail again in the first decade of the eighteenth century.

Even if the port act of 1691 or similar acts between the Interregnum and the first decade of the eighteenth century had been more realistically formulated and fully implemented, it is probable that the results would still have failed to fulfill the extravagant expectations of the Virginians. Yet the feasibility of altering the pattern of commerce by government action is indicated by the effects of the tobacco inspection acts enforced in Virginia after 1730. Designed to regulate the quality of tobacco rather than to centralize commerce, the tobacco inspection statutes established central warehouse storage of tobacco, and small commercial centers had often developed around these warehouses by the end of the colonial period. However, the persistent and conscious efforts in the seventeenth century to overcome the geographic forces which discouraged the growth of towns failed to produce even meager results. The failure was not caused by immutable environmental barriers; it was the result of a combination of factors which prevented a sustained and practical attack on the problem. An almost unlimited confidence, especially by the burgesses, in the ability of government to mold economic and social patterns by legislative edict led to the enactment of impractical programs. The tendency of the representatives to seek the benefits of commercial centers for their own counties resulted in laws creating an excessive number of ports. By attempting too much, nothing was accomplished; and the lack of tangible results produced hostility among the common planters who bore the taxes levied to support the town schemes. By the end of the century these inhibiting factors were reinforced by a fundamental conflict between the crown and its allies on the one hand and the burgesses on the other regarding the purpose of towns. This disagreement reflected both the crown's narrowing vision of Virginia's place in the empire and the expanding loyalty of the burgesses to Virginia as a "country" with distinct interests in conflict with those of the mother country.

NOTES

1. Letter of the Reverend John Clayton, August 17, 1688, read at the Royal Society, October 24, 1688, in Edmund Berkeley and Dorothy Smith Berkeley, eds., *The Reverend John Clayton: A Parson with a Scientific Mind: His Scientific Writings and Other Related Papers* (Charlottesville, 1965), p. 80.

2. Robert Beverley, *The History and Present State of Virginia*, edited by Louis B. Wright (Chapel Hill, 1947), p. 57; Stanley Pargellis, ed., "An Account of the Indians in Virginia," *William and Mary Quarterly* (cited hereinafter as *WMQ*), 3d Ser., XVI (April 1959), 237; William J. Hinke, ed. and trans., "Report of the Journey of Francis Louis Michel from Berne, Switzerland, to Virginia, October 2, 1701–December 1, 1702," *Virginia Magazine of History and Biography* (cited hereinafter as *VMHB*), XXIV (January 1916), 31; George Milner, Proposals in order to the Improvement of the Country of Albemarle in the Province of Carolina in point of Townes, Trade, and Coyne, n.d., Egerton Ms 2395, fol. 661 (British Museum, London; transcript in Library of Congress).

3. Philip Alexander Bruce, *Economic History of Virginia in the Seventeenth Century*, 2 vols. (New York, 1895), II, 523; Edward M. Riley, "The Town Acts of Colonial Virginia," *Journal of Southern History*, XVI (August 1950), 308. Riley notes (p. 323) that some Virginians desired towns, but he generally stresses the hostility of the colonists toward efforts to promote towns.

4. Bruce, *op. cit.*, II, p. 540; Thomas Jefferson Wertenbaker, *Norfolk: Historic Southern Port* (Durham, 1931), pp. 3–4; Riley, *op. cit.*, p. 308.

5. Robert Johnson, *Nova Britannia. Offring Most Excellent Fruites by Planting in Virginia* . . . (London, 1609), p. 9; Edwin C. Rozwenc, "Captain John Smith's Image of America," *WMQ*, 3d Ser., XVI (January 1959), 32–3; Treasurer and Council for Virginia to Governor and Council in Virginia, August 1, 1622, in Susan M. Kingsbury, ed., *The Records of the Virginia Company of London*, 4 vols. (Washington, 1906–1935), III, 669–70; John Chamberlain to Sir Dudley Carleton, July 13, 1622, in Norman Egbert McClure, ed., *The Letters of John Chamberlain*, 2 vols. (Philadelphia, 1939), II, 446.

6. Melvin Herndon, *Tobacco in Colonial Virginia: "The Sovereign Remedy"* (Williamsburg, 1957), pp. 46–8; Lewis C. Gray, "The Market Surplus Problems of Colonial Tobacco," *WMQ*, 2d Ser., VII (October 1927), 231–4.

7. Proposals Concerning Building of Towns in Virginia, n.d., Egerton Ms 2395, fol. 666; "Anthony Langston on Towns and Corporations; and on the Manufacture of Iron," *WMQ*, 2d Ser., I (April 1921), 101; Henry Hartwell, James Blair, and Edward Chilton, *The Present State of Virginia, and the College*, edited by Hunter Dickinson Farish (Williamsburg, 1940), pp. 8–11; Beverley, *op. cit.*, p. 319.

8. Treasurer and Council for Virginia to Governor and Council in Virginia, August 1, 1622, in Kingsbury, *op. cit.*, III, 669–70.

9. Thomas Ludwell to Lord John Berkeley, June 24, 1677, in Public Record Office, London, Colonial Office (hereinafter cited as PRO, CO), 1/21: 116–17; Thomas

Ludwell to Lord Arlington, July 17, 1671, *ibid.*, 1/27: 16; Richard L. Morton, *Colonial Virginia*, 2 vols. (Chapel Hill, 1960), I, 195–8; Bernard Bailyn, "Politics and Social Structure in Virginia," in James Morton Smith, ed., *Seventeenth-Century America: Essays in Colonial History* (Chapel Hill, 1959), pp. 90–115.

10. [Roger Green], *Virginia's Cure: Or an Advisive Narrative Concerning Virginia* (London, 1662), in Perer Force, comp., *Tracts and Other Papers* . . . , 4 vols. (Washington, 1836–46), III, no. 15, pp. 10–11.

11. [William Sherwood], "Virginias Deploured Condition . . . 1676," Massachusetts Historical Society, *Collections*, 4th Ser., IX (Boston, 1871), 163–5.

12. Philip Ludwell to Henry Coventry, June 16, 1679, in Henry Coventry Papers (Longleat, Wiltshire, England; microfilm in Library of Congress), LXXVIII, fol. 386; Proposals for Virginia, *ibid.*, fol. 258.

13. Nicholas Spencer to Henry Coventry, July 9, 1680, in PRO, CO, 1/45: 189.

14. [Green], *op. cit.*, p. 14.

15. [Francis Makemie], *A Plain & Friendly Perswasive to the Inhabitants of Virginia and Maryland for Promoting Towns & Cohabitation* (London, 1705), reprinted in *VMHB*, IV (January 1897), 258.

16. "London's Lotterie," *WMQ*, 3rd Ser., V (April 1948), 263–4.

17. William W. Hening, ed., *The Statutes at Large; Being a Collection of All the Laws of Virginia from the First Session of the Legislature in the Year 1619*, 13 vols. (Richmond, New York, and Philadelphia, 1819–23), I, 412–14; II, 172–6, 471–8; III, 53–69, 404–19; Fair Engrossed Bill for Ports, etc., PRO, CO, 1/58: 327–30.

18. Hening, *op. cit.*, I, 414; II, 474–7.

19. Berkeley letter of March 30, 1663, in Egerton Ms 2395, fol. 362.

20. John Pendleton Kennedy and H. R. McIlwaine, eds., *Journals of the House of Burgesses of Virginia* [1619–1776], 13 vols. (Richmond, 1905–15), *1659/60–93*, pp. 130–1, 137, 351; "Speech of Lord Culpeper to the House of Burgesses, 1680," *VMHB*, XIV (April 1907), 366–7.

21. Jacques Fontaine, *Memoirs of a Huguenot Family* (New York, 1853), 292–3.

22. "Petition of John Mercer," *VMHB*, V (January 1898), 278–9.

23. Report of the Commissioners of Customs, December 12, 1681, PRO, CO, 1/47: 252–3.

24. Hartwell, Blair, and Chilton, *op. cit.*, p. 12.

25. Mr. Clayton's Second Letter, containing his farther Observations on Virginia, in Berkeley and Berkeley, *op. cit.*, p. 53; [Mungo Ingles], "The Several Sources of Odium and Discouragement Which the College of Wm. & Mary . . . lyes under . . . 1704," *VMHB*, VII (April 1900), 391.

26. H. R. McIlwaine, ed., *Legislative Journals of the Council of Colonial Virginia*, 3 vols. (Richmond, 1918–19), I, 95–6.

27. "The Declaration of the People," *VMHB*, I (July 1893), 59.

28. *Ibid.*

29. Isle of Wight County Grievances, PRO, CO, 1/39: 223–7; An Exact Repertory of the General and Personall Grievances Presented to Us (His Majesty's Commissioners) by the People of Virginia, *ibid.*, 5/1371: 317.

30. Surry County Grievances, *ibid.*, 1/39: 207–8.

31. Council for Foreign Plantations to Virginia, February 18, 1660/61, in PRO, CO, 1/14; Letter from Mr. Povy concerning the natural products of Virginia in behalf of the Royall Society, March 4, 1659/60, in Egerton Ms 2395, fol. 296; Instructions to Berkeley, September 14, 1662, Coventry Papers, LXXVI, fols. 63–5; William Berkeley, *A Discourse and View of Virginia* (London, 1663), *passim*.

32. Edward Randolph to William Blathwayt, March 14, 1692/93, in Robert N. Toppan and Alfred T. S. Goodrick, eds., *Edward Randolph; Including His Letters and Official Papers . . .* , 7 vols. (Boston, 1898–09), VII, 435.

33. Kennedy and McIlwaine, *op. cit., 1702/3–1712*, p. 165.

34. Beverley, *op. cit.*, p. 319.

35. Order in Council, November 25, 1664, PRO, CO, 1/18: 323.

36. McIlwaine, *op. cit.*, I, 96; "An Account of Severall Things Whereby Illegal Trade is Encouraged . . .," October 16, 1695, Goodrick and Toppan, *op. cit.*, V, 117, 123–4.

37. Report of the Commissioners of Customs, December 12, 1681, PRO, CO, 1/47: 252–3.

38. Petition of Merchants, Owners, and Planters of Virginia and Maryland to the King, August 1687, *ibid.*, 1/63: 74; Some Reasons Why Bulke Tobacco from Virginia and Maryland Ought to Be Prohibited Being Exported Thence or Imported into England, *ibid.*, 76–7.

39. "Memorial to the Honorable Commissioners of His Majesty's Customs," in William Byrd, *History of the Dividing Line and Other Tracts*, 2 vols. (Richmond, 1866), II, 162–5.

40. Elizabeth Donnan, "Eighteenth-Century English Merchants: Micajah Perry," *Journal of Economic and Business History*, IV (November 1931), 73–81; William Byrd to Perry and Lane, March 5, 1688/89, and June 10, 1689, in *VMHB*, XXV (October 1917), 363; XXVI (January 1918), 25.

41. William G. Stanard and Mary Newton Stanard, comps., *The Colonial Virginia Register: A List of Governors, Councillors and Other Officials* (Albany, 1902), pp. 22–3, 25–6, 38–45; *VMHB*, I (January 1894), 244–6.

42. Louis B. Wright, "William Byrd's Opposition to Governor Francis Nicholson," *Journal of Southern History*, XI (February 1945), 76–8.

43. Nicholson to Lords of Trade, February 26, 1691/92, in PRO, CO, 5/1306, #89; H. R. McIlwaine, Wilmer L. Hall, and Benjamin J. Hillman, eds., *Executive Journals of the Council of Colonial Virginia*, 6 vols. (Richmond, 1925–66), I, 194 (the quotation is from this source); various letters of William Byrd, in *VMHB*, XXVI (April, July, and October 1918), 132–3, 250, 388; XXVII (April 1918; July and October 1919), 167, 273–8, 280, 286; XXVIII (January 1920), 14, 21. See also Byrd to William Blathwayt, October 30, 1690, in William Blathwayt Papers (Colonial

Williamsburg, Williamsburg, Va.), XIII; and William Fitzhugh to Nicholas Hayward, May 20, 1691, in Richard Beale Davis, ed., *William Fitzhugh and His Chesapeake World, 1676–1701: The Fitzhugh Letters and Other Documents* (Chapel Hill, 1963), pp. 290–92.

44. Nicholas Spencer to the Lords of Trade, April 29, 1689, in PRO, CO, 5/1305, #7; McIlwaine *et al., op. cit.,* I, 104–6; Spencer to Blathwayt, April 27, 1689, in Blathwayt Papers, XVIII; Edward Randolph to Blathwayt, March 27, 1690, in Toppan and Goodrick, *op. cit.,* VIII, 341.

45. Beverley, *History,* 97–8; Nicholson to Lords of Trade, June 10, 1961, in PRO, CO, 5/1306, #41; Nicholson to Blathwayt, June 10, 1691, in Blathwayt Papers, XV.

46. McIlwaine, *op. cit.,* I, 138–40; Kennedy and McIlwaine, *op. cit., 1659/60–93,* pp. 351–2, 359.

47. McIlwaine *et al.,* eds., *Executive Journals of the Council,* I, 212–13; Memorial from the General Assembly of Virginia, April 30, 1692, Blathwayt Papers, XV; Governor Effingham to Blathwayt, June 6, 1685, *ibid.,* XIV; Hening, op. cit., III, 58–60.

48. Kennedy and McIlwaine, *op. cit.,* 1659/93, p. 386.

49. Beverley, *op. cit.,* p. 100; Nicholson to Lords of Trade, July 16, 1692, in PRO, CO, 5/1306, no. 119; Nicholson to Nottingham, November 13, 1691, *ibid.,* no. 64.

50. Blathwayt to Nicholson, February 18, 1691/92, in Blathwayt Papers, XV.

51. Byrd, *op. cit.,* II, 162–5.

52. Order of Queen in Council, June 30, 1692, W. Noel Sainsbury *et al.,* eds., *Calendar of State Papers, Colonial Series,* 43 vols. (London, 1860–63), XIII, *America and West Indies, 1689–92,* 663; Report of the Commissioners of the Customs upon Certain Laws Past in the Assembly of Virginia, March 15, 1691/92, PRO, CO, 5/1306, no. 93; Journal of the Lords of Trade, June 27, 1692, *ibid.,* 391/7, pp. 104–6; Andros to the Earl of Nottingham, June 8, 1692, *ibid.,* 5/1306, pp. 433–4.

53. Andros to Blathwayt, November 3, 1692; January 16, 1692/93, in Blathwayt Papers, III; Andros to the Lords of Trade, November 3, 1692, in PRO, CO, 5/1306, no. 134.

54. Kennedy and McIlwaine, *op. cit., 1659/60–1693,* pp. 423, 436; Hening, *op. cit.,* III, 108–9.

55. McIlwaine *et al., Executive Journals of the Council,* I, 296–7.

56. Randolph to Blathwayt, October 30, 1693; Randolph to Povey, November 2, 1693, in Toppan and Goodrick, *op. cit.,* VII, 448, 452.

5. ECONOMIC DEVELOPMENT AND SOCIAL STRUCTURE IN COLONIAL BOSTON

James A. Henretta

A distinctly urban social structure developed in Boston in the 150 years between the settlement of the town and the American Revolution. The expansion of trade and industry after 1650 unleashed powerful economic forces which first distorted, then destroyed, the social homogeneity and cohesiveness of the early village community. All aspects of town life were affected by Boston's involvement in the dynamic, competitive world of Atlantic commerce. The disruptive pressure of rapid economic growth, sustained for over a century, made the social appearance of the town more diverse, more complex, more modern—increasingly different from that of the rest of New England. The magnitude of the change in Boston's social composition and structure may be deduced from an analysis and comparison of the tax lists for 1687 and 1771. Containing a wealth of information on property ownership in the community, these lists make it possible to block out, in quantitative terms, variations in the size and influence of economic groups and to trace the change in the distribution of the resources of the community among them.

The transformation of Boston from a land-based society to a maritime center was neither sudden nor uniform. In the last decade of the seventeenth century, a large part of the land of its broad peninsula was still cultivated by small farmers. Only a small fraction was laid out in regular streets and even less was densely settled. The north end alone showed considerable change from the middle of the century when almost every house had a large lot and garden. Here, the later-comers—the mariners, craftsmen, and traders who had raised the population to six thousand by 1690—were crowded together along the waterfront. Here, too, in the series of docks and shipyards which jutted out from the shore line, were tangible manifestations of the commercial activity which had made the small town the largest owner of shipping and the principal port of the English colonies. Over 40 percent of the carrying capacity of all colonial-owned shipping was in Boston hands.

Dependence on mercantile endeavor rather than agricultural enterprise had by 1690 greatly affected the extent of property ownership. Boston no

Reprinted from the *William and Mary Quarterly*, 3rd ser., XXII (January 1965), 75–92, by permission of the author. The author's notes have been deleted.

longer had the universal ownership of real estate characteristic of rural Massachusetts to the end of the colonial period. The tax list for 1687 contained the names of 188 polls, 14 percent of the adult male population, who were neither owners of taxable property of any kind nor "dependents" in a household assessed for the property tax. Holding no real estate, owning no merchandise or investments which would yield an income, these men constituted the "propertyless" segment of the community and were liable only for the head tax which fell equally upon all men above the age of sixteen. Many in this group were young men, laborers and seamen, attracted by the commercial prosperity of the town and hoping to save enough from their wages to buy or rent a shop, to invest in the tools of an artisan, or to find a start in trade. John Erving, a poor Scotch sailor whose grandson in 1771 was one of the richest men in Boston, was only one propertyless man who rose quickly to a position of wealth and influence.

But many of these 188 men did not acquire either taxable property or an established place in the social order of Boston. Only sixty-four, or 35 percent, were inhabitants of the town eight years later. By way of contrast, 45 percent of the polls assessed from two to seven pounds on the tax list, 65 percent of those with property valued from eight to twenty pounds, and 73 percent of those with estates in excess of twenty pounds were present in 1695. There was a direct relation between permanence of residence and economic condition. Even in an expanding and diversifying economic environment, the best opportunities for advancement rested with those who could draw upon long-standing connections, upon the credit facilities of friends and neighbors, and upon political influence. It was precisely these personal contacts which were denied to the propertyless.

A second, distinct element in the social order consisted of the dependents of property owners. Though propertyless themselves, these dependents —grown sons living at home, apprentices, and indentured servants—were linked more closely to the town as members of a taxpaying household unit than were the 188 "unattached" men without taxable estates. Two hundred and twelve men, nearly one sixth of the adult male population of Boston, were classified as dependents in 1687. The pervasiveness of the dependency relationship attested not only to the cohesiveness of the family unit but also to the continuing vitality of the apprenticeship and indenture system at the close of the seventeenth century.

Yet even the dependency relationship, traditionally an effective means of alleviating unemployment and preventing the appearance of unattached propertyless laborers, was subjected to severe pressure by the expansion of the economy. An urgent demand for labor, itself the cause of short indentures, prompted servants to strike out on their own as soon as possible. They became the laborers or semiskilled craftsmen of the town, while the sons of the family eventually assumed control of their father's business and a share of the economic resources of the community.

The propertied section of the population in 1687 was composed of 1,036 individuals who were taxed on their real estate or their income from trade.

The less-skilled craftsmen, 521 men engaged in the rougher trades of a waterfront society, formed the bottom stratum of the taxable population in this preindustrial age. These carpenters, shipwrights, blacksmiths, shopkeepers owned only 12 percent of the taxable wealth of the town. Few of these artisans and laborers had investments in shipping or in merchandise. A small store or house, or a small farm in the south end of Boston, accounted for their assessment of two to seven pounds on the tax list. (Table 3)

Between these craftsmen and shopkeepers and the traders and merchants who constituted the economic elite of the town was a middle group of 275 property owners with taxable assets valued from eight to twenty pounds. Affluent artisans employing two or three workers, ambitious shopkeepers with investments in commerce, and entrepreneurial-minded sea masters with various maritime interests, bulked large in this center portion of the economic order. Of the 275, 180 owned real estate assessed at seven pounds or less and were boosted into the third quarter of the distribution of wealth by their holdings of merchandise and shares in shipping. (Table 3) The remaining ninety-five possessed real estate rated at eight pounds or more and, in addition, held various investments in trade. Making up about 25 percent of the propertied population, this middle group controlled 22 percent of the taxable wealth in Boston in 1687. Half as numerous as the lowest group of property owners, these men possessed almost double the amount of taxable assets. (Table 1)

Merchants with large investments in English and West Indian trade and individuals engaged in the ancillary industries of shipbuilding and distilling made up the top quarter of the taxable population in 1687. With taxable estates ranging from twenty to 170 pounds, this commercial group controlled 66 percent of the town's wealth. But economic development had been too rapid, too uneven and incomplete, to allow the emergence of a well-defined merchant class endowed with a common outlook and clearly distinguished from the rest of the society. Only eighty-five of these men, one third of the wealthiest group in the community, owned dwellings valued at as much as twenty pounds. The majority held landed property valued at ten pounds, only a few pounds greater than that of the middle group of property holders. The merchants had not shared equally in the accumulated fund of capital and experience which had accrued after fifty years of maritime activity. Profits had flowed to those whose daring initiative and initial resources had begun the exploitation of the lucrative colonial market. By 1687, the upper 15 percent of the property owners held 52 percent of the taxable assets of the town, while the fifty individuals who composed the highest 5 percent of the taxable population accounted for more than 25 percent of the wealth. (Table 1)

By the end of the seventeenth century widespread involvement in commerce had effected a shift in the locus of social and political respectability in Boston and distinguished it from the surrounding communities. Five of the nine selectmen chosen by the town in 1687 were sea cap-

Table 1. Distribution of Assessed Taxable Wealth in Boston in 1687*

Total Value of Taxable Wealth	Number of Taxpayers in Each Wealth Bracket	Total Wealth in Each Wealth Bracket	Cumulative Total of Wealth	Cumu- lative Total of Taxpayers	Cumulative Percentage of Taxpayers	Cumulative Percentage of Wealth
£ 1	0	£ 0	£ 0	0	0.0%	0.0%
2	152	304	304	152	14.6	1.8
3	51	153	457	203	19.5	2.7
4	169	676	1,133	372	35.9	6.8
5	33	165	1,298	405	39.0	7.8
6	97	582	1,880	502	48.5	11.3
7	19	133	2,013	521	50.2	12.1
8	43	344	2,357	564	54.4	14.2
9	22	198	2,555	586	56.6	15.4
10	45	450	3,005	631	60.9	18.1
11	17	187	3,192	648	62.5	19.2
12	30	360	3,552	678	65.4	21.4
13	13	169	3,721	691	66.6	22.4
14	12	168	3,889	703	67.9	23.4
15	22	330	4,219	725	69.9	25.4
16	21	336	4,555	746	72.0	27.5
17	1	17	4,572	747	72.0	27.6
18	18	324	4,896	765	73.8	29.5
19	1	19	4,915	766	73.9	29.6
20	30	600	5,515	796	76.8	33.2
21–5	41	972	6,487	837	80.7	39.0
26–30	48	1,367	7,854	885	85.4	47.3
31–5	29	971	8,825	914	88.2	53.1
36–40	21	819	9,644	935	90.2	58.1
41–5	19	828	10,472	954	92.1	63.1
46–50	16	781	11,253	970	93.6	67.8
51–60	16	897	12,150	986	95.1	73.2
61–70	19	1,245	13,395	1,005	97.0	80.7
71–80	7	509	13,904	1,012	97.8	83.8
81–90	3	253	14,157	1,015	97.9	85.3
91–100	7	670	14,827	1,022	98.6	89.3
100–	14	1,764	16,591	1,036	100.0	100.0

* Money values are those of 1687. Many of the assessments fall at regular five pound intervals and must be considered as an estimate of the economic position of the individual. No attempt was made to compensate for systematic overvaluation or undervaluation inasmuch as the analysis measures relative wealth. The utility of a relative presentation of wealth (or income) is that it can be compared to another relative distribution without regard to absolute monetary values.

tains. This was more than deference to those accustomed to command. With total estates of £83, £29, £33, £33, and £24, Captains Elisha Hutchinson, John Fairweather, Theophilus Frary, Timothy Prout, and Daniel Turell were among the wealthiest 20 percent of the population. Still, achievement in trade was not the only index of respectability. Henry Eames, George Cable, Isaac Goose, and Elnathan Lyon, the men appointed by the town to inspect the condition of the streets and roads, had the greater part of their wealth, £105 of £130, invested in land and livestock. And the presence of Deacon Henry Allen among the selectmen provided a tangible indication of the continuing influence of the church.

These legacies of an isolated religious society and a stable agricultural economy disappeared in the wake of the rapid growth which continued unabated until the middle of the eighteenth century. In the fifty years after 1690, the population of the town increased from 6,000 to 16,000. The farms of the south end vanished and the central business district became crowded. In the populous north end, buildings which had once housed seven people suddenly began to hold nine or ten. Accompanying this physical expansion of Boston was a diversification of economic endeavor. By 1742, the town led all the colonial cities in the production of export furniture and shoes, although master craftsmen continued to carry on most industry on a small scale geared to local needs. Prosperity and expansion continued to be rooted, not in the productive capacity or geographic position of the town, but in the ability of the Boston merchants to compete successfully in the highly competitive mercantile world.

After 1750, the economic health of the Massachusetts seaport was jeopardized as New York and Philadelphia merchants, exploiting the rich productive lands at their backs and capitalizing upon their prime geographic position in the West Indian and southern coasting trade, diverted a significant portion of European trade from the New England traders. Without increasing returns from the lucrative "carrying" trade, Boston merchants could no longer subsidize the work of the shopkeepers, craftsmen, and laborers who supplied and maintained the commercial fleet. By 1760, the population of Boston had dropped to 15,000 persons, a level it did not exceed until after the revolution.

The essential continuity of maritime enterprise in Boston from the late seventeenth to the mid-eighteenth century concealed the emergence of a new type of social system. After a certain point increases in the scale and extent of commercial endeavor produced a new, and more fluid, social order. The development of the economic system subjected the family, the basic social unit, to severe pressures. The fundamental link between one generation and another, the ability of the father to train his offspring for their life's work, was endangered by a process of change which rendered obsolete many of the skills and assumptions of the older land-oriented generation and opened the prospect of success in new fields and new places. The well-known departure of Benjamin Franklin from his

Table 2. Distribution of Assessed Taxable Wealth in Boston in 1771*

Total Value of Taxable Wealth	Number of Taxpayers in Each Wealth Bracket	Total Wealth in Each Wealth Bracket	Cumulative Total of Wealth	Cumulative Total of Taxpayers	Cumulative Percentage of Taxpayers	Cumulative Percentage of Wealth
£ 3–30	78	£1,562	£1,562	78	5.0%	0.3%
31–40	86	2,996	4,558	164	10.6	0.9
41–50	112	5,378	9,936	276	17.9	2.2
51–60	74	4,398	14,334	350	22.6	3.5
61–70	33	3,122	17,456	383	24.7	3.8
71–80	165	12,864	30,320	548	35.4	6.5
81–90	24	2,048	32,368	572	36.9	7.0
91–100	142	13,684	46,052	714	46.1	10.0
101–10	14	494	46,546	728	47.1	10.1
111–20	149	17,844	64,390	877	56.7	13.9
121–30	20	2,570	66,960	897	58.0	14.5
131–40	26	4,600	71,560	923	59.7	15.5
141–50	20	2,698	74,258	943	60.9	16.1
151–60	88	14,048	88,306	1,031	66.6	19.1
161–70	11	1,846	90,152	1,042	67.4	19.6
171–80	18	3,128	93,280	1,060	68.6	20.3
181–90	10	1,888	95,168	1,070	69.2	20.7
191–200	47	9,368	104,536	1,117	72.2	22.7
201–300	126	31,097	135,633	1,243	80.4	29.4
301–400	60	21,799	157,432	1,303	84.2	34.1
401–500	58	24,947	182,379	1,361	88.0	39.6
501–600	14	7,841	190,220	1,375	88.9	41.3
601–700	24	15,531	205,751	1,399	90.4	44.6
701–800	26	19,518	225,269	1,425	92.2	48.9
801–900	20	17,020	242,289	1,445	93.4	52.6
901–1,000	16	15,328	257,617	1,461	95.4	55.9
1,001–1,500	41	48,364	305,963	1,502	97.1	66.4
1,501–5,000	37	85,326	391,289	1,539	99.5	84.9
5,001–	7	69,204	460,493	1,546	100.0	100.0

* The extant tax list is not complete. In ward 3, there are two pages and 69 polls missing; in ward 7, one page and 24 polls; in ward 12, an unknown number of pages and 225 polls. Only the total number of polls (224) is known for ward II. The missing entries amount to 558, or 19.3 percent of the total number of polls on the tax list. Internal evidence (the totals for all wards are known) suggests the absent material is completely random. Nevertheless, it should be remembered that this table represents an 80 percent sample.

The value of shipping investments and of "servants for life" was not included in the computation of the table as it was impossible to determine the assessor's valuation. Money values are those of 1771.

indenture to his brother was but one bright piece in the shifting mosaic of colonial life.

The traditional family unit had lost much of its cohesiveness by the third quarter of the eighteenth century. The Boston tax lists for 1771 indicate that dependents of property owners accounted for only 10 percent of the adult male population as opposed to 16 percent eighty-five years earlier. Increasingly children left their homes at an earlier age to seek their own way in the world.

A second factor in the trend away from dependency status was the decline in the availability of indentured servants during the eighteenth century. Fewer than 250 of 2,380 persons entering Boston from 1764 to 1768 were classified as indentured servants. These were scarcely enough to replace those whose indentures expired. More and more, the labor force had to be recruited from the ranks of "unattached" workers who bartered their services for wages in a market economy.

This laboring force consisted of the nondependent, propertyless workers of the community, now twice as numerous relative to the rest of the population as they had been a century before. In 1687, 14 percent of the total number of adult males were without taxable property; by the eve of the Revolution, the propertyless accounted for 29 pecent. The social consequences of this increase were manifold. For every wage earner who competed in the economy as an autonomous entity at the end of the seventeenth century, there were four in 1771; for every man who slept in the back of a shop, in a tavern, or in a rented room in 1687, there were four in the later period. The population of Boston had doubled, but the number of propertyless men had increased fourfold.

The adult males without property, however, did not form a single unified class, a monolithic body of landless proletarians. Rather, the bottom of society consisted of a congeries of social and occupational groups with a highly transient maritime element at one end of the spectrum and a more stable and respected artisan segment at the other. Although they held no taxable property, hard-working and reputable craftsmen who had established a permanent residence in Boston participated in the town meeting and were elected to unpaid minor offices. In March 1771, for instance, John Dyer was selected by the people of the town as "Fence Viewer" for the following year. Yet according to the tax and valuation lists compiled less than six months later, Dyer was without taxable property. At the same town meeting, four carpenters, Joseph Ballard, Joseph Edmunds, Benjamin Page, and Joseph Butler, none of whom was listed as an owner of taxable property on the valuation lists, were chosen as "Measurers of Boards." That propertyless men should be selected for public office indicates that the concept of a "stake in society," which provided the theoretical underpinning for membership in the community of colonial Boston, was interpreted in the widest possible sense. Yet it was this very conception of the social order which was becoming anachronistic under the pressure of economic development. For how could the growing number of propertyless men be integrated into a social order based in the first instance on the principle that only those having a tangible interest in the town or a definite family link to the society would be truly interested in the welfare of the community?

Changes no less significant had taken place within the ranks of the propertied groups. By the third quarter of the eighteenth century, lines of economic division and marks of social status were crystalizing as Boston approached economic maturity. Present to some degree in all aspects of town life, these distinctions were very apparent in dwelling arrangements. In 1687, 85 percent of Boston real-estate holdings had been assessed within a narrow range of two to ten pounds; by the seventh decade of the eighteenth century, the same spectrum ran from twelve to two hundred pounds. (Table 3) Gradations in housing were finer in 1771 and had social connotations which were hardly conceivable in the more primitive and more egalitarian society of the seventeenth century. This sense of distinctiveness was reinforced by geographic distribution. Affluent members of the community who had not transferred their residence to Roxbury, Cambridge, or Milton built in the spacious environs of the south and west ends. A strict segregation of the social groups was lacking; yet the milieu of the previous century, the interaction of merchant, trader, artisan and laborer in a waterfront community, had all but disappeared.

The increasing differences between the social and economic groups within the New England seaport stemmed in part from the fact that craftsmen, laborers, and small shopkeepers had failed to maintain their relative position in the economic order. In the eighty-five years from 1687 to 1771, the share of the taxable wealth of the community controlled by the lower half of the propertied population declined from 12 to 10 percent. (Table 2) If these men lived better at the end of the century than at the beginning, it was not because the economic development of Boston had effected a redistribution of wealth in favor of the laboring classes but because the long period of commercial prosperity had raised the purchasing power of every social group.

The decline in the economic distinctiveness of the middle group of property holders, the third quarter of the taxable population in the distribution of wealth, is even more significant. In 1771, these well-to-do artisans, shopkeepers, and traders (rising land values had eliminated the farmers and economic maturity the versatile merchant-sea captain) owned only 12½ percent of the taxable wealth, a very substantial decrease from the 21 percent held in 1687. These men lived considerably better than their counterparts in the seventeenth century; many owned homes and possessed furnishings rarely matched by the most elegant dwellings of the earlier period. But in relation to the other parts of the social order, their economic position had deteriorated drastically. This smaller middle group had been assessed for taxable estates twice as large as the bottom 50 percent in 1687; by 1771 the assets of the two groups were equal.

On the other hand, the wealthiest 25 percent of the taxable population by 1771 controlled 78 percent of the assessed wealth of Boston. This represented a gain of 12 percent from the end of the seventeenth century. An equally important shift had taken place within this elite portion of the population. In 1687, the richest 15 percent of the taxpayers held 52 percent of the taxable property, while the top 5 percent owned 26.8 percent. Eighty-five years later, the percentages were 65.9 and 44.1 (Tables 1 and 2 and Chart A)

Certain long-term economic developments accounted for the disappearance of a distinct middle group of property owners and the accumulation of wealth among a limited portion of the population. The scarcity of capital in a relatively underdeveloped economic system, one in which barter transactions were often necessary because of the lack of currency, required that the savings of all members of the society be tapped in the interest of economic expansion. The prospect of rapid commercial success and the high return on capital invested in mercantile activity attracted the small investor. During the first decade of the eighteenth century, nearly one of every three adult males in Boston was involved directly in trade, owning at least part of a vessel. In 1698 alone, 261 people held shares in a seagoing vessel. Trade had become "not so much a way of life as a way of making money; not a social condition but an economic activity." This widespread ownership of mercantile wealth resulted in the creation of a distinct economic "middle class" by the last decades of the seventeenth century.

A reflection of a discrete stage of economic growth, the involvement of disparate occupational and social groups in commerce was fleeting and transitory. It lasted only as long as the economy of the New England seaport remained underdeveloped, without large amounts of available capital. The increase in the wealth and resources of the town during the first half of the eighteenth century prompted a growing specialization of economic function; it was no longer necessary to rely on the investments of the less affluent members of the community for an expansion of commerce. This change was slow, almost imperceptible; but by 1771 the result was obvious. In that year, less than 5 percent of the taxable population of Boston held shares in shipping of ten tons or more, even though the tonnage owned by the town was almost double that of 1698. Few men had investments of less than fifty tons; the average owner held 112 tons. By way of contrast, the average holding at the end of the seventeenth century had been about twenty-five tons. Moreover, on the eve of the Revolution ownership of shipping was concentrated among the wealthiest men of the community. Ninety percent of the tonnage of Boston in 1771 was in the hands of those whose other assets placed them in the top quarter of the

Table 3. Real-Estate Ownership in Boston in 1687 and 1771*

1687			1771		
Assessed Total Value of Real Estate	Number of Owners	Cumulative Total of Owners	Assessed Annual Worth of Real Estate	Number of Owners	Cumulative Total of Owners
£ 1	0	0	£ 1	0	0
2	168	168	2	1	1
3	75	243	3	9	10
4	203	446	4	49	59
5	85	531	5	22	81
6	167	698	6	79	160
7	3	701	7	0	160
8	54	755	8	115	275
9	2	757	9	3	278
10	107	864	10	91	369
11	0	864	11	4	373
12	24	888	12	43	416
13	0	888	13	163	579
14	3	891	14	10	589
15	25	916	15	3	592
16	8	924	16	148	740
17	0	924	17	6	746
18	7	930	18	7	753
19	1	931	19	5	758
20	46	932	20	236	994
21–30	25	1,003	21–5	41	1,035
31–40	11	1,014	26–30	163	1,198
41–50	2	1,016	31–5	93	1,291
			36–40	92	1,383
			41–5	5	1,388
			46–50	42	1,430
			51–60	32	1,462
			61–70	10	1,472
			71–80	9	1,481
			81–90	3	1,484
			91–100	3	1,487

* The assessed annual worth of real estate in the 1771 valuation must be multiplied by six to give the total property value.

Data in Lemuel Shattuck, *Report to the Committee of the City Council Appointed to Obtain the Census of Boston for the Year 1845* (Boston, 1846), pp. 4–5, 43. The 1771 tax list indicates that only 17 of 318 Negro "servants for life" were held by persons whose property holdings placed them in the lower 50 percent of the distribution of taxable wealth; 70 by individuals in the third quarter of the economic scale; and 231 or 72.6 percent by the wealthiest 25 percent of the population.

population. With the increase in the wealth of the town had come a great increase in the number of propertyless men and a bifocalization of the property owners into (1) a large amorphous body of shopkeepers, artisans, and laborers with holdings primarily in real estate and (2) a smaller, somewhat more closely defined segment of the population with extensive commercial investments as well as elegant residences and personal possessions.

A similar trend was evident in other phases of town life. In the transitional decades of the late seventeenth and early eighteenth century, the fluidity inherent in the primitive commercial system had produced a certain vagueness in the connotations of social and economic status. Over 10 percent of the adult males in Boston designated themselves as "merchants" on the shipping registers of the period from 1698 to 1714, indicating not only the decline in the distinctiveness of a title traditionally limited to a carefully defined part of the community but also the feeling that any man could easily ascend the mercantile ladder. Economic opportunity was so evident, so promising, that the social demarcations of the more stable maritime communities of England seemed incongruous. By the sixth decade of the eighteenth century, however, rank and order were supplanting the earlier chaos as successful families tightened their control of trade. The founding in 1763 of a "Merchants Club" with 146 members was a dramatic indication that occupations and titles were regaining some of their traditional distinctiveness and meaning.

An economic profile of the 146 men who composed this self-constituted elite is revealing. Of those whose names appeared on the tax and valuation lists of 1771, only five had estates which placed them in the bottom three quarters of the distribution of wealth. Twenty-one were assessed for taxable property in excess of £1,500 and were thus in the top 1 percent of the economic scale. The taxable assets of the rest averaged £650, an amount which put them among the wealthiest 15 percent of the population.

That 146 men, 6½ percent of the adult male population, were considered eligible for membership in a formal society of merchants indicates, however, that mercantile activity was not dominated by a narrow oligarchy. The range of wealth among the members of the top quarter of the propertied population was so great and the difference of social background so large as to preclude the creation of a monolithic .class or guild with shared interests and beliefs.

Yet the influence of this segment of society was pervasive. By the third quarter of the eighteenth century, an integrated economic and political hierarchy based on mercantile wealth had emerged in Boston to replace the lack of social stratification of the early part of the century and the archaic distinctions of power and prestige of the religious community of the seventeenth century. All of the important offices of the town government, those with functions vital to the existence and prosperity of the town, were lodged firmly in the hands of a broad elite, entry into which was conditioned by commercial achievement and family background. The representatives to the General Court and the selectmen were the leaders of the town in economic endeavor as well as in political acumen. John Hancock's taxable wealth totaled £18,000; James Otis was assessed at £2,040, while Colonel Joseph Jackson had property valued at £1,288. Other levels of the administrative system were reserved for those whose business skills or reputation provided the necessary qualifications. Samuel Abbot, John Barrett, Benjamin Dolbeare, John Gore, William Phillips, William White, and William Whitewell, Overseers of the Poor in 1771, had taxable estates of £815, £5,520, £850, £1,747, £5,771, £1,953, and £1,502 respectively. All were among the wealthiest 7 percent of the property owners; and Barrett and Phillips were two of the most respected merchants of the town. John Scollay, a distiller with an estate of £320, and Captain Benjamin Waldo, a shipmaster assessed at £500, who were among those chosen as "Firewards" in 1771, might in an earlier period have been dominant in town affairs; by the seventh decade of the century, in a mature economic environment, the merchant prince had replaced the man of action at the apex of the social order.

Gradations continued to the bottom of the scale. Different social and occupational levels of the population were tapped as the dignity and

Chart A

Lorenz Curves Showing the Distribution of Wealth in Boston in 1687 and 1771 (Drawn from data in Tables 1 and 2.)

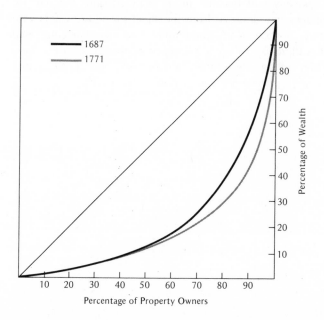

responsibility of the position demanded. It was not by accident that the estates of the town assessors, Jonathan Brown, Moses Deshon, and John Kneeland, were £208, £200, and £342. Or that those of the "Cullers of Staves," Henry Lucas, Thomas Knox, and Caleb Hayden, totaled £120, £144, and £156. The assumption of a graded social, economic, and political scale neatly calibrated so as to indicate the relation of each individual to the whole was the basic principle upon which the functioning of town-meeting "democracy" depended. William Crafts, with a taxable estate of £80, was elected "Fence Viewer." Half this amount qualified William Barrett to be "Measurer of Coal Baskets," while Henry Allen and John Bulfinch, "Measurers of Boards," were assessed at £80 and £48. The design was nearly perfect, the correlation between town office and social and economic position almost exact.

As in 1687, the distribution of political power and influence in Boston conformed to the standards and gradations of a wider, more inclusive hierarchy of status, one which purported to include the entire social order within the bounds of its authority. But the lines of force which had emerged on the eve of the American Revolution radiated from different economic and social groups than those of eighty-five years before, and now failed to encompass a significant portion of the population. The weakening of the "extended" family unit and the appearance of a large body of autonomous wage earners, "proletarians" in condition if not in consciousness, had introduced elements of mobility and diversity into the bottom part of society. Equally significant had been the growing inequality of the distribution of wealth among the propertied segment of the community, notably the greater exclusiveness and predominance of a mercantile "elite." Society had become more stratified and unequal. Influential groups, increasingly different from the small property owners who constituted the center portion of the community, had arisen at either end of the spectrum. Creations of the century-long development of a maritime economy in an urban setting, these "merchant princes" and "proletarians" stood out as the salient characteristics of a new social order.

6. THE CITY OF BROTHERLY FEAR
The Poor in Late-Eighteenth-Century Philadelphia

John K. Alexander

When the historian of early America attempts to study people near the bottom rungs of society, he is faced with the problem: "Poverty, thou hast no genealogies."[1] What he can discover about the poorer elements in society comes almost exclusively from governmental records, records of charitable organizations, and newspapers. If he wants to go beyond statistical studies of the poor, he is forced to focus primarily upon the attitudes and actions of the nonpoor. Our history must, unfortunately, be from the "top down" rather than from the "bottom up." In this paper we shall examine the views of the nonpoor of Philadelphia, especially their fear of the poor. In the late eighteenth century, established and respectable Philadelphians apparently believed that the actions of the poor endangered civilized society; control seemed to be slipping from their hands. The problems associated with the poor, while unquestionably real and even grave, might not have been as overwhelming as the nonpoor feared they were. Perhaps we will never know to what degree fiction blended with fact to cause this fear, for fear does not have to match reality. Realities are sometimes less real than fictions; incorrect perceptions sometimes *make* realities. Once the fear was born, it took on a life of its own.

In the last two decades of the eighteenth century, Philadelphia was a city in flux. Some historians have tended to conclude too readily that a situation of flux necessarily marks a socially and economically open society.[2] A city in flux can have a hardening of social and economic lines as well. Certainly not all Philadelphians viewed change as worthwhile, and some resisted it strongly. It is perhaps closer to the facts of the case to see Philadelphia not as an open society, but as a city deeply divided against itself. Philadelphians were, in many ways, fearful of the present and anxious about the future. And much of the fear that permeated society was a fear of the poor.

Philadelphia was a city steeped in fear in part because, by the late years of the eighteenth century, it was a cosmopolitan city. Walking through the streets and alleys, one could hear a mixture of languages and dialects. The number of German-speaking Philadelphians was large enough to necessitate the printing of signposts in both German and English. The Irish immigrants and descendants of Irish stock also formed a large segment of the population.[3] Toward the end of the period, refugees from the French Revolution and the 1794 revolt of blacks at Port-au-Prince in Haiti turned the city into "one great hotel or place of shelter for strangers."[4]

Philadelphians wanted immigrants in order to increase the city's population and power. Throughout this period, Philadelphia boosters painted a picture of glorious opportunities awaiting immigrants to the city and to Pennsylvania, and they carefully pointed out the dangers of settling in other parts of America.[5] But at the same time the booster literature made it quite clear that Philadelphia wanted only the right kind of immigrant. Tench Coxe, one of the city's leading boosters, pointed out that since the Revolution the state's policy was to receive all "sober" immigrants with open arms. The Pennsylvania Journal agreed, proclaiming its hope that the Pennsylvania area would always be "the asylum of peacable [sic] and honest emigrants." In tune with this view, the first arrival of the French "peasantry" in 1790 was applauded because of their "sobriety, honesty and industry."[6]

Well before the end of the eighteenth century many Philadelphians were not at all sure that living in an "asylum" was desirable. For these Philadelphians, there were clearly dangers in accepting immigrants unless their character and political views were carefully scrutinized. Charles Biddle, when he was Vice-President of Pennsylvania, claimed that the state needed a "mode" to be able to admit "the industrious and honest" while excluding "the idle and profligate" immigrant.[7] And it was not only the idle and profligate who were viewed with alarm. Irish and French immigrants—even when industrious—often came under attack for their politics. In a time of great political ferment, Philadelphians who feared democrats knew that these two national groups would rarely be their allies. And they did not hesitate to paint the Irish and French as bloody Jacobins who wanted nothing more than to subvert any political system that stressed order and stability.[8]

If some questioned the wisdom of calling for immigrants to choose Philadelphia as their new home, no one questioned the fact that the boosters had done their work well. From the end of the Revolution to the beginning of the nineteenth century, the population mushroomed. In the first federal census (1790), Philadelphia's population was listed as slightly more than 42,500; by 1800 it was almost 72,000.[9] As the city's population increased, so did its total wealth. But many observers felt that far too much of that wealth was being squandered on needless luxuries which weakened the city's moral fiber. Vocal critics pointed out, often in print, that while many Philadelphians basked in luxury, many others lived in want.[10] Calls for economy constantly appeared in print. The same critics were often quick to point out that poverty too was on the increase.[10]

In contrast with the growth in population and the increase in total wealth was the fear of decline. After the great yellow fever epidemic of

1793, and with the regular reappearance of the yellow death, Philadelphians dreaded the approaching autumn. Each new bout with yellow fever seemed to lessen the city's chance for urban dominance.[11] And although Philadelphia was the nation's capital during the 1790s, in 1800 the capital was to be moved to the banks of the Potomac. Many established Philadelphians may have feared that economic and political dominance would move with the capital.[12]

The specter of economic decline and ruin reached into even the best Philadelphia homes, for a constant theme of the period was how easily one could fall from the pinnacle of prosperity to the depths of debtor's prison.[13] It is no accident that calls for charity were often couched in statements such as, "It is a prudent foresight of the disasters which may happen to our selves, which induces us to assist others: that they may be willing to return the favor to us on a similar occasion." The concept of charity as insurance was an organic part of the whole scheme of poor relief.[14] Thus, when even the most prosperous of Philadelphia's citizens looked around them, they saw much to fear. One special focus of their fear and anger was the poor.

For the Philadelphians of this period, as for most Americans of the time, the disadvantaged were of two types. There were the "industrious" or "deserving" poor. Their chief characteristics were industry and, in most cases, sobriety. These were people who worked when work was available, but who lived close to the subsistence level. They were the citizens who, if unemployed for long, were at most a few weeks from entering the House of Employment, which was the public almshouse. The industrious poor were the people for whom subscription charities were almost annually established during the winter when the weather deprived them of work. They were the Philadelphians who were especially hard hit by yellow fever, because they could not afford to flee the city and could not find work. Immense relief funds were necessary to save them from starvation.[15]

Below the industrious poor, in the estimation of prosperous Philadelphians, were the "indigent" or "vicious" poor. Their chief characteristic was a lack of industry often caused by intemperance or "vicious" upbringing. They were seen as "worthless," "vagabond" types, and as "Drunken; Rioting, Skulking Lazy fellow[s]."[16] Prosperous Philadelphians were constantly reminded of their duty to help the industrious poor while spurning aid to the indolent poor. Despite the rhetoric, when the nonpoor Philadelphians wrote of the dangerous actions of the poor, the distinctions between the industrious and the worthless tended to melt away.[17]

Given the eighteenth-century definition, how many Philadelphians were poor? This is a critical question, but unfortunately one that is impossible to answer with precision. We can say how many people were in the House of Employment at any given time, but this only shows us the very bottom level of poverty, for as the overseers of the poor noted, "the better sort of poor"—the "honest" poor—refused to go there.[18] The essential question is how many industrious poor there were in the city.

The poorer element was not listed in city directories; and although census returns usually listed occupations, in lower-class areas occupations often were not given.[19] And many poor people may not have appeared in the census at all. In 1790 an observer noted that the census population of the city was too low because "the smaller and poorer families" often hid members, fearing they would be taxed by the size of their family. The poor also moved frequently, which made it easier for recording agencies to overlook them. In the winter, country laborers came to the city to find work and probably increased the number of poor.[20]

One of the best sources we have for determining the number of poor people was the record of charity dispensed in the winter. During the winter of 1783–4 a private subscription fund provided wood and other "necessaries" to "the poor labouring people" of the city. Approximately 1,600 families, a total of 5,212 people, were aided. This means 1 in every 7 Philadelphians was helped by this charity alone. When we add to the total aided by subscription the number helped by public funds, immigrant aid societies, and church charity, and also allow for the fact that some may have been denied aid because they were not "labouring poor," more than 1 in every 6 Philadelphians needed assistance during that winter.[21]

Other indicators suggest a maldistribution of wealth in the city. In 1793 Philadelphia numbered 7,088 taxables among its population. By 1800 the number of taxables had fallen to 6,625.[22] This decline was even more dramatic when compared to the city's sharp rise in population during the 1790s. If we cannot say precisely how many Philadelphians were poor, we can say that the number was significant.

What did it mean to be a poor person in the Philadelphia of this period? It meant above all else that employment was uncertain. What good were high wages if one could not get a job? If winter came early, many jobs literally ceased to exist. Day laborers were not the only ones hurt. Mechanics were usually referred to as part of the "common people" and linked with laborers as part of the industrious poor because of the uncertainty of their employment. It was not just chance that appeals to support American manufacturers repeatedly stressed the need to provide employment for the industrious poor.[23] Thus to be poor meant one had to plan ahead, be frugal, and practice the difficult necessity of deferred consumption.[24] And since employment was often uncertain, the poor had to work even under harsh conditions that were clearly dangerous to their health. One commentator noted that "in this climate most who are used to hard labor without doors begin to fail soon after thirty, especially if they have been obliged to live on poor diet."[25]

To be poor was, for many, also to be visible. Common seamen not only spoke distinctively, they dressed distinctively. Servants dressed in such a noticeable way that when describing a runaway servant or criminal, a Philadelphian could speak of him as having a "servant-like" dress.[26] And because the poor always paid a housing price for their poverty, they were also visible in a geographic sense. Since Philadelphia was still a walking city, the least desirable housing areas were at a distance from the center of activity. It should therefore not surprise us that the poor often lived on the outskirts.[27] Certainly the Philadelphians of the day were aware that the poor people normally lived at or near the outer edges of the city.[28] In fact, almost no poor people (such as laborers) lived in the central part of the city. If laborers did live in central areas, they usually lived together or next to each other.[29] And the dwellings of the poor were often located in the alleys of the city. If you had walked into Apple Tree Alley in the early 1790s, you would have found 23 working adults, of whom 10 were laborers.[30]

Distance was not the only housing price the poor paid. Philadelphia as a whole was not a clean city, but almost everyone agreed that the outskirts were the most "noxious" and unhealthy areas.[31] The smaller alleys—again often the home of the poor—were also offensively dirty, as were the cellars the poor occupied. During the yellow fever scourges, these alleys and cellars were death traps that often caught the poor who could not afford to flee the city.[32] For the poor, life in the cellars and alleys could indeed be nasty, brutish, and short.

To be poor also meant one needed to be deferential and of good character, for charity of any kind required recommendations. Even in the chaos that marked yellow fever epidemics, people seeking relief were expected to procure a recommendation from a "respectable" person.[33] While it was not explicitly so described by the participants, the recommendation system probably served as a means of social control. Presumably only the better sort of poor—that is, the industrious, sober, and orderly—could get a recommendation. Some groups dispensing charity clearly stated that they intended to "superintend the morals, and general conduct" of the people to whom they gave assistance. And part of this supervision was to see that the recipients of aid gained "a deep impression of the most important, and generally acknowledged moral and religious principles."[34] When winter charity was a regular occurrence and when even artisans were unemployed during yellow fever periods, the ability to receive a recommendation was essential.[35] Certainly, having a reputation as a respectable poor person and exhibiting a properly deferential demeanor enhanced one's chances of receiving aid. It was therefore not surprising that charity-dispensing groups expected and usually received "a becoming deference" from the poor.[36]

But the poor were not always respectable and deferential. Self-styled respectable citizens complained constantly of disorder in the streets, especially near the outskirts of the city inhabited by the poor. The streets were filled with vicious children making it "next to impossible in the crouds [sic] of Vice to preserve the morals of children." The district of Southwark found it necessary to establish a Society for the Suppression of Vice and Immorality. But even with such measures, people feared that where the "Vices of *Whoring, drunkenness, swindling, fraud,* and *daring impiety* abound to the extent they do in this city," success against these evils was "not possible." The public press felt the need to denounce the person who "joins in mobs, beats down the watchman, breaks open doors, takes off knockers and disturbs the quiet of honest people."[37]

Not only were the streets scenes of disorder, they were also too often the places of crime. Especially during slack times or during the yellow fever periods, the crime rate was viewed as dangerously high. Philadelphians even felt there were times when people would resort to arson to be able to "plunder" the ruins. It was noted that after each fire, "the ruined buildings are generally over-run with boys and idle people, scrutinizing, not without risk, the scenes of destruction and probably secreting any small article which they find uninjured."[38]

The fear of the poor and the immigrants was not without some foundation. Records from the city court indicate that for the period 1794–1800, at least 68.3 percent of the criminals convicted were either born in Ireland or were black. Less than 12 percent of the criminals were born in Pennsylvania, and less than 6 percent were born in Philadelphia.[39] Not only were convicted criminals often foreign born or black, they were also from the poorer element of Philadelphia. The vast majority of the blacks in the city were, all observers agreed, members of the lower class, and at best, members of the industrious poor. (The majority of blacks appear to have been laborers, servants, and seamen.)[40] That blacks accounted for almost 32 percent of all convictions indicates that a large number of criminals came from the poorer classes. The occupations of the criminals also attested to their poverty. For those convicts who had a listed occupation, 26.3 percent were laborers. The next highest groups of offenders were mariners, shoemakers, and carpenters. Few men whose occupations indicated a possible high income were convicted in the city court. Further, the items taken were often not those one would pawn. Richard Butcher stole a salmon; Oliver O'Harra took one pair of boots; Ann McCoale stole four pieces of muslin. In at least half the cases, such items suggested that hunger or need for clothing was the force that pushed these people into crime.[41]

The poor did indeed appear to form a dangerous class. Philadelphians clearly saw the link between poverty and crime. Writing in 1797, *Gale's Independent Gazetteer* pointed out that "the most afflictive and accumulated distress" in Philadelphia existed "amongst the *Irish Emigrants* and the *French* Negroes," which led the editor to note:

... it may not perhaps, be unworthy of public attention, to enquire how these people are generally supported, and whether many acts of depredation, and many scenes of horror which have occurred in this and neighboring States, may not, in some degree, be traced to the extreme poverty of this distressed class of people; for, where there is no hope there can be but little exertion, and it requires something more than common abilities to struggle against the accumulated miseries of Poverty, Sickness and Contempt![42]

It was not simply the physical and criminal violence of the poor that made them a dangerous class; their very language was considered violent. Swearing was far too common, and it was noted that among "the lower sort of People . . . there is a want of good manners."[43] Benjamin Rush, a driving force behind education for the poor, argued that the "ignorance and vices" of the children of the poor "contaminated" the children who came from "the higher ranks of society." Only by educating the children of the poor, who form "a great proportion in all communities," could the "profane and indecent language" that abounded in "every street" be stopped. Moreover, education would reduce the number of poor and lower the crime rate. It was essential not to "exhaust" charity funds on health care because "their [the poor's] morals are of more consequence to society than their health or lives."[44] Thus the poor were to be educated not so much for themselves as for society's needs. Rush was not alone in fearing what he called the "vulgar habits" of the poor.[45] Urging the need to educate the poor as well as the rich, one writer maintained that "ignorance, generally speaking, is the cause of almost all the evils we feel or fear." Another observer noted that "seveu-eights [sic] of the wretches who suffer punishment for crimes, are destitute of learning." Time and again the point was made that once the children of the poor were educated, "then our streets will be no more crouded [sic] with the votaries of ignorance or vice, nor our persons endangered by the midnight robbers or assassin."[46]

Philadelphia responded to such appeals by establishing numerous charity schools. The Society of Friends increased its already impressive efforts to provide education for blacks. The Sunday School Society opened its first school in March 1791. By 1800 it had provided schooling for over 2,100 poor children. Church groups also opened their own charity schools. Efforts to educate the poor were truly charitable, but not disinterested. The people who supported these charities were thankful that the children of the "poorer part of the community who would otherwise have been running through the streets habituating themselves to mischief, are rescued from vice and innured [sic] to habits of virtue and religion." These charities seem clearly designed not so much to elevate the poor as to keep them orderly.[47]

Not all Philadelphians agreed that education was the road to a tranquil society. Those who wanted to educate the poor noted that their opponents often contended that "the poor ought to be ignorant—that learning makes them idle, vicious and proud." And some coupled a call for education with a demand that youths who could not pay for their education should be forced to work to learn habits of industry.[48] Still, even the opponents of education were dominated by fear—the fear that an educated but poor person would be discontented with his lot. Clearly the whole public debate on educating the poor reflected the belief that the poor formed a dangerous class. The primary question was how best to keep them in check.

Fear of the poor also clouded politics. Throughout the period, almost all public comments on political questions bristled with statements that reveal class antagonisms. Specific appeals to the poor were also commonplace.[49] The governance of the city itself created a political battle liberally sprinkled with appeals to save the poor from oppression. In 1783, when a plan for incorporating the city was before the state legislature, approximately 1,400 Philadelphians signed a petition against incorporation, because it would subject them to "an aristocratic police." When the issue came up again in 1786, citizens noted how "distressed" Philadelphians would be if the people should once again be subjected to "an aristocratic common council, who may extend it[self] at their pleasure."[50]

But in 1789 Philadelphia was incorporated. The basis of the new city government was a fifteen-man aldermanic council elected by freeholders worth 50 pounds and a thirty-man common council elected by all freemen.[51] The protests and attacks on this city government continued loud and long. A nonfreeholder urged the freemen to elect common councilmen who "are in your own situation of life—men who will not *betray*, but *feelingly support,* your interest." In a later essay he expressed his fears more explicitly, arguing, "as a *freeman,* I abhor the odious distinction which the constitution holds out upon the present occasion. It not only *deprives* the *poor* of a vote in the election of Aldermen, but it places the *Aldermen* in a state of *dependence upon the rich only*; and this *dependence* may induce them to disregard and *oppress the poor,* who have the misfortune to contend for *their rights with the rich.*" Throughout the 1790s, the poor were told their interests were being sacrificed to benefit the rich.[52] If the rich feared the language and viciousness of the poor, the poor and even the middle classes feared the political power of the rich.

The experience of Israel Israel as a candidate in Philadelphia offers a clear picture of politics based on class appeals and fear of the poor. During the yellow fever epidemic of 1793, Israel, a leader in the Democratic Societies, was one of the people who stayed in the city and helped distribute relief to the poor. Using this relief work as a key point in his campaigns, he ran for the Pennsylvania Senate in 1793 and 1795, losing each time. In both campaigns he stressed the fact that the Philadelphia government was an aristocratic government which disregarded the needs of the poor. As one of his supporters argued, "let the poor wretch agonized with disease and ab[a]ndoned by the world say whether *Israel Israel* has not a soul above the common part."[53]

The election of 1797 was a different story. The vote for state senator occurred while many affluent Philadelphians were out of the city because of a recurrence of yellow fever. Israel carried only 2 of the 12 city wards— North and South Mulberry—but these were the wards with the highest percentages of lower-class residents. And by winning slightly more than 82 percent of the vote in the Northern Liberties and almost 87 percent of the vote in Southwark, both lower-class suburban areas, Israel was able to win by a margin of only 38 votes out of 4,010 cast.[54] The supporters of his opponent, Benjamin R. Morgan, denounced the election and argued that Israel won only because the yellow fever had driven "the freeholders and other respectable inhabitants" away, allowing "the citoyens of Irishtown [in Southwark] and the Northern Liberties" to elect him. Only his appeal to the "deluded masses" and chance had allowed him to win.[55]

There is no question that Israel used class appeals and his relief work for the poor to achieve victory. As one of his supporters noted, "the *well born*" of Philadelphia opposed Israel because he was a tavern keeper, "but as the right of suffrage is fortunately *not yet* confined to the gentlemen of the *learned professions*, it is not to be [but] imagined, that this objection will have little weight with the useful classes among us, the artisans and mechanics have too much respect for themselves to object to Israel Israel because he is not a merchant or a lawyer."[56]

Morgan's supporters were not to be done in so easily. They petitioned the Pennsylvania Senate, claiming Israel's election was illegal because people in the Northern Liberties and in Southwark had been allowed to vote without proving that they had taken the required oath of allegiance. The Senate committee agreed, and ordered a new election.[57]

From the middle of January 1798 until the new election of February 22, the press was filled with charges and countercharges. Both sides denounced the violence of the opposition. Both sides claimed the opposition would use fraud, intimidation, and "dark schemes" to win.[58] "A Friend to Justice," claiming he had not voted for Israel in October, declared he would do so now because the committee had proved the right of suffrage "to be of *sportive* value." He argued that since 1790 a certificate of allegiance was unnecessary and not needed to vote "until lately, when party purposes were to be answered by the exaction." And he agreed with Israel's supporters that if such a voting rule were to be uniformly required, not a single legislator could claim to be legally elected. "A Republican" bitterly argued that Israel's election was not put aside for irregularities. The truth of the matter was that Israel's opponents objected to "his being a zealous defender of, and advocate for liberty and equality amongst men, disapproving of all distinctions, titles, excises and stamp acts, with every other political measure which lays a burden on the common and poor people for the benefit of the rich." Israel's supporters stressed the fact that he was "a true republican" and a friend to the poor, as his relief work indicated. Using such appeals, the pro-Israel group hammered home the theme that the rights of the people had been taken away when he was denied the Senate seat.[59]

The Morgan forces depicted Israel and his followers as riotous Jacobins. Time and again it was charged that Israel's followers used violence to take over or to disrupt Morgan endorsement meetings. The pro-Morgan press carried dire predictions of what an Israel victory would mean. They warned that "the hour of danger is come— . . . our country is struggling in the deadly gripe [*sic*] of disorder and rapine, and the contest is doubtful. Our government and laws totter under the unremitting exertions of ruffians panting for tumult, plunder and bloodshed . . . and in hellish anticipation [they] view your property as already their own." Other Morgan backers urged all to vote for Morgan lest "the lawless sons of anarchy and mis-rule" steal the people's property. And realizing the appeal of Israel to the poor, the Morgan forces attempted to counter it by reminding the voters that "the enemies of the rich, are the enemies of the poor." They denounced all "demagogues" who drew "a political distinction between the rich and the poor." Since the interests of the rich and the poor were identical and since Morgan was the man who supported the Constitution, Morgan was the only choice.[60]

When the votes were in, Morgan had won by 357 out of 8,723 votes cast. Israel won only a third of the votes cast in the city wards. As in the first election, the only city wards he carried were North and South Mul-berry wards. And he again won handily in the lower-class areas of the Northern Liberties and Southwark. He won 69 percent of the vote in the eastern Northern Liberties, 76 percent in the western Northern Liberties, and just less than 75 percent of the vote in Southwark.[61] Not without reason did William Cobbett claim that many of "the ignorant and indigent" were won to Israel's cause by his relief work.[62]

When the victory for Morgan was assured, Cobbett gloated that "the friends of government [that is, Morgan backers] have proved themselves, not only the most rich and the best informed, but also the most *numerous.*" Still he had to concede that Morgan was able to win only because the Quakers, who normally did not vote, had supported him. Had the Quakers —as a group among the most prosperous Philadelphians—not supported Morgan, Philadelphia would have had "the mortification to see a grogshop man fixed in the Senate." And with special relish he told his readers an election story that revealed the deep class divisions in the election. A Quaker on his way to vote asked a man walking along the road if he wanted a ride. But he also asked the man for whom he was going to vote. When the man said Israel Israel, the Quaker told him to walk. Cobbett noted: "This is a good example. Let no one give them a lift.— Let them trudge through the dirt, without shoes or stockings, 'till misery and pain bring them to their senses."[63]

The pro-Israel *Aurora* agreed that the vote was cast along class lines. It argued that Israel had done very well "not withstanding all the influence of wealth was exerted in his [Morgan's] favor." And the editor added that the closeness of the election "must strike terror into the hearts of aristo-crats." The *Aurora* closed the books on the election by claiming that Morgan people "have threatened and deprived of bread those who are in their employ if they did not vote with them."[64] To the last, the election of Israel was conducted with an eye to the position of the poor and with bitter class antagonism.

The case of Israel Israel demonstrated that many Philadelphians feared the political power of the poor, and that the poor would respond to a man who had helped them in time of need. Israel was not the equal of the city or ward bosses of the nineteenth century, but he too gave assistance and asked for votes in return. And he got them.[65]

The attempt to control the poor or dangerous class went beyond Sunday schools and alliances to defeat candidates who courted their votes. The Philadelphia press printed countless items that offered psychological inducements to the poor to suffer their woes quietly, contentedly. Appeals extolled the joys of poverty, labor, and adversity while pointing out the miseries of being rich. The poor were reminded that "the mind that's contented, from ambition free/Tis that man alone which can happiness see."[66] It was often claimed that "Riches bring Cares," and that while contentment "seldom makes her home/In proud grandeur's glided dome," she "loves to visit humble cots."[67] To be rich was dangerous, for "Prosperity best discovers Vice, but Adversity, Virtue!" Occasionally, the theme was varied to say that while people in "the higher departments of life" had more pleasure, they also had a greater measure of pain.[68]

Tied to the listing of the joys of poverty were reminders "to suffer what we cannot alter and to pursue without repining the road which Providence, who directs every thing, has marked to us." Since all men suffer "misery and misfortunes," we should suffer "willing[ly] what we cannot avoid." And there are rewards if one suffers quietly. For "to be good is to be happy," and "Virtue alone, has that to give/which makes it joy to die or live." If one was contented and virtuous, but poor, he would surely receive his reward in Heaven, for God loves the poor.[69] Of course if a man was sober, respectable, and industrious, he could expect to advance.[70] And if he suffered misfortunes, such as being out of work, he could expect to receive charity. Still, one should be contented with his lot and not expect advancement to come quickly.

We cannot be sure that these psychological appeals were caused solely by fear of the poor. Still, they must be examined within the context of the fear of the poor that did exist. Surely, mere chance did not dictate such a high number of calls to suffer in orderly quiet. And it is revealing that even with the controls the nonpoor had over jobs and charity, even with the power of government to aid them, established Philadelphians felt the need to add this psychological weapon to their arsenal. A man does not constantly plead with you to be orderly and to stay in your place when he can, without violence, force you to do so. The constant use of these appeals seems to show just how terribly unsure the prosperous were of being able to control the poor.

The Philadelphia we have been examining seems, in many ways, to be a very modern city. Was the eighteenth-century city really so different from that of the nineteenth or even the twentieth century? Certainly we need to examine the story of the poor and their place in early American society far more than we yet have. And certainly before we proclaim that early America was basically a happy, socially open society, we had better do some more excavating. In excavating the bedrock of the urban social structure in young America, we may uncover some strikingly familiar artifacts. We may find that time has wrought few changes in American urban life. Even this preliminary examination apparently supports historians' claims of continuity in American history,[71] although that continuity may well be far different from what is normally depicted. At least for urban America, there is the real possibility that among the most persistent elements have been a high degree of residential segregation, a large measure of poverty, and a deep fear of the poor.

NOTES

1. Quoted in "The Memorial of Poverty, Infirmity and Old Age," *Aurora. General Advertiser,* July 28, 1796. Hereafter cited as *Aurora.* Some personal accounts can be found, and in some cases historians can make the poorer elements of early American society speak for themselves. See Jesse Lemisch, "Jack Tar in the Streets: Merchant Seamen in the Politics of Revolutionary America," *William and Mary Quarterly,* 3rd Ser., XXV (July 1968), 371–407. But in most cases we cannot find enough personal material to undertake a full study. (In this note, as in those that follow, the citations are to representative selections. No attempt has been made to exhaust the possible examples that might be cited.)

2. Sam Bass Warner, Jr., *The Private City: Philadelphia in Three Periods of Its Growth* (Philadelphia: University of Pennsylvania Press, 1968), pp. 5, 8, 17; but cf. p. 45. And see also Jackson T. Main, *The Social Structure of Revolutionary America* (Princeton, N.J.: Princeton University Press, 1965), pp. 194–5.

3. Philadelphia City Archives, "Sentence Docket December 2, 1794 to February, 1804," pp. 3, 48, 72. The city archives will be abbreviated hereafter as PCA. See also "A Citizen of Pennsylvania," *The Pennsylvania Packet, and General Advertiser,* April 7, 1790. Hereafter *Penn. Packet.* Henry Wansey, *Journal of an Excursion to the United States of North America* (Salisbury, Eng.: n.p., 1796) pp. 184–5; Benjamin Rush to Charles Nisbet, August 27, 1784, in L. H. Butterfield, ed., *Letters of Benjamin Rush,* 2 vols. (Princeton, N.J.: Princeton University Press, 1951), I, 336.

4. Samuel Hazard, ed., *Register of Pennsylvania, Devoted to the Preservation of Facts and Documents, and Every Other Kind of Useful Information Respecting the State of Pennsylvania,* 16 vols. (Philadelphia: Hazard, 1828–36), II, 22–3.

5. Isaac Weld, *Travels Through the States of North America, and the Province of Upper and Lower Canada, During the Years 1795, 1796, and 1797* (London: John

Stockdale, 1799), pp. 438–9; *The Pennsylvania Mercury and Universal Advertiser,* June 29, 1787. Hereafter *Penn. Mercury.* Benjamin Rush to James Currie, November 20, 1801, in Butterfield, *op. cit.,* vol. II, p. 839. See also "To American Farmers . . . ," in *ibid.,* vol. I, pp. 503–505; Tench Coxe, *A View of the United States of America* (Philadelphia: Hall and Wrigley & Berriman, 1794), pp. 61, 94–5.

6. Coxe, *op. cit.,* p. 74; *Penn. Mercury,* June 3, 1790; *The Pennsylvania Journal and the Weekly Advertiser,* February 4, 1789. Hereafter *Penn. Journal.*

7. *Penn. Packet,* March 1, 1786.

8. "Charlotte," *The Pennsylvania Evening Post and Daily Advertiser,* August 10, 1785. Hereafter *Penn. Post. Gazette of the United States, & Philadelphia Daily Advertiser,* November 8 and December 17, 1798. Hereafter *Gaz. of U.S.* "Irish Rebels," *Porcupine's Gazette,* November 28, 1798; "Comparison," *ibid.,* December 6, 1798. For a relevant study of the Irish and politics in Philadelphia, see Edward C. Carter, II, "A 'Wild Irishman' Under Every Federalist's Bed: Naturalization in Philadelphia, 1789–1806," *The Pennsylvania Magazine of History and Biography,* XCIV (July 1970), 331–46.

9. Philadelphia at that time included the district of Southwark and the township of the Northern Liberties. While not legally a part of the city, they were considered integral parts by all Philadelphians. See *A Century of Population Growth* Washington, D.C.: Government Printing Office, 1909), pp. 11, 13; and Evarts B. Green and Virginia D. Harrington, *American Population Before the Federal Census of 1790* (New York: Columbia University Press, 1932), pp. 117n, 118; *Return of the Whole Number of Persons . . . for the Second Census . . . One Thousand Eight Hundred* (Washington, D.C.: Apollo Press, 1802), p. 49. It is possible that the population count for 1790 is too low. See *Aurora,* November 19, 1790.

10. [J. P. Brissot De Warville], *New Travels in the United States of America 1788,* Durand Echeverria, ed., (Cambridge: Harvard University Press, 1964), p. 253; Eugene Chase, ed. and trans., *Our Revolutionary Forefathers: The Letters of Francois, Marquis de Barbe Marbois . . . 1779–1785* (New York: Duffield and Company, 1929), p. 133; "A New Catechism," July 14, 1789, and "X.Y.," October 26, 1793, in *The Independent Gazetteer; or the Chronical of Freedom.* Hereafter *Indep. Gazetteer.* "On the Times," *The Philadelphia Minerva,* July 9, 1796. Hereafter *The Minerva. The Pennsylvania Herald, and General Advertiser,* June 9, 1787. Hereafter *Penn. Herald. Penn. Packet,* December 9, 1784.

11. John H. Powell, *Bring Out Your Dead* (Philadelphia: University of Pennsylvania Press, 1949); *Claypoole's American Daily Advertiser,* November 8, 1798. Hereafter *Claypoole's ADA.*

12. *The Freeman's Journal: or the North-American Intelligencer,* April 7, 1784, and August 24, 1791. Hereafter *Freeman's Journal. Penn. Journal,* August 26, 1789; *Gaz. of U.S.,* September 1, 1790.

13. "On Benevolence," *Penn. Packet,* August 17, 1787; "Delia," *ibid.,* February 28, 1787; *Indep. Gazetteer,* January 20, 1787; "Effects of Misfortune," *The Minerva,* April 22, 1797; Thomas Scott, *A Sermon Preached at St. Peter's Church, on Sunday the 26th of August, 1792* (Philadelphia: Stewart & Cochran, 1792).

14. "Humanity," January 2, 1796, and "Pity," January 27, 1718, in *The Minerva;*

"Monitor," *Indep. Gazetteer,* November 9, 1793; *ibid.,* May 18, 1793; "The Beggars," *The Federal Gazette, and Philadelphia Evening Post,* June 27, 1789. Hereafter *Fed. Gazette.*

15. *Gaz. of U.S.,* April 7, 1796; *Penn. Journal,* March 17, 1790; *Indep. Gazetteer,* December 31, 1785, July 10, 1787, January 8, 1791, and April 16, 1794; *Freeman's Journal,* June 25, 1783; *Penn. Packet,* August 26, 1785; *Porcupine's Gazette,* October 23, 1797, and November 29, 1798; *Fed. Gazette,* September 6, 1791, and May 2, 1794; Powell, *op. cit.,* pp. 57–8.

16. PCA, "Guardians of the Poor: 'Daily Occurrences' at the Alms-house March 26, 1792 to June 7, 1793." See entries for April 22, 1792, and March 26, 1792. See also *Penn. Packet,* November 9, 1786; *Penn. Mercury,* June 21, 1788; *Aurora,* November 1, 1790; *The Pennsylvania Gazette, and Weekly Advertiser,* October 1, 1788. Hereafter *Penn. Gazette.*

17. *The Minerva,* February 3, 1798; *Penn. Journal,* July 18, 1781; *Freeman's Journal,* September 24, 1788; *Indep. Gazetteer,* February 28, 1789; *Claypoole's ADA,* October 7, 1797. Some refused to accept such a distinction and called for charity for all in need. See "Charity," *The Minerva,* April 11, 1795; *Fed. Gazette,* June 13, 1789; "Benevolus," *Freeman's Journal,* September 24, 1788.

18. The records of the House of Employment and Alms-House are remarkably complete. See PCA, various kinds of records listed under Guardians of the Poor and Managers of the Alms-House. The figures were normally printed in the newspapers each year. On the attitudes noted, see PCA, "Minutes of the Overseers of the Poor of the City of Philadelphia MDCCLXXII [to September 27, 1787]," entries of February 15 and August 18, 1785; "Managers of the Alms-House Minutes May 1788 to March 1796," pp. 422–3.

19. On the lower classes being excluded from directories, see the good short comment by Stuart Blumin in Stephan Thernstron and Richard Sennett, eds., *Nineteenth-Century Cities* (New Haven, Conn.: Yale University Press, 1969), pp. 170–71.

20. *Aurora,* November 19, 1790; "The Durid, No. V," *Penn. Journal,* May 9, 1781; and Weld, *Travels,* p. 72; "An American," *Indep. Gazetteer,* August 14, 1787; and cf. "The Discontented Villager," *The Minerva,* January 28, 1797.

21. "To the Public," *Penn. Packet,* March 11, 1784. The ratio of 1 in 7 is based on the assumption that Philadelphia's population in 1783 was 33,870. See *A Century of Population Growth,* pp. 11, 13. During that winter public charity alone relieved 117 out-pensioners and an average of 230 in the almshouse, and this total does not include the "great" number of beggars and "vagrants" who were in the city. See PCA, "Managers of the Alms-House Minutes May 1780 to May 1788," entry of March 3, 1784.

22. While the number of taxables was declining in the city, the number of taxables in Philadelphia County was increasing. See "Return of Taxable Inhabitants," *Aurora,* December 31, 1800; and Hazard, *op. cit.,* vol. II, p. 352.

23. "Communication," *Aurora,* October 28, 1796; *Penn. Mercury,* June 29, 1787; "Thoughts on Good Times," *Freeman's Journal,* July 9, 1788; Jacob C. Parsons, ed., *Extracts from the Diary of Jacob Hiltzheimer of Philadelphia, 1765–1798*

(Philadelphia: Wm. F. Foll & Co., 1893), p. 204; "On American Manufacture," *Penn. Packet,* August 26, 1785; "The American Cotton Manufactory," *ibid.,* November 12, 1788; Historical Society of Pennsylvania, Pennsylvania Society for the Encouragement of Manufactures and the Useful Arts, entry of December 21, 1787. Hereafter the Historical Society will be abbreviated HSP. "An Old Whig," *Indep. Gazetteer,* October 10, 1785; *Penn. Herald,* January 18, 1786, and July 22, 1786; *Fed. Gazette,* March 9, 1792; *Aurora,* September 29, 1797. Charles S. Olton, who has made a detailed study of Philadelphia artisans, believes the mechanics were more of an "entrepreneurial" than a "dependent" class. See his "Philadelphia Artisans and the American Revolution" (unpublished Ph.D. dissertation, University of California at Berkeley, 1967), pp. 3, 15–16. I am less sanguine about the place of mechanics in the social structure.

24. "Oeconomy," *Penn. Herald,* May 30, 1787; and "C," Fed. Gazette, September 6, 1791.

25. *Penn. Gazette,* February 2, 1780.

26. *Indep. Gazetteer,* May 15, 1784, and January 15, 1785; *Aurora,* March 16, 1793; *Penn. Packet,* April 27, 1785; *The New World,* January 6, 1797; and cf. John F. Watson, *Annals of Philadelphia and Pennsylvania in the Older Time* . . . , 3 vols. (Philadelphia: Edwin S. Stuart, 1905), I, 189, 191–2.

27. Warner, *op. cit.,* pp. 13–14, but cf. p. 17. And, for example, in 1780 West Mulberry ward had 527 taxables, of whom 104 were laborers. In 1781 Southwark had 723 taxables of whom 101 were laborers. In centrally located wards in 1780, the figures run: Chestnut ward, 103 taxables of whom 1 was a laborer; Lower Delaware ward, 104 taxables of whom 3 were laborers; High Street ward, 175 taxables of whom 4 were laborers. (I am responsible for all of these figures, which were obtained from the Constable's tax returns in PCA where the returns are listed by ward and date.) When the federal census was taken in 1790, the occupations of 827 residents of Southwark were listed. Two hundred of the 827 were "laborers, porters, helpers," or held other menial jobs. In the more centrally located area between South and Race Streets, there were 2,758 residents with their occupations listed. But only 239 residents of this area were "laborers, porters, helpers, etc." Considering only people whose occupations were listed, the ratio of residents of the more central area to Southwark is about 3.5 to 1. But the ratio of doctors is 12 to 1, the ratio of merchants and dealers is 13 to 1, and the ratio of lawyers is 12 to 1 (all ratios approximate). Southwark obviously had much less than its share of professional people *(A Century of Population Growth,* pp. 142–3). In 1800 in the eastern Northern Liberties, 378 of 1,734 taxables (approximately 22%) were laborers. In the western Northern Liberties, 469 of 1,788 taxables (approximately 26%) were laborers. In eastern Southwark the percentage of laborers was only about 10% because eastern Southwark had a high concentration of sailors, seamen, and mariners (approximately 26%), many of whom were members of the lower class. In the western area of Southwark, over 10% of the taxables were laborers. HSP, "Enumeration of the Taxable Inhabitants within the County of Philadelphia 1800." (I am responsible for the listing of total number of laborers and for the percentages.) Cf. also Norman J. Johnston, "The Caste and Class of the Urban Form of Historic Philadelphia," *Journal of the American Institute of Planners,* XXXII (November 1966), 334–50, esp. 340–41.

28. See entry of February 5, 1798, in HSP, "Philadelphia Poor House 1765–68," in the Edward Wanton Smith Collection; and PCA, "Managers of the Alms-House Minutes May 1788 to March 1796," pp. 82–3.

29. For example, three of the four laborers who lived in High Street ward in 1780 lived together or next to each other. See PCA, "Constable's Tax Return for 1780," p. 120, and cf. pp. 116–22 *passim*. Warner claims that "variety best characterizes the occupational structure of the [Middle] ward as it did all the other wards of the first Philadelphia" (*The Private City*, p. 17). Yet, in the Middle ward Warner was studying, almost 50% of the laborers lived in Elbow Alley or in the extreme western part of the ward (see PCA, "Constable's Returns of the City of Philadelphia for 1775").

30. See Powell, *op. cit.* There were 24 householders, but in all records Peter Mercer is merely listed as "Negroe." (See PCA, "Constables Returns for South Mulberry Ward, 1791," pp. 36–7.) The census listed 14 heads of households, of whom 3 were laborers. See *Heads of Families at the First Census of the United States Taken in the Year 1790 Pennsylvania* (Washington, D.C.: Government Printing Office, 1908), p. 232.

31. "Truth," *Fed. Gazette*, July 10, 1799; *ibid.*, February 5, 1796, and June 5, 1799; *Penn. Packet*, May 24, 1787; *Carey's United States' Recorder*, February 17, 1798. Hereafter *U.S. Recorder*.

32. Mathew Carey estimated that seven-eighths of the people who died during the yellow-fever epidemic of 1793 were poor (cited in Powell, *op. cit.*, p. 91). See also *Porcupines' Gazette*, August 9, 1788; HSP, Ebenezer Hazard to Robert Ralston, September 13, 1797, in Gratz Collection; HSP, Margaret Morris to M. M. Moore, October 2, 1800; HSP, "Ann Parrish Visitations to the Sick 1796," in Parrish Collection, p. 7. HSP, Samuel Duffield to Alexander Dalles, July 27, 1794, in Gratz Collection.

33. "Tents," *Porcupine's Gazette*, September 25, 1798; PCA, "Minutes of the Board of Health Beginning 26th July 1796 and ending the 3d of May 1788," entry for September 21, 1797; HSP, St. George's Society Minutes for April 23, 1772 to December 17, 1812, *passim*.

34. HSP, "Penn. Abolition Society Committee for Improving Condition of Free Blacks, Minutes, 1790–1803," entry of April 10, 1790. Hereafter "Penn. Abo. Soc."

35. Mathew Carey, *Short Account of the Malignant Fevers Lately Prevalent in Philadelphia*, 4th ed. (Philadelphia: M. Carey, 1794), p. 17.

36. HSP, "Penn. Abo. Soc.," p. 35, and cf. pp. 59–60. See also W. E. B. DuBois, *The Philadelphia Negro* (New York: Shocken Books, 1967 [original 1899]) pp. 83–4.

37. For the quotations, see "Honestus," *Penn. Packet*, September 3, 1785; *Porcupine's Gazette*, January 16, 1798; "The Picture," *Penn. Packet*, August 20, 1785. See also Hazard, *Register, op. cit.*, vol. II, p. 326; "A.B.," *Indep. Gazetteer*, November 8, 1783; "M," December 23, 1788, and October 16, 1790, in *Fed. Gazette; Penn. Journal*, August 10, 1798: *Penn. Gazette*, August 17, 1791; *Claypoole's ADA*, December 17, 1790; "To the Orderly," *Aurora*, August 24, 1795; "An Enquiry," *Penn. Packet*, June 11, 1787. Riotous people were not necessarily poor, but the link was often made.

38. *Penn. Herald,* November 11, 1786; *Indep. Gazette,* November 12, 1785; *Penn. Journal,* February 8, 1780, and August 10, 1791; *Porcupine's Gazette,* September 15, 1797; *Gale's Independent Gazetteer,* December 23, 1796; *Claypoole's ADA,* January 17, 1797; *The New World,* January 6, 1797; "A Citizen," *Penn. Packet,* November 28, 1789.

39. The source for the construction of these figures is in PCA, "Sentence Docket for December 1794 to February 1804," and "Philadelphia County Inspectors of the Jail and Penitentiary House—Prisoners for the Third Docket 1790–1797." The percentages are based on 320 prisoners convicted in the Mayor's Court of Philadelphia from 1794 through 1800. (We have no similar sentence dockets from earlier periods. Twenty-eight criminals who were repeat offenders were counted only once.)

The percentages given are a very conservative estimate of the percentage of immigrant and black crime, because the figures reflect only place of birth. Also, when a person was not specifically described as a black, he was put in the white category. Thus three convicts born in Guinea and one man described as being "a yellowish man" were not included in the totals for blacks. However, using a list of convictions may somewhat overstate the degree of crime by the poorer element. It is quite possible that the more prosperous Philadelphians, even if engaged in crime, avoided conviction.

40. See Dubois, *op. cit.,* pp. 17, 22–3; Wansey, *Journal,* p. 184; HSP, "Penn. Abo. Soc.," pp. 112, 219–20; *Gale's Independent Gazetteer,* January 3, 1797.

41. Only 57 of the 320 criminals had an occupation listed, and 15 of the 57 were laborers. See PCA, "Sentence Book for 1794–1804," pp. 22, 29, 182, and *passim.*

42. January 3, 1797; see also *Penn. Herald,* September 18, 1787; *Porcupine's Gazette,* September 15, 1797; *U.S. Recorder,* June 7, 1798.

43. Weld, *Travels,* p. 17. See also *The Philadelphia Monthly Magazine, or Universal Repository of Knowledge and Entertainment,* II (July 1798), p. 22; and *The Minerva,* April 11, 1795.

44. Benjamin Rush, "To the Citizens of Philadelphia," dated March 28, 1787, in Butterfield, *op. cit.,* vol. I, pp. 412–15 and *passim.*

45. *Penn. Herald,* July 18, 1787; *Indep. Gazetteer,* August 28, 1789; *Penn. Journal,* January 27, 1790; *Penn. Packet,* January 21, 1790.

46. *Claypoole's ADA,* February 9, 1796; *Gaz. of U.S.,* January 9, 1796; "Z," *Fed. Gazette,* November 20, 1788.

47. DuBois, *op. cit.,* pp. 83–4; *Penn. Mercury,* November 22, 1788; James Mease, *The Picture of Philadelphia* (Philadelphia; B. & T. Kite, 1811), pp. 251, 261, 262–3; *Fed. Gazette,* December 2, 1793; *Aurora,* February 12, 1791, and May 17, 1796; James Hardie, *The Philadelphia Directory and Register,* 2nd ed. (Philadelphia: Jacob Johnson and Company, 1794), p. 212; *Gaz. of U.S.,* July 18, 1787, and August 27, 1796; *Gale's Independent Gazetteer,* April 21, 1797.

48. *Gaz. of U.S.,* August 2, 1796; *Penn. Packet,* May 21, 1787; *Aurora,* December 15, 1791.

49. *Freeman's Journal,* August 8, 1781, October 23, 1782, September 29, 1784, and

January 28, 1789; *Indep. Gazetteer,* September 16, 1786, May 5, 1789, and
January 30, 1790; *Fed. Gazette,* April 8, 1789, October 7, 1799; *The New World,*
November 1, 1796.

50. "A.B.," *Penn. Packet,* April 30, 1786; and *Penn. Journal,* September 10, 1783;
cf. *Indep. Gazetteer,* January 13, 1786; and *Penn. Herald,* November 30, 1785.

51. Edward P. Allinson and Boies Penrose, *Philadelphia 1681–1887* (Philadelphia:
Allen, Lane and Scott Publishers, 1887), pp. 9, 19, 60–62.

52. "No Freeholder," *Indep. Gazetteer,* March 26, 1789; "An Old Mechanic,"
March 28, 1789, December 1, 1792, in *Fed. Gazette; Aurora,* March 26, 1794, March
28, 1794, July 8, 1794, October 5, 1795, and January 30, 1796.

53. Quote from "Justitia," *Aurora,* October 5, 1795. See also *ibid.,* March 21, 1795;
Indep. Gazetteer, December 14, 1793; *Fed. Gazette,* October 26, 1793, and
December 19, 1793; *Penn. Gazette,* May 15, 1793, and May 7, 1794.

54. *Porcupine's Gazette,* October 10, 1797, November 13, 1797, February 7, 1798,
Gaz. of U.S., February 21, 1798, October 9, 1797; *Fed. Gazette,* October 9, 1797;
Claypoole's ADA, October 10, 1797; *Aurora,* February 24, 1798.

55. *Porcupine's Gazette,* October 13, 1797; see also notes 63 to 65, below.

56. *Aurora,* October 9, 1797; cf. "Humanitus," *Fed. Gazette,* October 24, 1797.

57. The pro-Morgan argument also included the claim that the election in
Southwark was not held at the legally designated polling place. See *Fed. Gazette,*
January 23, 1798, January 25, 1798; *Aurora,* January 26, 1798, February 8, 1798;
Claypoole's ADA, January 27, 1798.

58. "A Republican," *U.S. Recorder,* February 17, 1798; "A Democrat," *ibid.,*
February 20, 1798; "Truth," *Gaz. of U.S.,* February 20, 1798.

59. Quotes from *Fed. Gazette,* February 13, 1798, and *U.S. Recorder,* February 17,
1798. See also *Fed. Gazette,* February 17, 1798; *Aurora,* January 18, 1798; *Claypoole's
ADA,* February 19, 20, and 21, 1798.

60. Quotes from "Foresight," *Gaz. of U.S.,* February 21, 1798; *Penn. Gazette,*
February 21, 1798; *Gaz. of U.S.,* February 16, 1798. See also *ibid.,* February 17 and
21, 1798; *Penn. Gazette,* February 21, 1798.

61. *U.S. Recorder,* February 24, 1798; *Aurora,* February 26, 1798.

62. *Porcupine's Gazette,* February 24, 1798.

63. *Ibid.,* and February 26, 1798.

64. *Aurora,* February 24 and 26, 1798.

65. Israel was elected Sheriff of Philadelphia County in 1800.

66. "Contentment," *Penn. Mercury,* August 24, 1787; see also *Penn. Packet,*
November 24, 1785.

67. Quotes in *The Mail: or Claypoole's Daily Advertiser,* April 1, 1793, June 17,
1793. Hereafter *The Mail.* See also *Penn. Packet,* July 23, 1789, July 28, 1789,
July 17, 1790; *Penn. Mercury,* August 26, 1785, August 24, 1787; *U.S. Recorder,*
March 13, 1798; *The Minerva,* January 9, 1796.

68. *The Minerva,* February 20, 1796, October 7, 1797, and April 15, 1797. I have found only one item in the press that calls the idea of the rich being less happy or having more misery absurd. See "Reflections," *Freeman's Journal,* February 8, 1786.

69. Quotes from *Penn. Packet,* January 16, 1790; *Penn. Mercury,* August 29, 1785; *Penn. Packet,* September 4, 1790; *Penn. Mercury,* August 28, 1787. See also *The Minerva,* February 28, 1795, and October 29, 1796; *Claypoole's ADA,* December 29, 1800; *The Mail,* February 25, 1792; *Freeman's Journal,* October 26, 1785, March 7, 1787, and October 6, 1790; *Penn. Packet,* November 24, 1785, January 11, 1786, June 21, 1787, July 5, 1788, and October 13, 1789; *Aurora,* March 3, 1795.

70. *Claypoole's ADA,* October 7, 1797; *Aurora,* September 14, 1791; *Indep. Gazette,* January 7, 1788; *The Minerva,* January 16, 1796; *The Merchant's Daily Advertiser,* July 19, 1797.

71. John Higham, "The Cult of the 'American Consensus' Homogenizing Our History," *Commentary,* XXVII (February 1959), 93–100, and his "Beyond Consensus: The Historian as Moral Critic," *American Historical Review,* LXVII (April 1962), 609–25.

PART THREE

CITIES IN AN EXPANDING NATION, 1780-1865

"I view great cities as pestilential to the morals, the health and the liberties of man," Thomas Jefferson declared in 1800. Had Jefferson lived through the next half-century, he would have had ample grounds to alter or confirm his view. For the United States, from the turn of the new century to the outbreak of the Civil War, underwent an amazingly rapid transformation from an agrarian, landlocked nation, hugging the Atlantic coastline, to a mercantile and manufacturing nation, traversing inland waters and mountain ranges and assuming the shape of a continental empire. The most dynamic process in this nation building was urbanization. The great cities that Jefferson had feared grew ever larger, while upstart cities in the East and the West challenged the commercial, cultural, and political supremacy of older, established communities.

Three of the nation's four largest cities in 1800 had shared the same distinction in the colonial period: New York, with a population of nearly 61,000; Philadelphia, with some 41,000; and Boston, with almost 25,000. The fourth city, Baltimore, was a recent entry in the urban race; its population had grown to over 26,000, having doubled its size in a single decade. Between 1790 and 1830 all four cities experienced a population explosion of astounding magnitude; percentage increases were, respectively, 548.9, 265.7, 397.1, and 497.1. Nor were these cities unique. Minor Eastern seaports north and south—Norfolk, Savannah, and Salem— grew at a rapid clip. Eastern interior cities like Lancaster, Pennsylvania, expanded, while a number of new cities in the West outdistanced even the fondest dreams of their most ardent supporters.

Between 1820 and 1860 American urban growth progressed more rapidly than at any other time in the country's history. For each decade between 1820 and 1860 the total national population increased by over 30 percent; the urban population (places of 2,500 or more) expanded at three times the rate of the total. Despite Jefferson's view, one of the most important developments in the nation's economy, in its social development, indeed, in its very sense of "nationhood," was urbanization.

As noted by George Tucker, a professor of political economy at the University of Virginia in the 1840s, "the proportion between the rural and town population of a country is an important fact in its interior economy and condition. It determines, in a great degree, its capacity for manufactures, the extent of its commerce, and the amount of its wealth. The growth of cities commonly marks the progress of intelligence and the arts, measures the sum of social enjoyment, and always implies increased mental activity, which is sometimes healthy and useful, sometimes distempered and pernicious." If urbanization was not yet the controlling factor in national life that it seemingly became in the post-Civil War period, the growth and diffusion of cities nonetheless altered the physical, economic, and social landscape of ante-bellum America.

The importance of urban growth in national expansion early became evident in the West. Although American historians have traditionally seen in the ante-bellum decades "the rise of the Old West," it has become clear that cities were, in Richard C. Wade's telling phrase, the "spearheads of the frontier." By 1800 newcomers had surveyed, cleared, and begun the settlement of every major city in the Northwest except Chicago, Milwaukee, and Indianapolis. By 1803, when Ohio became the first state admitted to the Union under the Northwest Ordinance, Cincinnati had been incorporated and already was on the threshold of rapid population growth. By 1810 visitors to Pittsburgh had dubbed it the "Birmingham of America," a center of mills, shops, and small factories. A journalist traveling the Ohio River in 1815 astonishedly discovered its banks "sprinkled with towns." St. Louis, born in the 1760s of a French merchant company's lust for pelts, already had matured into the nation's center for the lucrative fur trade, a city whose commerce stretched west nearly to the Pacific and north to the border of Canada.

While none of these towns and cities were large by modern standards, there were two ways in which they were vitally important in the expansion of the nation westward. First, they hastened the agrarian development of the West. For many men less adventuresome than the pioneer farmer of legend, the lure west was the presence of already settled towns and the promise of future growth. Farmers of the Ohio Valley moved principally into agricultural areas that had a local town where they could satisfy their economic needs and barter whatever surplus they might produce. Others moved first to cities like Buffalo, Cincinnati, or Detroit, and only subsequently took up farming. Second, the frontier towns and cities offered, for settlers who were not interested in an agricultural existence, the inducement of starting life over in a new urban setting with fresh economic opportunities.

The entire period saw a succession of "urban Wests," moving, from St. Louis and Cleveland, to Chicago, to Abilene, to Denver and the mining camps of the Rockies. On the Pacific coast the lure of gold contributed to the settlement and growth of San Francisco. To the north during the 1850s, Portland continued to grow in size and population, while the new town of Seattle began to take shape amid the pine forests bordering Puget Sound. In 1861 lobbyists succeeded in cajoling legislators into granting acreage for a territorial university in primitive Seattle. Local citizens cleared the land and jerry-built an Ionic-columned structure, complete with a picket fence designed, as one cynic put it, "to keep the stumps from getting out of the yard." The "university," together with a brothel begun by an ambitious San Franciscan, symbolized urban culture in the northern wilderness.

The "Wests" were not the sole beneficiaries of urban growth. The South, though primarily rural, nonetheless had important cities throughout the period. On the eve of the Civil War the influential journalist J. D. B. DeBow, observing the vast changes in Southern life that had occurred over the previous forty years, noted that the country had become "more and more dependent on the town. Whether in pursuit of business, pleasure, or information, men leave the country and visit some neighboring city. Our bodies are in the country, our souls in town." DeBow's emphasis on the growing significance of cities was accurate; by 1860 the census numbered thirty urban places in the South with a population of 8,000 or more. While many of these were small towns, crossroads trading centers, and state capitals, others were major cities. Washington, the capital of the nation, remained very much a regional Southern city, along with St. Louis, Louisville, New Orleans, Mobile, Savannah, Charleston, Richmond, and Baltimore. All of these, except Charleston, were actively growing communities during the ante-bellum years. Indeed, the South as a whole lagged behind only the North and Great Britain, among the regions of the Western hemisphere, in its rate of urbanization.

The growth of Memphis was only an exaggerated example of Southern urban development. Founded in 1819, Memphis followed the life of a sleepy flatboat town until the late 1840s. Then, aided by a vigorously prosperous cotton economy in its hinterland and by railroad connections with Charleston, Memphis experienced a population boom and expanded by over 155 percent during the decade of the 1850s. Although native critics like Hinton Rowen Helper denounced the South for its lack of mercantile and manufacturing cities and direly predicted an impending crisis with the North, Southern towns and cities played vital roles in the region's economic and intellectual life.

The process of nationwide urbanization relied largely upon the transportation revolution that between 1800 and the Civil War drastically altered the physiognomy of the United States. Even before the War of 1812 Eastern urban leadership had tried to generate a national system of roads. The most successful of the new highways was the Lancaster Turnpike in Pennsylvania, financial profits from which spurred other road-building enterprises. By 1815 reasonably good highways linked together eastern Pennsylvania, New York, New Jersey, and southern New England towns and cities. British blockades of the Atlantic coast during the War of 1812 and the need for a revitalized commerce following the war led to the building of more turnpikes. New England, Pennsylvania, and New York interests vied for advantage by building new roads to join East and West with commercial ties. Road-building fever occasionally gripped Southerners and Westerners, too, although both their areas trailed the East Coast in the financing of proposed highways. By the 1830s the days of turnpikes were drawing to a close. In the meantime, urban merchants and investors gradually had turned their attention to new means of transportation. Water, not land, was to provide new highways to the West.

The era of canal construction began in the years immediately following the War of 1812 and continued unabated until the Civil War. Commercial interests in New York City financed the spectacularly successful Erie Canal. The canal, begun in 1817 and opened for trade in 1825, quickly justified the hopes of its promoters. De Witt Clinton, mayor of New York City and commissioner of the canal, best summarized the reasons for building it: "As an organ of communication between the Hudson, the Mississippi, the St. Lawrence, the great lakes of the North and West, and their tributary rivers, it will create the greatest inland trade ever witnessed." But most important, Clinton stressed, the canal, stretching 364 miles through the wilderness between Albany and Buffalo, would open up the trade of the West to New York City. "That city will, in course of time," Clinton confidently predicted, "become the granary of the world, the emporium of commerce, the seat of manufactures, the focus of great moneyed operations." Clinton's prediction proved accurate, and other cities quickly followed New York's lead in canal building. In the East, Philadelphia and Baltimore interests struggled with each other and with New York rivals for dominance of the Western trade, while worried Bostonians actually surveyed means of laying a canal across the Berkshires to the Hudson River. To the West, urban promoters in Illinois, Ohio, Indiana, Michigan, and Wisconsin jockeyed for commercial advantages by lobbying canal schemes through their legislators. The Illinois and Michigan Canal, for example, connected Lake

Michigan with the Illinois and eventually the Mississippi River and tremendously boosted the growth of the new city of Chicago. Even the tidewater districts south of Virginia and North Carolina were involved in the water race westward. Although little came of numerous ambitious schemes, the country as a whole experienced a speculative craze for canal construction that fostered urban growth and expanded the national economy.

A chief reason for Western support of canals was the steamboat. In 1815 the *Enterprise* puffed upriver from New Orleans to Pittsburgh, demonstrating the usefulness of steam navigation on Western waters. The dream of an inland continental empire loomed as a reality once Westerners saw the trade and manufacturing possibilities of a vigorous commercial flow up and down inland waterways. Over the next twenty years, as Richard C. Wade has observed, steam navigation "telescoped a half-century's development into a single generation." New towns sprang up as if by magic along navigable rivers, while already existent cities burgeoned. As a French foreign minister testified of the steamboat in 1824, "In the brief interval of fifteen years, many cities were formed . . . where before there were hardly the dwellings of a small town. . . . A simple mechanical device has made life both possible and comfortable in regions which heretofore have been a wilderness." By 1830 steamboats plied all the main rivers of the West and many of the principal tributaries, structuring, from passenger and commercial traffic, the first truly regional economy. Together with canal construction, steam navigation promoted the urbanization of the West.

If turnpikes, canals, and steam navigation fostered urban growth, the most influential innovation of the transportation revolution was the railroad. Steamboats and canals had to follow natural routes, but the railroads could follow any routes created for them. For a nation looking westward across unbounded prairie horizons, railroads offered a means of leapfrogging vast distances. They were supremely adapted to American needs during the 1830s when the Atlantic states financed the construction of over 3,300 miles of track, which tied together with short lines most of the major urban centers. Again, the race to the West proved the most dynamic element in the expansion of a transportation network. Boston, Baltimore, and Charleston, each lacking significant inland waterway connections, produced the vanguard of railway developers. As early as 1828 Baltimore business interests secured a charter for the Baltimore and Ohio Railroad, designed to reach westward to the Ohio River. Philadelphia joined the struggle during the 1840s and Boston, with a flurry of construction during the early 1850s, enjoyed a brief reputation as the nation's largest railroad center. Within the West itself, urban rivalries led to a surge of railway building. Promoters of Sandusky, Ohio, for instance, lost to Cleveland interests a battle for domination of lakeshore trade when the ill-fated Mad River and Lake Erie Railroad project ran afoul of legislative machinations. While the new urban giants Milwaukee and Chicago battled with veteran St. Louis for control of the Mississippi Valley during the 1850s, a host of other towns in the West fought for new railroad construction and a share in an increasingly lucrative trade market.

Depending upon the routes taken, new railroads either spurred the founding of entire new communities or left in their wake ghost towns as remnants of the shattered schemes of urban boosters who had promised the railroads would pass. Certainly the famous Andrews Report on Transportation (1853) was not far off the mark in predicting for America that "railroads will chain all the several parts each to each; the whole people from the Pacific to the North Atlantic ocean, from the Great Lakes to the Gulf of Mexico, . . . incited by a genuine rivalry for the accomplishment of the real mission of the American people." By 1860, as economic historian George Rogers Taylor has observed, railroads had come of age, "had built great cities, hastened the settlement of the West, made farming practicable on the prairies, and greatly stimulated the flow of internal commerce." A transportation revolution had created physically a "nation," an interlocking directorate of major cities and growing towns.

The process of nineteenth-century urbanization, accelerated by transport innovations, revealed a quickening faith among Americans in the promise of their own future. Beginning in the seventeenth century, settlers on New World shores had poured forth an immense variety of advertisements for life in a "new Eden." The subsequent history of the country may be traced in an ever-growing body of promotional literature that reflected the ambitions and aspirations of men who knew what they wanted America to become.

During the first half of the nineteenth century much of this booster mentality focused on the planting and cultivation of cities and produced a new breed—the urban promoters. Some of these early businessmen concerned themselves principally with broadening their city's already prominent base in trade, manufacturing, and the arts. Others hoped to transform barren prairie land and swampy ground into a new Philadelphia, New York, or (as was most common) a "new Athens" in the West. Early in the century Daniel Drake, a Cincinnati physician, prophesied that the small villages squatting on the banks of the Ohio and Mississippi would one day become "populous and magnificent cities." Later propagandists such as Jesup W. Scott, a Toledo newspaperman, and William Gilpin, a Missouri explorer and land speculator, explained the natural and historical necessity of great cities springing up in the interior of the nation.

The career of a man like William B. Ogden demonstrates the work of the city booster. He was born in a small New York town in 1805. At the age of fifteen he became fascinated with real-estate speculation. In 1835 he joined a group of investors and moved to the new community of Chicago. On his arrival he discovered a town of some 3,200 residents. Two years later those residents elected him as their first mayor. Shrewdly investing in land and perceiving the importance of railroads to the town, Ogden helped to bring about a period of fantastic growth for the city, as well as for his personal fortune. By 1850 Chicago had expanded to almost 30,000 citizens; by 1860, to more than 109,000. Ogden became a millionaire several times over. But like the best of the city boosters, Ogden's first loyalty was not to himself, but to Chicago. As one of his contemporaries recalled, "Chicago booming or Chicago in ashes, its great future was to him a fixed fact."

For every William Ogden and every Chicago, there was a small-town counterpart. Unlike Ogden, many of the boosters were little more than urban con artists. Slick salesmen would search for any spot they could build up as the destined site of a great metropolis. After buying a thousand acres or more along a stream or road, they laid out plots for schools, churches, and opera houses and then left it "to any man of sense and candor to say whether any point upon our continent has ever presented a fairer prospect of a greater inland commercial city." Such projects lasted but a few months, but they represented the pattern of booster promotion at the time. Many prospective settlers, lured by the promise of city development, would respond to advertisements in Eastern and Western newspapers, buy lots, then move themselves and their families, only to discover that their lots lay under ten feet of swamp water or that the "city" consisted of one muddy street, a saloon, and a newspaper with a distribution of twenty or thirty families. According to a sadder-but-wiser investor in the new city of "Franklin, Illinois," in the early 1830s, it was "the era of imaginary villages," a time when great cities and thriving commercial centers existed primarily on lavishly printed maps— and nowhere else.

Whether in imagined villages or real communities, the philosophy of boosterism was that urban growth and the diffusion of cities over the landscape was infinitely desirable, was probably inevitable, and could be summed up in the belief, "if our city does not outdistance all others, it surely will wither away." Among responsible and irresponsible promoters alike, the notion that a community could reach a maximum, satisfactory level of development and then stabilize seemed unheard-of. Boosters of new towns in the West and those of well-established cities in the East took the path of least resistance and courted unplanned and unfettered growth. They showed a lust for progress that perceptive observers said characterized the nation as a whole. As a Scotsman, James Stirling, observed during his travels between 1856 and 1857, "The American flies at everything. 'Go ahead anyhow,' that is his motto. The characteristic of his civilization must . . . be extensiveness." British novelist Anthony Trollope visited Milwaukee in 1861 and noted that "a city at its commencement is laid out with an intention that it shall be populous . . . Men build on an enormous scale, three times, ten times as much as is wanted. The only measure of size is an increase on what men have built before." What was true of Milwaukee was true elsewhere.

Nineteenth-century Americans busied themselves, as historian Daniel J. Boorstin put it, in "packaging a continent" of vast, unsettled land. The rhetoric of expansionism argued that growth was good for business, good for employment, and good for its own sake. If America itself from its inception was a speculation, then land speculation was the principal enterprise of nineteenth-century Americans. In turn, city building was the chief activity of real-estate speculators. Federal land law after the Northwest Ordinance of 1787 ensured that town promotion would be the most profitable means of packaging the continent. Cities might come and go, but, as a contemporary exclaimed, promoters would "trumpet forth the qualifications of a town in the moon, if there was a chance of selling any of the lots." And the leaders of older, established communities were just as vigorous in boosting the commercial and cultural advantages of their own cities as were the Western promoters. Every promoter wanted his city to be bigger and better than the competition. Even the fact that New York outdistanced all its East Coast rivals during the period gave a positive incentive to other communities. If the leaders of other cties and towns could not hope to surpass the "emporium of the nation," they still could follow its lead by making their communities more successful, larger, and more culturally dynamic than they ever had been—and perhaps more so than neighboring communities down the road or the stream. Certainly the city mania and the feverish pace of boosterism helped to fill a continent, accounted for the unplanned nature of urban growth, and revealed a faith among nineteenth-century Americans in an urban future for the nation.

In the growth and diffusion of cities a curious paradox emerged. With all the opportunities for new beginnings offered by the country, with all the desires of urban imperialists to succeed where others failed, the fabric of national urban development unfolded, with very few alterations, from the same pattern. Imitation, not innovation, characterized governmental policies, social class structures, and urban life styles.

Those communities labeled by historian Bayrd Still the "mushroom metropolises of the West"—Buffalo, Cleveland, Detroit, Chicago, and Milwaukee—displayed a striking similarity in the forms and limitations of governmental powers. Their charters, granted at different intervals during the period, read almost like carbon copies of one another. Like colonial "cities in the wilderness," the lake cities were characterized by strictly regulated local economies, with public control exerted over private enterprise in such matters as prices, prohibitions against monopoly, false weights and measures, and adulterated foods. Both to promote commerce and to protect the citizenry, city fathers had charter authority to extend regulatory powers for preventing fires, sinking public wells, constructing and repairing streets, providing constabulary forces of some kind, establishing uniform building codes, and levying taxes for new docks, wharves, and warehouses. City communities endowed their annually elected councils with broad powers, but not until the end of the period did they grant strong executive powers to their mayors. Each community began with a property qualification for voting and office holding, and each set about to abolish such restrictions during the 1850s. With few exceptions the lake cities, and cities of the Ohio Valley such as Cincinnati, St. Louis, Pittsburgh, Lexington, and Louisville, had charters, forms of government, and regulatory powers modeled after the Eastern examples of Philadelphia, New York, and Baltimore. Except for their continued limitations on Negro suffrage and participation in local affairs, Southern towns and cities tended to follow the same patterns. Thus, the founders of Western and Southern cities relied upon the tested models and past experience of urban government in the East; they were not pioneering innovators in political institutions.

The new towns and cities did not radically depart from the traditional social structure of eighteenth-century urban America. Local boosters in Western cities talked a great deal about egalitarianism, but urban practice belied their rhetoric. Social lines developed quickly, even if they were never drawn as tightly as in Eastern cities. At the apex of a stratifying

society stood a merchant or businessman class. Until the 1830s the
merchants presided over the affairs and politics of Western towns. There,
as in the East and South, economic prowess meant social prestige and
political power. While challenges to the businessmen from workingmen's
organizations and parties East and West began eroding merchant
power, commercial interests largely continued to govern the cities until
the Civil War. In Eastern cities merchant-capitalists like Francis
Cabot Lowell and Nathan Appleton of Boston remained powerful. While
the wealthy of Philadelphia, New York, and Boston rarely numbered more
than 2 to 5 percent of their respective urban populations, they
exercised an inordinate amount of political and social power. In Southern
cities businessmen dominated community life and ruled the countryside,
especially in the "black belts" of the lower South where the leading
cotton capitalists depended upon credit and commercial facilities
for carrying on their extensive planting operations.

Closely allied with business interests, although separated by wealth and
background, were the professional classes in American cities. The
professionals, white-collar employees, small businessmen, and skilled
workers formed a growing urban middle class that began flexing
its political and social muscles in the early 1830s. The working class began
to swell in the early 1820s, when foreign immigration joined the native
rural migration cityward. Although many contemporaries saw the specter of
pauperism stalking city streets in the form of the urban workingman, most
wage earners were neither debtors nor paupers. They nonetheless lived
close to the level of subsistence, believing, with some justification, that
urban America held a class society dominated by the successful few. Even
a burst of urban prosperity beginning in the 1840s did not substantially
alter the occupational and living conditions of most urban workers. Skilled
workers, particularly in the building trades, made considerable wage
advances during the early 1850s, but factory operatives, clothing
workers, iron workers, and unskilled laborers in general failed to make
significant headway. At the bottom of the social structure in the cities
were free blacks and, in the South, free and slave blacks, working for the
most part as common laborers. Urban workingmen and free blacks enjoyed
some opportunities for economic and social mobility; class lines were
not so rigid that advancement was impossible. Still, such mobility had
its limitations, and occurred in small steps up the social ladder; rarely did
men leap from the bottom to the top, fulfilling the rags-to-riches success
story so dear to the hearts of nineteenth-century Americans.

While a nation of cities that were showing similar patterns of growth
and development emerged during the first half of the nineteenth century,
the cities themselves were undergoing dramatic and significant changes.

Until at least the mid-1820s American cities remained, as they had been in the colonial years, overwhelmingly preindustrial commercial centers. A Philadelphia in the East or a Pittsburgh or Lexington in the West might have enjoyed the reputation of a manufacturing center even before the War of 1812, but for the most part imported factory goods, funneled through Atlantic seaports, satisfied economic needs. The shift from a preindustrial to an industrial economy required large concentrations of capital, business skill, an adequate labor pool, a specialized work force, and extensive transportation facilities. After 1820 each of these factors became operative in the larger cities. Between 1790 and 1830 over 400,000 foreign immigrants entered American seaboard cities. Most of them tarried but a short time in Boston, New York, and Philadelphia, before traveling into the hinterland to meet the demand for farm laborers. But those who did remain were largely skilled laborers who brought with them from the Old World valuable experience in textile manufacturing, the machine and foundry trades, and the boot and shoe industry. A second tide of immigration flooded the cities in the late 1840s and early 1850s with over 4 million newcomers, swelling the unskilled labor pool and thus meeting the rising demands of urban manufacturing. In addition, merchant-capitalists joined forces, forming corporations to create substantial stockpiles of investment capital and to take advantage of innovations in transit. From the 1820s on, a "manufacturing revolution" began to alter the patterns of life and labor in urban America, and the preindustrial city began to dissolve under the pressures of economic progress.

The main solvent was the introduction of the factory system. The earliest example of this new method of business organization was the Waltham Plan, sponsored by Francis Cabot Lowell of Boston and a group of his fellow merchants. In 1813 the Boston Manufacturing Company founded a small textile mill in Waltham, Massachusetts, operating on the principles of a maximum use of mechanical power; specialization of low-cost, standardized fabric production; and heavy investment to provide working capital and funds for plant expansion. The striking success of the factory system in textile manufacture led to the establishment of new mill communities in New England such as Lowell (1822), Chicopee (1823), and Holyoke (1847); it also encouraged the adaptation of the system for other industrial purposes, and boosted the rate of industrial growth in numerous cities. Baltimore and Rochester, New York, became leading flour mill centers; communities in eastern Pennsylvania and western New Jersey became major sites of anthracite furnaces and iron-rolling mills; Philadelphia's machine-tool industry boomed; and Cincinnati took the lead in the manufacture of steamboats. The factory

system was an urban development that helped to account for the burst of
urban population between 1840 and 1860, when factories replaced home
and small-shop manufacturing in many industries. Although industrialization
alone did not explain the rate of urbanization during the period (cities
continued to grow on a commercial base), certainly the manufacturing
revolution greatly stimulated an increase in the density of population in
the larger cities and helped to diffuse towns over the American landscape.

Cities in the expanding nation became communities in motion. Everywhere
the pace of life picked up, and contemporaries both praised and damned
the "bustle, energy, and activity" of urban life. Just as external
migration to the city produced a population explosion, so mobility
within the city produced new social problems. Neighborhood instability
became a commonplace, with various areas experiencing extraordinary
rates of turnover in their class, income, ethnic, and racial compositions. A
working-class consciousness surfaced for the first time. And the "better
sort" of citizens discovered that "the poor" were possibly the permanent
offspring of commerce and industry. The increasing strength of
Roman Catholicism as an urban religion frightened Protestant city
fathers and aroused nativist ire. Religious, racial, and class riots underscored
the tenuousness of community harmony. And still the multitudes arrived,
compounding by their very presence already serious social tensions.
Newspaperman Horace Greeley caught the spirit of the times in the late
1850s when he observed that "we cannot all live in cities, yet
nearly all seem determined to do so."

During the ante-bellum decades of the nineteenth century, then, a
network of growing cities emerged in various sections of the country.
Sharing similar political institutions, economic organization, and social class
structure, these cities in effect helped to create an American "nation." A
national economy anchored by the larger cities, as historian George
Rogers Taylor has observed, had replaced the colonial orientation of the
late eighteenth century. Sectional divisions within the country—North,
West, and South—were neither as clear nor as significant for national
development as were the increasing differences in life styles and
goals between rural and urban America. By the eve of the Civil War only
some 20 percent of the nation's population was urban. But, while the total
population of the United States rose by 226 percent during the years
of 1820 to 1860, the number of people living in cities leaped ahead by
nearly 800 percent. Clearly the strength of the nation's present and the
promise of its posterity lay in its cities—and in the direction that
urbanization might take in the future.

7. MANUFACTURING IN THE AMERICAN MERCANTILE CITY, 1800–1840

Allan Pred

During the initial decades of the nineteenth century American manufacturing was characterized predominantly by an emphasis on consumers' rather than capital goods, by handicraft rather than machine techniques, by household and workshop rather than factory organization, and by rural dispersion rather than concentration in major urban centers. Even in the textile industries, where factories were the most important production units by the 1830s,[1] activity was largely confined to rural waterfall sites and mill towns recently superimposed upon the rural landscape. The factory and industrial capitalism had not as yet become the cornerstones of metropolitan growth. In other words, at a time when the economy of the United States was an agricultural economy, the industrial as well as the agrarian population was preponderantly rural.

Within the framework of these commonplace facts, it is perfectly logical that the magnitude of absolute population growth in rural areas completely overshadowed relative urban advances during the early nineteenth century. Certainly, New York, Boston, Philadelphia, and Baltimore thrived commercially and expanded rapidly in size, but whereas the total 1840 population stood at 17,120,000, and thereby surpassed the 1800 total by nearly 12 million, the number of inhabitants in "urban places" only increased from 322,000 in 1800 to 1,845,000 in 1840.[2]

Rural dominance however, was to be of short duration. Subsequent to the financial panic and depression of the late 1830s a series of developments, which had previously been set in motion, began to gain the momentum that ultimately shifted the locational spotlight of manufacturing from a rural to an urban proscenium. The railroad network, which consisted of a mere 2,800 miles of disjointed trackage in 1840, mushroomed into a well-articulated system exceeding 30,600 miles in 1860,[3] and began to facilitate the long-distance raw material assembly and finished product distribution which was so vital to urban-industrial growth. In addition, the score of years preceding the Civil War were marked by a perceptible diffusion of uniform production based on interchangeable parts and of the factory system outside the textile industries, a gradual replacement of

Reprinted from the *Annals* of the American Association of Geographers, LVI (June 1966), 307–325, by permission of the publisher.

waterpower by steam-driven engines, an increased use of coal rather than wood fuels, a critical expansion of machine tool output, a growing stream of European migrants and a consequent enlargement of the domestic market and labor pool, and an increasing popularity of the joint-stock and limited liability corporation. The panic of 1837 itself was partly instrumental in provoking some of these post-1840 urban-industrial adjustments, since that commercial and financial fiasco terminated the conditions which forced American merchants to make unnecessarily large imports of foreign factory production.[4] In short, between 1840 and 1860, the principal functions of the country's major cities were still mercantile, but changes were under way which were bringing the phenomena of urban growth and industrial growth into closer association, an association whose culmination has permitted us to interpret metropolitan size-growth from 1860 to 1910 as a circular and cumulative process, in which successive manufacturing thresholds were fulfilled and the possibilities of industrial invention and innovation were continuously enhanced.[5]

Since it was prior to the transition period 1840–60 that manufacturing occupied its most subordinate position in the urban economy, since industrialization and initial advantage were apparently the keys to the growth of the United States' highest-order urban centers in the post–Civil War era, and because zones of manufacturing became such an important component in the internal structure of metropolises, a series of economic-geographical questions arises regarding the role of industry in the American mercantile city during the formative years of the early nineteenth century. What factors militated against the location of additional manufacturing activities in the larger commercial cities? Why were existing industries located in New York, Boston, Philadelphia, and Baltimore? What forces operated in shaping the intraurban locational patterns of specific industries?

These questions are important not only because they promise to clarify subsequent patterns of urban-industrial growth and internal metropolitan structure, but also because they look into the spatial prism of early-nineteenth-century manufacturing through the face of urban units, rather than through the face of individual industries, as Clark and others have done. These same broad queries require an expansive canvas upon which to depict their answers. Although some of the more subtle strokes can be painted with the delicate brush of primary sources, the grosser splashes of color must derive from the varied palette of secondary classics by economic historians and other students of the early nineteenth century.[6]

THE ECONOMIC FUNCTIONS OF THE MERCANTILE CITY

The logical pondering of the above questions is extremely difficult without first establishing some frame of reference, and therefore, a sound interpretation requires at least an outlining of both the economic functions of the mercantile city and the relative importance of manufacturing within that city's overall economy.

A contemporary portrayed New York City as a "mercantile town" with "the character of a general mart for the exchange of foreign and domestic productions."[7] On a smaller scale, the other major Atlantic ports and New Orleans also performed as "hinges," linking the national agricultural economy with Europe through a "network of trade relationships on the continent and on the high seas."[8] (See Tables 1–3 for some indication of the relative importance of the leading mercantile cities.) Dominance of internal trade by the "hinge" cities was almost complete. Until agents became nearly ubiquitous, shop and store keepers from throughout the country created "a great concourse of persons at the principal sea-ports, to purchase groceries, woolens, cotton goods, etc."[9] Most of the merchandise sold in the young interior river ports of St. Louis and Cincinnati,[10] and in lesser centers west of the Alleghenies, came from New York, Baltimore, and Philadelphia; whereas Boston compensated for its physically restricted hinterland by channeling much of its commerce to Fall River, Lowell, and the smaller rising textile mill towns of the Merrimac Valley.[11] Domestic coastal interaction, as well as inland hinterland trade, accounted for a considerable portion of the economic activity and external relations of the mercantile port-cities. Indicatively, in 1835, the tonnage, if not the cargo value, of a fraction of arriving coastal vessels surpassed the tonnage of all arriving foreign-trade vessels in New York, Boston, and Philadelphia (the tonnage ratio of long-distance coastal to foreign-trade arrivals was at least 1.03 to 1.00 for New York, 1.69 to 1.00 for Boston, and 2.45 to 1.00 for Philadelphia).[12]

With the possible exception of Philadelphia (Table 3), the wholesaling-trading complex and retailing were the two most prominent economic functions of the leading mercantile cities, even in 1840, when the secondary

Table 1. Population of Major U.S. Cities: 1800–1840[a]

	1840	1800
New York (Manhattan)	312,710	60,515
Baltimore	102,313	26,514
Philadelphia[b]	93,665	41,220
Boston	93,383	24,937
New Orleans	102,193	——[c]

[a] Source: Bureau of the Census, *1960 Census of Population,* vol. I, Part A.

[b] Not including the unincorporated Northern Liberties, Spring Garden, Kensington, or Southwark. These suburbs, whose growth was inseparable from that of Philadelphia, had a combined 1840 population slightly in excess of 100,000. The failure to include these later incorporated suburbs, while admittedly detracting from the scale of Philadelphia's early-nineteenth-century increase, is justified by similar omissions for New York, Boston, and, to a lesser degree, Baltimore.

[c] Not available. In 1810 New Orleans had a population of 17,242.

position of manufacturing was likely to be considerably less pronounced than it had been in earlier decades.[13] The dock, the wharf, the counting house, and the warehouse were the principal foci of the urban economy; and the merchant middlemen (shipping merchants and importers), and agent middlemen (brokers, auctioneers, commission merchants, and factors), were the city's primary capital accumulators, in most instances cumulatively assessing "a mark-up of 100–150 percent on the cost of imported merchandise."[14] In acting as generators of urban growth the mercantile element directly or indirectly provided jobs for a large portion of the city's working population. As a striking example, as early as 1800 there were nearly 1,000 persons licensed as carters to transfer merchandise to warehouses and to tranship import and export commodities on the streets of New York City,[15] and by 1833 the number of carts operating on the city's thoroughfares was approaching 2,500.[16]

Of course, it was in New York, the largest of the mercantile cities, that the wholesaling-trading function was most articulated (Tables 2 and 3). In 1832, when the value of foreign goods arriving at Manhattan was less than one-half of that imported during the boom of 1836,[17] it could be said that:

The amount of merchandise of every description sold [principally on credit] in
one year by New York to supply the other cities, towns and villages of the country,
from Maine to New Orleans, may probably be estimated at $100,000,000.[18]

In the same year of modest activity New York merchants were involved in an additional $26 million of foreign-export transactions.[19] By 1841, no less than 59.1 percent of the nation's foreign imports, as well as 43.5 percent of the nation's total foreign trade, was passing through the control of New York merchants.[20] The road to this position of dominance had been paved by the collective decisions of British manufacturers to dump their accumulated surpluses in the port following the end of the War of 1812, by establishment of regular packet service to Liverpool and other European cities subsequent to 1818, by the construction of the Erie Canal, and by the aggressive action of New York commercial agents in detouring the cotton trade of the South through their harbor.

Table 3 crudely reflects the subservient role of manufacturing in the economy of the mercantile city, particularly in New Orleans where the ratio of investment in the mercantile sectors to investment in industrial activities exceeded fifteen to one, and in New York and Boston where the ratio was at least on the order of five or six to one—despite the exclusion of "commercial houses in foreign trade" and the inclusion of sizable construction investments in each city's manufacturing category.[21] The low-ebb position of urban manufacturing during the opening decades of the nineteenth century is well reflected by the fact that in 1810 only 230 of 13,241 structures enumerated within the municipal boundaries of Philadel-

Table 2. Selected Trade Statistics for Leading Mercantile Cities[a]

	New York	Boston	Phila-delphia	Baltimore	New Orleans	Total U.S.	Selected ports as a % of U.S.
	Exports (millions of dollars)						
1815	10	5	4	5	5	52	55.8
1820	13	11	5	6	7	69	60.9
1825	35	11	11	4	12	99	73.7
1830	19	7	4	3	15	73	65.8
1835	30	10	3	3	36	121	67.8
1840[b]	34	10	6	5	34	132	67.9
	Imports (millions of dollars)						
1821	23	14	8	4	3	62	83.9
1825	49	15	15	4	4	96	90.6
1830	35	10	8	4	7	70	91.4
1836[b]	118	25	15	7	15	189	95.2
1840	60	16	8	4	10	107	91.6

[a] Source: Albion, (see note 12), pp. 390–91. Compiled from *Reports on Commerce and Navigation* issued annually by the Secretary of the Treasury.

[b] Peak year 1800–40.

phia were classified as "manufacturing buildings,"[22] and by a Baltimorean's 1825 observation that manufacturing had yet "to become a powerful and certain auxiliary in contributing to the wealth, prosperity, and advancement of the city."[23]

Prior to the 1837 panic there were discernible urban-industrial increases, e.g., by the initiation of the 1830s the annual value of Baltimore's manufacturing was hazarded at "five millions of dollars,"[24] and similar figures for Boston and Philadelphia were correspondingly in the vicinity of $13,400,000[25] and $20 million.[26] However, these increments ought not be exaggerated because many of the establishments placed in the manufacturing category either combined production and retailing or wholesaling functions, as in the case of the food-processing industries, or devoted most of their efforts to making repairs.[27] Furthermore, the value added by production, generally regarded as the best measurement and indicator of manufacturing activity, was naturally far less than the annual value of output.[28]

Although the unimposing role of manufacturing in the urban economy doubtlessly had its roots in the eighteenth century, when industrial growth was hampered by British restrictive policies, it seems that some further amplification of the facts is necessary in order to comprehend the inhibited scale of urban-industrial output in an era when population was expanding

Table 3. Selected Economic Characteristics of Major U.S. Cities: 1840[a]

	Commercial houses in foreign trade	Commission houses	Commission houses	Capital Invested (1,000's of dollars)			Construction employment
				Retailing	Manufacturing[b]		
New York (Manhattan)	417	918	45,941.2	14,648.6	11,228.9		4,033
Baltimore	70	108	4,404.5	6,708.6	2,730.0		845
Philadelphia[c]	182	35	1,944.5	15,177.6	5,387.5		713
Boston	142	89	11,676.0	4,184.2	2,770.3		524
New Orleans	8	375	16,490.0	11,018.2	1,774.2		1,001

[a] Source: "Sixth Census of the United States, 1840" (see note 65).

[b] These figures are probably exaggerations since they include all capital invested in the construction sector of the urban economy.

[c] See note 13 for remarks on the striking aberrations of the Philadelphia statistics.

and supposedly beneficial import-restricting legislation and protective tariffs were in effect (the Embargo and Non-Intercourse acts functioned as protective measures between 1808 and 1815, and levies that were imposed on imported manufactures in 1816 persisted in altered form throughout the period).[29] Thus, an earlier posed question may be reiterated: What factors militated against the location of additional manufacturing activities in the larger commercial cities?

RESTRAINTS ON EARLY-NINETEENTH-CENTURY URBAN MANUFACTURING

It is reasonable to contend that the limited dimensions of manufacturing in the American mercantile city were attributable to shortages of capital and labor, the state of technology, an expensive and inadequate transport network, and the restricted size of the accessible market.

Factor Shortages

In 1810, Gallatin argued that "the want of a sufficient capital" was one of the "most prominent of those causes" impeding the growth of manufacturers in the United States.[30] Better than forty years later a Philadelphian could still bemoan a situation where "bank officers, in distributing their loans, have not yet exercised a wise discrimination" in favor of manufacturers.[31] Adequate capital supplies frequently existed, but the problem most often confronting the factory or workshop owner was that of obtaining a portion of those excess mercantile funds. Since it was in the larger cities that the potential investor encountered the widest spectrum of financial outlets and opportunities, the development of large-scale, capital-intensive urban industries was particularly hampered under the prevailing conditions of investment capital scarcity.

Although merchants became somewhat more sympathetic toward industrial investments during the 1820s, for a number of decades the majority still "preferred to speculate in land purchases or to enlarge their spheres of trade rather than to back manufacturing projects."[32] (Mercantile conservatism regarding industrial investments had been briefly interrupted by the War of 1812, when American ports were cut off from British manufacturers; but even this turn of events tended to favor the textile mills of Massachusetts and Paterson rather than the manufacturing of the larger cities, and much capital began to be rechanneled into its normal outlets immediately ensuing the war when English competition was renewed, industrial prices fell while currency problems pushed the general price level upward, and poor harvests in Europe increased the value of American agricultural commodities considerably.) Enlarging the sphere of trade normally meant that mercantile earnings were ploughed back into expanded wholesaling, or related retailing, banking, and insurance activities. However, as hinterland competition intensified, a growing share of the financial resources available in the major cities was diverted into a less direct path of commercial promotion, namely turnpike, canal, and railroad development. Investment in transportation projects usually took the form of subscription to state-sponsored bonds, was not accompanied by great expectations of direct profit, and was based on the "economic principle . . . that a town must create trade rather than have trade come to the commercial seat of its own accord."[33]

If the merchant's predisposition toward investment in his own sector of the urban economy is almost self-evident, his preference for real estate and construction speculation over support for manufacturing can only be fully appreciated through the depiction of specific details. A competent chronicler noted that "in New York, Philadelphia, Boston, or Baltimore, the value of building lots is fully as high as it is in Liverpool, Glasgow, etc.; but if we travel about a mile from an American city, the value rapidly decreases; when at two miles, it would not sell for one-quarter as much as land would produce within the same distance of a large town in Great Britain."[34] The combination of a steeply declining gradient of land values outward from the urban core and exuberant population growth provided an alluring capital outlet for the seeker of quick gains. And quick gains there were to be made in profusion. By 1823 there were streets in New York which had front-lot values of $1,000 per foot,[35] and from that year onward the total assessed value of Manhattan's real estate spiraled dizzily from $50 million to over $76 million in 1829, to slightly more than $104 million in 1833, to $253,201,191 in 1836.[36] Real estate in New York had become "by means of hypothecations familiar to the common course of trade, . . . a circulating capital, which is constantly changing its form, and yielding at every conversion a profit to its employers";[37] and in the other mercantile cities the maneuvering of property proceeded with equal fervor. In Boston a single $443,883 sale could net close to $100,000,[38] or, on a more ambitious scale, areas as large as East Boston or the South Cove could be manipulated with "cupidity";[39] and in Baltimore, long before land values peaked, a meager 19 × 63 foot (unoccupied?) lot could bring $27,200.[40]

Construction and rent profiteering went hand in hand with climbing land values, the former involving the demolishment and replacement of older structures, as well as the perpetual erection of new wharves, warehouses, and dwelling units. An active year could see Philadelphia become richer by 1,300 buildings, or as many as 2,000 houses built in New York at a cost in the vicinity of $5 million;[41] whereas a single Boston project costing about $450,000 could be considered "a small thing compared with others which have been accomplished, or are about to be done!"[42] The temptation to speculate in properties, and to appropriate investments to build upon them, was compounded by the promise of high rental returns held out by an often inadequate supply of living quarters.[43] In addition, the possibility of the manufacturer securing available mercantile capital was further diminished by the siphoning off of funds into land purchases in upstate New York and the developing agricultural areas west of the Alleghenies.

Although the prospects of assembling capital sufficient to establish larger industrial enterprises were dimmed, but not made impossible, by the prevalent pattern of investment behavior amongst the merchant class, relatively small-scale urban manufactories were able to originate or expand on the basis of funds secured from accumulated firm savings, surplus mercantile capital, or even from artisan savings. Industrial capital was its own progenitor to the extent that a Boston participant in the U.S. Treasury Department's 1832 survey of manufacturing could state:

... as a general rule, I am inclined to think that few manufacturers rely upon permanent loans from banks or individuals, the capital invested being their own property.[44]

Of course, urban industry could perpetuate itself only because it was overwhelmingly comprised of small-scale establishments requiring small-scale monetary injections. Characteristically, when commercial capital was relegated to manufacturing projects it was more likely to be in the form of credits than in the riskier form of direct investment.[45]

The prevailing forms of business organization and proprietorship multiplied the difficulties of initiating large-scale urban manufacturing. Regardless of the increasing number of modern industrial corporations in the 1830s, a division between ownership and control was the rare exception rather than the rule, and most urban workshops and factories remained under the aegis of an individual owner, a small partnership, or an unchartered joint-stock company.[46] These bases of organization usually imposed a severe limitation on the capital horizons of any specific project. Moreover, the scale of urban-industrial undertakings was further inhibited by the general practice of confining investment solicitations to proximate sources, for "this was the period of the 'parochial point of view,' when the scope of businessmen's decisions was local or regional and when they could not easily change the locus of their activities."[47]

The fiscal predicament of urban manufacturers was complicated additionally by a number of other local and general factors. The volume of traffic moving to the interior from New Orleans and Baltimore was disproportionately small in comparison to the flow of agricultural produce and other commodities down the Mississippi and the Susquehanna, and as a consequence mercantile capital was detoured into purchasing upstream products which otherwise might have been secured by payment in goods.[48] In mercantile city and mill town alike, scanty capital "forced many factory-owners to put up with poorly constructed machinery that required continual attention and repairs."[49] Such inefficient production conditions doubtlessly reduced profit margins (endowing the capital problem with a self-generating quality), and thereby curtailed the feasibility of expansion through reinvestment. Finally, capital difficulties were occasionally magnified when industrial investment funds were absorbed by the initiation of unprofitable undertakings during short-lived booms.

Until the enormous migrations of the late 1840s, the problems of capital availability were intensified by the costliness and inelasticity of labor supplies. Economic historians have repeatedly demonstrated that the abundance of cheap and frequently fertile land led to a high output per man in early-nineteenth-century American agriculture, and that these productivity conditions exerted a negative effect on industrial wage levels and the quantity of labor available for manufacturing purposes. Although American urban-industrial salaries were high by the standards of English and other European competitors, Clark has stated that:

even a temporary cessation of work caused employees to scatter widely in search of other employment, and even to leave permanently the occupations in which they previously had been engaged.[50]

Nonetheless, this phenomenon does not require us

to suppose that large numbers of industrial workers moved. It is sufficient if 'the abundance of western land drew many thousands of potential wage earners . . . who might otherwise have crowded into the factories.'[51]

The shortage of labor was particularly acute in Boston where "there were no appreciable numbers of men ready and willing to work at wages low enough to foster the establishment of profitable new enterprises," and "a constant deficiency of labor had seriously hampered the growth of industry until the forties." Between 1837 and 1845 few Boston industries underwent sizable growth

and many actually declined. The prospective manufacturer desiring a site for a new establishment, or the capitalist with an 'abundance of money seeking an outlet' found little encouragement. And even those already established who wished to expand were inhibited by the apparently inflexible labor supply.[52]

Boston boot and shoe entrepreneurs found it ameliorating to maintain workshops outside of the city where labor was more plentiful, and similarly, at one time, 75 percent of the city's hat dealers had the making of their millinery put out to neighboring towns.[53] These conditions persisted in Boston and the other major Atlantic ports despite the waxing flow of migrants being funnelled through these cities (especially New York, through whose portals roughly 58,000 individuals entered the country in 1836).[54] The bulk of the alien newcomers were either attracted away from the urban labor market by the lure of possible agricultural prosperity, or did not possess the skills requisite to participation in most of the city's handicraft and workshop industries.

The State of Technology

It appears incontrovertible that the state of technology impeded the spatial concentration of manufacturers in the mercantile cities; but the extent of this interference, and the manner in which it operated, is in some ways not entirely clear. The muddy waters overlying this problem issue from the fact that industrial-technological innovation is at least a two-stage process requiring entrepeneurs sympathetic to the adoption of production improvements, in addition to the actual occurrence of invention or technical modification. Thus, a given level of locally *adopted technology* need not have been synonymous with the level of *technical knowledge* achieved locally. For example:

During the years 1800–1850 Philadelphia provided for some industries a nourishing environment for technological innovation; for others it passively received new technology which had been introduced and demonstrated elsewhere; in still other industries the city successfully resisted change for several decades.[55]

Regardless of the presence or absence of resistance to the adoption of innovations, and regardless of the argument propounded by Habakkuk and others to the effect that labor problems acted as an inducement to American manufacturers to implement capital-intensive production techniques, it remains indisputable that by 1840 the machine had not yet superseded the hand tool. In fact, in some of the largest urban-industrial employment categories, such as the manufacture of shoes and ready-made clothing, inventions had not appeared by the onset of the forties which under any circumstances would have permitted the substitution of the factory system for workshop and domestic production. Quite revealingly, the available evidence for New York City indicates that, as late as 1840, the total number of machinists, or machine fashioners and operators, probably did not exceed 300.[56]

Another indication of the inability of technology to facilitate concentration is the fact that the limited number of mechanized urban establishments was small in size by modern standards. Establishments were particularly small previous to the War of 1812; e.g., as of 1811 the most imposing, if not the largest, plant in Philadelphia employed "about thirty-five workmen."[57] Subsequent decades saw the appearance of larger manufactories in the mercantile cities, but few, if any, provided work for more than 200 individuals. In the early 1830s New York's biggest industrial facilities were apparently the famed Allaire ironworks, which had 200 laborers in its service,[58] and the Harper Brothers' publishing house, with its 17 presses and 140 employees. At the same date, Boston had no industrial unit employing as many as 100 workers,[59] and somewhat later the vast majority of people engaged in manufacturing there "were employed either in establishments of ten or less or were unclassifiable, that is, worked in their homes."[60] An anomalous cotton mill in Baltimore employed 200 persons as early as 1824, but it appears as if the only other operations notable for their scale within the city itself were a coach "factory," which had 80 hands in 1831, and a carpet "factory" with about 90 employees in 1833.[61]

Equally significant, the urban productive units utilizing machinery were usually characterized, in contrast to their counterparts of that late nineteenth century, by a relatively small volume of undifferentiated, unspecialized production. For instance, the "Mars Works" of downtown Philadelphia were described in 1811 as consisting of "an iron foundry, mould-maker's shop, steam engine manufactory, blacksmith's shop, and mill-stone manufactory." These same works were described as producing cast and wrought work

for machinery for mills, for grinding grain or sawing timber; for forges, rolling and slitting mills, sugar mills, apple mills, bark mills, etc. Pans of all dimensions used by sugar boilers, soap boilers, etc. Screws of all sizes . . . , and all kinds of small wheels and machinery for cotton and wool spinning etc.[62]

The "Eagle Works," another Philadelphia enterprise of the same period, turned out sugar kettles, sugar-mill rollers, sugar-mill pumps, soap boilers, cannon, cylinders for steam engines, other machinery parts, and "iron castings of every description."[63] Likewise, a plant of somewhat later origin in New York was the producer of printing presses and equipment, sawmill machinery, "and machinery generally"; and a Baltimore concern manufactured chemicals, paints, medicines, and other items simultaneously.[64] Although these multifunctional plants substantiate the contention that the state of technology had not advanced to a point where many individual urban units could turn out uniform products on a mass production scale, it should be pointed out that these same shops and "factories" often contributed to future urban-industrial growth by acting as seedbeds for dovetailing cumulative inventions of eventual widespread applicability.

The most persuasive point in this whole line of reasoning regarding the state of technology and its deleterious effect upon the spatial concentration of industry in the mercantile cities is the simple fact that water power, then the most important source of energy used to drive factory machinery, constituted an immobile raw material. Just as the mountain could not be moved to Mohammed, water power could not be moved to the city. The mechanized cotton textile industry could flourish in Waltham, Paterson, or the Schuylkill suburbs of Roxborough, Spring Garden, and Kensington, but not in Boston, New York, or Philadelphia proper.[65] Similarly, factories utilizing water power functioned profitably beside the Patapsco Falls, and at the foot of at least nine other falls within a thirty-mile radius of Baltimore, but no large-scale water-driven machinery operated within the corporate limits of that mercantile center.[66]

Steam power, the only alternative to water power, was not yet suitable to intensive utilization in the country's largest cities. It is true that steam engines were employed as early as 1801 for grinding plaster of paris in Philadelphia and for sawing lumber in New York City, that New York printing presses began using steam power in 1823, and that there were isolated cases of steam-driven cotton mills in Philadelphia and Baltimore.[67] However, by 1832 only four of Boston's 95 industrial categories were evidently utilizing steam engines,[68] and six years hence no more than 429 horsepower could be generated by *all* 46 of the city's steam-powered manufactories.[69] The 1838 picture was little different in Baltimore, whose 45 steam-using industrial establishments had a total capacity of 562 horsepower, or in Philadelphia, whose 59 plants with steam engines were capable of generating 477.5 horsepower.[70] Moreover, it is unlikely that the entire horsepower potential of the country's industrially employed steam engines was equivalent to that of 200 contemporary American automobiles.[71]

Cost was the greatest constraint on the adoption of steam power in the mercantile city. The efficiency of steam engines was such that: "By 1839, at Easton, Pennsylvania, *a point accessible to coal,* the relative annual cost per horse power for water and steam was $23 and $105."[72] Of course, neither Boston, New York, New Orleans, or Baltimore possessed immediate accessibility to coal, and thus the expense of steam power in those cities was compounded by transport outlays for either coal or wood. The volume of coal consumed, as well as the cost of moving it, was such that even the steam engines of Philadelphia were still quite dependent on wood in the thirties—despite the relative ease with which Lehigh Valley anthracites could be procured by an all-water route.[73] Significantly, in 1838, two places with populations much smaller than those of the mercantile cities, but situated directly upon major coal deposits, surpassed their larger urban brethren in the exploitation of steam power. Specifically, Wheeling, whose 1840 population was 7,885, had steam engines which could generate 768 horsepower; and Pittsburgh, with an 1840 population of 21,115, had steam-mechanized factories and workshops with a total capacity of 2,651.5 horsepower (considerably more than Boston, Baltimore, and Philadelphia combined).[74] In the formal terminology of Weberian and neo-Weberian location theory, coal-burning steam engines were highly concentrated in coal-field cities because in most of the industries using such engines the fuel constituted a "dominant weight-losing raw material" (i.e., its weight consumed per ton of product was equal to or greater than the weight of the product plus the weight of any other localized materials), and thereby was almost an automatic locational determinant.

We can, therefore, conclude that the immobility of water power, the inefficiency of steam power, and the dominant weight-losing character of coal temporarily prevented the development of urban industries whose scale economies would have stimulated further metropolitan growth by facilitating the extension of market areas, i.e., by permitting the substitution of production economies for the transport diseconomies of larger shipments.

The Transportation Network and the Size of Markets

Irrespective of the state of industrial technology, the costs of shipment on the prerailroad transport network were in themselves a formidable obstruction to the growth of manufacturing in the larger urban centers. The cost of overcoming distance by any means of overland transportation other than fragmentary rail routes must have been staggering to an entrepreneur contemplating market area expansion; for road and turnpike transport, which was often impractical on a year-round basis, varied in cost from twenty to sixty cents per ton-mile. Representatively: during the century's first decade, the cost incurred in hauling a ton of goods nine miles on inland roads was equivalent to that of importing the identical weight from Europe; in spite of a water leg between Albany and New York, the 1817 charge for freighting a ton from Buffalo to Manhattan was $100, or about twenty-five cents per ton-mile; and in the thirties, a charge of one dollar per ton was imposed for moving merchandise within a radius of a few miles from Boston.[75]

Industrial commodities could move with somewhat greater freedom on riverways and on the canals that began to mushroom in the 1820s. The canals offered ton-mile tariffs which were usually considerably lower and, on occasion, drastically less than turnpike rates. Illustratively, in 1829, the governor of Massachusetts estimated that the Blackstone Canal permitted vessels to haul goods from New York to Worcester for half the levy charged on overland carriage between Boston and Worcester.[76] However, in 1840 inland waterway transportation still cost five cents per ton-mile and required large blocks of time for lengthy shipments (after completion of the Erie Canal one week was still necessary for shipments to journey from Detroit to New York, and about thirteen days were needed to go by steamer from New Orleans to St. Louis).[77] The temporal dimensions of inland-waterway freighting made it quite difficult for urban manufacturers to respond to demand fluctuations in the nonlocal market, and forced such entrepreneurs to manacle capital to goods in transit. Furthermore, transshipment tariffs frequently added significant sums to the cost of movement; e.g., goods shipped over the mongrel water and rail Mainline from Philadelphia to Pittsburgh in 1838 had to be unloaded and reloaded at Columbia, Hollidaysburg, and Johnstown at a cost of roughly $2.50 per ton, or the equivalent of an additional fifty miles of movement.[78] Because of the rapidity with which total transport outlays were multiplied by transfer and overland movement, prospective market and supply areas were confined to a limited radius around river and canal routes. The disadvantages of canal and river transportation were complicated additionally by winter freezing, the desiccation of locks during summer droughts, and sometimes excessively circuitous routes. In short, even if technology had somehow advanced to a late-nineteenth-century level, where agglomeration economies could be substituted for these transport diseconomies, the geographical extent of the area in which most urban industrialists could compete with the products of rural mill and domestic manufacture would not have been very great in the prerailroad era.

This last observation is not to be interpreted as meaning that the manufacturing potential of each of the four infant metropolises on the Atlantic seaboard and New Orleans was equally handicapped by the prerailroad transport network. New Orleans was singularly beset with obstacles to upstream navigation (so much so that her northward shipments, most of which were confined to Louisiana and Mississippi plantations, "never exceeded one-half the volume that came downstream"),[79] and this circumstance was a primary contributor to the inordinately small scale of manufacturing in the Crescent City (Table 3). Baltimore, although plagued by similar difficulties in ascending the Susquehanna, and its roundabout route to the North and Europe, could tap the National Road, as well as the limited trackage of the B. and O. Railroad, and was admirably situated for coastwise shipping to the South and exporting to the West Indies. Most importantly, the completion and opening of the Erie Canal in 1825 dramatically expanded New York's hinterland and conferred upon some of its manufacturers competitive advantages that did not exist in other ports.

On the one hand, the Erie Canal merely reinforced New York's existing transport advantages, its nearness to the sea as compared to Baltimore and Philadelphia, its proximity to the South as compared with Boston, its magnificent harbor, and its access to the valleys of the Hudson and the Connecticut.[80] But, on the other hand, the canal represented a major initial line of penetration and its construction brought with it an "ideal-typical sequence" of transport developments; i.e., market area expansion possibilities were compounded by the establishment of feeder routes and the occurrence of "hinterland piracy."[81] In other words, it may be argued that the relatively large volume of capital invested in New York manufacturing in 1840 (Table 3) was partially ascribable to the spatial lengthening of production made possible by the Erie Canal. However, even "Clinton's Big Ditch" could neither negate the previously mentioned shortcomings of inland waterway transportation, nor overcome factor shortages and the state of technology, to thus promote manufacturing from its secondary position in the most important of the mercantile cities.

Inasmuch as the broader transportation network had virtually no effect on finished product distribution within the contiguously built-up area of each city, a final word ought to be injected regarding the ramifications of local market size, and by indirect extension, aggregate market or population accessibility (potential). The number of inhabitants in each of the mercantile cities under consideration was not very impressive by modern metropolitan standards (Table 1), and their accessibility to population was meager, even if 1860 is used as a gauge (Fig. 1). At the same time, evidence seems to indicate that, under conditions of mechanized industrial tech-

nology, urban manufacturing diversity is to some degree a function of population and market or population accessibility. This implies that large-scale
industrial diversity would not have been feasible in the presence of a
technology considerably more advanced than that which prevailed in the
major urban centers of 1840. If, because of the inadequate local market
population and a low index of accessibility to population, a number of
large-scale manufactures could not survive, the mercantile city was nonetheless more diversified industrially than its similarly sized counterparts of
more than a century hence.[82] This was so because small-scale handicraft
and unmechanized production units had low threshold requirements. It
should be emphasized however, that the aggregate output of these low
threshold units was not only stunted by the absolute size of the local
market, and by the other restraining factors already elaborated upon, but
also by the generally low purchasing power of much of the urban population.

THE MANUFACTURES OF THE MERCANTILE CITY

The subsidiary role of manufacturing in the mercantile city is entirely
logical within the framework of the restraints and obstacles depicted on

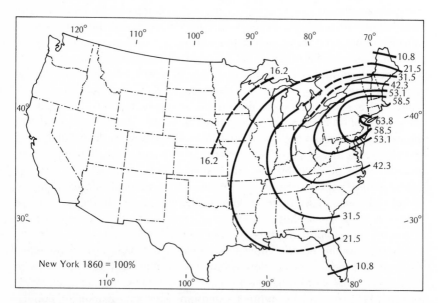

Figure 1. Accessibility to population: 1840 Adapted from J. Q. Stewart and
W. Warntz, "Macrogeography and Social Science," *Geographical Review*, XLVIII
(1958), 181; and J. Q. Stewart, "Empirical Mathematical Rules Concerning the
Distribution and Equilibrium of Population," *Geographical Review*, XXXVII (1947),
479.

the foregoing pages. But it is certainly obvious that the presence of obstructions failed to completely eliminate manufacturing from the urban scene, and thus there remains the question: Why were existing industries located in New York, Boston, Philadelphia, and Baltimore?

In 1827 it was observed that:

the city of New York has no manufactures, excepting such as are altogether independent of local facilities [raw materials], and such as are likely to grow wherever there are large accumulations of men and means.[83]

One can be more explicit, and concurrently substantiate the appropriateness of the term "mercantile city," by demonstrating that an overwhelming portion, perhaps virtually all, of the industrial activities located within the confines of New York, Boston, Philadelphia, and Baltimore were either directly or indirectly linked to the mercantile functions of those cities.

Entrepôt Manufactures

The most direct and significant linkages were those which existed between the mercantile city's foreign and domestic commerce and the entrepôt manufacture of consumers' goods. Those merchants who were less hesitant than their colleagues to invest in industrial ventures had, from an early date, "tended to confine their interests and capital to enterprises which combined a mercantile and manufacturing interest, or to those which grew naturally out of their course of trade."[84] The preference for processing import and export commodities with which the merchant class was already familiar was in most instances founded on the security derived from dealing with already known markets and previously established distribution channels. From a purely theoretical viewpoint, entrepôt manufacturing was also rational because it eliminated the additional set of terminal costs which would have been incurred if the particular raw materials were processed at some point other than that where their transshipment was made almost mandatory by a break in bulk or a change of ownership.

The apparently modest preeminence of entrepôt manufactures in New York in 1810 serves as one indication of prevailing conditions in the other mercantile cities during the period 1800–1840. Ten years after the turn of the nineteenth century, sugar refining, tanning and leather processing, and tobacco milling numbered amongst Manhattan's most prominent industries, with a combined output approaching or perhaps surpassing $800,000 per annum.[85] The American sugar refining industry reputedly traces its origins to New York in 1730; and, one century afterward, Philadelphia, Baltimore, and Boston were important competitors (as of 1813, there were 11 sugar refineries in New York, 11 in Philadelphia, 8 in Baltimore, 3 in Boston, and only 38 in the entire country).[86] Characteristically, at the end of the period, the industry was undergoing technical changes which would later permit it to operate on a truly large scale; e.g., in the late 1830s one New York firm increased its daily output to 12,000 pounds by introducing steam power, and shortly thereafter, in the early 1840s, centrifugals were installed in New York plants to separate sugar from molasses.[87] Although similar scale shifts were not incipient in the New York tanning and tobacco-processing industries, a growing trade in hides and tobacco had embellished the importance of these two manufactures (over 700 people were employed in New York's tanneries and related leather-working establishments in 1840, and by then the city was well on its way to becoming "the largest emporium of foreign hides in the world").[88] More significantly, the inability of high raw-material assembly costs to interfere with the port location of trade-linked or entrepôt industries is dramatized by the perpetuation and expansion of urban tanning in an era when it was necessary to consume between five and eleven tons of oak or hemlock in order to produce one ton of leather.[89]

A more complete, if somewhat imperfect, image of the stature of entrepôt industries in a mercantile city can be derived for Boston from McLane's 1832 "Report on Manufactures."[90] According to this document, entrepôt manufactures accounted for a minimum of 20 percent of both Boston's industrial value added and employment (Table 4). The magnitude of this percentage would be considerably augmented if it were somehow possible to sort out value added and employment associated with retailing in non-entrepôt categories that either combined retailing and manufacturing functions, as did the "shoe and boot making" industry (Table 5), or coupled production and repairing activities, as did the "cabinetmaking" industry. Since all clothes-making establishments were assigned to the "local" group in Table 4, an even more impressive percentage increase could be gained if it were possible to segregate that portion of the tailoring industry (Table 5) which catered to the Boston market from that which made "slop clothing for navy and merchant ships."[91] Classificatory problems aside, the most noteworthy aspects of Boston's entrepôt production were the dimensions of its distilling (similarly important in New York, Philadelphia, and Baltimore), and the exotic variety of raw materials used. Strikingly, the umbrella and cane industry alone utilized imported ivory, silks, buckhorn, linen, rattan, ebony, and boxwood.

Several other manufactures, thus far unmentioned, were also directly associated with the primary trading function of the mercantile cities. One of these, flour milling, was especially articulated in Baltimore and its vicinity, and until the Erie Canal commenced operation the inhabitants of the Chesapeake Bay city boasted that theirs was "the largest flour market in the world."[92] More importantly, and almost ironically, the largest single industry growing out of urban commercial activity, the integrated power-driven cotton textile industry, was located in Boston's hinterland and the suburbs of Baltimore and Philadelphia, but with the exception of the aforementioned anomalous steam-powered plants, not in the city proper.[93]

Table 4. The Structure of Boston's Manufacturing: 1832[a]

Industry group[b]	Number of establishments	Number employed	Percent	Value added	Percent
Entrepot	201	1,794	20.8	$ 974,774[c]	20.0
Commerce-serving	232	2,599	30.2	1,355,125	27.8
Local market	561	4,214	49.0	2,553,385	52.2
Construction materials	55	400	4.7	286,935	5.8
Other[d]	506	3,814	44.3	2,266,450	46.4
Total	994	8,607[e]	100.0	4,883,284[c]	100.0

[a] Source: (see notes 25 and 90), pp. 432–69.

[b] As implied in the text discussion of tailoring, industries fitting the criteria for two groups were classified entirely into the more appropriate alternative.

[c] Incomplete data, minor omissions.

[d] This category particularly, and thereby the total, is exaggerated by the unavoidable inclusion of retailing and repairing functions.

[e] Slightly over 40 percent of this total (3,460) was comprised of boys under sixteen years of age, and women and girls.

Francis C. Lowell, P. T. Jackson, Nathan Appleton, and many of the other individuals backing the early cotton spinning and weaving factories in New England, southeastern Pennsylvania, the Baltimore area, and Paterson, had been urban merchants. As active participants in the trade of Boston, Philadelphia, Baltimore, and New York, a number of merchants were acquainted with the market, made familiar to them through the wholesaling of English dry goods, and with the raw material sources, made intimate to them through the re-export of cotton. Because face-to-face contacts were so vital within the context of an essentially primitive communications system, merchant capital was rarely risked in nonlocal industrial projects; and as textile factories were anchored to immobile water-power sources, it may be conjectured that large-scale integrated cotton spinning and weaving would have initially emerged as a major industry in the mercantile city if an alternative economical energy source had existed (although admittedly, Boston then contained little if any space for large factories).

Commerce-serving Manufactures

In addition to the entrepôt industries, a second group of manufactures was directly linked to the commerce of the mercantile city. Shipbuilding, printing, coopery, and other industries had grown in the larger Atlantic

Table 5. Selected Characteristics of Boston's Leading Industries: 1832[a]

Industry	Number of establishments	Number employed	Cost of domestic raw materials	Cost of foreign raw materials	Value of production	Value added
Printing and publishing	91	1,309	$583,700	$ 65,100	$1,426,300	$777,500
Tailoring	100	1,700[c]	400,000	1,500,000	2,600,000	700,000
Shipbuilding and repairing[b]	102	795[c]	542,440[c]	500,850[c]	1,436,125[c]	392,835[c]
Iron foundries	9	320	700,000	20,000	1,100,000	380,000
Boot and shoe making[d]	200	500[c]	200,000	20,000	500,000	280,000
Baking	40	126	187,775	2,550	400,000	209,675
Distilling	20	80	190,000	1,000,000	1,371,000	181,000
Subtotal	562	4,830	2,803,915	3,108,500	8,833,425	2,921,010
Total for all industries	994	8,607	4,099,820	4,459,941	13,321,595[e]	4,883,284[e]
Subtotal/Total	56.5	56.1	68.4	69.7	66.3	59.8

[a] Source: McLane (see notes 25 and 90), pp. 432–69.

[b] Includes the independent production of sails, masts, pumps, and blocks, etc.

[c] Estimated.

[d] Some establishments with repairing and retailing functions included.

[e] Incomplete data, minor omissions.

ports in response to the demand created by local commercial activities. Periodic increases in the volume of trade required corresponding increments in vessel carrying capacity, and therefore, during prosperous years, shipbuilding thrived on a noteworthy scale in New York, Baltimore, Philadelphia, and Boston. (Output was also encouraged after the War of 1812 by the termination of European restrictions on the purchase of American-built ships.) Although New York outdistanced its rival ports in vessel construction (Table 6), Baltimore was renowned for the grace of her slender schooners and larger "clippers," and Philadelphia was respected for the shape, speed, and quality of her products—despite a slump of the city's yards during the thirties.[94] Boston's commitment to shipbuilding (Table 5) was supplemented by launchings and repairs at Medford (five miles north of the city), where twenty-three ships and eight brigs were completed in 1832 and part of 1833, and at Charlestown (eventually incorporated into Boston), where 100 men were involved in the industry during 1832.[95]

Table 6. Selected Shipbuilding Statistics for Leading Mercantile Cities[a]

(in thousands of tons)

	New York	Boston	Philadelphia	Baltimore	U.S. total
1833[b]	22	16	3	8	161[c]
1837	20	6	3	5	122
1841	16	15	5	7	118

[a] Source: Albion (see note 12), p. 406. Compiled from Reports on Commerce and Navigation issued annually by the Secretary of the Treasury.

[b] First year for which statistics are available on a port-by-port basis.

[c] Virtually none of the total for all three years was accounted for by New Orleans.

The shipbuilding market functioned in such a manner that it was essentially obligatory for some production to coincide with the major centers of consumption, even though it was frequently necessary at the leading ports to assemble live oak, white pine, and pitch pine timbers from distant points in the Carolinas, Georgia, Florida, and Maine. Advertisements for individual vessels were usually placed in the local newspapers when the planking state of construction was attained in the urban shipyards, for most purchasing merchants "preferred to order vessels from builders who were known to them, and whose yard they could visit" in order to dictate structural specifications, insure quality, and cut costs.[96] Significantly, when New York displaced Philadelphia as the nation's leading commercial metropolis after the War of 1812, it also surpassed the latter city to become the foremost shipbuilding center.

A similar exchange of positions occurred concomitantly in the printing industries, whose size, aside from book publishing, was basically a function of the local demand for newspaper advertising, handbills, business papers, printed blanks, and legal forms. The leading daily newspapers in early-nineteenth-century New York carried such banners as "The New York Gazette and General Advertiser," "The Commercial Advertiser," "The Mercantile Advertiser," and "The Public Advertiser," and thereby emphasized the relationship between the printing industries and the primary mercantile functions of the city. The publication of *Niles' Weekly Register* in Baltimore, and the appearance elsewhere of lesser known, more short-lived periodicals, such as Philadelphia's *Archives of Useful Knowledge*, was another manifestation of the strong bonds between commerce and urban printing. If numbers employed can be accepted as a valid indicator, then printing and publishing, with over 2,000 workers, was New York City's single most important industry in 1840.[97] If the preferable but usually impractical value-added gauge is used, then the same indications of primacy are obtained from the most nearly complete set of data available, for the value added by Boston's printing and publishing industries[98] in 1832 was greater than that of any other manufacturing class (Table 5).

The assembly of barrels, boxes, kegs, casks, and other items of cooperage was a less imposing, but still important, industrial servant to commerce. Despite the absence of census materials, we do know there were already upwards of 150 coopers on Manhattan in 1800, and at least 220 similar craftsmen in Boston as of 1832.[99] The localization of the coopering industry in the mercantile city derived largely from the handcuffing of much of its output to uniquely specified orders, and the producer's need to avoid the unnecessary transportation costs normally associated with shipping space-consuming vacuous containers.

Remaining Manufactures

An overwhelming percentage of the manufacturing in the major urban centers which neither fell into the entrepôt category nor responded directly to commercial demands was at least obliquely related to the mercantile aspect of those cities. In more specific terms, the production of construction materials, such as glass, nails, paint, "paper hangings," and plaster of paris, and the manufacture of beer, baked goods, furniture, clothing, carriages, and other consumers' goods was ubiquitous to New York, Boston, Philadelphia, and Baltimore, because of the aggregate demand precipitated by the local mercantile population and the classes serving that population. The evidence that can be ferreted out would seem to indicate that these local-market and threshold manufactures were larger as a group than the entrepôt and commerce-serving industries. However, the local-market industry figures for Boston in Table 4 should be interpreted with caution. There is little, if any, reason for doubting the magnitude of the construction material industries in that table,[100] but the same cannot be said of the residue of the local market group. We have already alluded to the unavoidable inclusion of some retailing and repairing in this balance, as well as to the classificatory problems associated with tailoring. Furthermore, testimony from the Philadelphia record suggests additional obfuscation of retailing by the four furniture establishments subsumed under the table's local-market residue.[101]

Certainly, some of the remaining urban manufactures were not embraced firmly by the broad local-market category, or by the entrepôt and commerce-serving groups. The machinery and locomotive plants of downtown Philadelphia spring immediately to mind as refractory anomalies. However, closer examination reveals that these deviant examples are not as unruly as their initial impressions might imply. Unless the census for 1840 is grossly inaccurate on the point, there were less than 400 people employed in Philadelphia's machine-making shops and factories at that time.[102] A portion of this small number were occupied in the manufacture of machinery for cotton and woolen textile mills, much of which was distributed to a market within a few miles of the city. While other machinery industries and locomotive production did not necessarily cater to such a blatantly local market, they originated for the most part rather late in the 1800–1840 period under consideration. For example: the famed Baldwin Locomotive Works did not go into full operation until 1833–1834; the Norris Locomotive Works were established in 1834, "in a small shop, employing but six men"; and the Southwark Foundry, a relatively large producer of "heavy machinery," originated no earlier than 1836.[103] In short, the late arrival and magnitude of these and other apparent exceptions present insufficient cause to refute the premise that manufacturing in the mercantile city was basically an adjunct of the city's dominant commercial functions.

NOTES

1. By 1831, when U.S. cotton textile production was slightly in excess of $40 million, factories accounted for $26 million of the total value of output. In contrast, Gallatin had claimed that roughly two-thirds of the clothing worn by the rural populace in 1810 was the product of domestic family industry. T. Pitkin, *A Statistical View of the Commerce of the United States of America* (New Haven: Durrie and Peck, 1835), pp. 472, 482–4.

2. U.S. Bureau of the Census, *Historical Statistics of the United States: Colonial Times to 1957* (Washington, D.C. 1961), pp. 7, 14. It is quite likely that these figures understate urban population, as the data compiled by the Bureau of the

Census refer only to places with a population in excess of 2,500. Cities, particularly in the early stages of economic growth, ought to be defined in functional and structural terms, and not by arbitrary demographic limits.

3. *Ibid.,* p. 427.

4. In respect to these conditions Clark commented: "British mercantile houses had allowed American importers to pyramid credits in England by accepting their bills, with an understanding that before maturity bills signed by other parties might be substituted for those falling due. As this practice stimulated undue purchases of foreign manufactures, it was evidently unfavorable to American industry, and its termination by the panic was a compensating feature of that event." V. S. Clark, *History of Manufactures in the United States* (New York: McGraw-Hill, 1929), I, 380.

5. For more specific details regarding a descriptive model of urban-industrial growth and the evolution of the American system of cities between 1860 and 1910 see A. Pred, "Industrialization, Initial Advantage, and American Metropolitan Growth," *Geographical Review,* LV (1965), 158–85.

6. Scholars of the stature of Schumpeter have insisted that the development of theory to some degree depends on the syntheses and generalizations to be constructed from secondary works. See J. A. Schumpeter, "Economic Theory and Entrepreneurial History," in R. R. Wohl, ed., *Change and the Entrepreneur* (Cambridge: Harvard University Press, 1949), p. 83. Also note the introductory remarks on "Analytical Models in the Study of Social Systems," in E. E. Hagen, *On the Theory of Social Change: How Economic Growth Begins* (Homewood, Ill.: The Dorsey Press, Inc., 1962), p. 505.

7. J. A. Dix, *Sketch of the Resources of the City of New-York* (New York: G. and C. Carvill, 1827), p. 14.

8. J. Gottmann, *Megalopolis* (New York: The Twentieth Century Fund, 1961), p. 103.

9. I. Holmes, *An Account of the United States of America, Derived from Actual Observation, During a Residence of Four Years in that Republic* (London: The Caxton Press, 1823), p. 355.

10. R. C. Wade, *The Urban Frontier: Pioneer Life in Early Pittsburgh, Cincinnati, Lexington, Louisville, and St. Louis* (Chicago: The University of Chicago Press, 1964), pp. 54, 62. The difficulty of ascending the Mississippi prior to the introduction of the steam boat, and the city's subsequent tardiness in promoting internal improvements resulted in New Orleans having relatively restricted sales in the upper Mississippi Valley.

11. O. Handlin, *Boston's Immigrants 1790–1880* (Cambridge: Harvard University Press, 1959), p. 7.

12. R. G. Albion, *The Rise of New York Port 1815–60* (New York: Scribner, 1939), pp. 394–7. These figures do not by any means give full measure to the importance of coastal movements since Albion's sources forced him, in each case, to omit the voluminous short-distance arrivals of wood and produce from the same state and the two adjacent states. Some have said: "Over most of the antebellum period the coastwise trade was the most important artery of interregional commerce." [See A. Fishlow, "Antebellum Interregional Trade Reconsidered," *American Economic Review,* LIV (May 1964), 362.]

13. Although it is generally acknowledged that Philadelphia was relatively the most industrialized of the nation's largest cities in 1840, there are a number of grounds upon which to question the dwarfed position of the city's wholesaling as indicated by Table 3. Firstly, our suspicions are aroused by the purported scale of retailing and the incongruously small number of "commission houses" in Philadelphia. It is most unlikely that Philadelphia, with a population equivalent to that of Boston, and one-third that of New York, would have more capital invested in retailing than the latter, and more than three times as much as invested in the former, even if Philadelphia's populous suburbs were brought into the picture. Secondly, there is considerable confusion regarding the term "commission houses," as it seemingly included auction houses and other firms performing quasi-retailing functions plus establishments that could be placed in the category of "commercial houses in foreign trade." Typically, in New Orleans "one is confronted with a situation in which many business houses advertised as wholesalers or were referred to in that capacity, but actually may have been carrying on considerable retailing business. . . . Occupational functions were very flexible among early wholesale middlemen . . . , and consequently occupational titles must not be accepted without reservation." [H. A. Mitchell, "The Development of New Orleans as a Wholesale Trading Center," *The Louisiana Historical Quarterly,* XXVII (1944), 947, 950.] Therefore, since it is known that local census marshals often resolved these ambiguities by making their own arbitrary classificatory decisions, it may be concluded that much of Philadelphia's 1840 wholesaling and auctioning is masked by its abnormal retailing statistics. Perhaps it may also be surmised that similar discrepancies, but of a lesser dimension, exist in the data pertaining to Baltimore.

14. H. J. Habakkuk, *American and British Technology in the Nineteenth Century* (Cambridge: The University Press, 1962), p. 41. For a thorough discussion of the roles and operations of individuals in the various urban mercantile professions see F. M. Jones, *Middlemen in the Domestic Trade of the United States: 1800–1860* (Urbana: Illinois Studies in the Social Sciences, 1937).

15. *Longworth's American Almanac, New-York Register, and City Directory* (New York: Thomas Longworth, 1800), pp. 92–107.

16. *Niles' Weekly Register,* XLV (September 21, 1833), 56.

17. According to Albion's compilations the value of foreign goods entering the port of New York in 1832 and 1836 was respectively $53 million and $118 million. Albion, *op. cit.,* p. 391.

18. *Niles' Weekly Register,* XLIII (December 8, 1832), 241. Since imports for that year only totalled $53 million, it may be reasonably assumed that the remaining value of New York City's domestic trade was derived from markups and the merchandising of commodities associated with coastal arrivals and local manufactures.

19. Albion, *op. cit.,* p. 390. Figures of this sort are only one reason for arguing that Albion's work probably represents the most detailed scholarly account of the economy of a mercantile city during the period in question.

20. Albion, *op. cit.,* pp. 390–91.

21. If one follows Marburg's rather conservative precedent, and allocates an investment for each "commercial house in foreign trade" equal to the national average invested in "commission houses" ($41,000), then the 1840 ratio of mercantile to local industrial investments was better than seven to one in New York and Boston. If one makes the alternative assumption that average investments in "commercial houses in foreign trade" were on a par with those in *local* "commission houses," then the ratio for Boston jumps to 12.4 : 1, and New York's increases more modestly to 7.3 : 1. See T. F. Marburg, "Income Originating in Trade, 1799–1869," in *Trends in the American Economy in the Nineteenth Century* (Princeton: Princeton University Press, 1960), p. 318.

22. J. Mease, *The Picture of Philadelphia* (Philadelphia: B. and T. Kite, 1811), p. 32. Some small-scale manufacturing probably also occurred in an additional indeterminable number of buildings which were categorized as "work-shops."

23. J. Sparks, "Baltimore," *North American Review*, XX (1825), 124.

24. *Niles' Weekly Register*, XL (August 20, 1831), 433.

25. Compiled from L. McLane, *Report on Manufactures* (Washington, D.C.: House Document No. 308, 22nd Congress, First Session, 1833), I, 432–69.

26. *Niles Weekly Register*, XXXVII (January 30, 1830), 379. This source is unclear as to whether the sum given refers to the city or the county of Philadelphia.

27. For example, many of the coopers in Boston were "fish dealers and exporters," and in 1832, roughly 95 percent of the value of production in that same city's cabinetmaking industry was comprised of repairs. McLane, *op. cit.,* pp. 435, 441.

28. When Boston's annual production was valued at approximately $13,400,000 the value added for the city was less than $5 million. McLane, *op. cit.,* pp. 432–69.

29. Although the intricacies of the tariff question are not central to the matters under discussion, reference should be made to Taussig's classical assertion that the limited progress in the early-nineteenth-century American manufacture of cotton and woolen textiles, iron, and other products was not attributable so much to the tariff as to inventiveness and resources. See F. W. Taussig, *The Tariff History of the United States,* 8th rev. ed. (New York: Capricorn Books, 1964 [originally published 1892]), pp. 8–67. Also note Clark, *op. cit.,* pp. 283–7, 308–12.

30. A. Gallatin, *Report on Manufactures: American State Papers, Finance* (Washington, D.C., April 17, 1810), II, 430.

31. E. T. Freedley, *Philadelphia and Its Manufactures: A Hand-book Exhibiting the Development, Variety, and Statistics of the Manufacturing Industry of Philadelphia in 1857* (Philadelphia: E. Young, 1859), p. 128.

32. C. McL. Green, "Light Manufactures and the Beginnings of Precision Manufacture," in H. F. Williamson, ed., *The Growth of the American Economy* (New York: Prentice-Hall, 1951), p. 195. The attitude that "investment in manufacturing enterprises . . . was a third choice at best" existed among many American merchants from a period at least as early as the 1770s. See V. D. Harrington, *The New York Merchant on the Eve of the Revolution* (New York: Columbia University Studies in History, Economics and Public Law, 1935), p. 145

33. J. W. Livingood, *The Philadelphia-Baltimore Trade Rivalry 1780–1860* (Harrisburg: The Pennsylvania Historical and Museum Commission, 1947), p. 161.

Even the Baltimore and Ohio Railroad, the most celebrated of the private ventures, received considerable funds from the municipal government of Baltimore.

34. Holmes, *op. cit.,* pp. 151–2.

35. *Niles' Weekly Register,* XXV (December 27, 1823), 259.

36. *Niles' Weekly Register,* XXXVII (November 7, 1829), 164; XXXVIII (March 27, 1830), 85; XLIV (May 11, 1833), 163; and LI (November 12, 1836), 167, 176.

37. Dix, *op. cit.,* p. 41.

38. *Niles' Weekly Register,* XLIX (October 17, 1835), 98.

39. Handlin, *op. cit.,* p. 4.

40. *Niles' Weekly Register,* XXXV (September 27, 1828), 68.

41. *Niles' Weekly Register,* XXXIII (January 26, 1828), 356; and XIV (June 27, 1818), 310. The volume of construction activity fluctuated violently from year to year. In an extreme instance, the number of new buildings erected in New York City slumped off from 1,826 in 1836 to 840 in 1837 [*Niles' Weekly Register,* LVIII (May 16, 1840), 164].

42. *Niles' Weekly Register,* XLV (November 2 and 9, 1833), 148, 165.

43. Rents in Baltimore at times surpassed the "excessively high" sums paid out in New York [Holmes, *op. cit.,* pp. 268–73], and housing shortages attained proportions similar to those which prevailed during New York's boom of 1825. It was said of the New York crisis "that a furnished house, without a tenant, is not to be found in this great city, and that well dressed families are observed to be occupying houses of which the builders do not appear to have accomplished the work so far as to have fully closed them in by doors and windows." *Niles' Weekly Register,* XXVIII (August 27, 1825), 415.

44. McLane, *op. cit.,* p. 471.

45. Clark, *op. cit.,* p. 368.

46. For dated but relevant discussions of corporate enterprise and industrial organization see Clark, *op. cit.,* pp. 440–63; and G. S. Callender, "The Early Transportation and Banking Enterprises of the State in Relation to the Growth of Corporations," *Quarterly Journal of Economics,* XVII (November 1902), 111–62.

47. J. Rubin, *Canal or Railroad? Imitation and Innovation in the Response to the Erie Canal in Philadelphia, Baltimore, and Boston* (Philadelphia: Transactions of the American Philosophical Society, New Series, Vol. 51, part 7, 1961), p. 14.

48. In contrast, the constriction of Boston's hinterland released considerable sums for industrial investment. However, as the subsequent pages will indicate, neither the labor situation nor the state of technology permitted much of these capital resources to remain within the legal limits of Boston.

49. Clark, *op. cit.,* p. 370.

50. Clark, *op. cit.,* p. 244. Quite differently: "The temporary suspension of a factory in Great Britain did not mean the dispersion of all available labor for operating it. A plant could resume operation at any time with a full complement of qualified workmen."

51. Habakkuk, *op. cit.*, p. 12. Habakkuk quoted from C. Goodrich and S. Davidson, "The Wage-earner in the Westward Movement," *Political Science Quarterly,* LI (1936), 115.

52. Handlin, *op. cit.*, pp. 11, 74. Significantly, industrial investments did begin to stay in Boston to a much larger degree when the Irish eventually provided the city with a cornucopia of cheap labor.

53. McLane, *op. cit.*, pp. 444, 468–9.

54. A total of 80,972 migrants entered the United States in 1836. Approximate disembarkations at other Atlantic Coast cities were as follows: Baltimore, 6,000; Boston, 3,000; and Philadelphia, 2,000. See U.S. Bureau of the Census, *op. cit.*, p. 62; and Albion, *op. cit.*, p. 418.

55. S. B. Warner, Jr., "Innovation and the Industrialization of Philadelphia 1800–1850," in Oscar Handlin and John Burchard, eds., *The Historian and the City* (Cambridge: The M.I.T. Press and Harvard University Press, 1963), p. 64.

56. *Longworth's American Almanac, New-York Register, and City Directory* (New York: Thomas Longworth, 1840). It is apparent from the 37,125 entries, the prevailing size of family, and the total population of Manhattan (Table 1), that the completeness of this directory, which lists 103 machinists, in all likelihood exceeds 33 percent.

57. Mease, *op. cit.*, p. 76.

58. McLane, *op. cit.*, II, 115; and *Niles' Weekly Register,* XLIV (August 17, 1833), 404. New York's second largest ironworking firm employed no more than 90 men in 1832, and the total number of workers in nine similar establishments, including the Allaire Works, was only 465. An identical number of foundries in Boston had an even less impressive employment of 320.

59. McLane, *op. cit.*, I, 432–69.

60. Handlin, *op. cit.*, p. 10.

61. Sparks, *op. cit.*, p. 128; *Niles' Weekly Register,* XL (August 20, 1831), 433; and *idem,* XLV (October 5, 1833), 83.

62. Mease, *op. cit.*, p. 76.

63. T. Scharf and T. Westcott, *History of Philadelphia* (Philadelphia: L. H. Evarts and Co., 1884), III, 2,251.

64. *The Great Metropolis; or Guide to New-York for 1846* (New York: John Doggett, Jr., 1845), p. 117; and J. L. Bishop, *A History of American Manufactures from 1608 to 1860* (Philadelphia: Edward Young & Co., 1861, 1868), II, 231.

65. At least two attempts were made to establish a water-powered textile industry on Manhattan in the 1790s, but both were unsuccessful, and in at least one instance failure was ascribed to the inadequacies of the power site. A futile effort was also made to harness Boston's Mill Dam for manufacturing purposes.

66. There were 34,102 spindles operating in the cotton mills of Baltimore County in 1839, but only 3,600 of these were within the city proper, and they in a solitary steam-powered manufactory which by this time only employed 120 people. The situation was nearly identical in Philadelphia County where only 3,120 of 40,862 spindles fell within the city boundaries—and these too were presumably all steam-driven. *Aggregate Value and Produce, and Number of Persons Employed in Mines, Agriculture, Commerce, Manufactures, etc:* ["Sixth Census of the United States, 1840"] (Washington, D.C., 1841), pp. 169–71, 217.

67. L. Woodbury, *Report on Steam Engines* (Washington, D.C., House Document No. 21, 25th Congress, Third Session, 1838), pp. 160, 210; and Bishop, *op. cit.,* pp. 91, 205, 286, 336.

68. McLane, *op. cit.,* pp. 432–69.

69. Woodbury, *op. cit.,* pp. 41–4.

70. Woodbury, *op. cit.,* pp. 159–67, 210–11. Numerous small-scale industrial users of steam were also to be found in the remainder of Philadelphia County, and immediately outside of Boston and Baltimore. Woodbury's Treasury Department report gave no detailed statistics for New York City.

71. Woodbury, *op. cit.,* p. 10, wrote that: "The power employed in all steam-engines in the United States is ascertained and estimated at 100,318 horsepower; of this 12,140 only is in engines estimated and not returned. . . . Of this force, 57,019 horsepower is computed to be in steamboats; 6,980 in railroads, and the rest, being 36,319, in other engines [including those used for pumping water and other non-industrial uses]."

72. Clark, *op. cit.,* p. 410. Italics added by the author.

73. Of the 90 to 100 steam engines operating in Philadelphia County during 1831, approximately 60 were fed by anthracite coal. *Niles' Weekly Register,* XL (July 16, 1831), 344.

74. Woodbury, *op. cit.,* pp. 191–4, 224–5; and U.S. Bureau of the Census, *1960 Census of Population* (Washington, D.C., 1961), Vol. 1, Part A, pp. 1–66, 50–9.

75. Livingood, *op. cit.,* p. 88; I. D. Andrews, *Report . . . on the Trade and Commerce of the British North American Colonies* (Washington, D.C., Senate Document No. 112, 32nd Congress, First Session, 1853), p. 278; and McLane, *op. cit.,* p. 470.

76. Rubin, *op. cit.,* p. 90.

77. *Niles' Weekly Register,* XXIX (October 8, 1825), 96; and Clark, *op. cit.,* p. 350.

78. W. H. Dean, Jr., *The Theory of the Geographic Location of Economic Activities* (Ann Arbor, Mich.: Edwards Brothers, 1938), p. 45. Testimony by an engineer before the Pennsylvania House of Representatives complained of the repeated delays and the high incidence of lost and damaged goods caused by the transshipments [Rubin, *op. cit.,* p. 18].

79. Mitchell, *op. cit.,* p. 941.

80. For a more detailed discussion of the relative situational merits of New York, Baltimore, Boston, and Philadelphia, see R. G. Albion, "New York Port and Its Disappointed Rivals," *Journal of Economic and Business History,* III (August 1931), 602–629.

81. See E. J. Taafe, R. L. Morrill, and P. R. Gould, "Transport Expansion in Underdeveloped Countries," *Geographical Review,* LIII (1963), 503–505. Also note

A. Pred, *The External Relations of Cities during 'Industrial Revolution'* (Chicago: University of Chicago, Department of Geography, Research Paper no. 76, 1962), pp. 42–3.

82. In 1832, Boston had 95 distinct industrial categories, many of which, as indicated above, produced a wide range of products. It is difficult to conceive of a contemporary U.S. city of comparable size (about 65,000) having as diversified an industrial structure.

83. Dix, *op. cit.,* p. 44.

84. Harrington, *op. cit.,* pp. 145–6.

85. *Third Census of the United States, 1810: A Series of Tables of the Several Branches of American Manufactures* (Washington, D.C., 1811), pp. 34–8. The possible relevance of this figure is undermined by the incompleteness and inaccuracy of the Census of 1810, as well as by the drawbacks inherent in using value of production as a measure for industrial comparisons.

86. Bishop, *op. cit.,* pp. 359–60: The 1840 census, the most comprehensive and reliable manufacturing inventory to that date, indicated that the value of Philadelphia's sugar processing production($585,000) overshadowed the city's reported output of machinery and related products ($379,500). [*"Sixth Census of the United States, 1840,"* *op. cit.,* p. 169.] Even if concessions are made with respect to possible data deficiencies and differences in the value added ratio of the two industries, there remains little room for disputing sugar refining's position of relative importance within Philadelphia's total manufacturing structure.

87. Bishop, *op. cit.,* Vol. 3, p. 150; and Clark, *op. cit.,* p. 491.

88. *"Sixth Census of the United States, 1840,"* *op. cit.,* p. 128; and Bishop, *op. cit.,* II, 425. Tobacco processing and tanning were also still among the leading industries of Baltimore and Philadelphia in 1840.

89. A. F. Weber, *Report on the Growth of Industry in New York* (Albany: New York State Department of Labor, 1904), Second Annual Report, Part 5, p. 274. In other words, contrary to the basic precepts of industrial location theory, the dominant weight-losing character of the bark did not confine production completely to forested areas. Admittedly, a good number of persons and workshops assigned to the tanning classification must have practiced currying, or the combing, smoothing, and dressing of leather already tanned in the Catskills and elsewhere.

90. McLane, *op. cit.,* pp. 432–71. The statistical and descriptive materials presented on these forty pages provide unquestionably the most detailed account available of urban manufacturing in a mercantile environment. The source is not, however, without flaws and idiosyncrasies. Much of the data is in rounded figures, and occasional estimates were inserted where firms or individuals refused to comply with the request for information. With reference to the latter shortcoming, the marshal reported in somewhat comic fashion that: "This class of manufacturing [millinery] has been found difficult to estimate, as women are not generally accountants, and therefore it is not easy for them to answer the questions proposed. Many of them decline giving any answers, apparently from the apprehension that their statements may be considered absurd; others refuse, for the usual woman's reason, 'because.' This estimate here given is believed to be rather within the actual amount, than to exceed it."

91. McLane, *op. cit.,* p. 465. The market area estimates provided for most other industries are sufficient enough to remove any problems of distinction between predominantly local and predominantly nonlocal markets.

92. Sparks, *op. cit.,* p. 123. Naturally, much of the wheat arriving from the interior had already been transformed into flour.

93. In 1840, the city of Philadelphia employed as many as 474 laborers in its cotton textile industry, a larger number than was to be found in any of the other mercantile cities. However, the majority of these workers were apparently associated with dying and printing establishments, rather than with integrated spinning and weaving mills. *"Sixth Census of the United States, 1840,"* op. cit., p. 169.

94. In 1828, when construction was more active, Philadelphia shipyards created 11 ships, 5 brigs, 5 schooners, 15 sloops, and one steamboat, or a total of 6,516 tons. *Niles' Weekly Register,* XXXVI (July 18, 1829), 334.

95. *Niles' Weekly Register,* XLV (October 26, 1833), 130; and McLane, *op. cit.,* pp. 316–17. It is very difficult to assess the total number of people linked with shipbuilding at any given date in any of the mercantile cities. Problems arise because some occupations, such as glazing and painting, involved part-time work in the shipyards, and therefore defy the clear-cut assignments which are possible with sailmaking, sparmaking, shipcarpentry, and other trades.

96. J. G. B. Hutchins, *The American Maritime Industries and Public Policy, 1789–1914* (Cambridge: Harvard University Press, 1941), p. 194.

97. Census statistics, which may not have been complete, indicated 1840 employment in the printing and publishing trades as follows: New York, 2,029; Philadelphia, 904; Boston, 437 (compare Table 5); and Baltimore, 279. *"Sixth Census of the United States, 1840,"* op. cit., pp. 54, 129, 169, 217.

98. Includes lithography, engraving, copperplate printing, type founding, stereotyping, bookbinding, and the production of blankbooks, newspapers, books, pamphlets, and miscellaneous printed items.

99. *Longworth's American Almanac, New-York Register, and City Directory, 1800,* op. cit., and McLane, op. cit., pp. 434–5. Presumably, there were additional individuals listed or enumerated as carpenters who indulged in coopery on a part-time basis.

100. The dimensions of construction material production obviously must have oscillated with the rate at which new buildings were put up. In an active year (such as the one Philadelphia had in 1827, when an estimated 40 million bricks were consumed locally), the numbers of workers and value added involved elsewhere in the building material industries almost certainly surpassed the corresponding figures for 1832 Boston. *Niles' Weekly Register,* XXXV (September 6, 1828), 19.

101. According to one account: "In 1840 there were but few Furniture stores in Philadelphia, and they mostly small ones; keeping samples of the styles of goods, but relying mainly on orders from their customers to supply work for their employees." Freedley, *op. cit.*, p. 272.

102. The census reported 337 males working in the machinery industries of Philadelphia. *"Sixth Census of the United States, 1840," op. cit.*, p. 169.

103. Freedley, *op. cit.*, pp. 306, 309, 434.

8. SAN FRANCISCO, 1846–56
The Patterns and Chaos of Growth

Roger Lotchin

The discovery of gold in California guaranteed that the San Francisco Bay area would become urbanized at least in some degree, because of the transportation facilities of the day and California's geography. The two main distributing points to the mining regions were Sacramento and Stockton, located on the Sacramento and San Joaquin rivers, respectively. Both waterways were navigable to vessels drawing ten feet of water or less. Those which drew more than that, and this group included all the clipper ships, had to reload their cargoes onto smaller boats, which in turn carried them to the interior. The transfer point was San Francisco. Therefore, the Bay City was the beneficiary of a "transportation break" in the gold-mine commerce.

However, if this theory explains how there came to be cities on the bay, it does not demonstrate why urbanization began exactly where it did, for there are no overwhelmingly convincing reasons why the metropolis of the bay area should have been situated where it is. In fact, throughout the period under study here, no one considered what is now San Francisco a very eligible site for a great city. The many hills complicated construction and transport. There was a large mudflat immediately in front of the town, but very little level ground on shore. Besides all this, the area did not have a good supply of water, and its climate was less salubrious than that of other places on the bay, especially the Contra Costa. In San Francisco it was colder and the winds blew much harder, bringing in dense clouds of fog and filling the air with dust and sand from the largely treeless, chaparral-choked site. These disadvantages may not now seem very great; indeed, some of them, such as the hills and the mist, may even be charming. But for settlers without the means to surmount heights easily, overcome a lack of water, cope with the pulmonary disorders caused by winds and damp, or keep out dust, they were formidable.

Despite the sand bar on San Antonio Creek, the Contra Costa shore, with its superior weather and more level land and timber resources, would have been a better place for a city. So would the Benicia-Vallejo area at the north end of San Pablo Bay. That the metropolis was planted where it was and not at one of these other spots was the result of a number of peculiar and transient developments, plus some other long-range ones.

The Mission of San Francisco and the Presidio, founded primarily to promote and protect Spanish imperial interests, were established in 1776. A town (or pueblo) grew up around the Mission, usually called the Mission Dolores, and by 1845 had a population of 150, though both Mission and Presidio were then virtually defunct.[1] Besides colonizing San Francisco, the Spaniards had founded other missions and pueblos around the bay: San Jose, Santa Clara, San Rafael, and San Francisco de Solano at Sonoma. With the passage of years, a number of ranches appeared in between these places. It was to capitalize on the commercial possibilities of this thin line of settlement that modern San Francisco was founded.

In 1835 an Englishman named William Richardson settled on the Cove of Yerba Buena, an inlet on the northeast side of the peninsula several miles distant from the Mission Dolores, which was in the Mission Valley. Richardson chose this spot in order to trade with the Mexican population scattered about the bay. Since the harbor was less exposed than that opposite the Presidio, whalers and other ships had for some time been in the habit of anchoring there. Using two schooners belonging to the missions of Dolores and Santa Clara, Richardson carried on a commercial exchange between these vessels and the people around the bay.[2] He was soon followed by other merchants—including for a while those of the Hudson's Bay Company—and by the agents of the Boston hide traders. Thus the future city of San Francisco had a distinctly commercial origin, but it was a commerce based on Spanish-Mexican (plus an increasing American) settlement, not on gold.

The liquidation of the Latin part of this heritage was the second critical factor in fixing the urban demography of the bay area. The military phase of the Mexican-American War of 1846–8 in San Francisco was almost comic, but it was a crucial event for urbanization. Since the village of Yerba Buena was the largest on the bay, it was there that the American flag was raised, the United States Quartermaster's Store established, the troops quartered, and the customs house located. This government patronage gave a decided impetus to the economic life of the town and more than made up for the disruption of the hide trade caused by military operations.

The third development which helped root the city on its sandy peninsula was a religious one. In the summer of 1846, a ship carrying about 200 Mormons landed at Yerba Buena, thereby doubling the population. These people were seeking a refuge from religious persecution; but instead of joining their brethren at Salt Lake, many of them stayed on at the bay hamlet.

Together the Mormons, the Mexican War, and the desire for commercial profits caused a modest growth in Yerba Buena. In 1848 the population on the cove numbered between 850 and 1,000. By the time the Gold Rush enormously stimulated the commerce of the area, therefore, San Francisco was enough of a city to attract this increase and benefit from it.

Still another pre-1848 circumstance helped San Francisco profit from the Gold Rush. Before early 1847 the city was known as Yerba Buena rather

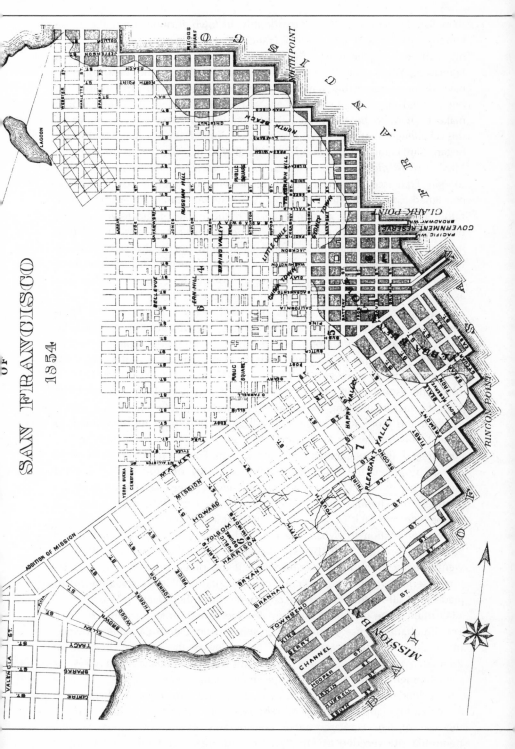

SAN FRANCISCO
1854

than San Francisco. In order to identify its own fortunes with the more famous mission and bay of San Francisco, which appeared on maritime maps throughout the world, the cove settlement changed its name to San Francisco. Yerba Buena's rival was a tiny hamlet at the head of ship navigation on San Pablo Bay, the gateway to the interior. This place had been called Francesca by its owners, also in the hope that the title would make it seem to be the principal city on the bay. It was in response to this challenge that the new name was adopted. When the Gold Rush began, San Francisco benefited considerably. Since San Francisco Bay and Mission were widely known, Eastern shippers merely sent their merchandise to San Francisco. The change of name ensured that goods would be consigned specifically to the formerly unknown hamlet of Yerba Buena rather than to the bay area in general. If the name of the town had not been so closely identified with that of the better-known mission and bay, it is quite possible that much of the cargo sent out in the early years of the Gold Rush would have ended up at rival Francesca (shortly renamed Benicia), and given a strong impetus to urbanization on a site that was as much (or more) suited to it than San Francisco.

It is ironic that several of the important reasons that gave San Francisco its preeminence were of little or no significance after 1848. The trade with the "Californios" was dwarfed by the gold commerce; the Mexican War came to an end; and the Mormons as a group were not prominent in the city's growth between 1848 and 1856. Yet from 1835 to 1848, and especially in the last two years of that period, these were three powerful factors in fixing the urban configuration of the bay area.

When the Gold Rush occurred, still other developments combined to protect this modest urbanization. The great impetus to economic life encouraged the appearance of rivals to San Francisco at the same time that it propelled the small hamlet into an orgy of growth. The cost of landing goods quickly rose to absurd levels. Because there were no wharves, merchandise had to be lightered ashore. With mining keeping wages high and lack of space doing the same for storage costs, there was a great temptation to bypass the city and ship directly to Sacramento and Stockton. Through 1849, barks, schooners, and other smaller craft often went directly to the interior entrepôts, but this practice was abandoned before it seriously cut into San Francisco's prosperity. Wildly fluctuating prices made time all-important in river commerce; and the advent of steamers in 1849 offered the merchant both greater speed and larger carrying capacity. The simultaneous rise of the clipper ship in the California trade provided much the same advantages on the ocean leg of the journey. Because of their size, however, clippers could not navigate inland waterways. A transshipment therefore had to be made somewhere on the bay. The natural tendency was to make this transfer at the most developed spot; and as technology supplied more warehouses and wharves, the deterrents to the use of San Francisco were considerably eased. The threat to the peninsula site receded as rapidly as it had arisen, and the chief point of urbanization on the bay remained fixed. Curiously enough, it was the introduction of more modern commercial facilities—wharves, streets, warehouses, steamboats, and clippers—that reinforced and protected the rather primitive urban arrangement of San Francisco Bay.

It was entirely accidental that American imperial aspirations should have coincided with the Mormon desire for religious freedom in such a way as to bring men of both ambitions to the northern end of San Francisco Peninsula at the same time that commercial fortune seekers located there. It was equally fortuitous that the Gold Rush should have poured a stream of men into San Francisco just one short year after the city had claimed the name for that very reason and before any other town on the bay was well enough known to compete with it. If these were not coincidences enough, there was also the almost contemporaneous invention of the clipper ship, which reinforced the transshipment break at the bay. The nearly exact coincidence of a war, a religious migration, a shrewd commercial decision, a Gold Rush, and a new discovery in ocean transport, combined with the presence of a certain level of river transportation technology and a desire to exploit the commercial possibilities of a given situation, are not the stuff out of which exact sciences are made. But they are the very essence of history—very odd, very lucky, and very human.

In the years immediately after 1848, the pattern of growth was seemingly quite random. In fact, one it tempted to conclude that there was no order, only chaos. The shuttling back and forth to the mines, the filling of the cove, and the rapid growth created a great deal of flux. Again and again one is impressed with an extraordinary sense of motion in the city—of men, businesses, and institutions.

The record for transiency and uprootedness in a city built for the worship of Mammon perhaps was set by a congregation dedicated to the glorification of God. The Reverend Albert Williams of the First Presbyterian Church began his meetings in the public school on Portsmouth Plaza in 1849; but between then and 1851, he and his flock were in near perpetual motion. After leaving the school, the assemblage met successively in the district court room on Dupont between Jackson and Pacific, in the second story of another structure on the latter street, and in a tent which had formerly been the marquee of a Boston military company. When the heavy rains of 1849-50 drove the worshippers from this refuge, they adjourned to the church of their Baptist rivals. Following a short tenure there, they moved to the U.S. Customs House, then to the superior court room at City Hall on Pacific and Kearny, and finally to a new house of worship built for them on Stockton between Broadway and Pacific. When this burned in 1851, the congregation found shelter, successively, in the supreme court room in the Marine Hospital on Stockton, in the superior court room in the St. Francis Hotel, and again with their Baptist competitors. Finally, late in that year, the group settled on the site where they remained through the period.[3]

Not everyone had the same experience as these Presbyterian nomads;

yet this wandering was only an extreme case of the flux that gripped the city after the discovery of gold. As each year passed, however, San Francisco settled down somewhat; under the surface evidences of confusion, a surprising degree of order began to emerge. Although the expansion of the city was without plan, it was not without pattern. But hardly any of this pattern was imposed by public authority. The street plat was set aside for transportation; slaughterhouses, stockyards, chandleries, hospitals, soap-making establishments, and other enterprises were banned from certain parts of town; and a few square blocks, including Portsmouth Plaza, were reserved for open space. Yet despite this lack of central responsibility, San Francisco did have a number of striking patterns. One of the most important of these was natural. To a very considerable extent the initial growth of the metropolis was decided by its geography; yet, to an equally impressive degree, its geography was determined by its growth.

Throughout the years between 1846 and 1856, especially at first, there was a decided preference for low ground. Both the original settlements, Yerba Buena and Mission Dolores, were situated on or near water, next to the cove and Mission Creek, respectively. The Gold Rush added several more small colonies, also on low land. New concentrations grew up at Happy and Pleasant valleys south of Market Street and St. Anne's Valley and Spring Valley north of that future artery. West of the hills, the Washer-woman's Lagoon settlement augmented this group. By 1856 a continuous line of dwellings linked these initially isolated clusters. Moreover, several new additions had been laid out, in each case avoiding the heights: Hayes Valley, just west of the present Civic Center Plaza; Horner's Addition, immediately south of the Mission Dolores; and the Potrero Nuevo, east of that. Population in the north spread westward along the foot of the range of hills fronting the bay.

The low and relatively level ground soon ran out and forced the inhabitants to eliminate the hills they could remove and scale the ones they could not. A steam shovel—known contemporaneously as the "Steam Paddy" or "Vaporific Patrick" after the Irishman it presumably replaced—scraped off the sand hills, and railroad cars deposited them in the cove. A similar operation was carried out at the bayward base of Telegraph Hill, where the rock of that bastion was blasted away. These projects created new areas of level land in both directions; and so for a time technology was able to ease the restraints of geography. Yet neither blasting nor the "Steam Paddy" was capable of entirely removing Russian, Nob, and Telegraph hills. The high ground could not be avoided indefinitely.

As late as 1853, however, the line of settlement had not yet come very close to the more elevated portions. In the north, population flowed into the declivity between Telegraph and Russian hills, again sticking to the lower ground. This march of improvement skirted Telegraph Hill to the west, reaching close to Kearny Street. On North Beach, the heights of

Russian Hill were flanked by a five-block-wide salient extending as far west as Jones Street between Union and Chestnut. To the south, settlement also avoided the heights by going down the line of Market and Mission streets, thus bypassing Nob Hill. In 1853, therefore, there was still a striking correlation between low geography and high density, with Rincon, Russian, Telegraph, and Nob hills the least crowded areas. The farther one got from these great works of nature, especially the northern trio, the closer he came to those of man.

Due to the scarcity of level ground, however, the march to the sea was soon matched by one into the hills. This movement was already underway in 1851. "Two years ago," explained the *Alta* in that year, "the property there [that is, on the elevated places surrounding the cove] was considered almost worthless, as it was hardly supposed that anyone would travel up there to live so long as there were any level spaces left." But an astonishing growth and its accompanying congestion soon caused the hills to be valued as "airy" places to settle.[4] Shortly thereafter the city marched straight over the heights, and San Franciscans began their long tradition of cliff dwelling. Once again, it was technology that freed the metropolis for further growth, as thoroughfares were blasted out of the high ground and plank streets were laid to ease the burden of ascent.

In 1853 the urban frontier north of Market was about a half block west of Mason on the east side of the hills; by 1857 the vanguard of settlement had reached beyond to Larkin, five blocks to the west, and in some places exceeded that line. The majority of residences and economic activities were clustered in and around the northern part of the old Cove of Yerba Buena. The southern part of the cove beyond Market was not yet as intensively used. The mission was still the southern outpost of the newly created urban empire, as Washerwoman's Lagoon was the northern; but in 1857 both were linked directly to the rest of the city.[5]

Besides the geographic, a number of other land-usage patterns, both residential and economic, emerged during these ten years. While San Francisco still reeled under the impact of the Gold Rush, the retail, wholesale, manufacturing, and middle-class residential sections were packed closely together downtown. These were flanked by the workingmen's neighborhoods; but with that exception, there was relatively little specialization in land use. For the most part, the city was compact and undifferentiated. Some retailing, especially grocery, was done in other parts of town, but most of this trade took place within one area. The retailing, wholesaling, manufacturing, and middle-class residence section was a half-moon-shaped area fronting the old cove in the north part of town. The outstanding characteristic of these locations was proximity to the waterfront and to each other. Lower-class residences tended to be on the periphery of this indiscriminate grouping, although they too were close to the water.[6]

Much of this pattern had changed by 1857. Most of the working classes were still anchored to the outskirts of the central business district, but little else remained the same. What had happened in the interim was the sorting out and separating of the various activities that had in 1850 been located contiguously. The wholesaling part of the business community had migrated eastward toward the water. The middle classes had erupted over the hills to the west and, to a lesser extent, into the Rincon Hill area south of Market. The retailing section tended to stay where it had been or to spread out to the west and south, following its retreating customers. The resettling gave the retailers a position between the wholesalers and the middle-class residences. Unlike retailing, petty manufacturing, such as blacksmithing and coopering, did not follow the middle-class ascent of Russian and Nob hills. Instead, the migration of these artisans was north and south, away from the central position they had formerly held. In general, petty manufacturing located in the working-class districts, which had always been on the periphery of the main original settlement. And even the lower class tended to migrate out, though their base remained fixed.

In addition, a new element entered the picture: relatively large-scale manufacturing. This too was set up in a part of the working-class district south of the original area of settlement, but not in the same section as petty industry. The iron foundries, ship builders, flour and saw mills, and gas works were established either south of Market on First Street, on Market itself, or close to this part of town.

Thus, by 1857 there was a decentralization of economic and residential patterns. Accompanying this trend was considerable specialization of land use. Hand in hand with decentralization of the various categories of activities went a greater concentration within each. For example, the commission merchants were congregated on the angle of Front and California; the produce merchants were segregated together on Clay Street or close by; the lumber dealers were in an odd-shaped linear district along Steuart, California, and Market; the clothing and dry goods merchants were on Sacramento; the lawyers, on Montgomery or Merchant; the large-scale manufacturing, south of Market, and so forth. This differentiation was not complete by any means, but it was definitely present and growing.[7]

Many of the economic spatial relationships within the city can be explained by reference to a number of urban boundaries. American historical scholarship has traditionally emphasized the importance of the frontier to national development, and there can be little doubt that it had a great influence on San Francisco.[8] However, there were a number of significant frontiers within the city itself which played a role in determining patterns of land usage. The areas of relative safety from fire, of high rent and land prices, of minimum drayage rates, of planked streets, of newly made land, and of accessible water supply all had considerable meaning in the metropolis. They are not an entirely sufficient explanation for the placement of economic activities, but they do reveal quite a bit of the rationale underlying the pattern.

It would be difficult to overestimate the influence of fire in the total development of San Francisco. In the matter of building location, it was crucial. Yet this impact was not uniform, and often set in motion contradictory tendencies. In some cases, conflagrations caused dispersal of economic operations. One man purposely built his three buildings in different parts of town to avoid losing all of them in one blaze; and the warehouse of the merchants Crosby and Dibblee was erected in an uninhabited area of South Beach in order to utilize cheap wood construction.[9] But dispersion was only one way in which flames helped set up the spatial relationships of San Francisco. Concentrations could come from the same cause. Before 1851 the town was built largely of wood; but after the terrible fires of that year, brick became considerably more popular. The practice of erecting brick structures close together grew up, for the less wood in an area, the better its chance in the next holocaust.[10] Well before 1856 this hiving had progressed far enough to include most of the central business district within the "brick frontier," one of the most important in the city.[11]

The blazes that so often engulfed the metropolis also stimulated the eastward drift of its wholesaling district by serving as a liberating force. "The merchant who was content to do business in Sacramento Street as long as his old building stood," explained the *Picayune*, ". . . when he was compelled to move [by being burned out], preferred the more eligible sites which the steam excavator [was] continually making in the harbor, and even at a higher rent erected his warehouse in the deep water."[12] So the fires at once freed the merchant from his old, less advantageous business location and put him on piles over the water, where goods could be exchanged more easily and fires combated more readily.

The aftermath of a conflagration usually featured considerable switching around, and at least one part of the city suffered drastically from it. Long Wharf and its "hinterland" was originally the busiest part of the waterfront, but the holocaust of 1851 hurt it badly. The pier itself was partially consumed in the flames, and both it and the real estate in its vicinity were damaged. Still another contribution of fires to the reshuffling of economic activities had to do with the availability of water. Since few artesian wells were located west of Montgomery, and since the area east of that street was also closer to the bay, it was easier to fight blazes in that section. For the many who rigged up their own private water supply as well as for those who did not, the presence of water was crucial.

The supply of land was even more influential in determining spatial arrangements. New land, lower and closer to the wharves, was continually becoming available; and even when there was no fire, merchants kept drifting down toward the bay. Planked streets enabled them to take advantage of the newly created land, and proximity to the ships and wharves supplied them with a reason to do so. Yet transportation did not determine the initial pattern in this case. It was businessmen, through financing of both street improvements and wharves, who dictated their location rather than vice versa. Transportation was a "function" of urbanization, or rather, of urban economics.

Once the original investment had been made in the planking and paving, however, the lower sites were more desirable. Thereafter, transportation became a significant variable in its own right, drawing business activity down toward the waterfront or into the planked section. In 1854 Battery Street, for example, was the only artery that connected the central business district with the warehouses in the north end of the city. Proximity to Battery thus was obviously important. The popularity of the area of improved thoroughfares was further revealed by high rents and land prices, which were always above those in other sections of town.[13]

In the beginning, the very lack of street improvements caused an important trend in land usage. Early in 1850 it looked as if the city would not get its thoroughfares planked before another rainy season set in. That prospect prompted many merchants to locate on piles over "water lots," using the bay as a substitute for improved streets. This movement led the *Picayune* to predict that "the heavy amount of commercial and mercantile business will be likely to be done over the tide water next winter."[14]

The importance of transportation appeared again in drayage rates. Here, too, there was an urban frontier of some significance. The teamsters set different prices for various distances. For example, in 1850 the charges for anything hauled outside the territory of Stockton, Pine, and Pacific were 50 cents to a dollar higher.[15] Given the scale of some merchants' operations, the stiff competition they invariably faced, and the additional fact that the wharves and streets were built in the first place to bring down lightering and hauling charges, it is safe to assume that the "low cartage frontier" was of some consequence in the location of business.

The great wharves that jutted out into the bay illustrate the importance of transportation even more graphically. These piers, like the streets, had been built to serve the needs of urbanization. Once in place, however, they too became an independent force in setting up spatial relationships. "The great strides which business has taken towards Happy Valley within the last few months . . . puts the success of the Market Street wharf, as a speculation beyond doubt," explained the *Picayune*. "As is, however, always the case, the wharf will react to the improvement of the Valley."[16] Thus, the building of a wharf obviously could encourage the development of its "hinterland" and vice versa.

Harbor customs were also a part of the wharves' influence upon urban land usage. To an extent, the docks, like the central business district, were subject to specialization of function. The *Herald* noted as early as 1853 that "the business [of the wharves] has been classified, and particular kinds are now carried on in particular localities."[17] That specialization, in turn, affected what happened in their immediate hinterlands. The Clay Street Wharf, for example, was usually the one to which small craft from around the bay came with produce. Clay Street below Front was the area where nearly all the commission produce merchants were, and those who were not on Clay were located close by. This same artery between Leidesdorff and Montgomery, was also the site of four of the city's largest markets.[18] The concentration of warehouses at the base of Telegraph Hill probably owed something to the customs of the harbor, too. The wharves around the north part of the city were "preferred for the accommodation of the heavy shipping from distant ports."[19] Since cargoes had to be landed from these ships and duty paid on them, a storage area close to the large docks was a definite advantage.[20]

Exactly why the various wharves concentrated on certain kinds of activity is not wholly clear. The location of steamship facilities was probably determined by the inducements offered to the companies, since it was usual for the various piers to compete for their custom. The northern wharves specialized in landings from ocean-going vessels because "the deep water in the vicinity of North Point gives this section a decided advantage over all others."[21] Yet whether the produce and lumber dealers drew the schooners and coasters to the Clay and Steuart Street wharves or vice versa is not known. Whatever the order, the arrangement, once established, attracted other merchants.

If the customs of the harbor explain some of the spatial relationships in the city, business mores and the level of communications technology illuminate still others. In the San Francisco business arena, face-to-face contact was considered an imperative. "There is probably no city in the world in which the peculiarity of the market so emphatically calls for a constant and unremitted intercourse between the merchants as in San Francisco," wrote the *Picayune*. "If a person in San Francisco happens to become the possessor of any lot of goods, he is obliged to traverse the whole city before he can either determine on the state of the market, or know who is in want of the commodity."[22] An economic map of the Bay City indicates rather clearly how highly desirable person-to-person contact was.

The lack of telephones or modern means of transportation, however, should not be overemphasized as a cause of concentration in the center city. There were ways the requirements for information could have been met—through commercial exchanges, trade associations, and monopolies; even by 1856 San Francisco was not yet so large a city that only the wonders of science could provide it with communication. The important point is that these institutions either did not exist or did not work. Commercial information was a jealously guarded commodity among many merchants. Therefore, the need for personal contact and the economic specialization that stemmed from it were as much the product of trade mores and the absence of modern forms of business organization as they were the result of the lack of the telephone. Moreover, to a very considerable degree, the system was both unnecessary and inefficient. There were dozens of big merchants in the metropolis, and traveling about to see each of them was not an effective way to get the necessary data.

The level of technology did not have a uniform impact upon spatial arrangements. In fact, like fire, its influence was somewhat contradictory, since the same reasons that led the wholesalers to crowd onto the corner of California and Front persuaded the retailers to scatter westward toward Stockton and southward past Market. Their trade required proximity to their customers up the hill just as that of the importers and jobbers demanded contiguity with others of their kind and with the improved streets, wharves, and watercraft that conveyed their orders, their customers, and their commercial correspondence.

Petty manufacturing, like retailing, was influenced by the need for proximity. Although small manufacturers as a group were dispersed, they often congregated by trades outside the central business district, though not as compactly as the enterprises within that section. For example, jewelers, wagonmakers, and coopers were near others of their kind. Often different but allied crafts associated, such as blacksmiths and the carriage makers who were partly dependent upon them. Obviously, artisans derived benefit in the form of external economies from a location close to those whose trades were related or whose skills were needed to supplement their own.

Much of the explanation for the distribution of artisans outside the downtown area can be found in land values. Small operators could not afford to pay either the high rents or the higher prices for center city lots. Therefore, steadily rising real-estate costs were a strong centrifugal force, expelling people, institutions, and businesses from the heart of the city.[23] Churches, for example, moved to the periphery very early, even though few people lived there, in part because their budgets could not stand the strain of a central site.[24]

The resources of land, as well as the price, determined some of the economic spatial arrangements. The clay of Mission Creek, for instance, soon attracted a colony of brickmakers. Powder magazines went out of the city by municipal request, since they were a menace in a thickly populated area. The ropewalk joined the trek to the suburbs because 2,600 feet of clear space were required to make cordage.[25] Other economic activities also left the metropolis behind them because of crowding. Slaughterhouses, charcoal burners, and soap manufactories were constantly subject to nuisance prosecution; and soap making and slaughtering were eventually banned within certain limits, making their exodus mandatory.

The residential configuration of San Francisco, like its economic pattern, was relatively segregated. The separation was not complete by any means, but it too was clearly present and growing. For the middle class, the continuing specialization of land use meant an increasing distance between home and work.[26] In 1850 this group lived in the center city. A small vanguard had migrated as far west as Stockton and Powell, but most resided close to their places of employment downtown. Eight years later, the proportions were reversed. By then, the city's bankers, clerks, merchants, and doctors looked down on the remnants of their fellows in the central business district from the heights of Nob and Russian hills. A few others had passed beyond Market to the South Park neighborhood (Bryant, Brannan, Second, and Third), but this was a fairly small contingent.

As the desertion of the center city north of Market progressed, a central bloc of middle-class preponderance developed. Bounded by the waterfront, Sutter, Gough, and Greenwich streets at its farthest extremities, this section was based upon the central business district, from which it had grown, and ran from the harbor to the periphery. Within this part of the city, the demographic mixture varied, but everywhere the working class was in a minority.[27] East of Montgomery in the central business district, this group came closest to holding its own at 47 percent; but from there to Taylor the proportion lessened. In the area between the downtown section and Dupont, the middle class held a lead of 65 percent. This predominance dipped to 60 percent on Dupont, rose to 67 percent on Stockton (the most densely populated and the longest part of the middle-class section), and finally soared to 75 percent on Powell. The next two streets, Mason and Taylor, were 60 and 75 percent, respectively.

The prevalence of the middle class in this area was striking because of their minority status in the population as a whole. Of the approximately 50,000 people living in the city, only 39 percent belonged to the middle class; but within its special preserve, this sector of society was a majority.[28] Moreover, the minority of lower-class people living among their "betters" were those closest to them in income and status—artisans, skilled laborers, and so forth.

The workingmen's part of the metropolis flanked the middle-class preserve. The workingmen held sway north of the Jackson Street boundary of the central business district and east of the Dupont frontier of the middle classes. From Montgomery to the waterfront their lead was better than 2 to 1; but west of that street their prevalence diminished as one neared Dupont. South of the California Street wholesaling concentration, beginning at the shoreline, and north of Howard, the working class enjoyed its greatest superiority. Closer to the bay and downtown, that lead was longest. In the area bounded by Market, Mission, Steuart, and Second, it was 89 percent to 11. In the parts of the city surrounding this great concentration, the workingmen predominated by 3 to 1. Between Market, California, and Dupont, this preeminence was not so great; but it still ranged from 2 to 1 to 3 to 1.

Thus the lower orders in San Francisco, like the upper, had their own areas of settlement where they were an absolute majority and where their numbers were significantly disproportionate to their share of the population as a whole. On the outskirts of town—that is, in the suburbs, beyond

Leavenworth and in some places Larkin—population density diminished very greatly, but there seems to have been the same configuration. The working class lived west of its downtown concentrations and the middle class dwelt west of its own group. Yet beyond these suburbs, where farms mingled with city dwellings, settlement was really quite sparse.

Within the district of working-class ascendancy, there were still other divisions based on income and employment. Artisans, for example, tended to live farther out from the center city and water line and closer to the ranks above them than did others in their group. Occupation also played a role. Carpenters, teamsters, laborers, and those whose work was not necessarily done in a particular part of town resided throughout the lower-class sections. However, machinists, blacksmiths, and those in water-related trades, such as boatmen, sailors, shipwrights, shipsmiths, and stevedores, congregated close to their jobs in the part of the city which specialized in that activity. In addition, workingmen generally resided in areas of considerable small- and large-scale manufacturing or close to the central business district, and they therefore did not experience the same degree of separation between home and work as the middle class.

Although the segregation was not complete, the sorting out of classes had begun. The bulk of the middle-class residents was clearly drifting toward the periphery, and the largest concentration of workingmen was anchored near the center city. The middle class had pushed westward out of their 1850 downtown location to the edge of the heavily settled section and were spreading out north and south from there. Numerically and proportionately, the middle-class lead was greatest in the area geographically farther from the center city; the working-class predominance was just the reverse. The separation of classes was most evident where population was heavily concentrated. Dense settlement and segregation of social groups clearly went together.

It is impossible to state definitively whether this pattern amounts to a "new" or "old" city center and periphery pattern, but the old arrangement seems least likely. The heaviest working-class preponderance was closer to downtown than the largest middle-class block, and the metropolis definitely did not break down into a middle-class core and a working-class ring. It is possible that the new arrangement was in the process of being born, but this pattern had not yet fully emerged by 1868, almost ten years after horse-car mass transit had been introduced into the city.[29]

There are many reasons for the distribution of San Francisco's population. The working class, however, had little choice; the prevailing high land and rental rates caused both concentration and scattering. "The laborer, at present, to obtain a building at a rental consistent with his means," explained the local voice of the workingman, "must either go beyond the city limits or stow himself and family into some dilapidated building, located in one of the filthy lanes or alleys with which this city abounds."[30] From the very beginning of the Gold Rush, Happy Valley had been the center of the working-class district; the high rents downtown were one of the principal reasons for this development.[31] To a certain extent, the same factors affected the residential choices of other social groups. Yet for the middle class, whose incomes allowed greater flexibility, the matter was more complex.

Transportation contributed significantly to the desertion of the center city. As early as 1852, regular—though somewhat precarious—steamboat connections were established with the infant town of Oakland, and other areas around the bay eventually followed this lead. As a result, a small contingent of San Franciscans filed out of the city to these "steamboat suburbs." Plank roads and streets facilitated on land what the ferries did on the bay. From 1850 on, these improvements covered an increasing proportion of its thoroughfares, and their impact upon decentralization is obvious. The plank roads, especially those on Mission, Folsom, and Brannan, together with the bridge over Mission Creek, channeled settlement toward the Mission Dolores.[32] An omnibus service, beginning in 1850 and running over the first of these routes, encouraged the same demographic distribution.

North of Market, however, the sequence of events was different. South of that artery and in the suburbs, settlement was more the result of these technological innovations, since the plank roads, omnibus, and steamboats began operations before many people lived in the sections serviced. In the remainder of San Francisco, the pattern was reversed. There the population was relatively dense before any of the improvements that came after 1850 were made. In fact, though Powell Street had inhabitants as early as 1847, it was not until 1852 that a limited omnibus service was begun in this middle-class stronghold and it was 1854 before street planking was widespread.[33] Therefore, the initial configuration of residences determined the transportation arrangements—whether planked streets or omnibus service—rather than vice versa. Once established, of course, these transit facilities reinforced the trend.

Street planking, omnibuses, and private carriages, then, provided San Franciscans with a "mass transportation" system adequate to their needs. In the distribution of population, the planking seems to have been more important than the omnibuses. The latter, which in 1854 began to operate between North Beach and South Park via downtown, served two middle-class areas as well as a working-class section in between. Both ends of the route were in middle-class areas, but middle-class settlement was not strung out just along or predominantly along the omnibus routes. Rather, residence had a much higher correlation with the street planking.

Improved methods of conveyance, however, provided only the means of migration from downtown rather than the motivation. "Status" considerations undoubtedly drove some from the city center to the outskirts of town or the suburbs. South Park and Stockton Street both were widely acclaimed as "fashionable" living places.[34] Yet one should not exaggerate

the significance of this factor in changing the residential make-up of the
center city. There were many solid, prosaic, and even more compelling
reasons for such a change. Safety was an important one of these. Some of
the downtown districts, such as Sydney Valley north of the central business
district, were quite disorderly, rowdy at best and lethal at worst. For a
middle-class woman such as Mrs. Benjamin Butler, who witnessed a throat
slitting from her own window, this area could be quite terrifying. "In the
morning the Policemen were up there. We were very careful not to say
anything. It was a coman [sic] occurance [sic].³⁵ Just as undesirable was
the constant specter of fire. People deserted the downtown section, where
conflagrations usually originated; and often their institutions, such as the
churches, went with or even ahead of them.³⁶

Comfort and economy entered into consideration along with security.
The regions closer to the waterfront were increasingly cluttered with the
paraphernalia of commerce or manufacture. While desirable for the economy, these things were not so conducive to pleasant residential living. For
those who left the metropolis entirely, the better climate at other spots on
the bay was an important inducement. The Contra Costa, the Santa Clara
Valley, and San Mateo, for example, each had more sunshine and less fog
and wind.³⁷ Moreover, the price of downtown land, for rent or purchase,
had risen enormously. Literally fantastic rates prevailed in the city center
in the first years of rapid growth; and though these declined somewhat,
they were still high.³⁸ The cost of a residence in the central business district was usually prohibitive, even for the bankers.

Much of the motivation for the trek to the suburbs was the now-
common phenomenon of ambivalent attitudes toward urban living and
urban values. Despite a fascination with the Golden Gate City, there were
many who were willing to praise its antithesis. In fact, the "rural ideal"
found fairly frequent expression. "It is a sententious truth that 'man made
the city, but God made the country.' " wrote the Alta in 1852. "The utilitarian [way] in which we live, and the practical, work-aday life which we
Californians lead, do not altogether deprive us of sweet visions of green
fields, wholesome country air, and retired rural homes." "With none,"
added the city's leading daily, "would the change from the hustling hours
of a business day in the crowded streets of a city, to the evenings and
mornings of retirement in a suburban retreat, be more grateful than to the
business men of San Francisco."³⁹ Outside the metropolis, one could have
"plenty of room without being elbowed by rude neighbors" or troubled
by contact with what the Alta called "an accumulation of a class that always becomes numerous in every large and old city, and from whose
presence all who can hope to escape."⁴⁰ Other men were fleeing different
things. "Usually on Saturday I drive out to San Mateo only too glad to be
under the necessity of looking after the farm, glad to be far away from

the constant strife of the city life," George Howard wrote to Agnes Howard. "I picture to myself for you the life of the country that we are so charmed with among the English gentry, free from the forced, false life of the city."[41]

These examples are sufficient to demonstrate what was being sought and what avoided in the hegira to the suburbs. Pure air, living space, beauty, trees, solitude, retirement, and a respite from the dust, bustle, conflict, crowds, artificiality, utilitarianism, and practicality of a growing city were desired by the weary metropolitan. In short, man and his works were being shunned.

It is worth emphasizing that this set of desires cannot very well be separated into rural and urban ones, for they do not make any sense by themselves. The attractions of the country were potent only to one who had endured the reverse in the city. What this means for urban history, at least for San Francisco, is that the "rural ideal" had an *urban* origin. The notion was not an argument of embattled yeomen farmers who were striving to preserve and extend rural values. Neither was it the construct of Jeffersonian theorists who disliked the city, nor of those who wanted to recapture the lost "glories" of the small town. Real estate men, editors, and ordinary people concocted these ideas in response to urban pressures, not rural attractions. The suburbs were not desired because they were like some rural or small-town past, but rather because they were more "natural" and therefore less like the big-city present.

As the constant repetition of the longing for solitude, retreat, and retirement indicates, the suburbs were valued as a haven. They were a place of temporary escape from the "ceaseless activity" of Montgomery, California, and Front streets. "Let the Bay City keep its business, its bustle, toil, and mammon-worship," urged the *Chronicle*, "and [let] Oakland be an occasional refuge for its disappointed, heart-sick workers."[42] Yet very few San Franciscans seriously intended to take up dirt farming or even, for the most part, to become full-time gentry. What they wanted was a periodic break that would make life in the city more endurable. The regenerative qualities of the suburbs were described in an 1851 letter. William Weston invited his aunt to take an imaginary journey with him "out where morning Breaks and look at those magnificent flower gardens of nature—now in full bloom, and they will fill the soul with enough of love and poetry to enable thee to withstand the rough passes of city life, with its turmoil and vexation, for a whole week. . . ."[43]

In other words, San Franciscans, like many other nineteenth-century American city dwellers, wanted to share the best of both worlds.[44] Residents of the Golden Gate City were lucky, the *Alta* commented, to live in an area where "the commercial advantages of the Emporium can be so readily united [with] those of the peaceful and retired home," where one could be "removed from the bustle of the city, and yet within a few minutes' ride of it."[45] As more and more people came to appreciate this happy combination of opportunities, the separation of residence and work continued.

Taken out of the total context of public opinion, such stress on the "rural ideal" might seem to indicate a widespread aversion to urban life. Nothing could be more misleading. From the authors of the *Annals* (the city's first history) on down, San Franciscans were endlessly fascinated with their city. Ironically enough, nothing was more common than to hear praised those very qualities that in the context of the "suburban ideology" were damned. When speaking of a move to Hayes Valley or South Park or Oakland, press and people treated the bustle, confusion, struggle, crowdedness, artificiality, noise, and "ceaseless activity" as disadvantages. Yet when noting the splendid growth of the city, they pointed to these same characteristics with pride. At first glance, then, inconsistency or ambivalence would seem the proper term for the prevailing attitude, and since the metropolis was the prime symbol of progress, toward progress as well.

There is, however, a much more rational and persuasive explanation. Throughout these ten years, the community's quest for wealth was accompanied by a search for values, an attempt to define the rules of living. In this effort it was quite typical of San Franciscans to try to reconcile different and often directly contradictory ideals. The nineteenth-century American love of progress is well known, and residents of the Bay City were enamored of this doctrine. At the same time, and often for the same people, there existed a worship of primitivism—as the "suburban ideology" indicates.

Yet it was certainly not inconsistent for them to embrace these seemingly contradictory attitudes, for most of the values the community admired and the rules of living to which they subscribed were not absolutes. In the field of economics, it was generally held that competition was the life of trade; but that did not mean unlimited competition. The same was true in the matters of progress and primitivism, of the city and country. Most men did not intend to forego permanently the "advantages of the Emporium" for the "sweet visions of green fields, wholesome country air, and retired rural homes." The idea was to enjoy a bit of both. A return to chicken raising, like a steady life in the center city, was too much of a good thing. The suburb was a symbol of primitivism, a residential expression of the desire for a refuge from urban progress, but only a part-time refuge, not a permanent one.

By the year 1856 the success of San Francisco was virtually assured. Despite the inauspicious location, a great city had grown up on the north end of San Francisco Peninsula. Nourished by the farmers of California and the world, enriched by the Gold Rush, and spurred on by competition with its neighbors as well as among its own sections, San Francisco had spread out over a relatively large expanse of land. After the initial chaos of the

Gold Rush had subsided, the growth of the metropolis attained a noticeable degree of order. Land differentiation had begun to produce specialized areas for both business and residence. And in only eight years the city had grown from around 1,000 to about 50,000 people, from a bustling but fairly simple town to a complex city without peer on the West Coast of the United States. Portland, San Jose, Sacramento, Stockton, and San Diego were small towns; Seattle was a mere hamlet; and Los Angeles was a rowdy cow town economically in thrall to the Golden Gate City. San Francisco stood alone as the "Great Commercial Emporium of the Pacific," dominating, influencing, and directing an entire region.

NOTES

1. Hubert Howe Bancroft, *The History of California*, IV (San Francisco: The History Company Publishers, 1888), p. 664.

2. Frank Soule, John H. Gihon, and James Nisbet, *The Annals of San Francisco* (New York: D. Appleton and Co., 1855), p. 163.

3. Rev. Albert Williams, *A Pioneer Pastorate and Times* (San Francisco: Bacon and Company Printers, 1882), p. 61.

4. *The Alta California*, September 9, 1851. Cited hereafter as *Alta*.

5. See United States Coast Survey maps for 1853 and 1857 (Bancroft Library, University of California).

6. These and other conclusions about land use have been drawn largely from residential and economic maps made by the author and based upon the various city directories: Charles P. Kimball, comp., *San Francisco Directory for 1850* (San Francisco: Charles P. Kimball, 1850); J. M. Parker, comp., *San Francisco Directory for 1852* (San Francisco: J. M. Parker, 1852); S. Colville, comp., *San Francisco Directory for 1856* (San Francisco: S. Colville, 1856); Henry G. Langley, *San Francisco Directory for 1857–58* (San Francisco: H. G. Langley, 1857–8).

7. Since it is difficult to tell exactly what the norms of specialization were at that time or how they compare with the degree of specialization today, I will merely describe what I found. Probably more comparison will be necessary to determine just how specialized the city was compared with a modern metropolis. "Significant" in this context means that I found a high degree of specialization that was noticeable, even to the residents of the city themselves.

8. For example, influencing wages in the city.

9. Letter of Albert Dibblee to John N. Hicks, San Francisco, April 16, 1853, pp. 1–2, in Albert Dibblee Correspondence and Papers (Bancroft Library, University of California).

10. *Daily Evening Picayune*, November 1, 1851. Cited hereafter as *Picayune*.

11. *San Francisco Daily Herald*, September 25, 1853. Cited hereafter as *Herald*.

12. *Picayune*, September 24, 1851.

13. *Ibid.*, December 14, 1850; October 15, 1851.

14. *Ibid.*, August 7, 1850.

15. *Daily California Courier*, July 20, 1850. Cited hereafter as *Courier*.

16. *Picayune*, August 23, 1851.

17. *Herald*, October 28, 1853.

18. *California Chronicle*, May 10, 1856. Cited hereafter as *Chronicle*.

19. *Herald*, October 28, 1853.

20. Other wharves also had their own specific functions. Pacific Street Wharf was the terminus of the river steamers that would take the goods from the city to the interior; Jackson Street Wharf was the host for the Nicaragua steamers; and Vallejo Street Wharf performed the same function for the Pacific Mail steamers. *Chronicle*, May 10, 1856.

21. *Herald*, October 28, 1853.

22. *Picayune*, September 8, 1851.

23. Letter of David Fay to his brother, San Francisco, March 31, 1853, p. 2, and Logan Fay to Patrick Fay, San Francisco, May 16, 1853, p. 1, in Fay Collection (California State Library at Sacramento).

24. *Chronicle*, April 25, 1856.

25. Alfred L. Tubbs, *Recollections of Events in California*, Bancroft Library MSS.

26. These conclusions are based on random and other samples of the various city directories as well as on maps based upon them and on land-use maps made in 1853, 1857, and 1869 by the United States Coast Survey, plus verbal comments of contemporaries.

27. My definition of class is a catalog of those who would have been considered to be in one group or another rather than a list of supposed characteristics of a social stratum. For the most part, I have tried to let contemporaries do their own defining; I have merely listed the results. Artisans, laborers, sailors, longshoremen, etc., were considered working-class; merchants, clerks, lawyers, middle-class.

28. These estimates are based on a 10 percent sample of the 1857–8 city directory compiled by Langley.

29. An 1867–8 demographic map reveals about the same configuration as the 1857–8 one. In some places the middle class was on the periphery and in some places the working class; but nowhere was a ring and core pattern very clear. The transportation facilities definitely affected the city, but they seem to have had their greatest impact on the working-class district south of Market, which stretched far to the west along the car lines. The map was based on a 3 percent sample of the 1867–8 city directory compiled by Langley. For 1857–8, the presence of the Chinese neighborhood at Dupont and Sacramento further skews the pattern; but it is hard to tell how much, since the Chinese were hardly represented in Langley's directory. Possibly the four square blocks bounded by Dupont, Montgomery, Clay, and California would have been working-class if the Chinese were included. This estimate is based on a 10 percent sample of the 1857–8 city directory compiled by Langley.

30. *Daily Morning Call,* December 5, 1856.

31. William Redmond Ryan, *Personal Adventures in Upper and Lower California, 1848–49;* . . . (London: William Shoberl Publishers, 1851), pp. 271–5.

32. See United States Coast Survey maps for 1853 and 1857 (Bancroft Library, University of California); *Annals,* p. 298.

33. Roy S. Cameron, *History of Public Transit in San Francisco, 1850–1948* (mimeographed copy, San Francisco: San Francisco Transportation and Technical Commission, 1948), pp. 1–2. There was no correlation between class and the plank roads south of Market either. For a view which stresses the role of the omnibus in promoting differentiation of land uses, see Charles N. Glaab and A. Theodore Brown, *A History of Urban America* (New York: Macmillan, 1967), p. 147.

34. *Annals,* p. 452.

35. Benjamin Franklin Butler, Papers (California Historical Society).

36. *Chronicle,* April 25, 1856.

37. *Alta,* June 9, 1852.

38. *Annals,* p. 254. The complaints in the press thereafter about exorbitant rents were quite frequent.

39. *Alta,* June 9, 1852.

40. *Ibid.,* August 29, 1852; *Chronicle,* October 23, 1854.

41. Letters of George Howard to Agnes Howard, San Francisco, July 14, 1855, February 11, 1855, February 25, 1855, in W. D. M. Howard Papers (California Historical Society); see also *Alta,* February 23, 1853; July 1, 1856.

42. *Chronicle,* April 10, 1854.

43. Letter of William Weston to his aunt, San Francisco, March 30, 1851, in William K. Weston Papers (California Historical Society).

44. Glaab and Brown, *op. cit.,* p. 154.

45. *Alta,* June 9, 1852, February 5, 1855, August 28, 1856; *Picayune,* November 8, 1851.

9. THE EMERGENCE OF CENTRAL IMMIGRANT GHETTOES IN AMERICAN CITIES, 1840–1920

David Ward

During the three generations of sustained and heavy European immigration into the United States, which preceded the immigration restriction legislation of the early 1920s, congested ghettoes of foreign immigrants assumed substantial dimensions within the residential structures of American cities. Most immigrants settled near the sources of unskilled employment and, although suburban industrial districts attracted considerable numbers of immigrant laborers, the majority of newcomers concentrated on the margins of the emerging central business districts. The central business district provided the largest source of unskilled employment opportunities, and many of the adjacent residential quarters had been abandoned by their original residents because of the threatened encroachment of commercial activities. Although some districts retained their middle- and high-income occupants, most residential areas adjacent to the central business district were abandoned to immigrants. Vacated houses were converted into tenements and rooming houses, while vacant lots and rear yards were filled with cheap new structures. On some margins of the central business district newly established immigrant concentrations were rapidly displaced by expanding commercial activities; but because the specialized functional areas of the central business district expanded at different rates in different directions, many adjacent residential districts survived and exhibited striking variations in their relative longevity, physical quality, and social composition. Indeed, the selective adoption and subsequent characteristics of immigrant residential locations were primarily determined by the timing, dimensions, and direction of the expansion of the adjacent specialized business activity. This paper proposes, first, to examine in general the competing and at times complementary claims of immigrants and commerce for central urban locations between 1840 and 1920, and second, to illustrate the relationship of immigrant residential locations to different adjacent business activities in the particular instance of Boston, Massachusetts, during the same period.

Reprinted from the Annals of the American Association of Geographers, LVIII (June 1968), 343–51, by permission of the publisher.

IMMIGRANT RESIDENTIAL LOCATIONS AND THE URBAN RESIDENTIAL STRUCTURE

The settlement of newly arrived immigrants on the margins of the central business district has for long been closely associated with the blighting effects of commercial encroachment into adjacent residential districts. The uncertain timing and quality of future commercial developments encouraged the neglect of existing property and the departure of the more prosperous members of the resident population. Once abandoned by their original populations, central residential districts were most frequently adopted by low-income immigrants, and the deterioration of the physical quality of the dwellings was assumed to encourage the social disorganization of the new residents. Blighted conditions thus implied not only bad housing but also pathological social repercussions. Even today, however, blighted conditions do not prevail on all margins of the central business district, and many observers have documented the considerable variations in the social and physical characteristics of the central residential districts. Although a zone of blight adjacent to the central business district formed an integral part of Burgess's concentric scheme of the urban residential structure, he was impressed by the apparently anomalous location of central high-income apartment districts and by the belt-like distribution of Negroes across the otherwise concentric arrangement of urban social groups.[1] Zorbaugh examined the development and survival of the "Gold Coast" apartment district of Chicago alongside the central business district and the slums of the Near North Side, and Hoyt recognized similar high-rent areas near to the business districts of other American cities.[2] Zorbaugh suggested that the "Gold Coast" was artificially protected by lease conditions and would eventually yield to the competitive demands of commerce. In contrast, Hoyt proposed a sector hypothesis of the residential structure of the city which was in part an effort to recognize the variations in the quality of residential districts on the margin of the central business district.

Since surviving middle- and high-income residential districts occupy only a small segment of the residential fringe of the central business district, they are often regarded as local exceptions to the widespread blighted conditions created by the threat of commercial expansion. Reevaluations of the social organization of low-income neighborhoods have, however, also enlarged our conceptions of the physical and social conditions of central residential districts. It was for long assumed that all low-income neighborhoods were afflicted by pathological social conditions which were directly related to the unhealthy and congested living conditions of tenement housing and to the breakdown of the traditional social organization of rural people in the impersonal and anonymous world of the city.[3] Relatively few immigrants escaped the material and social discomforts of congested urban living conditions, but some immigrant groups were able to reestablish parts of their ancestral social organization in the New World and thereby facilitate their adjustment to the unfamiliar scale of American urban life. For example, Ware demonstrated that the institutions and values of the native American society seemed remote and confusing to most immigrant groups and, therefore, it was the survival of the extended family, along with local political and religious allegiances, that facilitated the adjustment of immigrants and their descendants to American urban life. Similarly, Whyte identified the distinctive internal structure of the street corner society and suggested that earlier observers had failed to recognize the presence of social organization among low-income people largely because their customs and values were different from those of the more familiar society of suburban America.[4]

The suburban movement has severely depleted the populations of the original ghettoes of European immigrants; but quite recently Glazer and Moynihan have suggested that ethnic origin has also partly influenced the suburban residential choices and social life of the descendants of immigrants,[5] while immigrants from Puerto Rico and from the American South have partly compensated for the population losses created by the suburban movement. Since, however, the central business district has lost its former preeminence as a source of unskilled employment and since low-rent housing is no longer confined to central residential districts, the more recent immigration has had more modest effects upon the central residential pattern than that of the nineteenth century. Although urban renewal schemes have diminished the extent and capacity of many tenement districts, some authorities have suggested that the material and fiscal priorities of most public improvement schemes have obscured the social attractions of many low-rent districts to their resident populations.[6] A preoccupation with the vitality of local neighborhood life has at times degenerated into an uncritical admiration of the culture of poverty; but nevertheless there is a need to identify variations in the social and living conditions of low-income residential areas.[7] Some original ghettoes have survived for several generations on the margins of the central business district and, in spite of considerable depopulation, remain attractive to the resident population. Other districts have housed either a rapid succession of diverse immigrant groups or the most impoverished and discriminated social groups in the city and, under these circumstances, pathological social conditions tend to compound the material inadequacies of the housing and neighborhood.

Firey, and Jones, in their respective studies of central parts of Boston and Belfast, have related the survival of middle- and high-income districts and the development of different types of low-income areas to the sentiments and values of the occupying social groups.[8] Although this perspective provided many new insights into the attachment to a given district of a particular social group, the effect of changes in the central business district upon the original adoption and subsequent survival of the adjacent residential districts remained obscure. Indeed, most recent contributions to our understanding of the residential structure of American cities have acknowledged the locational implications of cultural preferences in their developments of an explanatory focus pioneered some fifty years ago and based upon measures of site costs and of accessibility of home to employment.[9] These considerations have provided the most satisfactory principles for an interpretation of the extensive suburban residential additions to American cities since the turn of the century. The emergence and diversification of central residential districts, however, occurred during the course of the second half of the nineteenth century when the suburban alternative to central tenement residence was available only to limited numbers of immigrants and their descendants and when the growth and differentiation of the central business district most profoundly affected the adjacent residential quarters.

IMMIGRANT CONCENTRATION IN CENTRAL URBAN LOCATIONS

The dense central concentrations of immigrants were thus established at a time when the distributional implications of accessibility were determined not only by the extent and density of the streetcar network, but also by the long working hours, low wages, and unpredictable tenure of unskilled employment.[10] Most newly arrived immigrants sought cheap accommodation partly because of their poverty and partly because of their desire to accumulate savings to finance the passages of relatives. The central tenement districts provided by far the largest supply of cheap living quarters, but because most tenements were overcrowded, badly designed, and poorly—if at all—endowed with sanitary facilities, even low rents were exorbitant. Tenement accommodation, however, could be obtained by the room at fractional rates, whereas self-contained dwelling units which possessed only the minimum requirements for the comfort and health of their occupants rented at rates far beyond the means of new immigrants.[11] Towards the end of the nineteenth century, legislation was introduced in many cities to improve the living conditions in newly constructed tenements, but even modest structural refinements increased minimum rents and failed to enlarge the supply of low-rent housing.[12] The housing choices of most immigrants were thus largely restricted to central residential districts until either a rise in real incomes made possible suburban residence or public funds were provided to subsidize rent payments.[13]

The central tenement districts also possessed the advantage of convenient accessibility to the growing employment opportunities of the emerging central business district. Although the facilities for local transportation were improved and enlarged during the second half of the nineteenth century, many immigrants were employed in occupations with long and awkward hours and, therefore, preferred a short pedestrian journey to work. The tenure of unskilled employment was also characteristically uncertain, and daily hiring was the common procedure in general laboring and portering. Consequently, immigrants not only faced the problems of numerous changes in the location of their work, but also suffered from frequent spells of unemployment. Under these circumstances, employment in the central business district had the advantage of a wide range of alternative opportunities when regular work was abruptly terminated. Suburban industrial districts also attracted considerable numbers of immigrants, and cheap housing was built in adjacent locations; but the variety of both industrial and commercial employment within and near to the central business district supported far larger numbers of immigrants in central residential locations. The central business district offered the largest and most diverse source of unskilled employment opportunities, and the adjacent tenement districts provided uncomfortable but conveniently located residential quarters which were within the limited financial means of new immigrants.

The first generation of immigrant groups who arrived in American cities in large numbers often provided almost the entire labor force of some activities conducted within the central business district. Irish immigrants first helped to build, and later found employment in, the warehouses and terminal facilities of the business district, whereas German immigrants found employment in the sewing machine and port supply trades which were housed in the upper stories of warehouses.[14] Italian immigrants in part replaced the Irish as general laborers, but the distribution of fresh food also attracted Italians in large numbers.[15] Jewish immigrants, equipped with long experience in the handicraft industries and local commercial life of their East European homelands, rapidly developed many branches of merchandising at a time when the retail and wholesale segments of marketing were first firmly separated and established as distinct specialized areas within the central business district.[16] Jewish immigrants also adopted the ready-made clothing industry and, in order to achieve economies of rent and labor, reorganized production within their own residential districts. The clothing industry needed close and immediate contact with the credit and informational facilities of the central business district, and the central tenement districts possessed the advantage of adjacency to the commercial facilities of the city.[17] This ethnic division of labor was neither rigid nor exclusive but, nevertheless, encouraged the concentration of immigrants in those residential districts where they could most effectively obtain employment from their compatriots. Many immigrant business enterprises, which later served the entire city or national market were, moreover, originally founded upon the provision of the distinctive material and dietary needs of the immigrant community.

Group conciousness, as well as economic necessity or advantage, stimulated the concentration of immigrants in the central tenement districts; for once established, the ghetto provided institutions and neighborhood life familiar to the immigrant. Indeed most immigrants preferred to spend their early years in a new country and unfamiliar city in a district which housed their fellow countrymen or coreligionists if not their immediate family and friends. Many contemporary observers were inclined to ignore the positive social attractions of the tenement districts to the newly arrived immigrants, for it was assumed that the congested living conditions resulted in the social disorganization of the resident population and that the concentration of immigrants delayed and discouraged their assimilation into the native American society. In spite of the adverse living conditions, however, some immigrant groups established stable local communities and attracted deservedly laudatory reports upon the stability and moral orthodoxy of their family and neighborhood life.[18] Moreover, in the absence of effective public welfare, residential concentration provided immigrant communities with their share of the patronage of local politics, for the heavily populated ethnic wards provided a major source of voting strength in the civic elections.[19] The development of local communities within the tenement districts attracted the majority of newly arrived immigrants of similar ancestry and assisted their adjustment to the unfamiliar scale and conditions of American urban life.

The social attractions and political advantages of residential concentration were not, however, characteristic of all tenement districts, nor were they shared by all immigrant groups. The adjustment of different immigrant groups to the changing conditions of residence and employment in American cities was rarely repetitive. Although southern Italian immigrants had lived in large unsanitary villages, and Jewish immigrants had lived in the congested towns of Eastern Europe, many immigrants had no previous experience of crowded living conditions. Certainly relatively few immigrants had faced the problems of residence in cities as large and as complex as those of industrial America, and some groups lacked the numbers to support their own institutions or to lay claim to their proportionate share of political patronage. Moreover, most small immigrant groups were composed of young single men who eventually hoped to return to their homelands with the assumed profits of their American employment and, consequently, with neither a family structure nor a permanent commitment to residence in the United States, some degree of social disorganization did compound the material discomfort of their residential quarters.[20] Although the marginal economies and social advantages of scale insulated most large and well-established immigrant groups from the problems faced by small groups, all central concentrations of immigrants faced the disturbing effects of displacement by the expansion of the adjacent commercial activities. Even the largest and most organized immigrant groups were unable to establish enduring communities in those tenement districts which suffered from the continuous invasion of business premises. The specialized functional areas of the central business district, however, emerged and expanded at different rates at different times and, accordingly, the effect of the central business district upon the adjacent residential areas was neither continuous nor uniform.[21]

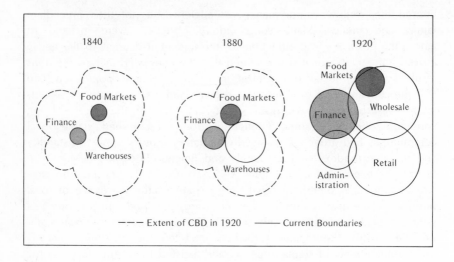

Figure 1. Generalized stages in the development of the CBD

THE EFFECT OF BUSINESS EXPANSION ON IMMIGRANT CONCENTRATION

Thus, although the residential choices of immigrants were largely restricted to central locations, and although the tenement districts fulfilled many of their more immediate social and economic needs, the development and survival of central concentrations of immigrants was primarily dependent upon the rate and dimensions of expansion of the adjacent segment of the emerging central business district. The invasion of business activities into adjacent residential districts occasionally followed so closely upon the departure of the original population that the immigrant newcomers had neither the time nor the incentive to develop a stable neighborhood life. The warehouse quarter, for example, housed both expanding small-scale workshop industries and a large proportion of the growing commercial activities of the city and, during the middle decades of the nineteenth century, made greater claims upon the adjacent residential quarters than all the other segments of the central business district combined[22] (Fig. 1). Towards the turn of the century, the demands of regional distribution had displaced most of the workshop industries and stimulated a separation of the retail and wholesale segments of marketing within the central business district (Fig. 1). The emergence of a retail quarter and the continued expansion of the warehouse district as the seat of wholesale distribution increased even further the rate and scale of expansion of business premises into a broader segment of the residential fringe of the central business district. Central residential districts adjacent to these rapidly expanding segments of the central business district were most frequently occupied by the smallest or poorest immigrant groups along with remnants from older groups which had moved on to securer residential locations.[23] The residents of these districts did suffer from the social disorganization created by the problems of eviction and residential relocation.

There were, however, central residential districts which failed to attract anticipated commercial developments once they had been abandoned by their original populations. Because of the improvement in the facilities for local movement and the increase in the scale of business organization, the location of the greatest constructional activity and commercial expansion within the central business district tended to shift during the course of the nineteenth century.[24] Consequently, residential districts adjacent to older centers of growth lost their attractiveness for commercial development. Moreover, the most attractive locations for business had often been preempted early by commercial activities which were unable to maintain their original choices in the face of the expanding needs of more competitive activities. Financial and administrative functions for long occupied separate and diminutive quarters, and only late in the nineteenth century coalesced and expanded their accommodations into premium locations within the existing limits of the central business district rather than at the expense of peripheral residential locations (Fig. 1). Other business activities retained their small quarters throughout the nineteenth century and eventually reorganized their facilities by decentralization rather than by central expansion. The distribution of fresh food, for example, was conducted in extremely congested quarters and expanded only slightly into adjacent residential districts, partly because nearby tenements provided convenient housing for laborers who worked in the early hours of the day.[25] Under these circumstances of limited commercial expansion into the adjacent residential districts, the immigrant newcomers were able to establish enduring ghettoes which not only served their own immediate residential needs but also those of later immigrant arrivals. Districts which housed Irish and German immigrants in the middle decades of the nineteenth century gradually passed into the possession of Italian and Jewish immigrants towards the turn of the century.[26]

The subdivision of abandoned housing and the construction of cheap new tenements in their vacant grounds were designed to extract a marginal rental income from buildings and land during the period of uncertain property values which preceded their adoption by commercial activities. Thus, the housing of immigrants was at first regarded as a temporary expedient, but it soon became clear that as long as immigrants arrived in large numbers, the provision of their housing needs would be a source of substantial profit. Once established under favorable conditions on the edge of the central business district, immigrant ghettoes resisted or at least retarded the rate of any subsequent commercial claims upon their quarters.[27] Not all central districts were converted into tenement areas, for it was also possible to obtain a substantial income from lodging or rooming house accommodation. Conversion into rooms was, moreover, less costly than the modifications required for tenement residence, whereas lodging houses tended to maintain the status of an area by catering to the needs of single white-collar people.[28] Although many single foreign immigrants were housed in the lodging and rooming house districts, the relatively high proportions of native Americans clearly distinguished the populations of these areas from those of the tenement districts and, for a brief time, the lodging house districts were able to escape the popular and often erroneous identification of depravity and delinquency with immigrant tenement districts.

Although almost the entire residential fringe of the central business district eventually housed low-income immigrants, lodgers, or commerce, one segment occasionally retained its original high-income population and resisted the competitive demands of business and immigrants. The survival of high income residential districts in part depended upon favorable site conditions and long-established status. Many central locations which were at one time endowed with advantages of site and status failed to retain their original population, for the quality and needs of the adjacent business activity in part influenced the status of central residential quarters. Financial institutions and the seats of public authority attracted rather than discouraged adjacent residence by people of wealth and status. Throughout the nineteenth century many established families valued their proximity to the sources of political and economic power and the historic status of the adjacent residential quarters. Financial and administrative activities offered only limited unskilled employment opportunities and, consequently, the demand for low-rent housing was more limited than on those margins of the business district adjacent to abundant sources of unskilled employment. The different directions and characteristics of the expansion of the central business district directly affected the selective adoption of central residential districts by immigrants and also in part influenced the abandonment of these districts by their original populations. Thus, during the course of the nineteenth century, not only tenement districts of varying quality but also lodging houses and substantial town houses developed on different margins of the central business districts of large American cities.

THE RESIDENTIAL STRUCTURE OF CENTRAL BOSTON

As both the first receiving stations of foreign immigrants and the earliest beneficiaries of American industrial and commercial growth, the major seaports of the Northeastern coast most clearly exhibited the effects of sustained immigration and of the expansion of the central business district upon the emergence of the central residential districts of large American cities. In Boston, for example, an enduring and diversified residential pattern developed on the edge of the central business district between 1840 and 1920. By 1920, Italian and Russian Jewish immigrants occupied tenements in the North End and in adjacent sections of the West End; smaller

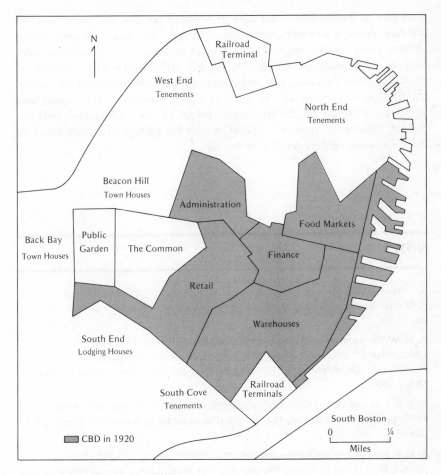

Figure 2. Central Boston in 1920

and poorer immigrant groups were housed in rather more sordid tenements in the South Cove district, and single men of both immigrant and native American parentage lived in lodging and rooming houses in the South End (Fig. 2). Although immigrant settlement and business expansion affected almost the entire fringe of Boston's central business district, Beacon Hill and the adjacent Back Bay continued to house wealthy and socially prominent people in town houses (Fig. 2).

Over the past fifty years depopulation and redevelopment have only partly altered the residential pattern established on the edge of the central business district during the nineteenth century. Although many of the tenements in the West End and the South Cove have been demolished and their populations relocated, the North End continues to house a flourishing but much diminished population of Italian-Americans. Beacon Hill and the

Back Bay no longer house the elite of Boston's society, and some sections are now devoted to professional offices or specialty retail activities; nevertheless, many of the original town houses maintain their residential function as apartments or rooms. The South End has in part retained its rooming house function, but large sections are now occupied by a substantial Negro community. In spite of these changes in the extent and social composition of the residential fringe of Boston's central business district, substantial remnants of the residential pattern established during the nineteenth century remain to this day.

NOTES

1. E. W. Burgess, "The Growth of the City," in R. E. Park, E. W. Burgess, and R. D. MacKenzie, eds., *The City* (Chicago: University of Chicago Press, 1925), pp. 47–62.

2. H. W. Zorbaugh, *The Gold Coast and the Slum* (Chicago: University of Chicago Press, 1929), pp. 1–16; H. Hoyt, *The Structure and Growth of Residential Neighbourhoods in American Cities* (Washington, D.C.: U.S. Government Printing Office, 1939).

3. R. E. Park and H. A. Miller, *Old World Traits Transplanted* (New York: Harper, 1921), pp. 60–80; O. Handlin, *The Uprooted* (Boston: Little, Brown, 1951), pp. 259–85.

4. C. F. Ware, *Greenwich Village: 1920–1930* (Boston: Houghton Mifflin, 1935), pp. 3–8, 81–126; W. F. Whyte, *The Street Corner Society* (Chicago: University of Chicago Press, 1943), pp. 94–104, 255–78.

5. N. Glazer and D. P. Moynihan, *Beyond the Melting Pot* (Cambridge: MIT Press, 1964).

6. H. J. Gans, *The Urban Villagers* (New York: The Free Press, 1962), pp. 3–41; B. J. Frieden, *The Future of Old Neighbourhoods* (Cambridge: MIT Press, 1964), pp. 1–5.

7. G. C. Homans, *The Human Group* (New York: Harcourt, Brace & Co., 1950), pp. 334–68; W. I. Firey, *Land Use in Central Boston* (Cambridge: Harvard University Press, 1947), pp. 170–97, 290–313.

8. W. I. Firey, *op. cit.;* E. Jones, *A Social Geography of Belfast* (London: Oxford University Press, 1962).

9. W. Alonso, *Location and Land Use* (Cambridge: Harvard University Press, 1964); L. Wingo, Jr., *Transportation and Urban Land* (Washington: Resources for the Future, 1961); R. M. Hurd, *Principles of City Land Values* (New York: The Record and Guide, 1903).

10. D. Ward, "A Comparative Historical Geography of Streetcar Suburbs in Boston,

Massachusetts and Leeds, England: 1850–1920," *Annals,* Association of American Geographers, LIV (1964), 477–89.

11. E. R. L. Gould, "The Housing of the Working People," *8th Special Report of the Commissioner of Labor* (Washington, D.C.: U.S. Government Printing Office, 1895), p. 419.

12. E. E. Wood, *The Housing of the Unskilled Wage Earner* (New York: Macmillan, 1919), p. 21.

13. E. Abbott, *The Tenements of Chicago: 1908–1936* (Chicago: University of Chicago Press, 1936), pp. 481–3.

14. R. Ernst, *Immigrant Life in New York City: 1825–1863* (New York: King's Crown Press, 1949), pp. 17, 61–77; O. Handlin, *Boston's Immigrants: A Study in Acculturation* (Cambridge: Harvard University Press, 1959), pp. 54–87.

15. R. F. Foerster, *The Italian Emigration of Our Times* (Cambridge: Harvard University Press, 1919), pp. 332–44.

16. S. Joseph, *Jewish Immigration to the United States from 1881 to 1910* (New York: Columbia University Press, 1914), pp. 42–6.

17. J. R. Commons, "Immigration and its Economic Effects," *Report of the Industrial Commission XV* (Washington, D.C., 1901), pp. 316–26.

18. W. T. Elsing, "Life in New York Tenement Houses," in *The Poor in Great Cities* (New York: Scribners, 1895) pp. 42–85.

19. T. J. Lowi, *At the Pleasure of the Mayor: Power and Patronage in New York City, 1898–1958* (New York: The Free Press, 1964).

20. Zorbaugh, *op. cit.,* pp. 142–51.

21. Information on the timing and scale of the expansion of the component specialized areas of the central business district during the nineteenth century is widely scattered and rarely related to the fortunes of adjacent residential districts. J. E. Vance, "Emerging Patterns of Commercial Structure in American Cities," in K. Norburg, ed., *Proceedings of the I.G.U. Symposium in Urban Geography* (Lund: Gleerups, 1962), pp. 473–83, and D. Ward, "The Industrial Revolution and Emergence of Boston's Central Business District," *Economic Geography,* XLII (1966), pp. 152–71, give some indication of the developmental aspects of the problem, whereas R. E. Murphy and J. E. Vance, "Delimiting the CBD," *Economic Geography,* XXX (1954), 189–222, and D. W. Griffin and R. E. Preston, "A Restatement of the Transition Zone Concept," *Annals,* Association of American Geographers, LVI (1966), 339–50, from an essentially contemporary perspective indicate the diverse characteristics of different edges of the CBD.

22. N. S. B. Gras, "The Development of the Metropolitan Economy in Europe and America," *American Historical Review,* XXVII (1922), 695–708.

23. Zorbaugh, *op. cit.,* p. 127.

24. L. Grebler, *Housing Market Behavior in a Declining Area* (New York: Columbia University Press, 1952), p. 113 on the up-town shift of retailing on Manhattan Island and the effects on the residential districts near to the original center of growth.

25. Zorbaugh, *op. cit.,* p. 166; F. E. Bushee, "Italian Immigrants in Boston," *Arena,* XVII (1896–7), 722–34.

26. W. L. Warner and L. Srole, *The Social Systems of American Ethnic Groups* (New Haven: Yale University Press, 1945), pp. 33–52; K. H. Claghorn, "The Foreign Immigrant in New York City," *Report of the Industrial Commission XV* (Washington, D.C., 1901), pp. 471–2.

27. Grebler, *op. cit.,* pp. 106–16.

28. R. A. Woods, ed., *The City Wilderness* (Boston: Houghton Mifflin, 1898), pp. 35–39; Zorbaugh, *op. cit.,* pp. 69–86.

PART FOUR

IMMIGRATION, MIGRATION, AND MOBILITY, 1865-1920

In 1890 the Bureau of the Census announced that the Western frontier was no more. The plains Indians, outnumbered and decimated after numerous encounters with the United States Cavalry, had been pressed onto reservations; the thundering buffalo herds had been replaced by the belching steam engines of transcontinental railroads; the great open spaces, testaments to the world of American opportunity, had been largely filled in. Now, as the Reverend Samuel Lane Loomis told the graduating class of that year at Andover Theological Seminary, Americans were living in "an age of great cities." In that year, the nation's population was already one-third urban and the population in the Northeast was well over one-half urban. With 2 million inhabitants, New York was already the second largest city in the world, and Chicago and Philadelphia each contained about a million inhabitants. Places like Minneapolis, Denver, Seattle, San Francisco, and Birmingham, which hardly existed in 1840, had become major regional metropolises. Only the South, whose population would remain three-fourths rural as late as 1920, seemed to be running counter to the national trend, but even there, in Houston, New Orleans, Atlanta, Memphis, and Dallas, the foundation was being created for more substantial expansion later in the century.

The enormous growth of American cities between the Civil War and 1920 can be attributed largely to the quickening pace of the Industrial Revolution. In 1860, when about one American in five lived in communities of more than 2,500 inhabitants, the United States was a secondary industrial nation, and its largest cities owed their success primarily to commerce; in 1920, when more than half of the American population was urban, the nation had achieved a position of industrial preeminence. Urbanization and industrialization seemed to be mutually reinforcing processes. Organized means of production led to larger factory complexes and to larger urban centers; in turn, the building of homes and offices and streets and sewers in those centers fueled the industrialization trend. The largest cities remained multifunctional—that is, their economies continued to be based upon a combination of manufacturing, trade, and services—but others became closely identified with specialized manufacturing processes—Minneapolis with milling, Milwaukee with beer, Dayton with cash registers, Detroit with motor cars, Rochester with photographic equipment, and Pittsburgh and Birmingham with steel.

The huge increase in urban population that provided both the market and the brawn for an industrial economy derived from three sources: an excess of births over deaths, a migration from farm to city, and immigration from Europe. The increase in births was less dramatic than migration and immigration but equally important. Prior to 1850, population experts commonly reported that cities were unable to reproduce themselves. Birth rates were lower and life expectancy shorter in congested than in rural areas. However, improvements in urban sanitation and public health in the second half of the century closed the gap between city and country and enabled natural increase to account for about 35 percent of the urban population growth between 1860 and 1920.

The exodus from the farms is not normally considered significant before the twentieth century. As a partial result of the Homestead Act of 1862, which made available 160 acres of free land to citizens after five years of residence upon it, the number of farms increased from 2 to 5.7 million and the number of farm workers from 6.2 to 10.6 million in the four decades between 1860 and1900. The consequent increase in the amount of acreage under cultivation made it possible for the American farmer not only to feed the United States population but also to produce a large surplus year after year.

However, farm conditions worsened in the generation after the Civil War. As productivity increased, agricultural prices declined, with the result that farmers labored longer hours for less remuneration. Rural families, depressed by the poverty, monotony, and loneliness of farm life, began an exodus that continues even today. For every urban dweller who took up the plow between 1860 and 1900, twenty farmers moved to the city. In demographic terms, this meant that large areas of the nation were losing their population. Between 1880 and 1890, for example, almost all of Nevada as well as most of New York, Maine, New Hampshire, Vermont, Ohio, Illinois, Connecticut, and Maryland lost residents. Famed New York newspaper editor Horace Greeley, who coined the phrase "Go west, young man, go west," noted ruefully that with "millions of acres" awaiting cultivation, "hundreds of thousands reject this and rush into the cities."

Greeley was not alone in puzzling over the migration of rural families to congested areas where there was scarcely room enough for half of those already there. Ministers, politicians, and authors by the hundreds contrasted the pure air and clean living of rural America with the saloons, impersonality, and degeneracy of the post-Civil War city. Why should the sturdy yeoman barter, in Lewis Mumford's words, "all his glorious heritage for gaslight and paved streets and starched collars and skyscrapers"? Precisely because the music, dancing, and lighted taverns seemed more attractive than barnyard mud and village monotony. Speaking of the wonder that resides in a city, Richard Harding Davis said: "Any man who can afford a hall bedroom and a gas stove in New York City is better off than he would be as the owner of 160 acres on the prairie."

Even more attractive was the city's promise of a range of economic and social choices, a spectrum of possible lines of action that farm life could not offer. Theodore Dreiser, looking backward to earlier days, reported that he "loved Chicago. It was so strong, so rough, so shabby, and yet so vital and determined." A *Harper's New Monthly Magazine* inquiry into continuing migration to New York in 1882 concluded:

A great city always exercises a strange, well-nigh inexplicable fascination on the multitude not less than on individuals. The former like it for its bigness, its bustle, its movement, its variety, its fluctuations. Where there is so much of everything, they are likely, they believe, to get their share. At any rate, they want to be in the tumble and the tide. Having no inward resources, they hunger for tumultuous externals.

The city was the lodestar of immigrants from Europe even more than of native-born farmers. Although the bulk of the English, Scottish, German, and Scandinavian newcomers scattered throughout the country, there were large immigrant contingents in cities as early as 1850.

In the last two decades of the nineteenth century the sources of immigration underwent a drastic shift. On the one hand there was a fall in the size of the annual contingent from northern and western Europe. In 1882 German arrivals amounted to 250,000 and Scandinavians to 105,000. Fifteen years later, the annual total from Germany had fallen below 40,000 and the number from Scandinavia had become almost negligible. There were many reasons for the precipitous drop: a decrease in the homeland's birth rate, a labor shortage caused by rapid industrialization, and military rivalries (Great Britain, for example, sought to divert emigrants to colonies in her overseas empire where they might be available to the mother country in an emergency.). But at about the same time that England, Germany, and Scandinavia were sending fewer sons to these shores, conditions in southern and eastern Europe were making possible a new wave of immigration to America. For the first two-thirds of the nineteenth century most countries in that region had placed heavy restrictions upon emigration. In Italy, it was the success of the unification movement of 1859–60 that brought about the removal of restraints; in large parts of the Balkans the right to leave came after the Russo-Turkish War of 1877, when Serbia, Bulgaria, Bosnia, and others were liberated from Turkish rule. Impoverished and usually uneducated, citizens of this region answered the call of the American Statue of Liberty:

Give me your tired, your poor
Your huddled masses yearning to breathe free
The wretched refuse of your teeming shore.
Send these, the homeless, tempest-tost to me
I lift my lamp beside the golden door.

The newer immigrants came over in unprecedented numbers. Whereas in 1880, 12,000 Italians and 5,000 Russians had landed in the United States, the corresponding figures for 1907 were 286,000 and 259,000. Moreover, these immigrants were much more likely than old-stock Americans to live in cities. At a time when less than half the national population was urban, more than five-sixths of all first-generation Russian-Americans and Irish-Americans lived in cities. Among immigrants from Italy and Hungary the proportion was more than three-fourths. This urban concentration was especially marked in the twenty-eight largest cities, which in 1890 contained less than 13 percent of the native-born and more than 33 percent of the foreign-born population in the United States. In that same year New York City, with more Germans than Hamburg, more Jews than Warsaw, and more Irishmen than Dublin, contained more foreign-born residents than any other city on earth.

Because the urban population expanded so rapidly after the Civil War, neither in New York nor in any other large American community was there room for the new arrivals. Developing forms of mass transit— horsedrawn streetcars, cable cars, steam railroads, trolleys, and finally automobiles—provided the middle and upper classes with the option of moving to larger homes on generous lots well away from the noise and confusion of the inner city. But the poor, as David Ward notes in his article "The Emergence of Central Immigrant Ghettoes in American Cities," took the dark, filthy, and crowded shanties and apartments that were within walking distance of employment. Inner-core neighborhoods took on national and even provincial casts, so that one could walk for blocks without hearing a word of English spoken. Jacob Riis wrote of New York in 1890 that "A map of the city, colored to designate nationalities, would show more stripes than on the skin of a zebra, and more colors than any rainbow."

The most famous of all ethnic neighborhoods was the Lower East Side of New York. Between 1870 and 1914, a million-and-a-half Jews left their eastern European ghettoes for the promised land; more than two-thirds of them streamed into a twenty-block section of Manhattan bordering the East River. Parks and playgrounds were nonexistent; residential densities reached half a million per square mile, the highest degree of congestion the world has ever known. In such circumstances, even the infamous "dumbbell tenement," described and diagramed by Moses Rischin in his article "The Lower East Side," was viewed as an improvement over the miserable, windowless apartments already occupied. Disease, of course, was a frequent visitor; the mournful cry was *"Luft, gib mir luft"*— "Air, give me air."

What is perhaps most significant about the Lower East Side is not the existence of ghetto conditions—on a different and slightly smaller scale the same story could be told of dozens of other communities—but the speed with which those conditions were abandoned by successive immigrant groups. Irish and German in 1870, solidly Jewish in 1910, the area is now Puerto Rican and black. Harry Golden has said of the Jews that "The second generation came along and soon the sons took the old folks away, out to Brooklyn, or up to the Bronx, and thus they made room for new immigrants. America gave them all life and hope, and they repaid America. There has never been a more even trade."

The story is not all that simple, of course. In an excellent study of Newburyport, Massachusetts, in the late nineteenth century, Stephan Thernstrom probed more deeply into the rags-to-riches myth than anyone had before. His research touched off a whole series of quantitative investigations into the residential, social, and economic mobility of the common man, as well as of various racial and ethnic groups. Two of the essays in this section, one by Humbert Nelli on Italians and one of Richard J. Hopkins on mobility in Atlanta, study the questions of ethnic adjustment and residential dispersal.

In their desire to get ahead and in their tendency to move frequently, native Americans and recent immigrants shared similar traits. But the differences between them were sharp. Not only were the "newer" immigrants two or three times as likely to live in large cities as were native-born citizens, but they also retained Old World customs and languages and held fast to their Roman Catholic or Jewish religious beliefs.

Nativists were upset by the immigrants' reputation for heavy drinking and by their support of big-city political machines. As early as the 1850s, New York socialite Philip Hone stuffily noted in his diary that the Irish "increase our taxes, eat our bread, and encumber our streets, and not one in twenty is competent to keep himself."

The notion that certain immigrant groups constituted a collective entity different from and inferior to white, Anglo-Saxon Protestants gained currency in the 1880s and 1890s when race-conscious New England intellectuals formed the Immigration Restriction League and militant Protestants organized the American Protective Association. These groups argued that the declining native birth rate was due to immigrant competition and that the national culture was being submerged beneath a sea of foreigners. According to sociologist Edward A. Ross, Eastern European immigrants were "the beaten members of beaten breeds."

Attempts to reduce the size and alter the composition of the immigrant tide were not successful until the early 1920s, when the Ku Klux Klan recruited all over the country and especially in cities on the strength of an imagined racial and religious threat. The racial purists finally won with passage of the Johnson-Reed Act of 1924, the avowed purpose of which was to maintain the "racial preponderance of the basic strain of our people." It adopted the "national origins" principle and reduced the amount of immigration by 75 percent, effectively shutting off a major source of urban population growth.

The decline of European immigration was an important factor in the twentieth-century movement of blacks from farm to city. In 1900, about four-fifths of the nation's blacks lived in the South and about the same proportion lived on farms. Their ability to leave the land was hampered by their status as tenant farmers or sharecroppers for white landlords. Because black field hands often found it necessary to borrow money or to accept advances to meet family needs, they were frequently in debt to whites who charged high rates of interest. It was an impossible position. Effectively deprived of political rights and the protection of the law, blacks were held in a virtual state of peonage. Those who protested the injustice of what euphemistically was termed the "Southern way of life" often met violent deaths. Lynchings claimed more than 3,000 Southern blacks between 1880 and 1919 and not a single white person was ever executed for the crime. As a migrant from Houston wrote, "I would like Chicago or Philadelphia. But I don't care where so long as I go where a man is a man."

In the hope that the North was "a land of freedom," or that any city,

North or South, was better than the agricultural "black belt," more than 600,000 blacks moved away from the farm in the single decade from 1900 to 1910. The exodus assumed larger proportions during World War I, when a combination of poor agricultural conditions in the South and a labor shortage in the North loosened the hold of plantation life. Usually moving by rail along meridians of longitude, blacks from the Gulf and South Atlantic states tended to move toward Baltimore, Philadelphia, and New York, while those from Mississippi and Alabama were more likely to choose St. Louis, Chicago, or Detroit. Thus the shift of blacks ran counter to that of whites; while the national center of population was moving south and west the black population was moving north and slightly east.

Although Northern cities afforded him more economic and political opportunities than were available in the South, the black migrant soon found that the North was not the promised land. There the nature of discrimination toward him was far more profound and devastating than that encountered by the white immigrant. When the European arrived in Northern cities, provisions were often made to provide him with food, clothing, shelter, and employment. There was prejudice, of course, but there was help. Southern blacks found no such courtesy, and what recognition they did get was calculated, as novelist Curtis Lucas put it, "to remind them that white Americans may fight among themselves, but in the clutch know how to stand together as a race." Blacks were unable to enter basic trades except as strikebreakers and were generally confined to jobs as domestic workers or unskilled laborers. When nondiscriminatory unions such as the International Ladies' Garment Workers Union organized blacks, many employers refused to hire them unless they could pay them lower wages. And discrimination pervaded every aspect of their lives outside their work. They were refused admittance to most hotels, were served salted drinks in saloons, were assigned to balconies in theaters, were greeted by doctors' signs reading "white patients only," and were charged exorbitant rates for housing and insurance.

Residential segregation, perhaps the most pervasive type of discrimination in the North, increased with the cityward migration of blacks. Anxious whites even sought to legalize a restrictive housing pattern. In 1910 citizens of Baltimore, unhappy because a portion of the northwest residential area known as Druid Hill had been converted into a black neighborhood, called protest meetings that led to a municipal ordinance providing for the official designation of all-white and all-black street blocks. In the next six years, similar laws were adopted in Richmond,

Louisville, Norfolk, St. Louis, and Oklahoma City. When the United States
Supreme Court ruled against such measures, white homeowners turned
to the restrictive covenant, which was written directly into the individual
deed. And if that did not work, violence was a last resort. As William M.
Tuttle, Jr., points out in his essay "Contested Neighborhoods and Racial
Violence," fire-bombings were common in Chicago during and after
World War I. The tension resulted in a vicious riot in 1919 which left
twenty-three blacks and fifteen whites dead.

Conditions did not improve in the 1920s, and the recommendations of
the Chicago Commission on Race Relations in 1922 were quietly shelved.
Blacks did not forget what it meant to be denied equal treatment. The
plight of the black man in America was bitterly described by
one of the main characters in Curtis Lucas' novel *Third Ward Newark*,
published in 1946:

Hunger makes hustlers and double crossers and Uncle Toms out of anybody. White
people are the same way, only they're on top and they can say to us, "Do this, or do
that, or starve." They got us by our breadbaskets and that's where it counts most.
It goes on like this year after year. It's like this all over this goddamned country.

10. THE LOWER EAST SIDE

Moses Rischin

From their homes they come rosy-cheeked and with health and Spring. They have had little fish, little meat, little bread, and it is to get more that they come hither. But they have had air and light. . . . Air and light, and water have been from all time the heritage of man and even of the animals.

Evening Journal (1903)

By the first decade of the twentieth century, the Lower East Side had become an immigrant Jewish cosmopolis. Five major varieties of Jews lived there, "a seething human sea, fed by streams, streamlets, and rills of immigration flowing from all the Yiddish-speaking centers of Europe." Clustered in their separate Jewries, they were set side by side in a pattern suggesting the cultural, if not the physical, geography of the Old World. Hungarians were settled in the northernmost portion above Houston Street, along the numbered streets between Avenue B and the East River, once indisputably *Kleindeutschland*. Galicians lived to the south, between Houston and Broome, east of Clinton, on Attorney, Ridge, Pitt, Willett, and the cross streets. To the west lay the most congested Rumanian quarter, "in the very thick of the battle for breath," on Chrystie, Forsyth, Eldridge, and Allen streets, flanked by Houston Street to the north and Grand Street to the south, with the Bowery gridironed by the overhead elevated to the west. After 1907 Levantines, last on the scene and even stranger than the rest, for they were alien to Yiddish, settled between Allen and Chrystie streets among the Rumanians with whom they seemed to have the closest affinity. The remainder of the great Jewish quarter, from Grand Street reaching south to Monroe, was the preserve of the Russians—those from Russian Poland, Lithuania, Byelorussia, and the Ukraine—the most numerous and heterogeneous of the Jewries of eastern Europe.

The leading streets of the Lower East Side reflected this immigrant transformation. Its most fashionable thoroughfare, East Broadway, bisected the district. To the north lay crammed tenements, business, and industry. To the south lay less crowded quarters where private dwellings, front courtyards, and a scattering of shade trees recalled a time when Henry, Madison, Rutgers, and Jefferson street addresses were stylish.

Reprinted by permission of the publishers from *The Promised City: New York's Jews, 1870–1914* (Cambridge, Mass.: Harvard University Press, 1962), chap. 5, pp. 76–94. Copyright 1962 by the President and Fellows of Harvard College. The author's notes have been deleted.

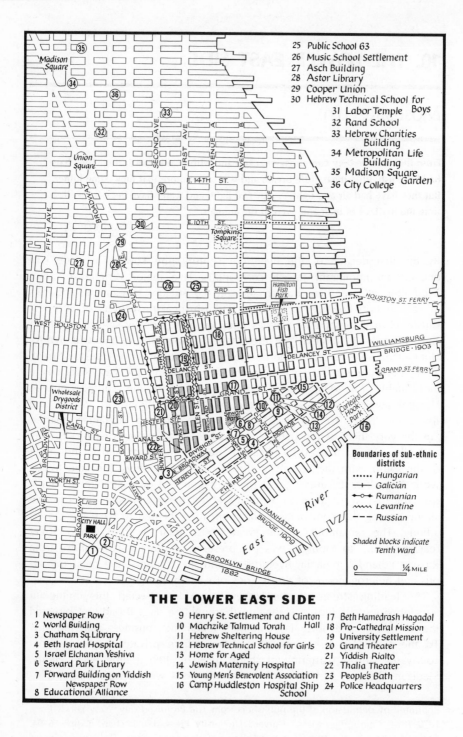

25 Public School 63
26 Music School Settlement
27 Asch Building
28 Astor Library
29 Cooper Union
30 Hebrew Technical School for Boys
31 Labor Temple
32 Rand School
33 Hebrew Charities Building
34 Metropolitan Life Building
35 Madison Square Garden
36 City College

Boundaries of sub-ethnic districts

······ Hungarian
———†— Galician
●—○—● Rumanian
〰〰〰 Levantine
— — — Russian

Shaded blocks indicate Tenth Ward

0   ¼ MILE

THE LOWER EAST SIDE

1 Newspaper Row
2 World Building
3 Chatham Sq. Library
4 Beth Israel Hospital
5 Israel Elchanan Yeshiva
6 Seward Park Library
7 Forward Building on Yiddish Newspaper Row
8 Educational Alliance
9 Henry St. Settlement and Clinton Hall
10 Machzike Talmud Torah
11 Hebrew Sheltering House
12 Hebrew Technical School for Girls
13 Home for Aged
14 Jewish Maternity Hospital
15 Young Men's Benevolent Association
16 Camp Huddleston Hospital Ship School
17 Beth Hamedrash Hagadol
18 Pro-Cathedral Mission
19 University Settlement
20 Grand Theater
21 Yiddish Rialto
22 Thalia Theater
23 People's Bath
24 Police Headquarters

The Russian intelligentsia, for whom the Lower East Side was New York, fancied East Broadway as New York's Nevsky Prospect, St. Petersburg's grand boulevard. In addition to the physicians and dentists who occupied the comfortable brownstone fronts that lined its shaded curbs, an ever-growing number of public and communal buildings came to endow it with a magisterial air. By the second decade of the twentieth century, the ten-story edifice of the *Jewish Daily Forward*, set off by Seward Park on Yiddish Newspaper Row, loomed commandingly over the two Carnegie-built libraries, the Educational Alliance, the Home for the Aged, the Jewish Maternity Hospital, the Machzike Talmud Torah, the Hebrew Sheltering House, the Young Men's Benevolent Association, and a host of lesser institutions.

Only second to East Broadway was Grand Street. Long a leading traffic artery and a major retail shopping center of lower New York, Grand Street fell into eclipse after the turn of the century with the widening of the Delancey Street approach to the Williamsburg Bridge and the comparative decline in ferry traffic. Grand Street's popular department stores, Lord and Taylor's, Lichtenstein's, and O'Neill's, moved uptown, and Ridley's closed, leaving the way open for conquest by the newcomers. Bustling Delancey Street lined with naphtha-lit stalls crammed with tubs of fish; Hester Street with its agents on their way to becoming bankers after the example of Jarmulowsky's passage and exchange office; and the Bowery, with the largest savings bank in the world, symbolized the district's new retail character.

Only after 1870 did the Lower East Side begin to acquire an immigrant Jewish cast. In the early years of the century a small colony of Jewish immigrants had lived there. Dutch, German, and Polish Jews had settled on Bayard, Baxter, Mott, and Chatham streets in the 1830s and 1840s. Shortly thereafter, German and Bohemian Jews took up quarters in the Grand Street area to the northeast and subsequently Jews of the great German migration augmented their numbers. Except for highly visible store fronts, Jews made little impress on the dominantly German and Irish neighborhood. But practically all east European immigrants arriving after 1870 initially found their way to the Lower East Side. Virtually penniless upon their arrival in the city, they were directed to the Jewish districts by representatives of the immigrant aid societies, or came at the behest of friends, relatives, or employers.

The changes brought about by the great Jewish migration forced the district's middle-class Germans and Irish, living in predominantly two- and two-and-one-half-story dwellings, to retreat to less crowded quarters. By 1890 the Lower East Side bristled with Jews. The tenth ward (loosely coinciding with the Eighth Assembly District), closest to the central factory area, was the most crowded with 523.6 inhabitants per acre; the adjacent wards, the thirteenth and seventh, numbered 428.6 and 289.7 persons per acre respectively. Exceeding 700 persons per acre by 1900, the tenth ward was the most densely settled spot in the city; residential block density was even more appalling as factories and shops crowded tenements. In 1896 a private census counted 60 cigar shops, 172 garment shops, 65 factories, and 34 laundries in the tenth ward. In 1906, of fifty-one blocks in the city with over 3,000 inhabitants each, thirty-seven were on the Lower East Side. On Rivington Street, Arnold Bennett remarked, "the architecture seemed to sweat humanity at every window and door." Hardy, older, or improvident remnants of the region's earlier Irish residents and a floating seafaring population still clung to the river edges along Cherry and Water streets; at the turn of the century, Italian immigrants crossed the Bowery on Stanton and East Houston streets and crowded into the lower reaches of East Broadway. But in the second decade of the new century, the Lower East Side, from the Bowery to within a stone's throw of the East River, and from Market Street to 14th Street, had become a mass settlement of Jews, the most densely packed quarter in the city. In 1914 one sixth of the city's population was domiciled below 14th Street upon one eighty-second of the city's land area; most of New York's office buildings, and factories that employed over one half of the city's industrial workers were located in this district.

Once the immigrants had come to rest on the Lower East Side, there was little incentive to venture further. Knowing no English and with few resources, they were dependent upon the apparel industries, the tobacco and cigar trades, and other light industrial employments that sprang up in the area or that were located in the adjacent factory district. Long hours, small wages, seasonal employment, and the complexity of their religious and social needs rooted them to the spot. It was essential to husband energies, earnings, and time. Lodgings of a sort, coffee morning and evening, and laundry service were available to single men for three dollars a month. Bread at two and three cents a pound, milk at four cents a quart, a herring for a penny or two, and apples at from one to five for a cent, depending on quality, were to be had. Accustomed to a slim diet, an immigrant could save much even with meager earnings and still treat himself to a bracing three-course Sabbath dinner (for fifteen cents). Thrift and hard work would, he hoped, enable him in time to search out more congenial and independent employment. Until new sections of the city were developed at the turn of the century only country peddlers were to stray permanently beyond the familiar immigrant quarters.

There was a compelling purpose to the pinched living. Virtually all immigrants saved to purchase steamship tickets for loved ones and many regularly mailed clothing and food parcels to dependent parents, wives, and children overseas. The power of home ties buoyed up the spirits of immigrants wedded to the sweatshop and peddler's pack, whose precious pennies mounted to sums that would unite divided families. Among the early comers women were relatively few, but the imbalance between the sexes soon was remedied. In 1890 an investigation by the Baron de Hirsch Society into the condition of 111,690 of an estimated 135,000 Jews on the Lower East Side counted 60,313 children and 22,647 wage earners, with 28,730 unspecified, mostly women. Undoubtedly, the proportion of women and children in New York was far greater than it was elsewhere. In 1910 women exceeded men among Hungarians and Rumanians, were equal among Austrians, and made up 47 percent of the Russians. As non-Jews from these countries were heavily male, Jewish women clearly outnumbered men, accentuating the group's domesticity. Among the major ethnic groups of New York, only the Irish, 58 percent female, exceeded the Jewish ratio.

A nondescript colony of Jews in the 1870s swelled into a center of Jewish life by the turn of the century, the drama of whose fortunes and passions was closely followed by fellow immigrants throughout the country as well as by those in the lands they left behind. A highly visible knot of Jews "huddled up together" around Baxter and Chatham streets had been engulfed by an influx that saturated the whole region with its flavor and institutions.

THE TENEMENT BOOM

Ever since the 1830s New York's housing problem had been acute. Manhattan's space limitations exacerbated all the evils inherent in overcrowding, and refinements in the use of precious ground only emphasized the triumph of material necessities over human considerations. New York's division of city lots into standard rectangular plots, 25 feet wide by 100 feet deep, made decent human accommodations impossible. In order to secure proper light and ventilation for tenement dwellers twice the space was needed, a prohibitive sacrifice considering real estate values. No opportunity was overlooked to facilitate the most economical and compact housing of the immigrant population. To the improvised tenements that had been carved out of private dwellings were added the front and rear tenements and, finally, the dumbbell-style tenement of 1879.

With the heavy Jewish migration of the early 1890s, the Lower East Side, still relatively undeveloped compared to the Lower West Side, became the special domain of the new dumbbell tenements, so called because of their shape. The six- to seven-story dumbbell usually included four apartments to the floor, two on either side of the separating corridor. The front apartments generally contained four rooms each, the rear apartments three. Only one room in each apartment received direct light and air from the street or from the ten feet of required yard space in the rear. On the ground floor two stores generally were to be found; the living quarters behind each had windows only on the air shaft. The air shaft, less than five feet in width and from fifty to sixty feet in length, separated the tenement buildings. In the narrow hallways were located that special improvement, common water closets. In 1888 a leading magazine described typical dumbbell tenements on Ridge, Eldridge, and Allen streets.

They are great prison-like structures of brick, with narrow doors and windows, cramped passages and steep rickety stairs. They are built through from one street to the other with a somewhat narrower building connecting them . . . The narrow court-yard . . . in the middle is a damp foul-smelling place, supposed to do duty as an airshaft; had the foul fiend designed these great barracks they could not have been more villainously arranged to avoid any chance of ventilation . . . In case of fire they would be perfect death-traps, for it would be impossible for the occupants of the crowded rooms to escape by the narrow stairways, and the flimsy fire-escapes which the owners of the tenements were compelled to put up a few years ago are so laden with broken furniture, bales and boxes that they would be worse than useless. In the hot summer months . . . these fire-escape balconies are used as sleeping-rooms by the poor wretches who are fortunate enough to have windows opening upon them. The drainage is horrible, and even the Croton as it flows from the tap in the noisome courtyard, seemed to be contaminated by its surroundings and have a fetid smell.

As if the tenement abuses were not degrading enough, the absence of public toilet facilities in so crowded a district added to the wretched sanitation. It was reported that "in the evening every dray or wagon becomes a private and public lavatory, and the odor and stench . . . is perfectly horrible."

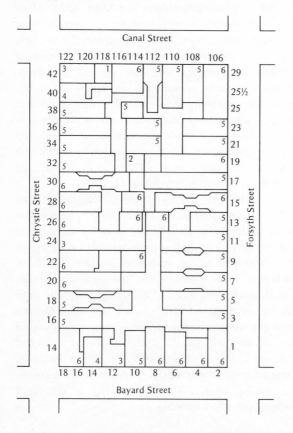

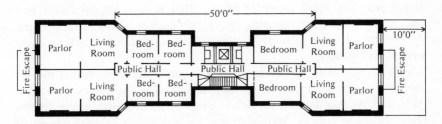

A typical dumbbell tenement

Conditions became almost unendurable in the summer months. Bred in colder and dryer climates, tenement inhabitants writhed in the dull heat. Added to the relentless sun were the emanations from coal stoves, the flat flame gas jets in lamps, and the power-producing steam boilers. Inevitably, roofs, fire escapes, and sidewalks were converted into sleeping quarters, while the grassed enclosure dividing Delancey Street and Seward Park supplied additional dormitory space. Late July and early August of 1896 were especially savage. Between August 5 and 13, 420 New Yorkers perished from the continuous heat, "the absolute stagnation of the air, and the oppressive humidity," noted Daniel Van Pelt, although the temperature averaged 90.7 degrees and never reached 100.

Fire and the possibilities of fire brought added terror to the inhabitants of overcrowded tenements. "Remember that you live in a tenement house," warned insurance agents. In 1903, 15 percent of the tenements in the district still were without fire escapes. Of 257 fatalities in Manhattan fires between 1902 and 1909, 99, or 38 percent, were on the Lower East Side, all victims of old-law tenements.

Few families could afford the privacy of a three- or four-room flat. Only with the aid of lodgers or boarders could the $10 to $20 monthly rental be sustained. The extent of overcrowding in the tenements, reported a witness before the United States Immigration Commission, was never fully known.

At the hour of retiring, cots or folded beds and in many instances simply mattresses are spread about the floor, resembling very much a lot of bunks in the steerage of an ocean steamer ... The only way to properly determine the census of one of these tenements, would be by a midnight visit, and should this take place between the months of June and September, the roof of the building should not be omitted.

However trying tenement living proved to be for adults, for children it was stultifying, concluded a settlement worker. "The earlier years of the child are spent in an atmosphere which . . . is best described by a little girl, 'a place so dark it seemed as if there weren't no sky.' "

Evictions for nonpayment of rent and rent strikes were perennial. Uncertainty of employment, nonpayment of wages, unexpected obligations, dependents, and adversities contributed to the high incidence of evictions.

In the year 1891–1892 alone, in two judicial districts of the Lower East Side, 11,550 dispossess warrants were issued by the presiding magistrates. In 1900 the absence of mass evictions was regarded as a mark of unexampled well-being.

Earlier residents of the Lower East Side and hereditary property owners profited from the overcrowding. The rise in real estate values, exorbitant rents, and the low upkeep provided tenement owners with ample returns upon their investments. Even allowing for losses due to nonpayment of rent and an average occupancy of ten months in the year, landlords earned 10 percent. By more studied neglect, a resourceful agent might reap even higher returns. The Lower East Side tenements soon came to be recognized as the most lucrative investment in the city. Nowhere else did the speculator's market in tenement properties flourish as luxuriantly as it did here, where earlier immigrants had learned to exploit the misery of later comers.

In 1901 the further construction of dumbbell tenements was prohibited. The Tenement House Law of that year set new standards for future housing and attempted to correct the worst abuses in the existing buildings. All new tenements were to have windows that opened at least twelve feet away from those opposite. Toilets and running water in each apartment, unobstructed fire escapes, and solid staircases were required. In the old buildings modern water closets were to be installed in place of the outside privies. Finally, a Tenement House Department was established to supervise and enforce the provisions of the law. While the law never was effectively enforced, its initial achievements proved encouraging.

Many new tenements were quickly built according to the new specifications. In the fiscal year ending July 1, 1903, 43 percent of New York's new tenements were located on the Lower East Side. Its inhabitants eagerly welcomed the brightly lighted rooms, bathtubs, and other improvements. At first, landlords on the Lower East Side were more prompt to make alterations in old-law tenements than landlords elsewhere in the city, for the heavy pressure of population made even remodeled properties attractive. The years 1905 to 1909 saw an unparalleled boom throughout the city with houses to fit every taste, from tenements to palatial mansions for chance customers, at unprecedented prices ranging up to $500,000. "It is doubtful if New York City, or in fact any other city of the world, ever before witnessed the expenditure of so many millions of dollars in the construction of tenement houses during a similar period."

While new housing was on the rise, the fast-developing clothing trades also were relocating and building. As the heavy settlement of East Europeans decisively affected the housing of the city's earlier residents, so the new growth of the apparel industry, manned by Lower East Side Jews, helped to transform the city's business districts. Once legislation and the advent of electric power combined to reduce Lower East Side sweatshops, thousands of garment shops and factories pushed up the axial thoroughfares of Lower Manhattan. By 1910 the continued march uptown found the garment industry intruding upon once fashionable Madison Square, the site of New York's tallest skyscrapers. Brownstones and brick residences were razed to be displaced by sixteen- to twenty-story steel-girdered loft buildings trimmed with granite and marble and housing scores of clothing shops. In the course of this displacement, the city's central retailing district and its theater and hotel district were forced northward. The main retailing center, at 14th Street in 1880 and at 23rd Street in 1900, became anchored at 34th Street by 1910.

DISEASE AND CRIME

Superficially, East European Jews seemed ill-prepared to contend with the demands that tenement living thrust upon them. "Their average stature is from five feet one inch to five feet three inches, which means that they are the most stunted of the Europeans, with the exception of the Hungarian Magyars." Shortest were the Galicians; tallest and sturdiest, the Rumanians. Undersized and narrow-chested, a high proportion were described as "physical wrecks." Centuries of confinement, habituation to mental occupations, chronic undernourishment, and a deprecation of the physical virtues ill-fitted them for heavy labor. Between 1887 and 1890 nearly five thousand immigrants were returned to Europe labeled physically "unfit for work." Seemingly helpless and emaciated, they were to exhibit exceptional capacity for regeneration; traditional moral and religious disciplines were to serve them in good stead.

Despite the trying conditions under which the immigrants lived, they showed a remarkable resistance to disease. With the highest average density of tenants per house in the city, the tenth ward had one of the lowest death rates. Indeed only a business ward and a suburban ward surpassed it in healthfulness. Dr. Annie Daniel, a pioneer in public health, volunteered her interpretation of this before the Tenement House Committee:

The rules of life which orthodox Hebrews so unflinchingly obey as laid down in the Mosaic code . . . are designed to maintain health. These rules are applied to the daily life of the individuals as no other sanitary laws can be . . . Food must be cooked properly, and hence the avenues through which the germs of disease may enter are destroyed. Meat must be "kosher," and this means that it must be perfectly healthy. Personal cleanliness is at times strictly compelled, and at least one day in the week the habitation must be thoroughly cleaned.

True, only some 8 percent of Russian Jewish families had baths, according to a study of 1902, and these often without hot water. Yet the proliferation of privately owned bathhouses in the city was attributed largely to the Jewish tenement population. "I cannot get along without a 'sweat' (Russian bath) at least once a week," insisted a newcomer. In 1880, one or two of New York's twenty-two bathhouses were Jewish; by 1897, over half of the city's sixty-two bathhouses (including Russian, Turkish, swimming, vapor, and medicated bathhouses) were Jewish. If standards of cleanliness were not as faithfully maintained as precept required, the strict regimen of orthodoxy, even when weakened, contributed to the immigrant's general well-being.

Nevertheless, close crowding and unsanitary conditions made all communicable diseases potentially contagious. Despite great apprehension between 1892 and 1894, Jewish immigrants did not carry to New York the cholera and typhus epidemics raging at the European ports of embarkation. But in 1899 the United Hebrew Charities became alarmed by the Board of Health's report of the mounting incidence of tuberculosis in the city. That Jewish immigrants might become easy victims of the "White Plague" was hardly to be doubted. "As many as 119 Jewish families have lived in one tenement house on Lewis Street within the past five years." Hundreds of flats had been occupied by fifteen successive families within a brief period. "Many of these houses are known to be hotbeds of the disease, the very walls reeking with it." Increasingly, the dread disease with its cough and crimson spittle took its toll. Ernest Poole, an investigator, frequently heard the plea of the afflicted. "Luft, gibt mir luft—Air, give me air." Especially susceptible were the intellectuals, whose often shattered spirits, overwrought minds, and undernourished bodies fell prey to the killer. Yet so great was the immigrant's concern for health that the mortality rate from tuberculosis was lower on the East Side than in the city's prosperous districts. Venereal diseases, previously almost unknown among Jews in Eastern Europe, became progressively more common among young men, as restraints were weakened by exposure to new temptations.

Alcoholism, a prime contributor to poverty, ill-health, and mortality among other national groups, was unusual among Jewish immigrants. As Jews replaced the earlier inhabitants, the many saloons of the Lower East Side, trimmed with shields that proclaimed them "the workman's friend," declined. Those that survived drew few clients from a neighborhood addicted to soda water, "the life-giving drink"; they depended on the throng of transients that passed through the district. Jews did not abstain from drink. Yet only upon religious festivals and during the Sabbath ritual when the Kiddush cup was emptied did alcohol appear in the diet of most immigrants. In 1908, $1.50 a year for holiday and ritual wine seemed adequate for a family of six. "The Day of Rejoicing of the Law and the Day of Purim are the only two days in the year when an orthodox Jew may be intoxicated. It is virtuous on these days to drink too much, but the sobriety of the Jew is so great that he sometimes cheats his friends and himself by shamming drunkenness," Hutchins Hapgood noted. Jews habitually imbibed milder beverages. Russians were notorious tea drinkers. Hungarians were addicted to coffee. The less austere Galicians and Rumanians tippled mead and wine respectively. But in the New World all fell victim to the craze for seltzer or soda water with its purported health-giving powers. In his long experience, reported the president of the United Hebrew Charities in 1892, he had known only three chronic Jewish drunkards.

Neurasthenia and hysteria, however, took a heavy toll of victims. Their sickness was the result of a history of continual persecution and insecurity, intensified by the strains of settlement in unfamiliar surroundings. Diabetes, associated with perpetual nervous strain, was common. Suicide, rarely recorded among the small-town Jews of Eastern Europe, also found its victims in the tenements of New York. Despair, poverty, and the fears generated in the imagination led some immigrants to take their own lives. "Genumen di gez" (took gas) was not an uncommon headline in the Yiddish press. Yet in the late 1880s only the city's Irish showed a lower suicide rate than did Russian Jews.

However desperate the straits in which Jewish immigrants found themselves, confirmed paupers among them were few. The rarity of alcoholism, the pervasiveness of the charitable impulse, the strength of ties to family and *lanslite,* and a deep current of optimism preserved the individual from such degradation.

Prior to the 1880s only the Rubinstein murder case spotted the record of New York's Jews. Upon the testimony of doubtful witnesses, Rubinstein was sentenced to death for the slaying of his girl cousin, but cheated the hangman by taking his own life. The first crime of violence attributed to a Jew in the city's annals, its very novelty gave rise to the popular street song, "My name is Pesach Rubinstein." So unassailable was the peaceful reputation of the Jewish districts that it was a matter for continual commendation. In 1878 Jews numbered 7 in a workhouse population of 1,178; 8 among 485 prison inmates; and 12 among 1,110 house-of-correction inmates.

The obloquy attached to the strident Jews of Baxter and Chatham streets; to the Canal Street clothing shop puller-in and the Division Street millinery shop pulleress; to Michael Kurtz, better known as "Sheeney Mike," reputedly the "champion burglar of America"; and to "Marm" Mandelbaum, unmatched receiver of stolen goods, did not detract from the high repute of the city's Jews. The two dozen Bowery pawnshops were owned by Americans or earlier immigrants who catered to the needs of a heterogeneous population and were not part of the immigrant community.

The major crime and violence in the area did not stem from the immigrants. They were its victims. The Lower East Side had always attracted much of the city's criminal element to its margins. By the last decades of the nineteenth century, it had shed the ferocity of earlier years when the "Bowery B'hoys" and the "Dead Rabbits" terrorized the area. But Mayor Hewitt's reform drive in 1887 inadvertently reinforced the district's frailties by forcing criminals and prostitutes from their accustomed uptown resorts into the less conspicuous tenements of the tenth ward, where they remained, undisturbed even by the Parkhurst crusade. The Raines Law, which provided that only hotels could serve liquor on Sundays, worsened the situation. In 1896, of 236 saloons in the tenth ward, 118 were Raines Law hotels, while 18 were outright houses of prostitution. In the first decade of the twentieth century, crusading District Attorney William Travers Jerome kept open house in his special office on Rutgers Street, at the hub of the Lower East Side, and the most salient features of criminality were forced underground. By 1905 the "peripatetic sisterhood" had been driven from the Bowery, and Captain Godard's Anti-Policy Society's campaign banished gambling from the thoroughfare. But the criminal elements soon returned.

Crime was endemic to the Lower East Side. The close collaboration between police officers, politicians, and criminals, revealed in detail in the Lexow and Mazet investigations of the 1890s, had turned the district into a Klondike that replaced the uptown Tenderloin as a center of graft and illicit business. Invariably the culprits in these activities were not immigrants, but Americanized Jews learned in street-corner ways and shorn of the restraints of the immigrant generation. "It is not until they have become Americanized, have adapted themselves to the environment of the district and adopted its ways and vices, that they become full-fledged wretches," commented Dr. I. L. Nascher. In the early years of the twentieth century the effect of such conditions upon the young deeply disturbed those anxious for the public weal. In 1909 some 3,000 Jewish children were brought before Juvenile Court and in the next few years Jewish criminals regularly made newspaper headlines. The appearance of an ungovernable youth after the turn of the century was undeniable and excited apprehension.

The violations of the law that characterized the immigrant community differed from the crimes of the sons of the immigrants. The former were an outgrowth of occupational overcrowding, poverty, and religious habits. Straitened circumstances contributed to the large number of cases of family desertion and nonsupport. Concentrated in marginal commerce and industry, Jews were prone to transgress the codes of commercial law. "The prevalence of a spirit of enterprise out of proportion to the capital of the community" gave rise to a high incidence of felonious larceny, forgery, and failure to pay wages. Peddlers and petty shopkeepers were especially vulnerable to police oppression for evading informal levies as well as formal licensing requirements. Legislation controlling business on Sunday found Jewish immigrants natural victims. In so congested a district, the breaking of corporation ordinances was unavoidable and the slaughtering of chickens in tenements in violation of the sanitary code proved to be a distinctly Jewish infraction.

The Bowery, way station of derelicts, transients, and unsuspecting immigrants, attracted the less stable and wary of the immigrant girls. The dancing academies that sprang to popularity in the first decade of the twentieth century snared impetuous, friendless young women. Lured by promises of marriage, they soon were trapped by procurers for the notorious Max Hochstim Association and other white slavers who preyed upon the innocent and the unsuspecting. The appearance of prostitution, previously rare among Jewesses, alarmed the East Side.

The Lower East Side, girded by the Bowery with its unsavory establishments and Water Street with its resorts of ill-fame that catered to the seafaring trade, was surrounded by violence. Bearded Jews often were viciously assaulted by young hoodlums, both non-Jews and Jews, the area adjacent to the waterfront being especially dangerous. In 1898 and 1899, the newly organized American Hebrew League of Brooklyn protested a rash of outrages in the wake of the Dreyfus affair. Nevertheless there was only one instance of mass violence: the riot of July 30, 1902 at the funeral of Rabbi Jacob Joseph. This incident, the only one of its kind, can be attributed to the stored-up resentment of the Irish who were being forced out of the area by the incursion of Jews.

SIGNS OF CHANGE

Gradually the miseries and trials of adjustment were left behind. For those who had inhabited the hungry villages of Eastern Europe, the hovels of Berditchev, and the crammed purlieus of Vilna and Kovno, the factories and sweatshops of New York provided a livelihood and possible stepping-stone. Despite unsteady and underpaid employment, tenement overcrowding and filth, immigrants felt themselves ineluctably being transformed. The Lower East Side, with its purposeful vitality, found no analogue in the "leprous-looking ghetto familiar in Europe," commented the visiting Abbé Félix Klein. Physical surroundings, however sordid, could be transcended. Optimism and hope engulfed every aspect of immigrant life. For a people who had risen superior to the oppressions of medieval proscriptions, the New York slums acted as a new-found challenge. Each passing year brought improvements that could be measured and appraised. Cramped quarters did not constrict aspirations. "In a large proportion of the tenements of the East Side . . . pianos are to be seen in the dingy rooms." And soon the phonograph was everywhere. "Excepting among the recent arrivals, most of the Jewish tenement dwellers have fair and even good furniture in their homes."

The East Europeans began to venture beyond the boundaries of the Lower East Side into other areas where employment was available on terms compatible with religious habits. Brooklyn's German Williamsburg district, directly across the East River, where Central European Jews had been established for some decades, was settled early. In the late 1880s a few clothing contractors set up sweatshops in the languid Scottish settlement of Brownsville, south and east of Williamsburg. The depression delayed further expansion for a decade despite the extension of the Fulton Street El in 1889. Then the tide could not be stemmed. Between 1899 and 1904 Brownsville's population rose from 10,000 to 60,000. Land values soared as immigrants came at the rate of 1,000 per week. Lots selling for $200 in 1899 brought $5,000 to $10,000 five years later. As the real-estate boom revolutionized land values, many a former tailor was suddenly transformed into a substantial landlord or realtor who disdained all contact with shears and needles of bitter memory.

The mass dispersion of Jews from the Lower East Side to other parts of the city was in full swing in the early 1890s, as the more prosperous pioneers hastened to settle among their German coreligionists in Yorkville between 72nd and 100th streets, east of Lexington Avenue. For many a rising immigrant family in this period of swift change, it was judged to be a ten-year trek from Hester Street to Lexington Avenue.

The unprecedented flow of immigrants into the old central quarter, exorbitant rents, and the demolition of old tenements incidental to the building of parks, schools, and bridge approaches drastically reduced the area's absorptive capacity and spurred the search for new quarters. The construction of the Delancey Street approach to the Williamsburg Bridge in 1903 displaced 10,000 persons alone. The consolidation of the city and the growth and extension of rapid transit facilities connected what were once remote districts with the central downtown business quarters. In the new developments, cheaper land made possible lower rents that compensated for the time and expense of commuting. On Manhattan Island, the construction of underground transit opened to mass settlement the Dyckman tract in Washington Heights and the Harlem flats. The new subway also opened the East Bronx to extensive housing development. In Brooklyn, in addition to the heavy concentrations in Brownsville, Williamsburg, and South Brooklyn, Boro Park with "tropical gardens" and "parks" became increasingly accessible. Even distant Coney Island was brought into range by improved transit facilities.

With 542,061 inhabitants in 1910, the Lower East Side reached peak congestion. Thereafter, a decline set in. By 1916 only 23 percent of the city's Jews lived in the once primary area of Jewish settlement, compared to 50 percent in 1903 and 75 percent in 1892. By the close of the first decade of the twentieth century the Lower East Side had lost much of its picturesqueness. In tone and color, the ghetto was perceptibly merging with the surrounding city. East European Jews had scattered to many sections of the city and were swiftly becoming an integral, if not as yet a fully accepted, element in the life of the community.

In 1870 the Jews of New York were estimated at 80,000, or less than 9 percent of the city's inhabitants. By 1915 they totaled close to 1,400,000 persons (nearly 28 percent), a number larger than the city's total population in 1870. Before 1880 the Jews of the city were hardly more than a subject for idle curiosity. But thereafter, the flow of East European Jews quickened the city's industrial life, helped to transform its physical shape, and contributed a varied and malleable people to the metropolis. Despite poverty and great numbers, these immigrants created no new problems. But their presence accentuated New York's shortcomings in the face of unprecedented demands upon its imagination and resources. In the early years of the new century, their voice would be heard. The problems of industrial relations and urban living accentuated on the Lower East Side were to become the focus for major reforms.

11. ETHNIC GROUP ASSIMILATION
The Italian Experience

Humbert S. Nelli

I

In the decades between 1880 and World War I, European immigrants and their children comprised the major part of the population of the large industrial cities of the East and Middle West. Concerned contemporaries saw in this mass of human beings a preponderance of gangsters, paupers, illiterate peasants and illegal contract laborers, packed together into colonies where they poisoned American life with their Old World habits and aggravated urban problems with their teeming families. Few observers saw that their location in the city profoundly affected the newcomers themselves.

In 1880, some 12,400 Italians entered the United States; by 1900, the yearly minimum from Italy totaled 100,000 and it soared to a peak of 285,731 in 1907. The earliest Italian immigrants came from the northern parts of the peninsula. The flood of migrants leaving southern Italy and Sicily reached its greatest proportions after the turn of the century: between 1899 and 1910, when 372,668 northern Italians reached the United States, 1,911,933 arrived from the southern regions.[1]

The pattern of Italian settlement in cities east of the Mississippi and north of the Ohio began with the founding of the immigrant community by northern Italians, who tended to predominate until the 1880s. The original enclave started in or near the center city—that is, the business area—and was characterized by the movement of economically successful newcomers out of the ethnic district and into the wider American community. New arrivals from overseas swarmed into the colony, filling vacancies and creating or contributing to overcrowded, rapidly deteriorating neighborhoods.[2]

In general, the settlement patterns in Chicago typified the Italian experience in urban America. Northern Italians, most of them from Genoa and Tuscany, formed the early colony in the years after 1850. Whether from the northern provinces or from the southern areas and Sicily, newcomers at first settled along the same streets and in the same tenements, and sought jobs where others from their own province worked. This early concentration broke down as the immigrants met and mingled with newcomers from other towns and provinces and with non-Italians who lived and worked in close proximity. In the process, they began for the first time to think of themselves as Italians rather than as members of a particular family. Whereas in Sicily and southern Italy life centered around family needs and goals, in the United States the family was neither large enough nor sufficiently powerful to ensure aid in all emergencies. Hence in this new world a community identity and an ethnic consciousness evolved, one that bore little resemblance to the family-dominated society of the Italian South. Rather than being an importation, this community feeling and awareness of being Italian developed in the United States as a response to changed surroundings.[3]

The community of the immigrant generation served as a staging ground where newcomers remained until they absorbed new ideas and values that facilitated their adjustment to urban America. It thus fulfilled a vital function both for its inhabitants and for the receiving society by bridging the gap between rural traditions and the city. Italians lived and worked in this community with compatriots from all parts of the Kingdom, as well as with Irish, Germans, Poles, Scandinavians, and others; many went to church with these "foreigners," and their children attended the same schools. In contrast to the homeland tradition of seeking a spouse from the same place of birth, they began to intermarry with "outsiders" from elsewhere in Italy.

Continuing the pattern set by their northern predecessors, southern Italians and Sicilians whose economic position improved moved away from the colony. If migration from the ethnic settlement—a sign of economic mobility and an indication of a desire for better housing and living conditions—did not take place in the first generation, it generally occurred in the second or third. Contemporary American observers, who did not realize that successive waves of newcomers filled the vacancies left by departing immigrants, concluded that Italians, their children and their grandchildren after them, remained on the same streets and in the same tenements from the time they arrived until they died. Americans also assumed that compact, unchanging colonies remained grouped according to place of origin—as, indeed, they were during the early years of immigration. This cohesion, however, soon broke down. The composition of Italian colonies (like that of other ethnic groups) was in constant flux, with at least half the community changing place of residence each year, some to other housing within the colony, others to entirely different areas.

Contrary to popular belief, Chicago, like other urban localities, contained few blocks inhabited exclusively by Italians, and even fewer such neighborhoods. Between 1890 and 1920, only limited sections of certain Chicago streets held a 50 percent or higher concentration of Italian immigrants and their children. The population density of Italians in most of the city's various Italian districts fell considerably below 50 percent. Even the Near West Side community in the vicinity of Hull House, which between 1880 and 1920 made up the largest and most heavily concentrated Italian group in the city, had only a few blocks where Italians constituted

50 to 70 percent of the inhabitants; and they made up only one-third of the area's total population. Nevertheless, newspapers, social workers and the general public characterized this community, and others like it, as "Italian."

Observers of immigrant life in Chicago and other cities ignored or did not recognize the gradual shift in the location of Italian districts. Thus the area discussed in one study often differed from that in another, even though the colony in both instances might be labeled "the West Side" or "the North Side" community. And because the composition of Italian districts underwent rapid and continual change, the miserable, poorly fed residents described in one survey probably were not the same people examined in subsequent studies of the same area.

II

Americans concerned over slums and the self-perpetuating misery in which newly arrived Italians lived sincerely believed that urban difficulties could be alleviated by encouraging immigrants to move to rural areas. Because most of the newcomers had engaged in farm labor in Italy, it seemed logical that they should hope to settle on farms in America. Shifting Italians into agriculture appeared to be "the natural solution of the problem of Italian concentration in the slums," wrote sociologist I. W. Howerth in 1894, "henceforth the tendency of Italians to congregate in large cities will decrease."[4]

To promote the movement of Italians to farms, the Italian and United States governments, individual states, and even private agencies supported the establishment of agricultural colonies throughout the country, and especially in Texas, Arkansas, Mississippi, Louisiana, and Alabama. Despite auspicious beginnings and official support, most of these rural ventures failed. One visitor to an early farming settlement noted not only "poorly constructed houses" with few weatherproof features, where "members of the colony sleep together without distinction as to age and sex," but also a total lack of sanitation facilities and a financial organization whereby the colonists remained "eternally deeply in debt."[5]

Distasteful as these conditions appear, their impact on the immigrants was slight. Robert Foerster has shown that factors like ignorance of opportunity, unfamiliar climate, squalid living conditions, and cost of land did not deter colonists who wanted to farm. In Argentina, for example, Italians overcame similar obstacles and farmed to great advantage, adapting without difficulty to new crops, soils, markets, and living conditions. A more important factor caused immigrant unwillingness to settle in the country in the United States: most Italians simply did not emigrate to North America with hopes or intentions of farming. Like the majority of immigrants to this country, they arrived seeking economic opportunities.

In the last decades of the nineteenth century and the early ones of the twentieth, prospects of financial gain in the United States existed not in agriculture, but in the commercial and industrial centers of the East and Middle West. It was this fact that led to the failure of agricultural colonies. The U.S. Industrial Commission recognized the desire for economic betterment in its summary volume, published in 1902, in which it examined the factors responsible for immigrant concentration in cities. The commission noted first "the general movement of all modern industrial peoples toward urban life—a movement quite characteristic of the American people themselves." For the foreign-born, additional factors reinforced this trend: the isolation of farm life in the United States, in contrast to agricultural areas of Europe; immigrant memories of the "hardships and oppression of rural life from which they are struggling to escape"; and ready employment in cities directly upon arrival and for higher wages than those paid to farm laborers.[6]

Immigrant difficulties in America stemmed from the cultural problem of adjusting to new living patterns, the result of moving from a rural to an urban environment. Contemporaries were convinced that Italians would become Americanized more rapidly in a country setting than they would in a city. Commissioner-General of Immigration Frank Sargent maintained that "if, instead of crowding into our large cities," immigrants would go to farms, "there would be no need to fear for the future." Yet assimilation slows or halts in a rural environment, where the community is forced in upon itself by the lack of outside contacts, and local customs can be preserved almost intact. In cities, on the other hand, the intermingling and outside influences that encourage the assimilation process are inevitable.[7] Adjustment would have been necessary had the Italian villagers migrated to a city in Italy or to some other European city rather than across the Atlantic. And Americans of farming background who moved to urban areas faced many of the same problems encountered by immigrants from Italy.[8]

III

Italians who in Italy never considered the possibility of cooperation with compatriots from other towns and provinces found that in the United States, in the absence of the old family ties and services, they could solve many problems only as members of organized groups. In forming these groups, newcomers modified familiar institutions (like the Church), adapted some that had scarcely touched their lives in Italy (such as the press and mutual benefit societies), and established agencies that did not exist in the home country (notably the immigrant bank). Although some immigrant institutions had counterparts in the Old World, southern Italians and Sicilians generally first came into contact with them in America.

Many newcomers sought to alleviate life's complexities by joining mutual benefit groups. These were not "transplanted" institutions. In southern Italy and Sicily the family provided aid in times of need; group life consisted of a few small and unimportant social clubs featuring recreational activities. By the 1890s, mutual aid groups began to appear in the Italian South and in Sicily (but not in those portions from which emigration flowed) and were closely involved with the growth of labor unions. Societies in the United States concentrated on insurance and social functions, aiding newly arrived immigrants to deal with sickness, loneliness, and death rather than with labor organization. Benefit societies existed in this country before Italians arrived in large numbers, apparently an outgrowth of the English friendly societies, although American groups developed a stronger social and fraternal character. The lodge filled a great social and psychological void for those uprooted from familiar surroundings and life patterns; and the practice of "passing the hat" for unfortunate group members guaranteed help in need at minimum expense for all concerned, at least during the early years of the society when most members were young and vigorous.[9]

Immigrants (and native Americans) who joined mutual benefit organizations contributed small monthly sums, usually between 25 and 60 cents, to guarantee that the group would look after them when they were sick and bury them when they died. Regulations required all members to attend funeral services or pay a fine; thus the organization assured each contributor of a proper burial and a well-attended service. Societies also handled other related activities, particularly the payment of sickness and accident expenses.[10]

At first, societies were formed on the basis of place of origin, either town or province of birth; this basis itself was a significant movement away from Old World distrust of anyone outside the family circle. A number of societies were formed to satisfy political, religious or military needs and desires, and the bases of organization varied—sometimes confining membership to residents of a particular street or building. In time, small units consolidated or joined larger ones, and Italian heritage rather than place of birth or residence became the prerequisite.

The function and value of the immigrant press were temporary, specialized, and vital only so long as a large group needed its services. The press saw itself as an indispensable ally and friend, offering newcomers "wise advice, moral and material assistance, true and ardent fraternal love —for their success and triumph" in a new world.[11] The real contribution of Italian-language journals was on a less exalted but undeniably important level: They eased the first critical years of immigrant adjustment to the United States. Articles about events in Italy and in the home towns and provinces, news of other immigrant communities, reports of societies and listings of collections for needy newcomers—all helped Italian-Americans to develop and nurture a sense of belonging in their new surroundings. Information about local and national American events, emphasis on the importance of education and the benefits accruing from participation in politics, and advice regarding behavior acceptable to

Americans served to point the way toward assimilation in an urban world. The press functioned as a crutch for many immigrants who felt a nostalgia for homeland traditions. To many of the second generation (and a number of self-reliant newcomers), immigrant tabloids offered little of interest or value. Readership therefore reached its height during the first two decades of the twentieth century, the time of arrival of great masses of immigrants desperately in need of the services provided by the press.

During the period of large-scale Italian immigration, the ethnic press copied American newspapers in style and content. To attract attention and hold readers, Italian-language journals featured sensational headlines, brief articles in simple language, specialty columns (concerning opera, events in Italy, the papacy, and other topics of particular interest to readers) and many illustrations. They quickly lost any resemblance to homeland journals. Editors who valued literary excellence over titillating news items, pictures, and frequent protestations of loyalty to Italy quickly went out of business. Because of inadequate staffing, all immigrant journals were filled with typographical errors, slang, plagiarisms and unverified news reports.[12]

Unlike other institutions, the Church existed for newcomers before they left Europe. In Italy the Church formed an integral part of life; in America, Italians found the Church to be a cold, remote, puritanical institution, controlled and often staffed, even in Italian neighborhoods, by the hated Irish. Devout Catholics and atheists alike resented Irish domination of the institution, demanded Italian priests, and sought to control the churches in their communities. Liberals and nationalists decried the Church's opposition to Italian unification and its refusal to recognize the Kingdom of Italy. By 1900, Italians appeared to be so dissatisfied that many Catholics believed the situation posed a serious threat to the Church's future in the United States, and in following years the "Italian problem" became the "biggest Catholic question."[13]

Protestants seized the opportunity to seek converts. They publicly supported the Italian Kingdom and denounced papal intransigence. Some Protestant sects, especially Methodists, Baptists, and Presbyterians, worked actively among Italian immigrants in urban America. They supported 326 churches and missions with more than two hundred pastors, and printed numerous Italian-language newspapers, books, articles, pamphlets, and leaflets in English and Italian.[14] Protestant settlements and missions, evangelizing social workers, public school teachers and ministers all influenced some Italians to turn toward Protestantism. It seemed to be a quick road to Americanization. As one minister proclaimed in 1906, "If the immigrant is evangelized, assimilation is easy and sure." Despite costly and prodigious efforts by non-Catholic churches and settlement houses, however, relatively few Italians converted; those who did usually transferred to congregations in American neighborhoods.[15]

Although most Italian immigrants remained nominally or actually loyal to Catholicism, their loyalty differed from that of other Catholic groups such as the Irish- or Polish-Americans. National consciousness, which developed among all three groups in the United States, strongly influenced ethnic attitudes toward religion. Irish and Polish nationalists saw Catholicism as a central part of their loyalty; for Italians, Catholicism and nationalism exerted opposing forces (at least until the Concordat of 1929). Hence, at the same time that they raged against the Church both in Italy and the United States, Italian-American leaders urged compatriots to support the "Italian church" against Irish "usurpers" and Protestants, and to "stand fast to the traditions of their fathers' religion."[16]

The image worship and simple superstitions that made religion a daily part of life to the unlettered immigrant seemed, to more sophisticated American critics, to indicate an irreligious or pagan attitude. In the same way, observers considered the Italian addiction to festivals, processions, and feasts to be a perversion of religion, although to participants such celebrations formed a basic part of worship and an extension of much-loved homeland traditions. What Americans saw as a falling-away from religion was partly an adaptation of old habits to new conditions, and partly an effort to counteract the Irish influence in the American Church.[17]

In order to gain and hold the support of immigrants and their children, the Church in the United States found it necessary to offer a variety of services which were partly or entirely nontheological in nature, and which were unnecessary in the static homeland village. These new facilities included missions, lay societies, and Sunday schools, and they formed part of a general movement in the American Catholic Church during the period between 1890 and World War I toward meeting the needs of Slavic and Italian immigrants. Prior to 1921, nevertheless, the Church did not occupy the position of prestige among Italian-Americans it later assumed, particularly after 1945.[18]

Identification with the colony and use of its facilities and institutions signified not only a movement away from homeland outlooks, but also, for many newcomers, a necessary step in Americanization. Some immigrants ignored all community institutions and never expanded their loyalty or interest from their home village; even the Kingdom of Italy lay outside their comprehension. Some chose to make use of a few or all existing community institutions and gradually identified themselves with the "Italian" group, a concept that did not exist for them before their emigration; others saw immigrant churches, journals, and societies as intermediaries through which to learn American customs and ideas. Often members of this assimilation-oriented group arrived as children or young adults and absorbed (or consciously adopted) American habits and speech from the outside community—from schools, settlement houses, criminal gangs, and political organizations.[19]

Social workers reached and influenced many through classes in English, sewing courses, handicraft activities, Italian theater groups, summer camps, and the sponsoring of political and social clubs. Along with public schools, social workers and settlement houses offered alternate channels of contact with the American community to those provided by American political bosses, Italian "prominenti," bankers, and *padroni*. Some reformers sought to establish and support free employment agencies for immigrants and to destroy the *padrone* labor system, while others worked to procure the passage of child labor laws and strict observance of compulsory education legislation.[20]

Italian immigrants won notoriety (and the wrath of social workers) because they seldom permitted their children to obtain adequate schooling. While complaining that their own lack of education kept them from getting better jobs, parents sent their offspring out to work in order to supplement family incomes. Although in time most Italians complied with the minimum requirements of compulsory education laws, they secured jobs for their children after school hours. When Italian children reached the legal withdrawal age of fourteen, they were "to an alarmingly high degree" withdrawn from school and put to work.[21]

IV

Despite dire predictions that Italians, caught in a "cycle of poverty," would remain destitute and a burden to society, by 1900 they had begun to move from unskilled labor into commercial, trade, and professional work, including printing, bricklaying, carpentering, import and export, banking, law, and medicine. Notwithstanding the complaints of reformers and the laments of immigrant workers about education, financial success at this time did not depend entirely upon schooling; ambition, hard work, and cunning could, and did, overcome illiteracy.[22]

Crime, one means of economic advancement independent of education and social background, provided all classes of Italians opportunities for quick and substantial monetary gains and sometimes for social and political achievements as well. Within the colony, bankers and *padrone* labor agents, blackhanders and other lawbreakers realized small but important profits by terrorizing or swindling compatriots. Organized criminal operations reaped tremendous profits from the American community and offered almost limitless opportunities for wealth and prestige.

Americans reacted to Italian crime with a frenzy of emotion aroused by no other immigrant activity. In the thirty years following 1890, the word "Mafia" and stories about Italian criminals filled American newspapers. Italian leaders responded by denying the presence of the Mafia, and some insisted it did not exist even in Sicily. In order to make clear to Americans that Old World criminal patterns did not carry over into immigrant colony crime, Italian-language newspapers began, shortly after the turn of the century, to use the term "Black Hand" to identify crimes within the community. It was this label that then was picked up by the

American press in the first two decades of the twentieth century.

Whichever label they used to describe the crime, Italian colony newspapers at first denied the existence of organized gangs. With the passage of time, the press attributed an increasing number of crimes to the Black Hand, and deplored the growing rate of "bombings, murder, and blackmail" within the ethnic district. As the colony grew in size, crimes increased in number, although few contemporaries recognized the relationship between crime and population growth. Community leaders blamed the "lack of capacity shown by the police" and the silence of victimized Italian-Americans who, "when they are questioned by the police . . . become as dumb as fish." Chicago's *L'Italia* described a typical Black Hand "job": the hoodlums would demand money from a victim—usually by letter—and if he ignored their threats and demands, they would kill him; should they spare his life, they would bomb his home. As larger numbers of southern Italians and Sicilians migrated to American cities, they became ever more tempting sources of money, for they were readily intimidated by threats because of the reputation of the Mafia in Sicily.[23]

These Black Hand crimes were limited almost entirely to the Sicilian and southern-Italian neighborhoods. Writing in 1909, Arthur Woods, Deputy Police Commissioner of New York City, reported that "in almost every case" Black Hand operations were committed by men who had been involved in criminal activities in Italy and who had emigrated to New York in order to continue "fattening off the main body of their fellow-countrymen." During this period, such gangsters had not joined any tightly organized, centrally directed structure. "The Black Hand is not a cohesive, comprehensive society, working with mysterious signs and passwords," maintained Woods. "Given a number of Italians with money, and two or three ex-convicts, you have all the elements necessary for a first-rate Black Hand campaign."[24]

Black Hand activities virtually disappeared in the 1920s, for several reasons. First, the supply of simple, pliable victims dwindled after the termination of immigration during World War I and by subsequent restrictive legislation. Second, enforcement of laws prohibiting the use of the mails to defraud forced personal delivery of threatening Black Hand notes. Neighborhood hoodlums, craving anonymity, found this activity to be too risky. While these factors limited opportunities for criminals within the ethnic quarter, at the same time, a new field of endeavor had sprung up in the wider American community. Before January 16, 1920, when the Volstead Act prohibited the manufacture and sale of alcoholic beverages in the United States, most Italian criminals worked within the colony. American drinking habits did not adjust to the new regulations, and lawbreakers saw their chance to profit. Former blackhanders, unemployed immigrants, and restless youth gangs turned to the lucrative liquor business, which they eventually dominated in New York, Chicago, and other large urban centers. Hence immigration restriction and Prohibition marked the end of the Black Hand era and introduced many Italian newcomers into the mainstream of American gangsterdom.[25]

"Prohibition is a business," maintained Alphonse Capone. "All I do is to supply a public demand. I do it in the best and least harmful way I can." He and others like him could see themselves as hardworking executives catering to those urban dwellers, rich and poor alike, who desperately sought and willingly paid for the finished product, because Prohibition "opened up a new criminal occupation, with less risk of punishment, with more certainty of gain, and with less social stigma than the usual forms of crime like robbery, burglary, and larceny."[26]

Black Hand activities—mainly extortion and terrorism—received the most publicity inside and outside the immigrant community until Prohibition eclipsed other types of lawbreaking, but many varieties of crime existed within the colony, often committed by men who shunned Black Hand methods. Labor agents prospered in cities like Chicago that served as transportation centers. These agents, or *padroni*, brought together American businessmen and unskilled immigrant laborers (to the advantage of both), but generally did so by cheating and shortchanging their less knowledgeable compatriots until effective safeguards hampered their operations.[27]

Immigrant bankers flourished in every part of the country where newcomers from Southern and Eastern Europe gathered in considerable numbers. Their principal function was to receive deposits and send money abroad. Immigrants transmitting cash provided bankers with lush opportunities to defraud, either by using the money for personal investments—with the intention of sending some overseas when investments paid off—or else by keeping it outright. Because they operated freely outside legal controls, worked with a minimal accumulation of capital, and had little experience in business methods, many immigrant bankers went bankrupt; others absconded with customers' savings. The defrauded immigrants had no legal recourse.[28]

Other businessmen in the colony supplied services and products and lined their own pockets by overcharging or otherwise cheating their compatriots. Among these were quack doctors, unscrupulous lawyers, and merchants who adulterated their wares and adjusted their weighing scales. Italian-language journals reported other non-Black Hand crimes, including robbery, embezzlement, arson, counterfeiting, election fraud, and a number of rackets executed by peddlers, restaurant owners, and community businessmen, all contrived to relieve the inexperienced newcomer of his money. In addition, corruption and violence often marked the organization and operation of Italian labor union locals.

Despite the wide range of immigrant community illegalities, most southern Italians and Sicilians in urban America led law-abiding lives. The majority of arrests and convictions involving them resulted from minor offenses (misdemeanors), particularly violation of city ordinances. The average immigrant often faced arrest and severe punishment for ignoring ordinances about which he, and most other newcomers, knew nothing. If the immigrant spoke no English, he labored under an additional disadvantage because most court interpreters (when they were available) lacked knowledge of court procedures, were unacquainted with the various dialects used by Italian residents of the city, and often themselves had a limited familiarity with English. In some courts, "interpreters" were bystanders, clerks or policemen who claimed to speak Italian.[29]

V

From politics, Italians gained patronage jobs, a voice in city government, and neighborhood conveniences like bath houses. In the early years of settlement, Italian "political influence" consisted of delivering the vote for Irish politicians (who generally controlled "new" immigrant wards) in exchange for occasional machine support for Italian candidates seeking precinct or ward positions. Over the years, Italians won control of Italian wards, and even a few victories in city-wide elections, but real successes occurred regularly only during and after the 1930s and 1940s.[30]

In center city wards, where the ethnic composition was undergoing rapid and extensive changes from Irish, German, and Scandinavian to Italian, East European Jewish, and Slavic, methods that seemed corrupt to reform-minded residents simply facilitated achievement of the ward boss's principal goal—political power through winning elections. Bargains, compromises, connections, patronage, and favors were essential ingredients of practical politics, then as now. Ward politicians found jobs and did favors for constituents, obtained franchises for companies, and reimbursed themselves at public expense. They also used intimidation, bribery, violence, trickery, and the services of criminals in their wards to prevent the rise of rivals who might threaten their own positions.[31]

Newspaper editors and other leaders in the Italian colony seemed unable to recognize the realities of urban politics. Regarding politics as a struggle between good and evil, they achieved relatively little at the practical level. To many immigrants, politics represented a way of getting jobs and community facilities. Machine politicians recognized these expectations and fulfilled them.

In nearly forty years as a ward boss in Chicago, John Powers (like most core area bosses in American cities) concentrated on retaining his political control. His base of support lay in the Nineteenth Ward, where he resided, attended church, and operated a saloon. In the community's value system, he rated as a respectable and friendly man. Jane Addams challenged Powers' control of the ward from her position at Hull House, and discovered that "the successful candidate must be a good man according to the standards of his constituents. He must not attempt to hold up a morality beyond them, nor must he attempt to reform or change the standards. If he believes what they believe, and does what they are all cherishing a secret ambition to do, he will dazzle them with his success and win their confidence." He will also win their votes.[32]

Miss Addams found that Powers remained at the head of ward politics because of the services he rendered. Most important, he used his prominence in city politics and his influence with businessmen to get jobs for constituents. "An Italian laborer wants a 'job' more than anything else," wrote Miss Addams, "and quite simply he votes for the man who promises him one." Besides jobs, Powers provided other factors and services. He furnished bond for ward residents charged with crimes; obtained exemptions from city ordinances for community businessmen; distributed turkeys at Christmas; gave presents at weddings and christenings; sponsored ward dances, parades, and picnics; supported church bazaars and other church functions; and attended funerals (thereby winning himself a nickname, "The Mourner"). In return for his many kindnesses, Powers asked only for votes.

Despite his highly efficient ward machine, Powers did not preside effectively over all aspects of his constituents' well-being. He used force and fraud without hesitation at elections, and utilized the promise of political office to buy opponents. Hull House investigators found public schools badly overcrowded and poorly equipped, with 3,000 more children in the schools than there were seats available for them. Dirt and refuse filled streets and alleys. The area badly needed parks and bath houses. Hull House women determined to improve the situation by opposing Powers and his henchmen, but found themselves easily outmaneuvered by the boss. Powers won the election of 1898, when Hull House and the Italian community organized to fight him. He lost but one of thirty-three precincts, the seventeenth, which contained the highest concentration of Italian voters in the ward. Oscar Durante, editor of L'Italia, claimed that this vote equaled a declaration of war against Powers on the part of the ward's Italians. From that year until 1921, La Tribuna Italiana Transatlantica, L'Italia, La Parola dei Socialisti, and other Italian-language journals worked to bring about Powers' defeat.

Only one Italian-American leader arose to offer an effective challenge to the ward boss, and that political duel lasted from 1915 until the final defeat of the anti-Powers forces in the aldermanic election of 1921. The Italian leader, Anthony D'Andrea, was a convicted counterfeiter, unfrocked priest, and frequenter of bawdy houses; his political strength lay in the union organizations he headed or managed, and his weakness in his unsavory background. The women of the ward—who were enfranchised in 1913 in Illinois—repudiated him in favor of Powers, who posed successfully as a humble, church-going family man. Powers won the male vote with a plurality of 124 and the female vote by 257, out of a total of 7,587 votes. D'Andrea died of shotgun wounds in May 1921, a grim warning to other ambitious Italians.

Reapportionment provided an even more effective way of silencing vote-seeking Italians. In 1921, the city council passed legislation (to become effective in 1923) that increased Chicago's wards from thirty-five to fifty, and changed the boundaries of existing wards. Powers saw to it that the huge West Side Italian community, which provided a majority of votes in the old Nineteenth Ward, was carved up and distributed among four new wards, where Italians formed a minority of ethnic residents. Despite this setback, Italians from the West Side won elections to the city council from the Twentieth Ward before the end of the decade, but their successes did not come through reform programs and activities; they made use of the old machine methods, both legal and illegal.

There were other responses to urban politics. Chicago's Seventeenth Ward lay about a mile north of the Hull House district, and contained the Chicago Commons settlement house, under the direction of Graham Taylor. Although Taylor and his Commons supporters did not face so effective a leader as Powers, they had to overcome (in Taylor's words) "an Irish boss and his organization [which] dominated politics" in the ward. Taylor also had to convince a variety of ethnic groups—Norwegians, Swedes, Poles, Germans, East European Jews, Irish, and Italians—to submerge their antagonisms and join in support of candidates who were not of their own background. In 1901 the Chicago Commons group endorsed a Polish lawyer, John F. Smulski; in 1902, an Irish tanner, William E. Dever, who later became superior court judge, appellate court judge, and eventually mayor; and in 1903, Lewis D. Sitts, a German. Graham Taylor, a shrewd political realist, attracted a group of aggressive, intelligent, and dedicated young reformers, among them John Palmer Gavit, Allen T. Burns, James Mullenbach, and Raymond Robins, who provided powerful aid in reforming politics within the ward. According to Taylor's son, by 1906 Italian voters in the Seventeenth Ward were refusing "to be delivered in the customary way, but went upon record for independence, as the Scandinavians have before them during the past successes of the Community Club." This Community Club formed the Chicago Commons equivalent of the Hull House Men's Club.

In spite of the fact that she faced a more securely entrenched rival than did the Seventeenth Ward reformers, Miss Addams after 1910 might have realized considerable success against Powers and his cronies if she had concentrated upon a single ethnic group—the Italians—and exploited the antagonisms, rivalries, and suspicions that existed between them and the Irish who controlled ward politics. It is possible, of course, that Miss Addams, her supporters, and the hopes of reform might also have suffered greater defeats at the hands of the Powers element. From the standpoint of ward residents and the cause of local and city-wide civic reform, the possible gains would have made the effort worthwhile. In their "struggle for self-determination," Nineteenth Ward Italians fought to displace the Irish leader who had first come to power during the heyday of the preceding wave of immigrants. Because of the absence of reform candidates or backers with city-wide prestige (after Miss Addams turned away from local politics), in the words of John Landesco of the Illinois Crime Commission, "only a D'Andrea, willing to use force without stint or limit, could rise to leadership against the use of fraud, the connivance and protection of politics, and the highly developed qualities of 'ward heeler' leadership which John Powers possessed along with the availability of protected, armed partisans."

VI

Willingly or unwillingly, immigrants began the process of assimilation as soon as they arrived in the city. The community and its institutions fulfilled the function not of prolonging Old World traits and patterns, but of providing important first steps in introducing newcomers to American life. Schools and settlement houses helped many to adjust to middle-class ideas and habits, and served as outside forces influencing the second generation and the more independent newcomers. Economic achievement, both legal and illegal, played a vital role in furthering assimilation as well as in spurring movement out of early ethnic districts. Newcomers and their children gradually moved up the economic ladder, progressing from unskilled labor into business, trades, and the professions, as well as into organized labor, politics, and crime. Critics complained of the slow rate of immigrant adjustment, and compared Italians unfavorably with their predecessors, ignoring the fact that the "old" elements had been assimilating in Chicago, New York, and other northern cities considerably longer than southern Italians, East European Jews, Poles, Lithuanians, and Greeks.[33]

Like most later immigrants, the Italians appeared to move outward from the urban core more slowly and reluctantly than had the Irish, the Germans, and other older groups. Contemporaries did not see the extensive residential mobility among Italians. From the early years of settlement, movement took place not only inside colonies and from one colony to another, but also from the centrally located districts toward outlying areas of the city and even into suburbs. By the 1920s the suburban trend was noticeable and significant. When World War I and the immigration laws of 1921 and 1924 closed the sources of additional immigration, Italian districts declined immediately. Depression in the 1930s and housing shortages in the 1940s slowed the rate of this dispersion from the ethnic colony, but since 1950 it has again accelerated.

NOTES

1. U.S. Senate, *Reports of the Immigration Commission,* I (1911), p. 104.

2. George La Piana, *The Italians in Milwaukee, Wisconsin* (Milwaukee: The Associated Charities, 1915); Frederick A. Bushee, "Italian Immigrants in Boston," *Arena,* XVII (April 1897), 722–34; Walter I. Firey, *Land Use in Central Boston* (Cambridge, Mass.: Harvard University Press, 1947), chap. 5; Charlotte Adams, "Italian Life in New York," *Harper's Magazine,* LXII (April 1881), 676–84; Charles W. Coulter, *The Italians of Cleveland* (Cleveland: Cleveland Americanization Committee, 1919).

3. For a detailed discussion of the points presented in this and following paragraphs, and full documentation, see Humbert S. Nelli, *Italians in Chicago, 1880–1930: A Study in Ethnic Mobility* (New York: Oxford University Press, 1970), chaps. 1 and 2.

4. I. W. Howerth, "Are the Italians a Dangerous Class?" *Charities Review,* IV (November 1894), 40.

5. Giovanni Preziosi, *Gl'italiani negli Stati Uniti del Nord* (Milan: Libreria Editrice Milanese, 1909), p. 81.

6. Robert F. Foerster, *The Italian Emigration of Our Times* (Cambridge, Mass.: Harvard University Press, 1919), pp. 370–71; U.S. Congress, *Reports of the Industrial Commission,* XIX (1902), pp. 969–71.

7. Frank E. Sargent, "The Need of Closer Inspection and Greater Restriction of Immigration," *Century Magazine,* LXVII (January 1904), 470; Robert E. Park, "Cultural Aspects of Immigration: Immigrant Heritages," *Proceedings of the National Conference of Social Work,* XLVIII (1921), 494; John Foster Carr, "The Coming of the Italian," *Outlook,* LXXXII (February 24, 1906), 429.

8. Pauline Young, "Social Problems in the Education of the Immigrant Child," *American Sociological Review,* I (June 1936), 419–29. See especially the discussion of urban adjustment problems of rural Americans on 420.

9. William E. Davenport, "The Exodus of a Latin People," *Charities,* XII (May 7, 1904), 466; J. S. McDonald, "Italy's Rural Social Structure and Emigration," *Occidente,* XII (September–October 1956), 443–6; J. Owen Stalson, *Marketing Life Insurance: Its History in America* (Cambridge, Mass.: Harvard University Press, 1942), pp. 446–9.

10. Antonio Mangano, "The Associated Life of the Italians in New York City," *Charities,* XII (May 7, 1904), 479–80; Grace Abbott, *The Problems of Immigration in Massachusetts* (Boston: Wright & Potter, 1914), pp. 202–206.

11. Luigi Carnovale, *Il Giornalismo degli emigrati italiani nel Nord America* (Chicago: L'Italia, 1909), p. 34; also pp. 33, 74, 77.

12. These remarks refer specifically, of course, to the bourgeois press. Anarchist, religious, and socialist papers reached a very small and specialized audience.

13. Laurence Franklin, "The Italian in America: What He Has Been, What He Shall Be," *Catholic World,* LXXI (April 1900), 72–3; D. Lynch, "The Religious Conditions of Italians in New York," *America,* X (March 21, 1914), 558.

14. Aurelio Palmieri, "Italian Protestantism in the United States," *Catholic World,* CVII (May 1918), 177–89; Antonio Mangano, *Sons of Italy: A Social and Religious Study of the Italians in America* (New York: Missionary Education Movement, 1917).

15. Howard B. Grose, *Aliens or Americans?* (New York: Missionary Education Movement, 1906), p. 256.

16. A. Di Domenica, "The Sons of Italy in America," *Missionary Review of the World,* XLI (March 1918), 193.

17. On the situation in Italy, see Joseph M. Sorrentino, S.J., "Religious Conditions in Italy," *America,* XII (October 17, 1914), 6–7.

18. François Houtart, *Aspects sociologiques du catholicisme américain, vie urbaine et institutions religieuses* (Paris: Editions ovrières, 1957) pp. 204–06.

19. Park, *op. cit.,* p. 495; C. A. Price, "Immigration and Group Settlement," in W. D. Borrie, ed., *The Cultural Integration of Immigrants* (Paris: UNESCO, 1959), pp. 267–8; Foerster, *op. cit.,* p. 395.

20. Coulter, *op. cit.,* pp. 32–4; Edward Corsi, *In the Shadow of Liberty* (New York: Macmillan, 1935), pp. 25–28; Jane Addams, *Twenty Years at Hull House* (New York: Macmillan, 1910), chaps. 10 and 13.

21. Alberto Pecorini, *Gli Americani nella vita moderna osservati da un italiano* (Milan: Fratelli Treves, 1909), pp. 397–8; Sophia Moses Robison, *Can Delinquency Be Measured?* (New York: Columbia University Press, 1936), pp. 143–4.

22. Carr, *op. cit.;* Alberto Pecorini, "The Italians in the United States," *Forum,* XLV (January 1911), 21–4; U.S. Congress, *Industrial Commission,* XV, pp. 435–6; Filippo Lussana, *Lettere di illetterati* (Bologna, Nicola Zanichelli, 1913); Letter from Grace Abbott to Julia Lathrop, January 14, 1913, in the Papers of Edith and Grace Abbott (University of Chicago), box 57, folder 7.

23. *L'Italia* (Chicago), February 4, 1911, April 1, 1911; The Italian "White Hand" Society in Chicago, Illinois, *Studies, Action and Results* (Chicago: *L'Italia,* 1908), pp. 25–6.

24. Arthur Woods, "The Problem of the Black Hand," *McClure's Magazine,* XXXIII (May 1909), 40.

25. John Landesco, "Prohibition and Crime," *Annals of the American Academy of Political and Social Sciences,* CLXIII (September 1932), 125.

26. Edward Dean Sullivan, *Rattling the Cup on Chicago Crime* (New York: Vanguard, 1929), esp. chaps. 4, 5, 6, 18; Denis Tilden Lynch, *Criminals and Politicians* (New York: Macmillan, 1932), chaps. 6, 10.

27. For a detailed examination of *padrone* methods as well as the factors responsible for the system's decline, see Humbert S. Nelli, "The Italian Padrone System in the United States," *Labor History,* V (Spring 1964), 153–67.

28. U.S. Senate, *Immigration Commission,* XXXVII, pp. 203–25.

29. Gino Speranza, "The Relation of the Alien to the Administration of the Civil and Criminal Law," *Journal of the American Institute of Criminal Law and Criminology*, I (November 1910), 563–72; Kate Holladay Claghorn, *The Immigrant's Day in Court* (New York: Harper and Bros., 1923), pp. 205–206, 209–10, 222–3.

30. John Palmer Gavit, *Americans by Choice* (New York: Harper and Bros., 1922), p. 372; Arthur Mann, *La Guardia: A Fighter Against His Times: 1882–1933* (Philadelphia: Lippincott, 1959), pp. 109–16; Samuel Lubell, *The Future of American Politics,* 3rd ed. rev. (New York: Harper & Row, 1965), pp. 77–83.

31. J. T. Salter, *Boss Rule* (New York: Whittlesey House, 1935), pp. 17–21.

32. This and the following paragraphs are based on Humbert S. Nelli, "John Powers and the Italians: Politics in a Chicago Ward, 1896–1921," *Journal of American History*, LVII (June 1970), 67–84.

33. Richard C. Ford, "Population Succession in Chicago," *American Journal of Sociology*, LVI (September 1950), 160.

12. STATUS, MOBILITY, AND THE DIMENSIONS OF CHANGE IN A SOUTHERN CITY
Atlanta, 1870–1910

Richard J. Hopkins

Two of the most fundamental experiences of a man's life are his job and his residence. Rarely is he away from either for more than a short time, and usually he leaves one only for the other. The human geography of the modern American metropolis indicates that there is a significant connection between occupation and habitat. Individuals with low incomes are forced to live in the congestion and decay of the least desirable residential areas, whereas people whose occupations provide high incomes usually are to be found residing in roomy new homes in the outer suburbs. Between the slums of the central city and the wealthy suburbs lie the homes of families whose incomes vary widely from moderately low to moderately high. These families, too, live in neighborhoods of similar income and occupational status, with moderately high-income sections located farther from downtown than moderately low-income areas. The final result is an urban residential structure composed of socioeconomically segregated neighborhoods, ranging outward from the lowest at the center to the highest on the periphery.

Neighborhoods in the modern city, however, are not static. Continuous outward migration from the center has turned the central middle-class neighborhood of yesterday into today's lower-middle-class section, and the outward pressure has created a ripple effect felt all the way to the outer limits of the city. Urban families have had to remain on the move just to maintain an environment with neighbors of similar occupations, incomes, and status. Moreover, individual success creates further residential movement, as the man who is promoted seeks out a "better" neighborhood that is more in keeping with his higher occupational and economic circumstances. People in the modern city, then, are on the move and neighborhoods are changing, but the current residential structure remains essentially the same—the best areas tend to be farthest out and the worst are nearest to the core.[1]

Movement and change have always been characteristic of the American city, but today's socioeconomically segregated residential structure has not. This pattern, in fact, emerging only since the 1850s, has resulted from millions of individual decisions to seek a "better" residential environment for self and family. This desire for more space and less congestion has been continuous in the history of American society; even colonial cities had "suburban" developments.[2] But large-scale suburbanization occurred after the 1850s with a dramatic innovation in urban transportation. The age of the street railway began with large-scale expansion of the horse car on the streets of New York City in the early 1850s, and this odd-looking conveyance permitted the systematic and rapid movement of much larger numbers of people over greater distances than ever before possible in the city.[3] The result was the transformation of the historic "walking city" into the modern metropolis.

More significant in the longer term, perhaps, than the increased territorial coverage was the spatial distance that population dispersal added to traditional social distinctions. In the walking city no significant amount of geographical distance had separated persons of high, middle, and low social status. In the later nineteenth-century residential pattern of the emerging metropolis, however, socioeconomic rank could be fairly reliably determined by the distance from the home to the central city: the greater the distance, the higher the rank. The individual now could gauge his relative social position in the directly measurable terms of distance and time from downtown. In the daily commuting process to his in-town job, he could see what had been left behind, and on the occasional Sunday excursions to the outlying districts, he got some notion of what remained to be achieved. If this were not enough to convince him of his present station, further confirmation was readily found in his neighborhood, for his neighbors were quite apt to be of a status similar to his.

Those who traveled the suburban route had occupations that met both the income and time requirements of suburban living. A man's job (or the jobs of the family) had to provide both an income high enough that a suburban residence could be afforded and sufficient flexibility and predictability of working hours and location to permit the expenditure of time in commuting. These occupational requirements tended to reinforce the traditional factors that had distinguished among occupations as more or less desirable. The major status distinction between white-collar and blue-collar jobs, between brain and brawn, became more important, and the more subtle rankings of employments within these two broad classes were strengthened. The clerk in a downtown office, for example, might not earn much, if any, more than a skilled building trades worker. Yet the clerk's place of work was fixed and his hours were predictable, whereas the skilled construction employee probably would be required to work wherever in the city his employer needed his skill at a particular moment and for as long as the weather permitted. The clerk's position more adequately met the requirements for suburban living. Consequently, even lower white-collar occupations became preferable to higher-paid manual positions. During a slack period in the economy in 1884, for example, an editorial writer for the Atlanta *Journal* talked about those distinctions, although he exaggerated them for effect, when he advised:

The number of unemployed men in Atlanta is one of the evidences of business inactivity. However, there is no necessity for any man to be out of work. The trouble with most unemployed men [is] that they find it difficult to obtain the kind of work they most prefer. If a bookkeeper finds no opening in the counting room and the dry goods clerk no place behind the counter, they should seek other employment, and determine to accept even a hod carrier's position.[4]

A man's occupation was always an important element in the national folklore of opportunity and success in the open society of America, and work was a crucial element in the residential restructuring of the historic city. As the editorial writer implied, many employees thought it better to be out of a job temporarily than to slide down the occupational ladder to a lower position, just for the sake of being employed. The folklore of the American success story emphasized mobility, but only in an upward direction. If one could not move up at the moment, he had to guard his present position very carefully. To backslide would be to lose. The folklore, then, emphasized the positive. In America even the poorest man could succeed by adhering closely to the middle-class virtues of diligent hard work, frugality, and the proper moral outlook. And the efficacy of the success formula was proved by the careers of thousands of annual migrants who departed the central city for the suburbs. As Professor Sam Bass Warner, Jr., has pointed out regarding Boston:

In an important way the suburbs served the half of Boston's population which could not afford them . . . [by giving] aspiring low-income families the certainty that should they earn enough money they too could possess the comforts and symbols of success. Even for those excluded from them, the suburbs offered a physical demonstration that the rewards of competitive capitalism might be within the reach of all.[5]

Many historians and observers of American society have accepted the historical openness of the American occupational structure as a fact. Yet it has been only in the last few years that any systematic investigation of this "fact" has been undertaken.[6] From the slowly accumulating body of material we know the occupational experiences of large numbers of men from various levels and starting points in the occupational structure of a few cities. The studies reported on so far, however, involve northeastern cities which had high proportions of foreign-born stock in their populations and which were more industrial than commercial in their economic life. Moreover, these cities had widely disparate growth experiences. Boston and Philadelphia already were large cities at the beginning points of the respective studies, and the other cities never came close to succeeding in the urban race for glory and power.

If historians are to understand occupational mobility, they need to study the careers of men in cities of various sizes and growth rates and with differing social and economic characteristics. The South long has been recognized as a special section in America. It remained overwhelmingly, almost oppressively, rural long after the Northeast and Midwest were predominantly urban. Moreover, the section's social traditions and population components varied from those of other parts of the country. Atlanta, which became the dominant city in the Southeast, shared in much of the uniqueness of the South; the city therefore is a logical choice for an examination of occupational mobility.

Atlanta began its rise to dominance in the Southeast rather inauspiciously. From its beginning in the middle 1830s until the eve of the Civil War, it had grown to only fewer than ten thousand inhabitants. The changes brought on by war needs, however, foretold the future. Only three years after the 1860 federal census enumerators counted 9,554 persons, the city was reported to contain over 20,000. General Sherman put an end to this boom period late in 1864, however, and after the destruction it seemed as if Atlanta would have to begin anew. The rebuilding process required great amounts of both time and money, but by 1870 the city's original urban renewal task was largely completed. The population then stood at 21,789, the town was the state capital, the railroads were operating normally again, and dislocations of the economy had been largely corrected. The future seemed brighter. The growth of the town over the next three decades was sufficient to produce a city of 90,000 people at the turn of the century; by 1920 the number had surpassed 200,000.[7]

The rapid growth rate of Atlanta in the decades after the Civil War paralleled that of several other cities in the nation, but the human components of its increase differed in one important respect from the non-Southern experience. Since the 1870 census, blacks have formed a sizable minority of the population, while immigrants from abroad have constituted a negligible component. Exactly the reverse was true for cities outside Dixie. Atlanta also differed from most other cities in the relationship between manufacturing and trade-and-transportation in its economy. The number of men engaged in trade-and-transportation occupations consistently outnumbered employees in manufacturing and mechanical industries from 1870 to 1930. In such towns as Louisville and Indianapolis, by contrast, the number of trade-and-transportation workers consistently trailed manufacturing hands. As early as 1880 even the great railroad and distribution center of Chicago employed only 33.5 percent of its male labor force in the trade-and-transportation category, as against 39.2 percent in manufacturing.[8] Did the unusual occupational and demographic structure of Atlanta affect the upward and downward mobility of the labor force as compared to other cities?

To determine the career patterns of component groups of the Atlanta population, a sample of three racial-nativity groups was selected from the enumerators' manuscript schedules for the 1870 federal census of the city. Every tenth native-born white and black male over fifteen years of age, and every second foreign-born male over fifteen, was included in the sample. This procedure provided the names and occupations of 258 native whites, 226 blacks, and 208 immigrants. Subsequent occupations and continued residence in the city in 1880 and 1896 were determined from Atlanta city directories for those years.[9] The occupations of the men in the sample then were classified according to a skill-status scale into unskilled, semiskilled, and skilled manual or blue-collar categories, and white-collar employee and proprietor-professional nonmanual categories, in order of increasing skill-status rank. Rates of occupational mobility in the following discussion refer to movement among these occupational classes.

The picture of occupational mobility this procedure revealed shows substantial differences in career patterns in Atlanta, as compared to the experiences of workers in other cities. Elsewhere, for example, members of ethnic minority groups found ways to escape their ghettoes over a generation or two. But Atlanta blacks did not share in this immigrant experience. The Atlanta evidence suggests that the only similarity between blacks there and immigrants elsewhere (but not Atlanta immigrants) was that both groups began at the bottom of the occupational ladder. Seventy-two percent of the black males in the 1870 sample were unskilled laborers, 6 percent held semiskilled jobs, 19 percent followed skilled trades, and only 3 percent were found anywhere among the nonmanual occupations. It should not be too surprising to find most freedmen in 1870 holding the most menial jobs, for most of them had been emancipated only recently and were making the adjustment from a rural existence to an urban one. It is significant, however, for any assessment of the condition of the urban black after the Civil War, that he found it very difficult to escape his lowly position over the next two and a half decades. Of the seventy-one unskilled black males in the 1870 work force who remained in 1880, nearly 90 percent were still at the bottom of the occupational hierarchy. Seven percent had crossed the hazy line between unskilled and semiskilled employment, 3 percent had achieved skilled occupations, and 1 percent had left the manual ranks for the nonmanual. If we give the laborers more time to rise up the ladder, the percentage results seem a bit brighter. Over the twenty-six years fom 1870 to 1896, some 11 percent of the unskilled blacks became semiskilled workers and 4 percent rose to the nonmanual category; none of the unskilled attained skilled employment in 1896. Yet this indication that access to semiskilled and nonmanual positions was becoming easier probably is misleading because of the small number in the sample who remained for the entire period.[10]

The same problem of small sample numbers plagues any analysis of the mobility patterns of semiskilled and skilled black men, yet the results over the first decade are suggestive. Seven of the ten (70 percent) semiskilled who remained until 1880 maintained their positions; one (10 percent) rose to a skilled job, but two (20 percent) fell to the bottom rank. Although only half the men (five) stayed in the city until 1896, the pattern of lost status appears more pronounced. By that time, none had bettered his position, but three had fallen to unskilled jobs. The mobility of the skilled blacks of 1870 exhibited similar downward trends in 1880 and 1896. Seventeen of the twenty-one (81 percent) who remained in 1880 maintained their positions and three (14 percent) fell all the way to unskilled jobs; only one (5 percent) had bettered himself with a nonmanual occupation by that time. Moreover, the experience of the few skilled workers who stayed for the full twenty-six years did not vary from the 1870–80 pattern.

The evidence bearing on the occupational careers of black Atlantans during the late nineteenth century is somewhat mixed. About 10 percent of the unskilled blacks who remained in the city found it possible to take that very small and poorly defined step upward to a semiskilled job. But rising any higher than that was nearly impossible.[11] Moreover, the greater downward mobility of higher-status manual workers indicates that blacks found it difficult to hold onto the better jobs even when they could get them. The traditional accounts of white workers pushing blacks out of the more desirable occupations have some basis in fact in the Atlanta experience.

It is clear that emancipation and Reconstruction did not win the black wage earner in Atlanta any measurable participation in the American success story. The labor market in the city was the province of the white man. And, unlike the Northern pattern in which foreign-born blue-collar whites were at a distinct disadvantage in competing with the native-born, Dame Opportunity was much more sensitive to the color line in Atlanta than to differences in ethnic background. Immigrant manual workers held lower status jobs than native whites in 1870, but the mobility experiences of both groups over the next twenty-six years were very similar. Momentarily ignoring the subtle status distinctions between unskilled and semiskilled jobs and looking for "significant" mobility (that is, movement from an unskilled or semiskilled position to the skilled or nonmanual categories), we find that 21 percent of the native whites and 10 percent of the immigrants advanced significantly within the blue-collar occupations by 1880. The fact that one of every five natives and immigrants alike left behind manual jobs for white-collar occupations is more meaningful. Moreover, by differentiating again between the unskilled and semiskilled strata, the dimensions of the mobility within the blue-collar ranks increase. Fifty percent of the native whites and 33 percent of the immigrant unskilled workers rose to higher positions by 1880. By 1896 the pattern of higher blue-collar upward mobility remained intact, with 52 percent of the natives and 57 percent of the immigrants holding higher-status jobs. Just as significant as the rather impressive upward movement of both groups, however, was their absolute lack of downward mobility. None of the skilled or semiskilled native whites or immigrants slid to a lower occupational status in 1880 or 1896. If all these men did not rise, at least those who did not were successful in maintaining their starting ranks.

The careers of nonmanual native whites and immigrants of 1870 show somewhat different patterns of success. Over 40 percent of the native-born and 45 percent of the immigrant clerks, bookkeepers, salesmen and other white-collar employees were able to become businessmen in 1880, and by 1896 the respective figures were 56 and 60 percent. But members of both nativity groups also experienced some difficulty in maintaining their particular nonmanual stations. About 10 percent of the native-born fell to lower ranks in each time period, and nearly half of these men ended in blue-collar jobs. The rate of occupational status loss for immigrants was slightly higher (17 percent in each time period). At least part of the greater downward movement of nonmanual native whites and immigrants can be attributed to the fact that they had, by definition, fewer places to which to rise and a greater distance to fall. Many higher-status occupations also were harder to maintain because of the greater demand for training, talent, and financial resources of business ownership. Immigrants had somewhat more difficulty in meeting these demands for maintenance of high occupational status.

It nevertheless is quite surprising, in light of Thernstrom's study of Newburyport, to find such similarities in the mobility rates of native whites and immigrants in Atlanta. The sharp contrast presented by the mobility rates of blacks clearly indicates that color was more important than ethnic background in determining who could improve his occupational status and who could not. The great disparity between the immigrant and black experiences, coupled with the small proportion of foreign-born and high proportion of blacks, suggests two things. First, the heavy concentration of blacks in the least desirable jobs and their inability to advance to better positions created a black proletariat against which low-skilled foreign labor perhaps did not wish to compete. Second, selective forces served to bring southward only a small number of the foreign-born, and they tended to be of a "better sort" than the masses who were crowding into Northern cities during these years. It required at least two moves over long distances—migrating from the homeland to the United States, then traveling against the grain of the dominant east-west transportation routes from New York City or some other point to the South—for a foreigner to settle in Atlanta. Only immigrants with some money or needed skills, or both, sought out the city. The Atlanta *Constitution* arrived at similar conclusions in 1883:

Foreign immigrants do not come to the south simply because they do not want to. There is very little inducement in this section for mere laborers, and those that come generally become disgusted with the methods employed. The sort of immigration that the south needs is coming rapidly enough, and it is making itself felt. It is composed of men with capital enough to set up small industries or make investments in mining lands or real estate of some character. Should there chance to come here an influx of laborers such as frequently pour into the west, the result would be pitiful indeed. There is little that they could do, and nothing that our people would want them to do. On the whole, everything is working out right in the south.[12]

And so it was in Atlanta—except for the black.

The achievement of some degree of success or improvement in occupational status was fairly common for white Atlantans in the later nineteenth century. This success obviously involved change of jobs. Yet it only begins to suggest the extent of change that was so characteristic of urban life in these years. If we think of occupational mobility as movement from one job to another, rather than as a rise or fall in skill-status categories, then the dimensions of change in the city become a bit clearer. Among the native whites, immigrants, and blacks in the 1870 sample who remained at least ten years, fewer than 10 percent had the same occupation or continued to work for the same employer in 1880. And nearly all those whose positions did remain constant were professionals or successful businessmen. Moreover, tracing many of the men in the sample through the many removes they made during the 1870s and 1880s shows that job identification was extremely fluid. Only the men at the top of the occupational pyramid remained stable. The experiences of most Atlantans in one of the central facts of life, work, was that of frequent change.

As important as the shifting occupational picture was the geographical instability of the Atlanta population. This type of change took two forms: leaving the city or moving from place to place within the city. The picture that emerges from an examination of the experiences of individual people in the city, rather than a reliance on statistical summaries of federal or state censuses, is a moving picture, not a still life.

The growth of the city from 1870 to 1880 is a good case in point. The 1870 population of 21,789 increased to 37,409 by 1880. These figures indicate a net addition to the city of 15,620. Yet it is apparent from tracing the men in the same samples drawn from the 1870 federal census manuscripts that fewer than half of the 1870 population remained in the city in 1880. This figure provides a persistence rate of under 50 percent for the decade. Only about 10,000–11,000 people, then (fewer than 30 percent of the 1880 population), had been there for at least ten years. More than 26,000 were newcomers. Over the twenty-six years examined, the persistence rate was less than one in four of the 1870 residents, while the total population of the city was in the vicinity of 85,000 in 1896. Moreover, the samples covered only those who lived in Atlanta in 1870; the statistics therefore cannot deal with the many thousands of people who came and went after that date, but it is reasonably certain that several hundred thousand different people lived in Atlanta between 1870 and 1896.[13]

The persistence rates cited here have referred thus far to the aggregate population of Atlanta. A clearer picture of the process of migration out of the city emerges, however, if we divide the population into the three racial-ethnic groups, native-born whites, immigrants, and blacks. Surprisingly, blacks stayed in the city until 1880 more often than either of the white groups. Their persistence rate of 48 percent compares favorably with the rate of 45 percent for the native whites. Immigrants were the most prone to move on to another place; only 41 percent remained until 1880.[14] The greater tendency of immigrants than native whites to move on might have been expected, for immigrants were cultural outsiders. They had moved several times to appear in Atlanta at all, and they usually had fewer ties than the natives. Many of them undoubtedly also became "disgusted with the methods employed," to repeat the words of the editor quoted above.

The unexpectedly high persistence rate of the blacks does not fit the traditional accounts of very high black mobility after the war. Professor E. Merton Coulter, for example, has written that " . . . the records of a Negro's life were . . . unfixed and his moving around was . . . constant," and that "An important element aiding the growth of Southern cities and contributing to their problems was the Negroes. Many who first went to the towns after their freedom later drifted back to the country, but a large number remained permanently."[15] Undoubtedly, the freedmen did become much more migratory after the war, and the nearly 10,000 blacks who lived in Atlanta in 1870 proves that members of that group were moving to the towns. Of the 52 percent of the black workers who left Atlanta by 1880, many undoubtedly returned to rural life. To say that blacks were in constant movement, however, without pointing out that the movement of native whites and immigrants was as high or higher, is most misleading. Granted that blacks did move a great deal, they still were the most stable segment of the city's population in the 1870s.

The blacks' greater stability, moreover, is even more pronounced if we compare their persistence rates for the blue-collar occupational categories with the rates of similar native white and immigrant workers. In the 1870s 44 percent of the unskilled blacks remained in the city, compared with 24 percent of the native whites and 38 percent of the immigrants. In the semiskilled and skilled categories black stability was even greater: 77 and 50 percent, respectively. The native white rates were 26 and 38 percent, while the figures for immigrants were 39 and 40 percent. By 1896 the relationships had not changed. For the unskilled, semiskilled, and skilled blacks, persistence rates were 17, 30, and 20 percent; for native whites, 12, 13, and 19 percent; and for immigrants, 10, 15, and 15 percent.

The number of blacks in nonmanual occupations in the 1870 sample, unfortunately, is not large enough for any meaningful calculation of their persistence. But the rates for native whites and immigrants are both meaningful and important. The correlation between persistence rate and occupational status for blue-collar native whites was noted above. Twenty-four percent of the unskilled, 26 percent of the semiskilled, and 38 percent of the skilled native whites remained in the city throughout the 1870s. For the entire twenty-six-year period after 1870, the positive correlation between job status and persistence continued, although the rates are only half as high as for the first decade. In the nonmanual occupations native whites exhibited somewhat higher persistence. Fifty-seven percent of the white-collar employees and 59 percent of the business and professional men stayed through 1880, and over the full twenty-six years the respective rates were 29 and 33 percent. For the native whites in the occupational structure, then, the correlation is positive over the entire range of skill-status categories. The tendency of nonmanual immigrants to remain in the city for ten years, however, is little greater than for blue-collar immigrants: the range was only from 38 percent for the unskilled to 47 percent for businessmen. Over the longer period to 1896, the range broadened to from 10 percent (unskilled) to 24 percent (businessmen), but immigrants still had somewhat lower persistence rates than native whites of the same occupational categories.

These persistence rates suggest at least two things about workers in Atlanta. First, blue-collar native whites were apt to quit the city more often and more quickly than their foreign-born counterparts. This fact perhaps reflects the inability or reluctance of low-skilled white labor to compete with blacks. Second, the rates confirm the expected positive correlation between a person's status or "stake in the community" and the length of time he remains in that community. The correlation is more obvious for the native whites, but it also seems to have been true for the immigrants as well, although over a longer period of time.

The high degree of movement into and out of the city after 1870 adds further to the characteristics of movement and change that conditioned individual Atlantans in the late nineteenth century. One final dimension, spatial change within the city, remains to be considered. For this portion of the study a sixteen-square-block area on the south side was selected, and the residents on the forty face blocks[16] involved were listed according to the street directory portion of the 1890, 1900, and 1910 city directories.[17] The section, just southeast of the main business district, included some of the finest older residences in the city on its western boundary, while the eastern limit consisted largely of black shanties. Between these two extremes were modest one- and two-family dwellings, a sprinkling of businesses, a public school, a few churches, and some scattered vacant spaces. Splitting the area was one of the city's earliest street railways, built in the mid-1870s. In 1880 the southern boundary was only a short distance from the outer edge of settlement, but the clear outlines of future peripheral growth could be seen fanning out on either side of the car line. By 1890 the sixteen square blocks already were beginning to become a transitional area, and over the next two decades their complexion changed noticeably.

Some of the most prominent families of Atlanta lived on Washington Street, the western boundary, in 1890. The estate of Joseph E. Brown, Confederate governor of Georgia, chief justice of the state supreme court and president of the Western & Atlantic Railroad after the war, and U.S.

Senator in 1890, occupied an entire block on the west side of the street. On the east side his neighbors included Julius Brown, lawyer and master in chancery of the United States District Court, and Junius G. Oglesby, partner in a large wholesale grocery business and president of the Atlanta Chamber of Commerce. In the face block to the north lived three wholesale merchants, a bank executive, a city judge, a partner in the city's largest cotton brokerage firm, and a retired merchant. Altogether the street directory listed fourteen heads of households on these two face blocks, and all were of the top rank in occupational and socioeconomic status. Five of the fourteen had lived in the same houses in 1880, and four of them (or their widows) remained in 1900. Only one widow stayed until 1910, and she died shortly thereafter. Seven of the nine who moved into the two blocks in the 1880s stayed until 1900, and four of them (including two widows) lasted until 1910. By 1900, however, the number of families living here had increased from fourteen to twenty-nine. The twelve continuous residents, therefore, had seventeen new families as neighbors, as older dwellings were subdivided and new houses filled in vacant spaces. The occupational status of the newcomers of the 1890s tended to be high, but somewhat lower than that of the older residents. By 1910 the number of families listed here had fallen to twenty-one because of the conversion of some buildings into a social club and a Catholic convent. One of the twenty-one families had lived here for at least ten years, five household heads (three widows included) had lived on the street since 1890 or before, and fifteen had become residents after 1900. Moreover, the occupational status of the newcomers was distinctly lower than that of the older residents.

These two face blocks on Washington Street, inhabited in the 1880s and part of the 1890s by some of Atlanta's occupational and social elite, were the most stable of the forty face blocks studied between 1880 and 1910. None of the other blocks even came close to equaling the 86 percent stability the two Washington Street blocks showed between 1890 and 1900. And that 86 percent was the highest rate even for these blocks; fewer than 25 percent of the 1900 residents remained in 1910. Moreover, the large influx of new families in the 'nineties meant that the older residents constituted but 40 percent of the new neighborhood of 1900. The other thirty-eight face blocks, which were inhabited in 1890 mostly by white small businessmen, white-collar employees, and skilled workers, and low-skilled blacks on the eastern fringe of the section, were in constant flux. A rate of stability as high as 40 to 45 percent over a decade was indicated for a very few blocks on which families of relatively high socioeconomic rank lived—notably the two blocks of Crew Street adjacent to the two Washington Street blocks. For the remainder, a turnover rate of 75 percent or more every ten years was characteristic. A few blocks turned over completely after 1890, as all of their residents either left the city or moved to another area.

As with the persistence rates earlier, there was a direct correlation between occupational rank and residential mobility. Those individuals at the top of the occupational hierarchy were most likely to live in the same house over a decade or more. These men for the most part were well-established professionals and large businessmen. Small businessmen, with the exception of neighborhood grocers, were considerably more mobile, as were such white-collar employees as clerks, bookkeepers, and traveling salesmen. The few blue-collar whites, all skilled workmen, who lived in this section in 1890 or 1900 were the most mobile of all the occupational categories. Only one plumber, who lived in the same house from 1900 to 1910, was stable for at least ten years. Among the blacks of all occupational ranks, residential mobility also was pronounced. Only about 10 percent of the blacks remained in the area for at least a decade, and many of those who did lived in a different house in the same or adjacent block.

For none of the forty face blocks studied did the occupational status of the block increase with residential turnover, and only a few even maintained approximately the same rank as newcomers replaced out-migrants.[18] In short, the complexion of most blocks declined in terms of job status. The area, then, clearly was a transitional one, and high turnover of residents might well have been expected. Yet the subsequent high mobility of residents who moved elsewhere in the city is instructive. Nearly all the white-collar employees, small businessmen, and less well-established professional men who moved elsewhere followed the lengthening street railway tracks to newer residential sections. The two favorite destinations were the developments several blocks south of the area examined and the rapidly growing Boulevard-Highland Avenue area of northeast Atlanta. For the few prominent businessmen and professional men who moved out, and especially for their sons, the destinations were the newly fashionable section extending northward on Peachtree Road and the Inman Park section on the east side created by real estate and traction magnate Joel Hurt. Except for those at the top of the occupational pyramid, however, the new homes were no more permanent than had been the ones in our sixteen square blocks. Within another decade most had moved again to newer neighborhoods still more distant from downtown. Moreover, the few men who achieved noticeable upward occupational mobility tended to move to somewhat nicer neighborhoods than did their former colleagues who remained behind in the status race. The blacks, just as mobile residentially as most of the whites, did not move in the same outward directions. Indeed, the blacks in the sixteen-square-block area usually moved to the growing black section on the eastern fringe of downtown or to the black area on the west side between downtown and Atlanta University.

It is clear, then, that constant movement and change dominated the occupations and habitats of most Atlantans in the later nineteenth century. And there seems to be no reason to expect that the Atlanta milieu was atypical. Most historians of this period of American history have recognized and described the larger trends of change and transformation: the development of a national economy, the rise of big business and the growing complexity of business organization, the beginning of labor unions, and the migration to the city from the American and European countrysides. These certainly were far-reaching alterations that directly or indirectly affected the jobs and residences of individual people. What is not as well appreciated, however, is that urban life itself was a continuous series of individual changes, movements, and adjustments in two of the most central experiences of life, and these changes were far more personal and immediate for the many thousands of persons involved than were the more general national trends.

Moreover, the conditions of flux varied considerably from one group to another in Atlanta society. Black Atlantans changed residence within the city as often as most whites, but blacks left the city less often than all whites. In addition, blacks changed jobs frequently, but found it very difficult to rise and quite easy to fall in occupational status. By contrast, both native white and immigrant blue-collar workers found that the opportunities to progress were relatively open. The breadth of opportunity for immigrants was somewhat less than for native whites in the nonmanual occupations; yet foreign-born men as a group remained upwardly mobile to a surprising degree. No distinction by country of birth can be made for the analysis of residential mobility, but the rates of turnover of whites for most of the forty face blocks from 1890 to 1910, and the subsequent pattern of further residential changes for the people who left this area, clearly show that there was very little residential or neighborhood stability for most white families. Only the white occupational elite remained in the same place and the same job for any extended period of time.

It is reasonable to expect that the constant alterations in urban lives affected the attitudes and behavior of the people who experienced them, but much more work has to be done in this area before any definite conclusions can be reached. One of the major problems in attempting to assess the effects of the changes is that our subjects are dead and have left no personal recollections. Many of the conclusions, therefore, will have to be pieced together from other evidence from the period and from insights of social scientists. Social psychologists have determined, for example, that a man's occupation influences his attitudes, and many analysts of today's "urban crisis" contend that the ghetto environment affects the attitudes of those who live there. It seems reasonable, then, to expect that such an important variable as residence, dependent to a large extent on occupation, influenced thinking in the late nineteenth century as well. No doubt then as well as now children of middle-class families who grew up in a succession of newer, class-segregated residential areas were accustomed to moving, to newness in environment, and to basically similar people whose attitudes were very much like their parents' and their own. When such children became adults, they were much more likely than children reared in the walking city to accept life in terms of insulated middle-class attitudes that emphasized environmental novelty and comfort, material progress, and other indications of the efficacy of the so-called Protestant, middle-class virtues as the road to success.

Some facts we do know from historical material. It is not entirely coincidental, for example, that the increased sensitivity to occupational identity and standards, which Professor Robert Wiebe has discussed in the context of the emergence of the "new middle class" at the turn of the century,[19] should appear after a generation or two of increasing urban differentiation and socioeconomic segregation. Further, such exercises in local history as this one can provide new insights, or new evidence to support older views, into the nature of such diverse political and social reform "movements" as Progressivism. Some Progressives saw a root of early twentieth-century social problems in the lack of stability of lower-class and ghetto neighborhoods. From the perspective of the occupational and residential instability of most Atlantans in the late nineteenth century, it seems clear that such reformers were operating on assumptions which stemmed not from the experience of the middle class, but from that of the socioeconomic urban elite.

Much more needs to be done, however, to define and refine these conclusions about the relationships between the quality of urban life in the late nineteenth century and its many and varied effects on mass attitudes and behavior. If we remember that one of the most constant characteristics of life in the city was continuous occupational and residential change, then perhaps we can better understand other aspects of urban life during these years.

NOTES

1. Professor Leo F. Schnore has shown that this pattern is applicable mainly to the nation's larger and older cities. For smaller and newer cities, the reverse is still prevalent. See Leo F. Schnore, *The Urban Scene* (New York: The Free Press, 1965), Part Four.

2. Carl Bridenbaugh, *Cities in the Wilderness: Urban Life in America, 1625–1742* (New York: Ronald Press, 1938), p. 306, and *Cities in Revolt: Urban Life in America, 1743–1776* (New York: Knopf, 1955), pp. 24–5, 218, 230–32, 236.

3. For an entertaining account of early methods of urban transportation, see John Anderson Miller, *Fares Please! A Popular History of Trolleys, Horse-Cars, Street Cars, Buses, Elevateds, and Subways* (New York: Appleton-Century, 1941).

4. *Atlanta Journal,* February 6, 1884.

5. Sam Bass Warner, Jr., *Streetcar Suburbs: The Process of Growth in Boston, 1870–1900* (Cambridge, Mass.: Harvard University Press, 1962), p. 157.

6. Some tentative conclusions about occupational mobility in the later nineteenth century, however, are beginning to emerge from what has been published, notably in the work of Professor Stephan Thernstrom, and from preliminary results of work still in progress or unpublished. See Stephan Thernstrom, *Poverty and Progress: Social Mobility in a Nineteenth Century City* (Cambridge, Mass.: Harvard University Press, 1964); "Urbanization, Migration, and Social Mobility in Late Nineteenth-Century America," in Barton J. Bernstein, ed., *Towards a New Past: Dissenting Essays in American History* (New York: Pantheon, 1968), pp. 158–75; and "Immigrants and WASPs: Ethnic Differences in Occupational Mobility in Boston, 1890–1940," in Stephan Thernstrom and Richard Sennett, eds., *Nineteenth-Century Cities: Essays in the New Urban History* (New Haven, Conn.: Yale University Press, 1969), pp. 125–64. These are Thernstrom's major contributions to date, although his full-scale study of occupational and social mobility in Boston, 1880–1968, is nearing publication. *Nineteenth-Century Cities* also contains essays on occupational mobility in Poughkeepsie, New York, by Clyde Griffen; Paterson, New Jersey, by Herbert Gutman; and Philadelphia, by Stuart Blumin.

7. Two of the more useful histories of Atlanta are Franklin Garrett, *Atlanta and Environs,* 3 vols. (New York: Lewis Historical Publishing Co., 1954), which summarizes the more important events year by year, and Workers of the Writers' Program of the Work Projects Administration in the State of Georgia, *Atlanta: A City of the Modern South* (New York: Smith & Durrell, 1942).

8. For Atlanta, the percentages of manufacturing employees and trade-and-transportation employees for selected years were: 1880, 28.7 and 34.7%; 1900, 27.9 and 43.4%; 1930, 32.5 and 35.2%. For Louisville: 1880, 40.5 and 30.0%; 1900, 37.3 and 34.3%; 1930, 42.3 and 32.4%. For Indianapolis: 1880, 38.4 and 30.4%; 1900, 37.6 and 33.5%; 1930, 43.2 and 32.4%. For Chicago: 1880, 39.2 and 33.5%; 1900, 36.9 and 35.1%; 1930, 42.5 and 30.3%. The figures were compiled from the population summaries of the federal census reports, 1880–1930.

9. To guard against inaccuracies in the city directories, the editions of 1879 to 1881 were consulted to determine continued residence and occupation in 1880 of sample members. Similarly, the 1895 to 1897 directories were used for 1896. If a man appeared in any one of the three editions, he was considered to have resided in the city in 1880 or 1896. This precaution was especially necessary for the blacks, for the directory publishers were quite careless about the listings of this segment of the population.

10. When the base number for calculating percentages is small, a change of one or two in the dividend can result in rather dramatic changes in the percentage figures. With a group of twenty-seven, as in the case of the unskilled blacks who remained in the city from 1870 to 1896, the shift of two men from the unskilled to a higher category would result in a total change of 16%; i.e., a drop of 8% for the unskilled category and a gain of 4% for each man in the higher categories.

11. The upward mobility of unskilled immigrants in Newburyport was nearly three times as high during the first ten years (28%) for the 1850 cohort as the upward movement of Atlanta blacks. The 1860 and 1870 cohorts for the Newburyport study showed smaller rates of 17 and 16%, respectively. The lesser mobility in the 1860s and 1870s is explained by the shrinking opportunities for immigrants in the semiskilled occupations. Thernstrom, *Poverty and Progress,* pp. 100–102.

12. *Atlanta Constitution,* April 11, 1883.

13. Peter R. Knights has calculated, for example, that the *annual* turnover in Boston's population during the years 1830 to 1860 was between 30 and 40%. See his "Population Turnover, Persistence, and Residential Mobility in Boston, 1830–1860," in Thernstrom and Sennett, *Nineteenth-Century Cities,* p. 263.

14. Death obviously removed some members of the sample after 1870, but it should have been only a small factor by 1880.

15. E. Merton Coulter, *The South During Reconstruction, 1865–1877* (Baton Rouge: Louisiana State University Press, 1947), pp. 54, 261.

16. As used here, one face block includes both sides of a street from one intersection to another.

17. The samples used for calculating occupational mobility and persistence rate were not used for the residential mobility portion of this essay because of the problems of finding home addresses for many of the members of the sample. The federal census manuscript schedules do not list address in 1870, and the 1870, 1871, and 1872 city directories often did not list a person's home address—if indeed they listed the person at all. Most blacks and many low-skilled whites were not included in these directories. The editions of the early 1880s also did not include a street directory that showed residence numbers and main occupants. Therefore, the 1890 directory was used as the starting point, and residents of each block were checked back in the 1880 directory to determine their addresses for that year. Unfortunately, unlike the census manuscripts, the city directories did not list a person's birthplace. It was impossible, therefore, to separate the whites into native-born and immigrant groups.

18. A few blocks in the center of the area, particularly on Capitol Avenue, maintained their occupational complexion because of the influx of some of the more successful immigrants and their children around the turn of the century.

19. Robert H. Wiebe, *The Search for Order, 1877–1920* (New York: Hill and Wang, 1967), chap. 5.

13. CONTESTED NEIGHBORHOODS AND RACIAL VIOLENCE
Chicago in 1919, A Case Study

William M. Tuttle, Jr.

The "18th birthday party given by Mrs. R. B. Harrison in honor of her daughter," the *Chicago Defender* reported in the late autumn of 1918, was "one of the social events of the season among the younger smart set. . . ." Held at Ogden Grove pavilion, the party featured an orchestra and a grand march. A half-year later, however, in May 1919, there was sadness in the Harrison family, as part of their house on Grand Boulevard lay in ruins, windows shattered, after a bombing.[1]

Best known for his role of "de Lawd" in *The Green Pastures* in the 1930s, R. B. Harrison was a black actor whose forte in 1919 was Shakespeare and readings from the poetry of Paul Laurence Dunbar. During World War I he was frequently on the road entertaining, part of the time at Liberty Loan rallies, and as a result his family was alone in the new house he and his wife had purchased. Shortly after moving to Grand Boulevard in March, Mrs. Harrison heard rumors that "the colored lady's house would be bombed." Warned by a black janitor that there was a plot to destroy her home, Mrs. Harrison telephoned the police, who casually rebuffed her and characterized her fears as "idle talk." The following evening, a Saturday, the bomber struck. At 11:00, a Yellow Cab pulled up to the curb in front of the Harrison house, the door sprang open, and a man jumped out and ran to the front porch. There he deposited a package before dashing back to the cab. Minutes later, an explosion rocked the house. Anger swept the black community. "This recent explosion could have been easily prevented by the police," exclaimed the *Defender*. But not only did the police seem to be uninterested in protecting the property of blacks, "It really appears" that they have been "giving aid and comfort to a certain element of violators of the law." The police belatedly detailed a squad to protect the family, but the very next night the bombers lobbed explosives from a vacant apartment next door onto the roof of the Harrison house. The skylight was destroyed and more windows shattered. Someone had unlocked the apartment to admit the bombers and locked it afterward, but the police did not question the occupants of the adjacent building or those leaving it after the explosion. "Neighbors Planned Bombing," charged the *Defender*. "The people in the block appeared to have information as to the exact time the explosion would occur."[2]

Nor was this the end of the story. The Harrisons had bought the property from a white realtor, William B. Austin, a man who apparently was sympathetic to equal access to adequate housing for both blacks and whites. After the two bombings, Austin began to receive anonymous letters assuring him that police guards would be useless and promising that the bombing campaign had only begun. The Harrisons moved from Grand Boulevard in mid-June 1919, just a couple of weeks after "a man on a bicycle" hurled a bomb at Austin's Lake Shore Drive home as he rode past.[3]

The Harrison and Austin bombings were not isolated occurrences. From July 1917 to the eruption of the Chicago race riot in late July 1919, no less than twenty-six bombs were exploded at isolated black residences in once all-white neighborhoods and at the offices of certain realtors who sold to blacks. Over half these bombs were exploded during the tense six months leading up to the riot.[4] According to the virulent denunciations by the black press of both the bombers and the police who failed to apprehend them, the single most important cause of the riot was housing. Out of the interracial conflict over housing there arose in the black community a marked lack of faith in the willingness and ability of the police to provide impartial protection. This sentiment, based in some cases on reality and in others on hearsay, led blacks to depend more and more on their own resources for protection. Furthermore, participation in the war, a recently realized and potent political voice in Chicago's affairs, and the self-respect of a courted wage earner had kindled a "New Negro" attitude. The "New Negro" was resolved to defend his family and home with militance. The housing crisis also stimulated the formation of property owners' associations avowedly hostile to blacks. The threats of these organizations and the bombings accentuated black racial solidarity, thus retarding even further the possibility of interracial accord through mutual interchange.

It is ironic, in light of the strident contention of numerous white property owners that blacks were alien to Chicago's institutions, that the city's first resident was apparently Jean Baptiste Point du Saible, a San Dominican black who built a trading post at the mouth of the Chicago River in 1779 and lived there for sixteen years. Despite this beginning, only a few blacks trickled into Chicago before the Civil War, largely because of laws excluding blacks—slave and free—from the state of Illinois. From 1860 to 1870, however, Chicago's black population rocketed by 285 percent, although nationwide the increase was 9.9 percent. Most of the new arrivals obtained domestic employment, and although there was no one black settlement, concentrations of black servant residences grew in areas near the homes of their wealthy white employers. After the Great Fire of 1871, a second fire in 1874, and the dispersal of blacks as well as whites to the undamaged areas, the concentration of blacks and their social institutions on the South Side took vague shape.

Chicago was expanding with such rapidity after 1870 that the black influx, though proportionately large, little more than kept pace with the flood of white immigrants. The new residential districts that emerged were often segregated, so that the black arrivals gravitated to their own increasingly dense settlements, especially the major concentration on the South Side. At the turn of the century, there were still black residences scattered throughout the city. A black studying in Chicago reported, however, that "no large Northern city shows a greater degree of segregation."[5]

As shown by several incidents in the 1890s and the first few years of the twentieth century, the most effective enforcer of residential segregation in Chicago was organized white resistance. In 1897, for example, Woodlawn property owners met and "declared war" against the small colony of blacks living in the neighborhood. Owners who rented to blacks were angrily denounced as "enemies" who "should be tarred and feathered." Intimidated by threats of violence, blacks often chose to move. Five years later, whites in Woodlawn succeeded in having construction stopped on an apartment house being remodeled for black occupancy. Celia Parker Woolley, the founder of a black settlement house, noted at this time that she could not obtain property for the venture. Realtors "were not averse to Negroes living on the premises if they were servants," she reported, "but so soon as they heard that the Negroes were to be considered on a par with white people they refused to lease the property."[6]

By 1906, well over half of Chicago's blacks lived in the South Side "black belt" between 12th and 57th Streets, and Wentworth and Cottage Grove Avenues. And while blacks, as one of their leaders wrote in 1905, did "not occupy all the worst streets and live in all the unsanitary houses in Chicago, what is known as the 'Black Belt' is altogether forbidding and demoralizing." The next largest settlement was on the West Side, and blacks had also filtered into Englewood, the near North Side, and Hyde Park. Between 1906 and 1912, the black belt and its satellite areas absorbed almost 10,000 new black residents. By 1912, many of these neighborhoods were saturated.[7]

A. P. Comstock, a sociologist who surveyed housing conditions in 1912, particularly in the South Side enclave, outlined the debilitating effects of such human density. On the South Side, he reported, most buildings were of pre-1902 vintage—that is, built before the city ordinances governing the construction of tenements had imposed specific, encompassing restrictions on builders. More toilets were outside the apartments than inside; they were in hallways, yards, and basements—and there were even some "privy vaults," which the city had outlawed in 1894. Sleeping rooms were overcrowded, usually because black tenants paying appreciably higher rents than whites took in lodgers to compensate for the racial differential. Outside stairways and porches were falling apart; lighting and ventilation were inadequate. The residents complained to Comstock that since black quarters were nearly always rentable, landlords refused to make necessary repairs. Other social investigators corroborated his findings. "In no other part" of the city, wrote S. P. Breckenridge of the University of Chicago, "was there found a neighborhood so conspicuously dilapidated as the black belt on the South Side. No other group," she added, "suffered so much from decaying buildings, leaking roofs, doors without hinges, broken windows, insanitary plumbing, rotting floors, and a general lack of repairs." This was the deplorable state of black housing in 1912, several years before a migration that more than doubled the city's black population.[8]

As the influx increased during the war, the disquieting aspects of the housing situation multiplied. Expansion of the areas of black residence was negligible; migration resulted instead in the drastically intensified density of the existing areas. On the South Side, for example, within the same spatial boundaries the black community almost tripled in numbers from 34,335 to 92,501—close to 90 percent of Chicago's black population. None of Chicago's blacks in 1910 had lived in a census tract that was more than 75 percent black; in 1920, 35.7 percent of the black population did. Only 30.8 percent in 1910 had lived in one that was more than 50 percent black; in 1920, 50.0 percent did.[9] Rents soared, moreover, since the demand for housing in the black belt far exceeded the supply. As before, rents for blacks were 15 to 25 percent higher than they were for whites, a fact that prompted the *Defender* to protest: "The principal idea . . . of some of these rent vampires is to gouge, gouge, gouge."[10] In addition to the excessive rents levied by black and white landlords alike, the migration accentuated both the overcrowding and the shabbiness of the facilities and militated against their being corrected.

Numerous blacks naturally wanted to escape these surroundings. Not only was the black belt dilapidated, decaying, and overcrowded, with landlords who overcharged and were obdurate in their refusal to make needed repairs, it was also a breeder of disease and the city's officially sanctioned receptacle for vice. Medical authorities boasted of statistics showing that Chicago's death rate was the lowest of any city in the world with a population of over one million. The statistics told another story as well, however; Chicago's blacks had a death rate twice that of whites. The still-birth rate was twice as high; the death rate from tuberculosis and syphilis was six times as high; and from pneumonia and nephritis, it was well over three times as high. The death rate for the entire city was indeed commendable. But the statistics indicated that the death rate for Chicago's blacks was comparable to that of Bombay, India.[11]

Vice and crime, which were controlled by men of both races, proliferated in the black belt. Such infamous operators as "Teenan" Jones, "Red Dick" Wilson, "Yellow Bill" Bass, "Mexican Frank," "Billy" Lewis, and Isadore Levin conducted their lurid businesses apparently without restraint before the migration—and, if anything, vice did not abate in the black belt during the war and in 1919. Guides to Chicago's night life boasted of the city's " 'black-and-tan' cabarets," establishments like The Pekin, The Entertainers, Dreamland, and The Panama, where "promiscuous dancing and the intermingling of the races may be observed . . . freely." Reformers, on the other hand, castigated these biracial houses of amusement, bemoaning that "the patrons were negroes and whites who danced together in a most immoral way." Whether friends or foe of this entertainment, there was no denying the abundance in the black belt of houses of prostitution, saloons, cabarets, billiard rooms, and gambling establishments.[12] Petty crime abounded. Boys, for example, would steal lead pipe and other salvageable items from vacant houses and then sell them to junk dealers. The incidence of more serious crime—murder, assault and battery, and arson—in the black belt spiraled during the migration.[13]

Whether this aggressive and disruptive behavior was a function of over-crowding, of social disorganization, or of despair, or perhaps of combina-tions of all these, the net result was the same: the desire of countless blacks to move away and leave the black belt far behind. Despite a natural preference to live near familiar social, economic, and religious institutions, numerous blacks with the financial resources sought sanitary, adequately maintained homes elsewhere.[14] In addition, vacancies in the black belt were practically nonexistent. In the spring of 1917, the Chicago Urban League, which met many of the migrants at the train station and was more instrumental in securing homes for them than any other agency, noted sadly: "It is impossible to do much else short of the construction of apart-ments for families and for single men." That summer, the Urban League canvassed the real estate dealers who supplied dwellings to blacks to ascertain the seriousness of the shortage. The dealers replied that of 664 black applicants, they were able to assist only 50. Since the migrants ordinarily could not afford to move into white neighborhoods, and since they were probably apprehensive of direct social contact with whites, it seems apparent that those who sought to leave the black belt behind them were generally the city's earlier and more prosperous black residents. In a sense, the migrant, whom the more established residents felt to be an undesirable neighbor, and with whom they increasingly identified such distasteful traits as prostitution, gambling, juvenile delinquency and illegiti-macy, was forcing the old settlers out, just as their own "invasions" would subsequently encourage whites to move.[15]

The directions in which the black belt could expand were few; it was in "the zone of transition—the interstitial region between residence and industry."[16] To the north were many of the city's light factories and busi-nesses. Although this was a run-down district, real estate prices were far beyond the reach of the ordinary househunter due to the industrial potential of the property. To the west, across Wentworth Avenue, were the Irish, whose hostility excluded blacks from that market. This hostility was so intense that the population in one Irish-dominated neighborhood bordering on Wentworth would tolerate only 29 blacks out of 3,762 residents, while in the neighborhood just on the other side of Wentworth, 1,722 out of 3,711 residents were black.[17] To the east, blacks could move into the limited area from Wabash Avenue to Lake Michigan. But as soon as they had occu-pied it, the only other direction for sizable expansion was southward—to the Hyde Park and Kenwood neighborhoods.[18]

Being immediately adjacent to the black belt, Hyde Park was the inevitable destination of numerous blacks. It was also a deteriorating neighborhood, one whose homes blacks could afford. Of the over 900 black property owners there in 1920, scarcely 10 could have purchased their properties at the original prices. For several decades property values had been declining because of the odor of the stockyards, the smoke and soot of the Illinois Central trains, the conversion of large homes into apartment buildings and flats, and the fear of an "invasion" of blacks from nearby areas. The residents of Hyde Park fled to escape further depreciation, and in 1916, just as the migration from the South was gaining momentum, an estimated 25 percent of the buildings in the district stood vacant. The older city residents and the few migrants who brought money with them or united with others to purchase properties at the prevailing low prices streamed into Hyde Park to join the few blacks who had moved in earlier almost unnoticed. Other blacks rented in the neighborhood. This process of expansion continued for nearly two years.[19]

During the war, residential construction largely ceased in Chicago, as elsewhere. In the early months of 1918 came the first effects of a housing shortage that was soon to be acute. The demands of whites for dwellings began to exceed the supply. Ugly interracial competition for homes broke out, as enterprising realtors touched off artificial panics with rumors that the blacks were "invading," and then proceeded to buy the properties of whites at low prices and sell them to blacks at sizable profits. Many whites soon blamed blacks for the vagaries of property values, the scarcity of housing, and urban decay.[20]

Although blacks seemed to blight the neighborhoods they inhabited, these neighborhoods were generally run down before their arrival. It was natural, moreover, that black rentees and lessees should exhibit a lack of respect for properties which their landlords were actually allowing to deteriorate further. In addition, because of excessive rents and exclusion from adjoining areas, blacks overcrowded both their buildings and their districts.

To be sure, the migrants were unaccustomed to city living. When it was hot, they paraded without shirts or shoes; they hung their wash on stoops to dry; they loitered on street corners. But no one more fully appreciated the incompatibility between this behavior and the higher aspirations of the race than other blacks. The *Defender,* the black belt's aldermen and churches, and the Wabash Avenue YMCA and other social service agencies staged such events as Clean Up and Grass Seed Weeks in 1918, and a Tin Can Day and Health Week in 1919. Saturday, April 26, was Tin Can Day, and hundreds of boys and girls combed the alleys and back yards. "Old trunks, suitcases, tubs, baby carriages, push carts, and wagons were commandeered for hauling cans." Five dollars in gold was the prize, and the minimum entry was 300 cans. This minimum figure, as it turned out, was superfluous, for the winning entry was 6,840 cans, and altogether 100,587 were turned in.[21]

The *Defender* featured a column entitled "Neighborhood Improvements," and the Urban League issued to migrants a "creed of cleanliness" that sought to appeal to the blacks' national pride. "I AM AN AMERICAN CITIZEN," the creed proclaimed. "I AM PROUD of our boys 'over there' who have contributed soldier service." These soldiers had learned "NEW HABITS OF SELF-RESPECT AND CLEANLINESS," habits which the migrants then vowed to observe for themselves. "I WILL ATTEND to the neatness of my personal appearance on the street or when sitting in front doorways. I WILL REFRAIN from wearing dust caps, bungalow aprons, house clothing and bedroom shoes out of doors. I WILL ARRANGE MY TOILET within doors. . . . I WILL INSIST upon the use of rear entrances for coal dealers, hucksters, etc. . . . I WILL DO MY BEST to prevent defacement of property either by children or adults." Two photographs accompanied the creed, one of a slovenly front porch, strewn with articles of clothing; the other of a clean, well-polished front porch. Seated on the first porch were three women in houserobes and kerchiefs; one of them peeled potatoes while the second combed the third's hair. The four women on the other porch entertained themselves by reading and engaging in polite conversation; they were neatly dressed, all with their buttons buttoned and without kerchiefs on their heads. These efforts at neighborhood and personal improvement were continued despite the unabated influx of migrants and the sustained demand for dwellings even approaching habitability. But for many if not most of the migrants, the adjustment to their new status as citizens of the North proved to be herculean. "During their period of absorption into the new life," Walter F. White of the NAACP wrote after the riot, many of the migrants tended to be "care-free, at times irresponsible and sometimes even boisterous," and this "conduct caused complications difficult to adjust."[22]

Several white property owners' associations, most of which had organized initially for responsible community projects and beautification, now focused their efforts on forcing out the blacks already residing in their neighborhoods and on ensuring that no others entered. The activities of these associations were conspicuous in the contested districts lying between 39th and 59th streets, and State Street and Lake Michigan. They consisted of mass meetings to arouse their neighbors against the blacks and of the publication in their journals of scathing denunciations of the race. The Community Property Owners' Protection Association, for example, was organized in September 1917. Its constituency was the district bounded by 39th and 51st streets, and Cottage Grove and Michigan Boulevard; its purpose was "keeping 'undesirables' out." "We don't want any gentlemen of color or gentlemen off color in our midst," declared one of the association's organizers, a local realtor.[23]

From early 1917 the property owners' associations and most realtors attempted to restrict the blacks to the black belt. In April 1917, a committee of seven representing the Chicago Real Estate Board, including four realtors in contested neighborhoods, estimated that the "promiscuous sales" to blacks of residences on all-white blocks had brought about immense property depreciation ranging from $5,000 to $360,000 per block. The committee recommended two courses of action to obviate the alleged decline in values.[24] First, it urged the property owners' associations to build up neighborhood solidarity so that no more defectors would sell out to blacks. It then called for a meeting with the blacks to discuss the practicability of block-by-block segregation. The same month the Real Estate Board committee met with Jesse Binga, Chicago's leading black banker, Robert S. Abbott, editor of the *Defender*, A. L. Jackson, and other black leaders, and asked them to persuade black realtors to "desist" from selling houses to their people in white neighborhoods. The blacks refused.

Several months later, the committee of white realtors adopted a resolution calling upon the Real Estate Board to prevent "race hatred, violence, and blood-shed" by appealing to the city council to enact legislation prohibiting further immigration of blacks to Chicago "until suitable provisions are made and such reasonable restriction of leasing or selling be enforced as to prevent lawlessness, destruction of values and property and loss of life." No such legislation was considered by the city council; but news of the realtors' appeal did serve to outrage leaders in the black community. "At this time," complained Binga loudly, "when the black men and the white men are asked to do their bit, it is nothing less than a crime . . . for real estate men . . . to begin an agitation on Race segregation." Black men would hesitate to enlist in the army if they suspected that their wives and children would be "subject to designing promoters, who are conspiring to develop race hatred in their neighborhood. . . ."[25]

Two obstacles blocked the legislative quarantine of blacks. In order for the Chicago City Council to enact zoning legislation, racial or otherwise, it first had to obtain an enabling act from the Illinois General Assembly, which was dominated by representatives from southern Illinois whose antagonism toward Chicago was renowned.[26] The second roadblock was a decision the United States Supreme Court delivered in 1917. In *Buchanan v. Warley*, the court invalidated a Louisville, Kentucky, racial zoning ordinance.[27] As a direct result of this ruling, restrictive covenants came into being, but these efficacious instruments of segregation did not gain currency in Chicago until the mid-1920s.[28] Lacking the voluntary or legal means to isolate blacks, white Chicagoans resorted to extralegal or illegal methods—intimidation and bombings.

In November 1917, just days after the Supreme Court announced its *Buchanan* v. *Warley* decision, the Chicago Real Estate Board reaffirmed the need for founding property owners' associations. The board resolved to "start a propaganda through its individual members to recommend owners societies in every white block for the purpose of mutual defense."[29] Of these organizations, the Kenwood and Hyde Park Property Owners' Association, which first gained notice in the fall of 1918 for its agitation to "make Hyde Park white," was perhaps the largest and undoubtedly the most vocal. "WE want you to join our organization," began the letter of solicitation: "Hyde Park is the finest residential district in Chicago," and in spite of "the weak-kneed [who] think it is too late," "WE are going to keep it that way." Joining this "red blooded organization," the letter continued, would put "big money in your pocket besides preserving our homes for ourselves and children."[30] The association launched a series of protest meetings at which racial antagonism permeated the speeches, and at which the audiences applauded inflammatory rhetoric promoting the use of bombs and bullets. "The depreciation of our property . . . has been two hundred and fifty millions since the invasion," one of the association's speakers declared in the spirit of World War I. "If someone told you that there was to be an invasion that would injure your homes to that extent, wouldn't you rise up as one man and one woman, and say as General Foch said, 'They shall not pass'?"

The avowed purpose of the organization was the prevention of the alleged depreciation of property by blacks, although from the speeches and editorials it was apparent that the implication of an inferior status for whites residing near blacks grated on the members. The *Property Owners' Journal,* the organ of the Hyde Park–Kenwood Association, inevitably linked aspirations of social equality to the blacks' quest for better housing: "The effrontery and impudence that nurses a desire on the part of the Negro to choose a white as a marriage mate will not result in making the Negro a desirable neighbor. . . ."[31]

As a solution to the black "invasion," bombing might have been viewed as a last resort, but it was attempted early. The first of the bombs arrived in July 1917, when one crashed into the vestibule of the home of Mrs. S. P. Motley on the South Side. Mrs. Motley and her family had moved into the house in 1913, the first black family on the block, and they had been living there peacefully for four years. The property had been purchased from a Mrs. Hughes, who, blacks charged, was a "nigger hater" and "an ardent supporter" of the Kenwood–Hyde Park Association. What seemed particularly to rankle Mrs. Hughes, in addition to her hatred of blacks, was that a white agent had negotiated the transaction for Mrs. Motley, and she had not discovered that blacks had been the buyers until the Motleys moved in. When several other black families joined the Motleys on the block in 1917, their white neighbors denounced Mrs. Motley for enticing them there and for operating a rooming house. Fortunately, the bomb claimed no victims, but a family residing in a first-floor flat barely escaped injury when the bomb was detonated, showering them with plaster, blowing out part of the parlor wall, and demolishing the vestibule and porch.[32]

After an eight-month hiatus during which the black expansion continued, the bombers returned in earnest. From March 1918, to the outbreak of the riot, twenty-five bombs rocked the homes of blacks and the homes and offices of realtors of both races. Of the eleven bombings in 1918, four were of properties merely held by black real estate agents, while the other seven were of black-inhabited dwellings. Moreover, mobs brandishing brickbats and other weapons and missiles stoned buildings, and intimidation and threats of further violence burgeoned as well. "Look out; you're next for hell," read a "black hand notice." Another was addressed to the black tenants on Vincennes Avenue: "We are going to BLOW these FLATS TO HELL and if you don't want to go with them you had better move at once."[33]

Realtors persisted in commercializing racial antagonism in 1919. Panicky whites focused their wrath on the black race; and blacks, suffering increasingly from the police department's failure to discourage the bombers, viewed the whites with suspicion and made ready to defend their homes and families against further violence. During the first six months of 1919, the bombers struck on fourteen occasions, and one of their bombs killed a six-year-old black girl. In January, explosives damaged the offices of one white and one black realtor, and on March 20 bombs exploded in the doorway of Jesse Binga's real estate office and that of an apartment building for which he was the agent.[34]

Early the next month, explosives tore a gaping hole in the hallway of an apartment building in Hyde Park which a black, J. Yarbrough, had purchased from Binga scarcely three months before. The Defender intimated that Yarbrough's white neighbors knew of the bombers' plans and were possibly conspirators. "It is strange . . ." noted the newspaper, that even though "the explosion occurred at 2 A.M.," the whites on the block "were up and fully dressed and over to inspect the damage." Since any neighborhood explosion would no doubt rouse nearby residents out of bed and into their clothes in less then ten minutes, the Defender betrayed an understandable bias in its indirect accusation. Yarbrough, however, agreed with the Defender's suspicion, for he filed a $300,000 damage suit against the Hyde Park–Kenwood Association, citing by name four real estate brokers, including the president, secretary, and a former secretary of the association. In filing the suit, Yarbrough's attorney explained: "We believe the men who placed this bomb are in the employ of real estate men and that the purpose of their work is to frighten Negroes out of . . . the neighborhood."[35]

Possibly there was substance to Yarbrough's claims. The Chicago police arrested only two suspects in connection with the siege of bombings, one of whom was a clerk in the real estate firm of Dean and Meagher in Hyde Park. Both Dean and Meagher were members of the Hyde Park–Kenwood Association, and Dean put up bond for the suspected bomber. White homeowners and real estate dealers of the Hyde Park–Kenwood Association had earlier threatened to "bomb out" blacks residing there. In addition, although two other predominantly white neighborhoods in Chicago were in the "reaction" or conflict stage of residential transition, the agitation against blacks where there was no Hyde Park–Kenwood Association was unorganized and assumed no more violent form than that of warning letters. As to motive, the association was dominated by realtors who held extensive property in Hyde Park and who affirmed unequivocally that blacks and property depreciation were synonymous. They endeavored, therefore, to preserve their interests by encouraging blacks to move away and by discouraging any future influxes.

Some residences were bombed just after blacks purchased them, but months before occupancy and before the public learned of the sales; probably only realtors, along with mortgage bankers, deed registrars, and the principals had occasion to know of these transactions. Finally, the waves of bombings ensued straightaway after, and apparently as a result of, the association's virulent protests against black occupancy.[36] Whether or not the realtors of the Hyde Park–Kenwood Association conspired to bomb out the blacks, two facts were evident: The bombings usually occurred shortly after speakers at association meetings had denounced blacks in vitriolic language (four bombs followed the organization's May 5 meeting); and these denunciations were becoming decidedly more vitriolic that summer.

"PREVENT FURTHER INCURSION BY UNDESIRABLES," proclaimed a poster announcing the June 6 meeting of the Hyde Park–Kenwood Association. No doubt the association would have been shocked to discover that blacks, among them the white-skinned, blue-eyed Walter F. White of the NAACP, had infiltrated the meetings, and that White would attend on June 6. White's description of the meeting's "inflammatory and incendiary remarks" was corroborated by Mrs. Meta Harvey, a black who attended the June 20 and 27 gatherings. When she entered the June 20 meeting, which was convened at a bank, she heard the speaker outlining a plan for removing a black hospital from the South Side within the next two months. A voice from the floor interrupted to demand action, not talk; and there were other references to the need for "pep" in forcing the hospital's removal within thirty rather than sixty days. Mayor William H. Thompson and the city's health commissioner were castigated for "their favorable attitude" toward blacks and for "assenting to the location of the hospital where it was." Some voices urged caution, but their advice was ignored. Blacks had armed, said one man; they had bought 800 rifles and buckets full of ammunition at a local department store; there would be bloodshed "if they went at the matter the way they were talking about." "Bloodshed, nothing!" another man shouted in anger. "Let them step on my corns and I'll show them what I'll do." "If we can't get them out any other way," agreed a voice in the rear, "we are going to put them in with the bolsheviki and bomb them out." Throughout the evening, speakers referred to blacks as "niggers" and "undesirables." One speaker told what he had done to three blacks "hanging around his place." He had put a "bolt" in his fist and knocked one down; "that's the way to treat the 'niggers'," he added. The association's officers, practically all of whom were local realtors and officials of the Chicago Real Estate Board, reported that any real estate agent who did not refuse to rent or sell to blacks would be blacklisted; that block captains had been selected to report any attempts by blacks to move into the district; and, finally, that three hotels in the neighborhood had agreed to cooperate in a plan whereby black employees who did not consent to vacate their residences in the district would be discharged. With these announcements, the meeting was adjourned.[37]

And, indeed, blacks repeatedly advocated arming themselves in the summer of 1919. For the flagrant negligence and indifference of the police had convinced them that they would have to provide their own protection against the property owners' associations and the bombers. Even when blacks reported bomb threats, for example, and the police staked out the buildings beforehand, they made no arrests afterward. A delegation twice attempted to file a complaint with Mayor Thompson in June 1919, but the mayor's secretary refused to permit the blacks to see him. The *Defender* expressed the consensus of the black community when it protested: "Police activity has been so deliberate and brazenly neglectful that one might construe that they are working in harmony with the bomb throwers."[38] The following week the *Defender* offered the only practical solution it saw to such one-sided law enforcement when it asked: "Why do these things go on unchecked and the perpetrators not apprehended? . . . Something must be done, and something will be done. If we must protect ourselves we shall do it with a vengeance. . . . this is nature's first law."[39]

The *Whip* also espoused self-defense. A newspaper that had begun publication in the summer of 1919, the *Whip* voiced the attitude of the "New Negro," the militant, intensely race-conscious black who felt acutely the blighted hope of heightened status for blacks after the war:

The *Whip* informs you, the whites, that the compromising peace-at-any price Negro is rapidly passing into the scrap heap of yesterday and being supplanted by a fearless, intelligent Negro who recognizes no compromise but who demands absolute justice and fair play. . . . WE ARE NOT PACIFISTS, THEREFORE WE BELIEVE IN WAR, BUT ONLY WHEN ALL ORDERLY CIVIL PROCEDURE HAS BEEN EXHAUSTED AND THE POINTS IN QUESTION ARE JUSTIFIABLE. . . . THE BOMBERS WILL BE BOMBED.[40]

With the advent of summer, the housing situation appeared still gloomier. The shortage in Chicago approached 50,000 apartments and houses, affecting upwards of 200,000 people; this, in turn, created boosts in rents from 10 to 30 and, in some cases, up to 100 percent.[41] Returning servicemen aggravated the scarcity. Worse yet, expectations of an enormous summertime construction program to offset at least part of the dearth of dwellings disappeared in mid-July when Chicago's contractors locked out 115,000 building tradesmen. The racial bombings were an accurate gauge of the multiplying housing scarcity; seven explosions punctuated the six sultry weeks preceding the riot. This was the most intensive rash of bombings yet, and it underscored the blacks' distrust of the police and their need for solidarity.

The hostility of the fearful white residents meanwhile proceeded to fuse with antipathy to blacks in other spheres, thus creating a more nearly unbroken white front. The property owners' associations, for example, espoused the battle cry of those who denounced black political power. Undoubtedly reflecting white anger over the April 1919 mayoralty election in which William Hale Thompson was reelected with only 38 percent of the total vote, the *Property Owners' Journal* carried scathing denunciations of blacks whose bloc support accounted for much of Thompson's plurality. "This vote situation," declared the *Journal*, "is the foundation of the Chicago Negro's effrontery and his evil design against the white man's property." Holding the balance of power, the black vote "can dictate the policy of any administration that happens to be elected by his controlling vote . . . Wake up, white voters!"[42]

The apex of racial antagonism—the summer of 1919—was in part a conjunction of elements antithetical to black aspirations. Conflict over housing, when fused with bitter competition over jobs, political power, and facilities for education, transportation, and relaxation, set the stage for the tragedy that was to follow—the bloody Chicago race riot of 1919.

On a crowded South Side beach on the afternoon of Sunday, July 27, 1919, white and black swimmers clashed in savage combat. Sparked by this clash, during which a black youth drowned, the interracial resentment that had been smoldering in Chicago exploded in furious rioting. The violence raged uncontrolled for five days, as whites mauled blacks and blacks in turn assaulted white peddlers and merchants in the black belt. Members of both races craved vengeance as stories of atrocities, both real and rumored, rapidly spread throughout the city. White gunmen in automobiles sped through the ghetto shooting indiscriminately as they passed, and black snipers fired back. Roaming mobs shot, beat, and stabbed their victims to death. The undermanned, and in some cases unwilling, Chicago police force was an ineffectual deterrent to the waves of violence that soon overflowed the environs of the black belt and flooded the North and West sides as well as the Loop, the city's downtown business district. Only six regiments of state militiamen and a cooling rain finally quenched the passions of the rioters, but by then thirty-eight lay dead—twenty-three blacks and fifteen whites—and well over 500 others had sustained injuries.[43]

In the area of housing, the riot did not prove to be a cathartic, purging certain people of their desire violently to dislodge the blacks. Indeed, with even greater frequency after the riot than before, bombs demolished windows, porches, vestibules, and other portions of the homes of black people residing in contested neighborhoods. Also damaged were the residences and offices of the realtors of both races who sold and rented to blacks. One in August and five in December 1919; in 1920, six in February, one each in March, April, September, and December, and two in October—this was the toll of bombings. Other realtors, politicians, and even the coroner's jury investigating the deaths of riot victims advocated the residential segregation of the races as the solution to unrest in the city. The property owners' associations were more vocal than ever before. "EVERY WHITE PERSON" was the addressee of a poster which the Hyde Park–Kenwood Association had nailed on trees and poles in the district. There would be a meeting, "the most important meeting ever held in the history of Hyde Park," the poster announced, on the evening of October 20, 1919. "Protect your property. . . . Shall we sacrifice our property for one-third of its value? And run like rats from a burning ship?" the poster asked. "Or shall we put up a united front and keep Hyde Park desirable for ourselves?" The meeting drew 2,000 people, who at the end rose "with one accord," and shouted their intention "to free the district of Negroes." Pamphlets circulated in contested neighborhoods after the riot. One of them, "An Appeal of White Women to American Humanity," told of the "horrible conduct of [black] French Colonials on the Rhine and the abuse of German white women." Yet the police did little or nothing to protect black residents, despite the public threats of realtors and property owners' associations to rid certain areas of the "invaders." "Property is being destroyed and life endangered by bomb throwing," Francis W. Shepardson, a white member of the Chicago Commission on Race Relations, complained to Governor Frank O. Lowden in February 1920. "The facts are known to all. They are reported in the papers. But," he added, "there seems to be no authority interested in the protection of Americans whose skins are black. The condition is a disgrace to American citizenship"; and, Shepardson predicted, "Unless something is done soon another riot is certain."[44]

Shepardson's well-informed prediction proved to be incorrect. Even though the bombs continued to explode and the police continued to be ineffectual in their pursuit of the bombers, there was no further riot. It is at this point that the task of the historian becomes difficult. Given the continuing friction and unrest, why was there no riot? Perhaps the answer lies in a widespread but unexpressed revulsion, shared by black and white alike, at the excesses of the 1919 bloodshed. It is a fact that throughout American history major riots have seldom occurred in the same city within a short period of time. Whatever the reason, it seems clear that Chicagoans in the 1920s were fortunate to escape a recurrence of the bloodshed and violence that badly defiled their city's reputation in 1919.

NOTES

Scholars interested in more detailed documentation of this article should consult the author's *Race Riot: Chicago in the Red Summer of 1919* (New York: Atheneum, 1970), especially pp. 165–83.

1. *Chicago Defender,* November 23, 1918.

2. *Ibid.,* May 24 and 31, June 21, 1919; Arna Bontemps and Jack Conroy, *Anyplace But Here* (New York: Hill and Wang, 1966), pp. 175–6; Chicago Commission on Race Relations, *The Negro in Chicago* (Chicago: University of Chicago Press, 1922), pp. 128–9; *Chicago Daily Journal,* June 17, 1919; *Chicago Herald-Examiner,* June 17, 1919; Richard Bardolph, *The Negro Vanguard* (New York: Vintage, 1959), pp. 241, 242–3.

3. *Chicago Broad Ax,* June 22, 1918; clipping from *Chicago Post,* June 20, 1919, in NAACP Papers, collection of NAACP's regional Youth Division, Washington, D.C. (NAACP–2).

4. Figures and dates of the bombings vary, but see Interchurch World Movement, *The Inter-Racial Situation in Chicago* (no imprint); list of bombings in NAACP-2; Chicago Crime Commission, *Illinois Crime Survey,* part 3 (Chicago: Illinois Association for Criminal Justice, 1929), pp. 958–9; Chicago Commission on Race Relations, *op. cit.,* pp. 115ff, 596.

5. Thomas A. Meehan, "Jean Baptiste Point du Saible, the First Chicagoan," *Mid-America,* XIX (April 1937), 83–92; R. R. Wright, Jr., "The Negro in Chicago," *Southern Workman,* XXXV (October 1906), 554, 557; E. Franklin Frazier, *The Negro Family in Chicago* (Chicago: University of Chicago Press, 1932), pp. 90–97; Robert C. Weaver, *The Negro Ghetto* (New York: Harcourt, Brace, 1948), pp. 14–18; Monroe Work, "Negro Real Estate Holders in Chicago" (unpublished master's thesis, University of Chicago, 1903), *passim;* R. R. Wright, "The Industrial Condition of Negroes in Chicago" (unpublished D. B. thesis, University of Chicago, 1901), pp. 7–10; Bessie Louise Pierce, *A History of Chicago,* 3 vols. (New York: Knopf, 1937, 1940, 1957), I, 186, 413–18; II, 11–12, 33–34, 382–3; III, 480.

6. Memoranda in "Negro in Illinois," WPA Collection, files in George Cleveland Hall Branch, Chicago Public Library, quoting from *Chicago Record,* May 5, 1897; and from *Chicago Inter-Ocean,* September 28 and 30, 1894, August 19, 1900, February 12 and July 25, 1902, December 15, 1904; Allan H. Spear, *Black Chicago: The Making of a Negro Ghetto, 1890–1920* (Chicago: University of Chicago Press, 1967), pp. 21–23; Homer Hoyt, *100 Years of Land Values in Chicago, 1830–1933* (Chicago: University of Chicago Press, 1933), pp. 215–16.

7. Fannie Barrier Williams, "Social Bonds in the 'Black Belt' of Chicago," *Charities,* XV (October 7, 1905), 40–44; David A. Wallace, "Residential Concentration of Negroes in Chicago" (unpublished Ph.D. dissertation, Harvard University, 1953), pp. 67–9.

8. Tuttle, *op. cit.,* p. 163.

9. *Ibid.*

10. *Ibid.,* p. 164.

11. These figures are from 1925 Health Department records, but all data indicate that the health of blacks was no better and perhaps even worse in 1919: H. L. Harris, "Negro Mortality Rates in Chicago," *Social Service Review,* I (March 1927), 58–77.

12. Tuttle, *op. cit.,* p. 165.

13. National Committee on Law Observance and Enforcement, *Report on Crime and the Foreign Born* (Washington, D.C.: Government Printing Office, 1931), X, 112–15.

14. See the suggestive essay by George M. Carstairs in National Commission on the Causes and Prevention of Violence, *Violence in America,* prepared under the direction of Hugh Davis Graham and Ted Robert Gurr (New York: Signet, 1969), pp. 730–42; George E. Haynes, "Conditions among Negroes in the Cities," *Annals,* XLIX (September 1913), 109.

15. E. Franklin Frazier, "The Impact of Urban Civilization upon Negro Family Life," *American Sociological Review,* II (October 1937), 609–18; Chicago League on Urban Conditions Among Negroes, *Annual Report,* I (no imprint), 10; Emmett Jay Scott, *Negro Migration During the War* (New York: Oxford University Press, 1920), p. 105; George E. Haynes, "Negroes Move North," *Survey,* XLI (January 4, 1919), 459.

16. Ernest W. Burgess, "Residential Segregation in American Cities," *Annals,* CXL (November 1928), 108.

17. *Ibid.,* pp. 111–12.

18. Tuttle, *op. cit.,* p. 167n.

19. Howard R. Gold and Byron K. Armstrong, *A Preliminary Study of Inter-Racial Conditions in Chicago* (New York: Home Missions Council, 1920), pp. 7–8; Thomas W. Allison, "Population Movements in Chicago," *Journal of Social Forces,* II (May 1924), 529–33; Spear, *op. cit.,* pp. 145–6; Chicago Commission on Race Relations, *op. cit.,* pp. 118, 196–200, 205, 206, 211–13; Charles S. Johnson, *The Negro in American Civilization* (New York: Holt, 1930), p. 205.

20. Tuttle, *op. cit.,* pp. 168–9.

21. "Elements in the South Side Problem," undated memorandum in NAACP–2; *Chicago Defender,* April 12, 19, 26 and May 3, 17, 1919; Chicago *Broad Ax,* June 14, 1918.

22. National Urban League, "An Idea Made Practical . . . Annual Report, 1919," National Urban League *Bulletin,* IX (January 1920), 20–21; Walter F. White, "Chicago and Its Eight Reasons," *Crisis,* XVIII (October 1919), 293–4.

23. *Chicago Defender,* September 22, 1917.

24. On the subject of race and depreciation in Chicago, see Hoyt, *op. cit.,* pp. 97, 124, 312–17; Burgess, *op. cit.,* pp. 113–14; *Chicago Daily Tribune,* May 10, 1919; "The Housing of Colored People," City Club of Chicago *Bulletin,* XII (August 18, 1919), 169–70; Egbert Schietinger, "Real Estate Transfers During Negro Invasion" (unpublished master's thesis, University of Chicago, 1948), pp. 4–5ff.

25. Chicago Real Estate Board *Bulletin,* XXV (April 18, May 15, October 15, November 21, 1917), 313–17, 355, 551, 623–4; *Chicago Defender,* April 14 and 21, November 10, 1917.

26. Tuttle, *op. cit.,* p. 173n.

27. *Buchanan* v. *Warley,* 245 U.S. 60. See "Race Segregation Ordinance Invalid," *Harvard Law Review,* XXXI (January 1918), 475–9; Davis McEntire, *Residence and Race* (Berkeley: University of California Press, 1960), p. 258.

28. Tuttle, *op. cit.,* p. 173n.

29. Chicago Real Estate Board *Bulletin,* XXV (November 21, 1917), 624.

30. In NAACP–2, "By Laws Kenwood Property Owner's [sic] Association"; letter from W. H. Schendorf to "Fellow Members," March 24, 1919; and copy of solicitation letter quoted in undated memorandum.

31. Chicago Commission on Race Relations, *op. cit.,* pp. 118, 119, 590–92; Jesse Binga's article on the Association in *Chicago Defender,* March 1, 1919; excerpts from letter from Hyde Park–Kenwood Association to Mayor Thompson, undated, NAACP–2.

32. A. Clement MacNeal to John Shilladay, April 15, 1920, including four affidavits–case histories of bombings, in NAACP–2; *Chicago Defender,* July 7, 1917.

33. *Chicago Defender,* May 11 and 25, June 1, 8, 15, August 31, September 28, October 26, November 2, 1918; *Chicago Broad Ax,* May 25, 1918; Chicago Commission on Race Relations, *op. cit.,* pp. 31, 123–33, 536, 596.

34. *Chicago Daily Journal,* March 20, 1919; *New York Age,* July 12, 1919; *Chicago Broad Ax,* June 7 and 14, July 12, 1919; *Chicago Defender,* June 7, 21, 28, 1919; Bontemps and Conroy, *op. cit.,* p. 176; Chicago Commission on Race Relations, *op. cit.,* p. 539; list of bombings in NAACP–2.

35. *Chicago Herald Examiner,* April 7, July 13, 1919; *Chicago Daily Journal,* April 7, July 12, 1919; *Chicago Daily Tribune,* April 7, 1919; *Chicago Defender,* April 12, 1919.

36. Tuttle, *op. cit.,* pp. 178–9.

37. *Ibid.,* pp. 179–80.

38. *Chicago Defender,* May 31, June 21, July 12, 1919; *Chicago Broad Ax,* June 7, July 12, 1919; *Chicago Daily News,* June 4, 1919.

39. *Chicago Defender,* June 28, 1919.

40. *Chicago Whip,* June 28, 1919.

41. *Chicago Daily News,* June 3, July 24, 1919; Chicago Real Estate Board *Bulletin,* XXVII (September 25, 1919), 720; *Chicago Defender,* April 19, 1919; *The New York Times,* July 25, 1919.

42. Chicago Commission on Race Relations, *op. cit.,* pp. 591–2.

43. Tuttle, *op. cit.,* pp. 3–10, 32–66.

44. *Ibid.,* pp. 250–51.

PART FIVE

THE RECURRENT URBAN CRISIS

One of the alleged symptoms of a man's advancing age is a tendency to dream nostalgically about the distant past. Thus may a city dweller recall neighborhoods that were once quiet and friendly, parks that were clean and safe, and public services that were cheap and efficient. His nostalgia may be fed by the sight of two communities from the distant past, Colonial Williamsburg in Virginia and Old Sturbridge Village in Massachusetts, where streets that once were choked with mud or dust are now paved and there is no suggestion of the rancid odors of decaying garbage and fecal waste that pervaded most American cities before the Civil War. In most such restoration projects everything works. Everything is clean, everything is pleasant, and the temptation is to contrast the projects with more typical urban environments, where transit strikes, sanitation strikes, police strikes, mail strikes, teacher strikes, and air controller strikes, to say nothing of power failures, filth, pollution, narcotics, and crime, create a miserable contemporary image.

Although urban pathology was not "discovered" until the late nineteenth century, neither our cities' problems today nor our attempted solutions to them are unique. The city in America has always been the locus of major social problems. Boston, New York, and Philadelphia faced serious conflicts in their streets between wheeled and pedestrian traffic even before the Revolutionary War, when uncontrollable animals and unregulated humans often met head-on. Nineteenth-century American cities were neither attractive nor clean, and their slums, venal municipal governments, overpopulation, and windfall speculators matched anything the twentieth century has produced. The current urban crisis is much better understood against its background of undesirable conditions in the past and responses to them by individuals and communities.

In colonial times and well into the nineteenth century, the most dangerous of all urban problems was fire. Conflagrations were common and deadly, although the relatively small size of most structures usually made it possible for people to escape with their lives if not their belongings. Because houses and businesses were made of wood and were usually contiguous, fires were exceptionally difficult to extinguish—especially when needed wells proved to be inoperative or too far from the blaze. In New York City in 1796, for example, more than 900 buildings burned in a single holocaust.

So great became the concern with fire that most American cities passed ordinances outlawing wooden structures in central areas, regulating the condition of chimneys, and prohibiting the storage of gunpowder or highly inflammable substances within the city limits. Arson was an especially serious offense, punishable by long prison terms or even by death. Volunteer fire companies proliferated in the eighteenth century. In Philadelphia, for example, fire protection began with Benjamin Franklin's formation of the Union Fire Company in 1736. Successful and popular by reason of their general sociability and irrepressible camaraderie, twenty more volunteer companies were established in Philadelphia before the Revolution, and by the eve of the Civil War the number had grown to more than 160.

Voluntary firemen were often dashing and heroic, but on occasion rival groups engaged in street fighting and hooliganism on the way to the flames. Increasingly, the larger cities saw the need for full-time, professional fire forces. Boston created a truly municipal fire department in 1842; Cincinnati, in 1853; New York, in 1865; and Philadelphia, in 1871. The great Chicago fire occurred in 1871, but by that date fire was no longer so much of a threat to urban life and property.

Epidemics, while less physically destructive than fire, were even more dreaded by urban residents. Once inside a city, infectious diseases were difficult to stop; in fact, the best preventative was escape to the country. Epidemics of smallpox, yellow fever, and cholera took a heavy toll in every city, particularly in the warm summer months. It seemed as if the very survival of cities might be at stake. As a Philadelphia citizens group remarked in 1793, if "the fever shall become an annual visitant, our cities must be abandoned, commerce will desert our coasts, and we, the citizens of this great metropolis, shall all of us, suffer much distress, and a great proportion of us be reduced to absolute ruin."

Little was done to mitigate the suffering before 1850; the theory that germs caused disease was then unknown and most people were content to believe that sickness was an instrument used by the Almighty to punish the wicked. That epidemics struck hardest at the poor was but additional evidence that the lower classes were intemperate and largely responsible for their own miseries.

The basic health problem, largely unrecognized at the time, was filth and unsanitary conditions. Alleys were filled with garbage that even pigs and dogs refused, and streets were lined with refuse. In Cleveland, the Cuyahoga River was on open sewer running through the city, and in Chicago a local paper reported in 1880 that "the air stinks. . . . No other word expresses it so well as stink. A stench means something finite. Stink reaches the infinite and becomes sublime in the magnitude of odiousness." And a visitor to Memphis just after the Civil War described it as follows:

The streets were huge depots of filth, cavernous Augean stables, with no Tiber to flow through and cleanse them. Front yards, back yards, avenues, alleys, and gutters were full of garbage, refuse, dead animals, and stagnant water, all producing a stench which, but for the adaptation peculiar to the olfactory sense, would have driven human life from the town.

Improvements in sanitation in the nineteenth century did much to alleviate the threat of disease. Sewers, introduced in Boston in 1823, were installed in most major cities by 1870, although it was almost impossible to find the money and labor necessary to build the complicated sewerage systems fast enough to keep pace with population growth. The greatest single impetus to the public health of American cities was the organization of the Metropolitan Board of Health in response to the threat of cholera in New York City in 1866. The New York State legislature gave the new health board sweeping powers over the city and all but the New Jersey suburbs. Among the board's achievements were more regular and more thorough cleanings of city streets, the removal of 160,000 tons of manure from vacant lots, the prohibition of butchering and tanning within congested areas, the disinfection of privies throughout the city, and the burning of personal articles belonging to the victims of cholera. There was opposition to the board's broad powers, but that year New York City suffered only one-tenth as many deaths as in the previous cholera epidemic of 1849.

Despite the achievement of the nation's largest city in the summer of 1866, disease remained a major problem of urban life. In the 1870s the infant mortality rate in Holyoke, Massachusetts, a typical New England mill city, was 312 per 1,000 children under one year of age. And in Memphis in 1878, a disastrous yellow-fever epidemic killed 5,000 of the 7,000 whites who remained behind in the city (blacks were relatively immune to the disease), including most of the Irish population. But as Charles Rosenberg has noted in *The Cholera Years*, a portion of which is reprinted in this section, the achievement of the Metropolitan Board of Health has a historical significance transcending its undeniable importance to the development of public medicine. It was, like the reaction to the problem of fire, a successful response to a specific challenge of urban life. It was a recognition of the fact that New York and other great cities could not and should not be abandoned—that an urban society must somehow solve the problems that an urban society creates. It also gave meaning to the proposition that government has no larger responsibility than to preserve human life. As a Cincinnati health officer put it, "Good privies are far higher signs of civilization than grand palaces and fine art galleries."

Neither fire nor disease could have come under control without the development of an adequate and pure supply of water. Certainly no other substance is more vital to urban life. In its absence, breadstuffs, pastries, soups, vegetables, and stewed meats could not be prepared; beer, soft drinks, coffee, and tea could not be served; dishes and clothes could not be washed; and human and industrial wastes could not be removed from the city.

In the colonial period water was not particularly popular with the city residents; according to Professor Carl Bridenbaugh the customary table drink came from a brewery rather than a well. In large part this was because well water was notoriously bad. In the 1740s even the horses balked at drinking New York water, and one enterprising well owner, realizing that he could not even give away his foul-smelling liquid, decided to bottle it and peddle it as medicine. Water above ground was no better. In the 1780s the Fresh Water Pond, where New York's Chinatown is now located, became notorious as a common sewer where housewives threw their slop buckets and other people threw dead dogs and cats. Legend has it that the cocktail drink known as a "Manhattan" derives its name from the color of the local water in the eighteenth century.

The nation's first municipal water system, designed for Philadelphia by the brilliant architect and engineer Benjamin Latrobe, went into operation in 1801. In its first fifteen years the system cost six times as much to operate as it received in revenue, but Philadelphians did not look at it from the perspective of cost. The water system came to be regarded as a great source of civic pride, something that made Philadelphia stand out as a particularly progressive, urbane, attractive, and sanitary metropolis. The Centre Square System became famous all over the world; even New York City residents recognized the superiority of the Philadelphia experiment over their own Manhattan Company, which in 1800 won an exclusive private franchise to provide water to the city. In 1835 New York voters approved by a three-to-one margin the construction of the Croton Aqueduct System at city expense. The investment was excellent.

This far-sighted undertaking, which has since been applauded many times, provided the framework for the present New York City water system, which remains among the best in the world. Thus the nation's largest cities led the way for smaller communities. By 1861 there were eighty private and sixty-eight public systems in operation throughout the country, and by 1900 the American municipal water achievement, judged either in terms of consumption per capita or in terms of filtration and purification, had surpassed that of anyplace else in the world.

Law enforcement proved to be more difficult to provide than water. The reformer Josiah Strong proclaimed that "the first city was built by the first murderer, and crime and vice and wretchedness have festered in it ever since," while another Midwestern spokesman, Hamlin Garland, entertained lurid dreams of the dangers attendant upon a callow youth who might venture to walk across downtown Chicago even at midday. Though these men obviously overstated the case in their attempt to make farm life seem relatively more attractive, the enormous growth of cities in the nineteenth century brought to quick obsolescence the old informal methods of colonial protection. As Professor James F. Richardson notes in his essay on the New York police, the old watch could not cope with riots, gangs, and confidence men, and the urban leadership in almost every large city decided to organize a professional and full-time police force. Unfortunately, murders, thefts, muggings, and rapes continued to occur. And when trouble occurred on a very large scale, as in the New York Draft Riots of 1863, the police proved unable to bring the situation under control without help.

If the newly uniformed constables were unable to bring tranquility, they at least created in many minds the exciting prospect of a city free of vice and sin. Such freedom, of course, was a tall order, for prostitutes and saloons could not exist without the customers who patronized them in great numbers. Almost from the beginning of urban settlement in the New World, vice had been an integral part of the local scene. In every city grog shops were among the most popular of institutions, and even in colonial days ladies of easy virtue congregated by the score along the waterfront in Boston and Philadelphia or down by the Battery in New York City. By the late nineteenth century almost every city of any size had a "red-light district," and some had several. Many a house of ill repute, like that of the Everleigh sisters in Chicago, was famous and even issued a published brochure describing the premises and the offerings. New Orleans had so many bawdy houses that guides were issued for prospective customers; in San Francisco the Barbary Coast had a similar reputation. As Mark Haller demonstrates in his essay on the attempt to close down the vice resorts in Chicago, such unsavory conditions were offensive to large numbers of urban residents. Some reformers among them were motivated simply by the gnawing fear that someone, somewhere was having a good time, but others were motivated by sincere religious impulses. Saloons and brothels were regarded as threats to decent men and women and as "holes of viciousness." George Walling, the New York Chief of Police, wrote in 1886 of the ease with which a fair maiden could fall into wickedness:

A pure girl who visits the Haymarket [a brightly lit building at Sixth Avenue and Thirtieth Street], if such a one ever does visit it, attracted by the gay scenes and the fascination of the waltz, may feel sure of her own power to keep from going lower in the scale of sensuality; but as surely as a displaced stone goes tumbling down a hillside, she rushes on to the black fate which awaits her, and virtue, youth, beauty, health and soul are lost in the downward course to ruin. A terrible fate it is, yet many are they who reach it yearly.

Intelligent observers realized that prostitutes were not simply the victims of some individual act of sin, that often young girls sold their bodies because their alternative economic opportunities and personal rights were so exceedingly slim. One way to improve the city and to eliminate the cycle of poverty and vice, for boys as well as maidens, was education. As Stanley K. Schultz demonstrates in his essay on public education in Boston, schools were expected to provide an avenue for both economic and moral uplift.

Another reaction to the physical, moral, and educational problems of the city was escape to the less congested suburbs. For many people the city was simply too crowded or too evil to be endured. Such flight was made possible by a number of developments and innovations in mass transit—the omnibus in the late 1820s, the steam railroad in the 1840s, the horsecar in the 1850s, the electric trolley in the late 1880s, and most important of all, the automobile in the twentieth century. As Professor Glen Holt explains in his humorous and incisive account of the commuting experience a century ago, the homeward-bound traveler had no more comforts then than now. But the very existence of a method of travel led to an increase in the length of the average journey to work. In the 1800s George Pullman, inventor of the railway sleeping coach, built on the outskirts of Chicago an entire factory, complete with model housing for his workers, within reach of the big city yet ten miles distant from city congestion, brothels, and saloons. Pullman's effort ultimately failed as an experiment in social and industrial democracy, but his desire to build fresh on open land away from the crowds became a common impulse for many individuals and companies.

Hope for those who remained in the city lay in the rise of city planning as a profession and in the spread of the "City Beautiful" movement. From the conviction that the physical and sanitary setting of individuals tends to mold their characters, city planners sought to improve the urban environment through conscious, concerted action. They proposed to make the city more attractive and healthy through the creation of spatial order.

The man who led the city-planning movement and who fathered the modern park system was the architect and landscape planner Frederick Law Olmstead. After an eventful youth that included a voyage to China and ten years of experimental farming, Olmstead found his life's work in 1857 when he won a contest sponsored by the city of New York to produce the best design for a large park of approximately 150 acres. At the time, no American city had provided a significant area for people to play, partly because the poor conceived of parks as aristocratic preserves where royalty rode and because the rich thought of parks as refuges for idlers and hobos. But the need for open space was nevertheless desperate. The enormous growth of New York City was pushing the population northward and people had begun to wonder if anything would remain of the island's former beauty. In the built-up portions of the city, the average density was well over 100,000 per square mile, and in the poorer quarters the congestion was even more horrendous. Moreover, it was not easy before the introduction of the trolley in 1887 for a working-class family to get out of the city for a Sunday afternoon of solitude or recreation.

Olmstead's design for Central Park, as all the world now knows, was an enormous success. The park, twenty years under construction, required the labor of 3,800 men to dig out its lakes and ponds and to build up its hills and paths. But it was visited by 10 million people even before it was completed, and its form—the south end was given over to formal functions like concerts and fountains, and the north end was made as rugged and wild as possible—influenced cities and towns throughout the land. Olmstead himself went on to design more than eighty public parks after the Civil War.

Although Central Park, like most American parks, was more accessible to the middle classes than to the slum children who needed it the most, it was important for its demonstration that municipal government could create public amenities on a grand scale. Central Park stimulated interest in the preservation of urban land for general use and helped establish the principle that a large degree of collective community effort was necessary to make cities habitable. This idea was an important precursor to the City Beautiful movement, which won national attention at the famed Columbian Exposition in Chicago in 1893. At that spectacular world's fair, planners were given an opportunity to create an elaborate and full-scale model of their vision of the ideal city. The entire exposition was built around public edifices, monuments, and malls. Architecturally, the "white city," as it came to be called, was distinctly classical, and its imposing columns and great open spaces were interpreted as a critique of the dismal gray city all around them.

Although millions of Americans came away from Chicago in 1893 in awe of the enormous possibilities for urban society, most cities in the United States did not turn beautiful in the ensuing decades. Nor did the quality of urban life notably improve. As gains were made in public health, fire prevention, water supply, and sanitation, other crises rose to take their place. Air pollution, for example, worsened considerably. As early as 1880 a great pall of smoke regularly hung over Pittsburgh and garbage was being dumped from piers, tug boats, and steamers into the waters surrounding most East Coast cities. Half a century later, a billion gallons of sewage per day was being emptied into New York harbor by the Hudson, East, and Harlem rivers and another billion gallons was being added from the New Jersey side. Even noise was becoming a significant problem; an official New York City commission concluded in 1930 that "a tiger from Siberia or Bengal could roar or snarl indefinitely" on many streets "without attracting the auditory attention of passersby."

Considering the rapidity of urbanization in the United States since 1820, the failings of cities seem rather less significant than their accomplishments. In material and physical terms, urban centers did help to make life more productive and meaningful. At no other time was so much—schools, houses, mass-transit facilities, sewers, factories, hospitals—built so rapidly for so many. By and large, men in cities lived with more ease, with more comfort, and probably with greater physical safety than men in the country had. Innovations such as elevators, electric lights, telephones, and flush toilets, standard amenities to urban residents, were luxuries in rural areas. The use of structural steel made possible the first skyscrapers in Chicago and New York as well as engineering feats such as John Roebling's magnificent Brooklyn Bridge, which when completed in 1883 was regarded as a major monument of the age and the eighth wonder of the world. In lashing together the first and fourth

largest cities in the nation, the bridge gave meaning to the proposition
that "God made the country but man built the towns."

Moreover, the attempts to find solutions to the cities' problems led
eventually to a fundamental alteration in the American attitude toward
government. Whereas the typical rural or small-town attitude was that the
best government was the least government, W. Stull Holt has shown that
nineteenth-century urban reformers necessarily moved toward a posture
of cooperation and positive municipal action. They realized that in a close
agglomeration of people the artesian well and the cistern would have
to give way to a common water supply, a sewerage system would have
to be introduced, noises would have to be abated, and the liberty
of individuals would have to be curtailed. To quote Providence's Dr.
Chapin, a champion of public health, in 1889: "When 125,000 people are
gathered together on 10 square miles of land they must of necessity
give up certain of their liberties. It is the sacrifice they make for the
advantages of city life."

If urban communities required the restriction of some rights, they
nevertheless allowed the expansion of the human mind. They were the
places where people from widely differing backgrounds came to live in
close proximity, and out of the mingling and interstimulation of diverse
attitudes, beliefs, and knowledge came civilized growth and cultural
progress. Music, art, theater, literature, and medical advancement flourished
as nowhere else in the great cities of the land, and the spires, lecture
halls, and libraries of great universities—Harvard, Columbia, Chicago,
Johns Hopkins, Pennsylvania, M.I.T., Berkeley, Yale, and Northwestern,
to name but a few—were an integral part of the urban scene.

As all of the essays in this section demonstrate, cities of the American
past were never without problems. But neither were they without hope
or resources or men of vision. In the 1970s such qualities seem sadly
lacking, yet American cities cannot and must not be forsaken. As Lewis
Mumford has said, "That magnification of all the dimensions of life,
through emotional communion, rational communication, technological
mastery, and above all, dramatic representation, has been the supreme
office of the city in history. And it remains the chief reason for the
city's continued existence."

14. THE NATURE OF POVERTY AND THE PREVENTION OF DISEASE

Charles Rosenberg

To most Americans, poverty was still a moral, not a social, phenomenon—as was cholera. The vice, filth, and ignorance that bred poverty nurtured cholera as well. No longer, however, did a man's moral condition seem sufficient explanation of his immunity or susceptibility. Disease was becoming more and more a product of environment: the city and the tenement assumed leading places in the list of cholera's predisposing causes.

Not all poverty was unworthy. Nor did cholera attack the prudent and industrious workingman. The vicious poor, the drunkard and idler, the prostitute and thief, were its proper victims. The filth that surrounded these self-sentenced exiles from society mirrored accurately their inner decay; they, not "the virtuous and industrious poor," suffered disproportionately. If hard-working mechanics and artisans were stricken, most Americans believed, it was not because of their moral, but their temporal proximity to the vicious and dissolute.[1]

The labor of America's farmers, artisans, and mechanics had made and sustained the republic. The dignity of labor was secure in the formulas of conventional rhetoric; these "real people," these "noble men," were not society's lower classes, but rather its foundation classes. "On their foreheads and palms God has set his enduring seal of nobility, and the shifts of fashion, the voice of public opinion, and the assumptions of aristocracy can never obliterate it." Despite the disdain of the thoughtless, the mechanic in his city workshop was as indispensable to society as the farmer in his fields. And, moralists noted, St. Paul, a tentmaker, and Jesus, a carpenter, had both been mechanics.[2]

What could be more absurd than the pretensions of America's self-proclaimed aristocrats? Almost invariably they were men whose fathers had been farmers or artisans, and whose grandchildren would most likely fill the same humble place in society. The poor man was healthier, his step more sound than the careworn man of wealth, who lived out his

Reprinted from *The Cholera Years: The United States in 1832, 1849, and 1866* (Chicago: The University of Chicago Press, 1962), pp. 133–50, by permission of the publisher. Copyright 1962 by the University of Chicago.

hectic and unnatural life far removed from God's open fields. Real poverty lay not in lack of riches, but in discontent with one's lot. America was a land of opportunity and equality, in which productive work alone conferred genuine distinction.[3]

Or was it? Far more than in 1832, newspapers, magazines, and sermons self-consciously affirmed the dignity of the worker, deplored the pretensions and cares of wealth. The assumptions of Jacksonian rhetoric had become explicitly homiletic: exhortation replaced effusion as the divergence between image and reality in American society became increasingly disturbing.

In the categories of popular thought, the vicious were easily distinguished from the industrious poor. In practice, this was not so easily accomplished. The hard-working mechanic was likely to spend much of his wages on drink, was often, if involuntarily, unemployed, failed to attend church, and lived in crowded and filthy tenements. To respectable, servant-employing, churchgoing Americans, the city poor were a uniformly unappetizing group.

Americans were not surprised that such degraded souls should succumb to cholera. And despite bitter experience to the contrary, it was believed not only that the lower orders suffered severely from the disease, but that they suffered almost to the exclusion of the better sort.[4] Cholera among the respectable was, as in 1832, attributed to hidden vice or unaccustomed imprudence.

Famine and revolution in Europe crowded American cities with newly arrived immigrants. Poor, ignorant, friendless, and often unaccustomed to city life, they tenanted the dirtiest boarding houses and the most decayed tenements. They were the first to be attacked by cholera.

More than 40 percent of those dying of cholera in New York had been born in Ireland. The cities with the greatest immigrant populations—St. Louis, Cincinnati, New York, New Orleans—were those which suffered most severely during the epidemic.[5] The decimation of St. Louis and Cincinnati seemed, at least to some Americans, to be more attributable to the drinking and Sabbath-breaking of newly arrived immigrants than to any lack of sanitation in the cities themselves. Philip Hone agreed completely. The immigrants, he noted in his diary,

filthy, intemperate, unused to the comforts of life, and regardless of its proprieties . . . flock to the populous towns of the great west, with disease engendered on Shipboard, and increased by bad habits on shore, they inoculate the inhabitants of these beautiful Cities, and every paper we open is only a record of premature mortality.[6]

Cholera was an acute phase of a chronic malady; immigration had become a permanent threat to American institutions. Even in normal times, "degraded foreigners" populated almshouses and hospitals.[7] At election time, immigrant votes were sold to the highest bidder, while each week the Sabbath was profaned by their whiskey-drinking and carousing. How long, questioned a Congregational weekly, would our remaining Puritanism survive this process of dilution? Someday, these new citizens and their children would be as loud in asserting themselves as those Americans whose ancestors had landed at Plymouth Rock or Jamestown. But would they be fitted for such privileges? Only unceasing missionary activity among them, pious Americans were warned, would assure their virtue and good citizenship.[8]

Americans had always thought of their country as an "asylum for the poor, virtuous, and oppressed of other lands." But the founding fathers could never have foreseen that the deserving poor of an earlier day would have, in less than a century, become the degraded and criminal refuse that polluted American shores in 1849. Few Americans, even the most moderate, could deny that "a very large proportion of the foreigners that have come to this country for several years past are vicious and worthless." A victim in the Old World of too much law and too much restraint, the immigrant could not, it seemed, conceive of responsible citizenship or ordered liberty. In minds long fettered, liberty too often meant license and freedom irresponsibility.[9] The votes of foreigners already decided elections in New York, Pittsburgh, St. Louis, and other cities. Nativists warned that these foreigners would soon have "control of the ballot box; and when they [did], mobocracy would be the order of the day."[10]

The Irish presented the greatest menace. Even the Germans, with their beer-drinking, their freethought, and their Continental Sunday were not as great a threat to American institutions. That the Irish suffered severely from cholera was but additional testimony to their ignorance, their habitual filth and drunkenness; Irish wakes denied propriety even to death. Prosperous Americans knew Irish men and women only as servants, and as servants who often remained as strangers though living under the same roof. An Irish peasant, working in a well-scrubbed Protestant kitchen, must have often seemed to his masters dirty, resentful, wilful, and invincibly ignorant.

He was, moreover, the stubbornest kind of Catholic. They are, in the words of an alarmed New York minister,

Catholics to the back-bone: an Irishman as part of his religion must not eat meat on Friday; he must run loose all of the Sabbath, and also every evening of the week, and he must be allowed to deceive and lie, even when truth would answer his purpose better.[11]

At best, the devoted Catholic was to be pitied as a priest-ridden worshipper of the Beast. Evangelical ministers still assured their flocks that the Church of Rome was the Whore of Babylon, the Mother of Harlots foretold in Revelation. Nevertheless, only a few Protestant divines went so far as to interpret cholera as a deserved visitation upon the Catholics.[12] Those that did blamed the priests for the death of their parishioners. Had they not granted these poor helots a general absolution? And had this not been followed by the drinking and reveling which brought death?

Many Americans were prepared to pity the ragged and untutored Irishman, but not even the most understanding could condone the "cynical machinations" of the Catholic hierarchy (a position similar to that of many twentieth-century liberals who find this distinction a convenient compromise between liberalism and vulgar anti-Romanism). While his clergy labored among the dying in New York, Bishop Hughes was, according to James Gordon Bennett's *Herald* (August 8, 1849), luxuriating in the safety of Saratoga Springs. Dramatizing to most Americans the hierarchical and antidemocratic nature of the Roman church was the collection of Peter's Pence during the summer of 1849 for use in maintaining the temporal power and defeating the Roman republicans. It seemed strange that American citizens should help preserve arbitrary government, that their dollars should purchase the bullets with which patriots and republicans were slain.

The church did make concessions. For Catholics to be accepted as Americans like any others, they must conform to the moral precepts of American Protestantism. Thus, for example, in an effort to avert cholera, the Cincinnati *Catholic Telegraph* participated wholeheartedly in a campaign to encourage temperance and a stricter observation of the Sabbath. Nor, Catholic editorialists commented, were the Irish as ruffianly and ungovernable as their critics would have them. On the contrary, because of their Catholic habits of mind, they were "contented with their position and state of life."[13]

Not all accusations during the epidemic were made by Protestants. Catholics were quick to boast of the fidelity of their clergy—and to make pointed comparisons with those Protestant shepherds who had deserted their flocks. Many Catholics, they charged as well, were denied the consolations of religion in almshouses and hospitals by the "long-faced psalm singing bigots" superintending these institutions.[14]

The devotion of the Catholic clergy, and especially the Sisters of Charity, won the often reluctant praise of their Protestant neighbors. As Richard Henry Dana wrote to his orthodox and intolerant wife: "In spite of all you say, I believe that if anybody goes to Heaven from Boston it will be the Sisters of Charity and the Roman Catholic clergy."[15] Admiration of the Sisters was general and unqualified; their benevolence was of a practical sort, their lives not idled away in the convent's living tomb.

The Jews, like the Irish, were part of an urban America. But as was not true of resentment against the Irish, hostility toward the Jews was tempered by a peculiarly American ambivalence. Unresolved tensions in American life were faithfully mirrored in the contradictory, even paradoxical, image assigned to the Jew. He, like the American, was a pious Shylock, a venturesome conservative, an individualistic traditionalist. To reject him completely was to reject much that was American.[16]

It was also to reject Christ. For the Jews occupied a peculiar place in the chiliasm of pious Americans. Often contemptible, even loathsome, as individuals, the Jews had as a race been preserved for some great purpose. Their misery, persecution, and degradation bore witness to the fate of those who rejected Christ. Only the millennium would bring their conversion. "Their miraculous preservation is a standing proof of the verity of our holy oracles; and many of the glorious prophecies of the Bible are yet to be fulfilled by their restoration to national greatness, and God's favor."[17] The condition of the Jews was a carefully observed index to the proximity of the millennium.

America's cities were no longer American; with each decade they seemed more and more alien. Yet most Americans saw no need to either accept or reject immigration as such. The problem had not yet been formulated in terms so absolute. Most Americans were still able to maintain a serviceable ambivalence toward immigration and the new citizens that it brought to this country. Americans still had faith in their country and in its God-given mission. No matter how unpromising, how distasteful, Irishmen, or Germans, or Jews might be, all would eventually become Americans. Even those alarmed at the danger to American institutions presented by this immense influx of foreigners still wished to think of their country as a "refuge from European poverty, bigotry or despotism."[18] It was only right that those oppressed in foreign lands "should have better hopes for their children in this country." Providence had chosen this nation to carry out a glorious and peculiar mission. America was to be

an asylum for the oppressed from various parts of the earth—that they might meet here together, blend in one, combine their energies, and establish a more glorious system of society and government than the world ever saw, and throw back their rays of light and influence on the nations whence they sprung.[19]

Disease, most Americans still believed, was but an item in the sum of the immigrants' misfortunes. These foreigners were the victims of dirt and overcrowding, to be pitied not feared. If they were impoverished, it was because Americans allowed them to be exploited. If they died because of their filth and ignorance, it was the duty of Americans to educate and to cleanse them. These unfortunates must be received with charity and understanding, "as Christ commanded and philosophy enjoins." They had fled from man's persecutions to meet in cholera "a more ruthless enemy in a pestilence which preys upon the children of want."[20]

Perhaps the immigrant did find only misery in America's cities. But this was the inevitable result of having never left his port of entry; to remain in the city was to sink ever lower into poverty, crime, and vice. And the nation needed these "stout, strong, and hardy laborers, the very fellows to cut down our forests, cut our railroads, and excavate our canals." While misery increased along the seaboard, "the broad West invites, nay, urges, subsistence and comfort upon the thousands that linger on the spot where they landed."[21] The spot was often the southern tip of Manhattan Island. It was not surprising that New York suffered from cholera—and typhoid, smallpox, and fevers. "Of all the cities on this continent," wrote a future president of the American Medical Association, "New York stands foremost as the grand focus and receptacle of the poverty and filth of Europe." Disease and civic disorder were the inevitable result. If 1849 had brought cholera and the Astor Place riots, what might succeeding years not bring?[22]

Cities were unnatural and immoral; they bred disease and crime, attracted the vicious, and corrupted the virtuous. These were traditional views, unquestioned by most Americans. Young men were warned of the city's dangers, of evil companions, of drink, and of soul-destroying ambition. Even greater were the temptations faced by young women. Jefferson was very much a man of his time in his discomfiture at the moral perils of great cities. The dangers of urban life, so clear in 1800, seemed even more apparent a half-century later.

To such traditional anxiety for the souls of city dwellers had been added a new concern for their bodies. Medical science, with its new statistical tools, had demonstrated irrefutably that the dirt, the congestion, and the bad air of cities shortened men's lives. In England, physicians and social reformers such as Edwin Chadwick, William Farr, and John Simon had made their countrymen conscious of the dangers of poor drainage, foul water, and crowded tenements. Their work and the unashamed empiricism upon which their conclusions were based had, by 1849, helped convince many physicians of the futility of traditional remedies.[23] Disease could not be cured: it must—and could—be prevented through cleanliness and sanitation.

Such teachings seemed increasingly relevant to Americans; their nation was no longer one of farms and villages. America's newer slums already rivaled in filth their European counterparts—even London's notorious tenements harbored no pigs. American city dwellers now seemed less vigorous than their supposedly effete European counterparts. "There is something radically wrong," wrote an Indiana minister, "in the construction of our cities and villages."

The Creator never designed that man should be deprived of the air, and light of heaven. Imperfect ventilation, impure water, and a crowded population, necessarily induce fevers and pestilence; while evil pleasures and sensual pleasures corrupt the morals, and enfeeble the intellect; and generation after generation, fall victims to flagrant violations of the laws of health.[24]

Moral and material causes conspired to produce stunted and rachitic children, adult ill-health, and early death.

An earlier generation had hoped that America might escape such misery. Alexander Stevens, president of the New York State Medical Society, recalled in 1849 his studies in Europe as a young man. It seemed to him then, as he passed through the wards of the London and Paris hospitals, that

Americans were hardier and healthier, their climate more salubrious. Thirty-five years later, his opinion had changed: the foul air and filth of American cities and hospitals seemed to have produced the same state of things he had seen as a student in Europe. The continued growth of cities promised, moreover, not only a corresponding increase in bodily ailments, but a disproportionate increase in diseases of the mind.[25] Insanity would, in the city of the future, become as commonplace as malaria in the countryside. (Mental disease was, in the middle of the nineteenth century, frequently attributed to the "artificiality" of urban life.)

Cholera was an extraordinarily lurid sample of the perils that ordinarily menaced the health of tenement dwellers. Twenty Orange Street and the many houses like it merited no particular attention in ordinary times; in the summer of 1849 it was impossible to ignore them, impossible to ignore the connection between the fate of those who died in these tenements and the conditions in which they had lived. Twenty-two pigs made their home in one New York frame building from which five cholera cases were taken. In Philadelphia, "a free couple of color," dying of cholera, were removed from the four-and-a-half by seven-foot room in which they lived; in a Boston cellar, the tide rose so high that a physician could only approach a patient's bedside by means of planks laid from one stool to another. The dead body of an infant in its coffin floated in another part of the room.

It was never difficult to predict where, in a city, cholera would first appear. Cholera—and typhoid, smallpox, and typhus—flourished where the ground was low, where garbage was never collected, where there was no adequate ventilation. In Louisville, for example, those sections which suffered most severely in the cholera epidemic of 1833, but which had in the intervening years been cleaned and properly ventilated, suffered not at all in 1849. On the other hand, those squares which were still as dirty as they had been sixteen years before suffered as they had then. Conjectures as to the ultimate cause of cholera were superfluous, and physicians were rebuked for such fruitless disputes "much better calculated to bring ridicule upon the whole profession than to advance the interests of science." Whatever the cause of cholera, it was operative only in close and filthy locations. Epidemics were not inevitable; a perfect system of drainage and sewerage would, reported the secretary of the New Orleans Board of Health, "at once remove all the known causes of disease."[26] It would be cheap at any price.

Millions for defense was a national boast. Yet, charged a committee of the New York State legislature, Americans "grudge the cost of protection against a destroyer more fearful than any mortal foe." Sanitary reform, moreover, had proven its effectiveness. The laws of nature, though immutable, were "beautifully adopted to the welfare of mankind."[27] They had only to be obeyed. So long as city dwellers allowed filthy tenements and cold, hungry, unwashed people to exist in their midst, so long would they be scourged by pestilence. "How the lamp of life, under such circumstances, holds out to burn, even for a day, is, perhaps, as great a wonder as that such a state of things should . . . be suffered to exist."[28] Civilized man could embark upon no task nobler than that of sanitary reform.[29]

Science had demonstrated that the most malignant epidemics could be prevented, and it was the responsibility of the legal guardians of public health to see that they were prevented. Streets had to be cleaned, cesspools purified, pure water supplied. But no problem was more immediate than that of improving the housing conditions of the poor. Bishop Purcell of Cincinnati suggested leveling "the filthy and disgusting hovels where the poor are compelled to congregate, and where, disease is generated and whence it radiates to infect the surrounding atmosphere." These, the Bishop concluded, should be replaced by "whole streets of comfortable cottages." The Rochester Board of Health suggested the passage of an ordinance requiring all persons wishing to erect a dwelling place to submit the plans to some competent authority for approval.[30] Only by improving the living conditions of the poor, it seemed, could the community protect itself permanently against epidemic disease.

It was clear that the city poor did not live as Americans should. Perhaps, a few Americans suggested, cholera was a judgment demonstrating not that the poor were sinful, but that they were oppressed. That the disease fell most heavily upon the destitute, the intemperate, and the degraded showed not, said Professor Samuel Henry Dickson of New York University, that it was a punishment for sin, but rather that it was "a scourge of our vicious social state."[31] It was "just retribution," wrote the New York *Herald* (July 27, 1849), when cholera spread from "the huts of poverty" to the "palaces of the rich." To reformers, cholera preached a message of social reconstruction; men thought to stop the ravages of cholera

with pestles and mortars, when in deed and in truth the only effectual barricades of resistance were the statute books of nations made conformable to the statute books of Infinite Justice. It is in a nation's dens of poverty, where unrequited toil pines for its daily food, where nakedness shivers in the wintry air, where the miserable victims of an unjust condition of society hive together in damp cellars and unhealthy garrets, where the blessed air of Heaven is tainted by unventilated streets and dark and obscure lanes and alleys, where pure water is a luxury which the rich only can enjoy, that the cholera is engendered. . . . The great axe of *reform* must be laid at the root of the tree, and this is the lesson which we are to learn from the terrible experiences with which humanity now suffers.[32]

If all men were Christians there would be no cholera: many of those unfortunates dying of cholera were direct sacrifices to Mammon. Criticism of the materialism and amorality of mere wealth was traditional. The remedies offered by accepted wisdom were, however, equally traditional. God must bless the rich with honest and liberal hearts and the poor with patience and charity.

Fortunately, however, lives could be saved without disarranging society. Cleanliness, drainage, ventilation, and pure water were goals that could be endorsed by the most moderate. Not only physicians, but every well-informed citizen had been made conscious of the need for improving the conditions of urban life.

Souls as well as bodies would benefit, for physical and spiritual purity were one. Vice was filthy and cleanliness truly next to godliness; the famed piety of the Puritans and Quakers was equaled only by their deserved reputation for cleanliness.

All testimonies agree in affirming that there is scarcely anything more distinctive of paganism than its love of dirt. Catholicism, which is but one remove from paganism, shows much of this disgusting character, whether its votaries sun themselves in the streets of Naples, or crouch on the mud floor of an Irish cabin.[33]

"When the Divine Lawgiver communicated with his people by direct revelation," he had been careful to provide them with a complete sanitary code. The recommendations of sanitary commissions and boards of health invariably emphasized the moral benefits that would accrue from improved drains and cesspools. "Bad sanitary regulations," it could not be doubted, had "a certain tendency to degrade the finer moral feelings, and debase individuals towards the level of brute creation."[34]

Perhaps immorality was a product of poverty, of human circumstances rather than human nature. If so, the poor needed medicines, and pure air, and wholesome food before their spiritual regeneration could be attempted. By the same token, prayer and pious injunctions could not alone prevent cholera. Equally futile were the healthful diets, the warm flannels, the scrupulous cleanliness which physicians urged upon the poor; it was a mockery to recommend port, beef roasts, and clean woolens to people sleeping a dozen to a room and eating the refuse of the market places. "Be ye warmed, and be ye clothed," the poor were commanded. Or so it seemed to a growing number of Americans.

Changes in etiological theory also helped to undermine traditional acceptance of personal immorality as a cause of illness. A growing belief in the specificity—though not necessarily the communicability—of disease decreased the physician's reliance upon vague moral factors in explaining its etiology. If the poor suffered most severely from cholera, it was because they were most likely to be exposed to the specific poison. No one would contend that the Five Points [a major tenement district in Manhattan that derived its name from an intersection of five streets] had improved either in cleanliness or morality during the years between 1834 and 1849—yet there had been no cholera during these fifteen years despite rum, vice, overflowing cesspools, and manure heaps. Only when a specific material cause was present could cholera appear.[35] At least one rural physician noted that in small towns, where there were no crowded tenements to attract the disease, it was from the ranks of the better and "middling-sort" that cholera chose its victims.[36]

The city's dangers were not inescapable; the miserable and starving tenement dwellers had only to leave for the country to improve at once their own lot and the condition of the city they left. In the West, moreover, the labor of men idle and starving in city slums was desperately needed. It seemed odd that any at all of the laboring poor should remain in the city when the country promised the "certainty (almost) of health and competency." To till the soil was to be one of "nature's real noblemen," to fill "the position of a man in the social structure."[37] The moral advantages of a rural life were as undeniable as its economic ones. Americans were still concerned with individual and moral solutions to social problems. To flee the evils of the city was to solve them.

Few Americans in 1849 questioned the belief that "as a very general rule when a man gets sick it is his own fault, the result of either ignorance or presumption." Immunity from disease lay ultimately in personal habits.[38] Though convinced of the necessity for environmental reform, most thoughtful persons were unable to discard an accustomed belief in the role of moral failing in the causation of disease. To many Americans, for example, it was the slum dweller who was responsible for the filth in which he lived; landlords in more than one city were urged as a preventive of cholera to be more selective in their choice of tenants.

Men's faults were still a possible cause of cholera. Poverty was still, in the eyes of most Americans, a result—not a cause—of vice and imprudence. Cholera was still a judgment.

NOTES

1. *Richmond* (Virginia) *Religious Herald,* September 6, 1849. The few surviving hospital statistics that report the occupations of those dying of cholera show them to have been overwhelmingly servants and laborers. Cf. New York City Board of Health, *Report of the Proceedings of the Sanatory Committee* . . . (New York, 1849), pp. 70–71, 72–3, 83, 97.

2. "Facts for Mechanics," *Morning Star,* XXIV (August 8, 1949), 68; *New York Sun,* December 7, 1948; *New York Organ,* December 9, 1848, p. 189; *Herald of the Prairies* (*Chicago*), January 17, 1849; *Cumberland Valley Sentinel* (Chambersburg, Pennsylvania), December 25, 1849; George C. Foster, *New York in Slices* (New York, 1849), pp. 4–5; *Brownlow's Whig* (Knoxville, Tennessee), September 29, 1849.

3. *Covington* (Indiana) *People's Friend,* August 25, 1849; *Vincennes* (Indiana) *Gazette,* May 31, 1849; *New York Sun,* June 13, 1849; *Ohio Observer* (Hudson), December 13, 1848; *St. Joseph* (Missouri) *Gazette,* July 20, 1849.

4. Belief in personal misconduct as a cause of disease did not die easily, despite any amount of evidence to the contrary—for it was "a great consolation." Charles Anderson to Caleb B. Smith, July 3, 1849, Caleb Smith Papers, Manuscript Division, Library of Congress.
The dichotomy between the deserving and the vicious poor was well-nigh universal in nineteenth-century thought. Karl Marx's distinction between the "proletariat" and the "lumpen-proletariat" is simply another reflection of this pervasive assumption.

5. At the height of the epidemic in St. Louis, 1,182, or about four-fifths of the 1,556 who died, were Catholic. John Rothensteiner, *History of the Archdiocese of St. Louis* . . . (St. Louis, 1928), II, 18. A tabulation of hospital statistics from six cities (Cincinnati, New York, Buffalo, Brooklyn, Boston, and New Orleans) shows that 4,309 of 5,301 patients whose place of birth was known were born outside the United States. This tabulation of hospital statistics is based on published board of health and hospital reports. Since these are hospital statistics and since people of the "better sort" did not go to hospitals, these figures do not accurately reflect the absolute percentage of immigrants succumbing to cholera, though they do reflect clearly the low economic status of the newly arrived immigrant.

6. Diary of Philip Hone, June 30, 1849, Manuscript Division, New York Historical Society. Americans were especially shocked at the German diet of green vegetables, sauerkraut, and strong beer—a diet which seemed to invite cholera.

7. Many journalists and ordinary citizens were disturbed by the threat of immigration to the public health. "The bodies of the miserable outcasts are charged with infection on the voyage, and then they are turned loose here to spread ship fever, or whatever contagious disease they may have imbibed, or to occupy the fever wards of our hospitals to the exclusion of our own citizens." *New York Sunday Times*, March 11, 1849.

8. Portland (Maine) *Christian Mirror*, February 1, 1849. The pious deplored especially the role of immigrants as whiskey-sellers and consumers. They had, it seemed, "not been accustomed in their native lands to regard the business as disreputable." Richmond (Virginia) *Watchman and Observer*, March 22, 1849; Cincinnati (Ohio) *Central Watchman*, September 28, 1849.

9. Cape Girardeaux (Missouri) *Western Eagle*, August 3, 1849.

10. "R," *Boston Christian Register*, XXVIII (April 14, 1849), 59.

11. John Todd, "Christian Duties to Domestics," *New York Evangelist*, July 26, 1849. Reverend Todd suggested that domestics be required to save a portion of their salary as a condition of their employment, that they be urged to attend family worship, and that they be forced to eat meat on Fridays.

12. "Criticus," New York, *Christian Advocate*, July 12, 1849; *Cincinnati Nonpareil*, n.d., cited in the *Boston Pilot*, August 25, 1849.

13. *Cincinnati Catholic Telegraph*, May 10, 1849; *New York Freeman's Journal*, March 24, 1849. This appeal showed how far at least one Catholic publicist misjudged the American temper. A defense of the Irish as being "contented" served only to reinforce the contentions of those who attacked the traditional tyranny of the church. It was the reputed personal pugnaciousness of the Irish, not any political activism, which Americans found most distasteful.

14. *Cincinnati Catholic Telegraph,* July 12, 1849.

15. R. H. Dana to Mrs. Dana, August 11, 1849, Dana Papers, Massachusetts Historical Society. For other praise of Catholic benevolence, see, for example, *Springfield* (Illinois) *State Register,* August 16, 1849; Boston Board of Health, *Report on Asiatic Cholera . . .* (Boston, 1849), p. 24; W. T. Hamilton, "Cholera in New Orleans," *Mobile Alabama Planter,* January 1, 1849; *Nashville* (Tennessee) *True Whig,* August 24, 1849; *New York Sunday Times,* December 3, 1848.

16. Jews were active in the intellectual and political revolutions which convulsed Europe at this time, events which conservative Americans also regarded with some ambivalence. Though the Jews fought in a good cause, for freedom of mind and body, "these children of Abraham are for the most part Socialists and infidels —hating Christ with the habitual malignity of the Jew, and the fierce fury of the Jacobin." "Ezra," *New York Christian Advocate,* April 26, 1849.

17. "Present Influence of the Jews," *Boston Puritan Recorder,* June 14, 1849.

18. *New York Evangelist,* February 1, 1849. Yet less than a month earlier, the same paper had warned that "this increasing tide of foreigners pouring in upon us is to work changes in our social, moral, and perhaps our political conditions. . . . We are fast losing our identity as Americans, and shall soon fall into a meager and powerless minority. The reins of power and influence are passing from the hands of Americans to those of foreigners" (January 4, 1849).

19. "The Resources and Destiny of our Country," *Christian Magazine of the South,* VII (1849), 18.

20. Edward H. Dixon, *The Scalpel,* II (1850), 224–5; *New Orleans Daily Picayune,* January 2, 1849.

21. *Boston Watchman-Reflector,* July 5, 1849; *Boston Weekly Herald,* September 1, 1849.

22. The symptomatic nature of the Astor Place riots was not lost on conservatives. New York "abounds with the material for mobs and riots," commented a Boston clergyman. "A large proportion of the population is not homogenous—it comprises many men of all nations, and a very great number deplorably ignorant and consequently vicious." *Boston Olive Branch,* May 19, 1849. Many of the Americans who were alarmed at the dangers of cities took, at the same time, a natural pride in the size and wealth of their cities.

23. For a useful, brief introduction to the historical development of statistical analysis in medicine and public health, see George Rosen, "Problems in the Application of Statistical Analysis to Questions of Health: 1700–1880," *Bulletin of the History of Medicine,* XXIX (1955), 27–45.

24. Joseph G. Wilson, *The Voice of God in the Storm, A Discourse Delivered in the Presbyterian Church, on the Day of the National Fast, August 3, 1849* (Lafayette, Ind., 1849), p. 13.

25. Stevens, "Annual Address, Delivered before the New York State Medical Society . . . February 7, 1849," *Transactions of the Medical Society of the State of*

New York, 1849, 13–14. The first half of the nineteenth century saw much discussion of whether the growth of civilization increased or decreased disease. Cf., for example, E. H. Ackerknecht, "Hygiene in France, 1815–1848," *Bulletin of the History of Medicine,* XXII (1948), 140–41; Lloyd G. Stevenson, "Science down the Drain," *ibid.,* XXIX (1955), 5–6; Mark D. Altschule, *Roots of Modern Psychiatry* (New York and London, 1957), chap. vii, "The Concept of Civilization as a Social Evil in the Writings of Mid-Nineteenth Century Psychiatrists," pp. 119–39; George Rosen, "Social Stress and Mental Disease from the Eighteenth Century to the Present: Some Origins of Social Psychiatry," *Milbank Memorial Fund Quarterly,* XXXVII (1959), 5–32.

26. T. S. Bell, "Brief Notes on Cholera in Louisville in 1850," *Western Journal of Medicine,* VI (1850), 104; E. H. Barton, "Annual Report of the New Orleans Board of Health," *Southern Medical Reports,* I (1849), 91.

27. New York State Senate, *Report of the Majority of the Committee on Medical Societies and Colleges on So Much of the Governor's Message as Relates to the Cholera . . . ,* Doc. No. 92 (Albany, 1850), p. 3; Boston Board of Health, *op. cit.,* p. 176.

28. Boston Board of Health, *op. cit.,* p. 15.

29. The influential *New York Independent* (November 29, 1849), for example, warned that "the great practical lesson which the city should have learned from the cholera" was that ". . . an efficient sanitary police should be provided which would see to the sanitary condition of the poor, their tenements and their general physical condition. . . . This is demanded of us alike by the dictates of humanity and self-interest."

30. Pastoral Letter to the Clergy and Laity of the Diocese of Cincinnati, July 2, 1849, *Catholic Telegraph,* July 5, 1849; Rochester Board of Health, *Report . . . on Cholera, as It Appeared in Rochester . . .* (Rochester, N.Y., 1852), p. 41.

31. Samuel H. Dickson, "On the Progress of the Asiatic Cholera during the Years 1844–45–46–47–48," *New York Journal of Medicine,* II (January, 1849), 19.

32. Thomas Drew, "Our Fast Day Sermon," *Burritt's Christian Citizen* (Worcester, Massachusetts), August 11, 1849.

33. *Cincinnati Central Watchman,* July 16, 1849. *Hall's Journal of Health,* II (1855), 53–4, warned its readers, for example, never to give charity *"to any dirty person; . . . deserving poverty is not dirty; if but a rag to wear, there is a mark of care about that rag."*

34. *Western Lancet,* XII (1851), 173. Even so moralistic an improver of the condition of the poor as Robert Hartley, pioneer in urban social welfare organization, never questioned the existence of a connection between physical misery and moral delinquency. *"Social demoralization and crime,* as well as disease, originate and thrive amidst the festering corruptions and pollutions of the miserable accommodations afforded the poor. There is something so congenial in their nature, that 'dirt, disease and crime are concurrent.' "* New York Association for Improving the Condition of the Poor, *Eleventh Annual Report . . . for the Year 1854 . . .* (New York, 1854), p. 30.

35. Alexander F. Vache, *Letters on Yellow Fever, Cholera and Quarantine* . . . (New York, 1852), p. 61; New York State Senate, *op. cit.,* p. 30. It will be recalled that few physicians during the 1832 epidemic believed in the existence of particular disease entities.

36. Joseph C. Hutchinson, "Report on Malignant Cholera, as It Prevailed in Saline County, Mo.," *St. Louis Medical and Surgical Journal,* XI (November 1853), 489.

37. *American Model Courier* (Philadelphia), June 30, 1849; Joseph G. Wilson, *op. cit.,* p. 17; *Boston Recorder,* April 6, 1849.

38. *Hall's Journal of Health,* I (1854), 60. Dr. E. H. Barton, of the New Orleans Board of Health, cited earlier for his belief in the importance of sewerage and drainage improvement, wrote in the same article that every individual carries his safety in his personal habits. "The liability being individual, the municipal power can only aid by cleanliness and ventilation." *Op. cit.,* I, 83.

15. TO CONTROL THE CITY
The New York Police in Historical Perspective

James F. Richardson

I

Society—or rather the elites who mold public opinion and set public policy —have never agreed on the proper political and social role of the police. Competing sets of leaders have continuously wrangled over proper functions, composition, and methods. Indeed, for a long time, many citizens and politicians strenuously opposed even the establishment of an organized, bureaucratic department. The police force has never been in the position of the Department of Water Supply, Gas, and Electricity, which operates in an atmosphere of low public visibility and concern except when a water main breaks, and whose services are available to all residents of the city more or less equally. The police have the legal right to employ force and in some circumstances to deprive citizens of life and liberty; and they exercise these powers much more often on the poor and the alienated than they do on the prosperous and the contented. Their function has been to control behavior that the dominant groups in society have considered criminal and deviant; the people being controlled have thought themselves victims of arbitrary interference and oppression and have tried to limit the scope of police activity as much as possible. For these reasons, there have been recurrent political conflicts over the department's direction and goals, as well as major temptations to corruption and bribery.

The idea—and even the word "police"—did not find ready acceptance in England and the United States before the nineteenth century. Political theorists and ordinary citizens of both societies feared a standing army or any quasimilitary body that might constitute a threat to civil liberties. For Englishmen a standing army revived memories of oppression under Cromwell's rule, an oppression that extended even to such activities as theatergoing and visiting the local ale house. As part of the ideological legacy of the American Revolution, Americans conceived the basic problem of politics to be the preservation of individual liberty against the encroachments of organized power. Because they viewed liberty as static and passive, power as active and dynamic, power and those who wielded it had to be carefully watched and restrained. In this framework a standing army and an organized police that resembled a standing army constituted instruments of power rather than guarantors of liberty. Both Englishmen and Americans feared the administrative efficiency, the use of spies, and the employment of *agents provocateurs* of the French police and wanted to limit the ability of government to interfere with and control the daily activities of citizens. As a result, in the eighteenth and early nineteenth centuries, English and American cities relied on a patchwork of weak instruments—aided by the military at peak periods of tension—to deal with crime and disorder.

Both London and New York City used the medieval institution of the night watch to preserve the peace, control disorder, and warn of fires. Each parish in London maintained its own watch protection. Some parishes spent enough money to provide an adequate number of watchmen, while others employed only a few old and infirm men who then did not have to be supported by the parish poor rate. In colonial New York the number and caliber of watchmen varied considerably at different periods, depending upon whether the fear of disorder or the dislike of taxation was greater at any given time.

By 1800 New York's watch organization had achieved the form it retained until the establishment of the Police Department in 1845, although the watch did increase in numbers to attempt to keep pace with the city's burgeoning growth in both population and area. The Common Council divided the city into watch districts and appointed and removed at pleasure the commanders of each district. The men who served on the watch either had other jobs during the day and literally moonlighted as watchmen, or were men who had no other means of earning a living. Politicians treated watch positions as patronage plums and therefore made appointments on the basis of party affiliation rather than competence. Each change in party control of the Council meant large-scale changes in the personnel of the watch. Thus, while the size and responsibilities of the watch increased, its prestige and efficiency declined.

In addition to the watch, both London and New York had a number of police officers attached to the various courts who served warrants and attempted to recover stolen property at the behest of the lawful owner. Since these men earned their primary sources of income from fees and rewards, they acted more as private entrepreneurs than as public servants. The principle upon which they operated was fee for service. In New York the state legislature established a schedule of fees for such actions as serving warrants or conveying prisoners to jail, while victim and officer negotiated the reward for the recovery of stolen property. The easiest way to recover goods was collusion with the thief, such as granting him immunity in return for restoration of the property. In some instances the agreement between officer and thief may have been consummated even before the crime took place. The officer would agree to attempt to recover the property, for a liberal reward, and then give a portion of the reward to the thief. Some victims found it cheaper to advertise and try to deal directly with the thief rather than to go through the detectives. In any event, the New York newspapers of the 1830s and early 1840s are full of references to the return of stolen property without apprehension of the criminal.

The major impulse behind the establishment of an organized, bureaucratic police was not the ineffectiveness of the night watch or the corruption of the police officers, but rather the fear of riots and social upheaval. In the England of the late eighteenth and early nineteenth centuries, riots served as vehicles of political and social protest. Men and boys who did not want the political disabilities removed from Roman Catholics or who resisted the introduction of labor-saving machinery often made their feelings known with paving stones and torches. During the 1830s and early 1840s, racial and ethnic hostilities in New York City, such as those between Protestant and Catholic Irish and whites and blacks, erupted in several serious riots. Conservative and cautious men worried about the increasing disorder in the city and lamented the loss of social control. The establishment of a professional police force would provide a means of restoring social cohesion and ensuring that the poor remained deferent toward their betters. Those interested in police reorganization in New York City looked to the London Metropolitan Police Act of 1829 as their model. In 1845, after a decade and a half of debate, proposal, and counterproposal, they established the New York Police Department.

In 1844 the Democratic state legislature passed an act for the formation of a police force of 800 salaried men for New York City; however, it was stipulated that the statute would not go into effect until the municipal authorities approved. The dominant party in the city government in 1844 was the Native Americans, a group dedicated to curbing the actual and potential political power of foreign-born Catholics, and this group rejected the state law in favor of a police proposal of its own. The 1844 act became operative only when the Democrats regained control of the city government in 1845.

The party conflict surrounding the establishment of the police permeated its organizational structure. Policemen were appointed for terms of only one year by the mayor after nomination by the Council members and tax assessors of each ward. In 1846, the legislature increased the term of office to two years; in 1849, to four years; and in 1853, to good behavior. Before 1853, policemen appointed when the Whigs were in office were likely not to be reappointed if their terms expired when Democrats controlled the ward and vice versa. Each ward constituted a patrol district under the command of a captain appointed by the Council to serve at its pleasure. Captains were virtually autonomous, although the act did call for a chief of police who had his office in the basement of City Hall. One indication of the chief's lack of power is that George Matsell held the office under both Democratic and Whig administrations from 1845 until 1857.

Since policemen had to reside in the ward in which they served, they reflected the social characteristics of the people among whom they worked. Most of the guardians of the "silk-stocking" Fifteenth Ward were native-born Americans, whereas a large proportion of the men of the Sixth Ward, a high-crime area with a predominantly immigrant population, were Irish.

Unlike London, the New York police were not uniformed before 1853, although they were supposed to wear a small star-shaped badge to identify themselves.

The new police represented a considerable improvement over the part-time night watch and the unsalaried officers of the pre-1845 period, although the New York department never attained the degree of public support and prestige enjoyed by the London force. Patronage appointments and partisan removals meant a low standard of personnel and excessively high turnover. The absence of a uniform made it easier for policemen to avoid difficult situations and to spend their duty time in saloons rather than patrolling the streets. The lack of systematic training and drill limited police effectiveness in handling riots such as that at Astor Place in 1849, when the crowd intimidated the inexperienced police. The militia was called out and fired into the mob, killing some twenty people.

In 1853, the state legislature, under pressure from a City Reform party led by men such as Peter Cooper, rectified some of these weaknesses by providing for good-behavior tenure for policemen and by establishing a board of commissioners, consisting of the mayor, the recorder (a judicial official), and the city judge, to administer the department. The members of this body, it was hoped, would be more respectable and less partisan and parochial than the councilmen elected from the various wards. Charter changes in a number of American cities at this time transferred increasingly complex administrative functions from the city councils, now made more exclusively legislative bodies, to independent or ex-officio boards and commissions.

The new board made significant improvements in the department's efficiency and morale. The security of tenure helped, as did the adoption of a uniform. However, some policemen, fearing the public might ridicule them as "liveried lackeys," protested that the uniform infringed upon their rights as free-born American citizens. The values of efficiency and authority prevailed over policemen's sensitivities when the commissioners secured court approval for dismissing men who persisted in their refusal to wear the uniform.

These administrative changes left unanswered two basic questions: What was the proper relationship between the police and the political parties and major officeholders like the mayor? And what was the role of the police in relation to crimes without victims, such as prostitution, gambling, and Sunday drinking? Both questions figured prominently in the mayoralty of Fernando Wood, a Democrat who began his first term in January 1855. A self-made man, Wood had accumulated a considerable fortune in mercantile activities and real-estate speculation before retiring from business at the age of thirty-seven to devote his full attention to politics.

At the outset of his administration, Wood presented himself as a dedicated reformer, ready to use the power of the mayor's office to improve municipal government. Putting heavy emphasis on the necessity for a disciplined and efficient police, he promised members of the department that merit rather than political influence would be the road to advancement under his leadership. He launched an ostentatious campaign against prostitutes, saloonkeepers who sold liquor on Sundays in violation of the Sabbath laws, and gamblers, although it soon became obvious that those of his supporters who engaged in these enterprises were not being bothered by the police. In June 1855, the state legislature adopted a prohibition law which forbade the sale of alcohol for other than medicinal or sacramental purposes. Put on the defensive, Wood in effect told policemen not to enforce the law if they wished to remain in his good graces.

The state action and Wood's response raised two related issues. The first concerned the relative spheres of authority of state and city, and the second the role of the police in controlling or suppressing behavior many people, including policemen, thought harmless. One segment of the community, a minority in the city but part of a state-wide majority, wanted to use the law to coerce people to be decent, to respect the moral imperatives of middle-class Protestantism. The cosmopolitan urban majority considered this use of law to be an unwarranted interference with legitimate pleasures and personal liberty. Therefore, if they could not prevent such laws from being adopted, they wished to limit enforcement as much as possible. In such a case an ambitious politician like Wood acted on the wishes of the majority of his constituents rather than on the dictates of the distant legislature. Policemen themselves often had little sympathy for the attempt to close all saloons and willingly followed the mayor's lead. As a result, the prohibition law was never enforced in New York City, and no great adjustments were required when it was declared unconstitutional the following year.

Wood exploited to the full his control over the police to advance his political career. He used his position on the board of commissioners, with the help of another member, to remove his opponents and advance his supporters in the department. In 1856, when he ran for reelection as mayor, his tactics included forcing policemen to contribute or risk being removed for any offense, no matter how trivial; granting furloughs to selected members who spent this time campaigning for him; and using policemen on election day to dissuade citizens from voting for anyone else. Wood succeeded in his quest for a second term, but his attitude toward the prohibition law, his partisan administration of the police, and his campaign tactics supplied considerable ammuniton to those who wanted to make basic changes in the administration and direction of the force.

If a municipally controlled department meant that the liquor laws went unenforced, that only Democrats could be policemen, and that this partisan force would be used to perpetuate Democratic control, perhaps a state-created and -administered department could reverse these tendencies by giving the Republicans (who replaced the Whigs as the major opposition to the Democrats in the mid-1850s) both police patronage and a major voice in the conduct of New York City's elections. Thus in 1857, the Republican-dominated legislature brought in a bill to create a Metropolitan Police Department for New York City, whose commissioners would be appointed by the governor of the state, John A. King, a Republican.

This proposal encountered constitutional objections. According to the state constitution of 1846, officers of cities, towns, and villages had either to be elected by the voters or appointed by the elected officials of the local government in question. The legislature sidestepped this difficulty by enlarging the Metropolitan Police district to encompass the city of Brooklyn and the counties of Richmond and Westchester. The proponents of the measure argued that the London Metropolitan Police area included suburbs and therefore so could New York's. Furthermore, because this was a new district created by the legislature, the governor's appointment of commissioners would not infringe upon the constitutional rights of any established unit of local government. The act called for seven commissioners, five to be named by the governor, plus the mayors of New York and Brooklyn. There was no provision for approval by the municipal authorities or voters of the cities; the Republicans knew that such approval would never be forthcoming. By the terms of the act, all members of the New York and Brooklyn departments before the passage of the act became Metropolitan policemen.

Wood fought this innovation bitterly. One newspaper asserted he had spent $100,000 to prevent passage of the bill in Albany, and after its adoption he refused to recognize its validity. He began a test of its constitutionality in the courts, arguing that if the judiciary did not declare the act null and void, New York would be a "conquered city." He had the City Council adopt an ordinance for the creation of a municipal police, and he vowed to hold police property such as station houses and the telegraph for the use of his municipal force rather than turn these facilities over to the Metropolitan commissioners as the law required. Moreover, he told policemen that if they obeyed the new commissioners and the law were later declared unconstitutional, they would be removed from the department.

Of the 1,100 men of the New York Police Department supposedly absorbed into the new Metropolitan force, some 800 remained faithful to Mayor Wood and only 300 supported the new commissioners. For several weeks, New York City found itself in the anomalous position of having two police forces, each of which claimed to be the sole protector of life and property. Persons arrested by one force might be rescued and released by the other, and in June 1857, a full-scale riot broke out between the two groups. Only the fortuitous intervention of the Seventh Regiment, which happened to be marching nearby, prevented serious consequences. The controversy remained unresolved until the state's highest tribunal, the Court of Appeals, upheld the constitutionality of the Metropolitan Police Act in July 1857, whereupon Wood disbanded his municipal force.

The Metropolitan Police remained in existence from 1857 to 1870, although its governing body changed in size and mode of appointment at various times. In 1860 the legislature removed the mayors of New York and Brooklyn from the board and reduced the number of commissioners to three, all appointees of the governor. In 1864 the legislature increased the board to four members, who would now be named by the legislature itself rather than the governor.

The greatest test for the Metropolitans came not in the legislative or Council chambers, but on the streets of the city in the famous Draft Riots of July 1863. These riots, the most serious in the city's history, grew out of the hostility of the city's Irish population to its blacks. Irishmen and blacks competed for the same low-paying jobs, such as waiters and long-shoremen. When the Irish captured the bulk of the stevedoring on the docks, blacks could still be employed as strikebreakers. The onset of the Civil War intensified these racial and economic cleavages, which reached a critical stage with the introduction of emancipation as a war aim, the use of black troops, and the adoption of a discriminatory draft law that exempted anyone who could provide a substitute or pay a commutation fee of $300.

The draft began in New York City on July 11, 1863, a Saturday, and the following Monday mobs destroyed by fire a draft enrolling office and the Colored Orphan Asylum on Fifth Avenue, and looted and burned houses and stores. Before the restoration of order three days later, rioters had killed eighteen people, including three policemen and eleven blacks, some of whom were lynched from lampposts and then mutilated; savagely beat Superintendent of Police John A. Kennedy; and engaged in numerous individual acts of looting, robbery, and arson. The police and the military put down the riot with gun, club, and artillery. Although no one knows how many rioters were killed, an estimate of two to five hundred deaths and major injuries seems reasonable in light of contemporary accounts.

As there were few regular troops in the city and most of the militia proved unreliable, the burden of dealing with the riots fell primarily upon the police. The department concentrated its forces at its new headquarters building on Mulberry Street and relied upon its telegraph network to keep abreast of riot activity. The commanders could then dispatch men to trouble spots and also protect the downtown area, the center of the city's economic and political life. By Friday, July 17, the riots came to an end, and large numbers of troops sent from Pennsylvania, where the great battle of Gettysburg had recently been fought, patrolled the streets.

The defenders of the Metropolitan Police asserted that even though the state might have violated the city's home rule by establishing the Metro-politans, the act saved the city because a municipal police would never have acted as energetically in suppressing the riots. It is also possible that if the police had been closer to the community, and if many slum dwellers had not looked upon the Metropolitans as an alien army of occupation, the riots might either not have started or at least been brought under control without the trauma that four days of turmoil inflicted upon the city.

In addition to loss of life and property damage, the riots led to a major confrontation between Governor Horatio Seymour, a conservative Democrat, and the Republican police commissioners. Seymour had threatened to remove the commissioners from office as early as his first day as governor in January 1863, and he repeated those threats in June of that year. Now in January 1864, he did remove the commissioners because of his objections to their report on the Draft Riots. The commissioners refused to vacate their offices, and a stalemate seemed imminent. It was at this juncture that the legislature changed the number of commissioners from three to four and provided that the legislature rather than the governor would henceforth appoint police commissioners. Seymour accepted this compromise, since two of the four commissioners named in the text of the bill were Democrats acceptable to him.

In 1865 and 1866, the legislature established state commissions for New York City's fire protection and health and liquor traffic regulation. The Metropolitan Police provided the model for these new boards, whose districts and administrative structures paralleled those of the police. Republicans defended these acts on the grounds that they made the municipal government more efficient and less corrupt. Democrats, on the other hand, denounced them as infringements upon home rule and as partisan tools adopted solely to increase the power and patronage of the Republican minority in New York City. When the Democrats, led by William M. Tweed, elected John Hoffman as governor and secured a legislative majority in the fall of 1869, the state commissions were doomed. In 1870 Tweed drafted a new city charter and judiciously distributed $600,000 to ensure its passage through the legislature. Tweed's charter returned the control of the police and other agencies to municipal authorities. A board of four members chosen by the mayor for terms of six years made up the governing body of the police. The four-man board remained as the administrative head of the police until 1901, when the legislature adopted a bill for a single commissioner.

The board mechanism reflected the traditional fear of unitary power and also made it possible to divide police patronage—in the form of appointments, desirable assignments, and promotions—among the major political parties and the various factions within them. Thus, in the years after Tweed's downfall, the board might contain a Tammany Democrat or two, a non-Tammany Democrat, and one or two Republicans. Until 1895, there was no legal imperative that the board be bipartisan, although it was customary to have minority party representation. After 1890, however, Tammany's domination of the board became more pronounced; and the Republicans used the revelations of the Lexow Committee of 1894, which documented a dreary story of police corruption and brutality, to adopt a law for a mandatory bipartisan board.

In the early 1890s moral reformers came to look upon the Tammany-dominated Police Department as one of the city's more lawless elements. Men such as the Reverend Charles Parkhurst, the president of the Society for the Prevention of Crime, and Frank Moss, a public-spirited young lawyer, demanded an inquiry into the department. Parkhurst's tours of the city's red-light districts convinced him that the police were more devoted to the protection, for a price, of brothels, Sunday liquor sales, and gambling houses, than to their eradication. Thomas Platt, the Republican boss in the state, saw the possibilities an investigation offered to increase Republican strength in New York City. In 1894, he approved the establishment of a special Senate committee, chaired by Clarence Lexow of Rockland County, which conducted a sweeping muckrake of the department. The published testimony taken by the committee ran to more than 5,000 pages and showed a systematic and pervasive pattern of police corruption and brutality.

These sensational revelations helped to oust Tammany in the 1894 elections. William R. Strong, a respectable Republican businessman, became mayor and appointed Theodore Roosevelt as one of the four police commissioners. The other commissioners chose Roosevelt as president of the board and therefore spokesman for the department. The Roosevelt board consisted of two Republicans and two Democrats as the bipartisan law demanded. Although Roosevelt and his colleagues did improve discipline and morale among the police and made appointments and promotions on the basis of merit rather than political influence, still the board dissipated much of its energy in personal and partisan wrangling. In 1897, Tammany returned to power, and the Police Department reverted to its pre-Lexow mode of operation. In 1901, after further exposures of police corruption, the legislature replaced the board with a single commissioner.

II

As this brief review of the administrative history of the police indicates, the department was not an independent bureaucratic agency in the nineteenth century. Rather, the political parties viewed control of the police as crucial to their own well-being. The force provided patronage; it had a dominant role in the conduct of elections; and no one could operate outside the law without police approval. Therefore, the department remained an adjunct to the political organizations instead of becoming an autonomous body.

The pattern of systematic bribery and corruption that governed the relations among the police, the politicians, and the underworld heavily influenced the policeman's working life from the beginning of his career. A young man who wished to become a policeman had to pay $300 for the position; a patrolman who wished to rise in rank often had to pay much higher sums. Captain Timothy Creeden admitted to the Lexow Committee that he had paid $15,000 to a representative of one of the commissioners for his captaincy; since the salary was $3,000 a year, Creeden had to assess illegitimate enterprises in his precinct to recoup his investment.

He was not as successful in this endeavor as Captain, later Inspector, Alexander S. Williams, who in the 1880s was the precinct commander of the city's most fashionable red-light district, the Tenderloin. Williams owned a house on East Tenth Street and an estate at Cos Cob, Connecticut, complete with a fifty-three-foot steam yacht. Williams, known as "Clubber," once asserted that there was more law at the end of a policeman's night-stick than in all the statute books. Although almost unashamedly brutal and corrupt, he avoided expulsion from the department because of the strength of his political connections. By 1887 hundreds of complaints had been filed against him, many of which had resulted in fines. The commissioners included this material with a notice of Williams' promotion from captain to inspector. During the Lexow investigation, Captain Max Schmittberger testified that he had paid Inspector Williams a portion of his monthly col-lections from gambling houses. Williams explained to the committee that his considerable wealth came from speculating in Japanese real estate. In 1895, the Roosevelt board forced him to resign.

In the early 1890s Charles Parkhurst, the minister whose sermons on New York's corruption triggered the Lexow inquiry, fought a running battle with Captain William Devery, then commander of the Eldridge Street precinct on the Lower East Side. The commissioners removed Devery from the department for neglect of duty, but the courts later voided the removal and reinstated him. In 1898, after Tammany's return to power, Devery became Chief of Police. Lincoln Steffens and other reporters considered Devery a "magnificent villain," always good for another story about police graft and some laughs at the same time. Gamblers, saloonkeepers who opened on Sunday, prostitutes, and gunmen all found New York a pleasant place to work, especially since the risk was minimal. Under Devery, New York was a wide-open town.

Often drunk as he presided at the trials of erring policemen, the fat chief's advice to his men was, "when you're caught with the goods, don't say nothin'." He used his power of transfer to build Tammany's strength and to show policemen that the primary rule of life was, if you want to get along, go along. He transferred one man who resisted this message five times in twelve months. Devery's conduct as chief proved so outrageous that in 1901 the legislature, in substituting a single commissioner for the board, also abolished the office of Chief of Police and gave the powers of assignment and discipline the chief had exercised to the commissioner. But Devery remained influential in police affairs: he was appointed First Deputy Commissioner by the new commissioner, and in effect continued to run the department. He was close to Big Tim Sullivan, an East Side political power who had extensive interests in gambling and prizefighting, and to whom control of the police was vital. As in 1894, exposure of police corruption brought about a reform fusion movement in 1901 which elected as mayor Seth Low, former mayor of Brooklyn and president of Columbia University. Low's police commissioner removed Devery from office. Similarly, police scandals preceded the elections of John Purroy Mitchel and Fiorello La Guardia, great New York reform mayors elected in 1912 and 1933, respectively.

III

Police corruption arose primarily from the desire to punish and control behavior many people considered harmless. When the law attempted to make the sale of alcohol, sex, or betting slips illegal, it ran counter to the moral codes of sellers, buyers, and many policemen—who taken together constituted a sizable portion of the city's population. Those whom the law would regulate or suppress made every effort to capture control of or at least influence the police. Since policemen often had more in common with the gamblers and the drinkers than they did with the moral reformers, it is not surpising that they took money from the former to ignore violations of laws passed by the latter. The political masters of the department shared this conception of proper police performance.

However, the law could always be enforced *selectively*. If a saloonkeeper made the mistake of supporting Tammany's opponents, he could find himself arrested for selling on Sunday. Since the police had the legal right to raid or "pull" whore houses, they could set high fees for madams who wanted to avoid this unpleasantness. One has the impression, difficult to quantify, that reform crusades and shakeups were most likely when police commanders and the political district leaders had lost any sense of restraint and had raised the level of exaction beyond acceptable limits. Then reformers would find willing witnesses like madams who had been bankrupted by police rapacity. Certainly, Charles F. Murphy, Tammany's shrewd chieftain from 1902 until his death in 1924, tried to control the extent of police graft and prevent spectacular scandal. After Murphy's death, James J. Walker, New York's famous playboy mayor, said of him that "the brains of Tammany Hall lie in Calvary Cemetery." Walker's own career proved the truth of his comment, for the Seabury investigations of Tammany corruption in the police and other departments led to Walker's downfall and the first election of Fiorello La Guardia as mayor in 1933.

In the nineteenth century the men who set departmental policy, the captains and the inspectors, were those most likely to view their action or inaction as negotiable. Captains like Timothy Creeden had to exploit their official positions for personal gain; otherwise they would not have held those positions. If the essence of corruption in government is the use of public office for private gain, police commanders who had to pay for their promotions had little choice but to be corrupt. One may question, however, whether corruption was an entirely negative phenomenon. It helped modify official behavior to meet widespread private demands; it helped reward the politician for his public service; and it provided sufficient flexibility for people of widely varying backgrounds to live together without undue violence, if not necessarily in peace and harmony.

Yet corruption contradicted the official morality. In a capitalistic society each man supposedly followed his self-interest, and the functioning of the system was based on the rationality of economic man. Only the public servant was forbidden to pattern his behavior according to this model. He was to pursue the "public interest" in a coolly disinterested manner and to accept society's low valuation of his worth without question. But many of those who sought political office and power did so as a means of upward mobility. For ambitious young men of the slums, without capital or formal education, public office provided a way to escape poverty and insecurity and attain power. Many of the participants in the political and administrative structure did not share the conception of disinterested public service that the middle-class ethos presupposed, and the police acted according to the operative values rather than the official ones.

Although corruption may have been functional in providing for the adjustments necessary for a heterogeneous community, it could be dysfunctional for police-community relations. Being "on the take" made law officers into law breakers, and "crooked cop" was a pejorative term indeed. But although the department had the legal responsibility to uphold the official morality, any real attempt to live up to that responsibility brought charges of "rigid" and "harsh" conduct. Should the police ignore the law for a price, they would be charged with violating their trusts and presenting the spectacle of lawless law enforcement. Community hostility to the force increased the sense of separation from the community among policemen and made them defend each other against outside attack, no matter how justified. They committed perjury for each other as a matter of course, which in turn intensified public hostility and suspicion.

Police brutality and abuse of authority flourished in such an atmosphere. If civilians did not respond to the uniform as a legitimate symbol of moral authority and the patrolman had not established a network of relationships with the people on his beat to keep the peace peacefully, the alternative was the use of gun and club. The constant complaints and well-documented instances of brutality indicate that this was too often the case, although the surviving evidence does not allow any precise generalizations about the nature of the relations between individual policemen and their usual constituency.

Officers like George Walling, who served in the department for almost forty years, and Cornelius Willemse, who joined the force in the late 1890s, did comment that policemen and civilians more often interacted in an atmosphere of hostility and suspicion than respect and trust. As Walling put it in the late 1880s:

To such an extent is the public demoralized that they no longer consider the policeman in his true light, that of a preserver of the peace; but actually, and with some degree of justice, deem him a public enemy. This, of course, inevitably reacts on the police force itself, until a policeman very naturally comes to consider himself not unlike an armed soldier in the midst of a hostile camp. Further, the police are by no means supported by the authorities in the enforcement of law, and as a natural consequence, are sometimes dilatory in bringing culprits to justice, or, as has happened time and time again, mete out punishment themselves.

In his memoirs Willemse tells of being dressed down as a rookie by his sergeant for bringing in unharmed two robbers he had arrested. The sergeant had two older patrolmen work the robbers over so that if for any reason they managed to escape judicial punishment, they still would have bumps and bruises to remind them of their transgression. The police acted on the assumption of guilt, and they exhibited little concern for the civil rights of the poor and politically powerless. Above all else, the police wanted to be respected, and they could not expect that the authority of the uniform alone would earn them this respect; rather, they frequently resorted to force or at least the threat of force to accomplish this goal.

Parades, fires, and especially strikes and labor demonstrations provided the most likely occasions of hostile, violent confrontations between policemen and civilians. In these situations there were often no previous relationships to fall back on, and both sides might be operating under heightened tension and fear. Policemen could not be counted on to refrain from the use of unnecessary force when surrounded by people they disliked or who they knew despised them and who also lacked public support. Labor agitators qualified on every count. Union men objected to police graft and corruption and resented the force's role in ushering strikebreakers past picket lines and keeping streetcars running during strikes. Conversely, strikes meant long hours of extra duty for policemen, and labor unrest violated their desire for complete order and predictability.

In the nineteenth and early twentieth centuries, the political overlords of the police urged them to take a firm line in resisting disorder and anarchy, such as in the Tompkins Square affair of 1874, when police attacked a gathering of men, women, and children who had come to Tompkins Square Park to agitate for public works at a time of severe unemployment. Subsequently, the police arrested anarchists such as Johann Most and Emma Goldman for delivering speeches that challenged the existing order. When the department learned of a memorial meeting honoring the anarchists executed after the Haymarket bombing in Chicago, the commissioners reported, "a sufficient force was at once sent . . . with instructions to prevent the mock proceeding at all hazards."

The police possessed awesome discretionary authority. Their decision to shoot or not, or to make an arrest or let someone go with a warning and a box on the ears, determined whether a man or boy kept or lost his most precious possessions, his life and his liberty. The wider the gap between police and community, the more likely it was that this discretionary authority would be regarded as illegitimate and even tyrannous. In the 1860s and 1870s, people of Irish birth and ancestry constituted a majority both of the police force and of those arrested. In the last two decades of the nineteenth century, when many Italians and East European Jews came to New York, there were greater divergences between the police and the poor, since the Irish remained the dominant group in the department. Indeed, as late as the early 1960s, men of Irish ancestry made up about 40 percent of the force, about four times the Irish proportion of the total population of the city. The next largest group in the police are now the Italians. Recent immigrants, Puerto Ricans, and blacks have long complained that the predominantly Irish and recently Italian police have regarded them with contempt and treated them accordingly.

In the twentieth century the department has become increasingly independent, almost an autonomous, self-directing bureaucracy. Through the activities of organization politicians, the police themselves, and the reformers, many of the ties between the police and the district leaders have been broken. Charles F. Murphy's desire to avoid police scandals has already been noted. The force itself has come to realize that neutrality in the conduct of elections is in its organizational self-interest, although members, organized in such groups as the Patrolmen's Benevolent Association, recently have become more politically active. Traditionally, the PBA has concentrated on issues like salaries, pensions, and work schedules, but in 1966 the association organized a very effective campaign against a civilian review board for the department and defeated it in a referendum by a substantial margin.

The reformers put their emphasis on civil service procedures, on removing politics from the police. As legislators and city administrations built institutional safeguards against the evils of the nineteenth century, they unwittingly increased the bureaucracy's capacity to resist pressure and demands for change. Any concern on the part of civic groups or officeholders about the police can be attacked as political interference. Given the nature of the police–district leader relationships that prevailed for so many years (and which still may be present in some areas), this shibboleth has strong appeal. Opponents of change can point to the days when Tammany men like Tim Sullivan and their underworld allies determined police captaincies and assignments. But how desirable is an insulated bureaucracy more concerned about maintaining its traditional practices and prerogatives than examining and reappraising the role of the police in an age of social upheaval?

The civil service system has prevented some of the more egregious practices by which politicians rewarded their friends and punished their enemies; it has not always worked to improve police performance or to encourage innovation in a field that badly needs it. Since supervisors must work their way up through the ranks, a practice that dates from the late 1850s, men who become commanders spend long years being indoctrinated into the approved principles and practices, which are not necessarily those likely to be useful in the present and the future. A newspaper reporter of the 1890s noted:

The section room in a police-station is a great place for traditions. There walk the ghosts of men notorious in their time, whom the town has forgotten absolutely, and the stories about them affect the manner of grip with which the policeman swings his club, or the temper in which he blackmails disorderly women.

Even with the introduction of elaborate training programs in the twentieth century, the most important part of a rookie's education comes with his first assignment, when the oldtimers tell him to forget all the nonsense he was taught in the police academy and to listen to those who really know what it's all about. In this manner the "tough" approach common in the precincts continues despite the "professional" character of the academy faculty and curriculum.

In recent decades the bureaucracy has succeeded in getting the principles of career service and promotion from within accepted at the very highest levels of the department—the commissioner (who is known to all policemen as the P.C.) and the deputy commissioners. It has become rare for a mayor to appoint anyone other than a career police officer as commissioner. When Mayor John Lindsay wanted to move the department in new directions, he went outside the city for his police commissioner when he chose Howard R. Leary. Still, he minimized the challenge to the bureaucracy, because Leary had served twenty-six years in the Philadelphia police at all levels from patrolman to commissioner. These principles of career service and promotion from within ensure that the leaders have essentially the same perspectives as the rank and file—that the commissioner, the captains, and the patrolmen look at the world and their role in it in much the same way. Even if a commissioner wishes to be an innovator, he faces formidable obstacles. His most difficult task is gaining control over his own department, and often commissioners have come into office with great plans and ideas about reform and improvement that fade because of the opposition or indifference of the bureaucracy and the necessity simply to stay afloat in the midst of daily crises.

The department has traditionally recruited its new members from working- and lower-middle-class youth attracted by the security of a police career. In the 1930s, the depression made the force attractive to college-educated men, but in recent years only about one out of twenty recruits has had any college training at all. The police, then, who have to bear the brunt of attacks upon the established order and the growing demands for social change coming from the slums and the alienated affluent, themselves are members of those groups most passionately committed to the status quo and the most fearful of change, the working and lower-middle classes. Moreover, the policeman by definition is an authority figure, and who now has a harder time? The very men who by background, training, and role are most committed to the values of order and stability are those charged by society with dealing with disorderly outgrowths of poverty, discriminatory housing patterns, and political and social protest.

If urban society is not to disintegrate into mindless violence, the widening gap between the police and many segments of the population must be overcome. There seems little doubt that the attraction of the John Birch Society and other extremist groups for many policemen lies in their sense of public rejection. But many policemen have also rejected the city they serve. Like other members of the white middle class, they have voted with their feet and left the city. In contrast to the situation in Fernando Wood's day when policemen had to live in the ward in which they worked, many now commute from suburbs on Long Island or well north of the city limits in New York State. Suburban residence may be the middle-class ideal; its impact on police-community relations is questionable at best.

In 1874, Mayor William Havemeyer gave the New York Police Department the sobriquet by which it has since been known, "the finest." There is a long record of heroism to justify this term, from those killed and disabled in the line of duty to the men who put their lives in danger as a matter of routine to rescue people from fire or water. It would be easy to fill many pages with accounts of the heroic exploits of individual policemen; what would be more difficult would be to assess the impact of these feats on the public's view of the department and the police conception of their role in society.

If prestige and rewards came primarily for the "good collar" (the spectacular arrest), this is what most policemen would strive for, rather than for keeping the peace peacefully. Until very recently, the fastest way for a policeman to achieve promotion and recognition was to get into a gun battle. Unless one had a particularly strong "hook" or "rabbi" (a powerful patron in or out of the department), this was the classic method of getting out of the "bag" (uniform) and into the detective bureau. Police training programs have stressed law enforcement, the rules of evidence, and the use of weapons; yet most policemen spend most of their time providing aid to people in need or in "cooling" domestic disputes. But if the public image of the "good cop" is that of the gun-toting hero or the club-swinging suppressor of the "dangerous classes," whether they be striking laborers or rioting students, policemen are not going to be prone to conceive of themselves as mediators of domestic and social controversy, as harmonizers whose function is to minimize urban conflict and violence rather than to contribute to its existence.

For most people of power and influence, the key question has not been *what* the police have done, but *to whom* they have done it. The prosperous and the contented have demanded scrupulous police behavior toward the respectable elements of society; at the same time they have been ready to let the force "muss up the punks." Policemen get into trouble when they apply methods suitable to the "undeserving poor," to use a nineteenth-century expression, to those with some social standing and political influence.

Yet social hypocrisy is even greater than this, for society is not completely willing to admit even to itself that it does maintain this double standard of police performance. Americans are sometimes embarrassed by the contradictions between their rhetoric of freedom and respect for the rights of the individual and their demands for conformity and social control. So, while they want the police to suppress deviancy and delinquency, except when they are personally involved, they do not want to know too much about the methods employed. Some men, of course, are ready to turn the force loose with gun, club, and Mace on criminals, deviants, and dissenters without hesitation or apology; civil libertarians insist that the police treat all citizens with regard to their constitutional rights and the respect due them as human beings. The silent majority, however, seems unwilling to accept either position. It will not condone the rubber hose, but it has no objection to the use of psychological pressure to extract a confession. It may value the Bill of Rights, although it is not prepared to let Communists speak in local school auditoriums or to allow demonstrators much leeway in presenting their case.

When the crunch comes, most people seem to prefer order to freedom, and are therefore prepared to grant the police considerable autonomy in dealing with deviants, as long as questionable methods are not employed too blatantly or too publicly. Since society is inconsistent and hypocritical in what it expects of its police, it can hardly expect consistency, honesty, efficiency, and respect for civil liberties to be the dominant characteristics of police performance.

FOR FURTHER READING

1. Michael Banton, The Policeman in the Community (London: Tavistock, 1964), provides useful sociological insights and contrasts the situation in England, Scotland, and the United States.

2. David J. Bordua, ed., The Police: Six Sociological Essays (New York: Wiley, 1967), is a useful compilation reflecting the current interest in police and policing. James Q. Wilson's essay on the morale of the Chicago police is particularly good and blessedly free from jargon, which cannot be said for some of the others.

3. Paul Chevigny, *Police Power: Police Abuses in New York City* (New York: Pantheon, 1969), is a study of police abuse of authority by an attorney for the New York Civil Liberties Union. Chevigny recognizes that many abuses are condoned and even encouraged by public opinion.

4. Arthur Niederhoffer, *Behind the Shield: The Police in Urban Society* (Garden City, N.Y.: Doubleday, 1967), combines the findings of the author's Ph.D. dissertation on police cynicism with anecdotes and insights derived from his more than twenty years as a member of the New York Police Department.

5. James F. Richardson, *The New York Police: Colonial Times to 1901* (New York: Oxford University Press, 1970), surveys the development of the police until the adoption of the single commissioner in 1901. It attempts to relate that development to the social and political history of the city.

6. Wallace S. Sayre and Herbert Kaufman, *Governing New York City: Politics in the Metropolis* (New York: Russell Sage Foundation, 1960), is a full-scale examination of the city's government and politics with excellent bibliographies. There is considerable useful information on the police scattered throughout the book.

7. Emma Schweppe, *The Firemen's and Patrolmen's Unions in the City of New York: A Case Study in Public Employee Unions* (New York: King's Crown Press, 1948), is broader than its title indicates. It is especially good on the political context in which the police functioned.

8. Jerome H. Skolnick, *Justice Without Trial: Law Enforcement in a Democratic Society* (New York: Wiley, 1966), persuasively makes the case that law and order are antithetical, not synonymous terms; that in a democratic society the police must operate within the law rather than attempt to maintain social control through bureaucratic and ultimately totalitarian means.

9. Jerome H. Skolnick, ed., *The Politics of Protest* (New York: Clarion, 1969), has one chapter on "The Police in Protest" which discusses the extent to which the police have become increasingly alienated and at the same time more politically active to advance both their material interests and their conception of proper political and social policy. It is not a reassuring picture.

10. Bruce Smith, *Police Systems in the United States* (New York: Harper and Row, 1949), is a comprehensive study by the then foremost independent expert in police administration in the country. Smith emphasizes the necessity for the police to be an independent professional body, free from political interference and control. A second revised edition was published in 1960.

11. James Q. Wilson, *Varieties of Police Behavior: The Management of Law and Order in Eight Communities* (Cambridge: Harvard University Press, 1968), does not use New York City as one of his case studies, but he makes a number of useful generalizations that can be applied to police in any community.

16. URBAN VICE AND CIVIC REFORM
Chicago in the Early Twentieth Century

Mark Haller

The image of the city as a place of temptation and evil has been an enduring one in American history. In the city were the gambling halls, saloons, houses of prostitution, and burlesque shows. In the city were streets where decent citizens feared to walk even in daylight. In the city young girls became harlots and young men were tempted into a life of dissolution. And Chicago, very early in its history, developed a special reputation for sin and corruption.[1]

Chicago displayed, sometimes in exaggerated form, many of the social characteristics that underlay vice and crime in urban centers. A city of less than 30,000 in 1850, the population grew to more than 300,000 by the time of the Chicago fire in 1871, more than 1 million by 1890, more than 2 million by 1910, and more than 3 million by 1930. As a port city and later as a rail center, the city attracted a large transient population and developed the institutions that service such a population: cheap rooming houses, saloons, a skid row, and houses of prostitution. As a rapidly growing urban center, the city gathered a heterogeneous population uprooted from the nations of Europe and from the towns and countryside of the United States (persons of native white parentage were only 21 percent of the population in 1900). The migrants and their children, freed from many of the traditional controls of family, church, and neighborhood, faced the influences of a strange and dynamic urban society. Nevertheless, the amount of crime and social disorganization in the city was probably not unusual. If Chicago captured headlines, it was often because its civic reformers were particularly active.

The central concern of the reformers was the moral environment that shaped the lives of children and adolescents in the inner-city neighborhoods. A study of campaigns to reform the moral climate of the city illuminates two important aspects of urban life in the early twentieth century: the values and goals of the reformers and the patterns of street life and amusement among the city's lower-class youth.

The concern for the moral dangers of the city grew, at least in part, out of a moralistic value system shared by many Americans. There was, so they believed, a close connection between moral character and success in life. Young men who worked hard and did not squander their money on drink, gambling, and loose women would gain success and respect. Those who frequented saloons, gambling dens, and bordellos risked being drawn permanently into a life of dissolution and crime. The impetus for moral reform often came from those who accepted this value system. Although the leadership generally consisted of relatively well-to-do native white Protestants, their views were widely shared by German and Scandinavian Protestants, by German Jewish immigrants, and by some of the religious and professional leaders of the newer immigrant groups.[2]

Among the groups that shared the moralistic value system, reform movements drew chiefly upon those with direct experience of life in the city's ethnic and working-class neighborhoods. Jane Addams and other workers in the social settlements knew the anguish of immigrant parents whose children joined gangs and became recruits to delinquency or prostitution. They knew what happened when, in a family on the borderline of poverty, the husband spent his meager pay on drink and gambling in a local saloon. They knew that the centers for vice and gambling in Chicago were concentrated in the zones of transition between the Loop (the central business district) and the immigrant slums that encircled the Loop.

Campaigns for moral reform, then, were rooted both in a moralistic culture shocked by vice and crime and in direct knowledge of the quality of life in the impoverished neighborhoods of the city. Religious leaders, the business elite, settlement workers, professional organizations, and neighborhood groups in Chicago banded together in a bewildering variety of associations to improve the dynamic city that both fascinated and appalled them.

STREET LIFE

Boys in the ethnic slums developed a street life that was crucial in shaping their behavior and values. Crowded living conditions forced them to go outside the home to find places to be with their friends. Because of the poverty and long hours of work by one or both parents, boys were often thrown on their own, with little adult supervision. In a large and impersonal city, youthful gangs could easily evade the controls of school, church, or other local adults. They developed a street life and a value system that was passed on from older boys to younger, from older immigrant groups to newer immigrant groups. On the streets of the American city, the young created a life style of their own.[3]

An important feature of the late nineteenth- and early twentieth-century city was the large number of boys engaged in street trades—as bootblacks, fruit peddlers, delivery boys, errand boys, and newsboys. Often boys played hooky from school to work and live in the streets. Many worked late at night. And for many boys—even quite young ones—street trades sometimes provided enough income so that they could live away from home. With other boys, they evaded truant officers, amused themselves by gambling, and formed gangs for petty thievery, jackrolling (robbing drunks), or burglary. Some went to live in the skid row area along Chicago's West Madison Street, where food and lodging were cheap and a boy could lose himself among a crowd of homeless men.[4]

The news alley in the courtyard of the Hearst Building became a gathering place for unsupervised boys. The newsboys, many only ten or twelve years old, congregated there in the early evening hours to pick up the papers they would sell on the streets to the late-night crowds. At midnight or after, men and boys returned to settle their accounts, and perhaps two hundred would loaf or sleep there overnight. Gambling, smoking, and the organization of criminal activities were a common part of life in news alley. As one boy explained:

We had a regular racket of "jack-rolling" and breaking into homes, and made more money than we needed, . . . but we got rid of most of it . . . at the newspaper alley. This alley is usually filled with a large number of "newsies" and truck chauffeurs. . . . It proved to be a good place to lose money, as there was a continuous crap game going on there.

Being approached for homosexual purposes was a common part of street life. As one investigator discovered:

It even became the common thing for men wanting boys for homosexual practices to come to the news-alley to get them. Many boys added greatly to their income in this way as well as securing better sleeping quarters for the night. Many of these boys were not even ten or twelve years old.

By 1916, the Juvenile Protective Association, which was formed by women civic leaders and was the major Chicago group involved in delinquency prevention, periodically brought pressure on both the police and the newspaper management to cease allowing young boys to congregate in the news alley or to sell papers at night. By the 1920s, the association had launched a general campaign to regulate the street trades and to prevent boys under fourteen from engaging in them.[5]

VICE DISTRICTS

Part of Chicago's moral environment was the open prostitution that existed in many parts of the city but was concentrated and officially tolerated in three vice areas. The largest of these was the so-called Levee district south of the Loop. By the turn of the century, in every major city in the United States—from the Barbary Coast of San Francisco to the Tenderloin of New York—there were vice districts; and Chicago's Levee was one of the best. The quality of the vice resorts ranged from the world-famous Everleigh House to cheap brothels. The Levee district, though, was more than a center of prostitution. It was also an entertainment center, with saloons, cabarets, gambling dens, pool halls, and restaurants. It was also a social center for the city's underworld, where pickpockets, burglars, pimps, gamblers, and strongarm men met for relaxation and for business. Presiding over Chicago's Levee district, mediating protection and collecting the pay-offs, were two improbable aldermen, "Bathhouse" John Coughlin and Michael "Hinky Dink" Kenna.[6]

In Chicago, as in other American cities, segregated vice districts were supported by police officials, politicians, and other community leaders on the grounds that, as one newspaper editorial expressed it, "The disreputable women, the pickpockets and petty thieves are better 'bunched' in one section of the city than scattered all over it. The police know where to find them. Respectable people know how to avoid them." To counter such arguments, opponents of the vice districts argued that commercialized prostitution did great harm: It destroyed the moral quality of impoverished neighborhoods, spread venereal diseases, and recruited thousands of girls into a life of sin and degradation. In Chicago and across the nation, the heart of the campaign against prostitution was exposure and exaggeration of the evils of white slavery.[7]

Newspapers periodically reported stories of young girls recruited to prostitution against their wills through deception, drugs, or force. By 1908 a national campaign had been launched to wipe out the evils of white slavery. In city after city, there were cases of country girls or confused immigrant girls recruited to prostitution by professional white slavers who were believed to be organized into national and even international rings for the entrapment, transportation, and sale of girls. Many of the most exciting scandals arose in Chicago, where lurid headlines like the following appeared in the newspapers:

Girl Sold to Chinese
$125 to $200 Is Price Paid
Mabel Carson Says She Is One
of 100 or 200 Victims
Detectives Seek Others

Such stories spurred an ongoing campaign against white slavery and against the commercialized vice of which white slavery was a part.[8]

Alongside the image of the prostitute as an evil woman, the campaign put forward an image of her as a victimized young girl. In part, the image was based upon a general belief that girls were essentially innocent with regard to sexual passion, and girls were perceived to be not only innocent of sexual passion but also frequently ignorant concerning the perils of the city and the wiles of evil men.[9] Even a madam in the 1890s reportedly stated:

Girls, and I say this emphatically, are not seducers. They have innate delicacy and refinement. I say honestly that I do not believe that one woman in 10,000 would cast herself at the feet of lust except under duress or under the force of circumstance.

In addition to innocence and ignorance, there were economic factors that, in the city, turned girls to prostitution. Low wages in factories and department stores made the additional income of prostitution attractive. And the inexorable needs of commercialized vice demanded new recruits. If, as some believed, the average prostitute lived only five years after entering the profession and if there were more than 20,000 prostitutes in Chicago, then the economics of commercialized vice required that some 20,000 girls enter prostitution in Chicago every five years.

Listen, father, mother, there are twenty-two thousand poor, dearly-beloved young girls growing up in our midst today who within five years must under the present business system of white slavery, put aside father, mother, home, friends and honor and march into Chicago's ghastly flesh market to take the place of the twenty-two thousand helpless, hopeless, decaying chattels who now daily behind bolts and bars and steel screens, satisfy the abominable lust of (approximately) two hundred and ten thousand brutal, drunken adulterers.

In extreme form, this was what many reformers came to believe: that the segregated vice districts were a place of moral and physical ruin for thousands of innocent girls each year.[10]

Finally, commercialized vice activities clustered primarily in the area between the downtown business district and the ethnic and black slums that surrounded it, or else were scattered along the commercial streets in the slum neighborhoods. Well-to-do parents could raise their children in neighborhoods relatively free of vice; the poor knew that their children would be raised where vice was an everyday part of life. Indeed, the vice district had long abutted on the area of heaviest black settlement, so that in Chicago— as in many other cities—the vice district was, ironically, the most integrated aspect of city life. Blacks held many of the jobs as maids and entertainers in the district; and black madams and pimps occasionally managed white prostitutes, while black prostitutes sometimes worked for white madams or white pimps. As reformers pointed out: "the apparent discrimination against the colored citizens of the city in permitting vice to be set down in their very midst is unjust, and abhorrent to all fair minded people. Colored children should receive the same moral protection that white children receive."[11]

From 1907 to World War I, a coalition of reformers campaigned to reduce vice activities in the city. Some groups worked quietly to redeem prostitutes and to help them to return to legitimate society. Other groups led highly publicized campaigns to expose police and political corruption in order to create public support for effective law enforcement. In 1907 the business elite of the city formed a Joint Club Committee to support prosecution of white slavers. Religious leaders formed neighborhood associations and a city-wide Illinois Vigilance Association to combat white slavery, suppress obscene books and pictures, and prevent the spread of venereal diseases. As a result of pressures from civic leaders, gradually, from 1912 to 1914, the open vice of the Levee district was driven underground. It moved to working-class suburbs that lay west and southwest of the city, and was driven deeper into the South Side black ghetto.[12]

SALOONS AND LIQUOR

Reformers often found the saloon a more difficult issue than commercialized vice. In most cities laws requiring that saloons close at a certain hour each night and that they be closed on Sunday went unenforced. The issue of enforcement became a highly symbolic one. On the one side were the largely Protestant moral reformers for whom the failure of enforcement represented all that was evil in immigration: political corruption, control of government by liquor interests, and desecration of the Sabbath. For several immigrant groups, on the other hand, the protection of Sunday drinking and the saloon became a defense of social customs and personal freedom against the meddling of officious do-gooders.[13]

Although saloon closing laws were a highly symbolic and divisive issue, the general effort to control the abuses of saloons in residential neighborhoods had somewhat wider appeal. In many neighborhoods, saloons were perceived as centers of drunkenness, gambling, vice, crime, and demoralization of the home. During the late 1880s and 1890s, when Chicago more than doubled its area by annexing the residential towns on its periphery, the towns often insisted as a condition of annexation that they retain their own liquor laws, which either prohibited saloons or permitted local option on the issue. In the twentieth century, state law allowed neighborhoods, by petition and referendum, to vote themselves dry. By 1916, nearly two-thirds of the area of Chicago, consisting primarily of middle-class or well-to-do residential neighborhoods on the edges of the city, was either prohibition or local-option territory.[14] In many of these neighborhoods, local neighborhood associations carefully investigated violations and kept out saloons.[15]

Despite the fact that most of the area of Chicago was relatively free of saloons, most of the people lived in the densely populated inner-city neighborhoods where saloons were heavily concentrated. And, while many saloons functioned as social centers for workingmen, the abuses of the saloon were widely recognized. Many saloons sold liquor to minors, stayed open after hours, were criminal hangouts, and provided places for vice and gambling. In 1903 the City Council passed an ordinance forbidding the sale of alcoholic beverages to minors. In 1906, in order to reduce the density of saloons, the City Council passed ordinances raising the annual license fee for saloons from $600 to $1,000 and forbidding the issuance of any more licenses until the number of saloons in the city was reduced to one for every 500 persons. Under the ordinances, the number of saloons declined from 8,097 in 1906 to 7,094 in 1916. But because saloons remained concentrated in the inner-city areas, their density remained high. In the First Ward, which encompassed the Levee vice district, there were still 675 saloons in 1916, or one for every 77 persons (adults and children).[16]

The saloon and its relationship to vice, gambling, and corruption was therefore a central issue in the efforts of many civic reformers to create decent neighborhoods in the city. The issue became even more intense with the coming of prohibition after World War I. To moral reformers, prohibition at first held out great hope for the improvement of urban life. In the early years, many social settlement workers and other reformers reported that wife-beating and squandering of money by husbands had declined and that the quality of family life in inner-city neighborhoods had become better. With the rise of bootlegging gangs and the worldwide fame of Al Capone, the reformers themselves became divided: some pressed for stricter enforcement of prohibition laws; others reluctantly called for repeal of prohibition. But most agreed that the 1920s—with its speakeasies, cabarets, roadhouses, and the apparent sexual revolution among the young—had created a social climate dangerous for the young people of the city.

COMMERCIALIZED AMUSEMENTS

Movies were another commercialized amusement with a troubling impact upon city youth. Crude mutascopes—or "peep-through machines" —were known in the 1890s and continued into the twentieth century as a standard feature in the many penny arcades that provided entertainment for young people. Although brief movies, shown on a screen, were established features at vaudeville shows by 1900, not until 1904 did Chicago have its first theater devoted entirely to films. Thereafter, the five-cent theaters, or nickelodeons, proliferated rapidly and became a major amusement for young and old. By 1908, Chicago's theaters were showing 16,000 films a year; by 1913 there were 606 licensed nickelodeons seating 251,000 patrons. Many were set up in small stores, with a barker out front to attract customers and a piano inside to play along with the jerky, silent films that ran about seventeen minutes. Gradually, however, the length and quality of the films grew; gradually, too, the number of theaters declined as smaller ones went out of business to be replaced by large, modern theaters seating as many as 3,000 patrons. By the 1920s, the world of Hollywood had been created, with its movie stars, press agents, and scandal. In fan magazines such as *Screenland* or *Photoplay*, young persons could read about the glamorous world of stars like Rudolph Valentino or Mary Pickford. Many young people were entranced by both the fantasy world of the film and the fantasy world of Hollywood.[17]

The congregation of the young at the theaters, often without adult supervision, in itself seemed dangerous to some reformers. Adolescents sometimes used the theaters for flirting and necking. And many theaters near the Loop had become, like the news alley, places where homosexuals solicited teenage boys.[18]

The main concern of civic reformers, however, was the impact of the films themselves upon the young. The films often had scenes of crime and violence and sometimes showed crime in an attractive or humorous light.

The moral danger to the young seemed obvious. As a Catholic priest and sociologist explained in 1919:

When we go to our congested districts, to our slums and foreign settlements, you see how little is done for the people in the way of legitimate recreation. The movie is an indispensable means of supplying a need of that sort, and therefore it needs to be supervised just as we supervise our water supply and our milk supply.... Whatever is bad for moral health should be eliminated on the same principle, that we eliminate what is bad for physical health.

Furthermore, leading physicians and psychiatrists claimed that movies were harmful to children's eyes and caused nervousness, St. Vitus's dance, hallucinations, and mental disorder. Expert opinion, in short, held that movies threatened the moral and mental health of urban youth.[19]

The Chicago City Council acted decisively in response. An ordinance in 1907 required that each film receive a police license before being shown in the city. This was the first movie censorship law in the nation. At first, the police performed the censorship functions themselves, although they often turned to the leaders of the Chicago Woman's Club or the Juvenile Protective Association for advice in difficult cases. By 1911 the leaders of the Juvenile Protective Association, pleased with the results, declared that the police do "not allow scenes of murder or robbing or abduction to be shown upon the screens, and in consequence the motion picture shows of Chicago are now very decent." In 1912, reacting to further reform pressure, the City Council established the position of Second Deputy Superintendent of Police, with responsibility for enforcement of laws against prostitution and "the censorship of motion pictures and public performances of all kinds." Under the new system, the following scenes were deleted from films: a policeman in his underpants, a soldier drinking from a bottle, a ballet girl smoking a cigaret, and the stabbing scene from *Julius Caesar*. Although the policy later became more flexible, movie censorship continued to be a police function and to receive strong support from civic reform organizations.[20]

If movies were an immoral influence, dance halls led directly to improper and immoral behavior. Dance halls were numerous in the city at the turn of the century and were a major center for the social life of lower-class adolescents. In 1910, for instance, the Juvenile Protective Association investigated 266 licensed dance halls and about 100 unlicensed halls. "This investigation showed," according to the report, "that 240 halls sold liquor, that 190 had saloons opening off the halls, that 146 sold liquor to minors, that 187 permitted immoral dancing." Some dance halls catered to families and to the social activities of varied ethnic groups. Civic reformers were disturbed by much of the customary behavior—the ribald joking, the presence of small children while parents drank and danced, or the embracing and horseplay among adolescents and adults. But far more common and, to civic reformers, far more upsetting were the dance halls that catered to the young. At these halls, boys and girls, who usually arrived in separate groups, mingled in an atmosphere often made livelier by the availability of beer and liquor. Indeed, much of the profitability of dance halls derived from sale of alcoholic beverages. Girls sometimes started attending as young as twelve; boys, as young as fourteen or fifteen. The boys often attempted, sometimes with success, to pick up girls and take them elsewhere to engage in heavier sexual activity. Thousands of young persons in Chicago developed loyalties to particular dance halls, attended regularly, and made the dance hall the center of their social life.[21]

In the 1920s, with the decline of the segregated vice districts, the development of taxi dance halls added a new dimension to the dance hall problem. At a taxi dance hall, the girls were employees, while the young men bought tickets that entitled them to dance with a girl. A ticket usually cost 10 cents, of which the girl received half. For many young working girls, taxi dance halls were a way to supplement their incomes. The advantage for the man was that the girl, if not already spoken for, had to dance with him and, if she wished to be popular and earn money, to dance the way he wished. A number of taxi dance halls became places where, to reformers, the behavior was unspeakably vulgar. At the New American Dance Hall, for instance, an observer noted:

I saw more socking and rolling that night than I ever saw before. The young fellows use this socking for masturbation purposes. After a guy shoots off, he says, "another two bucks saved" and he transfers his money to his other pocket.[22]

Yet the taxi dance hall served an important social function in the heterogeneous city. For shy and awkward men, it provided a chance to dance with a girl. For many Chinese and Filipino men, working in a city where there were few girls from their place of origin and where prejudices against them were often strong, the taxi dance hall was the only place where they could find feminine companionship.

The tireless investigators for the Juvenile Protective Association took the lead in attempts to control abuses of the dance halls. By the 1920s, the association had persuaded a number of dance halls to hire women chaperones, and it worked closely with the National Association of Ballroom Proprietors and Managers in raising the moral standards of dance halls.[23]

YOUTH CULTURE

The early twentieth century was the gestation period for a new life style that in the 1920s became a major attraction for youth and a major concern for many social reformers. The youth culture developed around the new jazz music, dance styles, clothing, and dating customs. Jazz was a music that matured in the cities—and in its more artistic forms was rooted in the black experience. Its origin lay in part among the talented musicians —black and white—who played in the vice and entertainment districts of New Orleans in the 1890s and early 1900s. Soon the musicians and their styles spread to St. Louis, Memphis, Chicago, New York, and to the entertainment districts of other major cities. The lively ragtime tunes were widely popular in the 1890s and had become a nationwide craze by 1910. In subsequent years, ragtime and other varieties of jazz formed the basis for the popular hit tunes that were a crucial part of the youth culture.[24]

Development of various mass media in the twentieth century made possible the instantaneous popularity of the new tunes. The player piano (pianola) had a period of widespread use after 1900. The rolls for the player pianos included both classical and popular works, among which *Alexander's Ragtime Band* was a great favorite. More important in the long run, the phonograph after 1900 gained rapidly as a standard appliance in many homes. By 1921 over one hundred million records were sold annually in the United States, and Americans spent more for records than for any other type of recreation. Popular records easily outsold classical records, so that already the youth market was a major source of customers. By the 1920s, too, jukeboxes were available in restaurants and other public places. Finally, commercial radio broadcasting began after World War I. During the 1920s, music constituted over three-fourths of the programming, with varieties of jazz predominating among the music played. As a result especially of the radio and phonograph, a tune played by a particular musician might reach a larger audience through a single record or radio broadcast than he could previously have reached during an entire year. This led both to the rapid popularity of a tune and to the rapid exhaustion of popularity through repetition. In short, the phenomenon of hit tunes, known and shared by adolescents across the nation, made its appearance.[25]

Along with popular music went the development of new dance styles, known by such exotic names as the shimmy, camel walk, grizzly bear, or toddle. The dances, which often involved contortions that many adults found obscene, departed widely from the ballroom dancing accepted among respectable native Americans and the folk dances of immigrant groups, and thus were another factor binding youth together in a shared experience. Yet the new culture was more than music and dancing. Women —the flappers of the 1920s—wore a new style of clothing, interacted more freely with men, and in some cases even smoked cigarets in public (before World War I, only loose women smoked cigarets). There were signs of a freer attitude toward sex. Girls even in high school began to attend dances without wearing corsets, more afraid that a boy would call them "old ironsides" than that their parents would be shocked. The increasing use of automobiles during the same period not only meant that young people could travel farther in search of amusement, but also made possible lovers' lanes. In the 1920s there was much discussion of the "sexual revolution" and its meaning for the future of American morals.[26]

From the beginning, jazz music and the new dances were stigmatized because of their supposed origin in the vice districts, because of their association with blacks, and—most important—because of the apparent sensuality of the music and dances. By the early 1920s, Phillip Yarrow, an officer in the Illinois Vigilance Association formed by church people to fight vice and obscenity, summed up a widespread feeling:

Jazz music is obscene. Its influence in the dance is decidedly evil. It is scarcely possible to dance decently to the riotous strains of a jazz orchestra, blatantly blaring all the cries of the barnyard, united with the tumultuous noises of a boiler shop.

In the 1920s, in short, the campaign against the moral evils of the city became, in some ways, an opposition to a new youth culture that originated out of the commercial amusements of the city and the new mass media.[27]

The new music and dancing were often found in the dance halls and cabarets before World War I and in the cabarets and roadhouses that sprang up during the prohibition era of the 1920s.[28] In the 1920s the so-called "black and tan cabarets" came into their own. Just as Harlem became an entertainment center for New York City during prohibition, so the area around 31st and State streets—in the heart of Chicago's South Side black ghetto—became the center for vice, jazz, and entertainment. Of course, the association of vice and entertainment with black neighborhoods was not new, but the black and tan cabarets that flourished in the 1920s were visited by blacks, white college youths, and others in search of excitement. One investigator in 1922 reported:

A composite picture of these places would reveal a vile, disreputable dive in which colored and white races freely intermingle. All resorts were found to be very well patronized, in fact, so well patronized that in several places persons were found patiently awaiting an opportunity to secure admittance. In addition to the lawless element that frequent these places, slumming parties are also attracted. The indecent singing and dancing of the untalented performers is one of the main sources of attraction. The management of these resorts permits their guests to dance, and in no way attempts to restrict or to regulate their dancing. . . . Drunken white men and colored prostitutes, and white prostitutes with colored men were always in evidence in these places.[29]

The cabarets, in fact, varied considerably from those that offered good jazz entertainment to those that were mere fronts for prostitution.

If the cabarets were an outgrowth of the saloon, the roadhouses arose out of the twin influences of prohibition and the automobile. Outside the city limits—and thus outside the jurisdiction of city police—clusters of roadhouses sprang up in the early 1920s. Roadhouses varied in type. At one end of the scale were the large, modern buildings where food was served, music and dancing were available, and set-ups were provided for patrons who brought their own liquor. At the other end were the small places that served food and alcoholic beverages, provided private rooms for sexual intimacy, and ran various gambling activities. For young people of city and suburb, the roadhouses were places for drinking, dancing, and entertainment. And, as one investigator ruefully noted, "Wherever dancing occurred, the young people were repeatedly seen to press their bodies closely together and execute lewd, indecent and suggestive movements and contortions, provocative of and tending to excite the sexual impulse." Because bootlegging gangs arranged police protection for the roadhouses that purchased their booze, reformers had little success in persuading township and county authorities to move against them.[30]

· · ·

Many urban reformers, then, viewed the city as a dangerous environment for raising children. To some extent, their goal was to provide for the poor the same sort of urban neighborhoods that they had achieved for themselves. Their own neighborhoods were relatively free of the saloons, vice activities, and gambling dens; such activities were concentrated in or near the densely populated inner-city slums and victimized primarily the poor, the immigrant, and the black. In the inner-city neighborhoods were the delinquent gangs and the centers of street crime. Yet, to some extent, the moral dangers of the city appeared to entice all its adolescents. The street life and entertainment facilities of the city allowed young people to participate in a social life of their own. Regulation or elimination of these sources of entertainment became, then, a major goal of a wide range of civic reformers, including social settlement workers, religious leaders, women's clubs, business organizations, and professional associations.

The civic leaders who led crusades for moral reform in the cities were often the same people who backed many of the other reform goals of the day, including elimination of child labor, honest city government, tenement-house reform, and public health. An understanding of their moral vision has often been obscured by concentrating on the economic and political reforms and minimizing their moral reforms. For many reformers, there was no separation. In their view, the poor were victimized by bad housing *and* saloons, by lack of wholesome playgrounds *and* the presence of pool halls and gambling dens, and by both the economic and moral effects of child labor. The tragedy of poverty was its impact upon the character of children. The central thrust of urban reform was therefore to supervise and uplift the lives of the city's children.

The first thirty years of the twentieth century, especially within the larger cities, brought important changes in youth culture and adult taste. The commercialized amusements of the city, when combined with the mass media, provided the young with a common culture of popular music and dancing. They also created the movie stars and popular singers who became the idols for the young. By World War I, new styles of dating had become part of a growing youth culture. The myth—and perhaps the reality—of a sexual revolution among the young was as much discussed in the 1920s as in the late 1960s. In literature and art, too, the period brought a franker treatment of sex. To the extent that the moral vision of the reformers of the early twentieth century now seems antiquated, it is in part a reflection of the fact that the city provided an environment within which a new system of values arose. While moral reformers once spoke for a broad range of respectable and informed opinion, this became less and less the case.

From World War I to World War II, as a result, American social reform underwent a gradual, though crucial, change. Before World War I, a concern for moral reform was highly associated with a general concern for urban social and political reform. During the 1920s and 1930s, this association became less clear. By the period after World War II, moral reform— from movie censorship to temperance agitation—had become more closely associated with political opposition to economic and social reform. Urban reformers of the early twentieth century were the progenitors, at least in part, of both "liberal" and "conservative" traditions in contemporary America.[31]

NOTES

1. For discussion of the criminal image of Chicago and the American city, see Anselm L. Strauss, *Images of the American City* (New York: The Free Press, 1961), pp. 33–51, 169–79.

2. For a discussion of the moral value system, see Irvin G. Wyllie, *The Self-Made Man in America: The Myth of Rags to Riches* (New Brunswick, N.J.: Rutgers University Press, 1954), esp. chaps. 2–5; and Daniel J. Elazar, *Cities of the Prairie* (New York: Basic Books, 1970), pp. 223–30, 262–4, and *passim.*

3. The function of gangs is discussed in Frederic M. Thrasher, *The Gang: A Study of 1,313 Gangs in Chicago* (Chicago: University of Chicago Press, 1923); see also Clifford R. Shaw, *Delinquency Areas: A Study of the Geographical Distribution of School Truants, Juvenile Delinquents, and Adult Offenders in Chicago* (Chicago: University of Chicago Press, 1929).

4. See Clifford R. Shaw, *The Jack-Roller: A Delinquent Boy's Own Story* (Chicago: University of Chicago Press, 1930). A vivid fictional account of juvenile life in Chicago's skid row is Willard Motley, *Knock on Any Door* (New York: Appleton-Century-Crofts, 1950); see also Nels Anderson, *The Hobo: The Sociology of the Homeless Man* (Chicago: University of Chicago Press, 1923).

5. Quotations from Shaw, *op. cit.*, pp. 141–2, and Paul G. Cressey, "Report on Summer's Work with the Juvenile Protective Association of Chicago" (typewritten paper, October 1925), p. 37, in Ernest W. Burgess papers, University of Chicago Library, II-A, Box 39. Concerning street trades, see papers of Juvenile Protective Association, Library of University of Illinois at Chicago Circle, folders 84, 86, 88.

6. For descriptions of the vice districts, see Walter C. Reckless, *Vice in Chicago* (Chicago: University of Chicago Press, 1929); Charles Washburn, *Come into My Parlor: A Biography of the Aristocratic Everleigh Sisters of Chicago* (New York: National Library Press, 1936); Vice Commission of Chicago, *The Social Evil in Chicago* (Chicago, 1911); Lloyd Wendt and Herman Kogan, *Lords of the Levee: The Story of Bathhouse John and Hinky Dink* (Indianapolis: Bobbs-Merrill, 1943); and John Landesco, *Organized Crime in Chicago*, 2nd ed. (Chicago: University of Chicago Press, 1968), chap. 2.

7. Quotation from *Chicago Chronicle*, July 3, 1899, cited in Clark, "Newspaper History," p. 14. The nationwide campaign against prostitution is described in Roy Lubove, "The Progressive and the Prostitute," *The Historian*, XXIV (May 1962), 308–30; and Egal Feldman, "Prostitution, the Alien Woman and the Progressive Imagination, 1910–1915," *American Quarterly*, XIX (Summer 1967), 192–206.

8. Quotations from *Chicago Inter-Ocean*, May 21, 1890, and Frances Opal Brooks, "Crime in 1908" (typewritten paper, 1928), p. 17, in Burgess papers. Descriptions of white slavery can be found in Clifford G. Roe, *The Prodigal Daughter: The White Slave Evil and the Remedy* (Chicago: L. W. Walter Company, 1911), and in Jane Addams, *A New Conscience and an Ancient Evil* (New York: Macmillan Company, 1912). For white slavery in an earlier period, see Charlton Edholm, *Traffic in Girls and Florence Crittenton Missions* (Chicago: The Women's Temperance Publishing Association, 1893).

9. Quotation from William T. Stead, *If Christ Came to Chicago* (Chicago: Laird & Lee Publishers, 1894), p. 252. For a history of American attitudes toward prostitution, see Robert Riegel, "Changing American Attitudes toward Prostitution (1800–1920)," *Journal of the History of Ideas*, XXIX (July–September 1968), 437–52; also Margaret Wyman, "The Rise of the Fallen Woman," *American Quarterly*, III (Summer 1951), 167–77.

10. Samuel Paynter Wilson, *Chicago and Its Cess-Pools of Infamy* (Chicago, n.d.), p. 55. For a similar but more balanced view, see Jane Addams, *op. cit.*

11. Quotation from Vice Commission, *op. cit.*, p. 39. The relationship of blacks to vice activities is also discussed in Chicago Commission on Race Relations, *The Negro in Chicago* (Chicago: University of Chicago Press, 1922), pp. 342–8, 355–6; see also Ben L. Reitman, *The Second Oldest Profession: A Study of the Prostitute's "Business Manager"* (New York: Vanguard, 1931), esp. chap. 11.

12. Formation of the Vice Commission is described in Louise C. Wade, *Graham Taylor: Pioneer for Social Justice, 1851–1938* (Chicago: University of Chicago Press, 1964), pp. 199–200. The changing vice structure can be followed in Reckless, *op. cit., passim.*

13. See Alex Gottfried, *Boss Cermak of Chicago* (Seattle: University of Washington Press, 1962), pp. 53–60, 82ff; Eugene McCarthy, "The Bohemians in Chicago and

Their Benevolent Societies, 1875–1946" (unpublished master's thesis, University of Chicago, 1950), pp. 87–9; and Arthur Burrage Farwell, "Sunday Closing in Chicago," printed statement in Julius Rosenwald papers, University of Chicago Library, vol. XII.

14. Chicago Commission on the Liquor Problem, *Preliminary Report* (December 1916), p. 13.

15. See papers of the Hyde Park Protective Association, Chicago Historical Society.

16. Chicago Commission on the Liquor Problem, *Preliminary Report,* esp. pp. 3–17.

17. Lois Kate Halley, "A Study of Motion Pictures in Chicago as a Medium of Communication" (unpublished master's thesis, University of Chicago, 1924), pp. 12–50, 111; Chicago Motion Picture Commission, *Report* (Chicago, 1920), pp. 50–51; and Frederick A. Gordon, "The Movies in Chicago: Early Growth and the Rise of Censorship" (unpublished research paper, 1968), esp. pp. 1–12.

18. See "Memorandum for Miss Youmans," May 20, 1926, in Juvenile Protective Association papers, folder 1, and "Special Report on Investigation in Highland Park and Highwood, Illinois," [no date], folder 16.

19. Quotation from Chicago Motion Picture Commission, *op. cit.,* p. 75. For long quotations from leading experts concerning the dangers of films, see Halley, *op. cit.,* pp. 59–71; also Jane Addams, *The Spirit of Youth and the City Streets* (New York: Macmillan, 1910), esp. pp. 84–94.

20. Quotation from Louise de Koven Bowen, *Five and Ten Cent Theaters* (Chicago: Juvenile Protective Association, 1911). See also Chicago Motion Picture Commission, *op. cit., passim;* and Halley, *op. cit.,* pp. 21–8. For general studies of movie censorship, see Ira H. Carmen, *Movies, Censorship, and the Law* (Ann Arbor, Mich.: University of Michigan Press, 1966), and Richard S. Randall, *Censorship of the Movies: The Social and Political Control of a Mass Medium* (Madison, Wis.: University of Wisconsin Press, 1968).

21. Quotation from "Work of the Juvenile Protective Association" (1911), in Juvenile Protective Association papers, folder 15. For descriptions of dance halls, see Vice Commission, *op. cit.,* pp. 185–98; Louise de Koven Bowen, *The Public Dance Halls of Chicago* (Chicago: Juvenile Protective Association, 1917); and Constance Weinberger and S. D. Alinsky, "The Public Dance Hall" (typewritten research paper, 1928), in Burgess papers, II-D, Box 40.

22. Quotation from "An Evening in the New American Dance Hall" (typewritten paper, undated), in Burgess papers, II-D, Box 60. The best study is Paul G. Cressey, *The Taxi-Dance Hall: A Sociological Study in Commercialized Recreation and City Life* (Chicago: University of Chicago Press, 1932).

23. Quotation from report of Sybil L. Campbell, December 8, 1917, in Juvenile Protective Association papers, folder 104. For the campaign against dance halls, see correspondence in folder 102 and reports in folder 104 of Juvenile Protective Association papers.

24. See especially Neil Leonard, *Jazz and the White Americans: The Acceptance of a New Art Form* (Chicago: University of Chicago Press, 1962); also Joy J. Jackson, *New Orleans in the Gilded Age: Politics and Urban Progress, 1880–1896*

(Baton Rouge: Louisiana State University Press, 1970), pp. 273–82; Stephen Longstreet, *Sportin' House: New Orleans and the Jazz Story* (Los Angeles: Sherbourne Press, 1965).

25. Leonard, *op. cit.,* esp. pp. 91–4.

26. For a colorful discussion of the youth culture in the 1920s, see Frederick Lewis Allen, *Only Yesterday* (New York: Harper & Bros., 1931), esp. pp. 88–122; also Leonard, *op. cit., passim.*

27. Quotation from Phillip Yarrow, ed., *Fighting the Debauchery of Our Girls and Boys* (Chicago: Phillip Yarrow, 1923), p. 125.

28. For descriptions of cabarets see Louise de Koven Bowen, *The Road to Destruction Made Easy in Chicago* (Chicago: Juvenile Protective Association, 1916).

29. Quotation from typewritten report on "Commercialized Prostitution," December 10, 1922, in Juvenile Protective Association papers, folder 92.

30. Quotation from typewritten report on "Commercialized Prostitution," May 11–26, 1929, in Juvenile Protective Association papers, folder 99. Roadhouses are described in typewritten "Road-house Survey," July 25–August 31, 1929, *ibid.,* folder 106; and Daniel Russell, "The Road House: A Study of Commercial Amusements in the Environs of Chicago" (unpublished master's thesis, University of Chicago, 1931).

31. The increasingly marginal position of groups fighting obscenity in books is vividly chronicled in Paul S. Boyer, *Purity in Print: Book Censorship in America* (New York: Scribner, 1968). The movement of the temperance organizations toward a marginal and largely conservative position in American society is brilliantly analyzed by Joseph R. Gusfield, *Symbolic Crusade: Status Politics and the American Temperance Movement* (Urbana, Ill.: University of Illinois Press, 1963).

17. BREAKING THE CHAINS OF POVERTY
Public Education in Boston, 1800–1860

Stanley K. Schultz

Rather than being a stepchild of European Enlightenment theory, or the offspring of domestic democratic trends in the age of the so-called "common man," the public school movement in the United States matured in response to what contemporaries viewed as an urban crisis. Rising crime rates, increasing pauperism, and spiraling juvenile delinquency signaled a moral dislocation in cities undergoing commercial and industrial transformation. Swarms of foreign immigrants challenged their capacity to accommodate and assimilate newcomers, as did the influx of white and black native migrants from the countryside and small towns. Everywhere the orderly patterns of existence appeared interrupted; the cities seemed to be overwhelmed by the rush of social change. Cities lacking institutionalized systems of orderly government—police departments, fire departments, centralized governmental bureaucracies—had to forge new tools to hammer out an urban discipline.[1] A growing and ever more diverse population; new industrial demands on the time and energy of citizens; cities bursting at the seams of their former boundaries; and social institutions like the family and the church dissolving in the heat of economic progress—all these disparate elements of urban life had to be adjusted and accommodated to each other. Between 1800 and 1860 those seeking a new urban discipline created as one of their most useful tools a system of public education. City leaders championed education to secure social order in a disorderly age.

Of the various disorders in urban life, the most evident was poverty. While American cities always had known the poor, urban leaders of the past had believed in the transiency of poverty. In young and slowly expanding colonial cities, the economic horizons appeared limitless; the poor did not always have to remain poor.[2] But during the late eighteenth and early nineteenth centuries, these attitudes shifted dramatically. City officials and concerned private citizens began to suspect, perhaps already too late, that urban poverty was not a passing phenomenon but a permanent condition. A growing number of urban paupers presaged a day when cities might be divided sharply along class lines; when foreign indigents might threaten the hegemony of native Americans; and when public financial resources might be devoted more to charitable relief, to workhouses, and to prisons than to other needed public services. Many urban leaders saw in public education a form of social insurance against a possible tomorrow when the poor might dominate city life.

Systems of public schools did not arise solely as answers to the problems of poverty. As part of their heritage Americans had valued formal education for its uplifting, ennobling qualities and for its promised contribution to general social progress. Yet it was undeniable that nineteenth-century urbanites largely fashioned public schools in response to an alleged urban crisis—and that poverty played a primary role in their interpretations of that crisis. Boston, among large cities, enjoyed the highest reputation of caring for its poor. It also traditionally had led urban America in provisions for public instruction.[3] In nineteenth-century Boston, therefore, to a greater extent than in most other cities, citizens heralded public education as the most vital institutional answer to poverty and its related social problems. Boston hoped to master its urban crisis and to become a model for community growth.

"The poor were personally subjects of knowledge and cognizance to the more favored classes," reminisced a charity worker about the halcyon days of the 1820s. "Pauperism was a thing determinable in nature and quantity. . . . Every man was known by his neighbor, . . . none were overlooked, nor could escape in the crowd." Like many memories, the statement was partly romantic illusion. From the vantage point of the more troubled 1850s, the twenties looked like a time of close ties between the poor and the "more favored classes." But it was not. As George Ticknor, the cultural arbiter of mid-nineteenth-century Boston, recalled, certain events of the twenties destroyed the "compact, united, and friendly community" in which citizens "felt involved in each other's welfare."[4] Chief among those events was a change in the size and composition of Boston's poor population. Beginning in that decade, the poverty classes of the city underwent a significant transformation.

During the 1820s and early 1830s a large number of migrants entering the city came from the depressed rural areas of New England. In 1820, foreign residents comprised only 12 percent of Boston's total population, but over the following forty years, the immigrant population increased from roughly 5,000 to over 60,000. In the single decade of the 1840s, the immigrant percentage of the entire population jumped from 22 to over 45.7 percent. Between 1845 and 1850, the foreign populace boomed by over 70 percent, while the native population declined by 2.27 percent. By 1850, less than half the descendants of Bostonians alive in 1820 remained in the city. The portents were clear: Due to native migration from the city, alien immigration, and a much higher birth rate among foreign than among native residents, the population had become more mixed.[5] Many migrants, whether rural native Americans or foreigners, had swollen the ranks of Boston's poor. And as the number of the poor had increased, so had the social distance between them and the better sort. The complacency of middle- and upper-class Bostonians had given way to apprehension and then fear as the indigents had become more visible threats to social order.[6]

Beginning in the early 1820s, crimes common to the lower classes—drunkenness, assault and battery, "lewd" behavior, and vagrancy—accounted for a growing number of court convictions. After his election as mayor, in 1823 Josiah Quincy initiated a clean-up campaign of the city's most notorious districts. He proceeded "upon the principle that if in great cities the existence of vice is inevitable, that its course should be in secret, . . . not obtrusive, not powerful, not prowling publicity in the streets."[7] But if the vicious poor had become more visible, what of the less visible and vicious poor, those who did not appear in court or become identifiable public nuisances? Politicians, clergymen, charity workers, and educators felt a pressing need to identify those poor and to evaluate their potential threat to the safety of the community. Periodically between the 1820s and the 1860s concerned citizens conducted a bewildering variety of investigations into the problem. From their efforts emerged a composite portrait of the poor.

The poor were vicious (given to vice), ignorant, and lacking in habits of cleanliness and industry. They either were nonchurchgoers or Catholics, both unforgivable failings in the city of the Puritans. Identified by occupation and origin, the employed poor were white native-born, black, and alien laborers, working at the most menial tasks as domestics and unskilled hands in factories and building trades. For every employed poor person, however, far more remained unemployed. Within certain older areas of the city, the poor seemingly were more migratory than the rest of an astonishingly mobile population. Indigents and other members of the lower classes moved from street to court, from cellar to chamber to attic with a rapidity that defied the accurate keeping of records. They were residents of the city's foulest slums—former mansions, abandoned warehouses, and factories transformed into crowded and insanitary living quarters. Such breeding grounds of cholera, tuberculosis, and other diseases as "Jacob's Ladder," an alley tenement built into the side of Fort Hill, displayed living quarters littered with "putrefying vegetable matters" and "no small portion of substances still more loathsome." In a cellar room as many as thirty-nine men, women, and children might sleep together, often inundated by a flood tide that, as one doctor reported, rose "so high that it was necessary to approach the bedside of a patient by means of a plank which was laid from one stool to another; while the dead body of an infant was actually sailing about the room in its coffin." In such surroundings, visitors observed, "intemperance, lewdness, riot . . . enter in and dwell there."

As this portrait of the poor took shape in civic investigations and in the popular press, citizens began to notice a distinctively alien hue. Increasingly "the poor" and "foreign immigrants" became synonymous terms, used alike by those Bostonians who looked with compassion and those who viewed with contempt the growing numbers of indigents in their midst.[8] Foreigners afforded the most visible examples of those dwelling in poverty. Their styles of dress, their culinary customs, their speech mannerisms (and, for some, their completely alien tongues), and their personal habits all signaled their differences from the native poor. At the same time, their very distinctness made the immigrants appear to be the majority of the poor population of the city.

The "facts" of urban life catalogued in numerous public and private reports reiterated the central position of immigrants. The highest rates of unemployment and dependence on public aid seemed to be among the foreign classes. They filled the almshouses, the Houses of Industry and Correction, and other local public institutions. Bostonians professed to find an exact ratio between an increase in immigration and the size of the pauper rolls and charitable relief. In 1830 Boston spent slightly over $37,000 for poor relief; in 1840, over $43,000; in 1850, nearly $80,000; and, in 1860, over $168,000. Each year the number of foreigners receiving relief mounted proportionately. Boston mayors complained that immigrants, especially the Irish who were the majority, were draining the public treasury.

As relief costs soared, crime appeared to increase as well. Prostitution, especially in the city's North End where many new migrants settled, seemingly increased rapidly in the 1840s and 1850s. In those same decades burglary, with a low arrest rate during the 1820s, assumed the proportions of a crime wave. Arson was on the upswing. For city leaders who long had agreed that intemperance was a primary cause of poverty and crime, the major index of criminal activity was drunkenness. Of that crime foreigners, especially the Irish, were the most visibly guilty. From the late 1830s, arrests for drunkenness were concentrated among the immigrant poor, and during the 1850s the percentage of Irish arraigned rose ever higher. While a sympathetic newspaper editor pointed out that a poor Irishman was more likely to be arrested for drunkenness than was a poor or middle-class native simply because of a reputation for tippling, intemperance alone was enough to confirm the stereotype of the criminal immigrant held by many Bostonians.[9]

Those native and immigrant poor who did not join the criminal class or rely exclusively on the pauper rolls were little more acceptable to many Bostonians than their troublesome counterparts. Before the 1820s city leaders had feared that incoming foreigners would topple the experimental structure of republican government in America. Boston Federalists had urged that foreigners be kept out of the country, or at least that naturalized citizens be kept from holding office for fear aliens might contaminate the purity of the national character.[10] Throughout the 1820s —indeed for the remainder of the nineteenth century—this pathological suspicion of foreigners haunted many Boston leaders. In the late 1820s the foreigners' and native indigents' support of the "monster" Andrew Jackson alarmed the old Federalists and young Whigs of the city. Over the next three decades, a fear of class consciousness and class warfare troubled Boston's civic leaders. The slow emergence of working-class political involvement, a marked increase in the Roman Catholic population (by 1845 they numbered over one-fourth of the total population), and a rising incidence of riots during the 1830s and the 1840s only strengthened the grave concern of native citizens for the stability of their community.[11]

For a time, during the 1820s and early 1830s, most of the city's leadership class agreed that the dimensions of the threat were manageable. Those who proposed and carried to completion the construction of a new public workhouse in 1821–22 argued that such an institution meant an opportunity for useful labor and moral uplift. Neither economically nor spiritually need the poor remain poor—or so the city fathers affirmed. Harrison Gray Otis, inaugurated as mayor in 1830, noted of the city that "many of those who are in its first ranks rose from humble beginnings," and that mechanics and workingmen still could climb the economic and social ladders. Boston newspapers delighted in printing accounts of poor men whose careers demonstrated the unparalleled opportunities for advancement in the city. Yet, despite public rhetoric about an open and socially mobile city, astute observers suspected that all was not well. As early as the 1820s some Bostonians had begun to draw vague distinctions between "the poor" and "pauperism." In those distinctions lay their ultimate concern over the dangerous classes and the future of the city.

Josiah Quincy, mayor during most of the 1820s and nineteenth-century Boston's most vigorous leader, predicted that an inevitable result of the city's growth would be an increase in the number of those living in perpetual poverty. In two reports, issued in 1820 and 1821, Quincy noted differences between those he called the transient poor and paupers. The latter, he observed, were addicted to intemperance and to a lasting dependence upon public and private charitable relief. Paupers managed somehow to remain poor in spite of opportunities for betterment. A major concern of the city, he suggested, should be to prevent the temporary poor from falling into pauperism.[12]

Although Quincy's reports were illuminating, real enlightenment came through the efforts of a Unitarian clergyman, Joseph Tuckerman. In 1826 Tuckerman accepted a position as "minister-at-large" to the poor of Boston. During the ensuing decade, his work and writings changed the attitudes of Bostonians and other Americans toward the urban poor. Tuckerman sharpened current distinctions between the poor and paupers. The poor were individuals in temporary need of adequate subsistence; paupers were permanent dependents upon the largesse of society. "Ignorant" and "debased" as they were, paupers expected and demanded permanent social welfare subsidies. Tuckerman sought to isolate the causes of urban poverty and pauperism; to classify scientifically the various poor of Boston; and to help those whom aid would uplift, while finding ways of rendering the dangerous poor less threatening. Pauperism, or at least its chief cause, the minister found easy to explain and to solve. Intemperance, he declared, was the primary generator of pauperism and therefore of vice and crime as well. The able-bodied should be sent to workhouses. Manageable orphan children should be placed in male and female orphan asylums. "Vicious" children should be sent to reform schools. Rigorously enforced laws against intemperance should be passed. Tuckerman found the causes of poverty somewhat harder to define. His investigations, however, drove him to one certain conclusion: Various circumstances in contemporary urban life had forged links in a chain of poverty that extended over generations.

The real causes of poverty, Tuckerman suggested, were the "spirit of monopoly," the luxury and extravagance and "profligacy" of the "more favored classes," and the low estimation in which the more affluent held "the humbler of their fellow beings." The better classes of Boston society in the past had guaranteed the permanency of poverty by their refusal to recognize, as another contemporary writer put it, "how the other half lives." The result, as Tuckerman saw it and as he succeeded in bringing others to see, was that *"the poor, therefore, have lived and to a great extent are living as a caste, cut off from those in more favored circumstances; and doomed to find their pleasures, and sympathy in their suffering, alone among themselves."*[13]

By the early 1830s, then, Joseph Tuckerman and other Bostonians had become aware of an incipient culture of poverty developing within urban society.[14] In an expanding cash economy still largely dependent upon unskilled labor, both native and immigrant workers suffered from low wages, underemployment, and unemployment. The poor found themselves condemned for personal immorality and for failing in a society that claimed opportunity for all. As Tuckerman, other charity workers, politicians, and educators repeatedly emphasized, the poor had become a permanent urban class. They lived by their own values and standards rather than by those of the dominant middle and upper classes of Boston. The poor comprised a caste which promised to perpetuate itself over time as children trained in vagrancy, ignorance and crime reached maturity.[15]

The sudden arrival during the 1840s of hordes of foreigners, often desperately poor, only exacerbated an already serious problem. Slow to acclimate themselves to the moral chill of Puritan Boston, and even slower to infiltrate the economic and social life of the city, the foreigners cemented the probabilities of a permanent subclass among the urban poor. That class, declared numerous and diverse prophets of social catastrophe, eventually would destroy social harmony and urban order. As Horace Mann, first Secretary of the Massachusetts Board of Education, warned: "The favored classes may think they occupy favored apartments in the ship but, if it does founder, the state will go down with the steerage."[16]

But if the poor comprised a permanent social class in the city, that class could not be allowed to endanger social stability. For practical as well as humanitarian reasons, Boston's leaders determined to find a way to break the cycle of poverty. Among alternative methods of dealing with the "dangerous classes," urban leaders tended to follow four courses of action. One obvious answer was for the better sort to escape the city, and census takers during the 1840s discovered a mass exodus by native citizens to suburbs and surrounding towns.[17] A second solution was to remove the poor themselves from the city to the country, and various resettlement schemes were tried.[18] A third solution lay in giving huge doses of charitable relief to the worthy and incarcerating the unworthy in workhouses, debtors' prisons, and various asylums. In these endeavors Boston led all other American cities.[19] In the long run, however, most Boston leaders agreed that the best way to unlink the chains of poverty was to prevent their initial formation. If past circumstances could not be undone, the future might yet be salvaged. The means most favored by Boston leaders during the ante-bellum years for that task of prevention was public education.

When viewed as a cohesive and permanent social group, the poor and the immigrant represented a threat of class division and class warfare. Politicians, social reformers, and educators played upon the fears and hostilities of their contemporaries in gaining support for the common school movement. The presence of the poor and immigrant classes offered a perfect opportunity to the prophets of chaos, who argued that ignorance, vice, and crime would engulf the republic in waves of urban disorder. To be sure, the critics advanced differing justifications for their educational demands. Many hoped schooling would check the onrush of social upheaval by teaching the lower classes the responsibilities of citizenship; others, that public education would elevate the masses from lives of squalor and poverty by widening their economic opportunities and training them in the proper social habits; still others, that education would instill a much-needed respect for law and authority. Although the arguments for education shifted in emphasis from decade to decade, educators and reformers throughout the ante-bellum years relied upon the presence of the immigrant poor as one of their main advertising ploys.

Between 1800 and the 1860s, Boston leaders articulated a philosophy about the role of public education in securing urban stability. Public education was to be a form of social insurance against the real and imagined depredations of society by the native and foreign-born poor. On the one hand, an educator like E. C. Wines of Philadelphia and Boston could assert that the only practical antidote to the ills of immigration "is in so thorough an education of all our own citizens as shall nullify foreign influence, . . . and secure real personal independence in the natives of the soil." On the other hand, Horace Mann, the most important ante-bellum leader in the campaign for public education, argued that natives and foreigners alike had to be adjusted educationally to the rigors of urban life and to the responsibilities of being an American citizen. Foreigners, he admitted, remained unfit for America "until they have become morally acclimated to our institutions." But can it make any difference, Mann continued in his *Ninth Annual Report* (1845), whether an individual secured American citizenship from the bondage of an Irish lord or from that of an ignorant native parent or guardian? Mann answered that the person who was a serf up to the age of twenty-one, whether in Austria or the United States, still could not become a responsible citizen. And he was certain that urban poverty was a state of bondage from which all serfs should be liberated. Let education be expanded, Mann asserted, "and nine-tenths of the crimes in the penal code would become obsolete; the long catalogue of human ills would be abridged; men would walk more safely by day; every pillow would be more inviolable by night; property, life and character held by a stronger tenure; all rational hopes respecting the future brightened." If this was a large order for public schools to fill, Mann and others claimed that formal education could deliver the goods.[20]

By the early 1850s, Boston leaders stated categorically that without education, the difficulties of securing urban order and stability were insurmountable. Schooling was their panacea for all social problems. Samuel Bates, chairman of the public school Visiting Committees, explained that "our Public School System is a branch of the Government itself; as much so as are our courts, our police, criminal, and charitable regulations for the poor." The chief aim of city government in establishing and maintaining schools, therefore, "is its own preservation." He candidly admitted that the city sought "to train up all the children, within its jurisdiction, to be intelligent, virtuous, patriotic, American citizens."[21] When educators and politicians spoke of assimilating the native and foreign poor through the public schools, they were discussing ways and means of instilling in them a proper appreciation of American social values. They also were debating methods of adjusting the lower classes to the pace and demands of urban life. Due to population trends, the theory of education as social insurance was most clearly (and publicly) articulated during the late 1840s and early 1850s. But only the sense of urgency was new; educators had been working out the fundamental approaches for many years.

At the turn of the nineteenth century, Boston already enjoyed an enviable reputation for public schools. Children between the ages of seven and fourteen could enter any of several free public writing and grammar schools where they would receive a rudimentary education. For the more talented (and for those whose parents could send them on to college), a Latin Grammar School provided training in the classics during a four-year preparatory course. For school expenses and for the teaching masters' salaries, the Town Meeting annually voted over one-fifth of the public tax money. To be sure, the "public" being educated was small; the public school population of Boston numbered slightly over 12 percent of the total school-age population. These principally were children of the middle class. The offspring of wealthier parents enrolled in the many private schools that dotted Boston. The remaining children of the city either received instruction at home in the time-honored way, learned to read and write while apprenticed to a tradesman, or continued illiterate.[22] Among the latter category were most of the children of the poor.

Boston had not completely ignored the education of its lower-class poor. Individuals and philanthropic groups had provided charity schools in which indigent children could receive elementary instruction. But those schools, as in other cities, were not well-attended. Although the number of impoverished families increased yearly, those willing to label their children objects fit only for charity did not. If such children did not belong to a religious society (a customary agency for instruction), they were unlikely to receive any formal training in reading and writing. That instruction was vital for any child whose parents wanted him or her to enroll in the free public schools, for Boston law required a knowledge of reading and writing for entrance into the writing and grammar schools. Despite provisions for public education, then, the city effectively barred many children of the poor from attendance at the public schools.[23]

By 1816, a coalition of politicians, educators, social reformers, and other civic leaders had begun a campaign to expand the public school system. Building upon the experiences of the Boston Society for the Moral and Religious Instruction of the Poor—a group that had provided Sunday Schools to educate the poor—the coalition hoped to reach principally the youngest children. They reasoned that if children under the age of seven could be enrolled in a new class of public schools, the proportion of children in the grammar schools would increase. In the spring of 1817, the coalition petitioned the Town Meeting to provide public primary schools. The motives of the signers of the petition were not completely benevolent: Children under the age of seven attended no schools and thus were free to roam the streets as noisy, thieving, public nuisances. Still, the members of the coalition were aware of their responsibility to the poor, to the present Boston community—and to the future. Their attitudes received cogent expression in a newspaper letter by James Savage, a lawyer and antiquarian.

Savage already had demonstrated his social concern by helping to establish one of the first savings banks in the United States, an institution designed to encourage saving among the poor. Now, he stressed the right of the indigent to education. The children had a right to a "good bringing up and to a common school education." They had a right to "a common share of the friendship of the community." The poor and the rich, he argued, should have an equal chance to learn the nature and principles of republican government. And, he stressed, the children of the poor should be removed from the streets. Joining with Savage in arguing for primary schools were such notables as Elisha Ticknor, a renowned master of the grammar schools, a Federalist, and a devout Calvinist; William Ellery Channing, Boston's famed Unitarian minister; and Samuel May, later to become an ardent Garrisonian abolitionist.[24]

Although opponents of the primary school proposals included equally well-known Boston leaders, their arguments, based on the grounds of expense and of the current adequacy of the school system, failed to carry the day. The public, aroused by a brilliant propaganda campaign, backed the coalition. In June of 1818, the Town Meeting organized a Primary School Board and charged it to create primary schools throughout the city's wards. By 1820, there were thirty-four primary schools scattered throughout the town. Even before suspicions about the permanent poor had become certainties, Boston had organized the first system of urban primary schools in the nation and had taken a major step (or so its founders believed) in defending the city's future against the possible growth of an ignorant and indigent population. Those children who had not attended the charity schools or the public grammar schools because of literacy bars would now receive some public instruction. By the late 1820s the schools were well established. Out of an estimated 5,190 children between the ages of four and seven in the city, over 3,500 students came to school at least part of the year. More important to the founders, youth of foreign parentage accounted for more than half of the total enrollment, although the foreign population of the city was less than 20 percent. As a later historian of the city observed, this was "a fact of infinite moment, clearly showing that the city, even at that early date, was educating a host of aliens in the principles of our Puritan ancestors."[25] It was equally clear that not all the children of the city, either foreign or native, attended the schools, but a decade of operation had shown marked results. What more could one ask of public schools for the poor?

The good citizens of Boston and their leaders ultimately came to ask much more. Until all the children of poverty might be found in what Mayor Josiah Quincy called "these choice depositories of the hope of a free people," neither their moral uplifting nor the public order was assured. Over the following three decades, educators, politicians, and reformers undertook new additions to the system of public schools. Confronted with an expanding poor and foreign population, the city fathers increasingly turned to public education as the primary social institution for adjusting the newcomers to ;ban and to American ways of life.

Compared to other large cities, Boston was generous in its expenditures for education, yet the city's leaders constantly strove to hold expenses down. Financial resources had to go to other urban services—creation of fire and police departments, sanitation control, street construction—as well as to the public schools. To check expenditures while also extending the social reach of public education, they turned to new ways of organizing the schools. Having discovered a large body of children between the ages of seven and fourteen who did not attend the grammar schools, in 1820 educators opened the first of an anticipated system of "intermediate schools." This first school was housed in a basement room of the Boylston School House on Fort Hill, in the heart of the city's heaviest concentration of immigrant families. tI was the earliest example in the city of a recent innovation—the monitorial or Lancastrian school.

The introduction of a monitorial system in Boston and elsewhere was an early response to the challenge of mass urban instruction. The scheme was deceptively simple: A teacher would instruct older children in the first or second class of the school; these children in turn would repeat that instruction to younger pupils. Thus a school could accommodate a much larger than usual enrollment, and one individual could teach far more children than was customary. This assembly-line technique, so similar in conception to the "New England Idea" of interchangeable parts to increase factory production, had originated in England. An English Quaker schoolmaster, Joseph Lancaster, had experimented with the new method in English cities facing the same urban problems. The notion of mutual instruction appealed to American educators and politicians, to whom it seemed an ideal solution for providing instruction for the poor at the lowest cost.[26]

The Fort Hill school in Boston lasted less than two years. It had won high praise from Mayor Quincy, but the School Committee unaccountably dropped the effort. Members of the Primary School Board, however, unwilling to see immigrant and native poor children "abandoned to idleness, vagrancy, ignorance, and crime," supported the plan. Over the course of the twenties, the board repeatedly attempted to incorporate the monitorial system into the primary schools, and to foster as well the idea of the intermediate schools. In his election campaign of 1828, Mayor Quincy urged cost-conscious citizens to support monitorial schools. By 1829 there were twelve primary schools operating on the system and an undetermined number of grammar schools. Still, arguments by critics that the system's sole merit was saving money led to abandonment of the experiment. During the 1830s Boston, along with New York and Phila-delphia, shelved the Lancastrian schools. Workingmen and middle-class reformers alike decried the inadequacies of schools that held rows of orderly pauper children disciplined and instructed at the cheapest possible cost to the city. By the early 1840s Horace Mann found his contempt for the Lancastrian boast "give me twenty-four pupils to-day, and I will give you back twenty-four teachers to-morrow" shared by schoolmen in Boston and elsewhere. Cities would have to find some other way of mass instruc-tion for the poor.[27]

Educators continued to experiment with nonmonitorial intermediate schools, and throughout the 1830s citizens joined with schoolmen in advocating such schools for the children of the poor and the immigrant. The city refused to open special schools, but did allow unqualified children over the age of seven to enter already established schools on special permits. Once in the schools, however, these children found themselves segregated from the regular pupils, and taught by infrequent visits from the master and his helpers. Children who initially did not want to attend school were hardly encouraged by this practice. Catholic parents, already suspicious of Protestant educators, could not be expected to approve this evidence of inequity. By the late 1830s, surveys showed that few children availed themselves of the special permits. In 1838, the City Council authorized the Primary School Board to open four intermediate-school classrooms for children not educationally prepared to enter the grammar schools. The board located these rooms in areas containing the greatest numbers of immigrant and lower-class native children, since they were "only for the accommodation of those who, coming from abroad, or who, from misfortune or neglect, are excluded from the Grammar Schools." By the end of that year the special schoolrooms had proved so successful that nearly 1,000 children, or about 13 percent of the total school population, attended.

By the mid-1840s this special instruction seemed attractive enough that George B. Emerson, a friend of Horace Mann and the city's leading educator, spoke for the School Committee in urging its extension. With all good intentions, however, he was arguing for a kind of segregated school. Emerson did not realize—or, at least, did not admit—that he was advocating for poor and foreign children a system of schools much like those for Boston's black population. The city had provided a completely separate set of primary and grammar schools for the community's small number of black children. These institutions had developed not through law, but through custom. Now, although educators still hoped to assimilate lower-class white children into the mainstream of Boston life, Emerson and others implied that schools specifically created for those children and separated from the regular schools would best achieve that goal. A new note of ambivalence had thus entered into educational discussions. Referring to foreign children, in 1846 the School Committee harped upon the theme that "the bad boy at school acts on other boys susceptible of evil, and prompt to propagate it." While schoolmen still worked toward enrolling a mixture of rich and poor, native and foreigner, in the public schools, the idea of special schools increasingly appeared attractive.

Neither by law nor by publicly announced design were the special intermediate schools to enroll only the lower classes—educators could not just deny almost half a century of propaganda for public schools attended equally by all children of the city. But the natural process of selection—by age, intelligence, and residential location—effectively restricted enrollment to the native and foreign-born children of poverty. By the mid-1850s, the special schools had become almost exclusively provinces of the poor; the 1856 annual *School Report* testified that attendance had boomed among those deprived of proper parental care "through the vices of their parents, and the continual influx of strangers from foreign ports." Such de facto segregation along income, residential, and class lines did not bode well for the future stability of the city. Educators' beliefs that schooling per se would reduce class tensions and produce responsible citizens had fostered the special schools, but schools that became compounds for the poor could never create social harmony, as later generations of Bostonians would discover.[28]

While schoolmen experimented during the 1830s and 1840s, the primary and intermediate schools continued to increase in size, number, and enrollment. As the school system grew, so did the number of poor and immigrant children in the city. Determined to "domesticate them, and to give them American feelings, and identify them with ourselves as one people, with common interests," Boston educators diligently worked to increase immigrant attendance in public schools.[29] But their efforts were curiously misplaced. Even before the heaviest waves of immigration, schools throughout the city were becoming seriously overcrowded, and during the late 1840s overcrowding reached a near-crisis level. By 1850 there were over 11,000 children in the primary schools of the city, with an average attendance of 77 percent. Of these, more than half, or 6,130 children, were of foreign parentage. In addition, the schools suffered from an overburdening ratio of 1 teacher for every 55 students. An 1850 city census showed that the city-wide average of foreign children per ward was 29.3 percent, with the First, Fourth, Seventh, and Eighth wards (in the core of the old city) containing, respectively, 32.4, 34.4, 43.5, and 37.1 percent. To increase school attendance in these wards, with their large percentages of foreign population, was neither practical nor desirable, for it was in these schools that overcrowding was the most severe. To argue that children must continue to be packed into such schools on the grounds that attendance alone would accomplish the aims of education was to fly in the face of reality. Despite such difficulties, educators persuaded themselves, and attempted to persuade the public, that "our Primary Schools are doing more to *Americanize* that class of our population than all other classes combined."[30]

Nor were matters much different in several of the grammar schools located in or near the major centers of immigrant residence. The city had not overhauled its facilities to meet the needs of thousands of migrants fleeing the "Great Hunger" in Ireland. As late as 1848, the School Committee still expressed satisfaction with current conditions. "We shall have little to fear," predicted the committee, "from the much talked of dangers of immigration, if the rising generation of immigrants can thus be brought practically to understand . . . that the State will take care of them, as of the children of the soil." But to its dismay, the committee discovered in the early 1850s numerous institutions "composed in a great measure of foreigners, in the most humble and destitute circumstances." Population mobility had removed whole streets and neighborhoods of largely middle-class natives to the suburban outskirts of the city; in their places came the newcomers. There were now old schools (the city had constructed far too few new ones) surrounded by enclaves of immigrants in which classes held ratios of foreign to native children of over fifty to one. The city was reluctant to build new schools in neighborhoods that underwent population turnovers of three to four hundred families a year. Attendance would be irregular at best, argued the city fathers, and there was no way to guarantee that new schools would actually reach the immigrant masses. While the city and the state had adopted the nation's first compulsory attendance law in 1852, the machinery of enforcement had yet to be assembled. As with the primary schools, the School Committee pushed for heavier enrollment of the foreign poor in the grammar schools, while at the same time it complained of the congestion of some schools by too many "humble and destitute" aliens. The ambivalence went unresolved. By the mid-1850s, therefore, overcrowded and ethnically imbalanced grammar schools offered very little useful instruction to increasing numbers of foreign youth.[31]

Indeed, if alien children were learning any single lesson about America, it was that Americans believed in packaged and inadequate education. Though the schools might keep immigrant children off the streets, the educational value of overstuffed, understaffed, and ethnically homogeneous institutions was questionable. Attending school either regularly or, as was more common, on an irregular basis, immigrant children mingled largely with each other and less frequently with a few lower-class native children. By the eve of the Civil War, Boston schools reflected a paradox of urban public education that would continue to trouble American cities in coming generations. Schools had to reach children of all social classes and ethnic groups if they were to fulfill their function as a mediating force in urban disorder. If too many foreign and native poor children crowded out middle- and upper-class American youth, if schools became exclusive institutions for the poor, education could not create shared patterns of social behavior. It could neither offer social insurance nor foster any sense of community among city dwellers. But if mass education failed to include the poor and the strangers, it also would fail to accomplish its advertised social goals.

So the dilemma evolved, and so it persisted. Bostonians had discovered a cycle of urban poverty. Through preventive education, they had attempted to break that cycle. They had succeeded in enrolling many of the children of poverty in the schools. In fact, they had enrolled too many. After six decades of endeavor, the city had constructed a system of public schools that was the envy of urban America. Yet Bostonians remained frustrated in their best efforts to use public education to fashion an urban discipline and social order. The cycle of poverty, if bent, continued unbroken.

NOTES

1. See *The Charter of the City of Boston, and Ordinances Made and Established by the Mayor, Alderman, and Common Council* (Boston, 1827), and the similar volume for 1850; Oscar and Mary F. Handlin, *Commonwealth: Massachusetts 1774–1861: A Study of the Role of Government in the American Economy* (New York: New York University Press, 1947), pp. 72–80, 223–5, 253–5; and Roger Lane, *Policing the City: Boston, 1822–1885* (Cambridge: Harvard University Press, 1967), pp. 1–117.

2. Carl Bridenbaugh, *Cities in the Wilderness: The First Century of Urban Life in America 1625–1742*, 2nd ed. (New York: Knopf, 1955), *passim*.

3. See Robert F. Seybolt, *The Public Schools of Colonial Boston, 1635–1775* (Cambridge: Harvard University Press, 1935); Robert Middlekauff, *Ancients and Axioms: Secondary Education in Eighteenth-Century New England* (New Haven: Yale University Press, 1963); and Stanley K. Schultz, "The Education of Urban Americans: Boston, 1789–1860" (unpublished Ph.D. dissertation, University of Chicago, 1970), chaps. I–II.

4. Boston Society for the Prevention of Pauperism, *Annual Reports*, XXIII (Boston, 1858); George Ticknor, "Memoir of the Buckminsters," *Christian Examiner*, XLVII (1849), 173; Josiah Quincy, Jr., "Social Life of Boston: From the Adoption of the Federal Constitution to the Granting of the City Charter," in Justin Winsor, ed., *Memorial History of Boston*, 4 vols. (Boston: James R. Osgood and Company, 1881), IV, 2.

5. Percy W. Bidwell, "Rural Economy in New England at the Beginning of the Nineteenth Century," *Transactions of the Connecticut Academy of Arts and Sciences*, XX (1916), 383–91; Jesse Chickering, *Report of the Committee . . . and a Comparative View of the Population of Boston in 1850, with the Births, Marriages, and Deaths, in 1849 and 1850* (Boston, 1851), pp. 14–26; Lemuel Shattuck, *Report to the . . . City Council . . . Census of Boston for 1845* (Boston, 1846); *Report of the Special Joint Committee on the Census of Boston, May, 1855* (Boston, 1856).

6. While sociologists and social psychologists disagree about the mechanisms producing hostility and group prejudice, their work, if carefully used, provides insight for discussions about group conflict in nineteenth-century urban America. See, among others, E. S. Bogardus, *Immigration and Race Attitudes* (New York: D. C. Heath, 1928); G. Lindzey and S. Rogolsky, "Prejudice and Identification of Minority Group Membership," *Journal of Abnormal and Social Psychology*, XLV (1950), 37–53; Gordon W. Allport, *The Nature of Prejudice*, abridged ed. (New York: Anchor Books, 1958), pp. 3–65; M. and Carolyn Sherif, *Groups in Harmony and Tension* (New York: Harper & Brothers, 1953); W. D. Borrie, *The Cultural Integration of Immigrants* (Paris: UNESCO, 1959); Bruno Bettelheim and Morris Janowitz, *Social Change and Prejudice* (New York: Free Press, 1964); and Milton M. Gordon, *Assimilation in American Life: The Role of Race, Religion, and National Origins* (New York: Oxford University Press, 1964).

7. Massachusetts Temperance Society, *Plain Facts Addressed to the Inhabitants of Boston on the City Expenses for the Support of Pauperism, Vice, and Crime* (Boston,

1834); Josiah Quincy, *Remarks on Some of the Provisions of the Laws of Massachusetts Affecting Poverty, Vice, and Crime* (Cambridge, 1822); Quincy, *A Municipal History of the Town and City of Boston During Two Centuries* (Boston: Charles C. Little and James Brown, 1852), pp. 104–10; Lane, *op. cit.,* chap 2.

8. The patterns of investigation were established early by the Boston Society for the Moral and Religious Instruction of the Poor. See its *Annual Report, 1818* (Boston, 1818). Among others, see Joseph Tuckerman, *The Principles and Results of the Ministry-at-Large in Boston* (Boston, 1838); *Report of the Committee on the Expediency of Providing Better Tenements for the Poor* (Boston, 1846); *Report of the Committee on Internal Health on Asiatic Cholera* (Boston, 1849). See also Oscar Handlin, *Boston's Immigrants: A Study in Acculturation,* rev. ed. (Cambridge: Harvard University Press, 1959), pp. 54–87; Schultz, *op. cit.,* chap. 9.

9. *Annual Reports of the Directors of the House of Industry* (Boston, 1824–40); *Report of the Commissioners on the Pauper Surplus of Massachusetts* (Boston, 1833); "Public and Private Charities in Boston," *North American Review,* CXXVIII (July 1845), 135–59; *Massachusetts Senate Documents, 1850,* Doc. No. 12; *Twelfth Annual Report of the Executive Committee of the Benevolent Fraternity of Churches* (Boston, 1846); and *Boston Pilot,* May 12, 1849.

10. "An Act Providing for the Relief and Support, Employment and Removal of the Poor, February 26, 1794," *Laws of Massachusetts, 1780 to 1800,* II, 628–9; "An Act to Prevent the Introduction of Paupers from Foreign Ports or Places, February 25, 1820," *Massachusetts Laws, 1820,* chap. 290; Josiah Quincy, Jr., "Social Life in Boston"; John C. Miller, *The Federalist Era, 1789–1801* (New York: Harper & Row, 1960), pp. 230–31.

11. John Barton Derby, *Political Reminiscences, Including a Sketch of the Origin and History of the "Statesman Party"* (Boston, 1835); John R. Commons, *et al.,* eds., *A Documentary History of American Industrial Society,* 10 vols. (Cleveland: A. H. Stewart Co., 1910–11), VIII, 133–51; George H. Haynes, "Causes of Know-Nothing Success in Massachusetts," *American Historical Review,* III (1897); Robert H. Lord, *et al., History of the Archdiocese of Boston in the Various Stages of Its Development 1604 to 1943,* 3 vols. (New York: Sheed & Ward, 1944), I, 126, and *passim;* Ray A. Billington, *The Protestant Crusade, 1800–1860: A Study of the Origins of American Nativism* (1938; reprinted, Chicago: Quadrangle Books, 1964), pp. 53–84.

12. Quincy, *Remarks on . . . Poverty;* "Quincy" *Report on the Pauper Laws,* in *Report of the General Court of the Commonwealth of Massachusetts by the Committee . . . the Pauper Laws of the Commonwealth* (Boston, 1821).

13. Joseph Tuckerman, *Prize Essay on the Wages Paid to Females* (Philadelphia, 1830), pp. 40–54; Tuckerman, *First Annual Report, Association of the Delegates from the Benevolent Societies of Boston* (Boston, 1835), *passim;* Tuckerman, *Principles and Results,* pp. 166, 278–9, 286, 290–92; John H. Griscom, *The Sanitary Condition of the Laboring Population of New York with Suggestions for Its Improvement* (New York, 1845), pp. 5, 9; Edward Everett Hale, ed., *Joseph Tuckerman on the Elevation of the Poor* (Boston, 1874), p. 103; and Daniel T. McColgan, *Joseph Tuckerman: Pioneer in American Social Work* (Washington, D.C.: Catholic University of American Press, 1940), pp. 63–8; 117–33.

14. The concept of a culture of poverty recently has entered the literature of cultural anthropology, notably in the work of Oscar Lewis. See his *La Vida: A Puerto Rican Family in the Culture of Poverty—San Juan and New York* (New York: Random House, 1966), pp. xlii–lii, and *passim*. For debates on the concept see Lewis, et al., "The Children of Sanchez, Pedro Martinez, and La Vida: A CA Book Review," *Current Anthropology*, VIII (1967), 480–500; and Charles A. Valentine, *Culture and Poverty: Critique and Counter-Proposals* (Chicago: University of Chicago Press, 1968).

15. For example, see William Ellery Channing, *Memoir, with Extracts from His Correspondence and Manuscripts*, 3 vols., 2nd ed. (Boston: Crosby & Nichols, 1848), III, 39–42; Channing, "On Preaching the Gospel to the Poor," in *The Works of William E. Channing, D.D.* (Boston: American Unitarian Association, 1891), pp. 88–92; The Boston Society for the Prevention of Pauperism, *Constitution of the Boston Society for the Prevention of Pauperism, Nov. 5, 1835* (Boston, 1835); Tuckerman, *First Annual Report*, pp. 28–41; Theodore Parker, "Poverty," *Boston Daily Chronotype*, January 26, 1849.

16. *The Massachusetts System of Common Schools; Being an Enlarged and Revised Edition of the Tenth Annual Report of the First Secretary of the Massachusetts Board of Education* (Boston, 1849), pp. 85–6; Mann, *Ninth Annual Report of the Board of Education, Together with the Ninth Annual Report of the Secretary of the Board* (Boston, 1845), pp. 64–70, 94–6; *Twelfth Annual Report* (1848), pp. 57, 59, 78–89.

17. "Dr. Chickering's Report," in *Report and Tabular Statement of the Censors . . . State Census of Boston, May 1, 1850* (Boston, 1850), pp. 38–40.

18. *First Report on the Establishment of a Farm School* (Boston, 1832); *American Annals of Education*, IV (1834), 288; V (1835), 330, 461; VI (1836), 375. For similar actions in New York, see Miriam Z. Langsam, *Children West: A History of the Placing-Out System of the New York Children's Aid Society, 1853–1890* (Madison: University of Wisconsin Press, 1964).

19. For a convenient listing of numerous organizations, see McColgan, *op. cit.*, "Appendix 4," pp. 434–9.

20. Mann, quoting himself in his *Common School Journal*, VIII (June 1, 1846), 166–7. See also *American Journal of Education*, I, III (1826; 1828), 148, 158; 346–8; *American Annals of Education*, VI (1836), 163ff.; Robert Hall, "Opinion Upon Educating the Lower Classes," *New England Farmer* (February 13, 1833), p. 245; "Immigration: Its Evils and Their Remedies," *New Englander*, XIII (May 1855), 275, 264–76.

21. *The Report of the Annual Examination of the Public Schools of the City of Boston* (Boston, 1853), pp. 13–15, 20–21.

22. Manuscript minutes, bound as *Records of the School Committee of Boston, 1815–1836*, Special Collections, Boston Public Library; Joseph M. Wightman, comp., *Annals of the Boston Primary School Committee, From Its First Establishment in 1818, to Its Dissolution in 1855* (Boston, 1860), pp. 1–20; Arthur W. Brayley, *Schools and Schoolboys of Old Boston* (Boston: Louis P. Hager, 1894), pp. 1–40; Schultz, *op. cit.*, chap. 2.

23. "Boston School Law of 1789," in *Massachusetts Centinel*, September 19, 1789; Charles K. Dillaway, "Education Past and Present: The Rise of Free Education and Educational Institutions," in Winsor, ed., *op. cit.*, IV.

24. The *Christian Examiner*, XLIX (1850), 204–14; *Boston Columbian Centinel*, February 25, 1818; *Boston Daily Advertiser*, April 21, 1818; Wightman, *op. cit.*, pp. 20–36; letter of Savage, February 1841, quoted in *ibid.*, p. 65; *Records of the School Committee*, June 1818.

25. Wightman, *op. cit.*, pp. 36–61; *Report of the School Committee of the City of Boston on the State of the Schools, May, 1826* (Boston, 1826); Brayley, *op. cit.*, p. 51.

26. Charles P. Huse, *The Financial History of Boston: From May 1, 1822, to January 31, 1909; Harvard Economic Studies*, vol. XV (Cambridge: Harvard University Press, 1916), "Appendix I," p. 364; "Boston Public Schools," *North American Review*, LXVI (April 1848), 447ff.; Wightman, *op. cit.*, pp. 22–7, 53–4, 102–103, 297–8; *Barnard's American Journal of Education*, XXIV (June 1861), 716.

27. *Report of a Sub-Committee of the School Committee Recommending Various Improvements in the System of Instruction in the Grammar and Writing Schools of this City* (Boston, 1828), Wightman, *op. cit.*, pp. 89–116; *Records of the School Committee*, February 21, 1828; *Free Enquirer*, May 22, 1829; "Common Schools," *The New-England Magazine*, III (September 1832), 197–8; Mann, *Seventh Annual Report* (1844), p. 60.

28. Wightman, *op. cit.*, pp. 173–4, 210; Brayley, *op. cit.*, pp. 110–11; *Reports of the Annual Visiting Committee of the Grammar and Writing Schools of Boston for 1847* (Boston, 1847), pp. 53–5; David L. Child, "Report on African Schools," in *Records of the School Committee*, October 15, 1833; *Report of a Special Committee of the Grammar School Board, Presented August 29, 1849, on the Petition of Sundry Colored Persons, Praying for the Abolition of the Smith School. With an Appendix* (Boston, 1849); *Reports of the Annual Visiting Committees . . . 1846*, p. 34; *Reports of the Annual Visiting Committees . . . 1856.*

29. *Report of the Annual Examination . . . 1853*, p. 9; *Reports of the Annual Examination . . . 1848; 1849; 1850; Records of the School Committee, 1836–1850, passim;* John D. Philbrick, "Supplementary Report on Truancy and Compulsory Education," *Annual Report of the School Committee of Boston, 1861* (Boston, 1861); Schultz, *op. cit.*, chap. 11.

30. Wightman, *op. cit.*, pp. 175–6; "Semi-Annual Report of the Executive Committee of the Primary School Board, 1852," in *Boston City Documents, 1852;* John D. Philbrick, *Second Semi-Annual Report of the Superintendent of Public Schools of the City of Boston* (Boston, 1861), pp. 17–20; *Report and Tabular Statement of the Censors . . . State Census of Boston, May 1, 1850;* "Resignation Letter of Alvan Simonds, March 2d, 1852," reprinted in Wightman, *op. cit.*, p. 247.

31. *Report of the Annual Examination . . . 1853; Report of the Committee on Public Instruction Respecting the Consolidation of Grammar Schools* (May 1852), in *Boston City Documents, 1852;* Nathan Bishop, *First Semi-Annual Report of the Superintendent of Public Schools of the City of Boston* (Boston, 1852); Bishop, *Third Annual Report . . . 1853; Acts and Resolves of the General Court of Massachusetts, 1850*, chap. 294, and *1852*, pp. 170–71; quotation from *Report of the Annual Examination . . . 1848*, p. 22.

18. THE CHANGING PERCEPTION OF URBAN PATHOLOGY
An Essay on the Development of Mass Transit in the United States

Glen E. Holt

The street congestion of early-nineteenth-century American cities, or for that matter of any preindustrial city, was the result of men moving about on foot. Most men could not afford a horse or carriage, so the distance between residence and work was limited by their walking speed. The effect was to set the radius of a city at about 2 miles, or the distance a man could walk in about 30 minutes. As men went about their tasks on foot, they shared street space with a few men on horseback, some commercial carts and coaches, and the carriages of the wealthy. But congestion in this pretransit city was preeminently the friction of people coming into personal contact with each other as they walked about the city streets.[1]

In the decades after 1820, this internal congestion was compounded when America's largest cities began to grow rapidly. Between 1820 and 1830, New York City's population rose from 123,000 to 203,000; Boston's, from 43,000 to 61,000; and Philadelphia's, from 63,000 to 80,000. And in the following decades the increase was comparable or even more rapid. Associated with this population rise was a nascent suburban movement; many wealthy families gave up residential locations close to the noisy and crowded marketplaces, opting instead for houses in smaller peripheral towns. These suburbanites maintained their connection with the larger population center by water ferry and steam railroad, or they assumed the expense of providing their own carriages to conduct business and friendships in the city. Thus the residential movement away from the city center and into suburban areas predates the development of mass transit. Mass transportation innovation accentuated this thrust; it was not the seminal cause.[2]

THE BEGINNING OF MASS TRANSIT: THE OMNIBUS

Out of the period of dynamic urban growth between 1820 and 1860 came the development of the omnibus, the first mass-transit innovation used in this country. At first, the conveyance was merely a long-distance stagecoach used within the city or an enlarged version of a hackney coach. Within a decade, though, it had taken a fairly standard form: a rectangular box on wheels containing two lengthwise seats for from twelve to twenty passengers. The biggest and most congested cities led the way in adopting the innovation. By 1830 more than seventy of these clumsy carts navigated through the streets of New York, and more than a hundred were recorded two years later. Boston, Philadelphia, New Orleans, Washington, D.C., and Brooklyn all had omnibus or "urban stage" companies in operation by the mid-1830s, but because new cities continued to adopt them for the next twenty years, their peak period of use was not until the mid-1860s.[3]

The early popularity of the omnibus reflects the size of the potential transit market and provides a clue to understanding the character of the innovators. An 1849 observer summarized both points:

We have here in New York three hundred and fifty of these locomotive conveniences, coming into the City from every avenue, and all concentrating in the funnel-spout of Broadway below the Park. . . . Each stage makes ten trips a day, and takes in an average of twenty passengers up and down. Here are 70,000 sixpences, or four thousand three hundred and seventy-five dollars per day, paid for omnibus riding in the City of New York—amounting to over a million and a quarter per annum. How these sixpences count up when added together by thousands![4]

The innovators who captured this market were small businessmen, quite often those previously associated with livery stables, blacksmithing, or freight and baggage hauling. Their objective was to make unlimited profit; only secondarily, if at all, did they consider the public service aspect of the venture. The omnibus men therefore ran the first routes on those streets with the heaviest actual traffic and the most potential riders. Without fail, they tied one end of the route into a major traffic-generating point; ideally, the route had such a point at either end, whether it involved pairing a major business district and an outlying suburb (Boston and Roxbury) or, within a city like St. Louis, running between the wharf and the city's most opulent hotel.[5]

Primitive though they were, the little boxes on wheels were heralded as a new urban force. When the omnibus was introduced in Baltimore in 1844, a local newspaper, the Sun, lauded it as a significant improvement that enabled "persons to reside at a distance from their places of business in more healthy locations without loss of time and fatigue in walking."[6] The poorest workers never had the 5- or 10-cent fare to climb aboard public conveyances in any significant numbers, but people in better financial situations found within the crude bus a means of moving to residences farther from the downtown bustle.[7]

To a limited extent, the omnibus met public expectations of suburban growth. But another more idealistic expectation was doomed to inevitable failure. In the first decades of its use, several writers expressed the belief that omnibus riding might rub away class differences and breed "levelism" among urban citizens. An 1841 magazine article provides one example of such thinking:

Its levelism . . . [is the] chief beauty of the Omnibus. It ministers equally to all classes, and, as if the more fully to illustrate the republicanism of the thing, the little urchin who receives the sixpences at the door, is, without doubt, the most important personage of the company. . . . The statesman and politician . . . the greasy citizen who votes against him; and the zealots of different sectaries, dismounted of their several doxies, are compelled to ride, cheek-by-jowl, with one another. Such is the levelling and democratic Omnibus.[8]

Early observers both agonized and gloried over the omnibus's social effects. Both sides assumed that brief secondary contacts among different individuals would promote democratic tendencies. Actually, the riding experience was not conducive to the establishment of such attitudes; if anything, it promoted antagonisms. Riding public transportation was synonymous with the personal desire to get to a destination in the quickest way possible. With their minds on other concerns—jobs, shopping or family—riders were thoughtless and even rude in their relations with strangers in the bus. An 1860 article caught the nature of the human relationships that came out of the riding experience.

There is something irresistibly comic in an omnibusful of utter strangers. Face to face they sit, and their muscles are perfectly rigid; they nod forward, like an old dame dozing, at every jolt of the omnibus, and threaten each other with their noses; they stare vacantly at the brims of each other's hats or bonnets; their hands are crossed upon the handles of their sticks or umbrellas; and they speak never a word. . . . You there see man in his primitive state, not of nudity, of course, but of incivility; and you may form a notion, from the behavior of passengers, of the probable manners in the days of acorns.[9]

If there was a shared experience in omnibus riding, it was the together-ness of mutual discomfort and a common desire to reach individual destinations as quickly as possible. Interior fittings in most 'buses were primitive or rudimentary. Benches were usually unpadded, ventilation was poor, and straw thrown on the floor was the only early amenity against the cold. Passengers complained that the 'buses ran on irregular schedules, left the streets during inclement weather, shifted routings by fiat with no public announcements, and that drivers were rude, bad-tempered clods who insulted females and short-changed stalwart males. But the most frequent complaint concerned the crowding in the cars: a fare provided a passenger with the privilege of being sardined into either hot box or refrigerator and jerked and shaken to his point of destination.[10]

Rider complaints forced city councils to deal with the 'bus companies. The local assemblies narrowly defined their right to regulate a public carrier as "a private holder of privileges entitled to exploit a business for unlimited profits." The early legislation was usually elementary—a licensing tax, vehicle inspection or other rudimentary safety laws—and many con-tentious points were left unresolved.[11] But the public complaints contained a most significant implication: many people had begun to build the "riding habit" into their way of life. The urban mass commuter had been born, spawned by innovative businessmen who dragged wheeled boxes around with horses.[12]

THE HORSE RAILWAY

New York pioneered the next innovation in public conveyance. In 1832, the horsecar, still utilizing the stagecoach idea, but now riding on flanged wheels operating on iron tracks, made its first run on the street portion of the New York and Harlem Railroad. That brief run was portentous for many reasons, none more so than it was the occasion for the first street railway accident. The driver of the second car forgot to apply the brake at the end of the line and went crashing into the first car, which was filled with city dignitaries. After much untangling of harness, it was discovered that neither horses nor dignitaries were hurt. Even with the accident, the Mayor could declare: "This event will go down in the history of our country as the greatest achievement of man." Less limited in its generalization but more accurate about the effects of the innovation, the New York Courier and Inquirer predicted that it would "make Harlem a suburb of New York." Within the year, the specialized street railway, serving as a feeder to the larger steam railroad operation, began regular double-track service between Pine and 14th streets, a distance of about a mile.[13]

Other cities also experimented with horse railways in the 1830s, but it was not until after 1850 that the horsecar era really began. New York built lines rapidly in the first half of the decade, and other cities quickly followed: Boston's Union Railway Company began operations between the Bay City and Cambridge in 1856; the first Philadelphia line opened in 1858; Chicago, Baltimore, St. Louis, Cincinnati, Pittsburgh, and Newark began their lines a year later. The horsecars won immediate acceptance. In 1860, the largest horse railway in Boston carried nearly 6.5 million passengers, and together the various horsecar lines of the city carried over 13.5 million passengers. The horsecar dominated passenger service until the 1870s, and it was not seriously challenged until the next decade. Because of its introduction in medium- and smaller-sized towns in the 1880s (in terms of track mileage covered), this innovation did not reach its peak of popularity until 1890, when over 6,600 miles of horse railways were in operation.[14]

Placing the car on an iron rail increased the average speed of street transit by about one-third—to between 6 and 8 miles per hour. The rails also provided a smoother ride, lifting public conveyance out of the rutted and unpaved streets. And because of the minimal friction of iron wheels on iron rails, the same number of animals which had pulled an omnibus with seats for twenty passengers now pulled a horsecar that seated forty. At an average fare of 5 cents, with increased speed and double the capacity of an omnibus, the horsecars hastened the expansion of a city's dense, built-up area and acted as a separating agent that allowed middle- and upper-class citizens to move to their own fashionable neighborhoods.[15] A contemporary summarized the impact of the horse railway in an elegant left-handed compliment:

It is hardly too much to say that the modern horse-car is among the most indispensable conditions of metropolitan growth. In these days of fashionable effeminacy and flabby feebleness, which never walks when it can possible ride, the horse-car virtually fixes the ultimate limits of suburban growth.[16]

The iron rail innovation, however, brought as many problems as it solved. In order to raise money to purchase iron rails and horsecars, entrepreneurs utilized corporate organization. In St. Louis, for example, the typical horse railway company was a group of from eight to fifteen men, with all but a few from the city.[17] Forming a corporation, they sold stock to other citizens, with none more eager to buy than residents of neighborhoods who wanted the innovation to join their area with the city's major business district.[18] Competition for exclusive franchises to run on the best routes was always keen, with the potential profits to be made from fares the inducement. Horsecar companies maneuvered for exclusive monopolies using both legal and illegal tactics. In several cities the enfranchisement process was so fraudulent that reform movements were formed to cleanse the government.[19]

The impact of these mid-century reform efforts was slight, however, when matched against the voluminous complaints of contemporaries. These impeachments chiefly concerned the effect of the rails on the streets and the riding conditions. Laying track meant tearing up the streets, and sometimes it took a hard-pressed company a scandalously long time to make a single installation. Once laid, the rails continued to be an issue in litigation, originally because they were not set flush with the street, and later because they were poorly maintained. Accidents involving the rails and private vehicles were frequent—for example, when a fast-moving carriage caught a wheel too sharply against a raised spot, or when the wheel of a heavily-laden wagon got stuck in the space between the pavement and the track. If a set of horsecar rails was a symbol of progress in any small hamlet that wished to call itself urban, it was also increasingly the cause for city fathers acting under public pressure to make stringent regulations forcing the companies to maintain rights-of-way, pave the street space between their tracks, and pay taxes and use fees for the privilege of operation.[20]

The proliferation of horsecar lines within a city did not guarantee dependable transportation for all the people. The entrepreneurs who laid the rails wanted to minimize their investment risk. Beginning at the city center, they built their lines outward along the busiest streets and roads in the direction of the nearest marketing town or the largest suburban development. Once laid down, the early rail installations helped make permanent the dense urban travel corridors in today's cities. Subdividers nestled their developments close to the tracks, and horsecar lines, and the rail innovations that followed, tended to locate in the same corridors. The result was that transportation service was unevenly distributed throughout the city. Some sectors had excellent transportation; others, never adequately served, did not have any degree of commuting parity until the coming of the automobile. Nowhere in America is this uneven distribution clearer than in St. Louis. In that city, the first outward thrusts were in the northwest sector away from the downtown on the Mississippi. The southwest part of the city was always transportation-poor, and it was not until the automobile age that some of the areas within the southwest section—some 3 to 4 miles from downtown—had a time travel factor comparable to areas twice as far away in the northeast corridor when streetcars were the only method of commuting.[21]

Inside the iron-wheeled cars, passengers, who were as densely packed as they had been in the omnibus only now in larger clusters, complained frequently about crowding and riding conditions. Describing a typical ride in a New York car, one editorialist noted, "People are packed into them like sardines in a box, with perspiration for oil. The seats being more than filled, the passengers are placed in rows down the middle, where they hang on by the straps, like smoked hams in a corner grocery."[22]

Yet crowding itself was not the only concern; the character of the crowd was also an issue. The differences within city populations revealed themselves in cheap public conveyances, and class, ethnic, and racial differences became open controversies and the subject of legislation regulating public carriers. Examples abound: Gentlemen righteously refused to give up their seats to working-class women; men with muddy boots or those with hand tools were forced to ride on the platforms; the "better sort" of Philadelphia and St. Louis decreed that the workers could not have horsecars to the suburbs on Sunday because their noisy operation interrupted the hymns and prayers of the faithful in churches along the lines; black men had to conduct the equivalent of a modern sit-in in the 1870s before they were allowed to ride in Louisville, and in the City of Brotherly Love they had to go to court to obtain the same right.[23] The hope that public conveyances would somehow advance equality and democracy faded as the century aged. Too much had been expected of transit innovation; the horsecar and the omnibus were, after all, only crude attempts to provide transportation so that men did not have to walk.[24]

In place of the dream cherished by some that public conveyances would be a force for positive social uplift in urban society came the sad reality of strange people meeting in crowded public places. And to the congested spaces of the omnibus and horsecar came some of the most notorious and obnoxious of city dwellers. Pickpockets waited on car platforms, sometimes working in gangs to clean out the purse of an unsuspecting visiting yokel. Thieves occasionally committed armed robbery against the drivers, though safety fare boxes quickly eliminated most of that hazard. Street urchins peddled papers and grimy sweets to the passengers; drunks staggered in and out of the cars on their way home, trodding on well-shod toes and knocking hats awry; and obnoxious persons who refused to pay fares or annoyed passengers had to be ejected by force, sometimes creating a free-for-all in the process. Such activities were enough to make gentlemen write searing letters to the newspapers and to cause women of quality to fear for their own safety and to forbid their maiden daughters to ride the cars unescorted.[25]

MECHANICAL POWER AND TRANSIT INNOVATION

As the number of horsecar lines proliferated in the middle years of the century, experimental mechanical forms of propulsion were tried in an attempt to eliminate the expensive and street-dirtying horse from the public conveyance business. Many cities turned to the "steam dummy," a modified and smaller version of a large steam engine. Electric storage batteries, compressed air, internal combustion engines, and pneumatic tubes were all tested in an effort to find cheaper and speedier transit. A New Orleans company experimented with a walking-beam engine and a car that featured a mule trotting on a tread mill on one of its platforms in an effort to find a practical propulsion source. One inventor even patented a plan for a car driven by a large spring which, after being wound by a motor, would rewind itself as the car went downhill and unwind to provide power as the car ascended the next hill. All these innovations for one reason or another proved uneconomical, undependable, or more of a nuisance than the horses they were to replace.

These expensive experiments, however, were not made out of mere curiosity. All were attempts by inventors to cater to the insatiable travel need that existed in the cities. The omnibus and horsecar were insufficient to meet the existing demand, and the riding public was willing, even eager, to be part of any experiment that promised a smoother and quicker ride. Throughout the last half of the century, citizens proved their interest by subscribing stock in experimental motor companies and by supporting any number of quack inventors who promised cheaper and faster mass-transit devices. Nearly all citizens were captive riders, and if power sources could be found to meet their needs, an investor could grow wealthy from nickel fares.

In 1873 Andrew S. Hallidie made the first successful mechanically-powered innovation in mass transit when he introduced his cable car on the steep hills of San Francisco. By 1876, he had perfected the key feature of his device, the cable grip, and between 1882 and 1891, twenty-five other cities adopted his innovation; in some, it became the major form of transit. So rapid was its spread that by 1890, 5,089 "grip" passenger cars and their trailers carried approximately 375 million passengers in American cities. Although the cable car gained wide popularity, it had a number of drawbacks: A single break in the cable stopped all the cars on the line until time-consuming repairs could be made, and it had high construction costs. When the cable road was constructed in Washington, D.C., in 1890, it cost $125,000 per mile of double-tracked line. Adding the price of cables, cars, and power station put the mileage building figure at $183,500.[25]

Even while some entrepreneurs were substituting cables for horse power, a speedier device was already superseding it. The first experimental electric car was run in 1830, but it was not until 1886 that Charles J. Van Depoele built the first commercial trolley line in the United States in Montgomery, Alabama. Two years later Frank Sprague made a more ambitious installation. In Richmond, Virginia, he completed a railway system that served the entire city.[26] The switch to electricity was rapid. A 1902 census of electric railways showed that only 665 out of a total 22,577 miles of track was not electrified. On those rails, transit companies carried almost 7.8 billion passengers. A decade later, 9.5 billion passengers paid fares of over $567 million for the privilege of riding the cars. Translated into human terms, every person who lived in a city of 10,000 or more rode public transportation an average of 252 times a year.[27]

Electrification brought the speed of street transit to between 9 and 12 miles per hour, with even higher rates possible in low-density areas where stops were infrequent. Increased transit speed meant that the limits of the commuting city were again broken, and the radius of the densely built-up areas lengthened to 10 miles in cities like Boston and Chicago. After 1895, electric traction was pushed beyond adjacent suburbs to join with smaller neighboring towns previously served only by steam railroads. The building of the interurban lines made it possible for people who lived in these towns to work and shop in the central city, and generally at rates slightly lower and at speeds faster than those of steam railroads.[28]

Although mechanical power increased the possibilities for suburban expansion, streetcars were still bound by the same congestion factors—bridge openings, accidents, slow-moving vehicles, and wagons double-parked to load or unload—as the crudest horse cart. To avoid this congestion, entrepreneurs applied mechanical power sources on elevated or underground tracks. New York led the way in building such "rapid transit" lines. That city had an experimental cable-powered elevated in 1868. The line began successful steam operation in 1871 and was converted to electricity in 1902. Chicago had its first elevated in 1892; Boston followed in 1901, and Philadelphia in 1905. A subway experiment utilizing the principle of the pneumatic tube was carried out in New York in the late 1860s, but political opposition from other city carriers and financing problems held back a New York subway until 1904. Meanwhile, in 1897, Boston became the first American city to successfully tunnel underground to move its commuters; the Bay City ran its streetcars into tunnels as they entered the business district. Between 1890 and 1915 most of the larger cities in the country explored rapid-transit schemes, but fewer were built than were talked about. It took heavy densities to provide sufficient riders to pay for these expensive installations, and few cities except the very largest found the schemes practical. Most of the nation's urban commuters continued to ride the streetcar not so much by choice, but because no alternative was available.[29]

Because of continuing city growth, the carrying capacity of rapid-transit lines was quickly absorbed, and the streets seemed just as crowded, if not more so, than they had been before mechanical traction was introduced. George Hooker, a Chicagoan long associated with public transit, summed up the situation in 1904. Every city, he wrote, was "out of breath trying to catch up with its local transportation problem, and seems nevertheless to be scarcely gaining upon or even keeping up with it."[30]

As other transit innovations had done before, mechanically powered street railroads made city dwellers aware of problems connected with their operation. Rails still ran through major streets, and carts and buggies encountered difficulties where tracks were improperly maintained. Double-tracking—running a separate track each way on a single street—had begun in horsecar days, but the custom increased as more people rode. There were new mechanical hazards as well. The slot in the street through which the cable car grip passed seemed precisely sized to grasp the heel of a woman pedestrian's shoe, and small boys put more than one city's cable system out of commission by wedging sticks or rocks into the slot or "tieing on" their carts and wagons to the always moving cable. Where electricity provided the power source, thin high-voltage lines swayed a few feet above pedestrian heads, always a danger in a windstorm or when a vehicle accident tore down a supporting pole. At intersections, where two or three lines crossed, the sky was seen through a lace of electric lines, each with its thin supporting cable. Accidents were frequent, and since both cable and electric cars started quicker and ran faster than the lighter horsecars, their collisions were more spectacular. In a popular journal in 1907, a reporter noted the toll in life taken by the New York electric lines. He reported that "in 27 days there had been 5,500 accidents on the street railways of New York City; 42 people were killed outright, 10 skulls were fractured, 10 limbs amputated, 44 limbs broken, while 83 other passengers were seriously injured. In proportion to the traffic," he concluded, "the New York street railways killed eight times as many people as those in Liverpool."[31]

Rapid transit fared no better than surface lines when it came time for complaints. The elevateds closed out the sun on the streets where they ran, and land values in lots immediately adjacent to the lines were lowered by the nuisance factors of noise and dirt. The supporting structures were also seen as a hazard which slowed speeds and increased possibilities for accidents. Subways were maligned for different reasons. Criticism of underground transportation systems centered about their dreary interiors and the fact that they were cut off from sunlight and fresh air. Rapid transit was not seen as a cure-all, even if people were moved about somewhat faster.[32]

During the reign of the omnibus and horsecar, there had been those who had hoped the innovations might bring social improvements. With the development of the electrics, optimists again voiced their hope that the new mode would become a reforming force in society. Their grandest vision was that cheap electric transportation would open the suburbs to poorly paid workers and alleviate the terrible problems of the slum and the tenement house. The vision did not come true; the poorest remained the least mobile, locked into their ghetto areas.[33]

Few of the daily commuters shared any enthusiasm for the idea of street railway as a reform force, however. For fifty years citizens' groups had been asking a hard question: How could adequate transportation service be obtained from private monopolies that operated under exclusive franchises? By the turn of the century, their experience with the carrying lines brought a new conceptualization to the question: On what terms could a citizenry coexist with a "necessary nuisance"?[34]

THE LOSS OF CONSTITUENCY: PUBLIC MORALITY AND THE AUTOMOBILE

By 1900, electric street railways were the unchallenged rulers of urban passenger transit. The constant rider increase between 1900 and 1915 marked these years as the "boom days" of the industry. It was with great pride in their achievements that Frank Sprague, the "father" of the electric railway industry, spoke for all traction men in 1904:

The electric railway . . . has become a most potent factor in our modern life. . . . It has given us better paved streets, greater cleanliness, more perfect tracks, and luxurious, well lighted and ventilated cars. With the higher speeds it has made possible the extension of the taxable and habitable areas of towns and cities in a much greater ratio than is represented by the increase in speed. . . . It has built up communities, shortened the time between house and business, made neighbors of rural communities, and welded together cities and suburbs.[35]

Yet when Sprague painted this glowing picture of achievement, he omitted mention of the red ink which was already filling the profit and loss columns of some of the longest lines in the largest cities. The first factor in this business difficulty stemmed from the relationship between the fixed rate of fare and continuing urban growth. The mass-transit carriers had helped expand the residential portion of the city, but this expansion created a carrying problem. The suburban areas had low densities and fewer potential riders than the more heavily built up inner-city sections. And every rider who was carried to and from a distant suburb rode farther than an inner-city dweller for the same fare. Though the street railway companies applied for relief, until about 1918, city councils were usually reluctant to raise fares much over the basic 5 cents, the amount horsecars had originally charged for carrying people shorter distances at slower speeds. So traction companies were left to work out their financial problems without being able to raise their income except by carrying more passengers. Added to the burden of serving the suburbs was the fact that many lines had been overextended in anticipation of swift suburban growth. Some of these lines had to be closed down or, if they were kept in operation, supported by short-distance and downtown riders. The monetary losses associated with early overextensions also made the traction companies reluctant to build any new lines to unserved suburban areas, a reluctance manifested quite openly after 1912.[36]

A second factor had to do with the capital structure of the companies. Mechanical traction was much more expensive than horsecars, and required a sizable capital outlay for construction and initial operation. To obtain such financing, promoters turned to investment bankers and professional speculators who had access to investment houses throughout the country. Local men usually conceived the idea for a transportation scheme, but in order to fund construction of a lengthy electric car line or erect an elevated structure, they frequently had to sacrifice policy control to capitalists less interested in providing good local transportation service than in making a large percentage of profit on their investment. Whatever the nature of the control, it was too often true that excessive amounts of bonds and common stock were issued to pay for original construction. Companies then began actual operation with a huge lien against equipment and with stockholders anticipating high interest and dividends on the overabundant stock. This precarious financial condition was synonymous with disaster if riders did not materialize in huge numbers.[37]

A third factor had its heritage in the competitive nature of the line-building game. To win franchises from city councils, companies often assumed harsh financial and operating conditions in the form of high rents for use of other companies' lines, extensive commitments to a city for costly street maintenance, and the need to construct expensive bridges and tunnels. Moreover, the electric car companies, since they bought out previous franchises, had to pay off the watered stock earlier speculators had issued to build their conveyance systems. Electric car men ended up paying off the inflated construction costs of the horse railways and the cable lines. And usually their only strategy for getting out of these operating straits was to water their own stock and squeeze every nickel possible out of the public while spending the minimum on new cars, maintenance of track, further extensions, or added service. The financial quandary of many city railroads in the "boom days" of the industry was well illustrated by one Philadelphia company. Its owners found that after making required expenditures for fixed costs, they had only 40 percent of their gross revenue left to maintain their lines in daily operation. An absolute minimum of 50 percent was necessary if they intended to continue.[38]

The riding public was not very understanding about the financial problems of the companies. Daily commuters demanded fast and dependable service at a cheap price with basic amenities—a seat and heated cars. Too often the companies used strained finances and impossible street congestion as excuses for no action. Speculator-owners, who knew their conveyances had a captive audience, found it easy to be complacent in the face of criticism. The public cry was "a seat for every passenger"; the apocryphal company response was attributed to traction magnate Charles Tyson Yerkes, who was supposed to have declared, "The straphangers pay the dividends."[39]

The public's demand for better service and further extensions versus the strained capital position of the companies and the facts of ownership meant conflicts that had to be negotiated in the political arena. Local councils and state legislatures had been passing new legislation and codifying old regulations since the 1840s and 1850s, but after the mid-1880s, reformers began to discover that their city transportation problems were not solvable through the usual political processes. As the representatives of public improvement groups went before city councils and state legislatures to obtain improvements in service or to regularize operating practices, they discovered that the lawmaking bodies were involved through graft and boodle with the very companies they purported to regulate. There had been corruption connected with every transit innovation, but the "traction question" of the 1880s and after had a new vehemence about it: It was now preeminently a political question in which it was assumed that streetcar service for the community could not be improved until city and state government were cleansed of their collusion with the companies. The "traction question" became the catalyst that helped unite city reform groups to work for political change. In New York, Chicago, San Francisco, Cleveland, Toledo, Detroit, St. Louis, and elsewhere, the street railways' tactics of bribery and corruption of state legislatures and city councils were exposed and warred upon by angry reform groups.[40]

The violence of the attack startled the traction men, especially those who were attempting to work for the interests of the riding public. Frederick Whitridge, receiver of the Third Avenue Railroad in New York, understood the reaction better than most owners and managers. In a 1909 article, he noted that the heritage of poor service and bad financing had finally caught up with the transit companies. Taking the real advantages the public carriers had brought for granted, the public in a "reflex action" attacked the companies at their weakest points and at their time of greatest financial crisis. The citizens were prepared to bring the street railways to heel using any means at their disposal. Whitridge explained how the situation had developed in the history of his own company:

Nearly everything from an operating point of view which ought to have been done, was left undone, and very much was done which ought not to have been done. The property was not maintained, taxes were not paid, just claims were fought, the entire service deteriorated, till finally the collapse came, and the properties all passed into the hands of receivers.

The scandal of all this maladministration and rotten finance, the chagrin of the security-holders over their losses, and the denunciations of the press, united to form a public opinion which has visited upon the railroads and those in charge of them a good deal more than the just penalty of the sins of their financial fathers.[41]

Some of the transit men would claim that the riding public was over-reacting and that street railway nickels were buying more than any other 5 cents they spent.[42] Yet this argument missed the mark with those it was meant to influence. Citizens' groups and riders were not dissuaded from their reform programs by an enumeration of past achievements. Their indignation over poor riding conditions had been transformed into a new feeling that street railroads should operate under a code of public morality. As one student of street railway franchises put it, a passenger-carrying company was now regarded "as a contractor for the performance of a public service, rather than as a private holder of privileges entitled to exploit a business for unlimited profits."[43] Utilizing this theory, reform-minded citizens pushed legislatures to develop stringent regulations. This movement culminated in several states when street railroads were put under the supervision of specially appointed public service commissions which were given wide regulatory powers.[44]

With the public mood antagonistic and with possibilities for appropriate legitimate responses limited by economic conditions, the industry turned increasingly to cooperation and combination as a way to greater efficiency and lower costs. Boston was the first city to have combination on a large scale; by 1895 it was so complete in Philadelphia that only 24 miles of the city line was not under the control of a single monopoly; and in 1899, St. Louis consolidated all its lines, with the exception of one company, into the United Railways Corporation. Although the monopolistic tendency provided new business strength and in some cases improved the transfer system, the net effect was usually to lower the quality of service, thereby providing another point for public attack.[45]

Concurrent with the pressure for more regulation and the movement for consolidation was the pressure of municipal socialists for the development of publicly-owned traction systems. New York was one of the first cities to establish the legal right to "build, pay for, own and if necessary operate street railways," doing so between 1890 and 1895. Chicago, after a lengthy political battle, used the "purchase clause" in its franchise ordinances to buy its railways in 1907. Meanwhile, a nationally organized Public Owner-ship League propagandized for this development, furnishing information and legal advice to those pushing local ownership movements.[46]

Transit men, caught in a capital situation they had been instrumental in creating, hemmed in by regulation, with old equipment and no big profits in sight, were increasingly willing to let some public agency clean up the mess. Between 1917 and 1921, "137 electric railways, which operated over 9,000 single miles of track, and represented over $600,000,000 par value of bonds and over $500,000,000 par value of capital stock were thrown into bankruptcy." Eventually, in most cities, amid the inflation of World War I and the depression which followed, the alternative became either to have public ownership of a municipal rail system or to have no transportation at all.[47]

By 1900, two or three generations in every large American city had waited for the opportunity to break away from the crowded cars and the personal discipline imposed by the necessity of riding on a mass-transit system. The commuting public was certainly in the mood to try alternatives when Henry Ford introduced his cheap automobile in 1908. At first a trickle, the small cars were soon flooding the streets, or so it seemed to the men trying to run the traction systems. They estimated that there were over 1.5 million passenger cars and 136,000 commercial vehicles running on American streets by the end of 1914. Four years later, they counted over 6 million vehicles. More significant than raw figures, however, was the rate at which the number of automobiles increased in proportion to population. From 1914 to the beginning of 1919, the number of persons per auto dropped from 62 to 19, and the number of families per car fell from 16 to 5.[48]

But statistical growth did not tell the whole story of the demoralization of the street railway industry. A decade after the appearance of the mass-produced car, G. A. Richardson, Vice President and General Manager of the Chicago Surface Lines, explained its wide influence:

The automobile has encouraged people to move about as never before. Habits, customs, forms of entertainment, and the whole scheme of city life has been drastically altered. The new restlessness and roaming spirit have been developed by the freedom possible with the widespread use of automobiles for the amusement period of the day. Of course, the family car, or one of them, is also put to work on slight excuse as a carrier to and from work. The sense of luxury or of personal prestige derived from the use of an automobile appeals to many, and certainly has caused a decrease in the street railway riding from what otherwise would have resulted from the growth of population.[49]

More pointedly for the future of urban rail transportation, a spokesman noted in the transit industry's journal that each "cheap auto" meant "an average loss . . . of from three to five fares a day, because the man who owns the cheap auto not only goes back and forth himself, to and from his employment, but carries one or two of his neighbors."[50] "The automobile," another transit man noted sadly, "has come to stay. We cannot interfere with that. That is going to remain."[51]

The golden age of electric railways was killed by the automobile. But its demise was hastened by the attitudes and machinations of many owners and managers who acted as if no alternative would ever be found to mass-transportation devices. Few riders were ever satisfied with the way carriers treated them, and transportation men did little to alleviate real or perceived grievances. By the time the automobile was introduced in mass numbers, the riding public was more than ready to leave the streetcar behind. And the industry's response to the challenge of the automobile was hardly commendable. Too often, emphasis was put upon new public relations campaigns and "selling mass transit," rather than on meeting the commuting alternative the automobile provided. The last substantial technical innovation in the mass passenger-carrying industry occurred in 1897.[52] Certainly by 1920, the smart money had left a sinking industry. Municipalities were left to solve the problem of the few remaining captive riders in a climate of public opinion which held streetcars and buses to be nuisances impeding the movement of automobiles.[53]

With the decline in mass-transit riding, the nature of urban congestion was changed in a subtle way. In the pretransit city, congestion was primarily a matter of people moving about on foot. The mass-transit cars reshaped that congestion. Although they allowed many people to live in low-density suburbs, the commuter still had "to endure at least one or two hours a day of most uncomfortable and unhealthful congestion of population in the cars themselves."[54] When people moved out of mass-transit cars and into their own automobiles, they removed themselves from both older types of congestion. Not only did the automobile provide new freedom in controlling travel times and routing, but it also allowed the commuter to privatize his commuting experience. Within his automobile, he avoided the irritating or at least boring contacts with strange people in crowded public places. When the automobile came to dominate traffic, congestion became primarily vehicular. And within the automobile, the commuter faced congestion in a privately controlled setting walled off from the crowd. Commuting, which had been among the most public of daily experiences in the nineteenth century, became one of the most private in the age of the automobile.

NOTES

1. Gideon Sjoberg, *The Preindustrial City: Past and Present* (New York: The Free Press, 1960), pp. 92–3; Sam Bass Warner, *Streetcar Suburbs, The Process of Growth in Boston, 1870–1900* (Cambridge: Harvard University Press and M.I.T. Press, 1962), pp. 14–16; Adna Ferrin Weber, *The Growth of Cities in the Nineteenth Century: A Study in Statistics* (Columbia University Studies in History, Economics and Public Law, Vol. XI; New York: Macmillan, 1899), p. 471.

2. George Rogers Taylor, "The Beginnings of Mass Transportation in Urban America: Part I," *The Smithsonian Journal of History,* I (Summer 1966), 35–7; Charles V. Kennedy, "Commuter Service in the Boston Area, 1835–1860," *Business History Review,* XXXVI (Summer 1962), 153–70.

3. Arthur Krim, "The Innovation and Diffusion of the Street Railway in North America," (unpublished master's thesis, Department of Geography, University of Chicago, 1967), pp. 37–8; Taylor, I, *op. cit.,* pp. 40–46.

4. [George G. Foster,] *New York in Slices: By an Experienced Carver: Being the Original Slices Published in the New York Tribune* (New York: William H. Graham, 1849), pp. 64–5.

5. Taylor, I, *op. cit.,* pp. 43–6; Walter Barlow Stevens, *St. Louis, The Fourth City, 1764–1909* (St. Louis-Chicago: S. J. Clarke Publishing Co., 1909), I, 434–5.

6. John Anderson Miller, *Fares Please! From Horse Carts to Streamliners* (New York: D. Appleton-Century Co., 1941), pp. 9–10.

7. Kennedy, *op. cit.,* pp. 158–9; Taylor, I, *op. cit.,* p. 48.

8. Gilmore Simms, "The Philosophy of the Omnibus," *Godey's Lady's Book,* XXIII (September 1841), 105. See also Foster, *op. cit.,* p. 65.

9. "Omnibuses," *Chamber's Journal,* XXXIII, 3rd Ser., Vol. 13, (April 14, 1860), 228–30. The question of manners carried over into the horsecar era, especially the issue of giving seats to ladies when a car was crowded. See, for example, "Horse-Car Manners," *Every Saturday,* II (June 3, 1871), 523; "A Word from Colebs Pickle on Horse-Car Manners," *Every Saturday,* II (June 24, 1871), 595.

10. "The Omnibus" *Scientific American,* VII (May 22, 1852), 286; Miller, *op. cit.,* pp. 7, 13.

11. Delos F. Wilcox, *Municipal Franchises: A Description of the Terms and Conditions upon which Private Corporations Enjoy Special Privileges in the Streets of American Cities,* 2 vols. (New York: The Engineering News Publishing Co., 1911), II, 6. Wilcox's conclusion reinforces my own findings in studying regulatory ordinances of public passenger carriers in St. Louis. The examples in this paragraph are drawn from ordinances passed by the city council between 1843 and 1861.

12. Taylor, I, *op. cit.,* p. 48.

13. Miller, *op. cit.,* pp. 16–19.

14. Krim, *op. cit.,* pp. 36, 116–42; George Rogers Taylor, "The Beginnings of Mass

Transportation in America: Part II," *The Smithsonian Journal of History,* I (Autumn 1966), 39–43.

15. Humanitarians still objected to the hard lot of street railway horses. Taylor, II, *op. cit.,* p. 47; Warner, *op. cit.,* pp. 21–2.

16. Miller, *op. cit.,* p. 35.

17. St. Louis, *Ordinances of the City of St. Louis,* No. 4371, March 10, 1859; No. 4439, May 6, 1859; No. 4463, June 22, 1859, which chartered the first three successful St. Louis companies.

18. This neighborhood chauvinism was reflected in the extension of the People's Line to the Compton Hill Section of St. Louis. See *The Missouri Republican,* February 9, 1877, p. 8; February 18, 1877, p. 10; and Stevens, *op. cit.,* pp. 448, 452, for typical instances. The same sort of thing occurred in other cities for other innovations. For a neighborhood effort to secure the Chicago elevated, see John C. Spray, *The Book of Woodlawn* (Chicago: John C. Spray, 1920), p. 10.

19. On competition for horse railway franchises see Frederic W. Spiers, *The Street Railway System of Philadelphia, Its History and Present Condition* (Johns Hopkins University Studies in Historical and Political Science, Fifteenth Series, Vol. III; Baltimore: The Johns Hopkins Press, March-May, 1897), pp. 12–13; Harry James Carman, *The Street Surface Railway Franchises of New York City* (Columbia University Studies in History, Enocomics and Public Law, Vol. LXXXVIII; New York: Columbia University, 1919), pp. 48–9, 157–8; 183–5.

20. "City Railways—A New Method of Laying Them," *Frank Leslie's Illustrated Newspaper,* XXV (March 14, 1868), 402; Spiers, *op. cit.,* pp. 12–13.

21. In 1860 the Missouri State Legislature made an unsuccessful attempt to stop this clustering with the Third Parallel Law, which stated that street railways could not be laid closer than three blocks when they paralleled another set of tracks. The law was not effectively enforced, however. *Report on Rapid Transit for St. Louis, Submitted to the Board of Aldermen* (St. Louis: City of St. Louis, September 1926), pp. 35, 38; *The St. Louis Transit System, Present and Future* (St. Louis: City Plan Commission, 1920), Diagrams 2, 3, 4, 5.

22. Carman, *op. cit.,* pp. 29–30.

23. Harold E. Cox, " 'Daily Except Sunday': Blue Laws and the Operation of Philadelphia Horsecars," *Business History Review,* XXXIX (September 1965), 228–42; Harold E. Cox, "Jim Crow in the City of Brotherly Love: The Segregation of Philadelphia Horsecars," *Negro History Bulletin,* XXVI (1962), 119–23; Judith Walzer, "Segregation in Louisville, 1867–1890," (typescript; Chicago, 1966), pp. 24–8; Stevens, *op. cit.,* pp. 439–40; Spiers, *op. cit.,* pp. 18–27.

24. "Pickpockets at Work on the City Railroad Cars," *Frank Leslie's Illustrated Newspaper,* XXV (September 21, 1867), 3; "A Conductor Murdered on the Platform of his Car in New York City," *Frank Leslie's Illustrated Newspaper,* XXV (March 7, 1868), 398; "The Car Peddler," *Appleton's Journal,* XIV (October 2, 1875), 437–8; "How to Repress City Nuisances," *Appleton's Journal,* XIII (April 17, 1875), 498; "Our Country Cousins," *Frank Leslie's Illustrated Newspaper,* XXIII (January 5, 1867), 242.

25. Miller, *op. cit.,* pp. 35–46; Edgar M. Kahn, *Cable Car Days in San Francisco* (Stanford: Stanford University Press, 1940), pp. 27–42; Frank Rowsome, *Trolley Car Treasury* (New York: Bonanza Books, 1956), pp. 38–44.

26. Thorburn Reid, "Some Early Traction History" (Reprinted from *Cassier's Magazine,* August 1899, as *Traction Collector's Library,* XXI; Montreal: *Trains and Trolleys,* December 1968); Miller, *op. cit.,* pp. 54–69.

27. U.S. Department of Commerce, Bureau of the Census, *Central Electric Light and Power Stations and Street and Electric Railways with Summary of the Electric Industries, 1912* (Washington, D.C.: U.S. Government Printing Office, 1915), p. 184; U.S. Department of Commerce, Bureau of the Census, *Census of Electrical Industries: Electric Railways and Motorbus Operations of Affiliates and Successors, 1932* (Washington, D.C.: U.S. Government Printing Office, 1934), pp. 4, 7, 18. With the exception of the riding habit figure, these statistics do not separate interurban carrying from urban networks.

28. Warner, *op. cit.,* pp. 2, 153. George W. Hilton and John F. Due, *The Electric Interurban Railways in America* (Stanford: Stanford University Press, 1960), is the definitive study of interurbans.

29. Miller, *op. cit.,* pp. 70–98; William Fullerton Reeves, *The First Elevated Railroads in Manhattan and the Bronx of the City of New York* (New York: The New York Historical Society, 1936), pp. 9–12.

30. George E. Hooker, "Report to the City Council of Chicago on Local Transportation Development in Great Cities," (typescript; Chicago, February 1, 1904), p. 49.

31. Burton J. Hendrick, "Great American Fortunes and Their Making. Street Railway Financiers—III," *McClure's Magazine,* XXX (January 1908), 337; Spiers, *op. cit.,* p. 123, provides statistics demonstrating the increased number of serious accidents associated with mechanical traction.

32. Hooker, *op. cit.,* p. 59; "Sub-Sidewalk Railway Rapid Transit System" (Chicago: J. H. Farrar, 1907), pp. 1–5; Miller, *op. cit.,* p. 76.

33. Jacob Riis, *How the Other Half Lives: Studies Among the Tenements of New York* (New York: Scribner, 1890), p. 2; Carroll D. Wright, "The Ethnical Influence of Invention," *The Social Economist,* I (September 1891), 341–2; Frederic C. Howe, *The City: The Hope of Democracy* (New York: Scribner, 1905), pp. 203–204; Henry M. Boies, *Prisoners and Paupers, A Study of the Abnormal Increase of Criminals, and the Public Burden of Pauperism in the United States: The Causes and Remedies* (New York and London: Putnam, 1893), pp. 116–18.

34. Prentiss Cummings, "Street Railways of Massachusetts [, 1896]" (bound in George Hooker Scrapbooks, "Local Passenger Traffic, United States, 1895–1910," University of Chicago Library), p. 2113.

35. John H. Hanna, "Changing from Cable to Electricity," *Transit Journal,* LXXVIII (September 15, 1934), 323–7; Sidney Withington, "Railroad Electrification of 4,500 Miles: A Notable Record of Progress," *Electric Railway Journal,* LXXV (September 15, 1931), 537–41; Charles Rufus Harte, "Boom Days of the Electric Railways," *Transit Journal,* LXXVIII (September 15, 1934), 329–31. Sprague deservedly won the sobriquet for installing the Richmond system and for his many technical innovations in electric railways.

36. Adna F. Weber, "Suburban Annexations," *The North American Review*, CLXVI (May 1898), 614–15; G. Lloyd Wilson, *The Transportation Crisis* (New York: Sears Publishing Co., Inc., 1933), pp. 194, 200, 201. Delos F. Wilcox, *Analysis of the Electric Railway Problems: Report to the Federal Electric Railways Commission* . . . (Chicago: University of Chicago Press, 1921), pp. 77, 160–64.

37. Wilson, *op. cit.,* pp. 193–4; Wilcox, *Analysis, op. cit.,* pp. 22, 36–42.

38. Spiers, *op. cit.,* pp. 48, 53–72; Wilcox, *Analysis, op. cit.,* pp. 43–5; F. W. Doolittle, *Studies in the Cost of Urban Transportation Service* (New York: Bureau of Fare Research, American Electric Railway Association, 1916), pp. 5–7; Frank Parsons, *The City for the People*, rev. ed. (Philadelphia: C. F. Taylor, 1901), pp. 54–6.

39. On the character and thinking of street railway entrepreneurs, see Hendrick, *op. cit.,* p. 338; E. J. Edwards, "The Street-Car Kings," *Munsey's Magazine*, XXX (December 1903), 388–92; Charles B. Fairchild, Jr., *Training for the Electric Railway Business* (Philadelphia and London: Lippincott, 1919), pp. 115, 129, 338; Sidney I. Roberts, "Portrait of a Robber Baron: Charles T. Yerkes," *Business History Review*, XXXV (Autumn 1961), 344–71.

40. There is abundant writing that details transit corruption. Along with Spiers and Carman, principal works include Ralph Heilman, *Chicago Traction: A Study of the Efforts of the Public to Secure Good Service* (Princeton: American Economic Association, July 1908); James Blaine Walker, *Fifty Years of Rapid Transit in New York, 1864–1917* (New York: The Law Printing Co., 1918); Graeme O'Geran, *A History of the Detroit Street Railways* (Detroit: The Conover Press, 1931); Dallas M. Young, *Twentieth Century Experience in Urban Transit: A Study of the Cleveland System and its Development* (Cleveland: The Press of the Western Reserve University, 1960).

41. Frederick W. Whitridge, "Public Morality and Street Railways," *The Century Magazine*, LXXVII (March 1909), 788.

42. Cummings, *op. cit.,* p. 2115, for example of those who thought the public was overreacting.

43. Wilcox, *Municipal Franchises, op. cit.,* II, 6.

44. The regulation of street railways was part of larger movements to regulate railroads, common carriers, gas and electric companies. Wilson, *op. cit.,* p. 215. The period was also characterized by the first codifications of street railway law. See Andrew J. Nellis, comp., *The Law of Street Surface Railroads* (Albany: Matthew Bender, 1902); Henry J. Booth, *A Treatise on the Law of Street Railways* (Philadelphia: T. & J. W. Johnson & Co., 1892).

45. Spiers, *op. cit.,* p. 36; Delos F. Wilcox, *Report on the Transit Problems of Bethlehem, Pennsylvania, and Vicinity* (Bethlehem, Penn.: Times Publishing Co., 1918), p. 25.

46. Samuel Wilbur Norton, *Chicago Traction, A History Legislative and Political* (Chicago, 1907), pp. 203–40. Norton's history is really a political tract, an appeal for public ownership in the election of 1907. "Municipal Railways in the United States and Canada." Bulletin no. 18 of the Public Ownership League of America (Chicago: Public Ownership League of America, 1922).

47. Wilson, op. cit., p. 199; Wilcox, Analysis, op. cit., pp. 635–43.

48. Ralph C. Epstein, The Automobile Industry: Its Economic and Commercial Development (Chicago and New York: A. W. Shaw Co., 1928), pp. 317, 340, 344, for tables of statistics on number of automobile registrations and, after 1903, production figures of low-priced cars. Proceedings of the Federal Electric Railways Commission held in Washington, D.C., during the months of July, August, September, and October, 1919 (Washington, D.C.: U.S. Government Printing Office, 1920), pp. 425–6.

49. Thomas N. McCarter, "From Jitney Competition to Bus Coordination," Transit Journal, LXXVIII (September 15, 1934), 341–4.

50. Proceedings, op. cit., p. 139.

51. Ibid., pp. 1186–7.

52. In 1927 the annual publication of the electric railway industry was entitled Electric Railway Practice. In 1926 it became Making Transportation Pay, and in 1927 it was called Popularizing Public Transportation. In 1928 all subtlety was put aside and the title became Selling Transportation. Hilton and Due, op. cit., p. 41, argue that the multiple unit control which Frank Sprague invented in 1897 was the last major innovation of the electric railway industry.

53. Proceedings, op. cit., p. 1054; J. Borton Weeks, "Philadelphia's Traffic Problems and their Solution," Annals, CXVI (1924), 236–7, for streetcars as waste of space on public streets.

54. Wilcox, Municipal Franchises, op. cit., II, 7.

19. HOUSING REFORM AND CITY PLANNING IN PROGRESSIVE AMERICA

Roy Lubove

The initial spur to city planning in the United States came from the spectacular Chicago Fair of 1893. Chicago's "White City" has been aptly described as "a laboratory—a testing ground—not only for the problems of civic design but also for determining the best hygienic and protective methods for urban application."[1] Thanks to the skill of its chief architect, Daniel H. Burnham, and landscape architect, Frederick Law Olmsted, the planned unity and classic dignity of the fair became for Americans "a revelation" and "a benediction." Here, for the first time, they glimpsed "what an ideal city might be."[2]

The fair did not represent simply an experiment in civic art and architecture. Its organizers faced many practical problems: police and fire protection, the creation of water, sewerage, and transportation systems, the provision of cultural and recreational facilities. The Columbian Exposition suggested that the aesthetic and utilitarian could be coordinated to produce a higher form of urban civilization. That "glorious fairy city which sprung up almost overnight in Jackson Park, in Chicago"[3] was America's hope and promise of what the twentieth-century city might be.

The classic facade of the White City has been criticized by some, notably Lewis Mumford, as a dubious contribution to America's architectural and civic development. The architects had "chanted a Roman litany above the Babel of individual styles." The World's Fair triumph had "suggested to the civic enthusiast that every city might become a fair: it introduced the notion of the City Beautiful as a sort of municipal cosmetic."[4] Mumford's savage critique has validity. It is true that the classic vogue in architecture and the City Beautiful concept in civic design which sprang from the fair had certain baneful consequences.

But the dominating feature of the exposition, that which made the most lasting impression upon spectators, was its unity. "It remained for Chicago," the president of the American Civic Association observed, "to awaken our dormant sense of form and appropriateness in architecture and environment, and to show what planning could accomplish."[5] Never before, affirmed a contemporary, "was the unity of a single design so triumphant."

Reprinted from The Progressives and the Slums: Tenement House Reform in New York City, by Roy Lubove, pp. 217–30, 237–8, 243–5, by permission of the University of Pittsburgh Press. © 1962 by the University of Pittsburgh Press.

The lesson of the fair was the dependence of the city upon "proportion, balance, and ordered suitability of parts."[6] However one might disparage the somewhat sterile classicism of the fair, its ultimate influence was salutary. In contrast to the typically ugly, sprawling, squalid American industrial city of the nineteenth century, the White City was a beatific vision of blue lagoons, luxurious green lawns, and monumental splendor. Americans saw in its planned beauty, order and picturesque design an irresistible alternative to the dirt, monotony and pervading dinginess of their existing municipalities. This was the real meaning of the Chicago Fair; it created new ideals and standards by which to measure the quality of urban life.

Until about 1909 the City Beautiful was the principal expression of the newly discovered passion for planned civic growth.[7] Cities hired architects to produce elaborate schemes for civic centers, tree-lined boulevards in the European manner, parks, and a variety of other forms of ornamentation: public art, plant decoration, sculpture, street signs, even lamp posts. The City Beautiful also included several negative ideals, such as noise abatement and the control of street advertising.

Besides Daniel H. Burnham, the chief exponent of the City Beautiful for many years was Charles Mulford Robinson, a Rochester, New York, architect. A prolific author, Robinson labored to convert "the spirit of aesthetic renaissance," "civic art's transforming touch," into a secular municipal religion. For Robinson the City Beautiful was not merely an aesthete's delight, a genteel pastime, but an inspired social vision: "The moral and spiritual standards of the people will be advanced by this art, and their political ideals will rise with a civic pride and a community spirit born of the appreciation that they are citizens of 'no mean city.' "[8] This tenement population, particularly, would benefit from the sensual delights of the City Beautiful: ". . . to make the homes not only livable but attractive, to awaken ambition, to encourage the life of the beautiful—would not this, this glorious aggregate, be the first task that civic art would undertake?"[9] Robinson and other exponents of the City Beautiful interpreted civic art much as Jacob Riis interpreted nature; it was a moral force able to elevate the character and ideals of those touched by its magic wand.

In time the almost exclusive dominion of the City Beautiful was challenged. After 1909 the "City Useful" overtook, then surpassed the City Beautiful in the theoretical formulations of city planners, if not always in their actual plans.[10] The desire for urban unity and harmony aroused by the Chicago Fair achieved a more mature expression in the new utilitarian-oriented planning movement.

There were several reasons for the new point of view. The City Beautiful was a narrow and pathetically fragile ideal, remote from business, commerce, industry, transportation, poverty, and similar mundane but integral features of urban life. Once the glow of the White City had dimmed, the need to incorporate these features into a planning scheme became apparent. In addition, new men who achieved prominence in planning insisted that the City Beautiful must be subordinate to the City Useful if the goal of "a better, more orderly, more livable city"[11] was to be attained. Conspicuous among the champions of utilitarian planning was John Nolen, a Massachusetts landscape architect and founding father of modern planning in America. Very different from Robinson's ideal was the social and practical emphasis of Nolen. The absence of beauty troubled him less than the faulty street arrangement, the condition of the waterfronts, the uncoordinated transportation system, the "unsanitary and demoralizing influences of slums."[12] If housing reform in the broadest sense signified the belief that the health and welfare of the people in an urban–industrial society were too important to remain in the hands of the entrepreneur exclusively, the utilitarian-minded city planning movement after 1909 evolved from the conviction that urban growth in general was too important to continue unplanned and uncoordinated, the product of countless short-sighted and selfish private decisions.

Most significant in explaining the character of the planning movement after 1909, particularly in relation to housing, were two European developments. The City Beautiful remained dominant until planners and housing reformers had digested the implications of the garden city in England and the zoning program in Germany. The garden city was the product of a book by an obscure court stenographer named Ebenezer Howard; and Germany's zoning legislation unfolded from the experiments of Franz Adickes, Bürgermeister of Altona, a Hamburg suburb, and then of Frankfurt-am-Main. The concept of the garden city and zoning equipped American planners, for the first time, with a concrete formula for urban reconstruction based upon dispersion of population and industry.

In his book *Tomorrow* (1898), Howard proposed an alternative to city or country life possessing the advantages of both, but none of their inconveniences. The alternative would be a magnet, producing the "spontaneous movement" of people from crowded cities to the country. "Town and country *must be married*," Howard affirmed, for out of the union would "spring a new hope, a new life, a new civilisation."[13]

Howard outlined a plan for a garden city limited in population to about 32,000. Neither the first nor future garden cities would expand beyond that size, for any excess population would simply serve as the nucleus for an entirely new community. Each garden city would be surrounded forever by an agricultural belt producing food for the community and preventing suburban sprawl. Howard located factories, warehouses, and other business establishments in the outer ring of his circular city, separated from the people's homes in the inner circle. Besides homes, the inner circle would include attractive radial boulevards, parks, and civic, cultural, and shopping facilities.

Garden city was to be governed by a central council composed of the officers of various departments elected by the inhabitants. Its revenues depended entirely upon rents. Since the community as a whole owned the land, any increase in its value would revert back to the people. Thus no "unearned increment" would flow into the pockets of landlords and speculators as a consequence of the community's growth and prosperity.

A year after Howard's book appeared, a Garden City Association in England was formed to promote the plan. Its efforts resulted in 1903 in the formation of the First Garden City, Ltd., which purchased and developed on garden city principles a 4,000-acre estate at Letchworth. Letchworth suggested to planners and housing reformers in America and Europe that garden city was no idle, impractical dream fit only for a small cult of enthusiasts. It was a financial and social success.[14]

Garden city's appeal to reformers in England and America is not difficult to explain. On paper, at least, it was a simple scheme. One had only to grasp a few elementary principles, locate a site, and gather sufficient funds to purchase and develop it. The cooperative benefits of garden city impressed a generation of municipal reformers who attributed many of the evils of urban life to unsocialized individualism and private greed. Here at last was a way to insure that landed wealth created by the community would return to its source of benefit all the people instead of a few monopolists. At the same time, however, there was plenty of scope for private initiative in the agricultural, industrial, and retail trades integral to garden city's economy. The balance between industry and agriculture in Howard's machine-age utopia particularly interested a generation which feared that man was losing touch with nature, stifling himself in the smoke and soot of the great industrial city.[15] Finally, garden city was influential as a thoroughly planned community. In contrast to Chicago's White City, an ephemeral fairyland meant to vanish when the fair had ended, people actually lived and worked there. It was the most concrete example of the potentialities inherent in city planning for creating a new civilization.

Certain features of the garden city plan particularly impressed housing reformers. The limitations on population and the number of houses per acre seemed an ideal system for preventing the congestion out of which the slum had evolved. Equally important, the garden city program, revolutionary in principle but conservative in method, could be used against existing slums. It did not involve expensive and confiscatory slum clearance schemes in the core of the city where congestion had inflated land and property values. If enough of the urban population could be removed to garden cities, the inflated structure of values would collapse of its own weight. Land would become cheap enough to house people comfortably again, even in the heart of the city.

Although the garden city was the ideal goal, two modifications of its principles received even greater attention from planners and housing reformers in America. The garden suburb and garden village involved the identical end of urban decentralization, but were less ambitious in scope and thus were better suited for immediate application. The garden suburb was a planned residential community on the outskirts of a city. Although it was only an appendage which lacked the self-sufficiency of garden city, it seemed a practical way to house a sizeable percentage of the urban working population in attractive surroundings. The inspiration for the garden suburb also derived from England, where it formed a part of the great cooperative movement. In 1901 the Ealing Tenants, Ltd. had been formed by a group of cooperators to develop a suburban residential estate. Their success resulted in the organization of similar associations in English cities. The Co-Partnership Tenant's Council provided central leadership as an organizing and propagandizing agency; the associations themselves were affiliated in the Co-Partnership Tenants, Ltd. of London. By 1909 workers' cooperative associations owned almost $40,000,000 worth of property.[16]

There was also a middle road between the self-sufficiency of the garden city and the strictly residential character of the garden suburb. The garden village was a residential community organized around one or a few industries. The influence of two of the English garden villages upon planners and housing reformers in the Progressive era cannot be overestimated. In Port Sunlight and Bournville they say a brilliant alternative to the evils of crowded city life. Port Sunlight, a garden village located outside Liverpool, was founded by Sir William Lever, the soap manufacturer. Here was a planned community of winding, tree-lined roads, spacious parks, and handsome cottages with gardens. Lever operated the village for his employees at a loss, but found recompense in their contentment and good health. Observers were usually charmed by what they saw at Port Sunlight. One of them, prior to a visit, "had not known that there was anywhere in the world a village in which there was nowhere to be found one ugly, inartistic, unsanitary, or other demoralizing feature."[17]

Bournville was also an industrial village founded by a benevolent employer. It was developed as a model community after 1895 by George Cadbury, the cocoa manufacturer. In 1900 Cadbury turned over the property, located outside Birmingham, in trust to the nation. Besides its spacious, well-designed cottages, Bournville displayed such amenities as a meeting house; an institute containing a library, lecture hall, classrooms and similar facilities; children's playgrounds; wooded areas and village greens. According to Bournville's architect, it was the village of the future, "a village of healthy homes and pleasant surroundings, where fresh air is abundant and beauty present."[18]

After the inspiring examples of Port Sunlight and Bournville had permeated the thinking of American planners and housing reformers, they discovered that America actually had a tradition of industrial villages. Unfortunately, many of them were mining and cotton-mill towns, merely squalid caricatures of the English prototypes in physical layout and management. Not even the best specimens of the American industrial village, such as Pullman, Illinois, could compare with Port Sunlight or Bournville in the quality of planning or the benefits conferred upon their inhabitants.

Nonetheless, housing reformers were optimistic about the future of the industrial village. In model garden villages detached or row cottages, limited in number per acre, would provide excellent housing in contrast to the dreary flats or tenements to which so many workers were accustomed. The garden village was practical, for industrialists would surely find a contented and healthy working force to their advantage, not to mention the low taxes and land prices of suburban locations. It was not necessary or even desirable for a company to build and manage an industrial village. The work could be delegated to a subsidiary company or to private developers subject to strict standards of planning and design. In any case, the company must avoid both the paternalism which created resentment at Pullman and the despotism of most mining and cotton-mill towns.

A number of planned or semiplanned industrial suburbs had appeared before World War I. Gary, Indiana, one of the largest, showed little evidence of planning or the social responsibility reformers hoped to stimulate among companies engaged in real-estate operations. Within three years (1906–9), the United States Steel Corporation transformed marshland and sand dunes into a city of 12,000 equipped with paved streets, sidewalks, utilities, public schools, shops and residences; but since the Corporation had been more interested in expanding its steel production than in city-building it did not employ planners and it acquiesced in the speculative development of homes by private realtors on land south of the Wabash Railroad tracks. Hundreds of box-shaped, frame houses sprang up for unskilled workers, and no housing codes interfered with the builders.

More satisfactory specimens of industrial suburbs encouraged reformers to retain faith in the garden village. The Goodyear Tire and Rubber Company organized a subisidiary in 1912, which hired the landscape architect Warren H. Manning to develop a one-hundred-acre tract adjoining Akron, Ohio. About 250 brick and stucco homes of five to eight rooms had been erected by 1916 and sold to employees. Similarly, the Norton Grinding Company of Worcester, Massachusetts, commissioned Grosvenor Atterbury to develop a ninety-acre site. Under Atterbury's supervision, the Company built some sixty detached and semi-detached frame and stucco houses. John Nolen, a fervid champion of industrial housing, planned a garden village at Kistler, Pennsylvania, for the Mount Union Refractories Company. Nolen's plans for the fifty-acre tract included parks, playgrounds, and a school.

Emile Perrot, a Philadelphia architect familiar with the English garden village, helped plan Marcus Hook near Chester, Pennsylvania, for the Viscose Company. The Marcus Hook development included 215 brick row houses, a store, and a recreation building. Two additional experiments which aroused the interest of housing reformers were Morgan Park outside of Duluth, where the Minnesota Steel Company erected single-family detached and row houses for more than 400 families, and Eclipse Park, near Beloit, Wisconsin, where the Fairbank Morse Company built 350 detached houses for employees, ranging in price from $2,400 for four rooms to $3,100 for eight rooms.[19]

No garden cities appeared in America, and reformers could claim an extremely limited success in promoting the garden village. With a few exceptions like the Homewood project of the City and Suburban Homes Company, reformers could refer only to Forest Hills Gardens in Long Island to illustrate the planned garden suburb in America. Designed by Frederick Law Olmsted, Jr., and Grosvenor Atterbury, Forest Hills Gardens was sponsored by the Russell Sage Foundation in 1909. Its Tudor-style homes with spacious lawns, network of winding roads, shopping center, small parks and public schools illustrated the virtues of large-scale comprehensive planning. Yet Forest Hills proved nothing except the obvious— that attractive suburban communities could be created for those able to afford them.

In a report which appeared in the United States Bureau of Labor Statistics *Monthly Review* for November 1917, Leifur Magnusson examined 236 company housing projects. Few of the companies hired architects and planners of the caliber of Nolen, Atterbury, or Perrot. No American industrial communities matched Bournville or Port Sunlight, and many of them like Gary, or the mining towns of the Colorado Fuel and Iron Company, exhibited no housing or planning features worthy of emulation. For the reformer, however, the industrial village and garden suburb seemed in theory a promising alternative to the city tenement or flat. If only enough industrialists and philanthropists could be convinced of the economic and social advantages of the garden village and suburb, the reformer could strike at the heart of the housing problem by relieving the congestion of the industrial city. Here was a key point at which the housing and planning movements of the Progressive era intersected—relief of the congestion responsible for the tenement and slum through dispersion of work and population from the central city.

All progressive housing reformers endorsed the garden city program or its modifications. Even Lawrence Veiller, the leading exponent of restrictive legislation, could not resist the allure of planned garden communities. Although Veiller observed that workers in most American industrial towns "live in squalid and sordid surroundings," in time, perhaps, "far-sighted employers of labor" might "develop their community in such a way that it will not only furnish a delightful dwelling place for their workers, but will be a real asset to the industry."[20] Referring to the garden city, Veiller noted that by 1920 Letchworth contained eighty-two factories and workshops, 2,282 houses, and many shops and public buildings. It was a thriving community. England had demonstrated to his satisfaction that "the Garden City is a practical scheme; of benefit to the workers, of benefit to industry, of benefit to the community, of benefit to the nation."[21]

The COS Tenement House Committee promoted the garden city ideal and its variations whenever possible. It learned, for example, that Proctor and Gamble was planning to establish a plant in Staten Island, and offered some free advice to William C. Proctor. The Committee explained the merits of the industrial village, referring specifically to Port Sunlight, Bournville, and some American towns. It stressed its point by outlining the alternative to the planned, industrial village—the New York speculative tenement with its "increase in excessive drinking and gambling; over-indulgence in all the dissipations which gain influence as the home ceases to be attractive; increase in crime, and decrease in reliability, intelligence, contentment and efficiency."[22] Though nothing came of the Committee's proposal, it reflects the interest of the progressive housing reformer in directing the flow of population and industry away from the congested core of the city and into the country.[23]

The garden city program provided only for the planned development of new communities. It did not affect the expansion of existing municipalities or protect their better neighborhoods from future congestion. In zoning, housing reformers and planners thought they had found a device which would insure the orderly growth of existing cities. A planning weapon which had achieved maturity in Germany after 1900, zoning combined with the garden city movement after 1909 to enhance the utilitarian impulse superseding the City Beautiful. Although businessmen would promote zoning mainly to protect their financial interests, reformers viewed it in the broader perspective of the general social welfare; zoning would improve urban housing and living conditions by controlling population distribution.

German municipalities in rapid succession adopted zoning or districting regulations after 1900 in order to regulate expansion outward from the old (often medieval) central city.[24] The German zoning program consisted essentially of three series of restrictions over building development. First, the city was districted into specific use areas: residential, industrial, commercial, and mixed. In residential neighborhoods, protected against industrial or commercial invasion, property values would presumably remain stable because home owners were safeguarded against indiscriminate land use; property values would not fluctuate wildly, for speculators could not exploit the uncertainty and fears of home owners.

German zoning also involved the establishment of height districts. Building heights in designated areas were limited to a certain multiple of the street width. Height regulation had a dual purpose: it prevented congestion by limiting the number of people who could live or work in a particular area and simultaneously insured a minimum of light and air for all the structures. Height districting, in addition, protected property owners. A developer, for example, was prohibited from erecting a tall tenement in a neighborhood of one-family homes.

German zoning, finally, involved the creation of bulk or area restrictions. These regulated such items as court and yard sizes and the percentage of a lot which could be covered. Like height regulations, these area restrictions

also insured a minimum of light and air for commercial as well as residential structures, and reduced overcrowding by limiting the amount of
land which developers could improve.

American housing reformers and planners believed they had found in
zoning a tool with which to control land speculation, the fluctuation of
property values and, above all, congestion. Indeed, American municipal
reformers commonly assumed that if we imposed zoning regulations to
prevent overcrowding, we would plug the fountain from which many of the
physical and social evils of urban life flowed. No program of social betterment could achieve results unless "accompanied by a reasonably successful
attempt to lessen the congestion of population which now exists."[25]

. . .

. . . In 1916 New York City adopted America's first comprehensive zoning
code, enacted through the combined pressure of housing, taxation, and
other social reformers in alliance with conservative business interests.
Indeed, one small but powerful segment of New York's business community
triggered the events which resulted in New York's pioneering zoning
measure. The reformer was not isolated in his zoning campaign, for businessmen possessed a direct, tangible economic stake in zoning which they
lacked in the more visionary garden city ideal.

. . .

New York's zoning legislation was the product of many years of intensive
agitation and education by housing reformers, planners, and social workers,
reinforced by the costly experience of businessmen who discovered that
indiscriminate land use affected their pocketbooks. It is understandable
why real estate investors supported the zoning program of municipal
reformers in contrast to the garden city ideal. The latter had for its objective
urban decentralization, the radical deflation of those identical land and
property values which investors finally realized they could best protect
through zoning. In contrast to zoning, the garden city program represented
a kind of economic suicide both for real estate interests and the businessmen who profited from the concentrated urban population.

The New York zoning law of 1916, in which the interest of the social
reformer like Veiller or Purdy in promoting the general welfare coincided
with that of the businessman in protecting his investment, ranks with the
New York Tenement House Law of 1901 as among the most significant
municipal reforms of the Progressive era. By today's standards, certainly,
the zoning resolution was inadequate. In striving to win unanimous support and to insure that the restrictions would not discourage real estate
investment, the zoning commissions proved overgenerous to developers.
The 1916 measure with subsequent amendments permitted New York City
a potential resident population of more than 55 million.[26] Just as Veiller
had discouraged literal adoption of New York's housing laws, George B.
Ford in 1916 warned other cities against slavish imitation of New York's
zoning measure: "It would be most unfortunate if the law were applied as

it stands to other cities for it is full of unduly liberal provisions in the way of height and size that tend strongly to defeat the object of the law but were necessitated by the exceptional economic conditions of New York."[27]

The zoning legislation possessed a flaw, besides its liberality, which was not apparent to the housing reformers and planners of the early twentieth century. The zoning resolution of 1916 was a pioneering effort which aroused national interest and resulted in acceptance of zoning by hundreds of American communities in the following decade, but, like restrictive housing legislation, it was primarily negative in effect. Restrictive legislation and zoning provided municipalities with indispensable tools of control over physical development, and in this sense progressive housing reform and planning marks an important transitional era; the problem, however, was that such negative legislation in itself represented a dead end. It could not clear slums, nor provide adequate housing for those elements of the population whom the commercial builder could not profitably accommodate, nor establish criteria for satisfactory residential environments. The planner of the period was at heart a social reformer anxious to improve housing conditions, but he thwarted his own purpose by embracing a negative zoning program and a wistful garden city rhetoric, thus surrendering any hopes of dealing with housing directly. The response of the first generation of American planners to the urban housing problem was deconcentration attained through zoning and the garden city and its variations, a strikingly indirect approach which proved ultimately ineffectual. It left the slums standing, and although it pointed to the need for relating housing and planning, it provided no concrete, workable basis for the coordination of housing and planning policy.

NOTES

1. Maurice F. Neufeld, The Contribution of the World's Columbian Exposition of 1893 to the Idea of a Planned Society in the United States (Ph.D. thesis, University of Wisconsin, 1935), p. 133.

2. John Coleman Adams, "What a Great City Might Be—a Lesson from the White City," New England Magazine, XX (1896), 10, 3.

3. George B. Ford, "Digging Deeper in City Planning," American City, VI (1912), 557.

4. Lewis Mumford, Sticks and Stones: A Study of American Architecture and Civilization (New York: Dover, 1955), pp. 127, 130–31.

5. J. Horace McFarland, "The Growth of City Planning in America," Charities and the Commons, XVIX (1907–1908), 1525.

6. Alice Freeman Palmer, "Some Lasting Results of the World's Fair," *Forum,* XVI (1893–4), 520.

7. Consult the issues of *Municipal Affairs* (1897–1902) for many articles relevant to the City Beautiful.

8. Charles M. Robinson, *The Improvement of Towns and Cities or the Practical Basis of Civic Aesthetics,* 4th ed. (New York, 1913), pp. 211, 200, 292.

9. Charles M. Robinson, *Modern Civic Art or the City Made Beautiful,* 4th ed. (New York, 1918), p. 247.

10. In the plans made for cities after 1909, there are still many traces of the City Beautiful concept. However, the overwhelmingly utilitarian emphasis in theory can readily be ascertained by reference to National Conference on City Planning, *Proceedings,* 1910–17. Most of the articles and papers dealt with practical problems of city planning. Also, *American City,* 1909–17; *The City Plan,* and *Housing Betterment,* the organs respectively of the National Conference on City Planning and the National Housing Association; the papers of planners at the National Housing Association published in the annual *Proceedings; Charities and the Commons* and its successor, *Survey.*

11. Arnold W. Brunner, "The Meaning of City Planning," National Conference on City Planning, *Proceedings,* 1912, p. 22.

12. John Nolen, *New Ideals in the Planning of Cities, Towns, and Villages* (New York, 1919), p. 17.

13. Ebenezer Howard, *Garden Cities of To-morrow* (London, 1902), pp. 15, 18 (3rd ed. of *To-morrow: A Peaceful Path to Reform).*

14. For accounts of the evolution of the Garden City movement in England consult: C. B. Purdom, *The Garden City: A Study in the Development of a Modern Town* (London, 1913); E. G. Culpin, *The Garden City Movement Up-to-Date* (London, 1912); *Town Planning in Theory and Practice* (a report of a conference arranged by the Garden City Association, October 25, 1907).

15. In Howard's words: "It is well-nigh universally agreed by men of all parties, not only in England, but all over Europe and America and our colonies, that it is deeply to be deplored that the people should continue to stream into the already over-crowded cities, and should thus further deplete the country districts." Howard, *op. cit.,* pp. 10–11.

16. James Ford, *The Housing Problem* (Cambridge, Mass., 1911), pp. 15, 16 (A Summary of Conditions and Remedies Prepared to Accompany the Housing Exhibit in May, 1911 of the Harvard Social Museum).

17. Annie L. Diggs, "The Garden City Movement," *Arena,* XXVIII (1902), 627.

18. W. Alexander Harvey, *The Model Village and Its Cottages: Bournville* (London, 1906), p. 15. For the significance of the Garden Village as interpreted by Americans consult: Edward E. Pratt, "Garden Cities in Europe," *American City,* VII (1912), 503–10; Lyra D. Trueblood, "The Bournville Village Experiment: a Twentieth-Century Attempt at Housing the Workers," *Arena,* XXXIV (1905), 449–58; Robert Brown, "Progress of the Garden City Movement in England," *Arena,* XL (1908), 459–60; Carol Aronovici, *Housing and the Housing Problem* (Chicago, 1920);

Edith Elmer Wood, *The Housing of the Unskilled Wage Earner: America's Next Problem* (New York, 1919).

19. The American industrial village is discussed in Graham R. Taylor, *Satellite Cities: A Study of Industrial Suburbs* (New York, 1915); Leifur Magnusson, "Housing by Employers in the United States," National Housing Association, *Proceedings*, 1917, pp. 106–29; Grosvenor Atterbury, *Model Towns in America* (National Housing Association, Publications, No. 17, January 1913); E. R. L. Gould, *The Housing of the Working People*, Eighth Special Report of the Commissioner of Labor (Washington, D.C., 1895); Leonora B. Ellis, "A Model Factory Town," *Forum*, XXXII (1901–1902), 60–65, a favorable discussion of Pelzer, S. C. A detailed description of conditions in one of the most famous of American industrial towns is Margaret F. Byington, *Homestead, The Households of a Mill Town* (New York, 1910).

20. Lawrence Veiller, *Industrial Housing* (National Housing Association Publications, No. 36, June 1917), pp. 1, 25. A discussion of the practical problems of establishing an industrial village in terms of finance and design can be found in John Nolen, *The Industrial Village* (National Housing Association, Publications, No. 50, September 1918).

21. Lawrence Veiller, *Are Great Cities a Menace? The Garden City a Way Out* (National Housing Association, Publications, No. 57, February 1922), pp. 9, 10.

22. COS Tenement House Committee, Minutes, June 21, 1906.

23. See Carol Aronovici's plea for decentralization in "Suburban Development," *Annals*, LI (1914), 234–8.

24. Frank Backus Williams, "The German Zone Building Regulations," Heights of Buildings Commission to the Committee on the Height, Size and Arrangement of Buildings of the Board of Estimate and Apportionment of the City of New York, *Report*, December 23, 1913, 94–119.

25. Frank J. Goodnow, "Report of the Committee on Congestion of Population," First New York City Conference of Charities and Correction, *Proceedings*, 1910, p. 13.

26. *New York Times*, December 21, 1959, p. 22.

27. George B. Ford, "How New York City Now Controls the Development of Private Property," *City Plan*, II (October 1916), 3.

PART SIX

BOSSES, MACHINES, AND URBAN REFORM

He had Irish features, a derby hat cocked to one side of his head, a puffy cigar chomped between his teeth, his thumbs hooked into the pockets of a money-stuffed vest. Surrounded by loyal retainers, he carried on shady dealings with elected officials and wealthy businessmen and ruled the city like a medieval baron intent on pillage. Thus did late-nineteenth-century stereotypes depict the urban boss, that unique American contribution to the art and science of politics. The very term—denoting a professional politician in charge of a political machine— was a creation of nineteenth-century American political life. It was appropriate in cities undergoing an industrial transformation that the organization headed by the boss should be labeled in industrial terminology. A machine was a specialized tool designed to perform efficiently one industrial task in a factory that gathered together under one roof all the scattered operations of manufacturing. Likewise, the political machine organized and centralized all the bits of power scattered among far-flung precincts and wards. Its specialized function was to meet the specific personal and private problems of its constituents—needs and wants that more traditional forms of legitimate government either overlooked or ignored. To keep the machine in good working order and to make certain that its power remained centralized was the role of the boss.

At its core, boss politics was personal and practical. It did not involve the legal government of the city so much as it incorporated special-interest groups in a common cause, under leadership wielded by one man or a few associates. While the legitimate ruling groups expressed, at least in theory, a particular philosophy or ideology of government, bosses emphasized getting things done for the politically disaffected. Since an urban boss usually tried to cement a coalition of the unrepresented or the underrepresented, his efforts often took place on the fringes of the established parties of his day. In some cases the boss was an elected official, but more often he merely exercised influence and control over elected officials who were tied to him and to the machine by bonds of loyalty and job patronage. A boss rarely quibbled over party affiliation; he did business with Republicans and Democrats alike. And there was no predicting how he would conduct that business. In obtaining special privileges for himself and his followers he might act justly or unjustly. He might perform services directed toward the public good, or he might concern himself only with selfish gain. One fact was certain— whether in the public welfare or in private pursuits, the boss had to produce results. Either as an elected official or a private string-puller, the boss had to keep the machine well-oiled and his operatives working together in harmony. His own security, the life of the machine, and the centralized organization of power all depended upon it. And for much of the country's history boss politics, to achieve results, had to function outside the place of ordained government.

It was the function of the boss as an unofficial, irresponsible, invisible, actual governor behind the legal, constitutional "front" of municipal government that aroused the ire of a muckraking journalist like Lincoln Steffens. It was bossism in part that inspired Lord James Bryce, an observant Englishman, to claim in the 1880s that the government of the cities was "the one conspicuous failure of the United States." And it was boss politics that led the distinguished Andrew White, president of Cornell University, to remark that "with a very few exceptions, the city governments of the United States are the worst in Christendom, the most expensive, the most inefficient, and the most corrupt." Expense, inefficiency, and corruption were the charges that reformers hurled time and again at the system of boss politics. The "invisible government" that late-nineteenth- and early-twentieth-century reformers so condemned was, in Steffens' famous description, the "shame of the cities."

The municipal critics, reform-minded businessmen, and politicians who cried "shame" did so as though shocked by their discovery. The revelation that venality and inefficiency were the hallmarks of late-nineteenth-century urban government also has informed the writings of many American historians. These reactions suggest that never before had "politics" played a major role in municipal affairs, that "corruption"—or, more genteelly, the successful search for special privileges—rarely had characterized civic management, and that the reward-and-punishment system called "patronage" had not spread its tentacles throughout local big-city governments in the past. Presumably "bossism," "machines," "gangs," "rings"—whatever terms are used to denote organized political manipulation of the public for private profit—were products of urban America after the Civil War. But the historical record tells a different story. Bossism as an extralegal political tool for organizing and operating the everyday affairs of municipal life was as old as the cities themselves.

Colonial American towns and cities, in which British imperial policy presumably ordered political operations, offered numerous instances of boss politics.

In early-eighteenth-century Philadelphia, for example, the career of David Lloyd demonstrated the possibilities for personal politics. Lloyd was a brilliant lawyer and effective orator who held several public and proprietary offices during the 1690s in William Penn's Pennsylvania. In 1699, for various offenses and at the insistence of the Crown, Lloyd was removed from office by Penn. During the early 1700s Lloyd mounted an attack against proprietary government and promoted new powers for the Corporation of Philadelphia. By both design and accident Lloyd substantially altered the social bases of political activity and thrust himself into a position as champion of the "people" in his "Rattle of rights and Privileges." As historian Gary B. Nash has noted, Lloyd politicized a mass of individuals of mixed ethnic and religious backgrounds who occupied lower positions on the social and economic ladder than those held by the established Quaker leadership. His coalition exercised unchallenged control of Philadelphia and Pennsylvania politics for nearly a decade. While Lloyd failed to build a machine that perpetuated itself, his leadership exemplified the kind of personal politics that much later in American history would be labeled and libeled as bossism.

Economic conditions and anti-British sentiment in early-eighteenth-century Boston gave rise to that city's first political machine, led and dominated by Elisha Cooke, Jr., a physician, sometime lawyer, and shrewd politician. With several associates Cooke organized in the 1720s the Boston Caucus, later characterized by John Adams as a group that met in smoke-filled rooms to draw up slates of candidates before elections and to organize faithful supporters for the proposals that were to go before the Town Meetings. Since the caucus could not challenge royal appointments and patronage, its members relied instead on more devious means of grasping power. Speculative land operations that promised large profits, breaks in tax assessments to recruit and reward supporters, and gallons of free liquor to influence voters at election time were all levers the caucus used to pry its way into positions of importance. Although Cooke could not solidify political support outside Boston, he and the caucus were able to wield power within the city proper. Again, the machine did not sustain itself over time, but the lessons of organization that it taught were not lost on subsequent generations. It remained for the Society of Saint Tammany in New York City to found an organization that could and did perpetuate political leadership.

Established before the American Revolution, the Society of Saint

Tammany (named after a fabled Indian warrior who defeated the evil spirit in a series of battles) first helped to popularize revolutionary sentiment against the British. Largely composed of upper-class citizens, Tammany continued after the revolution as a social club that occasionally dabbled in city government. The political tendencies of the society and its partisan character became pronounced in the late eighteenth century when its members, under the patronage of Thomas Jefferson, opposed the aristocratic and allegedly monarchistic Hamiltonians of New York City. By the late 1820s an increase in immigration swelled the ranks of the city's lower classes and an extension of the suffrage widened the political base. Workingmen began organizing their own political clubs and parties. Keeping pace with the times, Tammany changed gradually from a group of Protestant upper-class conservatives to a group that organized and claimed to represent the poor and immigrant residents of the city. By the 1840s New Yorkers knew that Tammany and the Jacksonian Democratic party had meshed and the society already had acquired a reputation for political graft that would make its name synonymous with corruption in American political history. One of its leaders as Superintendent of the Almshouse had "borrowed" funds allocated for the poor, while another, serving as Collector of the Port of New York, had "collected" $1,250,000 and had fled the country. Already the society personified the characteristics of a "ring" or machine that would be offered some thirty years later by Presidential candidate Samuel Tilden: "The very definition of a 'ring' is that it encircles enough influential men in the organization of each party to control the action of both party machines; men who in public push to extremes the abstract ideas of their respective parties, while they secretly join hands in schemes for personal power and profit." Certainly the roots of boss politics ran deep in the soil of American municipal government.

But if civic corruption and personal politics were traditional in the urban past, beginning with the last half of the nineteenth century, there now was something new about their directions and extent of power. Both a consolidation and a diffusion of machine politics occurred in most major American cities. Existing political organizations during the 1860s and 1870s (insiders always referred to themselves as members of "the organization," not "the machine") tried to tighten their hold on city government, while other self-interest groups emerged either to take over the established machine or to build an organization of their own. Several conditions of life in post-bellum cities facilitated the rise of boss politics.

The growth of American cities between 1860 and 1900 was both rapid and disorderly. During the single decade of the 1880s, for example, New York's population increased from 2 to almost 3½ million, Chicago's grew from half a million to more than a million, and Detroit, Milwaukee, and Cleveland each doubled in size. Throughout those years the urban population of the nation as a whole jumped from slightly over 6 million in 1860 to over 30 million by 1900. During the last third of the nineteenth century American cities experienced an acceleration of the industrial takeoff that had begun before the war. Accompanying the increase in industrial production was a corresponding boom in commercial activity. Both population increases and economic expansion owed much to the arrivals of successive waves of foreign immigrants—from Ireland and Germany immediately following the war and from Austria-Hungary, Italy, Russia, Greece, Rumania, Turkey, and Poland as the century wore on. Indeed, by 1910, foreign-born residents and the children of foreign-born or mixed parentage accounted for the largest segments of urban populations throughout the nation. The presence of the immigrant masses complicated the already strained capacity of American cities to govern themselves in times of industrial and commercial growth.

Such rapid concentrations of people—both native and foreign-born— necessitated more efficient means of serving their wants and needs than former urban populations had required. Water supply and sewage systems had to be overhauled or newly created. Police protection of property and public safety had to be ensured. Streets had to be paved, lighted, and cleaned. Public utilities of light, gas, and transportation had to be provided, either by private enterprise or municipal ownership. Old housing had to be converted and reconverted to meet increasing demands, and new housing had to replace existing facilities. And businessmen, eager to profit from the urban boom, were ready to use any means of access to lucrative enterprises.

City officials were not prepared to respond to changing conditions. They most often found themselves unequipped, unwilling, or unable to meet the heavy demands placed upon them. Inadequate city charters long out-of-date, poor planning, and shoddy administration often combined with public apathy toward the problems of local government to produce serious political vacuums. To be sure, officials were not wholly to blame for sluggish responses to the new problems. Nineteenth-century democratic theory and practice militated against the kind of positive government required in the cities. Americans believed in a competitive marketplace, displayed a public commitment to minimal government interference in that marketplace, and retained their faith in a decentralized

decision-making process. Mid-nineteenth-century New York City, for
example, had governing powers fragmented among a mayor, a board of
aldermen, a board of councilmen, supervisors, a board of education,
separate police, park, port and fire commissioners, a board of health, and
a city comptroller. Some of these were elected officials, some were
appointed, and all served varying lengths of term in office. "Was there
ever," a contemporary wisely questioned, "such a hodgepodge of a
government before in the world?" Nineteenth-century cities exhibited,
in the telling metaphor of political scientist M. I. Ostrogorski, a "weakened
spring of government." To strengthen that spring, to bridge the gap between
rapid growth with its accompanying problems and the inability of urban
institutions to meet new challenges, untraditional forms of government
seemed necessary and even desirable. Personal and practical politics
became more vital than ever before and also more profitable. Following
the Civil War Americans witnessed, almost by default, the entrenchment
of a system of political rule centered on the figure of the urban boss.

The classic example of the modern urban boss, a professional whose
entire life was devoted to politics, was William Marcy Tweed, Democratic
leader of New York City's Tammany Hall in the decade following the
Civil War. Not every boss was a Democrat, nor the affable roughneck that
Tweed was, but Tweed's organizational ability and quality of leadership
typified later bosses in New York and other cities. The tactics employed
by the Tweed ring were representative of the fundamentals of successful
machine politics. Unlike the stereotype, Tweed came not from a poor
Irish background but from a respectable, native American, middle-class
family. He spent little time in formal education, working instead as a
carpenter's apprentice during his youth. Tweed entered politics by
joining a volunteer fire company, one of many such organizations taking
an active part in politics during the 1840s when he came of voting age.
As in carpentry, Tweed began in ward politics as an apprentice, rising
from an alderman to the United States House of Representatives and
returning to New York, where, through aggressiveness, good timing, and
luck, he achieved power in Tammany Hall. So effective was his use of the
organization that by 1865 he succeeded in gaining the election of his
candidate as mayor of New York City. By the late 1860s Tweed was the
unchallenged boss of the city, numbering among his followers the
governor of the state, the mayor, and numerous underlings on the bench,
the Board of Supervisors, the Board of Education, and in most other
branches of city government. His ties stretched from the legislature in
Albany to the local precinct in New York City. Like other city bosses,
Tweed allied himself with various business interests. At one time or another

he served as a partner of railroad magnates Jay Gould and Jim Fiske, occupied a seat on the Board of Directors of the Erie Railroad, acted as a director of the New York Railroad Company and the Tenth National Bank of New York City, and held widespread real estate.

As dictator of New York City politics, Tweed could directly influence or control half of the voters of the city through the various agencies at his command. His flair for leadership and executive ability was most evident in the efficiency he brought to ward organization. Political life in New York City and elsewhere was centered in the ward, where skillful captains dispensed favors and obtained jobs for the residents in return for votes. And the ward boss knew who voted for whom, who should be rewarded and who punished, for the secret ballot was not used widely in American elections until the early 1890s. Instead, parties or independent candidates printed up their own ballots, distributed them outside the polling places, and watched, with little or no pretense at secrecy, how the votes were cast. Thus ward politicians could know at a glance whether bargains were being kept or broken and whether votes they had paid for were being "honestly" cast. If matters were going badly, the efficient ward boss would send his "repeaters," men who went from polling place to polling place throughout election day, to vote for the machine's candidates. "Big Tim" Sullivan, one of Tweed's most reliable captains, preferred his repeaters to have beards. As he explained it,

When you've voted 'em with their whiskers on, you take 'em to a barber and scrape off the chin fringe. Then you vote 'em again with the side lilacs and a mustache. Then to a barber again, off comes the sides and you vote 'em a third time with the mustache. If that ain't enough and the box can stand a few more ballots, clean off the mustache and vote 'em plain face. That makes every one of 'em good for four votes.

It was such skillful organization as this that sustained the Tweed ring and other urban machines.

Like most later bosses, Tweed consolidated his power by attracting the votes of the immigrant masses that comprised nearly two-thirds of the electorate in New York City. Crowded together in "urban villages" within the larger city, the immigrants tried to adapt their rural institutions and cultures to the urban milieu. Untrained in democratic principles, usually deprived economically and socially, generally overlooked by the traditional ruling groups in the cities, and eager to take advantage of American opportunities, immigrants turned to the bosses for help and security. As one boss later put it, "I think that there's got to be in every ward somebody that any bloke can come to—no matter what he's done—and get help. Help, you understand; none of your law and your justice, but help." Who more natural to turn to than one of his kind?

One study of twenty leading city bosses demonstrated that at least half were Irish, Catholic, and Democratic—men who as second-generation immigrants had themselves "made it" in American life and yet remained with their people. Even those who were not first- or second-generation immigrants—Tweed, for instance—turned a sympathetic ear to the immigrants' problems, seeing in the newcomers a base for their own climb to power. And despite the cavils of contemporaries who scoffed at the food, fuel, and money given by ward politicians, the bosses did help immigrants adjust to life in the cities. The bosses found jobs for the unemployed, saw to it that the sick received medical care, built charitable institutions, public bathhouses, and parks, and in other ways attended to the physical and emotional needs of the immigrant poor. Above all, the bosses served as a personal reference point for immigrants who found themselves adrift in an unfamiliar, impersonal urban society. The bosses often were living proof that success could be grasped in the strange new world of America. The machine leaders and the immigrant followers shared a reciprocal relationship; each depended upon the other. The bosses provided for the foreign urban masses in a variety of ways, and all they asked for in return were votes.

To be sure, the machine turned votes to its own purposes. Only if its own men were in positions of influence could the machine sustain itself. It was not always necessary to capture the mayor's office; the decentralized nature of city government meant that the machine could lose the top spot on the ticket and still effectively control many of the city's operations. In cities undergoing vast physical expansion a chief source of job patronage and personal profit was the construction industry, and here the bosses used the immigrant vote to good advantage. Construction involved real-estate speculation and licensing; and bosses, working through their retainers in various city agencies, often gained the inside track on prospective building enterprises. Through fraud, the letting of contracts to friends, issuance of licenses, appointments to office, and other means connected with construction of public buildings and municipal facilities like sewer systems and horse-drawn railroads, bosses often succeeded in controlling the fiscal resources of the cities. By 1870 the Tweed ring had grafted up to 85 percent of the total city funds paid to public contractors. By Fall of 1871 the ring had swindled New York City out of an estimated $200 million. Like later bosses in other cities

Tweed and his associates amassed personal fortunes. The man who ran the machine and took the blame for its mistakes usually profited from his labors. Chris Magee of Pittsburgh acquired more than $4,450,000 in real and personal property; Richard Croker of New York probably made a fortune above $3 million; Roger Sullivan of Chicago left a will worth $1,503,607; and "King" James McManes of Philadelphia "earned" over $2,400,000. If not every boss fared so well, few died penniless.

The urban boss can be viewed as one of the successful businessmen coming to power and prominence during the late nineteenth century, and the machine as a prototype of the business corporations arising at the same time. The corporation and the machine were structured along similar lines: both were organizations of men linked together by desire for profit, both contained disciplined hierarchies of workers and executives, both endured and grew in strength only so long as they managed to anticipate and meet the needs of their respective "publics," and both retained a cadre of loyal supporters by offering psychic and material rewards. Both tried, and often succeeded in, manipulating the established branches of government to their own best advantage. Both bribed politicians and businessmen with contracts and orders for supplies, supported political parties to elect the "right" men, applied financial pressures to banks eager for their deposits, offered extensive advertising accounts to conciliate potentially hostile newspapers, and paid police, judges, and other public officials to ensure legal protection for their own interests.

It was no accident of history that both business corporations and political machines emerged during a period of great physical growth for the cities, rapid population increases, industrial transformation of the economy, and a public commitment to decentralized government. Like the corporation, the machine offered organization in the midst of disorder, and continuity in the face of disruptive expansion. And, like the corporation, the machine provided avenues of social mobility for certain groups in American society. For incoming foreigners, the urban machines often served as vehicles that enabled the immigrants to use their chief resource—sheer weight of numbers—to integrate themselves into the mainstream of American life. The major example was the Irish.

As described by Nathan Glazer and Daniel Patrick Moynihan in their book *Beyond the Melting Pot*, the Irish established in mid-nineteenth-century New York City a political system that, from a distance, looked like the social system of an Irish village. Certainly many nineteenth- and early-twentieth-century critics of bossism believed that the urban machine

was a creation of the Irish. While that was an exaggeration, there were
at least four features of machine politics that revealed the decisive
influence of Irish immigrants. First, because politics in Ireland were
thoroughly corrupt, stealing an election did not seem immoral as it did
to Americans. The Irish conceived of personal government and "influence
politics" as the natural order, and thus, upon arrival in the New World,
were indifferent to the proprieties of politics in America. Second, the
Irish brought in their cultural baggage a traditional view of formal
government as illegitimate and informal government as truly representative
of "the people." Third, mid-nineteenth-century Irishmen came fresh from
experience in the Catholic emancipation movement at home and therefore
saw the possibilities of politics for bettering their lot. Fourth, the Irish
displayed an amazing capacity for political bureaucracy, for a system of
predictable hierarchical relationships through which a person was bound
to progress over time. As Glazer and Moynihan observed, "the principle
of Boss rule was not tyranny, but order." Reformer Lincoln Steffens once
asked Tammany leader Richard Croker, "Why must there be a boss, when
we've got a mayor and—a council and—?" "That's why," Croker
interjected. "It's because there's a mayor *and* a council *and* judges—*and*
a hundred other men to deal with." The Irish perceived the chaos of
decentralized municipal government in the cities and so, to secure their
own best interests, imposed an effective, personalized bureaucracy upon
the existing political structure.

This brand of government might best be called "the politics of survival."
Certainly the Irish takeover of the political apparatus of New York City,
Chicago, and other cities enabled the immigrants to survive and prosper
in a new and often hostile environment. By the late nineteenth century
the Irish *were* Tammany Hall. "Honest John" Kelly succeeded Tweed,
and was followed in turn by Richard Croker and Frank Murphy. The Irish
ran the city until the end of the 1920s when Al Smith (by birth only
partly Irish but wholly so in spirit) ran for President and Mayor Jimmy
Walker "wore New York in his buttonhole." And Chicago was little different.
There, ward politicians like John Powers, "Bathhouse" John Coughlin, and
Michael "Hinky Dink" Kenna, among others, dominated city politics and
continued to rule into the 1970s in the person of "King" Richard J. Daley,
mayor of the city and a man described by political commentators as "the
last of the urban bosses." If not all cities were New Yorks and Chicagos
and not all machine politicians Irish, certainly the Irish were the most
dramatically successful of the various ethnic groups entering the cities in
the late nineteenth and early twentieth centuries. Their brand of bossism
with its in-group loyalty, its rewards for faithful service, and its sense of

community responsibility for residents of the wards shaped the directions taken by urban government in America and molded as well the experience of generations of newcomers to American cities. The political machine, as refined and tuned by the Irish, performed a positive function in American life at the same time that it created additional problems for a society struggling to come to terms with itself and its changing environment.

The spread of the "politics of survival" in American cities, with the attendant graft and corruption, brought forth an inevitable response. Critics of the political machine arose in righteous indignation, focusing attention on its negative functions. Reformers during the late nineteenth and early twentieth century fastened on bossism as the cause of every maladjustment in urban America. The corruption of the ballot box by hordes of ignorant aliens; the jerry-built slum districts of the cities which served as breeding grounds of crime, delinquency, and disease; illicit ententes between big business and self-serving politicians; monopolistic franchises for public utilities that failed to act in the public interest; the vast waste of money, time, and effort that appeared to characterize the unplanned physical expansion of the cities—all these evils the reformers charged to the bosses. To that exent, the reformers were correct. Irish and other ethnic ward and city bosses rarely viewed politics as a means of social change. To them, political activity was the best route to take in pursuing the traditional American goal of "getting ahead." In this sense, machine politics was the Horatio Alger myth fulfilled. To those immigrants determined to survive and succeed at all costs, social reform was not prized, but despised. For the reformers spoke in abstract terms about honesty and the ideals of the United States Constitution, while the urban masses sought physical survival and security. A characteristic exchange, revealing the gulf between the attitudes of reformers and ethnic politicians, involved Congressman Timothy J. Campbell of New York and President Grover Cleveland. Cleveland dismissed a personal request from Campbell, stating that it was unconstitutional. "Ah, Mr. President," Tim responded, "what is the Constitution between friends?" The reformers never understood the politics of nepotism and neighborliness that they so denounced. Their lack of understanding accounted for the plethora of reform organizations that sprang up in the late nineteenth century to challenge bossism and for the ultimate failure of reformers to destroy the urban machines.

The roster of reform enthusiasms and organizations in the late nineteenth century included a motley collection of ministers, educators, journalists, businessmen, newly emancipated college women, professionals like physicians and lawyers, politicians of a genteel, upper-class stripe, and some labor union leaders. Citywide charity organizations, formed on the "Buffalo plan" of 1877, which included private and public relief enterprises under one administrative umbrella, laid the groundwork for an extension of social welfare programs for the unemployed and working-class populations. A movement to reform tenement housing, carried on in the last two decades of the century, gained much of its impetus from charity organization activities. The writings of such students of poverty as Henry George (*Progress and Poverty*, 1879), Jacob Riis (*How the Other Half Lives*, 1890), and Robert Hunter (*Poverty*, 1904) also stirred the public conscience to an awareness of the plight of the urban masses.

In addition, a newly militant Christian church enunciated a new social gospel in the cities. Beginning in the 1880s, some Protestant clergymen effected a turnabout in the traditional stance of the church toward inhabitants of large industrial cities. Men like Washington Gladden, a clergyman who pioneered labor-management conferences in Ohio, and Walter Rauschenbush, a Baptist minister in Rochester, New York, denounced the excesses of capitalism and industrialization and called on urban churchmen to work for the salvation of society rather than the salvation of the individual soul. Their chief contributions lay in urging economic cooperation among all social groups and collective property rights to social wealth. Missionaries of the social gospel joined with other organizations, principally the newly formed Women's Christian Temperance Union and the Anti-Saloon League, in a crusade to close down the saloons and dry up the cities. And a social settlement movement, typified in the founding of Hull House in Chicago (1889) under the direction of Jane Addams, supported the cause of active local governments to aid the lower classes. Stressing the principle of "neighborhood sovereignty"—that is, mutual self-help and cooperation among immigrant residents of the urban villages—the settlement workers tried to teach the English language, offer training in labor skills for the unemployed, and instill respect for law and order and an understanding of the political workings of American democratic government.

From their own perspectives, all of these reform organizations challenged the dominance of the political machine and the "invisible government" of the bosses. Whatever their approaches, the reformers believed that no positive social changes could occur unless the strength of the machine and its strangle hold on the poor and immigrant classes could be broken. Starting usually from a middle-class economic base and sharing certain tenets about the need for pure, legitimate, democratic government, the reformers attacked the machine in a piecemeal fashion. While the bosses knew the art of coalition politics ("give everybody a little of what he wants") and daily practiced the politics of survival, the reformers talked about the integrity of the ballot box and generally shunned infighting in the political arena.

During the 1870s and 1880s a number of reformers followed the lead of citizens in Baltimore in organizing "good government" clubs in their respective cities. These were associations dedicated to rooting out the graft and corruption evident in the boss system and replacing the bosses with the "good people" of the city. "Restore honesty," they cried, "and all will be well." The highlight of the movement came in Philadelphia in 1894 with the National Conference for Good City Government. This meeting synthesized much of the reform activity of the previous two decades and at the same time pointed the way toward what would become known as national progressivism. Many of the representatives, including Jane Addams, Washington Gladden, and educator Edwin D. Mead, had been active in urban reform campaigns, and the keynote speaker was the man who later became the symbol of progressiveness on a national scale, Theodore Roosevelt. Roosevelt's message summed up the ambitions of the "good government" groups when he called upon his listeners to be disinterested, selfless, but also sincere, upright, and honest. Above all, he urged them not to give up the battle too easily. Out of this conference grew the National Municipal League, which served principally as an educational institution and a clearing house for the multitude of reform campaigns going on in the nation's cities.

Other reformers devoted most of their efforts to securing new franchises for public utilities, the old having served as lucrative props for boss government. Reform mayors like Tom Johnson of Cleveland and Hazen Pingree of Detroit joined with so-called sewer socialists like Frederick C. Howe, author of *The City: The Hope of Democracy*, in calling for municipal ownership of urban water supplies, sanitation facilities, and transportation companies. Thus, they argued, could the corruption inherent in the political machine be eliminated. Still other reformers looked at corruption on a cost-accounting basis and argued that the inefficiency and waste of bossism should be replaced with government by experts. The primary example of this approach was the "city manager" form of government, first worked out in Dayton, Ohio, in 1913.

So long as reformers could agree that the chief aims of government were limited and that city politics should perform only housekeeping chores, demands for efficiency, honesty, and the end of corruption appeared attractive. The reformers could soothe their troubled consciences and assure themselves that their forays into politics really accomplished something. But the bosses knew better. They knew that politics was an arduous job, demanding full-time effort. They also knew that government had to meet daily the needs of the urban masses, that it had to be positive and extensive in its services, and that mere housekeepers soon lost their jobs. Moreover, the bosses knew that they served their constituencies just as much as they helped themselves in return. As Boss Plunkitt of Tammany Hall put it: "nobody thinks of drawin' the distinction between honest graft and dishonest graft. There's all the difference in the world between the two." "Honest graft," as Plunkitt defined it, involved a politician serving the public by getting streets paved and parks constructed, while he and his friends profited financially from their part in the enterprises. No illegal shenanigans, no bribe-taking from gamblers or saloon-keepers, no actions harmful to his friends and constituents, ever sullied the reputation of a boss who engaged in "honest graft"—or so Plunkitt claimed. His commentary on human behavior in the exercise of political power was timeless in its implications. So was his classical explanation for the failure of reformers: "They were mornin' glories—looked lovely in the mornin' and withered up in a short time, while the regular machines went on flourishin' forever, like fine old oaks." "Say," he concluded, "that's the first poetry I ever worked off. Ain't it great?" If not poetic, his sentiments nonetheless were true.

20. THE SPECIALIZATION OF LEADERSHIP IN NINETEENTH-CENTURY PHILADELPHIA

Sam Bass Warner, Jr.

As businessmen abandoned the city's affairs and its politics new specialists assumed their former tasks. Politics became a full-time business and professionals moved in to make careers of public office. Although the first half of the nineteenth century was a transitional period, populated with many men and women who mixed old forms and modern roles,[1] two thoroughly modern types emerged in Philadelphia's pre–Civil War municipal politics—the boss and the gentleman-democrat. Both symbolized enduring experiences of a city which sought simultaneously to maintain an open society and to reward the successful pursuit of private wealth. The boss portrayed the self-made man; the gentleman-democrat portrayed the union of democracy and wealth.

The new city boss, or self-made politician, bore the marks of the steady battle for control of votes. Philadelphia's first boss, Joel Barlow Sutherland (1792–1861) lacked inheritance and outside income; he had to make politics pay. His plural office holding, his unscrupulousness, and his lack of imagination cast a shadow of uncreative, corrupt municipal management over the future of the city.

A Scotch immigrant's son, Sutherland graduated from the University of Pennsylvania Medical School the year of the opening of the War of 1812. He immediately joined a Philadelphia militia company and rose through militia politics to the rank of lieutenant colonel. Aided by such connections, Sutherland was three times elected to the state legislature. Peace, however, deprived him of the source of his popularity and power and he was forced to take the unglamorous job of doctor to the quarantine hospital of the port of Philadelphia.[2]

Reasoning correctly that law promised a better path to politics than medicine, he studied law and entered the bar in 1819. Two years later he was elected to the legislature and became Speaker in 1825. As Speaker he helped to promote the state canal project which was to give Philadelphia an economical transportation line to the west.[3] It was in these years, too, that he put together his southside political machine which grew in the next decade to be the major Democratic Party force in Philadelphia city and county. The southside of Philadelphia was a mixed area in the twenties and thirties. Sailors, shipyard workers, longshoremen, and the marine trades clustered along the Delaware shore, especially in the District of Southwark. The south edge of Philadelphia (the Cedar, New Market and Pine wards) bordered on the fashionable and also held the Negro ghetto. Few Negroes voted, however. Some Irish weavers settled in Moyamensing and an Irish colony grew in the western part of the area, along the Schuylkill wharves. Throughout the whole district lived large numbers of unskilled laborers, downtown workers, and local artisans.[4]

Political power centered around the two independent, self-governing Districts, Southwark and Moyamensing. During Sutherland's time both were intensely patriotic, white-equalitarian, anti-Negro, anti-foreigner, in short, strong followers of the old radical Revolutionary traditions of the city. Sutherland's strategy, like that of many Pennsylvania politicians, was to try to balance his constituents' enthusiasm for President Jackson and Jacksonian slogans with a steady support of his district's economic needs.

After two failures Sutherland, in 1826, was elected to Congress where he served for the next ten years.[5] This political success made it possible for him to garner the fruits of power, and during these years he held at intervals the additional offices of Prosecuting Attorney for Philadelphia County and Associate Judge of the Court of Common Pleas. In Congress, as a member of the House Commerce Committee, he promoted the Philadelphia Navy Yard, which was then situated on Federal street in Southwark, and helped to secure the federal appropriation for the important Delaware River breakwater.

In 1834 national events threatened Sutherland's ability to balance Jacksonian enthusiasm with support of Philadelphia's economic interests. The year 1834 saw the crisis of the Bank of the United States. President Jackson had consciously revived the old radical campaign against special privilege to the wealthy and championed the attack on the Bank's charter and federal deposits. In the banking capitals of the Atlantic seaboard municipal politics became strongly polarized between those who felt that a demagogue was attacking the sanctity of personal property and those who regarded Jackson as the savior of democracy. The division in Philadelphia, the home of the Bank of the United States, by no means cut neatly along class lines. Many workingmen joined Whig parades and memorials in defense of the Bank. All spring and summer the Whigs had been strong and active. The Bank, partly out of self-defense and partly in the hope of threatening Congress and the President with a depression, rapidly called in its loans and a severe, if brief, depression fell upon the city and the nation. In the face of these hard times men fell back upon their traditional voting patterns and few Philadelphia seats changed hands.

Spurred by the elections in New York, the Whigs of Philadelphia chose to attempt to unseat the southside Democratic boss, Joel Barlow Sutherland, even though Sutherland, otherwise an ardent Jacksonian, had announced himself in favor of the Bank. The Whigs devised the strategy of nominating an Irish mechanic, hoping to swing the election with a combination of native Whigs and new Irish voters. Sutherland's supporters countered with a strong anti-Irish campaign which seems to have united his following. The Whigs, in turn, seem to have expected a violent election; perhaps they intended using force at the polls. Nicholas Biddle of the Bank of the United States sent his family to the country because he feared violence on election day.

On Tuesday, October 14, 1834, balloting proceeded in an orderly way at the polls in the Southwark and Moyamensing parts of the congressional district. Moyamensing had just completed its Commissioners Hall and in front of the new polling place the Democrats had set up tents and the Whigs had rented a house for campaign headquarters. Toward evening as the voters queued up to cast their ballots a fight began in one of the lines and soon the Whigs in the crowd drove all the Democrats from the polls, flattened their tents and cut down the Democratic liberty pole. Since the Democrats were then a minority in Moyamensing, they sought help from adjacent Southwark. Men from this section ran into Moyamensing and soon drove the Whigs away from the polls and into their house. The mob then set about to destroy the Whig liberty pole which was partially sheathed in iron and could not be easily chopped down. While the Democrats milled around the pole some Whigs opened fire from the house, wounding fifteen or twenty in the crowd and killing one. The infuriated crowd surged on the headquarters, broke in, and beat persons they caught inside and heaped the furniture about the liberty pole to make a pyre. This street fire spread to a block of nearby houses. When the volunteer fire companies arrived, the mob set upon them, beating the firemen, cutting their hoses, and wrecking their carriages. The fire burned throughout the night unattended. Sutherland was re-elected.[6]

Two years later Sutherland fell victim to the continued confusions of Jackson's war on the Bank. He was caught in one of those painful moments in American political history when a politician cannot safely support both the popular enthusiasms and the economic interests of his constituents. Politics in Pennsylvania during the years 1834–6 fragmented over three issues: support of the law establishing free public schools, divisions over the location and number of state canals, opposition or sympathy for Jackson's attack on the Bank of the United States. All these issues split the Democratic party of Pennsylvania. Sutherland's wing of the party favored schools, canals, and the granting of a Pennsylvania charter to the Bank.

Many of the Whigs supported the same program. Because of the Democratic division in 1835 a Whig coalition swept the state's gubernatorial election. Sutherland, who had been under heavy attack from Jackson enthusiasts in Philadelphia, decided to try to switch party allegiance in the hope that he could ride a new wave. The state legislature assisted him by changing the First Congressional District so that it included new territory on the northwest side of town where native millworkers and shopkeepers should have responded to Sutherland's type of Whiggery. The Democrats responded by running a well-known Southwark District Commissioner, Lemuel Paynter (1788–1863), against him. Sutherland's machine delivered his old district to him. He carried Southwark and Moyamensing once more, but he lost in the newly annexed areas.[7] The district then alternated for sixteen years among Democrats, Whigs, and Native Americans until in 1850 a new boss, Democrat Thomas B. Florence (1812–75), took control by reviving Sutherland's old style of friendship to the workingman, attention to patronage and favors, and support for the basic economic interests of the city. Florence was succeeded in turn by the famous speaker of the House of Representatives Samuel Jackson Randall (1828–90), a skillful practitioner of the same style. Altogether, the bosses of Philadelphia's southside democracy, Sutherland, Florence, and Randall, held the Congressional district in steady professional control from 1826 to 1890 with but a single break of sixteen years.[8]

Sutherland's career suggests the new tensions of professional politics. To ensure repeated election to public office the professional must depend upon a mix of popular slogans, local patronage, party discipline, and support for local economic interests. Moreover the professional must maintain this mixture in balance, not being caught, as Sutherland was, with popular enthusiasms overrunning his loyalty to local economic interests. Such a precarious political balance promised weak government for the future of Philadelphia and suggested that such leadership would be slow to respond to change. On the other hand, the rising importance of the professional politicians also meant that it would become increasingly difficult for the city's businessmen to run for office for a term or two in order to accomplish some specific reform. Rather the business specialists would have to seek satisfaction from the political specialists.

Professionalism also manifested itself in the role of the gentleman democrat. The role was not a new one, having been followed by Washington and Jefferson and a number of national figures. In the nineteenth-century city, however, the role took on special significance as the compliment to the new professional boss. Richard Vaux (1816–95), frequent candidate and second mayor of the consolidated city of Philadelphia from 1856 to 1858 was such a figure. A Quaker whose parents were Friends, his father had retired early in life from a merchant career to become a philanthropist. The father is remembered today as a school and prison reformer. The son, Richard Vaux, was educated by tutors and at the Friends Select School, but the pacific teachings of Quakerism seemed to have passed him by. He was a vigorous, direct-action American of the kind so common in the early nineteenth century. After his schooling he read law with a well-known Philadelphia politician and lawyer, and at the age of twenty was admitted to the Philadelphia bar. Before beginning practice, however, he took the aristocratic tour of Europe. He served for a year as private secretary to the American minister at London, but diplomacy did not appeal to him.[9]

Upon returning to Philadelphia in 1839 he found that his friends had nominated him as Democratic candidate for state representative in a hopelessly strong Whig ward (Market Street). Though easily defeated in the election, he continued to be active in local and Democratic politics. After his defeat he became a member of the Board of Comptrollers of the Philadelphia public schools, and from 1841–7 held the judicial office of Recorder for the city. Soon after his appointment as Recorder, the Whigs in the city councils, in a partisan attack, abolished the fees and salary of the office, but Vaux stubbornly served on without compensation.

From 1839 to 1892 he served as an active member of the Board of Governors of the Eastern Penitentiary. His father had been a founder of this inhumane institution, which proved to be a misapplication of Quaker psychology. Richard, a believer in hereditary influence as the source of crime, continued his father's misguided advocacy of solitary confinement as a proper means of reforming criminals—despite mounting evidence that the system drove most prisoners into psychotic states or permanent insanity. A longstanding member of the Girard College board, Richard Vaux helped introduce vocational training into that school's curriculum. He was also an active Mason, eventually Pennsylvania Grand Master, and was a member of numerous organizations.

In politics Vaux was a gentleman champion of the common man and an upholder of the old radical animus against large merchant institutions. He made strong speeches against the "power of corporations," and the "Bank Party," and was always a good, orthodox supporter of President Jackson. Despite increasing criticism of the gang warfare among the fire companies, Vaux remained a staunch friend of these politically influential, working-class and lower-class groups. Indeed, while he was in politics municipal patronage was still too small to support many ward heelers, and as a result much of ward politics was organized around the fire companies. Though a friend of the common man, like most Philadelphians of his age, he was strongly prejudiced against Abolitionism and the Negro. Indeed, around the time of the Civil War he was nicknamed the "Bourbon War Horse" for his mildness towards the South.[10]

Although Vaux began in politics as a gentleman candidate who, the Democrats hoped, could attract votes of the well-to-do in the strongly Whig city, in the end he formed an alliance with Irish politicians and was elected mayor of the consolidated city as the leader of a coalition of local bosses. In style and manner, Vaux was a forerunner of such American gentleman-democrats as Theodore Roosevelt and John F. Kennedy. He favored the athletic image—took ice-cold showers, walked through the streets rather than take a streetcar, and went without a coat in rain and frost. The style suggested a man who would doff his coat, roll up his sleeves, and tackle the commonplace problems of his society.

Vaux's first campaign for mayor (1842) coincided with a nationwide, depression-inspired reaction to twelve years of Jacksonian hegemony in Washington. Moreover, in Philadelphia there had been bickering over the use of the King James Bible in the public schools and a summer race riot. Both these events favored the entrenched Whig party against the minority Democrats. The Democrats hoped that their gentleman candidate could attract some Whigs. His opponent was the incumbent mayor, John M. Scott (1789–1858), a lawyer, frequent city councilor, and the city's first popularly elected mayor. Scott carried all but three of the city's fifteen wards and won easily.[11]

In 1846 Vaux ran again. In this election he faced Philadelphia's perennial Whig mayor, John Swift (mayor 1832–8, 1839–41, 1845–9), a lawyer, club-man, and supporter of Henry Clay who had won respect for his forthright, if not effective, action as leader of the city's watch and constables in past riots.[12] The rise of nativism and the violent anti-Irish riots of 1844 had given rise to a new Native American party and had split off a good number of artisan votes from the Democrats' party. Finally, the preparations and news of the Mexican War during the spring and summer of 1846 over-shadowed local issues. The incumbent was easily swept in again.[13]

For the next few years Vaux ceased to be a candidate. He was not well connected to the rising state Democratic faction of James Buchanan,[14] and within the city of Philadelphia no Democrat could expect to be elected until the city Democrats could be counted with their fellows in the outer districts of Philadelphia County.

The consolidation of all the boroughs and districts of Philadelphia County into one city in 1854 gave Vaux a new opportunity. By this time the national issues of slavery and free soil had subsided briefly and a general revival of nativism stood in their place. Within Philadelphia native Protestant artisans, unskilled workers, and members of the new middle class were in steady conflict with Catholics in general and with the Irish in particular. The Irish had been identified with the violent riots of earlier years, and they were the opponents of temperance reform.[15]

The contest of 1854 was thus between Robert T. Conrad (1810–58), Nativist and former Whig who regarded immigrant paupers as the source of disorder in the city,[16] and Vaux, gentleman democrat, friend of the lower-class fire companies, ally of neighborhood Irish bosses, and symbol of the old radical Revolutionary and Jacksonian tradition of a democratic society open to all. Conrad defeated Vaux 28,883 to 21,020.[17] The day after his defeat Vaux climbed the old statehouse steps to shout his intention to run again.

Mayor Conrad proved a conscientious mayor. He addressed himself to the administrative problems of uniting all the districts of Philadelphia County and established the consolidated police force. He appointed none but native-born Americans to the force, however, a policy which height-ened the tensions between the police and the many Irish fire companies.

Moreover, Conrad's strict enforcement of the Sunday liquor laws aroused widespread resentment from native-born and foreign alike. After one term he retired from office.[18]

In 1856 Richard Vaux and the Democrats faced a winning situation. The Native Americans had aligned themselves with the temperance candidate in the election of county officers the year before and had been soundly defeated. The Whigs and Native Americans were splitting up under the pressure of national free soil and slavery debate. The Republican Party had just been established. Pennsylvania's leading Democrat, Buchanan, was on his way from England to the Democratic convention, where he would be nominated for President of the United States.

Vaux's opponent was Henry D. Moore (1817–87), a former Whig congressman (1849–53) who had been engaged in the mahogany and marble business and who was now running as the Native American candidate.[19] The Whigs at first nominated their own candidate and then withdrew, freeing their supporters to vote as they wished. The issues of Vaux's campaign had an unpleasantly modern ring. As an old Jackson supporter, he would be a friend to the common man. The taxpayer would remember him well because there would be no luxury and extravagance in his administration, only the strictest economy. Finally, while some of his firehouse leaders and local bosses labored in his behalf, his supporters, to show Vaux's opposition to corrupt boss government, picked out a notorious saloon keeper, William McMullen (1826–1901) of Moyamensing, as their target of attack. After his victory, lines of Vaux's supporters seeking jobs with the city filled the Chestnut street sidewalks.[20]

Vaux knew that he could do little as mayor beyond building up the police force. Many of the problems of municipal government lay beyond his reach in the ineffective management of semiautonomous boards for water, gas, schools, and hospitals. He did try to keep his pledge of economy, but when the panic of 1857 struck in the fall, throwing thousands temporarily out of work, he took the traditional mayoral position of approving expenditures for relief and public works to counteract a winter of unemployment.[21]

Most of all Vaux enjoyed his police work, which had been the motive of consolidation and became the specialty of his administration. He abolished his predecessor's objectionable native-birth requirement for police employment and introduced a number of permanent reforms: a police and fire telegraph system, a police section to investigate fires, military drill for the force, a uniform blue coat for all the men, and close inspection of their appearance and work. Vaux acted out the role which journalists later made part of the Teddy Roosevelt legend. He prowled the streets at night checking on his officers, and he joined with them in their legalized war to disperse the gangs of Philadelphia. In later years a story was told about the vigilante methods of his police, in this case an evening's bout with the notorious Schuylkill Rangers.

There was no formal arrest, there were few prisoners in the dock in the mornings; the justices of the peace were not much troubled, but the fellow who was caught never forgot until his dying day the time he fell into the hands of Dick Vaux's police. I remember one night three of the Rangers were surprised, and jumped into the river and swam to a tugboat in the middle of the stream. It was very cold, and they thought that Dick (I was there) and his men would not follow. They were never so much mistaken in all their lives. We got a boat and overtook them. The interview was more muscular than intellectual. The rascals were pretty well satisfied before it was over. So were we. They didn't trouble us again during the administration.[22]

Such a tale is hardly the story of a reformer of great thoroughness; it is the tale of a sporting gentleman doing his best to deal with what was then the most dramatic problem of this city. Yet "Dick Vaux's police" did enjoy some success: they broke up some of the most troublesome criminal gangs; they confined most crime and violence to small areas of the city; they brought the frequent gang fighting of the firehouses under better control, and they began with the police force to make an institution which under a strong management during the Civil War prevented the sort of outbreaks which wracked New York.[23]

In his campaign for reelection in 1858 opponents questioned the effectiveness of his police management. There had been complaints throughout his administration of police inefficiency and of the failure of the mayor to discharge incompetent officers. Some felt that a full-time police force cost more than they wished to pay in taxes. The traditional methods of the sheriff's posse and the watch were, after all, much cheaper. More important than such complaints was the fact that the anti-Democratic forces were recombining in a more effective political grouping. In the spring of 1858, there was a fusion of Republicans and Native Americans on a compromise platform which favored the tariff, free soil, restrained opposition to foreign paupers, and mild opposition to Negroes. A Whig, Alexander Henry (1823–83), defeated Vaux 33,159 to 29,120.[24]

On balance, Richard Vaux, though a professional who remained active in politics, did not enjoy a successful career. Compared to such later gentlemen professionals as Boise Penrose (1860–1921), who was to dominate all of Pennsylvania, Vaux's years as Recorder, school board member, and one term as mayor seem modest in the extreme. His contributions to the city, however, were substantial. During the years of Philadelphia's most intense nativism and anti-Catholicism he steadfastly played his role of gentleman-democrat, embodying by his candidacy and his actions as mayor his city's traditional goal of an open society. Though playing an old role, Vaux also was a creature of the transition to the new orientations of big-city politics. His active political years, from 1839 to 1858, coincided with the shift in ideology of Philadelphia politics from the old eighteenth- and early-nineteenth-century controversies over the representation of the mechanic and the laboring man in government to the new controversies over ethnic representation and ethnic power.

Vaux's career, like that of Joel Barlow Sutherland, also illustrates the growing constraints that professional politics were to impose on the city. Vaux's 1856 election resulted in large measure from a successful coalition of local bosses and firehouse gangs. To maintain such coalitions, lines of supporters seeking jobs had to be given work with the city. Neither Vaux nor his opponents could ignore that need. The price of such a pattern of professional politics is well known to American history: weak, corrupt, unimaginative municipal government. From the 1890s until the Great Depression reformers in every city in the nation labored against the consequences of this system of local government. As an old man Vaux himself led a group of citizens in an attempt to undo the then fully apparent disorders created by boss politics. A new charter was passed in 1885, but no basic reform resulted. No group of merchants came forward to lead the city. The new businessmen of the 1880s, like Jay Cooke before them, neither knew their city nor cared about it. Without such leadership, however, the voters of Philadelphia would not trust their government with large sums of money, big projects, or major innovations. Pinchpenny, corrupt, and unresponsive government ruled the city for the next sixty, if not one hundred, years.

NOTES

1. The lawyer politicians of the pre-Civil War era showed more local concern and were more closely tied to the city than later corporate lawyers. For example George M. Dallas (1792–1864) and John M. Read (1797–1874). The era of small-scale personal journalism also produced the transitional figures of journalist-politicians. For example, James N. Barker (1784–1858), mayor 1819–21; Robert T. Conrad (1810–58), mayor 1854–6; Joseph R. Chandler (1792–1880), congressman 1849–55.

2. Sutherland's biography must be patched together out of fragments. *Dictionary of American Biography;* Charles Sutherland, *A Memoir of the Life and Services of Joel Barlow Sutherland, First President of the Society of the War of 1812* (n.d., n.p.) pamphlet, Pennsylvania Historical Society, published privately by his son, pp. 5–9; Scharf and Westcott, *History of Philadelphia,* I, 588, 592, 604–8; John R. Commons, ed., *History of Labor,* I, 194–205; Snyder, *Jacksonian Heritage,* 48–50, 86; Louis H. Arky, "The Mechanic's Union of Trade Associations," *Pennsylvania Magazine,* LXXVI (April 1952), 165–74.

3. Richard I. Shelling, "Philadelphia and the Agitation in 1825 for the Pennsylvania Canal," *Pennsylvania Magazine,* LXII (April 1938), 175–204.

4. Until the boundaries were changed before the 1836 election Sutherland's First Pennsylvania Congressional District consisted of Southwark, Moyamensing, Passyunk, the west Philadelphia towns of Blockley and Kingsessing, and the three southside Philadelphia wards of Cedar, New Market, and Pine. *Congressional Directory of the Twenty-Third Congress, First Session* (Washington, D.C., 1834). The characterization of this district rests upon guesses from extrapolating back from the 1860 U.S. Census ward details to the thirties. In 1860 the Irish were still very much concentrated at the northern edge of the district in wards 4, 7, and 8. They had not penetrated the heart of Sutherland's old area of popularity. A sample of the occupations on the southside of Philadelphia taken from an 1840 street directory (Table XI) confirms the marine trade, artisan and unskilled characterization of most of the district. Similar hints can be found in *Hazard's U.S. Commercial and Statistical Register*, IV (January–July 1841), 394, and Norman J. Johnston, "The Caste and Class of the Urban Form of Historic Philadelphia," *Journal of the American Institute of Planners*, XXXII (November 1966), 334–9.

5. In his first attempt Sutherland was defeated by the well-known philanthropist and school reformer, Samuel Breck (1771–1862). Breck, a Federalist, served one term in Congress only.

6. Election, Snyder, *op. cit.*, pp. 46–9; Scharf and Westcott, *op. cit.*, I, 638–9. Two years later, as a result of this election riot, the state legislature passed an act indemnifying the owner of the houses that had been destroyed and making the city liable for all future damage to property caused by rioting. Act, March 11, 1836.

7. Snyder, *op. cit.*, pp. 53–60, 75–81, 85–6; district boundaries and votes, *Public Ledger*, October 13, 1836; Paynter, U.S. Congress, Joint Committee on Printing, *Biographical Dictionary of American Congresses 1774–1961* (Washington, D.C., 1961).

8. Paynter served only two terms and then retired because of ill health. He was succeeded by Charles Brown (1779–1883), Democrat, a cordwood dealer, city councilor and state senator. In 1842 Edward Joy Morris (1815–81), Whig, a lawyer and state representative, defeated Brown. In the next election, 1844, Lewis Charles Levin (1808–60), Native American, a lawyer and journalist, seized the seat and held it for three terms until he was defeated by Florence, a journalist, militia officer and professional Democratic politician. In 1862 Randall, who began his career in the legislature as a dealer in streetcar franchises, defeated Florence and held the seat until his death in 1890. It was, after the Civil War, the only Democratic seat in Philadelphia.

9. Vaux's biography must be patched together from fragments. *Dictionary of American Biography;* Richard Vaux, *Address on the Anniversary of the Victory at New Orleans, January 8, 1840* (Philadelphia, 1840, pamphlet, University of Pennsylvania Law Library), p. 6; Richard Vaux, *Address to the Philadelphia Hose Company* (Philadelphia, 1851, pamphlet, Pennsylvania Historical Society), p. 18; Scharf and Westcott, *op. cit.*, II, 1542–4; and the Pennsylvania Historical Society has some letters and odds and ends.

10. When Kansas exploded Vaux became a Douglas rather than a Buchanan Democrat, William Dusinberre, *Civil War Issues in Philadelphia* (Philadelphia, 1965), pp. 68–9, 78–9, 86–9, 107.

11. Scott 6,145, Vaux 5,137, *Public Ledger*, October 13, 1842. John M. Scott was a native of New York and Princeton graduate who came to Philadelphia in 1807 where he practiced law. He was a member of the Second City Troop, mayor 1841–4, and had been President of the Common Council. John R. Young, *Memorial History of the City of Philadelphia* (New York, 1895), I, 499.

12. John Swift (1790–1873), biographical sketch in Thomas Willing Balch, "The Swift Family of Philadelphia," *Pennsylvania Magazine,* XXX (April 1906), 150–52.

13. Swift 5,562, Vaux 3,402, Peter A. Browne, Native American, 3,164, *Public Ledger,* October 15, 1846. Vaux carried only the Upper Delaware Ward, Browne took the North Mulberry Ward where Vaux had been strong in 1844.

14. Vaux and John M. Read had attempted to start a Democratic campaign for General Zachary Taylor and when that failed they reluctantly supported Buchanan until the Kansas issue. Snyder, *op. cit.,* pp. 171, 209, 211.

15. Judges of the Quarter sessions had been complaining of "rum holes," while the commissioners of the Irish District of Moyamensing saw Sunday closing as the working of "the same fanatical, persecuting spirit . . . that prompted the Puritans of Massachusetts . . . to maim, maltreat, and murder those who differed with them in religious belief." *Public Ledger,* December 7, 1847; prohibition, Oberholtzer, *History of Philadelphia,* II, 318; resurgence of nativism, Sister M. Theopane Geary, *A History of Third Parties in Pennsylvania 1840–1860* (Washington, D.C., 1938), 166–9; Erwin S. Bradley, *The Triumph of Militant Republicanism* (Philadelphia, 1964), p. 32–3.

16. Howard O. Sprogle, *The Philadelphia Police* (Philadelphia, 1887), p. 100.

17. *Public Ledger,* June 7, 1854.

18. Scharf and Westcott, *op. cit.,* I, 718–20.

19. *Biographical Dictionary of American Congresses.*

20. McMullen, *Public Ledger,* obit, April 1, 1901; election, *Public Ledger,* May 7, 1856; Scharf and Westcott, *op. cit.,* I, 721–2.

21. Mayor of Philadelphia, *Second Annual Message of the Honorable Richard Vaux* (Philadelphia, 1858), pp. 6–13, 75–114; Benjamin J. Klebaner, "The Home Relief Controversy in Philadelphia, 1782–1861," *Pennsylvania Magazine,* LXXVIII (October 1954), 421–3; Austin E. Hutcheson, "Philadelphia and the Panic of 1857," *Pennsylvania History,* III (July 1936), 182–94; Scharf and Westcott, *op. cit.,* I, 721–7.

22. Quotation from Sprogle, *op. cit.,* p. 108.

23. *Ibid.,* pp. 105–13; Dusinberre, *op. cit.,* pp. 177–90.

24. Dusinberre, *op. cit.,* pp. 77–8; Scharf and Westcott, *op. cit.,* I, 728; vote, *Public Ledger,* May 12, 1858; Alexander Henry as mayor, Winnifred K. McKay, "Philadelphia During the Civil War," *Pennsylvania Magazine,* LXX (January 1946), 5–42.

21. BOSS COX'S CINCINNATI
A Study in Urbanization and Politics, 1880–1914

Zane L. Miller

Many observers of the turn-of-the-century urban scene have depicted bossism as one of the great unmitigated evils of the American city, as a tyrannical, authoritarian, relentlessly efficient and virtually invulnerable political system. Between 1904 and 1912, for example, George B. Cox was castigated by writers in four national magazines. Gustav Karger called him the "Proprietor of Cincinnati." Lincoln Steffens declared that "Cox's System" was "one great graft," "the most perfect thing of the kind in this country." Frank Parker Stockbridge claimed that "The Biggest Boss of Them All" had an organization "more compact and closely knit than any of the political machines which have dominated New York, Philadelphia, Chicago, St. Louis or San Francisco." And George Kibbe Turner concluded that in the 1890s "the man from Dead Man's Corner . . . seated himself over the city of Cincinnati. For twenty years he remained there—a figure like no other in the United States, or in the world." Yet these knowledgable and sensitive journalists obscured as much as they revealed about the nature of Queen City politics in the Progressive era. A new kind of city had developed, and "the boss" comprised only a fraction of its novel political system.

Paradoxically, Cox and his machine were produced by, fed on, and ultimately helped dispel the spectacular disorder which engulfed Cincinnati in the late-nineteenth century and threatened the very survival of the democratic political process. In these years, increasing industrialization, technological innovations in communication and transportation—especially the coming of rapid transit—and continued foreign and domestic migration had reversed the physical pattern of the mid-century walking city and transformed Cincinnati into a physically enlarged, divided, and potentially explosive metropolis.

Old citizens were shocked as familiar landmarks and neighborhoods vanished. By 1900, railroads and warehouses had monopolized the Ohio River bottoms. The financial and retail districts had moved up into the Basin around Fountain Square, the focus of the street railway system; new club theater, and tenderloin districts had developed; and industries had plunged up Mill Creek Valley, converting Mohawk-Brighton into "the undisputed industrial bee-hive of the Great Queen City of the West," surrounding once fashionable Dayton Street, creating a new community called Ivorydale, and reaching out to the villages of Norwood and Oakley in search of cheap land, ready access to railroads, and less congested and more cheerful surroundings.

The Over-the-Rhine entertainment section along Vine Street became tawdry with commercialism. It now had, complained one habitué, "all the tarnished tinsel of a Bohemianism with the trimmings of a gutter and the morals of a sewer"—a repulsive contrast, he felt, to "the old-time concert and music halls . . . where one could take wife, sister, or sweetheart and feel secure . . . that not one obnoxious word would profane their ears."

The fashionable residential districts which had flanked the center of the walking city began to disintegrate. One family after another fled the East End for the hills around the Basin, leaving only a small coterie led by the Charles P. Tafts to stave off the advance of factories and slums. The elite West End seemed to disappear overnight. "It "did not go down imperceptibly," recalled one old resident. "It went to ruin almost as if a bombshell sent it to destruction."

The Hilltops, at mid-century the private preserve of cemeteries, colleges, and a handful of wealthy families, became the prime residential district in the new city. The crush to get in generated new tensions. In 1899 one observer acidly remarked: "when rapid transit came the Hebrews . . . flocked to" Walnut Hills

until it was known by the name of New Jerusalem. Avondale was then heralded as the suburb of deliverance, but again rapid transit brought the wealthy Hebrews . . . in numbers greater than the flock of crows that every morning and evening darkens her skies, until now it has been facetiously said that the congregation has assembled in force and . . . when Avondale is roofed over the synagogue will be complete.

The diffusion of wealthy families, the reduction in casual social and business contacts, and the construction of new communities made ardent joiners of the Hilltops elite. Each neighborhood had an improvement association, and between 1880 and 1905 five new businessmen's organizations devoted to boosting the city's lethargic economy had appeared. In the same period six social clubs opened downtown facilities, and three country clubs were started. By 1913, moreover, there were twenty-two exclusive clubs and patriotic societies and innumerable women's groups. These developments helped counteract the disruptive effects of the "country movement," as one visitor labeled it, which was "so general that church-going became an affair of some difficulty" and "society itself . . . more or less disintegrated."

But not all those moving out were affluent. Liberated by rapid transit, skilled and semiskilled workers and moderately prosperous professional and white-collar men with life savings, the courage to take out a mortgage, an equity in a building and loan association, or a willingness to rent a flat in a double or triple decker, also fled the Basin. They took refuge in a no-man's-land between the center of the city and the Hilltops frontier which was similar to an area dubbed the Zone of Emergence by Boston social workers.

Zone residents formed what the Cincinnati *Post* referred to as "the so-called middle class . . . , the class that makes any city . . . what it is . . . [,] the class that takes in the great body of people between wealth and poverty" and builds up "many organizations, societies, associations, fraternities and clubs that bring together people who are striving upward, trying to uplift themselves, and hence human society."

They, too, found life in the new city a novel experience. A retired leather factory porter who moved into the Zone lamented:

When I lived down on Richmond in a little house we cooked the corn beef and cabbage in the house and ate in there, and when we wanted to go to the toilet we went out into the yard, now I live in a fine house, I am made to eat . . . out in the yard, and when I want to go to the toilet I have to go into the house.

Graham R. Taylor had noted that since most Zone residents commuted they suffered a severe "dislocation of the normal routine of factory and home": they had to adjust to "the need for travel and its curtailment of leisure and income . . . ," to eating lunches away from home, to doing without "customary city facilities," and to knowing the feeling of "isolation from their fellows." Price Hill—like the rest of the Zone a heavily Catholic area—felt itself conspicuously cut off. In the 1890s the editor of the *Catholic-Telegraph,* denouncing the traction company as the "octopus," joined the Price Hill Improvement Association in begging both city and traction company officials to bring the area "within range of the civilized world" and suggested secession as a means of dramatizing to the "people east of Millcreek" that a new public school, "granted by the unbounded munificence of the City of Cincinnati," did not amount to a redemption of the city's annexation pledges.

The exodus, however, did not depopulate the Basin. Instead, a great residential circle formed around the central business district. It filled with newcomers and those who lacked the means to get out—rural whites and Negroes from the South, Germans, Irish, Greeks, Italians, and Jews from Eastern Europe. Working at the poorest-paying jobs available, they were jammed into the most congested quarters. The Circle led all other areas of the city in arrests, mortality, and disease.

Although the pressure to escape was enormous, the barriers were formidable. Ignorant of the ways of the city, as an Associated Charities report put it, Circle dwellers had to be "shown how to buy, how to cook, how to make the home attractive, how to find employment." Many, "utterly friendless and discouraged," succumbed to "the damnable absence of want or desire" and grew "indifferent . . . to their own elevation." Plagued by "physical bankruptcy," they found it difficult to find and hold jobs, let alone form and maintain the kind of organizations which enabled Zone residents to shield themselves from economic disaster, legal pitfalls, social isolation, and apathy.

The immediate impact of the emergence of the new city pushed Cincinnati to the brink of anarchy. In March 1884, the *Enquirer* complained that the police had failed to choke off a crime wave although, in the last year alone, there had been twelve arrests for malicious shooting, twenty-nine for malicious cutting, forty-seven for cutting with intent to wound, 284 for shooting with intent to kill, ninety-two for murder and manslaughter, and 948 for carrying a concealed weapon. The total number of arrests came to 56,784. The city's population was 250,000. Later that same month, a lynch mob descended on the county jail. While police and militia fought off the mob, gangs looted stores and shops on the fringe of the downtown district. In three days of riot the courthouse was burned to the ground, fifty-four people were killed, and an estimated 200 people wounded.

During the fall elections, violence erupted in the lower wards; two policemen and one Negro were killed. Congressman Benjamin Butterworth remarked that he had "never witnessed anywhere such coarse brutality and such riotous demonstrations. . . ." Cincinnati, he concluded, "seems . . . doomed to perdition."

Less than two years later the city faced another major crisis. On May 1, 1886, Cincinnati workers joined in nationwide demonstrations for the eight-hour day. These were followed by a series of strikes. The militia was called out, and for two weeks the city resembled an armed camp. Only the show of force and, perhaps, the memory of the courthouse catastrophe prevented another riot.

Yet labor remained restive, and a rash of strikes followed. By 1892, the paternalistic system which had dominated the breweries was smashed. And in 1894, Judge William Howard Taft spent the hot days of June and July "trying to say nothing to reporters" and "issuing injunctions" in an effort to control and prevent the railroad strike from leading to mass violence.

The Sunday-closing question was another explosive issue. The *Post*, the *Catholic-Telegraph*, a Committee of Five Hundred, and many Protestant clergymen all leveled scathing attacks on the continental Sabbath. "Sunday in Cincinnati," asserted one Methodist minister, "is a high carnival of drunkenness, base sensuality, reeking debauchery and bloody, often fatal crime." Other spokesmen tied the open Sunday to anarchism, atheism, corrupt politicians, a decadent daily press, indifferent public officials, and the ruthless exploitation of labor. "The modern Puritan," insisted Charles P. Taft, "intends to rise up and oppose to the uttermost this kind of Sunday."

When, in 1889, the mayor announced his intention to enforce the Sunday-closing law for saloons, the city almost faced another riot. Some 1,000 saloonkeepers vowed to ignore the new policy. When a cadre of police and firemen marched over the Rhine to close Kissell's saloon, an unruly crowd gathered, epithets were hurled, but no violence occurred. Kissell's was closed; the "era of the back door," with "front doors locked and curtains up, but back doors widened," had opened.

These spectacular outbreaks plus other pressures overwhelmed city hall. Indeed, scarcely a residential area, economic interest, or social or occupational group was left unscathed by the multidimensional disorder. As the physical area of the city expanded, officials were besieged by demands for the extension, improvement, and inauguration of public services of all kinds and for lower taxes. Simultaneously, the relative decline of the city heightened the urgency of the agitation. Municipal institutions and agencies, established to meet the needs of the walking city, became overburdened, outmoded, and dilapidated.

The new city, with old ways shattered, provided a fertile breeding ground for turmoil and discontent and, as it turned out, for innovation and creative reconstruction. Initially, however, this unprecedented change accompanied by unprecedented demands for government action produced only the hope of reform. In 1885, on the eve of the repudiation of a Democratic administration, William Howard Taft predicted that "the clouds are beginning to break over this Sodom of ours and the sun of decency is beginning to dispel the moral miasma that has rested on us now for so many years. It's the beginning of an era of reform."

Yet for almost a decade no party could put together a decisive ruling majority. The city's political processes seemed frozen by a paralyzing factionalism. The division of the city into residential districts which roughly coincided with socioeconomic lines made it difficult for the wealthy and well-educated to keep in contact with and control ward politics. As a result, extreme factionalism developed which could, apparently, be surmounted only by appealing to a host of neighborhood leaders and by constructing alliances which crossed party lines.

According to close observers, the chief products of this system were the use of money in city conventions and the rise of what Charles P. Taft called the "bummer," a "queer creature" who "evolves somehow from the slums. . . ." In youth "a bootblack, a newsboy or a general loafer," he matured into "an Arab" who needed only "a good standing with a saloon that has a fine layout during the day." A "hustler at the polls and conventions," the bummer was in such demand that he could accept money from competing candidates, thus lengthening the convention and contributing to interfactional dealing. After studying the influence of the "bummer," Taft gloomily concluded that the "day of pure politics can never be . . . until a riot, a plague or flood kills off all the ward bummers."

By 1897, however, and without divine intervention, all this had changed. In January of that year, three months before the city election, the *Post* gravely announced its intention to describe "impassionately and without bias the means employed" in Cincinnati's "superior and unrecorded government." It was controlled by "the boss, whose power is absolute"—George B. Cox.

The *Post's* analysis closely paralleled those made after the turn of the century. It dissected the patronage system, outlined the sources of financial support, and noted the attempted appeasement of the city's various special groups—the soldiers, the Germans, the Republican clubs, the Reform Jews, the legal and medical professions, the socially prominent Hilltops businessmen, and certain cooperative Democrats. It excitedly reported the effectiveness of the organization's intelligence system, the way the "plugger" and the "knocker" wore "beaten paths to the office of the boss to urge the appointment of this man, the discharge of that [,] or to report some feature of misconduct or expression. . . ." The paper noted that Cox was always available for consultation with any citizen regardless of station or status and that he had been little more than one of several important factional leaders until, in 1886, Governor Joseph B. Foraker selected him to serve as chief adviser on patronage and political affairs in Hamilton County.

Foraker made a shrewd choice; Cox had grown up with the new city and received a liberal education in its ways. The son of British immigrants, he was born in 1853 and reared in the Eighteenth Ward, a district which by the 1880s contained fashionable as well as slum housing, factories, and its share of saloons and brothels. His father died when Cox was eight. Successively, Cox worked as a bootblack, newsboy, lookout for a gambling joint, grocery deliveryman, bartender, and tobacco salesman. His school principal, who later became superintendent of schools, claimed that Cox was frequently in boyish trouble in classes, exhibited an "undisguised love for his mother," and "never lied . . . bore malice, sulked, whined or moped." Cox had also been exposed to religion. Although not a churchgoer, as an adult he had, according to one journalist, "dormant powerful sentiments, which rest on foundations of the firmest faith."

In the mid-1870s Cox acquired a saloon in his home neighborhood. He entered politics and served on the city council from 1878 until 1885 when, after joining forces with the Republican reform mayoralty candidate, he ran unsuccessfully for county clerk. He tried for the same post in 1888, failed, and never again stood for public office.

At that time, moving away politically from the Circle, Cox worked with George Moerlein, perhaps the strongest of the GOP professionals in the Zone. In 1890, he and Moerlein quarreled over patronage; and in the city convention of 1891, Cox was able, with the support of the Blaine Club, a kind of political settlement house that he had helped to establish, to defeat Moerlein's candidate for police judge and nominate his own man. Moerlein men now became Cox men. So, too, did Charles P. Taft and the *Times-Star*, which had been one of the last, the most influential, and the most outspoken of Cox's critics in the Hilltops Republican ranks. It accepted Cox, the paper announced, to secure a "New Order" for Cincinnati. And the president of the gas company, sensing the political drift, confided to his diary that he had "concluded [an] arrangement with Geo. B. Cox for services at $3500 per year quarterly to last for three years." In the spring election of 1894 the Republicans carried the city with a plurality of over 6,500 votes, the first decisive municipal election in a decade. In 1897, Cox was the honest broker in a coalition composed of Circle and Zone Negroes, Zone politicians, the gas and traction companies, and Hilltops Republican reformers.

Election returns after 1885 disclose a clear pattern. The GOP won five successive contests by uniting powerful Hilltops support with enough strength in the Zone to overcome the Democratic grip on the Circle. Until 1894 the margins of victory were perilously thin. The substantial triumph of that year merely marked the completion of the alliance which pitted a united periphery against the center of the city.

The heart of the Republican "New Order" coalition, and the critical factor in the election of 1894, was its appeal to voters in the Hilltops fringe who demanded order and reform. To satisfy the Hilltops, Cox and his associates eliminated the bummer, provided brief and decorous conventions, enfranchised Negroes by suppressing violence at the polls, reduced the rapid turnover in office, and cut down the incidence of petty graft and corporation raiding.

Moreover, the "machine" heeded the advice of its reform allies from the Hilltops. Cox accepted the secret ballot, voter registration, and a series of state laws which, though retaining the mayor-council form of government with ward representation, were designed to give the city a stable and more centralized government. The administrations which he indorsed started to build a professional police force, expanded and reequipped the fire department, pushed through a $6 million waterworks program, renovated municipal institutions, supported the growth of the University of Cincinnati, launched extensive street-paving and sewer-constructing projects, and tried to reduce the smoke problem and expand the city's park acreage. They also opened the door to housing regulation, suppressed the Sunday saloon, flagrant public gambling and disorderly brothels (the city was never really closed), began to bring order into the chaotic public-utilities field by favoring privately owned, publicly regulated monopolies under progressive management, and succeeded in keeping the tax rate low. The Republican regime, in short, brought positive government to Cincinnati.

While this program also won votes in the Zone, it was not the sole basis for the party's popularity there. Many of the lieutenants and captains closest to Cox were Zone residents. They composed a colorful group known variously as "the gang," "the sports," or the "bonifaces"—a clique which met nightly Over-the-Rhine either at Schubert and Pels, where each had a special beer mug with his name gilded on it, or at the round table in Wielert's beer garden. Three of them owned or operated combination saloons, gambling joints, and dance halls; one was prominent in German charitable associations and the author of several textbooks used in the elementary schools; another served twenty consecutive terms as president of the Hamilton County League of Building Associations; and one was a former catcher for the Cincinnati Redlegs.

Their tastes, behavior, and attitudes were conveniently summarized in the biographical sketches of ward leaders and city officials in the 1901 *Police and Municipal Guide*. All were characterized as friendly, well-known, "All Around Good-Fellows" who liked a story, belonged to several social and fraternal groups, gave generously to charity, and treated the poor and sick with special kindness. They were all among the most ardent supporters of any project to boost the city.

Cox is pictured in the *Guide* as an adherent to the code of the Zone who had risen to the top. He was a *bon vivant* who enjoyed good cigars and good jokes, a man of wealth whose recently completed Clifton mansion was luxuriously decorated and adorned with expensive works of art, a man of impressive but quiet and private charity. Above all, he was true to his word, loyal to his friends, yet quick to reprimand and replace those who betrayed his trust by misusing public office.

Cox and his top civil servants—surrounded by a motley crowd of newspaper reporters, former boxers and ball players, vaudeville and burlesque performers, and other Vine Street characters—provided an attractive model for men awed by the glamor, wealth, and power which was so visible yet so elusive in the new city. Cox's opponents in the Zone seldom attacked him or this inside group directly. Even in the heat of the 1897 campaign, the *Volksfreund*, the German Catholic Democratic daily, carefully described Cox as an "amiable man" who had to be "admired" for his "success" and, either ignoring or unaware of the process of negotiation and mediation by which he ruled, criticized him only for his illiberality in imposing "dictatorial methods" on the GOP. Indeed, most Zone residents, like those of the Hilltops, found it difficult to object to a government which seemed humane, efficient, and progressive.

Yet it would be a mistake to overestimate the strength of the "New Order" Republican coalition. Its victories from 1885 to 1894 were won by perilously close pluralities. The organization, moreover, failed to carry a referendum for the sale of the city-owned Southern Railroad in 1896 and lost the municipal contest in 1897 to a reform fusion ticket, and the fall elections of 1897, 1898, and 1899 to the Democrats. In all these reversals, crucial defections occurred in both the Hilltops and the Zone. Skittish voters grew indignant over alleged corruption, outraged by inaction on the traction and gas questions, piqued by the rising cost of new city projects, annoyed by the slow expansion of the educational program, or uneasy over the partial sacrifice of democracy to efficiency within the Republican organization.

Thereafter, however, the Republicans rallied and won three of the next four city elections by unprecedented margins. The strategy and tactics remained essentially the same. Although not wholly averse to raising national issues, Cox's group gave local affairs the most emphasis. The organization was occasionally purged of its less savory elements. Cox and his Zone advisors continued to consult with their Hilltops allies on nominations. The party promised and, in fact, tried to deliver order and reform. Without abolishing ward repesentation in the city council, it strengthened the mayor and streamlined the administration. The party also broadened and deepened its program as civic associations, women's clubs, social workers, social gospellers, and spokesmen for the new unionism—all novel forces in urban politics—expanded and elaborated their demands.

But voting patterns underwent a fundamental and, for the GOP, an ultimately disastrous change. By 1903 the Republicans dominated the entire city, carrying not only the Zone and Hilltops but also the center. The Circle was now the invincible bulwark of Cox's power.

There were several factors involved in the conversion of Circle Democrats to Republicanism. First, Cox had extensive personal contacts with them which dated back to his unsuccessful races for county clerk in the 1880s. Second, the Democrats had been unable to put down factionalism. By the late 1890s there were two reform elements in the party, both of which belabored the regulars from the center of the city as tainted with corruption, too cozy with Cox, and perhaps worst of all, as a discredit and burden to the party because they wore the charred shirt of the courthouse riot.

In the wake of the fusionist victory of 1897, Mike Mullen, the leader of a riverfront Democratic ward, explained why he would henceforth work with the Republican party.

I have worked hard [for the Democratic party] have suffered much and have won for it many victories. Yet all the while there was a certain element . . . that looked on me with distrust. . . . [L]eaders of the Fusionist Party did not think enough of me to let me look after the voting in my own ward, but sent down a lot of people to watch the count. That decided me.

He was later joined by Colonel Bob O'Brien who, like Mullen, specialized in Christmas turkey, soupline, and family-service politics. These Democrats led their constituents into the Republican fold.

It was this alliance with the Circle which ultimately destroyed Cox. Anti-machine spokesmen were convinced that they had to educate the city before they could redeem it. They felt, too, that politics was a potent educational tool. But campaigns had to be spectacular in order to engage the voters' attention and participation. As A. Julius Freiberg notes, the "psychology" of the electorate was such that years of "speaking, writing, explaining, even begging and imploring" had been "to no purpose." The "reformer and his fellow students may sit about the table and evolve high principles for action, but the people . . . will not be fed by those principles unless there is a dramatic setting, and the favorite dramatic setting is the killing of a dragon." And all the people "love the dramatic; not merely the poor, but the rich, and the middle class as well." All that was needed was a situation which would enable the right man to "bring to book the boss himself."

Reformers hammered relentlessly at the theme that Cox was not a good boss; he was the head of a "syndicate" which included the worst products of slum life. In "that part of the city where vice and infamy hold high revel," went one version of the charge, "the boss-made ticket finds its most numerous supporters. Every dive keeper, every creature who fattens upon the wages of sin . . . , all the elements at war with society have enlisted." Men "who claim to be respectable," the chief "beneficiaries of this unholy alliance . . . , go down into the gutter and accept office from hands that are reeking with the filth of the slums." Worse still, this "alliance of the hosts of iniquity with the greed of special privilege and ambition for power and place" plays so successfully "upon the prejudices and . . . superstition of the many that wrong is often espoused by those who in the end are the victims of the wrong."

The reformers also impugned Cox's personal integrity. Democratic County Prosecutor Henry T. Hunt secured evidence that Cox had perjured himself in 1906 when he said he had not received a cent of some $250,000 of interest on public funds which Republican county treasurers had been paid by bankers. In the spring of 1911, Hunt and the grand jury indicted Cox and 123 others during a broad investigation of politics, corruption, and vice.

Finally, Hunt, stressing the issue of moral indignation, ran for mayor in the fall of 1911 on a Democratic reform ticket. Using the moral rhetoric of the muckraker, Hunt and his associates tied bossism, the chaos, poverty, and vice of the slums, and the malefactors of great wealth together and pictured them as a threat to the welfare of the whole city. Once again the Hilltops and Zone voted for order and reform. Hunt's progressive coalition swept the periphery, lost only in the Circle wards, and won the election.

By that time, however, Cox was no longer boss. President Taft and Charles P. Taft had wanted Cox to step aside as early as 1905, but they found him indispensable. After the grand jury revelations, however, they were able to convince the "bonifaces" that Cox was a liability. With the organization against him, Cox retired. For a time, he insisted that his two chief assistants, August Herrmann and Rudolph Hynicka, should also quit, apparently convinced that they, like himself, could no longer command the confidence of the periphery. Charles P. Taft's *Times-Star* agreed. The two men, backed by the Blaine Club, merely resigned their official party positions but refused to get out of politics entirely.

What, then, was Cox's role in politics and government in the new city? He helped create and manage a voluntary political-action organization which bridged the racial and cultural chasms between the Circle, Zone, and Hilltops. He and his allies were able to bring positive and moderate reform government to Cincinnati and to mitigate the conflict and disorder which accompanied the emergence of the new city. With the crisis atmosphere muted, ardent reformers could develop more sophisticated programs and agitate, educate, and organize without arousing the kind of divisive, emotional, and hysterical response which had immobilized municipal statesmen in the 1880s. In the process, while battering at the boss, the slums, and the special-privilege syndicate, they shattered the bonds of confidence which linked the Zone "bonifaces" and the moderate reformers of the Hilltops to Cox's organization. Cox, it seems, said more than he realized when, in 1892, he remarked that a boss was "not necessarily a public enemy."

22. SOCIAL AND STRUCTURAL REFORM
Mayors and Municipal Government

Melvin G. Holli

Hazen Pingree's brand of social reform—whose objective was to lower utility rates for the consumer and which attempted to place a larger share of the municipal tax burden on large corporations—was not the prevailing mood of urban reform in late-nineteenth- and early-twentieth-century America. Far more prevalent in the programs of large-city mayors who earned the epithet "reformer" was the effort to change the structure of municipal government, to eliminate petty crime and vice, and to introduce the business system of the contemporary corporation into municipal government. Charter tinkering, elaborate audit procedures, and the drive to impose businesslike efficiency upon city government were the stock-in-trade of this type of urban executive. Mayors of this kind of reform persuasion could be found in New York, Brooklyn, Buffalo, San Francisco, and countless other cities.

Although most of these structural reformers did not articulate their positions as eloquently as Seth Low or attempt to install business methods as ruthlessly as John Purroy Mitchel, they all shared a certain style, a number of common assumptions about the cause of municipal misgovernment, and, in some instances, a conviction about which class was best fitted to rule the city. Few of them were as blatantly outspoken in their view of democracy as Samuel S. McClure, the publisher of the leading muckrake journal. He instructed Lincoln Steffens to prove that popular rule was a failure and that cities should be run by a dictatorship of wise and strong men, such as Samuel S. McClure or Judge Elbert Gary. Similarly New York's former reform mayor Abram Hewitt asserted in 1901 that "ignorance should be excluded from control, [and] the city business should be carried on by trained experts selected upon some other principle than popular suffrage."[1]

None of the structural reformers had the unqualified faith in the ability of the masses to rule themselves intelligently that social reformers Hazen S. Pingree, Samuel "Golden Rule" Jones, or Tom L. Johnson did. "I have come to lean upon the common people as the real foundation upon which good government must rest," Pingree told the Nineteenth Century Club in

1897. In a statement that represented more than a rhetorical flourish, "Golden Rule" Jones chastised Reverend Josiah Strong for his distrust of the masses and told him that the "voice of the people is the voice of God." Tom Johnson, asserted Brand Whitlock, knew that "the cure for the ills of democracy was not less democracy, as so many people were always preaching, but more democracy." When Johnson was defeated by the Cleveland electorate at the very pinnacle of one of the most productive urban reform careers in the nation, he told Whitlock, "The people are probably right."[2]

The structural reform movement was in sharp contrast to the democratic mood of such a statement. It represented instead the first wave of prescriptive municipal government which placed its faith in rule by educated, upper-class Americans and, later, by municipal experts rather than the lower classes. The installation in office of men of character, substance, and integrity was an attempt to impose middle-class and patrician ideals upon the urban masses. The movement reached its height in the second and third decades of the twentieth century with the city-manager and city-commissioner forms of government, which called for the hiring of non-partisan experts to decide questions hitherto viewed as resolvable only by the political process. Like the structural reform movement of the late-nineteenth-century, the city-manager movement reflected an implicit distrust of popular democracy.[3]

New York's Mayor William F. Havemeyer was a prototype of the twentieth-century structural reformers. Having inherited a substantial fortune, he retired from the sugar refining business at the age of forty and devoted most of his career to public service. Elected mayor in 1872 during the public exposure of the Tweed ring, Havemeyer was a reformer who championed "clean government," "economy," and the business class point of view. Obsessed with tax cuts and retrenchment, he and his fiscal watchdog, city treasurer Andrew H. Green, cut wages on public works and demanded elaborate procedures to account for all petty expenditures of public funds. Green's painstaking scrutiny of every claim snarled the payroll so badly that the city's laborers rioted when their pay checks got lost in an administrative tangle.[4]

To practice economy, Havemeyer sacrificed important public services and, in the process, "crippled downtown development." During a three-month period in 1874 the Mayor vetoed more than 250 bills related to street grading, paving, and widening, board of education contracts, and appropriations intended for public charities. In justifying his liquidation of work relief, Havemeyer told the Harvard Association that contributions of private individuals and Christian and charitable associations were generous enough to meet the needs of the poor. According to Seymour Mandelbaum, the lower classes and the promoters of new areas of the city suffered most from Havemeyer's policies.[5]

During his second year in office, the aging Mayor fought with the city council and accomplished nothing of lasting importance. Havemeyer and the New York Council of Political Reform were so obsessed with "honest, efficient and economical government" that they indicted every public improvement as a "job" and labeled every politician who supported such measures as an "exponent of the class against which society is organized to protect itself." The Mayor's death in 1874 mercifully ended the agony of a reform administration which was strangling the city with red tape generated by its own economy programs. Ironically, Havemeyer helped to perpetuate the widespread belief that reformers were meddling, ineffectual reactionaries, or, as George Washington Plunkitt charged, "morning glories" who wilted in the heat of urban politics.[6]

Buffalo's "fighting mayor," Grover Cleveland, 1882, was another one of the progenitors of the structural reform tradition. Preoccupied as much as Havemeyer with cutting taxes and municipal expenditures, Cleveland had no positive programs to offer, with one notable exception: he fought and won authorization for a massive interceptor sewer system to diminish the dumping of refuse into the Erie Canal. He made his mark in Buffalo by the veto of a corrupt street-cleaning contract, the "most spectacular single event" of his administration in Allan Nevins's view. In addition, Cleveland fought to stop the constant proliferation of city jobs, exercised a Havemeyer type of vigilance over all claims made against the city treasury, and directed city employees to stop closing their offices at 4:00 p.m. and to perform a full day's work. His inflexible drive for economy and efficiency and his contempt for the dishonesty of city machines won him a reputation as a rugged veto and reform mayor.[7]

Seth Low, a wealthy merchant, philanthropist, and university president, was mayor of Brooklyn (1882–5) and later of New York (1902–1903). Perhaps more than any other American mayor, he possessed the qualities of a high-minded, nonpartisan structural reformer who attempted to infuse a large dose of businesslike efficiency into municipal government. He was widely recognized by his generation as one of the most prominent practicing reformers on the urban scene, but he also built a considerable reputation as a scholar of municipal affairs. In countless addresses, Low argued that the answer to urban problems was charter reform to bring nonpartisanship and a centralized administration into city government. Reform of this sort would arouse a new civic consciousness and create a cohesive corporate government that could be run along business lines, free from outside influences.[8]

Under the aegis of a silk-stocking Citizens' Committee, Low, with his refined eloquence and business support, had waged an effective campaign against political spoilsmanship and partisanship and won Brooklyn's mayoralty election in 1881. Low disregarded political affiliation and based his appointments on ability and merit. Although his two terms proved to be unspectacular, Low had advanced what he considered the cardinal principles of municipal reform: he had reduced the city's debt, tightened up the tax system, and conducted a vigorous campaign at Albany to stop special state legislation from interfering in Brooklyn's affairs. Such social questions as tenement-house reform and aid to the aged, the poor, or workingmen were for Seth Low but special benefits which could not be considered until local partisanship had been wiped out and municipal government had been reorganized along the lines of authority and responsibility. Low's name had become synonymous with efficiency, responsibility, and clean government.[9]

After a particularly flagrant period of municipal corruption under Tammany Hall, a reform-minded Citizens' Union, which counted J. Pierpont Morgan and Elihu Root among its founders, asked Seth Low to enter the lists as an independent candidate for mayor of New York against the Tammany favorite in 1901. Low ran on a platform of home rule and nonpartisanship, avoided the social-welfare planks endorsed by the Citizens' Union, and discussed honesty, economy, and responsibility in his speeches. Low was known to the voters because he had assisted in drafting the first charter for Greater New York, which consolidated hundreds of small towns and three large cities into one unit. Low's victory in 1901 was probably less an endorsement of his brand of reform than a public reaction against the excesses of Tammany.[10]

As New York's mayor, Low brought in experts to operate the various departments, pared away Tammany's payroll padding, and set himself up as the businessman in office. He cut salaries, increased the length of the working day for municipal employees, and reduced the city's annual budget by $1,500,000. In the public transit and utility field, Low saw to it that franchises were carefully drafted to safeguard the city's interests and to provide for additional revenue. He failed to press for lower rates, to agitate for a public rate-making body, or to instruct his district attorney to investigate the corrupt alliances between private business and politicians. He balked at appointing one of the best-qualified housing reformers, Lawrence Veiller, to head the tenement-house commission, apparently because Low did not wish to disturb the conservative real-estate interests. Low was willing, however, to use the full force of law against Sunday drinking, petty gambling, and prostitution, which were commonly found in the immigrant and lower-class sections of the city. The Bureau of Licenses also cracked down on the city's 6,000 pushcart peddlers who were operating without licenses, and the Department of Law prosecuted residents whose tax payments were delinquent. With similar zeal, the Department of Water raised nearly $1 million in income from overdue water bills.[11]

Low's tinkering with the machinery of government, his charter revision and rewriting, his regularization of tax collections, his enforcement of the city statutes, his appointment of men of merit, and his reduction of city expenditures were laudable actions by almost anybody's test of good government. Unfortunately, these measures bore most severely upon the lower classes. Low's structural reforms were also very impolitic, as his defeat in the election of 1903 demonstrated. Low never seemed to realize that his municipal reform had nothing to offer the voters but sterile, mechanical changes and that fundamental social and economic conditions which pressed upon the vast urban masses of immigrants and poor could not be changed by rewriting charters or enforcing laws.[12]

San Francisco's reform mayor James D. Phelan, a wealthy banker and anti-Bryan Democrat who held office from 1897 to 1902, was also a structural reformer like his model, Seth Low, whom Phelan frequently quoted. Phelan's program for reform included the introduction of efficiency and economy to ensure "scientific, systematic and responsible government," which was also the goal of the San Francisco Merchants' Association. Franchise regulation, lower traction rates, municipal ownership, and equal taxation were not part of Phelan's design for a better San Francisco. The distinguishing mark of the Phelan administration was its sponsorship of a strong mayor, and a short ballot charter that provided rigid fiscal controls over expenditures, city-wide elections for the council, and a merit system. Known as a "watchdog of the treasury," Mayor Phelan supported a low tax rate that forced the city to withhold schoolteachers' salaries, suspend many of the essential functions of the city health department, subject patients at the city hospital to inadequate care, and turn off the street lights at midnight. Phelan crippled his administration when he permitted the president of the police commissioners (who was also president of the Chamber of Commerce) to protect strikebreakers and club pickets during a teamsters' and a dock-workers' strike against the open shop. Although the eighteen unions lost their strike, they retaliated by forming their own political party and defeating the reformers in 1901. In the famous graft prosecutions after 1901, Phelan continued to act like a "member of his class" or, as Fremont Older put it, "a rich man toward a great business in which he is interested."[13] Like Low, Phelan failed to attack what social reformers recognized as the basic problems confronting the city.

Equally ineffectual in his attempt to make New York the best-governed city in the nation was Mayor John Purroy Mitchel, who served from 1914 to 1917. He was an "oddly puritanical Catholic" who represented the foibles and virtues of patrician-class reform. Mitchel's election in 1913 was the result of voter reaction to a decade of brazen looting by Tammany Hall. Like his reform predecessors, Mitchel was responsible for little of lasting importance and did not generate enthusiasm among the large mass of voters with his structural reforms.[14]

Mitchel's failure was due to his misconception that city government could be conducted by the "ledger book ethics of the corporation accountant." So dedicated was Mitchel to budgetary cutbacks that he adopted the Gary Plan of education, which enabled New York City to cram more children into the existing schools. He decreased appropriations for the city's night schools, thus seriously hampering the entire program; for the summer program, Mitchel asked the teachers to volunteer their services without remuneration. Mitchel also appointed cost-cutting charity agents who began either to return feeble-minded children to their parents or to threaten to charge the often hard-pressed parents if their children were kept in public-supported institutions. In addition, he instituted an investigation of the city's religious child care organizations, hoping thus to cut the city subsidy; but this action brought the wrath of the Catholic church down upon him.[15] Mitchel, although well-intentioned, had a kind of King Midas touch in reverse: everything he touched seemed to turn to ashes.

Robert Moses dismissed the Mitchel administration's efficiency drives as "saving rubber bands" and "using both ends of the pencil," but its flaws were much greater. The Mitchel administration and the structural reform movement were not only captives of a modern business mentality but sought to impress middle- and upper-class social values upon the urban community and to redistribute political power to the patrician class.[16]

Built upon a narrow middle- and patrician-class base and a business concept of social responsibility, the structural reform movement, with its zeal for efficiency and economy, usually lacked staying power. As George Washington Plunkitt pointed out, such crusaders were usually repudiated by lower-class voters after a brief tenure in office. Unlike the social reformers, who were also interested in economy, the structural reformers had a blind spot when it came to weighing the human cost of their programs. They failed to recognize that a dose of something as astringent as wage-cutting and payroll audits had to be counterbalanced with social welfare programs if the public were to be served effectively. Too often they blamed the immigrant for the city's shortcomings or directed much of the force of their administrations to exterminating lower-class vices, which they saw as the underlying causes of municipal problems.[17]

Unlike the structural reformers, social reform mayors such as Hazen S. Pingree (1890–97), "Golden Rule" Jones (1897–1903), Tom Johnson (1901–1909), Mark Fagan (1901–1907), Brand Whitlock (1906–13), and Newton D. Baker (1912–16) began with a different set of assumptions about the basic causes of misgovernment in the cities. They shared the view, which Lincoln Steffens later publicized, that big business and its quest for preferential treatment and special privileges had corrupted municipal government. The public service corporations, the utilities, the real-estate interests, and the large industrial concerns all had vested interests in urban America. They sought special tax advantages, franchises which eliminated competition, and other municipal concessions. They bought aldermen, councilmen, and mayors to protect these interests and, in the process, demoralized urban politics and city government. Mayor Tom Johnson's aide Frederic C. Howe was shocked when he was berated by his upper-class friends for opposing a franchise steal; they explained that the public utilities have "millions of dollars invested" and had to "protect their investments." "But I do say emphatically," declared Mayor Pingree in 1895, ". . . better take [the utilities] out of private hands than allow them to stand as the greatest corruptors of public morals that ever blackened the pages of history."[18]

The programs of the social reform mayors aimed at lower gas, light, telephone, and street railway rates for the community and higher taxes for railroads and business corporations. When they were unable to obtain the regulation of public utilities, these mayors fought for municipal ownership, the only technique to redistribute economic power available to them as urban executives. Establishment of free public baths, expansion of parks, schools, and public relief were similarly attempts to distribute the amenities of middle-class life to the masses. The social reformers recognized that the fight against crime in its commonly understood sense (i.e., rooting out gambling, drinking, and prostitution) was an attempt to treat the symptoms rather than the disease itself and that such campaigns would burn out the energies of a reform administration and leave the fundamental problems of the urban masses untouched. Pingree, like Jones and Johnson, believed that such binges of "Comstockery" were irrelevant to municipal reform. "The good people are always insisting upon 'moral' issues," asserted Toledo mayor Brand Whitlock, "urging us to turn aside from our large immediate purpose, and concentrate our official attention on the 'bad' people—and wreck our movement."[19]

The saloons where drinking, gambling, and other vices flourished, Pingree, Jones, and Johnson agreed, were but poor men's clubs and offered the workers but a few of the comforts that most rich men enjoyed. "The most dangerous enemies to good government are not the saloons, the dives, the dens of iniquity and the criminals," Pingree told the Springfield, Massachusetts, Board of Trade. "Most of our troubles can be traced to the temptations which are offered to city officials when franchises are sought by wealthy corporations, or contracts are to be let for public works." For refusing to divert public attention from the "larger and more complex immoralities" of the "privileged" interests, as Brand Whitlock put it, to the more familiar vices, the social reformers earned the bitter censure of the ministerial and "uplift" groups.[20]

The whole tone of the social reform movement was humanistic and empirical. It did not attempt to prescribe standards of personal morality, nor did it attempt to draft social blueprints or city charters which had as their goals the imposition of middle-class morality and patrician values upon the masses. Instead, it sought to find the basic causes of municipal misgovernment. Pingree, the first of the broad-gauged social reformers, discovered the sources of municipal corruption in his day-to-day battle with the light, gas, telephone, and traction interests, the latter represented at the time by Tom Johnson. Johnson, like Mayor Newton D. Baker, knew from his own experience as a utility magnate why municipal government had been demoralized. Mayor Mark Fagan discovered that Jersey City could neither regulate nor tax the utilities and the railroads because both parties were dominated by these interests.[21]

In attempting to reform the city, Pingree, Jones, Johnson, and Whitlock lost upper-class and business support and were forced to rely upon the lower classes for political power. The structural reformers, on the other hand, were frequently members of and sponsored by the very social and economic classes which most vehemently opposed social reform. "If we had to depend upon these classes for reforms," Pingree told the *Outlook* in 1897, "they could never have been brought about." "It is not so much the undercrust as the upper crust," asserted Professor Edward Bemis, who served as a Pingree aide, "that threatens the interests of the people."[22]

The inability of the structural reformers to pursue positive programs to alter the existing social and economic order was probably a reflection of their own business and class backgrounds. Their high regard for the sacrosanct nature of private property, even if obtained illegally, limited them to treating but one aspect of the municipal malaise, and then only when corruption by urban machines reached an intolerable point. This half-way attempt at urban reform prompted Brand Whitlock to observe in 1914: "The word 'reformer' like the word 'politician' has degenerated, and, in the mind of the common man, come to connotate something very disagreeable. In four terms as mayor I came to know both species pretty well, and, in the latter connotations of the term, I prefer politician. He, at least, is human."[23]

NOTES

1. Lincoln Steffens, *The Autobiography of Lincoln Steffens* (New York, 1931), pp. 374–5; Hewitt quoted in *Pilgrim*, III (December 1901), 4.

2. Hazen S. Pingree, "Address to the Nineteenth Century Club of New York," November 11, 1897, p. 7; S. M. Jones to Josiah Strong, November 15, 1898, Jones Papers; Brand Whitlock, *Forty Years of It* (New York, 1914), pp. 172–4.

3. Frederic C. Howe, *The City: The Hope of Democracy* (New York, 1913), pp. 1, 2. For the elitist views of reformers who overthrew Boss Tweed, see Alexander B. Callow, Jr., *The Tweed Ring* (New York, 1966), pp. 69–71, 265–7. Charles R. Adrian, "Some General Characteristics of Nonpartisan Elections," Robert C. Wood, "Nonpartisanship in Suburbia," both in Oliver P. Williams and Charles Press, eds., *Democracy in Urban America* (Chicago, 1964), pp. 251–66. For an exposition of the views regarding municipal government of one of the most prominent twentieth-century "structural" reformers, see Richard S. Childs, "The Faith of a Civic Reformer," *ibid.*, pp. 222–4. The "elitist commitments" of the city-manager system (as prescribed in city government textbooks) can also be seen in Lawrence J. R. Herson, "The Lost World of Municipal Government," *American Political Science Review*, LI (June 1957), 330–45.

4. Howard B. Furer, *William Frederick Havemeyer: A Political Biography* (New York, 1965), pp. 14, 144–54, 160; Seymour J. Mandelbaum, *Boss Tweed's New York* (New York, 1965), pp. 91, 97, 108, 111; Callow, *op. cit.*, pp. 253–86.

5. Mandelbaum, *op. cit.,* pp. 98–100, 111; Furer, *op. cit.,* pp. 156, 158, 160–61, 169.

6. *Ibid.,* p. 161; Mandelbaum, *op. cit.,* pp. 112–13; William L. Riordin, *Plunkitt of Tammany Hall* (New York, 1963), p. 17.

7. Allan Nevins, *Grover Cleveland, A Study in Courage* (New York, 1941), pp. 61–2, 83–94.

8. Harold Coffin Syrett, *The City of Brooklyn 1865–1898, A Political History* (New York, 1944), p. 134; Steven C. Swett, "The Test of a Reformer: A Study of Seth Low," *New York Historical Society Quarterly,* XLIV (January 1960) pp. 8, 9; Lincoln Steffens, *The Shame of the Cities* (New York, 1966), p. 201.

9. Syrett, *op. cit.,* pp. 104–106, 109–19, 134; Swett, *op. cit.,* pp. 7–9.

10. Albert Fein, "New York City Politics From 1897–1903; A Study in Political Party Leadership" (master's thesis, Columbia University, 1954), pp. 19–20; Swett, *op. cit.,* pp. 10–14, 16–18.

11. *Ibid.,* pp. 21–3, 26–31, 35–6; Roy Lubove, *The Progressives and the Slums, Tenement House Reform in New York City, 1890–1917* (Pittsburgh, 1962), pp. 153–4.

12. Swett, *op. cit.,* pp. 6, 32, 35–6, 38–41; Wallace S. Sayre and Herbert Kaufman, *Governing New York City Politics in the Metropolis* (New York, 1960), p. 695.

13. James D. Phelan, "Municipal Conditions and the New Charter," *Overland Monthly,* XXVIII (no. 163, 2nd series), pp. 104–11; Roy Swanstrom, "Reform Administration of James D. Phelan, Mayor of San Francisco, 1897–1902," (master's thesis, University of California-Berkeley, 1949), pp. 77–9, 80, 83, 85, 86; Walton Bean, *Boss Ruef's San Francisco: The Story of the Union Labor Party, Big Business, and the Graft Prosecution* (Berkeley, 1952), pp. 8, 9, 16, 17, 23; George E. Mowry, *The California Progressives* (Chicago, 1963), pp. 23–5; Fremont Older, *My Own Story* (San Francisco, 1919), pp. 27, 31, 65.

14. William E. Leuchtenburg, Preface to Edwin R. Lewinson, *John Purroy Mitchel: The Boy Mayor of New York* (New York, 1965), pp. 11–13; Lewinson, *op. cit.,* pp. 93, 95, 100, 102, 117, 124.

15. Leuchtenburg, *op. cit.,* p. 12; Lewinson, *op. cit.,* pp. 18, 151–69, 175–88.

16. Leuchtenburg, *op. cit.,* pp. 11–13; Samuel P. Hayes, "The Politics of Reform in Municipal Government," *Pacific Northwest Quarterly,* LV (October 1964), pp. 157–69.

17. Lewinson, *op. cit.,* pp. 11–13, 18, 93, 95, 102; Riordin, *op. cit.,* pp. 17–20; Swett, *op. cit.,* pp. 8, 9; Allan Nevins, *Abram S. Hewitt: With Some Account of Peter Cooper* (New York, 1935), pp. 515–16, 529–30; Seth Low, "An American View of Municipal Government in the United States," in James Bryce, *The American Commonwealth* (New York, 1893), I, 651, 665.

18. Hoyt Landon Warner, *Progressivism in Ohio 1897–1917* (Columbus, 1964), pp. 32, 70–72; Whitlock, *op. cit.,* pp. 211, 252; Clarence H. Cramer, *Newton D. Baker: A Biography* (Cleveland, 1961), pp. 46–7; Steffens, *op. cit.,* pp. 477, 492–93; Frederic C. Howe, *The Confessions of a Reformer* (New York, 1925), pp. 98, 102–108; Pingree, *op. cit.,* p. 196. For Mark Fagan, see Lincoln Steffens, *Upbuilders* (New York, 1909), pp. 28, 30, 33, 35, and Ransom E. Noble, Jr., *New Jersey Progressivism before Wilson* (Princeton, 1946), pp. 13–42. St. Louis Circuit Attorney Joseph W.

Folk (1901–1904), who began his career by investigating and prosecuting franchise "grabs," discovered that the real despoilers of municipal government were not minor city officials but promoters, bankers, and corporation directors who profited by misgovernment. After he became governor he dropped his crime-busting and supported progressive and urban reforms. Louis G. Geiger, *Joseph W. Folk of Missouri* (Columbia, 1953), pp. 32, 41, 81, 88, 93, 99–117. Robert Wiebe's assertion that the "typical business ally of the boss, moreover, was a rather marginal operator, anathema to the chamber of commerce" is at variance with what is known about the political influence wielded in Detroit by urban capitalists such as the Hendries, McMillans and Johnson or for that matter with the role played by Yerkes and Insull in Chicago, Mark Hanna in Cleveland, and the Huntington interests in Los Angeles, just to cite a few examples. Robert Wiebe, *The Search for Order, 1877–1920* (New York, 1967), p. 167.

19. Steffens, *Upbuilders*, pp. 3–45; Warner, *op. cit.*, pp. 71, 74; Cramer, *op. cit.*, pp. 50–52; Howe, *op. cit.*, pp. 90–93, 108–109; Carl Lorenz, *Tom L. Johnson, Mayor of Cleveland* (New York, 1911), p. 152; Steffens, *Autobiography*, p. 480; *Detroit Free Press*, March 14, 1896, P.S.; Samuel M. Jones to Henry D. Lloyd, April 16, 1897, Lloyd Papers; Samuel M. Jones to James L. Cowes, April 27, 1897; Tom L. Johnson to S. M. Jones, May 3, 1902, Jones Papers; Harvey S. Ford, "The Life and Times of Golden Rule Jones" (Ph.D. thesis, University of Michigan, 1953), pp. 185, 284–5, 330; Whitlock, *op. cit.*, p. 212. William D. Miller has argued that "Boss" Edward H. Crump, who was Memphis mayor from 1910 to 1916, stands with "Golden Rule" Jones and Tom L. Johnson as a typical progressive of the period, but an examination of Miller's book raises serious doubts about that judgment. Although Crump occasionally employed reform rhetoric, established a few milk stations for the poor, and put screens on public school windows, he used most of the energy of his administration to enforce the laws and instill efficiency into the municipal government in the structural-reform tradition. Crump wiped out "policy" playing by Negroes, eliminated loafing by the garbage collectors and street pavers, forced the railroads to construct eleven underpasses, lowered city taxes, reduced waste in municipal government by extending audit procedures even to the purchase of postage stamps, and increased city income by selling empty bottles, feed sacks, and scrap. William D. Miller, *Mr. Crump of Memphis* (Baton Rouge, 1964), pp. 79–113. Brooklyn's Mayor Charles A. Schieren (1894–5), who gained some stature as a reformer by defeating a venal Democratic machine, also followed a well-trodden path of cleaning out "deceit and corruption" and installing "integrity, nonpartisanship, and routine efficiency." Like most of the reform mayors of his period, Schieren failed to advance or support social reform programs. Harold C. Syrett, *The City of Brooklyn, 1865–1898, A Political History* (New York, 1944), pp. 218–32. Geoffrey Blodgett has tried to show that Boston became for "a brief time the cutting edge of urban reform in America" under Mayor Josiah Quincy (1896–1900), who established a publicly owned printing plant and expanded the city's playgrounds. Although the Dover Street Bath House may have been a "monument to municipal socialism" as Blodgett contends, Mayor Quincy stopped his programs short of anything that would have threatened the vested interests in the traction and utility business. Geoffrey Blodgett, *The Gentle Reformers: Massachusetts Democrats in the Cleveland Era* (Cambridge, 1966), pp. 240–61. For Quincy's absurd notion that regular bathing would cause the "filthy tenement house" to disappear, crime and drunkenness to decrease and the death rate to drop, see Josiah Quincy, "Municipal Progress in Boston," *Independent,* LII (February 15, 1900), 424. Henry Demarest Lloyd was critical of Mayor Quincy's failure to resist the traction interests and referred to the mayor's public baths as Quincy's "little sops." H. D. Lloyd to Samuel Bowles, December 13, 1898, Lloyd Papers.

20. Ford, *op. cit.,* pp. 151, 166, 339; Samuel M. Jones to Dr. [Graham] Taylor, October 5, 1897; S. M. Jones to L. L. Dagett, April 17, 1899, Jones Papers; Hazen S. Pingree address to Springfield, Massachusetts, Board of Trade, March 3, 1894, Ralph Stone Scrapbook; Whitlock, *op. cit.,* pp. 252, 254.

21. Robert H. Bremner, "The Civic Revival in Ohio: The Fight Against Privilege in Cleveland and Toledo, 1890–1912," (Ph.D. thesis, Ohio State University, 1943), p. 25; Hazen S. Pingree, "The Problem of Municipal Reform. Contract by Referendum," *Arena,* XVII (April 1897), 707–710; Cramer, *op. cit.,* p. 46; Steffens, *Upbuilders,* pp. 28–30, 33, 35; Noble, *op. cit.,* pp. 25–6, 35, 38.

22. Tom L. Johnson, *My Story* (New York, 1911), p. 113; Ford, *op. cit.,* pp. 136–7, 170, 339; Hazen S. Pingree, "Detroit: A Municipal Study," *Outlook,* LV (February 6, 1897), 437; Bemis quoted in *Detroit Evening News,* June 21, 1899, Stone Scrapbook; Whitlock, *op. cit.,* p. 221.

23. Whitlock, *op. cit.,* p. 221.

23. LA GUARDIA COMES TO POWER, 1933

Arthur Mann

Some men go to the top in politics when society seems to be a going concern and the people have need of an amiable figurehead who is content to stand still. It is usual for such a leader to avoid conflict, stress harmony, and celebrate what is: to assure and reassure the electorate that they've never had it so good. Government is not supposed to be an instrument for social change, it is considered an exercise in caretaking. Such is the leadership of normalcy.

Neither by temperament nor intellect was La Guardia the sort to administer a going concern. Unable to slow down long enough to stand still, he was inclined to shock and mock the celebrators of the status quo and to celebrate only the possibilities of the future. He throve on conflict, not harmony, in situations that made reform possible. It was no accident that the Anti-Injunction Act,* for which La Guardia and Senator George Norris had agitated futilely during the so-called normalcy of the 1920s, should suddenly have been passed by Congress at the beginning of the Depression. Fiorello was the kind of leader who comes into his own when a crisis in the old order creates opportunities for new directions.

Yet the laws of heredity and environment that produce a La Guardia have still to be discovered. His biographer can only call attention to his most important characteristics, infer their probable source from available evidence, and relate them to the culture in which they flourished. Three characteristics of the fifty-one-year-old man who entered City Hall in 1934 deserve special mention and elaboration: his hybridism, his ambition for power and fame, and his passion to do good.

His hybridism derived from an extraordinary mobility. Born in Greenwich Village but raised on Western Army posts and growing to maturity

*This milestone in social legislation, which President Hoover signed on March 23, 1932, restated the right of workingmen to bargain collectively and also declared that government had the responsibility to help them do so. Among other provisions, the Norris–La Guardia Act forbade federal courts to issue injunctions against a strike or against peaceful activities to carry on a strike unless the employer could prove that he had tried to settle the strike, been threatened, or that the strike would cause him irreparable harm.

in the Balkans, he returned to his native city at twenty-three and later spent much of his adult life in the nation's capital as a Congressman. All his life he had been learning how to live in someone else's culture and he acquired a working knowledge of half a dozen languages besides English: Italian, French, German, Yiddish, Hungarian, and Serbo-Croatian. He was a true cosmopolitan, which is to say that he was at home nearly everywhere, but without the roots that bind a true insider to the group and the place in which he was born.

His parentage foreordained that he would be what sociologists call a marginal man. Achille Luigi Carlo La Guardia and his wife Irene Coen emigrated to America in 1880 and returned to Italy with their children twenty years later. Theirs was a mixed marriage—Achille was a lapsed Catholic and Irene a lukewarm Jew—and while in the United States they raised their children as Episcopalians. When, in 1906, Fiorello returned to America, where everyone has an ethnic label or gets one, he considered himself an Italo-American. But his being a Protestant set him apart from his ethnic group, which was, of course, overwhelmingly Catholic.

Observers have asked why Fiorello did not identify himself as a Jew. His inheritance is again instructive. Irene Coen La Guardia, his Trieste-born mother, thought of herself as Austrian in nationality, Italian in culture, and Jewish only in religion. There was no Jewish community in the army towns where Fiorello grew up while his father was serving in the United States Army as a bandmaster. When Fiorello met Jews in large numbers—first as a consular agent in Fiume, then as an Ellis Island interpreter, and later as a labor lawyer on Manhattan's Lower East Side—he met Jews unlike his mother. They were Eastern European, not Mediterranean, Jews. They spoke Yiddish, their ritual was Ashkenazic, and they considered themselves a nationality and a cultural group as well as a religious body. Neither by descent nor religious upbringing was Fiorello one of them.

Nor was it expedient for him to be known as Jewish when he broke into politics in the 1910s. He started out with handicaps enough against him. His aberrant appearance and unpronounceable name put him at a disadvantage to the dominant Celtic and the vanishing Anglo-Saxon types who ran the city. Nativism was rising and would shortly culminate in restrictive legislation against the new immigrants from Eastern and Southern Europe. It was hard enough to be an Italo-American fifty and more years ago without inviting the derisive taunt—which his enemies would hurl at him in the 1930s after his mother's origins became known—"the half-Jewish wop."

So he made little of his Jewish background in public but exploited his Italian name and built a political base in Little Italy from which to launch a career. By 1934 not even Primo Carnera or Benito Mussolini exceeded the Little Flower as a popular idol in the colony. What is more, after establishing his public image as a Latin he championed a number of Jewish causes, sometimes in Yiddish, but as an understanding and compassionate *outsider*. This was smart politics in the largest Jewish city in the world (the

Jews and the Italians together constituted almost 45 percent of New York's population in the 1920s and 1930s). It was also, and nevertheless, sincere. Free from self-hatred, La Guardia was a man of mixed loyalties.

The son of Jewish and Italian immigrants who attended services in the Cathedral of Saint John the Divine, but who was married to his first wife in the rectory of Saint Patrick's and to his second wife by a Lutheran minister, was clearly the most remarkable hybrid in the history of New York City politics. Belonging, yet not fully belonging, to nearly every important ancestral group in the city, including the British-descended community of Episcopalians, Fiorello was a balanced ticket all by himself.[1]

His being marginal to many cultures had a deeper significance still. The mayor of New York, like the leader of any pluralist community, must be a political broker. This had been a familiar role to the hyphenated Congressman who started his career on the Lower East Side as a mediator between immigrant and native America, interpreting one to the other. A friend in court for the poor and the persecuted, he also had served as a go-between for reformers and professional politicians and a bridge connecting urban and rural progressives in Congress.* The mayoralty would enlarge the scope of previous experience. La Guardia would have to balance the demands of a variety of competing interest groups in the city, and also bargain and trade with borough, county, state, and federal officials whose power impinged on his own as chief executive.[2]

But an effective leader must not only mediate and negotiate, he also has to command, take the initiative, make policy, and break through channels when necessary to get things done. Such a leader seeks power, enlarges it, and enjoys its use. La Guardia was like that by 1934. One of the few pieces of sculpture the mayor owned was a bust of Napoleon that he first put on his desk when he began to practice law at twenty-eight. When he bought that object is unknown, but Bonaparte may have been his model at an even earlier age.

"Ambitious for promotion"—that is how the American Consul General of Budapest, who was given to the understatement of his New England birth and education, described his Italo-American subordinate in Fiume at the turn of the century. Commissioned a consular agent at twenty-one, Fiorello's pride of rank was inordinate. He expanded his jurisdiction whenever possible, breaking archaic rules and bringing them up to date on his own authority. The results of his innovations were often salutary, but his aggressiveness antagonized superiors. He quit in a huff after two and a half years, writing in 1906 to the State Department "that the service is not the place for a young man to work up . . . ."[3]

---

* John A. Simpson, president of the National Farmers' Union, described La Guardia to a colleague in these words: "Coming right out of the heart of the biggest city in the United States, . . . [he had] a sympathy and an understanding of farm problems that surpassed most of the Congressmen from agricultural districts." Simpson to Milo Reno, April 25, 1933, Milo Reno MSS. (privately held).

During World War I, as a major in command of American aviation in Italy, La Guardia was something of a virtuoso in running around, over, across, or simply straight through the protocol of two armies and one foreign government. Not having resigned his seat in Congress, he either impressed or intimidated higher ranking officers with his political connections. And forced to improvise on America's forgotten front, he improvised brilliantly, whether in training pilots, conferring with cabinet ministers, speeding up the production of planes, or rallying Italians to their own war effort after the disaster of Caporetto. "I love him like a brother," one Italian official exclaimed.[4]

Many voters in America felt much the same way. Between 1914 and 1934 La Guardia ran for office twelve times, and apart from a first and hopeless try, he lost only twice. His victories were particularly impressive in view of the fact that New York City was virtually a one-party (Democratic) town. Elected president of the Board of Aldermen in 1919, he was the first Republican to win a city-wide contest without Fusion backing since the creation of Greater New York by legislative act in 1897.* At one time during the 1920s La Guardia was the sole Republican Congressman from Manhattan outside the silk-stocking district.

His most obvious asset as a campaigner was his grasp of relevant issues and his ability to dramatize those issues, and himself as well, in colorful language and forceful terms. And once in office he was conscientious in serving his constituents. He was particularly popular with immigrants and their children, who accounted for 75 percent of New York's population when he was rising to power. He was fighting their battle, and his, too, for recognition and against bigotry. One of the few ethnic groups that could not claim the multi-hyphenated Little Flower through blood were the Polish-Americans, yet *Nowy Swiat*, a Polish-language newspaper, looked up to him as "head of the family . . . father, leader, judge, authority, and educator—like in the village . . ."

But there was a Machiavellian, even diabolical, side to La Guardia's melting-pot politics. When haranguing an audience, which he could do in any of seven languages, he was not above exploiting its fears, insecurities, prejudices, and hatreds. There were ways and ways of getting out the vote. After one such a harangue to an Italo-American crowd in the campaign of 1919, he turned in pride to an associate and said: "I can outdemagogue the best of demagogues."[5]

He justified such tactics by insisting that he had to fight the Tammany Tiger with its own weapons, and it was said of the Little Flower during his life that he was no shrinking violet. What a negative way of putting it! Fiorello was a superbly conditioned political animal who not only struck

---

* New York City was simply Manhattan until the annexation of the west Bronx in 1874. The rest of the Bronx was annexed in 1895, and two years later a state law added Brooklyn, Queens, and Staten Island. Today's boundaries of the city are identical with those established in 1897.

back when attacked but who really enjoyed the brutal struggle for office in the Manhattan jungle. No matter what he said in public to the contrary, La Guardia was a professional politician, bruising, cunning, tough, and with a strong stomach for the sordid methods and grubby details of election politics in his part of the world. "I invented the low blow," he boasted to an aide in the 1920s.[6] In East Harlem, which he represented in Congress for five terms until 1932, he commanded a superb personal organization of his own and gave lessons to Tammany at election time in machine campaigning.

The mayor knew how to get power, all right, and how to keep it, as his record for election and reelection proves. But why did he want it? There are very many gifted men, after all, for whom public responsibility is distasteful and whose main thrust is for money, leisure, travel, or women. Those had been the tastes of Mayor Jimmy Walker, who gladly let the Tammany bosses govern New York City while he relentlessly pursued pleasure on two continents.

Some of La Guardia's associates thought, and still think, that in reaching out for power he was compensating for feelings of inferiority deriving from a hypersensitivity to his size, his lack of formal education, and his origins. To reduce the complexity of Fiorello's behavior to an inferiority complex is too pat and too simple. His wife, who knew him as well as anyone, has dismissed the idea as preposterous. Yet it is a matter of historical record that the Little Flower *was* hypersensitive and, therefore, easily insulted and ferociously combative.

Who can forget the fury, for example, with which the mayor banned organ-grinders from the streets of New York? Those foreign-looking men, with their broken English, farcical little monkeys, and panhandling canned music, called attention to one of several disreputable Italian stereotypes that the Little Flower had labored all his life to refute and overcome. And although he himself might joke about his height and that of other men, no one else was allowed to do so in his presence. Once, when an associate made the mistake of being playful about a pint-sized applicant for a municipal job, La Guardia lost control of himself and screamed:

"What's the matter with a little guy? What's the matter with a little guy? What's the matter with a little guy?"[7]

The mayor was clearly a man of explosive resentments. They were long-standing and are a key to his personality. As a boy growing up on army posts he had resented the children of officers for lording it over the children of enlisted men. Why was he not as good as they? Later, in the Foreign Service or in the Army, on the Board of Aldermen or in Congress, he would resent superiors he thought intellectually and morally inferior to himself. By what rights should they be placed over him? To measure one's self against others is normal for competitive men, but in La Guardia's case it was excessive. His resentfulness heightened his competitiveness and his competitiveness intensified his resentfulness, so that he was constantly in rivalry with nearly everyone he met and forever proving that he was number one.

"I think he put on a great deal of his brutalities to test people out," C. C. Burlingham, who knew La Guardia well, has shrewdly observed. "If they could stand up against him it was all right, but if they couldn't they were in bad luck."[8]

That La Guardia was ambitious will surprise only those people who think that a stained-glass window of Saint Francis is really a sufficient monument to the mayor's memory. Yet only a mistaken realism would conclude that there was nothing more to his nature, and to human nature in general, than the promotion of self. Ed Flynn, the Democratic boss from the Bronx who prided himself on being a realistic judge of men, made that kind of mistake.[9] That is why Flynn was never able to understand and appreciate—or cope with—the *direction* of La Guardia's drive.

The direction was a liberal one. La Guardia wanted the power of public office not just to assert himself, it must be emphasized, but so that he could also be in a position to right social wrongs. Joining his resentments to a cause, he made a career for himself as a leader of the have-nots against the haves, or as he would have put it, the People against the Interests.

That was the image he had of himself—when he strove as a consul agent and interpreter to defend the humanity of immigrants against bureaucratic mindlessness and heartlessness; when he contributed his services as a lawyer and an orator to the trade unions that began to emerge in the 1910s from the squalid sweatshops of the Lower East Side; when as an over-age aviator he went off to war to make the world safe for democracy; when as president of the Board of Aldermen he defied the governor of New York State and fought against an increase of the five-cent fare on the subway (the poor man's ride) and the repeal of the direct primary (the people's defense against bossism); when as a Republican Congressman he bolted his party to join the Progressive party of 1924 in a crusade against the credo of the day that the business of America was business, not welfare. Had La Guardia done nothing else he still would have passed the bar of American liberalism in 1934 for the anti-injunction law he coauthored two years earlier with Nebraska's Senator Norris; it was the most significant piece of labor legislation passed by Congress up to that time.

La Guardia entered City Hall with a sense of injustice that was still bottomless, with a capacity for outrage that was still boundless, with a determination to reform society that was still enormous. His social conscience was as highly developed as his instinct for the jugular in political combat. The mayor's office, toward which he had reached out three times before finally capturing it, would give him the power he had wanted so long in order to realize his humanitarian goals.

The thrust of an enormous internal drive to establish his own high place in the sum of things carried La Guardia very close to the top in

American politics, and in that process he found more gratification in public fame than in the pleasure of private life.

When Fiorello returned to New York in 1906 after resigning from the consular service in Fiume ("Look here, Mother," he said in explanation, "I'm going back to America to become a lawyer and make something of myself."),[10] he arrived without friends or family. His father had been dead for two years and his mother chose to remain in Europe with her married daughter. The next decade and a half were devoted to the struggle to gain a foothold in the city he would someday rule. Not until 1919, when he was thirty-six, back from the wars as a hero, and finally established in his career, did Congressman La Guardia take a wife, an exquisite young blonde from Trieste by the name of Thea Almerigotti.

That marriage was, and would remain, the high point of La Guardia's private emotional experience. Setting up housekeeping in Greenwich Village, the couple enjoyed a semi-Bohemian life, one that was full of love and fun and music and good eating. La Guardia adored children, and in 1920 Thea gave birth to a daughter, who was named Fioretta after Fiorello's maternal grandmother. Yet La Guardia's personal happiness flickered for only a moment. Throughout 1921 he suffered the agony of watching his baby, and then his wife, waste away and die of tuberculosis. For the next eight years he threw himself into his work with an energy that can only be described as ferocious.

His second marriage in 1929 to Marie Fischer, his secretary since 1914, was a union of two mature persons. It was not blessed with children. The couple adopted a girl, Jean, in 1933 and a boy, Eric, the following year. At fifty-one, the Mayor was the foster father of very young children and had known married life for a total of only seven years.

In the nearly three decades he had lived in New York Fiorello acquired few personal friends, but rather many admirers, acquaintances, colleagues, allies, patrons, protégés, and advisers. He was too competitive to get along intimately with his equals. Only with children could he give himself completely. Hobbies he had none, other than a fondness for classical music. He was as mayor to surround himself with more intellectuals than any of his predecessors, but he had either no time or no taste for literature, not even for biography and history, and rarely read anything not directly relevant to his work.[11] He had lived, and would continue to live, mostly for his career and, what is equally important, for the affectionate acclaim that his public personality generated in a vast but impersonal audience. New York had in 1934 a full-time mayor.

La Guardia brought other qualities to the mayoralty in addition to his hybridism, his ambition, and his compassion for the oppressed. There was his gusto for work and his slashing wit, his quick but retentive mind and his theatrical flair. He also brought a considerable experience, stretching back to 1901 when he received his commission as consul agent from John Hay, Secretary of State under the first Roosevelt. By 1934 La Guardia had spent all but six years of his majority in one Government job or another. Public service was a way of life for him.

He clearly qualified for the office sometimes described as second in difficulty only to the Presidency as an elective office in American government. And by the late 1930s Republicans of the stature of William Allen White were booming him for the Presidency itself. Twelve years after his death in 1947, Professor Rexford G. Tugwell saluted him as "a great man in the Republic" and, excepting only F.D.R. among his contemporaries, as "the best-known leader in our democracy . . ."[12] Many people today accept that estimate as valid.

But the historian cannot stop there.

A NEAR MISS

The historian cannot stop there because La Guardia's career before he became mayor fell far short of greatness. He had been a good and even important consul agent, interpreter, deputy state attorney general, Army officer, president of the Board of Aldermen, and Congressman—but people of that sort, no matter how good and important, are hardly the sort whom the history books celebrate. La Guardia's renown dates from the mayoralty years, and we must therefore ask why a man of his obvious talent and ambition failed, except for the Norris–La Guardia Act of 1932, to make a major impression on American politics before then.

The answer lies in social forces beyond La Guardia's control, but also in serious defects of personality and character.

When he ran unsuccessfully for mayor in 1929, he faced a popular idol in Jimmy Walker, a fabulous machine given a respectable face by Al Smith, and Democratic registrations that outnumbered the Republican by better than three to one. The economy, moreover, was still prosperous. As for the positions La Guardia had won, none of them permitted him to make decisions of real consequence or to carry them out. Even when he held the balance of power in the 1932 Congress as the leader of a small band of progressives, he was more effective in blocking or modifying legislation than in pushing through his own bills, again excepting the Norris–La Guardia Act. Institutions had been beyond his control.

The times had been equally beyond his control. No one during the 1920s opposed more strenuously than Congressman La Guardia prohibition, privileged business, Yankee imperialism, and the Nordic nonsense that led to immigration restriction, or had worked so hard to enlarge the welfare functions of the federal government. One New York tabloid called La Guardia "America's most liberal Congressman." Yet the complacency and conservatism that dominated the nation's capital was too strong to overcome. Dissenter, critic, and gadfly—a fighter against the times—La Guardia said of himself during the Coolidge years:

"I am doomed to live in a hopeless minority for most of my legislative days."[13]

That was a strange thing for a man to say who had started his career as loyal Republican in 1910 and whose party controlled both the Congress and the Presidency during the 1920s. But by the latter decade La Guardia was so contemptuous of the moribund New York City organization and so hostile to the Old Guard leadership on the national level that he was a Republican only in name. In East Harlem, where his personal popularity and personal machine were stronger than any party label, he was some-times in and sometimes out of the GOP, usually running for office with the endorsement of other parties in addition to the Republican. "I would rather be right than regular," he said in 1924.[14]

His moralism was as genuine as it was courageous, but the hard fact was, and still is, that the big prizes in American politics usually fall to the men who play the game according to the rules of the two-party system. Except for unusual circumstances, i.e., New York City during the Depression and World War II, irregulars, insurgents, come-outers, bolters, and loners win only the contest for the minds of posterity—if they win even then. Congressman La Guardia lived in a hopeless minority not just because of his times, but also because his personal style unsuited him for the two-party system.

The unattractive features of that style gave the impression that Fiorello was erratic and unstable and therefore unreliable. His party infidelity, cockiness, truculence, irascibility, and demagoguery, not to mention his violent temper, played into the hands of enemies who wanted the public to believe that he was a crazy little wop. Men who disagreed with Fiorello were not merely wrong; he denounced them as betrayers of the public trust. Yet he himself was not free from lapses in disinterested high-mindedness. When a number of Congressmen in 1926 condemned Mus-solini as a murderous dictator, La Guardia, although privately loathing Italian Fascism, protested against the condemnation for fear of losing his seat from Latin East Harlem.[15] Those and other defects, particularly visible in a man with a naked ambition for high office, had caused New Yorkers of nearly every political persuasion to doubt, at one time or another in his career, that La Guardia was fit to govern the biggest city in America.

That was the sentiment of an ad hoc committee of reformers and Republicans that had been formed in the spring of 1933 to select a candi-date for mayor to head an antimachine ticket in the coming fall election. La Guardia wanted desperately to be their choice. The Seabury investi-gations of Tammany Hall had made New York ripe for a reform movement, and only through the mayoralty could La Guardia rescue a political career that his unexpected defeat for reelection to Congress the previous year had left dangling in the balance. But the committee bypassed him, offering the nomination to a number of men who declined it and finally designating a General John F. O'Ryan to make the race.

La Guardia ultimately made the race, not O'Ryan, and in retrospect one can agree that he was the logical one to do so.

But no one even vaguely familiar with American election politics can think that logic is the sole arbiter of conflict. Because politics is men leading other men, it is subject to the worst as well as to the best in human nature, not to speak of the caprice of chance, timing, accident, and just plain luck. And because politics can take place only in society, it is intertwined with social custom, tradition, habit, and institutions. The complexity and range of variables were such that historians can never fully know how La Guardia in 1933 came to be thought of as the right man for the right job at the right time, but the answer as to why he came to be thought so lies not only in himself but in the New Yorkers and the New York that grudgingly gave him his prize.

La Guardia entered City Hall at the head of a coalition comprising disparate elements. Yet there could be no mistaking what was essential in his mandate. If New York City was still a Democratic town in 1933, it was even more an anti-Tammany town. The vote for O'Brien and McKee may have been 327,000 more than for La Guardia, but that for La Guardia and McKee was 891,000 more than for O'Brien. Even in Manhattan, where the Curry incumbent ran strongest, six voters in ten decided that it was time for a change. New York City had given La Guardia a mandate to clean the Wigwamean Stables.

It came from voters of every sort and condition, but in largest proportion from the middle and wealthy classes. This fits what scholars have recently discovered and professional politicians have known for a long time—that both suburbs and silk-stocking districts generate the most power for anti-boss movements. That's how it was in 1933. Central Park East gave La Guardia and McKee their highest joint assembly-district return, and Queens furnished the two men their highest borough return.

The most suburban part of New York City, with the largest proportion of homeowners and native Americans, Queens housed the kind of voters who, uncontrolled by bosses and concerned with such problems as the tax rate and local improvements, responded in loudest voice (74.96 percent) to the La Guardia–McKee call that government by boodle and crony must go.

And just as Central Park East was the most Protestant assembly district in New York City, Queens was the most Protestant borough.[16] Not that all Protestants are or have been advocates of good government—witness the Huey Long movement—but the political expression of the Protestant ethic has always emphasized the application of private standards of rectitude to public affairs. Most of the men in La Guardia's inner circle, Berle and Burlingham, Seabury and Windels, Chadbourne and Blanshard, Tuttle and Macy, Morris and Howard, were Protestants. Nor was it a coincidence that the La Guardia administration would have more Protestant appointees than any administration since that of the Brahmin mayor Seth Low.

But the La Guardia administration would also include a large number of Jews, and that was not due to a mere political payoff. Davidson and Price, who at first opposed La Guardia but ultimately supported him, spoke for a significant segment of New Yorkers devoted to municipal reform. The Jewish middle classes were, and had been since the 1910s, partners with their Protestant counterparts in keeping the Protestant ethic alive in New York City. That more of them did so proportionately than Catholics may have been due to the fact that proportionately more Jews than Catholics had risen out of the immigrant proletariat to the great American middle class. The Protestant ethic is, after all, synonymous with the American creed and middle-class morality.[17]

But La Guardia had also asked for a mandate to build a local welfare state in the interests of the non–middle classes. Did he receive it? The voters who should have responded most positively to him in this connection voted instead for McKee in Greenpoint and the South Bronx and for O'Brien in Hell's Kitchen, the Lower East Side, and other slums rimming the city. In fact, to see at a glance where La Guardia's main opposition came from, turn the pages of *New York City Market Analysis* to the maps of the blue-colored districts whose residents lived below the poverty line. The chief exception was, of course, the Italians, most of whom were poor and many very, very poor. But apart from a few intellectuals and a minority belonging to the middle classes or the progressive trade unions of the garment industry, the Italo-Americans rallied to La Guardia because, like the Fascist Mussolini, he was a famous brother who made one proud to be Latin. Recognition, not reform, was their motive.

There was no questioning the mandate, though, from the 60,000 or so Norman Thomas Socialists who voted for La Guardia instead of Solomon and the larger number of Hillquit Socialists who declared for him. Although heavily Jewish, the Socialists ranks included New Yorkers of nearly every background. Not only that, the more doctrinaire Socialists like Abraham Cahan of the *Forward* denounced La Guardia as a servant of "the rich and the landlords," whereas the *Nation,* published by William Lloyd Garrison's grandson, backed La Guardia in the belief that he would turn New York City into a gigantic laboratory in social experimentation. "It may be that a certain percentage of my *Nation* following will be less likely to go Socialist if they know I am actively at work for you," Oswald Garrison Villard wrote to La Guardia.[18] The size of the left-of-center intellectual vote is unknown, but there can be little doubt that La Guardia got most of it.

But in terms of numbers, the La Guardia era began with less electoral support for promoting social justice than for throwing the rascals out of office. To that extent the 1933 Fusion movement was like those of 1913 and 1901: a crusade for what has been called good, not welfare, government. La Guardia therefore occupies a place in the Goo Goo tradition. But as a plain man from the plain people, Fiorello had only one thing in common with the likes of Seth Low: Protestantism.

Besides, he had talked enough about the need for social justice in the campaign to suggest the direction of his administration. It was to move to the left as the Depression deepened and the New Deal philosophy of government with a heart became the official philosophy of the 1930s. The times were to demand the social and economic liberalism La Guardia had been preaching for years. When he ran for reelection in 1937 he would again do so as a Republican, but also and more importantly with an endorsement from the newly founded American Labor party. Created by both New Deal Democrats and New York Socialists, that party would enlarge the limited mandate for social reconstruction that La Guardia had received in 1933.

To the extent that La Guardia received the support of Democrats, Socialists, and independents, he was elected mayor in spite of being a Republican. Therein lies the City Fusion Party's major contribution to the outcome of 1933. It made it possible for many people to vote for La Guardia without having to vote Republican. The widespread and long-standing dislike of New Yorkers for the Grand Old Party cannot be emphasized too much, for in the forty years since President Calvin Coolidge's election in 1924 Senator Jacob Javits has been the only Republican to carry the city in the Republican column alone.

But La Guardia, while overcoming the unpopularity of the GOP label, also capitalized on his affiliation with it. Contradictory as the statement sounds, the mathematics of 1933 were such that he would have gone down to defeat had not some 450,000 Republican voters remained loyal to their party's choice. In contrast to purists who court only one kind of voter on the theory that electoral politics is either a matter of blind political fealty or an exercise in applied ideology, La Guardia was a pluralist and a pragmatist who practiced the politics of coalition. The mechanics of his coalition are relevant to any Republican who hopes to duplicate Fiorello's feat in New York City: a firm base in his own party, an endorsement from a third party, defections from all other parties, and a divided Democratic party.

Tammany itself paved the way for La Guardia's chance to remake New York City. And here one must say that, while it is a mistake to underestimate the shrewdness of the old-line big-city professional politicians, it is also an error to make them brainier than they were. More concretely, La Guardia's debt to Tammany's stupidity was as enormous as that stupidity was monumental. Tammany was asinine, to leave aside the question of ethics, to swill at the public trough in so outrageous a manner as to invite the Seabury investigations. That was the beginning of the Hall's downfall. What completed it was the further absurdity of naming O'Brien as La Guardia's rival. Not only was the incumbent a preposterous figure in 1933, but his renomination resulted in the Roosevelt-Flynn-Farley conclave to run McKee. That intervention split the Democratic vote and, although it may not have been the President's intention, terminated in La Guardia's victory.

"The division in the party," Boss McCooey of Brooklyn complained bitterly, "cost us the election." Jim Farley said much the same though in a different spirit: "We lose but Tammany doesn't win." And this is how La Guardia put it shortly after the election in a speech before the Legislative Correspondents' Dinner in Albany: "Before I do anything or say anything here tonight, I want to thank one man who, more than any other man, is responsible for my election as Mayor—Jim Farley. Put it there, Jim." Farley flushed, then shook La Guardia's hand, while the room burst into laughter.[19]

The question has often been asked if La Guardia would have defeated O'Brien by a majority if McKee had not entered the race and taken anti-Tammany votes from La Guardia. The answer is probably yes. The *Literary Digest*, which successfully predicted the outcome of the contest in successive polls from September up to Election Day, had La Guardia way ahead of O'Brien before it became a three-way campaign. Roosevelt intervened, moreover, after the results of both the polls and the September primaries pointed toward the Democrats' losing the city to Fusion. But in the end none of this is conclusive, and it is doubtful if we shall ever be sure of what would have happened.

Nor can we be certain of the answer to a question still more intriguing but less often asked, namely, would La Guardia have beaten McKee had McKee been the incumbent in a two-cornered race? The question isn't altogether fanciful, for Flynn had sought McKee's nomination in both 1932 and 1933. By every rule of common sense he deserved it. The first concern of professional politics is to survive through a winning candidate, and McKee had proved a good vote-getter both as a state legislator and as president of the Board of Aldermen. Moreover, a political leader is supposed to please a variety of people, and McKee had done that as acting mayor. There was, finally, no reason to question his party loyalty in 1932 or before September of 1933, for he had said publicly that he was proud to be an organization Democrat. One can only suppose that Curry's choice of O'Brien over McKee manifested an oddly political form of the death wish.

Now, if O'Brien, an affable incompetent, could have been elected in 1932—with the stink of the Seabury investigations still burning in New York's nose—is it not possible that McKee would have done the same that year? And is it not even more within the realm of possibility that he would have given a less ludicrous performance as mayor and, therefore, have been a harder man for La Guardia to beat? Above all and beyond everything else, McKee would have been a formidable opponent, as La Guardia knew, if he had not had to share the party vote with another Democrat. There is, of course, no telling how many of his antimachine votes McKee, as a Tammany incumbent, would have lost to La Guardia, but it is still hard not to believe that 1933 *could* have been a horse race if Curry had shown more horse sense.

It is even harder to imagine Curry's comedy of errors being produced when Charles F. Murphy headed the Hall. The Gashouse boy had scrubbed the Tiger's face after the dirty Croker regime and, although he made mistakes, he judged men and events with extraordinary shrewdness. During the Progressive Era, when New Yorkers wanted reform, Murphy sponsored such outstanding Democrats as Al Smith and Robert F. Wagner, Sr. Even La Guardia admired Murphy for his understanding of what people wanted. Curry was an intellectual pygmy by comparison. Unimaginative, stubborn, rigid, and senseless, he ran the organization Seabury investigated. Jimmy Walker pronounced the epitaph for the local democracy when he said, of Murphy's death in 1924: "The brains of Tammany Hall lie in Calvary Cemetery."[20]

Much has been written about politics in terms of aspirations, but not enough has been said of the politics of resentment. We would miss the significance of 1933 if we failed to understand that resentment was the unifying element in the La Guardia coalition. Republicans, Democrats, Socialists, and Mugwumps, Anglo-Saxons, Jews, and Italians—all had their particular grievances against the ruling machine, and in La Guardia these groups found an appropriate leader. A master of the politics of resentment, he had been expressing for decades the frustrations, angers, and exasperations of people who had been looking in on things from the outside.

But he was also a political leader who converted resentments into aspirations. An angry man, La Guardia had a vision: an alternative to government by discredited district leader. It isn't often that voters of a big city are offered a referendum of such importance. And if he catered to passion and prejudice and flung buckets of mud, as he had in the past, he also appealed to reason. One of his admirers, Professor Berle, has summed up the matter this way: La Guardia "could be and was a gutfighter in New York politics," but "he knew the difference between gut-fighting and the society he hoped to create."[21]

And credit, too, to the men around La Guardia and his staff in the field. They created an organization almost overnight, coordinated it as well as was possible under the circumstances, arranged hundreds of meetings, prepared news releases and leaflets, solicited funds, answered the telephone, rang doorbells, policed the polls—they attended, in short, to the grubby but necessary details by which campaigns are won. Special credit goes, of course, to Seabury. He set the Tiger up. He chose La Guardia to make the kill. Together the Little Flower and the Mayflower prodded Gotham's conscience to throw out the ruling clique that had been misgoverning the city.

So, thanks to himself but also with the help of Seabury and the gratuitous aid of the dodos of Tammany Hall, La Guardia entered City Hall. The choice of a minority, he had received a conditional mandate. Whether he could consolidate his victory, and forge a wider political realignment against the united opposition he would face in 1937, would depend on how in the next four years he used the immense power he finally commanded.

NOTES

1. For the details concerning La Guardia's hybrid background, see Arthur Mann, *La Guardia, A Fighter Against His Times, 1882–1933* (Philadelphia, 1959), pp. 19–42, 100, 237, 246–56, and *passim.*

2. For a splendid account of the pluralist pressures on those who govern New York City, see Wallace S. Sayre, Herbert Kaufman, *Governing New York City* (New York, 1960), pp. 39ff.

3. Frank Dyer Chester to Robert Bacon, January 17, 1906, *Consular Dispatches,* vol. IV, Records of the Department of State, Record Group 59, National Archives; memorandum by La Guardia, enclosed with Chester to Bacon, March 8, 1906, *ibid.*

4. *The New York Times,* May 4, 1918.

5. *Nowy Swiat,* November 6, 1942; interview with Paul Windels, New York City, summer, 1956.

6. Interview with Joey Adams, New York City, December 13, 1958.

7. Quoted in Charles Garrett, *The La Guardia Years, Machine and Reform Politics in New York City* (New Brunswick, 1961), p. 123.

8. Charles Culp Burlingham, *Reminiscences* (Oral History Project, Columbia University, 1961), p. 34.

9. Edward J. Flynn, *You're the Boss* (New York, 1947), p. 138.

10. Interview with Mrs. Gemma La Guardia Gluck, La Guardia's sister, Long Island City, N.Y., July 19, 1956.

11. For the titles in La Guardia's personal library in 1933, see "Books Sent to 1274 Fifth Avenue," LGP.

12. Walter Johnson, *William Allen White's America* (New York, 1947), 466–7. For other expressions concerning La Guardia and the Presidency, see *The New York Times,* November 4, 7, and 21, 1937; *Current History,* XLVII (December 1937), 16–17; Karl Schriftgiesser, "Portrait of a Mayor, Fiorello La Guardia," *Atlantic Monthly,* CLXI (January 1938), 63; *Fortune,* XVII (January 1938), 92; John Chamberlain, "Mayor La Guardia," *Yale Review,* XXIX (September 1939), 27; C. B. Yorke to La Guardia, December 20, 1937, LGP; Eugene M. Elliott to La Guardia, March 24, 1938, *ibid.;* La Guardia to Elliott, April 4, 1938, *ibid.* For Tugwell's tribute to La Guardia, see his review of the first volume of this biography in the *The New York Times* book review section of Sunday, November 15, 1959, and his *The Art of Politics, as Practiced by Three Great Americans: Franklin Delano Roosevelt, Luis Muñoz Marin, and Fiorello H. La Guardia* (Garden City, 1958).

13. Quoted in Duff Gilfond, "La Guardia of Harlem," *American Mercury,* XI (June 1927), 155.

14. *New York Herald Tribune,* July 6, 1924.

15. *The New York Times,* September 26, 1926; *Congressional Record,* 69 Cong., Sess. I, pp. 2010–12, 2135.

16. Walter Laidlaw, *Population of the City of New York, 1890–1930* (New York, 1932), p. 275.

17. For similar views about Jews and Protestants in anti-boss movements, see Daniel P. Moynihan, "Bosses and Reformers," *Commentary,* XXXI (June 1961), 461–70; Theodore J. Lowi, *At the Pleasure of the Mayor: Patronage and Power in New York City, 1898–1958* (New York, 1964), especially pp. 36, 38, 197–9; Richard Skolnik, "The Crystallization of Reform in New York City, 1890–1917" (unpublished Ph.D. dissertation, Yale University, 1964), pp. 22–54, 386–7, and *passim;* James Q. Wilson, *The Amateur Democrat: Club Politics in Three Cities* (Chicago, 1962), pp. 2–58, 265–7, and *passim.*

18. Oswald Garrison Villard to La Guardia, August 28, 1933, LGP.

19. The quotations come, in order of appearance, from the *New York Daily News,* November 8, 1933; *New York Herald Tribune,* November 8, 1933; Reuben A. Lazarus, *Reminiscences* (Oral History Project, Columbia University, 1949–51), pp. 169–70.

20. Quoted in Gene Fowler, *The Life & Times of Jimmy Walker, Beau James* (New York, 1949), p. 11. For two illuminating assessments of Murphy's talents, see J. Joseph Huthmacher, "Charles Evans Hughes and Charles Francis Murphy: The Metamorphosis of Progressivism," *New York History,* XLVI (January 1965), 25–40; Nancy J. Weiss, "Charles Francis Murphy, 1858–1924: Respectability and Responsibility in Tammany Politics" (Smith College honors thesis, 1965).

21. Adolf A. Berle to Arthur Mann, March 31, 1965.

PART SEVEN

DILEMMAS OF METROPOLITAN AMERICA

"We're going to win. My God, we're going to win," shrieked an elderly man listening to the election returns in the Georgian Room of Newark's Robert Treat Hotel. "Black power," chanted the younger set, their fists raised. "Beep, beep make way." And they did win. In 1970 thirty-seven-year-old Kenneth Gibson became the first black mayor in the history of Newark, New Jersey. A few miles to the north in suburban Mahwah, the city council and the local populace were doing everything in their power to keep the poor, and especially poor blacks, out. And on the Great Plains, in hamlets such as Roundup, Montana, and Howard, South Dakota, disgruntled townspeople noted the 1970 census figures, which documented the departure of their young people for warmer climes and larger cities.

All three events were part of the widely recognized pattern of life in the United States in the 1970s—black and poor inner cities, white suburbs, and depopulated rural areas. Yet, as previously noted, all three trends began a century ago and have been especially noticeable since 1920. That year is often considered a watershed in American history because it marked the first time that the United States could officially be designated an "urban" nation. In 1920, 51.4 percent of all Americans lived in municipalities of 2,500 or more inhabitants; by 1970 the urban population had risen above 75 percent and the number of farmers had dropped to about 5 million.

Today the terms "urban" and "rural" no longer accurately portray the American profile. A century ago there was a sharp, visible, and easily understood difference between the "city" and the "country." A city, unlike the country immediately surrounding it, was compact and densely settled. And it offered social, cultural, and commercial interaction, which the country lacked. Since then the distinction between "urban" and "rural" has become blurred. Telephones, toilets, radios, and refrigerators—once symbols of an urban, if not an urbane, existence—are now commonly available in the remotest corners of the land. And no longer are the

visual differences between city and country quite so distinct. A century
or more ago, the traveler emerged from forests or prairies into a compact
community that stood out from the surrounding area. He knew when he
had come "to town." Long before the modern traveler reaches the city, he
is confronted by miles of motels, restaurants, service stations, and
billboards. The city of today is more readily identified by its welcome
signs and speed-limit notices than by any contrast with its environs.

Needless to say, the automobile more than any other single invention or
innovation has been responsible for the physical and social changes of
modern America. Only 8,000 of the curious vehicles were on the streets in
1900, but within the space of a single generation Henry Ford and his
Model T turned a novelty of the rich into a necessity of the middle class.
Automobile registrations climbed to 100,000 by 1906, to 1 million by 1913,
and to 10 million by 1922. By 1927 there was one automobile for
every five people.

Along with the automobile came a vast expansion of the nation's road
and highway system. In 1914 there were almost no decent roads outside
the East, and crossing the continent by automobile was a high adventure.
Change came rapidly. In 1916 the Federal Aid Road Act offered funds
to states that organized highway departments and launched programs,
and in 1925 the value of highway construction projects exceeded $1
billion per year for the first time. Most of the mileage consisted of
one- or two-lane roads. In heavily trafficked areas wider thoroughfares
seemed necessary. The Henry Hudson Parkway in New York City, the
first freeway to have limited access, no grade crossings, and service stations
of its own, was begun in 1934, and in 1940, the nation's first long-distance
superhighway, the Pennsylvania Turnpike, was opened. Finally, in 1956, the
greatest public works project of all time began with the passage of the
Interstate Highway Act.

Together the automobile and the highway have revolutionized life in the
United States. An initial concern was that passenger cars would become,
in the words of a judge, "houses of prostitution on wheels," because
they allowed men and women to be together far from the eyes and ears
of chaperones. But the most far-reaching effects have been upon the
day-to-day lives of a mobile citizenry. Neighborhood theaters have
given way to drive-in theaters, and the local soda fountain to drive-in
hamburger and hot-dog stands. Banks have added drive-in windows, and
small "7-11"-type grocery stores have opened that cater to motorists. In
suburban Garden Grove, California, a huge community church, situated
appropriately on twenty acres of land near a freeway interchange, offers
its 6,000 members the benefits of drive-in religious services. Ushers step

to the automobile window and direct the driver's attention to the announcement: "If you have a car radio, please turn to 540 on your dial for this service. If you do not have a radio, please park by the amplifiers in the back row."

Not least among the effects of the automobile age has been the changing pattern of retail shopping. During the time of the horse-car and the trolley, large department stores—John Wanamaker's in Philadelphia, Macy's and Gimbel's in New York, Marshall Field's in Chicago, Hudson's in Detroit, Jordan Marsh in Boston—grew up and prospered in downtown areas. A new method of retailing was presaged in the 1920s when Sears, Roebuck and Company embraced the concept of "America on wheels." The world's foremost mail-order house determined that because automobile registrations had outstripped the parking available in downtown areas, it would be sensible to build in outlying districts new outlets that would offer the advantage of lower rentals and yet, because of the great mobility of Americans, still be within reach of potential customers.

Another retailing development was the shopping center. The nation's first such center, a complex of stores with off-street parking, opened inside Baltimore's city limits in 1907. After Jesse Clyde Nichols built a similar complex in Kansas City in 1923, the former was designated a "neighborhood" center and the latter a "suburban" one. Then, shortly after World War II, the concept was further expanded by the erection of "regional" shopping centers, or self-contained business centers, remote from downtown. Prototypes like Northgate near Seattle, Shopper's World outside Boston, and Lakewood outside Los Angeles opened around 1950. By 1970 there were more than 13,000 shopping centers in the nation, and in some metropolitan areas, notably Boston and St. Louis, they were accounting for more than two-thirds of the local retail trade. As a suburban newspaper said of a shopping center near Detroit, "one could easily spend one's whole life in the Northland location and never want for anything."

The rise of the automobile, the highway, and the suburban shopping center has led to the collapse of all but a few mass transportation systems in the United States. Except for a brief period after World War II, the decline of trolleys, buses, and commuter railroads has continued since the Depression. The process of decline is circular: increasing reliance on automobiles leads to a decline in the availability and income of public transportation, which in turn increases reliance on the automobile. In New York City, which has the most extensive and heavily patronized mass transportation network in the world, as well as the most uncomfortable daily commuters, the system loses about $50 million per year despite a decrease in services. The Long Island Railroad, notes Columbia University economist William Vickrey, ran fifty or sixty trains an hour into Pennsylvania Station in the late 1930s; in 1971, with the commuter population on Long Island larger by 200 percent, the LIRR ran a maximum of thirty trains per hour into Manhattan. The situation is equally deplorable in Los Angeles, where those who do not have cars are totally cut off from jobs and those who do are caught in ever-larger traffic jams.

Forty-five years ago Henry Ford ventured the prediction that, because of the automobile, "the city is doomed." Certainly the city and the automobile are in many respects incompatible. Space simply does not exist for an ever-increasing number of cars and trucks in cities (one study has shown that if all of Manhattan's commuters arrived by automobile, five levels of parking space would be required over all the usable land from the Bowery to 52nd Street). Yet traffic engineers continue to widen streets or narrow sidewalks in the apparent conviction that machines enjoy a higher claim to space than people. Fifty percent of the total land area of most downtown areas is taken up by streets, parking lots, and expressways; in downtown Los Angeles the proportion under pavement is 65 percent. Mayors and downtown businessmen are themselves responsible for much of this folly. In the mistaken hope that new freeways will make the business center more accessible to commuters, businesses and homes are being bulldozed to make room for cars. The resulting loss of excitement is potentially devastating to a city. As Raymond Tucker, mayor of St. Louis and former president of the American Municipal Association, put it, "The plain fact of the matter is that we just cannot build enough lanes of highways to move all of our people by private automobile and create enough parking space to store the cars without completely paving over our cities and removing all of the . . . economic, social, and cultural establishments that the people were trying to reach in the first place."

Moreover, the internal combustion engine is the single largest contributor to urban air pollution. As Otis Dudley Duncan has said, "Where could one find a more perfect instance of the principle of circular causation, than that of the Los Angeles commuters speeding down their freeways in a rush to escape the smog produced by emissions from the very cars they are riding in?" Mass transit systems not only pollute the air less than automobiles, but also move people more efficiently, cost less per person and cause fewer deaths. Yet the trend toward paving over the nation continues. As of 1971 California, which has been called a large body of automobiles surrounded by highway signs, had lost more than 150 million acres just to freeways. That figure is expected to double in the 1970s. And surely the gasoline consumed by a car idling in a traffic tie-up is not the best possible use of America's limited petroleum resources. An encouraging, although grossly inadequate, first step to undo the urban snarl came early in 1971 when Congress finally approved a sweeping, twelve-year, $10 billion mass-transit program.

In the twentieth century people have been willing to suffer the frustrations of commuting because they have felt the alternative of living in the central city to be worse. Many have left the city for the pleasures of owning their own home, but others have been motivated by racial changes in their old neighborhoods. Of the nation's almost 11 million blacks in 1920, only 34 percent (compared with 53 percent of the whites) lived in cities and towns. The intervening half-century has seen dramatic changes in these statistics; as of 1970 more than 80 percent of the blacks (compared with 75 percent of the whites) lived in cities. The migration has generally been to inner neighborhoods. Atlanta, Washington, Gary, and Newark already have black majorities, and predications are common that half a dozen other core cities will join them by 1985.

Tragically, the continuing migration of black Americans from the plantation South has not significantly improved the basic quality of their lives. The pattern of the ghetto in 1920—residential segregation, underemployment, substandard housing, disrupted family life, inferior education, filth, and disease—has continued into the 1970s. Even racial violence, which in the "red summer" of 1919 claimed well over 100 lives in a dozen cities, has continued into the space age. As Richard C. Wade demonstrates in his essay "Violence in the Cities: A Historical View," rioting is a result of blacks being prevented from entering American society on the same terms as other groups before them. Thus the most striking feature of black life is not slum conditions, but the barriers that middle-class blacks encounter in trying to escape the ghetto.

In the catalog of current urban problems, crime has assumed an overriding importance. "Violence," observed H. Rap Brown, "is as American as cherry pie." Homicide rates suggest the accuracy of his claim. The United States is the world's most violent "advanced" country; its murder rate is four times as high as that of Canada, six times that of France, and seven times that of England. Houston, in fact, has in several years recorded more homicides than all of England, which has forty-five times as many people.

A common notion is that the middle-class white is the most frequent victim of criminal activity. Actually, crime is overwhelmingly a ghetto phenomenon. Because the poor, black and white, are concentrated there, and because unemployment rates, addiction to narcotics, and other indices of social dislocation are highest there, it is the slum dweller who suffers most and seems to receive the least protection. Blacks are more likely than whites to be victimized by forcible rape, aggravated assault, burglary, motor-vehicle theft, and willful homicide. In fact, a nationwide study by the Small Business Administration in 1968 demonstrated that ghetto businesses were burglarized, robbed, or vandalized about twice as often as stores in the suburbs.

State and federal governments give lip service to urban problems such as crime and poverty, but their response has been half-hearted and even counterproductive. Urban renewal and the Federal Housing Administration are only the most obvious examples.

To date, the basic urban-renewal statutes have been Title I of the Housing Act of 1949 and the Housing Act of 1954. According to the general principle of urban renewal, a city can acquire and assemble properties in a blighted area, using its power of eminent domain where necessary. Public funds are spent not as subsidies to redevelopers, who must pay the fair value of the cleared land, but as the cost of achieving a public purpose—the elimination of slums. Many of the "renewal" neighborhoods have experienced a renaissance; once block upon block of cancerous buildings, they are now impressive housing projects offering a better life to lower- and middle-income residents. In some instances, however, urban renewal has meant evicting people with no concern for their welfare or getting "undesirables" out of "desirable" neighborhoods by spot clearance. And even in the best of circumstances, the "new" housing usually has appeared several years after the "old" housing has been destroyed.

Even more damaging to the inner city has been the Federal Housing Administration, which between 1935 and 1967 issued more than $84 billion in mortgage insurance. These loans favored single-family construction in the suburbs, discouraged multifamily units through unfavorable terms, and discriminated openly against mixed neighborhoods. The FHA warned against "adverse influences" such as smoke, odor, and "inharmonious racial or nationality groups" and openly recommended "suitable restrictive covenants." Whole areas of large cities were declared ineligible for FHA loans because they were not expected to remain "suitable for residences." By becoming an active hindrance to the economic viability of urban neighborhoods, the FHA stripped American cities of much of their middle-class and middle-aged constituency, leaving them as havens for the very rich and the very poor, the very young and the very old. Jane Jacobs has commented that "Credit-blacklisting maps, like slum-clearance maps, are accurate prophecies because they are self-fulfilling prophecies."

Federal Housing Administration loans, like oil depreciation allowances, are not often thought of as giveaways to those who benefit from them. Instead, the middle class tends to accept grants from the federal government for schools and police and then protest "special pleadings for special interests." This double standard was what Martin Luther King had in mind when he said, "The rich man gets a subsidy and the poor man gets a handout."

Similar logic is behind the nation's current welfare policy, which regards public assistance as a local responsibility. Despite overwhelming evidence that unemployment is a national problem, New York City must support more than 15 percent of all the relief recipients in the United States, while several wealthy communities nearby need contribute nothing in local taxes to help.

The seeming ability of individual citizens to escape from crime, blight, and central-city tax burdens by the simple expedient of moving to the suburbs is among the major dilemmas of metropolitan America. There is nothing new about the drift of the middle class to the periphery; that has been the tendency for more than a century. What is new about their flight is the mental attitudes they display as suburban homeowners. Their sense of metropolitan identity is weak; they neither desire nor expect to remain a part of the central city. As Kenneth T. Jackson points out in his essay on suburban growth, the new pattern has fragmented local government to the point of absurdity. The New York metropolitan area alone includes more than 1,400 separate governments; the Chicago area has more than 1,000. Overlapping jurisdictions, inefficient public services, and unresponsive commissions are tolerated by the populace in order to maintain varying levels of homogeneity in the suburbs. Zoning in particular has become a highly arbitrary and discriminatory device for effectively preserving the status quo. While it benefits those who seek to retain at least a suggestion of rusticity, zoning penalizes the poor who are thereby effectively locked into old apartments in congested neighborhoods because of their inability to build, say, a detached, five-bedroom home on a two-acre lot.

Meanwhile the city-destroying cycle continues. First businesses, industries, and individuals move out of the urban core—some because of rising taxes, others for want of more space, still others out of fear of minority groups. Then property values decline, or at least fail to rise proportionately with prices, and low-income families move into the area. The new residents typically require more services from the city government than did the old. The city government must therefore increase expenditures. This in turn raises taxes, and the cycle repeats itself.

Thus, in an age of cities, our cities are dying. The nation sends astronauts to the moon and fights wars around the world but seems unable to rid its slums of rodents or build adequate housing for its poor. Crumbling tenements stand within blocks of gleaming skyscrapers. R. Buckminster Fuller and other visionary planners suggest that this is because the city is obsolete and that our energies might better be directed toward the creation of an environment more suitable to the space era. According to their view, the United States is entering a post-urban age.

The theory of a dissolving city is predicted upon the mistaken notion that telecommunications can substitute for that concentration of social and cultural forces which is so unique to cities and so necessary to civilization. The continuing growth of the suburbs threatens to rob the city of its diversity and excitement and the country of its serenity and beauty. But hopefully, Americans will realize that there is intrinsic value in the magnitude of great cities and that the intense human action of urban life stimulates creative thought. The city offers independence and wider intellectual horizons for the intelligent, the able, the talented, and the adventuresome, as well as encouragement and recognition for musicians, poets, dancers, actors, and philosophers. Man's greatest achievements have been realized not in the pastures and plains, but in the smelly streets of Pericles' Athens, Shakespeare's London, Rembrandt's Amsterdam, and Voltaire's Paris. History offers no examples of great societies that existed independently of great cities. The words of Eric Hoffer are apposite:

If this nation decays and declines it will not be because we have raped and ravaged a continent, but because we do not know how to build and run viable cities. America's destiny will be decided in the cities.

24. THE CITY COMES TO MAIN STREET

Lewis Atherton

Except for those towns that have grown spectacularly because of twentieth-century revolutions in transportation, management, and technology, the modern age has been unkind to country towns, unkind, that is, because they have refused in most cases to change their basic philosophies and their basic ways of achieving their desires. As in an earlier day, they still look to industrialization, improved transportation, exploitation of local mineral resources, and trade-at-home, hometown loyalty to bring them happiness. They still believe that the immediately useful and the practical must come first and that they must surpass all others in real-estate prices and population.

Early in the twentieth century, for example, the Brookfield, Missouri, editor published an article headed "Stand Up For Brookfield," in which he urged citizens to establish an "Improvement Association" to foster industry. In his opinion, Brookfield needed to start a pump or gasoline engine factory or to encourage the Burlington railroad to open a car manufactory locally. The local newspaper and the Brookfield Commercial Club were more than ready to act in 1907 when the industrial commissioner of the C. B. and Q. Railroad, which ran through Brookfield, announced that the Brown Shoe Company of St. Louis, Missouri, might consider establishing a branch plant locally capable of employing 500 workers. The local editor demanded immediate action to raise whatever subsidies might be necessary to bring the plant to Brookfield. Only a few months earlier he had printed a plea from the Mexico, Missouri, newspaper asking towns not to bid against one another for factories. Apparently, Moberly, Missouri, had found out how much Mexico had raised to obtain a branch of the Brown Shoe Company, and had then won the prize by offering $10,000 more. The Brookfield editor demanded an all-out effort to avoid a similar calamity.

The crusade opened in high gear. No one knew how large a bonus would be necessary but the local editor felt that future returns would justify any current sacrifice. Such a plant would boom the price of property; vacant houses would be filled; all would find employment at good wages.

From *Main Street on the Middle Border* by Lewis Atherton, pp. 338–48, 353–57. Copyright © 1954 by Indiana University Press. Reprinted by permission of the publisher.

The Commercial Club met daily to plan ways to raise the necessary subsidy. They bought land and divided it into lots for sale at $200 each. Buyers thus added to the bonus fund and provided themselves with real estate that was sure to boom in value when the new plant opened. Within two or three days after the campaign started, the Commercial Club sent a delegation to St. Louis to notify the shoe company that Brookfield was offering a free factory site and $40,000 in cash. Within a week, the local paper carried headlines, "Necessary Money Raised."

The shoe company prolonged local tension by examining competing sites. Chillicothe and Macon, Missouri, decided not to compete with Brookfield, a gesture which brought a "Thank you, Sisters" from the Brookfield editor and a promise to return the favor when they wanted something in the future. But Taylorville, Illinois, was still in the running.

Brookfield was not to be denied. She solicited congressmen and county officials for donations. When the venerable Dr. H. DeGraw, a local leader for many years, walked through the rain to address one of the mass meetings at Elks Hall, and then made a liberal contribution, others in the packed building doubled their pledges. Prospects of a factory employing 500 people to make "fine ladies' shoes" aroused hometown loyalty to feverish pitch. Week by week the cash bonus and other gifts increased in size. When the contract was signed in June of 1907, the bonus had reached $60,000, and the city also agreed to furnish free a factory site, water, and sewage disposal. In return, the shoe company promised to erect a three-story brick building 45 by 250 feet and to start making shoes as soon as labor could be obtained.

A few days after the successful campaign ended the local paper mentioned the suicide of H. B. Clarkson, an eighty-year-old resident. As a younger man, Clarkson had been a butcher, grocer, and livestock dealer, and at one time had been financially independent. Age and financial difficulties had reduced him to the extremity of paying out his last money for board and then to weighting his pockets with stones and drowning himself in Yellow Creek. In that age of rugged individualism, many people were embarrassed if offered public assistance but bonuses to industry were another matter.

The Brookfield branch of the Brown Shoe Company failed to reach the heights predicted for it by zealots during the bonus raising period. It has produced medium-priced and work shoes rather than fine quality products, mostly perhaps because unskilled labor in the Brookfield area could not handle quality production in the earlier years. In an early defense of the plant against its critics, the local editor granted that many employees received only a small weekly wage but pointed out that they were paid regularly. Without the factory, they would have had only intermittent work or none at all. In reality, many of them had come to Brookfield to work in the factory, and they probably cost the town more than they contributed in taxes from their meager incomes. In 1911, trouble of some sort developed between local workers and "foreigners" imported from St. Louis.

During World War I the plant was so embarrassed with unfilled orders that Brookfield's city fathers staged a campaign to recruit workers. When the plant reduced production in the hard times following the war and again in the early 1930s, Brookfield had a surplus of poorly trained workers to add to her problems. Machine shops erected by the C. B. and Q. Railroad helped Brookfield far more over the years, and they had cost the city nothing in the way of a bonus.

Nonetheless, Brookfield has been inclined to defend its investment in the shoe plant. In 1926, the city entertained officers from the mother company in St. Louis and local employees in honor of the plant's nineteenth anniversary. The occasion was marked by goodwill on all sides. When the president of the organization finished his address to plant workers assembled at one of the local theaters, a girl employed by the Brookfield factory proudly remarked to her boy friend, "He ain't a bit stuck up, is he?" Moreover, Brookfield continued to offer subsidies to prospective factories, although none comparable to the shoe plant in size was obtained.[1]

Experience of town after town in the Middle West shows the danger of subsidizing industry indiscriminately. Many promoters prey on small-town enthusiasm, with cash bonuses the real object in mind. As early as 1898, when Gower, Missouri, was said to be seeking a flour mill and a canning factory, the Brookfield editor sourly remarked that Gower might have trouble finding a flour mill, but that promoters kept canning factories and creameries in stock to unload on gullible communities.[2]

Enthusiasm would remain within bounds if city fathers would only remember that subsidized industries as a whole have low capital investments and depend on unskilled, low-paid labor. Towns made up of such workers lack the necessary tax structure to maintain adequate services for their citizens. While untrained workers may gain in skill, industries employing the unskilled will want to move on when that occurs. After towns have subsidized an industry, and have thus become emotionally involved, they often oppose efforts of their own unskilled workers to raise wages by unionization. When danger of unionization threatened a subsidized industry in Warsaw, Illinois, the following announcement appeared in the local paper:

To Warsaw Citizens

For several years citizens have put forth much effort and considerable expense in their endeavor to bring an industry to Warsaw. After several months of negotiation and investigation, the Mirro Leather Goods Company of Chicago has been induced to move its plant to our community. . . .

Unfortunately agitation and intimidation is being attempted by paid organizers who care nothing for our community and who are schooled and trained in the art of creating unrest.

The citizens of Warsaw are capable of handling any situation that may arise without the aid of outside paid agitators, who do not have the best interests of Warsaw and its people at heart. The local Factory Committee will be in constant contact with

the situation for the mutual benefit of the Mirro Leather Goods Company and
its employees.

Let us stand behind the Mirro Leather Goods Company and give them a chance
for our mutual success.

Warsaw Factory Committee[3]

Such touching loyalty appeals to industries anxious to escape the higher
wages demanded by unionized groups in cities.

Professional and literary people who grew up in small towns have
recognized the folly of trying to buy industrialization. Ed Howe's famous
Story of a Country Town, which appeared in 1882, suggested that factories
would seek out those towns suited to industrialization. Howe also spoke
of the disillusionment and frustration associated with poorly conceived
efforts to attract factories:

There was a very general impression that manufactories were needed, and this was
talked about so much, and so many inducements were offered, that the people
became discouraged, believing that the average manufacturer had a wicked heart
and a hollow head to thus wrong Twin Mounds . . .

The people were always miserable by reason of predictions that, unless impossible
amounts of money were given to certain enterprises, the town would be ruined,
and although they always gave, no sooner was one fund exhausted than it became
necessary to raise another. . . . I have thought that Twin Mounds would have been
a much better town but for the fact that it was always expecting improbable disaster,
but which never came, for the people were thus prevented from exercising their
energy, if they had any.[4]

Other perhaps less realistic critics have emphasized the destruction of
creative talent among small-town artisans when factories have taken over.
In his *Memoirs* Sherwood Anderson spoke of the "boss" in an Ohio
bicycle factory who was reduced to routine activity when once he had
been free to exercise some ingenuity in building carriages one by one:

"Here we paint these bicycles," he said. "Well, you see, we do not paint them.
We dip them in these goddamn tanks filled with this stinking stuff. It is true that
I do not myself dip them into the tanks. I stripe the damn things. You see how it is,
there are thousands and thousands and thousands of them, all striped just alike.

.   .   .

I tell you, boy, you get out of here as soon as you can. I am getting old and I have
to do what I can."[5]

Believing as they did in the immediately useful and the practical, townsmen, of course, paid no attention to people foolish enough to write
novels.

Country towns have found industrial opportunities in processing farm crops, and some have profited from diversified industries. Forty Wisconsin towns subsidized a total of 130 industrial plants between 1930 and 1945. An investigation of these subsidized industries in 1947 indicated that they had created a relatively satisfactory amount of new industrial employment and an increase in industrial payrolls. Nevertheless, subsidies were very large in comparison to results obtained in a number of towns, and perhaps improving economic conditions contributed to the favorable overall record. In Wisconsin, as elsewhere, success in subsidizing new industries has depended on the selection of stable firms suited economically to the local community, with financial aid limited to the amount necessary to overcome "economic immobilities and frictions which prevent the operation of basic economic forces."[6] When country towns depart from such principles they generally become involved in expensive and unprofitable undertakings.

Trade-at-home, hometown loyalty campaigns have grown in favor because of increased competition from mail-order houses and chain stores. Syndicates have thus found a market among country newspapers for long series of articles on the virtues of hometown loyalty. In the fall of 1935 the Clinton, Wisconsin, paper ran a series of twelve "editorials" on the virtues of "keeping money at home." These pictured Clinton merchants as the nucleus of a local network of community activities. Once the merchants disappeared, the cement binding the local community together would be gone. Many arguments were advanced to prove that it was cheaper to buy in Clinton stores. Rents and wages were said to be cheaper in smaller towns. Moreover, customers had to pay for the many services offered by city stores. In the end, they paid the salary of

the resplendent man with the brass buttons; of the fashionable information woman; of the floor walker with the wavy, blond pompadour; of the elevator starter with the natty uniform; of the demonstrator of the latest beauty preparations; of the attendant in nurse's uniform in the rest room; of the cash girls; of the force of plain clothes store detectives; of the credit department members with their extensive records that help them decide who shall not be permitted to run a bill and when they err to help them make good the loss.[7]

Such campaigns were never very effective. A comparison of prices and qualities of goods available locally and of those sold in cities and by mail-order houses convinced most customers that they suffered by slavish devotion to one town. When farmers of the Braham, Minnesota, community were asked about hometown loyalty in 1915, they answered: "Business is business; let the local storekeeper handle only those things that he can handle more cheaply than the mail-order houses." Likewise, in Pickaway County, Ohio, in 1927: "Farmers bought their supplies wherever they could get them most conveniently or most cheaply. They did not hesitate in going to distant towns or sending to mail-order houses if they thought that it would pay them to do so. When they traded near home they did so because it did not pay financially to go elsewhere, and not because of any recognition of mutual interest with the local dealer.[8]

Many outside organizations have been interested in helping country towns. National commissions, universities, and national foundations have all contributed ideas. Since so many different groups have been involved, and the movement has been in existence for so many years, on one agency can be credited with having developed a program strictly on its own. Suggestions have overlapped throughout the whole movement and have waxed and waned in no strict chronological order.

One of the earliest organized movements was devoted to beautifying country towns. Long before Hamlin Garland spoke of "barbed-wire" villages, Susan Fenimore Cooper urged citizens to form village improvement societies and to foster picturesque architecture, vine-covered stone bridges, brick and flagstone sidewalks, "overhanging trees," and street names with some originality.

At times, suggestions have bordered on the ridiculous. Mrs. Cooper thought that the name "Main Street" was fitting and proper, but that "Broadway" was an affectation. Perhaps, however, it served better than some of the names which she proposed to substitute. She preferred names of birds, trees, and animals, such as pewee, woodpecker, sparrow, chickadee, moose, bear, and stag. Midwesterners quite properly have balked at the idea of meeting friends on the corner of Chickadee and Moose or Pewee and Bear streets.

Similarly, so far as the writer knows, no one has ever complimented the architecture of the Midwestern Main Street. Highly utilitarian and nondescript, it has been both grim and drab. Nonetheless, it is better than the suggestion offered in *House Beautiful* for the improvement of Main Street, Wheaton, Illinois. An architect, Jarvis Hunt, was stranded in the local railroad station for a few minutes in 1909, long enough for him to observe the graceless and unimaginative store buildings along the main business street. Hunt submitted plans for altering this to the magazine. He proposed to use brick, cement plaster and wooden cross beams to change the appearance of all store fronts to a new type of architecture which he described as "A little English, a touch of German, all planned by a Yankee —perhaps just 'Wheatonesque.' " Whatever called, the form failed to touch a single indigenous strand in Midwestern history, as a glance at the before-and-after pictures will show, and thus failed to improve on the admittedly poor form which it was intended to replace.

Nevertheless, the Middle West had much to learn from Eastern sources about village beautification. Local improvement associations, starting with one in Stockbridge, Massachusetts, well before the Civil War, made their own communities beauty conscious. By the 1880s and 1890s periodicals like the *Chautauquan* were offering sensible and inexpensive suggestions for village improvement.[9] And, of course, the charm of old New England villages challenged "barbed-wire" Midwestern towns to seek a sense of beauty of their own.

The most popular and most effective programs depend on detailed surveys and detailed planning for more effective use of community resources. In 1917, for example, Bellville, Ohio, claimed credit for having made the first complete community survey, although other towns may have preceded it by as much as two or three years. Bellville felt sure that its revitalized church, school, and community program would make it a model American village.[10] In 1949, five small towns in central Illinois made a similar report on their joint activities during the preceding three years. In cooperation with newspaper editors and the University of Illinois they made detailed surveys of their needs and resources. Mass meetings gave citizens an opportunity to contribute toward the shaping of new programs. At such a meeting in Lexington, Illinois, a teenager impressed the group with her comment, "Speaking of *our children*, all you older people think it's wrong of us young ones to go off to Bloomington and Peoria to shows, dances and stuff. Well, what else are we supposed to do? What have *you* got to offer?"[11] Such challenges and much hard thought have stimulated the building of community houses, better farm–town relationships, and an educational curriculum adjusted to the needs of those intending to remain in the local community. Appreciation of relationships with the larger outside world, renewed hope, and energy have also resulted from the community survey movement.

Survey-planning programs have been particularly effective in making towns more conscious of the surrounding farm population on which their prosperity depends. After a survey and planning session in 1915 at Sauk City, Wisconsin, under the auspices of the state university, farmers and townsmen alike recognized the need for greater solidarity. Towns are learning that free picture shows, free band concerts, and giveaway contests and drawings will not win farm loyalty. Trite as it seems, the secret of improved relations lies in doing things *with* farmers rather than *for* farmers.

For sixty-nine years, St. Johns, Michigan, wanted to become an industrial city. Large sums of money were raised to subsidize industry but the results were disappointing. Local businessmen gave $150,000 toward the building of a local truck plant in the booming times just preceding the end of World War I, only to see this industry move to Detroit as soon as hostilities ended. Young people left St. Johns; population dipped below 4,000; and two new highways threatened to draw off much of the remaining trade to other towns. At the height of the emergency, in 1924, the town turned to the staff of the state agricultural college for advice. They told St. Johns that its location in the heart of rich agricultural land would guarantee its survival, and that it might grow if it would build first-class schools, up-to-date churches, a modern hospital, efficient wholesale and retail stores, sympathetic banking institutions, and ample recreational facilities.

The city fathers worked out a long-range program to achieve those ends.

They built a new community hospital. They constructed a new and modern high school with gymnasium and auditorium to serve a student body of which more than half lived on surrounding farms. They turned sixty acres of land, originally bought by the town for factory sites, into a park. They used brick from abandoned factory buildings to build pavilions, rest stations, and band shells. They dedicated the largest pavilion of all to the use of local 4-H clubs and encouraged country people to feel that the park belonged to them and to use its tennis courts and playing fields. In the eighteen years following inauguration of its new program, St. Johns achieved a new plateau of prosperity.[12] Though many country towns lack the necessary resources to provide all the services available in centers as large as St. Johns, numerous smaller places by conscious planning have increased their attractiveness markedly for the surrounding farm population.[13]

The twentieth century continues to be a revolutionary age. Americans now living have seen two world wars, revolutions in technology, management, and transportation, and tremendous upheaval everywhere. In such times, one normally can expect nothing but change. No one knows what atomic energy will mean to American civilization, and even minor influences like the proposed consolidation of high school districts may seriously affect numerous Midwestern towns. The road ahead keeps its own secrets.

As yet, most country towns retain their traditional philosophies of "progress." Town fathers continue to think in terms of population growth and rising real-estate prices. They stress the virtues of industrialization, of exploitation of local mineral resources, of improved transportation, and of trade-at-home, hometown loyalty as keys to "progress." In doing so, they are captives of their own past.

Cities, too, have worshipped material growth. By maintaining their phenomenal rates of increase beyond the golden age for village communities, they have bolstered hopes for similar "progress" elsewhere in America. As an integral part of American civilization, country towns, retaining these hopes, find it doubly difficult to change their patterns of thought. American civilization—urban and rural alike—dreads maturity.

Waves of national prosperity and of international calm strengthen America's urge for efficiency, for bigness, and for growth. In 1920s, for instance, Thomas A. Edison, high priest among American prophets, stressed the values of social engineering. In his opinion, the future lay with the city because people naturally would prefer the greater efficiency of urban ways. Edison suggested that benevolent nature would adjust mankind to city inconveniences, even to blessing them with deafness to shield their nervous systems from the noise of urban traffic.[14] Such ideas appealed in the roaring twenties.

Nevertheless, our national point of view has shifted. Much of our modern economic thinking rests on the premise that human material wants are limited. The great depression undermined convictions that full employment and an ever-expanding economy were our normal and inevitable destiny.

Perhaps we have reached the stage where we must invest in nonmaterial things to achieve full use of our resources. Perhaps necessity will compel us to concentrate on those spiritual ends toward which American effort supposedly has been striving all along. Public works in time of economic stress may set an example.

Necessity may compel Midwestern country towns to lead the way. Like the New England village of an earlier period, they seem to be passing from the growing pains of expansion to an ultimate stability. Farms and food and service centers for farmers must be maintained. Although additional declines may occur in farm population and in some rural towns, substantial losses seem unlikely. So, too, does growth. Mechanization and scientific methods now enable one farmer to feed several city people. Moreover, as national standards of living rise, relatively less of national income goes for food. Population growth itself perhaps will remain below the phenomenal increases recorded in earlier decades of American history, thus lessening the number of mouths to be fed. Since country towns have always depended on agriculture, they will probably share the farmer's declining but important part in American life.

In reshaping their thinking, small towns have much to learn from their past. Contrary to nostalgic memory they have lacked the stability, the changelessness, and the sense of continuity which people ascribe to them. They too have been buffeted by a revolutionary age. And yet, nostalgic memory is not wholly in error. Small-town residents have achieved a sense of stability through "belonging" to a community in its entirety. In the nineteenth century especially, people were born into the small town as they once were born into the church. They "belonged" by their very presence, and they had something larger than themselves to which to cling.

After declining temporarily in the early twentieth century, this urge to belong reasserted its appeal. As America's relations with the rest of the world expanded rapidly in World Wars I and II; as depression weakened the cult of self-reliance in the 1930s; and, most of all, as Americans became convinced that they really were a part of a world social order, the urge to belong to something a little less imposing and a little less impersonal was intensified. More and more, appreciation has arisen for primary groups, to which the individual can really belong, in which he can feel a sense of security, and in which he is not overwhelmed by the magnitude and the coldness of world citizenship. One writer in 1941 argued that Americans were more lonely and more unhappy than ever before. Radios, movies, and automobiles had not brought happiness. People found no real satisfaction in driving ten miles to sit among strangers in a movie audience. As a solution, the writer suggested neighborhood groups similar to those recently revived by the Ohio Farm Bureau. As one farmer participant said: "Our getting together and working together has made all of us realize that we have the best neighborhood in the country. I guess I'm kind of proud to belong."[15]

People cry out against overcentralization, even when it is in the interest of efficiency. Medical care is a case in point. Article after article in national periodicals stresses the decline in the number of doctors living and practicing directly in rural areas. Specialists thought for a time that hospitals were unnecessary within a fifty-mile radius of a large urban medical center, particularly if good roads and ambulance service were available. They thought of hospitals as workshops for doctors and as hotels for sick people needing bed service. In that opinion they ignored a wealth of evidence that many individuals refuse to patronize distant hospitals because in illness their need for families and friends becomes intensified. Community medical and health centers recognize that need.[16]

Bigness has many limitations. While county seats, like Webster City, have what sociologists call a "high service rating"—which enables them to gain trade at the expense of smaller towns—they almost invariably have a "low group identification." Growing social unity between farm and village has served partially to check trade encroachments from larger places. In this social identification of town and country lies much of the strength of small-town mid-America. Trade areas have become more stable in recent years, an indication that the automobile may have largely completed its work of reshaping trade and recreational patterns. Factual surveys also prove that individual initiative means much to town prosperity. One town may be in trouble while another of comparable size is fairly prosperous because its businessmen have adjusted to changing conditions. When country towns have held their own so well in a rapidly changing world, and have so many advantages in their favor, why should they distrust the future?

They need only to recognize that the time has come to stress ends rather than means. Like all Americans, villagers became accustomed to living in a feverish state of expansion, in which population, real-estate prices, and prosperity grew at fabulous rates. In the Middle West, as elsewhere, the first settlers stressed the immediately useful and the practical as necessary forerunners of arts, advanced learning, the humanities, literature, and "betterment." Some day, they said, their descendants could afford the better things. The Middle West has prospered greatly and its towns are approaching maturity. Unfortunately, they still spend relatively little of their time and their accumulated wealth on anything beyond the practical, which threatens to become an end in itself instead of a means to an end. The real problem of the country town thus demands only an honest answer to the Biblical question, "For what is a man profited, if he shall gain the whole world, and lose his own soul?"

NOTES

1. *Brookfield* (Missouri) *Gazette,* December 16 and 23, 1905; January 13 and June 9, 1906; April 13, 20, 27, June 1, 8, 15, 22, 29, and July 6, 1907. Additional reports on the shoe factory and on other industrial promotions will be found in the *Brookfield Gazette* for August 17 and October 5, 1907; March 14, 1908; November 20, 1909; October 28 and November 11, 1911; October 10, 1914; May 13, 1916; January 27 and September 29, 1917; August 24, 1918; December 6, 1919; and in the *Linn County Budget-Gazette* (Brookfield, Missouri), December 9 and 16, 1926; July 6, 1927; December 19, 1928; February 27 and March 1, 1929; January 3 and 5, 1940. For examples of industrial campaigns in other Midwestern towns see *Monroe* (Wisconsin) *Journal-Gazette,* June 5 and July 13, 1906; *Upper Des Moines-Republican* (Algona, Indiana), March 18 and April 22, 1908; *Montgomery News* (Hillsboro, Illinois), July 11 and 18, 1935; June 4 and 25, and November 8, 1945; *Hastings* (Michigan) *Banner,* January 12 and February 2, 1910; *Pickaway County News* (Circleville, Ohio), January 14, 1916; *Chatfield* (Minnesota) *News,* June 27, July 18, and August 15, 1946.

2. *Brookfield* (Missouri) *Gazette,* November 12, 1898.

3. Quoted in Dale Kramer, "Want a Factory?" *Survey Graphic,* XXIX (August 1940), 438–41, 446–7.

4. Ed Howe, *The Story of a Country Town* (New York, 1917), 228–9.

5. *Sherwood Anderson's Memoirs* (New York, 1942), p. 87. See also his story, *Poor White* (New York, 1920) for a similar novel-length theme.

6. W. D. Knight, *Subsidization of Industry in Forty Selected Cities in Wisconsin 1930–1946,* Wisconsin Commerce Studies, University of Wisconsin School of Commerce, Bureau of Business Research and Science, I, no. 2 (Madison, 1947).

7. *Clinton* (Wisconsin) *Times Observer,* series beginning November 21, 1935. The quotation is from the article which appeared in the issue of December 12, 1935.

8. Gustav P. Warber, *Social and Economic Survey of a Community in Northeastern Minnesota,* Bulletin of the University of Minnesota, Current Problems, no. 5, (Minneapolis, 1915), p. 61; Perry P. Denune, *The Social and Economic Relations of the Farmers with the Towns in Pickaway County, Ohio,* Ohio State University, Bureau of Business Research, College of Agriculture, (Columbus, Ohio, 1927), p. 60.

9. Susan Fenimore Cooper, "Village Improvement Societies," *Putnam's Magazine,* IV (September 1869), 359–66; "A Village Street—Before and After," *House Beautiful,* XXVII (April 1910), 127–9. Articles commonly credited Stockbridge, Massachusetts, with starting village improvement. See, for example, Anonymous, "Village Improvement Associations," *Scribner's Monthly,* XIV (May 1877), 97–107; Mary C. Robbins, "Village Improvement Societies," *The Atlantic Monthly,* LXXIX (February 1897), 212–22; Roger Riordan, "Village Parks and Gardens," *Chautauquan,* VIII (May 1888), 481–3; "Topics of the Hour," *Chautauquan,* XXXII (December 1900), 317–19. For expressed interest in village improvement associations in the Middle West see Susan F. Stone, "The Town Beautiful," *Craftsman,* VI (May 1904), 125–9.

10. "An Old Village on a New Model," *Survey*, XXXVII (March 24, 1917), 726.

11. Alfred H. Sinks, "The Old Home Town Fights to Live," *Collier's*, CXXIV (July 2, 1949), 28–9, 70–72.

12. M. T. Buckley, "The Linking of Village and Farm," *The American City*, Town and Country ed., XII (January 1915), 19–22; Delbert Clark, "This Town Went Rural," *Rotarian*, LX (February 1942), 41–2.

13. Innumerable articles telling how to build a better town or a better business have appeared throughout the course of the twentieth century. How to raise money for a community house; how to build up a great retail store in a small town; how the local chamber of commerce can be of service; how to operate a commercial club; how to meet mail-order competition; how to build a balanced program; how adult education can further hometown loyalty; how to increase recreational opportunities in the small town; how to build a community art center—these and other possibilities have been explained in article after article in periodicals ranging from those of limited circulation to others appealing to millions of Americans. See, for example, "How a Little Town Built a Community House by Getting 'Good and Mad,'" *The Literary Digest*, LXII (August 30, 1919), 98, 100; "A Community Center is the Hub of Town Progress," *The American City*, Town and Country ed., XIV January 1916), 10–11; Albert S. Gregg, "Three Young Men With Ideas," *The American Magazine*, LXXXII (October 1916), 30–32; "What Your Association Can Do for You," *System*, XXXII (August 1917), 256, 258, 260–63, and subsequent issues of the same periodical; Fred M. Hansen, "A Town Commercial Club Which Gets Results," *The American City*, X (March 1914), 259–61; W. C. Holman, "Keeping Retail Trade at Home," *System*, XXIII (January 1913), 13–20; John A. Piquet, "Opportunity Faces Small Cities and Towns," *The American City*, XLII (May 1930), 97–9; Grace M. Ellis, "Where Grownups Go to School," *Rotarian*, LX (March 1942), 40–43; "Some Small Communities at Play," *Recreation*, XXXVI (August 1942), 291–5; Bernard Ferguson, "Community Art Center Widely Used," *The American City*, LVI (August 1941), 85.

14. Edward Marshall, "The Scientific City of the Future, An Authorized Interview with Thomas A. Edison," *The Forum*, LXXVI (December 1926), 823–9.

15. David C. Coyle, "Belonging," *The American City*, LVI (August 1941), 71. Belief in this approach has led distinguished Americans like Arthur E. Morgan, former administrative head of the TVA, and a college president, to work ardently for the preservation of small communities. In 1940, Morgan took the lead in establishing "Community Service, Inc.," at Yellow Springs, Ohio, to provide information and help to small communities. In 1942, he published a book whose title indicates its theme: *The Small Community: Foundation of Democratic Life. What it is and How to Achieve It* (New York, 1942). For a well-reasoned statement of the values of community life see Baker Brownell, *The Human Community. Its Philosophy and Practice for a Time of Crisis* (New York, 1950).

16. "Rural Health: Vanishing Country M.D.'s," *Newsweek*, LVI (March 24, 1947), 58–60; Steven M. Spencer, "We Need More Country Doctors," *The Saturday Evening Post*, CCXXI (October 9, 1948), 36–7, 54, 59, 61–2, 64; A. R. Mangus, *Hospitals for Rural People in Ohio*, Department of Rural Economics and Rural Sociology, Bulletin 184, Ohio State University and Ohio Agricultural Experiment Station

(Columbus, Ohio, February 1945); Robert L. McNamara, *Illness in the Farm Population of Two Homogeneous Areas of Missouri,* University of Missouri College of Agriculture, Agricultural Experiment Station, Research Bulletin 504, July 1952; John H. Lane, Jr., *What Has Happened to the Country Doctor?,* University of Missouri College of Agriculture, Agricultural Experiment Station, Bulletin 594, February 1953.

25. METROPOLITAN GOVERNMENT VERSUS SUBURBAN AUTONOMY
Politics on the Crabgrass Frontier

Kenneth T. Jackson

The issue of the decentralization and dispersal of power at all levels of government is currently a popular one in the United States. In large metropolitan areas, especially, "power to the people" has become a common goal for blacks who seek greater control of their inner-city neighborhoods, for middle-class whites who want to protect a suburban way of life, and for professionals and intellectuals who fear that respect for institutions and authority is being eroded by mindless bureaucracies. In 1967 the borough president of Staten Island established a commission to study the possibility of secession from New York City. In 1968, the United Black Front of Roxbury, a predominantly black community, demanded independence from Boston. In 1969, small, middle-class property owners in Glen Park looked to secession from Gary as necessary for the protection of their housing investments. And in 1970, the Association of the Bar of the City of New York suggested the formation of up to forty-five new units of local government in the metropolis.

While the movement for neighborhood control gains adherents in some communities, the tendency in other cities is to pursue the opposite course —that is, to consolidate a larger geographical area and a greater number of people under a single autonomous government. Within the past half-dozen years, for example, Memphis, Indianapolis, Houston, and Oklahoma City have added huge expanses of land to their corporate limits (see Table 1). None matched the achievement of Jacksonville, however. In 1968 that Florida city became the largest municipality in the Western Hemisphere in area and joined the twenty-five largest cities in the United States in population when its government and territory were consolidated with almost all of Duval County.

These two generally opposite tendencies are simply recent manifestations of a dilemma that has confronted the residents of American cities for two hundred years. On the one hand, democracy seems to call for government to remain small and close to the people; on the other, efficiency and the regional character of many contemporary problems point to the necessity of government's becoming metropolitan in authority and planning.

Throughout most of American history, cities have grown steadily larger

Table 1. Territorial Size in Square Miles Since 1870 of the Twenty Largest American Central Cities That Have Continued to Gain Population Since 1950

Year	Los Angeles	Houston	Dallas	New Orleans	San Antonio	San Diego	Seattle	Memphis	Denver	Atlanta	Indianapolis	Columbus	Phoenix	Jacksonville	Portland	Fort Worth	San Jose	Milwaukee	Kansas City	Toledo	Total
1870	29	25	NA	16	36	74	11	4	4	9	11	12	NA	1	2	NA	NA	13	4	13	264
1890	29	9	9	196	36	74	13	4	17	9	11	14	NA	10	6	NA	NA	17	13	26	493
1910	85	16	16	196	36	74	56	19	58	26	33	23	NA	10	48	18	NA	23	59	29	825
1930	440	72	42	196	36	94	69	46	58	35	54	39	10	26	64	46	8	41	59	36	1471
1950	451	160	112	199	70	99	71	104	67	37	55	39	17	30	64	94	17	54	81	38	1879
1970	455	453	280	199	183	307	92	217	71	128	400	114	247	827	87	141	117	97	130	86	4631

Sources: Various City and County Data Books, various United States Census Reports, and Roderick D. McKenzie, The Metropolitan Community (New York: McGraw-Hill, 1933).

in area and in population. Of course, there were always a few small cities here and there that lost population, but most—and certainly all the larger ones—added residents between each decennial census. Historically, city fathers tended to be concerned with the *rate* of growth and with the relative standing of their community and rival cities.[1] We now know, however, that urban population growth is not inevitable. Boston, for instance, reached its maximum population in 1950, and since that time has had a net loss of 150,000 inhabitants. And the Hub is not unusual. Of the nation's twenty-five largest cities in 1960, seventeen have lost population in the past decade. In fact, this absolute decline is often cited as the most dramatic evidence that our cities are dying.

The large American cities that are losing residents are typically old and congested, and except for Birmingham and San Francisco, are located in the East and Middle West (see Table 2). It is often alleged, in fact, that the characteristics of these cities are themselves the reasons for their decline. In a youthful, mobile, and affluent society that seems to be looking toward the South and West, one would not expect ugly and crowded surroundings to be popular. But cities that are losing population share another more significant characteristic: their boundaries have not expanded in the last half-century. The municipal area of the twenty largest American cities that have experienced a net decline in permanent residents since 1950 has increased by only 13.7 percent since 1920. Individual cities have often expanded much less (see Table 2). Philadelphia, San Francisco, and Buffalo have not absorbed additional land since before the Civil War.

Those who have grown up in the suburbs or central cities of the East or Middle West find nothing very strange in all this. There is a Brookline as well as a Boston, an Evanston as well as a Chicago, a New Rochelle as well as a New York, and no one is likely to argue successfully that they should share a single municipal government. Yet the very fact that these dual communities continue to exist itself represents a break in the earlier urban tradition. When cities first experienced explosive growth in the nineteenth century, they expanded outward as well as in density. If the earlier pattern had continued, Boston would probably encompass the entire area circumscribed by Route 128, New York City would reach well into Westchester County and at least to the Suffolk County line on Long Island, and Chicago would stretch a quarter of the distance to Milwaukee. Those who find such assertions fantastic are reminded that dozens of American cities, including all of those that boast high population growth rates since World War II, have expanded their boundaries in just such a fashion.

THE NINETEENTH CENTURY

Without exception, the adjustment of local boundaries has been the dominant method of population growth in every American city of consequence. If annexation (the addition of unincorporated land to the city) or

Table 2. Territorial Size in Square Miles Since 1850 of the Twenty Largest Central Cities That Are Now Losing Population

Year	New York	Chicago	Philadelphia	Detroit	Baltimore	Washington	Cleveland	San Francisco	Boston	St. Louis	Pittsburgh	Minneapolis	Buffalo	Cincinnati	Newark	Louisville	Oakland	Birmingham	Rochester	St. Paul	Total
1850	22	10	2	6	13	60	5	5	5	14	2	—	39	6	15	5	5	NA	8	5	235
1870	22	36	130	13	13	60	12	42	13	61	23	8	39	20	16	12	5	1	8	6	540
1890	44	169	130	22	30	60	28	42	39	61	27	48	39	25	18	13	11	3	17	52	878
1910	299	185	130	41	30	60	46	42	39	61	40	48	39	50	24	21	46	49	20	52	1322
1930	299	207	130	140	79	62	71	42	44	61	51	54	39	72	24	38	53	50	34	52	1602
1950	299	224	127	140	79	61	81	45	46	61	52	54	39	75	24	38	53	50	35	52	1635
1970	299	224	127	140	79	61	81	45	48	61	52	54	39	78	24	57	53	76	35	52	1685

Sources: Various City and County Data Books, various United States Census Reports, and Roderick D. McKenzie, *The Metropolitan Community* (New York: McGraw-Hill, 1933).

consolidation (the absorption of one municipal government by another, usually adjacent) had not taken place, there would now be no great cities in the United States in the political sense of the term.[2] Only New York City would have grown as large as 1 million people, and it would have remained confined to the island of Manhattan.[3] Viewed another way, if annexation[4] had not been successful in the nineteenth century, many large cities would have been surrounded by suburbs even before the Civil War.[5] For example, the cities of St. Louis, Philadelphia, Pittsburgh, and Cleveland contained in 1970 less than one-half of the population of their standard metropolitan areas. Their boundaries have not been altered in almost half a century, and these cities are now extreme examples of core areas being strangled by incorporated suburbs. A St. Louis school administrator recently complained that suburbanites have "erected a wall of separation which towers above the city limits and constitutes a barrier as effective as did those of ancient Jericho or that of the Potsdamer Platz in Berlin." Yet if these cities had been unable to add territory before the Civil War, their central areas would have contained about the same percentage of the metropolitan population in 1850 as in 1970[6] (see Table 3).

If we consider the twenty largest American cities that lost population between 1950 and 1970, we find they had a very different experience in the nineteenth century.[7] Taken as a group (see Tables 2 and 4), they expanded their boundaries by more than 400 percent through the addition of more than 950 square miles of land between 1850 and 1900. In percentage terms, the decade of greatest gain was 1850 to 1860; in absolute terms, the premier decades were 1890 to 1900 and 1880 to 1890. At no time between 1850 and 1930, however, did these twenty cities in the aggregate annex less than 100 square miles in a decade.

Appropriately, the most significant annexations in the nineteenth century involved the nation's three largest cities: New York, Chicago, and Philadelphia. Philadelphia's mammoth consolidation of the city with Philadelphia County in 1854 is still the largest single such annexation. In one move, the City of Brotherly Love quadrupled its population, expanded its area from 2 to 129 square miles, and, until Paris annexed its outer arrondissements in 1859, became the largest city in the world in terms of area.[8] Included in the new city of Philadelphia were the formerly independent suburbs of Spring Garden, Northern Liberties, Kensington, Southwark, and Moyamensing, which in 1850 ranked as the ninth, eleventh, twelfth, twentieth, and twenty-eighth largest cities in the United States.[9] In terms of relative growth of population and area, the impact would be less today if Philadelphia were to annex the equivalent land area and population of Los Angeles, Detroit, and Boston.

Chicago's largest annexation took place in 1889, when 133 square miles and most of what is now the far South Side were added. The addition included pleasant residential villages between 35th and 71st streets like Hyde Park, Kenwood, and Woodlawn, as well as peripheral industrial com-

Table 3. Comparative Degree of Metropolitanization, 1850 and 1970

City	1850	1970
Philadelphia*		
City population	121,376	1,948,609
Metro population	371,860	4,774,000
City percentage	32.6	41.1
Pittsburgh†		
City population	46,601	520,117
Metro population	150,000	2,382,000
City percentage	31.1	21.8
Cleveland‡		
City population	7,977	750,903
Metro population	29,000	2,043,000
City percentage	27.5	36.8
St. Louis		
City population	25,000	622,236
Metro population	77,860	2,340,000
City percentage	32.1	26.6

* The Philadelphia metropolitan area is defined as Kensington, Northern Liberties, Southwark, Spring Garden, Moyamensing, South Penn, Richmond, West Philadelphia, Germantown, and Frankford.

† In 1850 the Pittsburgh boundaries were substantially extended. The figures reflect the situation before the addition of that year.

‡ The city of Cleveland is defined as the First Ward. Annexations of the 1840s are included in the metropolitan total.

Sources: Paul Studenski, ed., *The Government of Metropolitan Areas in the United States* (New York: National Municipal League, 1930), pp. 17–18; and Roderick D. McKenzie, *The Metropolitan Community* (New York: McGraw-Hill, 1933), pp. 194–7.

munities in the Calumet Region like Grand Crossing and South Chicago and the famed model town of George Pullman. At the time of annexation, only about 225,000 people lived in the area, and large stretches of the tract were rural or sparsely settled. Within thirty years, however, there were more than 1 million persons on the land added in 1889.[10]

The most important municipal boundary adjustment in American history occurred in 1898, when Andrew Haswell Green's lifelong dream of a Greater New York City was realized. Brooklyn, which at the time was the fourth largest city in the United States, joined Manhattan, as did Queens (with a portion withheld as the newly created Nassau County), Staten Island, and additional parts of Westchester County which came to be known as The Bronx. The size of the city increased from about 40 to 300 square miles and the population grew by almost 2 million, most of it as a result of the consolidation. Strangely enough, the impetus for the move came from a Republican governor and a Republican state legislature, who presumably meant to dilute the influence of Tammany Hall in the governance of the metropolis. There was hardly any public debate on the issue, and only in Brooklyn was an 1894 advisory vote close—65,744 to 65,467, a plurality of only 277 in favor of consolidation in a total vote of 131,000.[11] Nevertheless, the new city was created, and until the population spilled out for great distances into the surrounding areas, the government of the nation's largest city was a unique form of metropolitan organization.

Although smaller cities did not match the square-mile additions of Philadelphia, Chicago, and New York, every large city shared in the expansion boom. St. Louis increased its area from 4.5 to 14 square miles in 1856 and to 17 square miles in 1870. The biggest change came in 1876, when city voters overwhelmed the opposition of rural St. Louis County, and raised the municipal area to 61 square miles and created an independent city.[12] Boston added about 15 square miles by joining with Roxbury in 1868 and Dorchester in 1870, while New Orleans absorbed Carrolton in 1876, to give the Crescent City most of the area it occupies today.[13] Baltimore more than doubled its size in 1888; Minneapolis, Cleveland, Cincinnati, and Pittsburgh more than tripled through a series of small additions.[14]

MOTIVES FOR ANNEXATION

As Richard C. Wade, Robert Dykstra, Carl Bridenbaugh, Robert Albion, Daniel J. Boorstin, Wyatt W. Belcher, and a number of other authors have noted, American cities have been especially susceptible to the notion that "bigger is better." During the taking of the 1890 federal census, partisans of Minneapolis and St. Paul each accused the other community of falsifying the returns in order to appear larger. Investigators found the whole enumeration a frightful tangle, and a recount was made. The new census revealed that Minneapolis had enrolled the dead, while St. Paul's standing had been defended by the listing of hundreds of inhabitants who evidently lived in depots, barber shops, and dime museums.[15]

If counting the dead was frowned upon, annexing populous suburbs was a perfectly acceptable method of fueling the municipal booster spirit. Brooklyn gloried in its rise to third place among the nation's cities when it absorbed Bushwick and Williamsburg in 1855, and Chicago took pride in its second-place status after its massive annexation in 1889. In fact, it was partly the fear that Chicago would become the nation's largest city in 1900 or 1910 that prompted various factions to agree to the New York consolidation of 1898.[16] Not only would a city gain additional residents by expanding its borders, but the fact of growth often inspired citizens with renewed confidence in a community's future and spurred them to greater efforts in civic development. As a leading Philadelphia newspaper commented with regard to that city's successful consolidation of 1854:

All of us may feel today that we are citizens of a new city. The Philadelphia we have known heretofore . . . has undergone a transformation which at once not only magnifies it immensely in physical proportions, but invests it with a social spirit hitherto unknown in its experience.[17]

The desire to annex was inspired not only by the booster spirit, but also by the business idea that a large organization was more efficient than a small one and that substantial economies would accrue from a consolidation of municipal governments.[18] According to this view, even when suburbs were honestly governed, their management was inefficient; large cities, on the other hand, could be run by highly paid experts.[19] In what businessmen regarded as a typical and laudable development, the Philadelphia police department was reduced from 850 to 650 men after consolidation, presumably with no loss of effectiveness. On other occasions, annexationists pointed out that competing communities could sometimes offer mutual advantages. Thus, Los Angeles provided the resources and San Pedro the location for a new port; Cleveland provided the financing and Ohio City the site for a waterworks.[20]

In many cases, the cry for efficiency was a mask for the desire to exploit and to control: It might be termed the local or downtown brand of urban imperialism.[21] Often the large merchants and businessmen of the central business district sought to eliminate neighborhood governments that in their view inhibited progress. In Philadelphia, where wharfage taxes, railway rights, and water prices were among the issues of contention between the city and its suburbs, the supporters of consolidation were overwhelmingly middle- and upper-income residents of the core. Suburban supporters of the proposal tended to be well-heeled commuters to the central business district. Neither group was representative of the laboring and farming constituency of the outlying areas to be added.[22]

The business community also sought to regularize the relationship between Cleveland and Ohio City, two communities on opposite sides of the Cuyahoga River. Prior to their consolidation in 1854, partisans for each city disrupted trade by tearing down bridges thought to be advantageous to the other.[23] Brooklyn and New York fought for control of the lucrative ferry trade on the East River; Memphis and South Memphis for commercial trade on the Mississippi.[24] Through annexation, the strongest political unit could organize the government of a large area for its benefit.

The desire to regularize the economy was further buttressed by the felt need for greater social control. In New Orleans, the so-called "Spanish riot" of 1851 made clear to the city fathers the difficulty of police operations when law enforcement authority was divided among three separate corporations.[25] In Philadelphia, it was thought that a unified police force would eliminate undesirable conditions in districts then beyond the city limits. Riots in 1838, 1844, and 1849 had reduced city and suburbs to a garrison, and a group of leading Philadelphians proposed consolidation so that "the peace of our community will be preserved and the prosperity of its citizens protected without the unpleasant necessity of a resort to armed force."[26] Because the local constabulary of Southwark, Moyamensing, and the Northern Liberties proved unable to control the volunteer fire companies and the roving bands that moved back and forth across municipal boundaries, the *North American* said in 1850: "Philadelphia never before needed a stronger government nor ever possessed a weaker one."[27] According to a nineteenth-century historian of the Pennsylvania metropolis, "the miserable system of a city with adjacent districts each independent of each other was a protection to the disorderly and encouragement of them to unite together for the purpose of showing their disregard for the law."[28]

Land speculators also supported annexation, but they usually worked behind the scenes, and their precise role is difficult to measure. In a pattern familiar enough over the last century, real estate promoters purchased large tracts of rural land in the expectation that the advancing horse cars, steam railroads, and trolleys would make the area attractive to urban workers. In the absence of decent sewerage, water, and educational systems, land speculators looked to annexation as a sort of guarantee to potential buyers that the suburb would eventually possess the comforts of the city. The desire to turn a fast buck was undoubtedly an important reason why nineteenth-century urban boundaries were usually set far in advance of settlement. In Memphis, in Baltimore, in Cleveland, in Chicago, and in other cities, the municipality sometimes included land that had not even been surveyed, let alone laid out into streets.[29] In the Philadelphia consolidation of 1854, areas in certain parts of the county became officially part of the city although farmers continued to engage in agricultural pursuits there for more than a generation.[30]

THE NINETEENTH-CENTURY SUCCESS

What is most important about annexation in the nineteenth century is not motivation; rather, the important aspect is the single, overwhelming fact of area growth. With the exception of Boston, the thrust of municipal government was imperialistic, and the trend was clearly toward metropolitan government.

To the extent that historians have bothered with the history of annexation at all, their tendency has been to credit its early success to the sense of community or mutuality that supposedly existed between residents of the core and residents of the periphery.[31] Certainly, one could not deny that many suburbanites did regard the city as their achievement and were willing and even eager to be joined with it. But probably more important than such lofty notions were pragmatic, mundane considerations of sewers, schools, water, and police.[32]

Until at least the middle of the nineteenth century, the image of suburbia was not an attractive one. Partly because of a long tradition of forcing undesirable businesses such as slaughterhouses, leather dressers, curriers, and brothels out beyond the city limits, some suburbs were known for vistas of stagnant water, dead animals, and rotting garbage.[33] A visitor to Philadelphia at mid-century remarked that "nine-tenths of those whose rascalities have made Philadelphia so unjustly notorious live in the dens and shanties of the suburbs," and he labeled a suburban prostitution center as "the core of the rottenest and most villainous neighborhood ever peopled by human beings."[34]

As the centrifugal movement of the middle class gathered force after 1865, suburbia gradually shook off its reputation for vice and squalor.[35] But until late in the century, residential developments outside the cities normally could not offer a level of public services comparable to that of the core. Such considerations were apt to be important, particularly to newcomers who might have bought a house without water intakes or sewer outlets, on land that was overrun by snakes and rabbits, on a street that was neither paved nor served by storm drains nor watched over by the police. Thus, Roxbury joined Boston partly in an effort to gain relief from an intolerable sewerage situation;[36] Hyde Parkers looked to Chicago for better fire protection and cheaper gas rates; and residents of Kensington, Spring Garden, and Germantown were able to share more fully and economically in a Philadelphia water system that was rated among the best in the world.[37]

But then as now, many suburbanites were not swayed by the promise of better public services and preferred to retain their local autonomy. Few annexations were unopposed; some took place over the objections of as many as 90 percent of those concerned.[38] But in the nineteenth century, success depended much less on public than on legislative approval. Legally, of course, a city is a corporation that receives from the state government special powers of regulation over the residents of a precisely defined geographic area. Thus it normally remains within the power of the state to change the boundaries of governmental units under its jurisdiction.[39] In the nineteenth century, states tended to exercise this power without the advice of those who would be affected; that is, rarely were public referendums held on the issue. And when a vote was taken, it was often ignored if it was negative.

The predominant view in the nineteenth century was the doctrine of forcible annexation: No small territory should be allowed to retard the development of a metropolitan community; the most important consideration was simply the greatest good for the greatest number. The most recent articulation of this view came in 1917, when Judge Harlan of Maryland overruled the objections of Baltimore suburbanites and approved an annexation that tripled the area of the city. He declared:

Those who locate near the city limits are bound to know that the time may come when the legislature will extend the limits and take them in. No principle of right or justice or fairness places in their hands the power to stop the progress and development of the city, especially in view of the fact that the large majority of them have located near the city for the purpose of getting the benefit of transacting business or securing employment or following their profession in the city.[40]

Examples of forced annexations in the nineteenth century are numerous. In 1854, the consolidation of Philadelphia was approved not by sub-urbanites, who in fact sent delegation after delegation to oppose it, but rather by lawmakers in Harrisburg. Local referendums were not held on the San Francisco Consolidation Act of 1856 or on any one of the frequent annexations to Chicago and Baltimore prior to the 1880s.[41] Lawmakers added to both St. Louis and Boston three times before 1860, but the local electorate in each city rejected annexation measures submitted in 1853. A vote to reconsolidate the three municipalities of New Orleans met a popular defeat in 1850, only to be forced by special legislation in 1852; Louisiana also gave Carrolton to the Crescent City in 1876 without seeking the approval of the aroused residents.[42] The Ohio General Assembly added to Cleveland in 1829 and 1834, but when merger with Ohio City was first submitted to the voters in 1851, the total of the votes of the larger community was 1,098 to 850 against consolidation.[43] Some annexations did meet with popular approval, but it was in the legislative halls that the annexationists won their most important nineteenth-century victories.[44]

THE TWENTIETH-CENTURY FAILURE

For various reasons, then, the addition of peripheral land to cities was a normal process of urban growth in the nineteenth century. To most people, it seemed entirely logical and even inevitable that cities would add to their boundaries to accommodate a spreading and increasing population. In 1899, a suburban Chicago newspaper admitted, falsely as it turned out, that "the time may and doubtless will come when Oak Park will be swallowed up by the great city."[45] Several rash people even predicted that Minneapolis and St. Paul would come together "into one great city."[46] And the mayor of Newark in 1900, not foreseeing the day when his booming industrial city would be trapped by hostile suburbs within a minuscule 23 square miles, said: "East Orange, Vailsburg, Harrison, Kearny, and Belleville would be desirable acquisitions. By an exercise of discretion we can enlarge the city from decade to decade without unnecessarily taxing the property within our limits, which has already paid the cost of public improvements."[47]

But something has happened—or more precisely has failed to happen— in the twentieth century. For many cities, and particularly for the older ones now losing population, metropolitan government is a phenomenon of the past. Quite simply, they are no longer able to annex or to consolidate in order to keep pace with the overflow of population beyond established boundaries (see Tables 2 and 4).

Table 4. Comparison of Number of Square Miles Annexed by Twenty-Year Periods of Twenty Growing and Twenty Declining Cities, 1850–1970

Period	Square Miles Annexed	
	20 Declining Cities	20 Growing Cities
1850–70	305	NA
1870–90	338	229
1890–1910	444	332
1910–30	280	646
1930–50	33	408
1950–70	50	2,752
Cumulative Total Area in 1970 in Square Miles	1,685	4,631

Sources: Tables 1 and 2

The growing rejection of area expansion through annexation and consolidation can be seen in several ways. For the twenty largest cities in the United States now losing population, there is a marked percentage drop in the amount of territory added after 1900. The absolute number of square miles annexed remained over 100 per decade until 1930, however, after which time another drastic decline began (see Tables 2 and 4). Whereas the twenty cities added to their area by 400 percent in the last half of the nineteenth century and by 170 percent between 1870 and 1920, they have added less than 14 percent since 1920 and less than 6 percent since 1930.

The first really significant defeat for the consolidation movement came when Brookline spurned Boston in 1874.[48] Since that time, virtually every large city has been rebuffed: Chicago by Oak Park and Evanston; Rochester by Brighton and Irondequoit; and Oakland by the rest of Alameda County.[49] Some consolidation proposals, such as those of St. Paul in 1924, Cleveland in 1925, and Boston in 1931, have never even gained constitutional or legislative approval. Others, such as the proposals for Birmingham and Louisville, have been defeated by statewide public referendum.[50] And, as the suburban trend has gained momentum, state legislators have become increasingly reluctant to override the wishes of the voters concerned.

Because large cities have sometimes felt the need for financial retrenchment, the core areas have themselves occasionally rejected consolidation. In 1902, Mayor Carter H. Harrison of Chicago contended in his annual message that the city was too large to be administered efficiently. "An attempt to increase this territory," he said, "should meet with instant and emphatic discouragement. The ideal city is compact. With its area fully occupied, the care of all branches of administration can be applied to all sections expeditiously and well."[51] Particularly during the depression years of the 1930s, cities were not prepared to make the enormous capital expenditures annexation usually entails.[52]

But the inability of some of the older cities to grow in the twentieth century has not generally resulted from a lack of will on the part of the core area. In fact, the well-publicized consolidation attempts of St. Louis and Pittsburgh in the 1920s failed despite enormous campaigns on their behalf. The Greater St. Louis Conference attempted to enlarge borders that had been frozen since 1876, and it prophesied that failing such action, the Missouri city could only shrink in comparison with other cities of the nation and the world. The proposal won by a big majority in the city, but was rejected in the outlying areas by more than two to one.[53] The Pittsburgh vote came in 1928, following passage of an enabling amendment to the state constitution authorizing a federated city of Pittsburgh. It was approved in the statewide vote, but it failed to win the required two-thirds majority in a majority of communities. Like St. Louis, Pittsburgh did not expand in the 1920s and has not expanded since; it has suffered an enormous absolute loss of population in recent years.[54]

There are basically three reasons why America's older cities are now ringed by incorporated suburbs that emphasize their distinctiveness from rather than relationship with the metropolis: ethnic and racial distinctions, unworkable annexation laws, and improved suburban services. Most important is the changing reality and image of the periphery and the center, particularly with regard to population characteristics. With the vast increase in immigration in the late nineteenth century, the core city increasingly became the home of penniless immigrants from Southern and Eastern Europe. And of course, in the early years of the twentieth century increasing numbers of Southern blacks forsook the farms for a place where, they hoped, "a man was a man." In the view of most middle-class, white suburbanites, these newcomers were associated with and were often regarded as the cause of intemperance, vice, urban bossism, crime, and radicalism of all kinds. And as the central city increasingly became the home of the disadvantaged, the number of white-commuter suburbs rose markedly. These recent escapees from the central city were anxious to insulate their neighborhoods from the "liquor power" and other pernicious urban influences. An independent community offered the exciting promise of moral control. As the Morgan Park *Post*, a suburban Chicago weekly, remarked in an antiannexationist editorial on March 9, 1907:

The real issue is not taxes, nor water, nor street cars— it is a much greater question than either. It is the moral control of our village. . . . Under local government we can absolutely control every objectionable thing that may try to enter our limits —but once annexed we are at the mercy of the city hall.[55]

There were those who felt that the suburbs could best serve as a moral force by being annexed to the central city and then using the additional middle-class votes to crush the liquor and vice interests. As Zane Miller has noted of late-nineteenth-century Cincinnati, the successive enlargements of city boundaries kept the wealthy, highly educated, and politically sophisticated residents of the Hilltop suburban fringe firmly engaged in the city's affairs. And annexationists in Boston predicted that their city would share the fate of ancient Rome if the middle class, which had earlier provided reform leadership, was to separate itself from active involvement in municipal affairs.[56]

But even when annexations occurred, the political machines they were designed to unseat proved to have remarkable staying power. After all, argued the antiannexationists, how could the small suburbs possibly overcome the great city? "What influence would Oak Park have as the tail end of the 35th Ward?" asked one man at a suburban Chicago meeting. " 'About as much as the hair on a dog's tail,' shouted a citizen in the audience." Oak Parkers developed such an isolationist attitude that they even opposed cheap mass transit on the theory that undesirable elements might then find it possible to live among the chosen.[57]

These new middle- and upper-income suburbs had a much better chance of preserving their independence than did the low-status peripheral communities of the nineteenth century. Annexations have rarely affected prosperous towns, and it is no accident that places like Brookline, Newton, Evanston, Beverly Hills, and Shaker Heights have been able to resist consolidation for generations. A major reason for their success is that their representatives, together with those from rural areas, have moved state legislatures away from the doctrine of forcible annexation. With some notable exceptions in the South and West, where cities can sometimes annex without a popular referendum, it is now commonly held that annexation should be a voluntary affair which must gain the approval of the residents of an affected area. Even so, rigorous procedural and substantive requirements block the way, and special acts calling for annexation have been defeated by anti-urban state legislatures. Where annexation is provided for in a state constitution, as in the case of San Francisco, the relevant provision seems intended to thwart rather than to promote the process.[58] Conversely, it is a relatively simple matter legally to crank up and incorporate a new city, and some states even provide that central city services must be provided to the new communities at central city rates.[59]

A third factor causing the breakdown of annexation as a process has been the increased use of special service districts. This type of governmental structure was first used as an alternative to annexation in Philadelphia, where after 1790 special districts were established to administer prisons, schools, public health, and port administration.[60] Nineteenth-century examples were the New York Metropolitan Police Board (1857), the New York Metropolitan Board of Health (1866), the Massachusetts District Commission (sewerage, 1889; parks, 1893; water, 1895), and the Chicago Sanitary District (1889). To a man such as Andrew Haswell Green, these regional institutions emphasized the logic of complete consolidation.[61] But to most suburbanites, special service districts were an alternative rather than an avenue to metropolitan government. By bringing together suburbs that individually lacked the resources to provide high-quality sewerage, water, educational, or law-enforcement services, the special service district enabled suburbanites to have urban amenities without certain of the urban problems.

CONCLUSION

In summary, annexation is no longer a viable process for most of the old Eastern and Midwestern cities of the United States. Where once they moved their boundaries outward in a consistent pattern, they now lie surrounded by unfriendly suburbs. The metropolitan populations continue to grow, but the central cities decline in numbers of residents and in wealth because they are prevented from enlarging their boundaries.[62] Meanwhile, annexation remains a useful process for those cities that are growing in population, and it is in fact the reason they are growing in population. If we compare the twenty largest growing cities with the twenty largest declining cities (see Table 4), the significance of annexation becomes immediately apparent. Whereas the declining cities have grown by less than 6 percent since 1930, the growing cities have increased their area by an astonishing 201 percent in the same period through the annexation of more than 3,050 square miles.

Professor Kingsley Davis of the University of California at Berkeley has suggested that annexation is not a terribly important factor in the study of urban demography and ecology because the expansion of boundaries by political annexation tends to approximate the physical spread of the city. Thus, a city annexes because it becomes more populous. While that is to some degree a self-evident proposition, the data presented here suggest that cities also become more populous because they annex, and if they do not annex they will not grow. One could hardly argue that Broken Bow, Nebraska, can become a metropolis by annexing 500 square miles of Midwestern prairie. But the whole of the population growth of Memphis, Houston, Indianapolis, Phoenix, and many other cities has come from annexation. Within their 1940 boundaries, they lost population between 1940 and 1970.

If nothing more than civic pride were at stake, it would make little difference whether a given city were eighth or forty-eighth on the list of large cities. But there is abundant evidence to suggest that it makes a great deal of difference where the city limits are placed. In New Jersey, for instance, the suburbs flourish and try their best to ignore the fact that Jersey City and Newark, both densely settled and geographically extraordinarily small, must struggle with the whole range of contemporary urban problems. The rich have long since departed; the middle class is almost gone. Professor Scott Greer is correct when he says that the decline of American cities is really an optical illusion; only a small part of the city is suffering while most of it is relatively prosperous, particularly those parts on the edges. But in

Newark the area of decline is practically the entire city because annexation has not taken place on anything more than a small scale, and the city does not have a substantial middle-class zone. And assimilation is now more difficult for blacks than for immigrants, because movement from the ghetto involves movement into another governmental jurisdiction rather than simply movement into another neighborhood.

The answer to America's urban ills obviously does not lie solely in larger municipal governments. As New York City and especially its Board of Education so abundantly demonstrate, mere size is no guarantee of excellence or efficiency. More governmental functions than we perhaps realize can be handled only on a decentralized, almost neighborhood, basis. But our cities also face problems in transportation, pollution, and housing that are genuinely metropolitan in scope and that cannot be solved by having each community go it alone or by creating additional monstrous and self-serving public agencies like the New York Port Authority. Some sort of metropolitan or federated government whose planners recognize both the need to keep government human in scale as well as the need to develop citizen awareness of responsibilities beyond the local neighborhood or village is necessary if we are to continue to have great cities. As Tom Wicker noted in *The New York Times* of August 11, 1969:

The choice, in general, is not between the impersonal coldness of remote bureaucracy and a New England town government for every twenty city blocks. The choice is between a dangerously outmoded concept of the city, leading to abandonment and decay, and a rational development that would restore a congruence between the reach of government and the location of the governed.

NOTES

1. Boston and New Haven lost population temporarily in the eighteenth century, and Charleston, New London, Schenectady, and Newburyport in the nineteenth century, but such cases were rather unusual.

2. There is no general history of urban area growth. The best specialized studies are Richard Bigger and James D. Kitchen, *How the Cities Grew: A Century of Municipal Independence and Expansion in Metropolitan Los Angeles* (Los Angeles: Bureau of Governmental Research, UCLA, 1952); and Paul Studenski, ed., *The Government of Metropolitan Areas in the United States* (New York: National Municipal League, 1930).

3. By the terms of the Dongan Charter of 1686 and colonial legislation, the City of New York has been coterminus with Manhattan.

4. The terms *annexation* and *consolidation* will be used interchangeably.

5. If annexation had not occurred, the suburbs would have been growing faster than the cities by 1810 in New York, by 1800 in Philadelphia, by 1840 in Boston, and by 1850 in St. Louis and Cleveland.

6. Similar statements could be made about other large cities.

7. Some cities, notably Baltimore, added frequently to their boundaries before 1800, but most cities were stable or lost territory.

8. Of the present twenty *arrondissements* in Paris, the eleventh through the twentieth were taken in by the 1859 extension. Like Philadelphia, Paris has not been extended since that time. (Philadelphia did add 0.131 square miles from Montgomery County in 1916.)

9. Southwark, which was settled by Swedes in 1638, is older than Philadelphia, and like Spring Garden and Kensington is named for a London suburb. It was created a municipality in 1762 and incorporated in 1794. There were 28 other governments in Philadelphia County prior to consolidation. See William Bucke Campbell, "Old Towns and Districts of Philadelphia," *Philadelphia History*, IV (1942), 94–149; M. Antonia Lynch, "The Old District of Southwark in the County of Philadelphia," *Philadelphia History*, I (1909), 83–126.

10. There were 23 distinct communities in Hyde Park Township, which itself made up less than half the new area. Stanley Buder, *Pullman: An Experiment in Industrial Order and Community Planning, 1880–1930* (New York: Oxford University Press, 1967), p. 109.

11. In the 1870s and 1880s a Municipal Union Society agitated in behalf of consolidation and sent the legislature petitions and bills. As early as 1833, New York's mayor and aldermen opposed the incorporation of Brooklyn as a separate city on the grounds that it should be joined with Manhattan.

12. The county, which did not want to lose city tax revenue, voted 4 to 1 against the separation, but the total was 12,181 to 10,928 in favor of separation. It was the first home rule charter of its kind in the United States, but it unfortunately made no provision for future annexation—a policy of omission which was followed in the charter of 1914. Howard Lee McBain, *The Law and the Practice of Municipal Home Rule* (New York: Columbia University Press, 1916), p. 146.

13. Slight alterations were made in the Boston boundary by the legislature in 1836, 1838, and 1859.

14. In most communities, annexation maps may be consulted in the office of the city planner, city engineer, or city assessor.

15. Minneapolis demanded the removal of the capital from St. Paul, while St. Paul publicly regretted its forced connection with a city "that stands degraded and ashamed in the eyes of the nation." Minnesota Works Progress Administration Writer's Project, *Minneapolis: The Story of a City* (Minneapolis: Minnesota Department of Education, 1940), pp. 66–7.

16. The opening of the Brooklyn Bridge in 1883 was another powerful stimulus.

17. *Philadelphia North American*, February 4, 1854.

18. Paul U. Kellogg, "The Civic Responsibilities of Democracy in an Industrial District," in Kellogg, ed., *The Pittsburgh Survey,* 6 vols. (New York, 1910).

19. As Samuel P. Hays and others have noted, the desire to centralize also found expression in the elimination of ward representation in favor of "at-large" elections. If the neighborhood was not already inside the city, then the plan was to annex it. See Hays, "The Politics of Reform in Municipal Government in the Progressive Era," *Pacific Northwest Quarterly* (October 1964), 157–69.

20. Among other things, in Cleveland it was suggested that rents would fall, sickness would be reduced, and excess officials eliminated. *Forest City Democrat,* February 1, 1854; *Cleveland Leader,* April 3, 1844; Robert M. Fogelson, *The Fragmented Metropolis: Los Angeles, 1850–1930* (Cambridge: Harvard University Press and Joint Center for Urban Studies, 1967), p. 115; Studenski, *op. cit.,* p. 127.

21. In a recent volume entitled *Neighborhood Government: The Local Foundations of Political Life* (Indianapolis: Bobbs-Merrill, 1969), Milton Kotler argues that annexation was solely a device to exploit. He provides very little data to support that contention, however.

22. For instance, Philadelphia abandoned a plan to improve sanitary facilities and to rebuild rotting docks in 1820 when shipping interests threatened to move their business to neighboring Southwark and Northern Liberties. See J. Thomas Scharf and Thompson Westcott, *History of Philadelphia, 1606–1884* (Philadelphia: L. H. Evarts and Co., 1884), pp. 599–600; and Philadelphia Councils, Joint Special Committee on Removing the Railway on High, Third, and Dock Streets, *Report* (Philadelphia: L. R. Bailey, 1841), pp. 24, 28.

23. Their intention was to divert farm traffic to themselves.

24. Jacob Judd, "A Tale of Two Cities: Brooklyn and New York, 1834–1855," *Journal of Long Island History,* III (Spring 1963), 19–23; Edward F. Williams, III, "Memphis' Early Triumph Over Its River Rivals," *West Tennessee Historical Society Papers,* XXII (1968), 5–27; and Lois D. Bejach, "The Seven Cities Absorbed by Memphis," *West Tennessee Historical Society Papers,* VIII (1954), 95–104.

25. Kendall, *op. cit.,* p. 172.

26. *Philadelphia Public Ledger,* November 12, 1844. On the riots and subsequent consolidation, see Vincent P. Lannie and Bernard C. Diethorn, "For the Honor and Glory of God: The Philadelphia Bible Riots of 1844," *History of Education Quarterly,* VIII (1968), 44–106; Eli K. Price, *The History of the Consolidation of the City of Philadelphia* (Philadelphia: J. B. Lippincott, 1873); Harry Leffmann, "The Consolidation of Philadelphia," *Philadelphia History,* I (1908), 26–40; and Sam Bass Warner, Jr., *The Private City: Philadelphia in Three Periods of Its Growth* (Philadelphia: University of Pennsylvania Press, 1968), pp. 125–57.

27. Some early opponents of annexation, such as the chief editor of the *North American,* switched over after the second riot. The newspaper then called it "vital to the future progress and welfare of the city." The volunteer fire companies typically opposed consolidation, while an organization called the Friends of a Paid Fire Department supported it. See *Philadelphia Public Ledger,* August 10 and 29, 1853; *Philadelphia North American,* April 19, 1844.

28. Scharf and Westcott, *op. cit.,* p. 691.

29. The location of the line of settlement can either be calculated through an accurate knowledge of ward boundaries and ward population totals, or by reference to the Dynamic Factor Maps of Homer Hoyt or the Maps of the Enumeration Districts of the Various Censuses, both located in the Cartographic Division of the National Archives. In Memphis, for example, it is quite clear that the owners of land on the periphery were the prime movers in the areal growth of the city. In New York, Mayor Havemeyer opposed the annexation of part of the Bronx because it would serve only the interests of "speculators on both sides of the Harlem River." Seymour Mandelbaum, *Boss Tweed's New York* (New York: Wiley, 1968), pp. 109–10. And Sam Warner found that speculators were active in the annexation of West Roxbury to Boston in 1873. *Streetcar Suburbs: The Process of Growth in Boston, 1870–1900* (Cambridge: Harvard University Press, 1962), pp. 41–2.

30. As late as 1900 Byberry and Moreland were divided into farms of from 30 to 100 acres each. Joseph C. Martindale, *A History of the Townships of Byberry and Moreland in Philadelphia* (Philadelphia: G. W. Jacobs, 1900?), p. 148.

31. For example, see Warner, *Streetcar Suburbs,* pp. 163–4.

32. Most authors agree that newcomers to suburbia were more likely to support annexation than long-time residents. For example, of the 449 men who signed a petition for the annexation of Morgan Park to Chicago in 1914, 202 were not listed as living in Morgan Park in 1910. Hubert Morken, "The Annexation of Morgan Park to Chicago: One Village's Response to Urban Growth" (unpublished master's thesis, University of Chicago, 1968), p. 67.

33. For example, see I. N. Phelps Stokes, ed., *Iconography of Manhattan Island,* 6 vols. (New York: Robert H. Dodd, 1928), I, 162, 197.

34. George Rogers Taylor, ed., "Philadelphia in Slices," by George G. Foster, *Pennsylvania Magazine of History and Biography,* XCIII (January 1969), 34, 39, 41. Contrary to the popular image, the dance halls and brothels of early Wichita and Abilene were also on the outskirts. Robert R. Dykstra, *The Cattle Towns* (New York: Knopf, 1969), p. 233.

35. The outward movement of the elite is treated in Kenneth T. Jackson, "Urban Deconcentration in the Nineteenth Century."

36. Roxbury was threatened both by ocean storm tides and by high water in the Stony Brook.

37. In the newly annexed areas of Chicago, 16 new fire companies were formed in 1890, and fire alarm boxes were extended as far south as Pullman. And prior to annexation, most of the south suburbs in Chicago were still lighted by kerosene lamps. Studenski, *op. cit.,* pp. 117, 129–33. Suburban problems with water are highlighted by Nelson Manfred Blake, *Water for the Cities: A History of the Urban Water Supply Problem in the United States* (Syracuse: Syracuse University Press, 1956), pp. 87–9.

38. The estimate is that of John T. Scharf regarding an 1816 annexation to Baltimore. Scharf, *The Chronicles of Baltimore* (Baltimore: Turnbull Brothers, 1874), p. 61. The same thing still happens today. A straw vote recently indicated that residents of Whitehaven opposed annexation to Memphis by a 19-to-1 margin, but the 55,000-resident community was added to the Tennessee metropolis anyway.

39. The various types of legislative, popular, municipal, judicial, and quasilegislative methods of annexation are discussed in Frank Sengstock, *Annexation: A Solution to the Metropolitan Area Problem* (Ann Arbor: University of Michigan Law School Legislative Research Center, 1960), pp. 6–12. For the current annexation laws in each state, see National League of Cities, Department of Urban Studies, *Adjusting Municipal Boundaries: Law and Practice* (Washington, D.C.: National League of Cities, 1966).

40. *Daly vs. Morgan* (69 Maryland Reports, p. 461), quoted in Studenski, *op. cit.,* pp. 75–6.

41. An important source of resistance came from industries on the periphery that were especially anxious not to pay city taxes. Thus George Pullman fought for years to keep Pullman out of Chicago, and the big Birmingham consolidation of 1910 was carefully arranged to leave out the largest industrial plants so as "to relieve these huge enterprises of the burden of municipal taxation." The quote is from an otherwise worthless volume by John R. Hornady, *The Book of Birmingham* (New York: Dodd, Mead, 1921), p. 268.

42. Kendall, *op. cit.,* pp. 742–59.

43. The strongest opposition in Cleveland came from the Fourth Ward, which was most distant from the area to be added. The Third Ward, which included the retail and warehouse districts of the city, was the only section to vote in favor of the merger. James Harrison Kennedy, *A History of the City of Cleveland* (Cleveland: Imperial Press, 1896); and Bigger and Kitchen, *op. cit.,* pp. 145–6.

44. For instance, Roxbury voted for annexation to Boston in 1857 (no action taken however); Cleveland approved the merger with Ohio City in 1854; and St. Louis was enlarged by popular vote in 1856.

45. *Oak Park Reporter,* November 16, 1899; quoted in Arthur LeGacy, "Improvers and Preservers: A History of Oak Park, Illinois" (unpublished Ph.D. dissertation, University of Chicago, 1967).

46. Isaac Atwater, ed., *History of the City of Minneapolis* (New York: Munsell and Company, 1893), p. 87; and Lucile M. Kane, *The Waterfall That Built a City: The Falls of St. Anthony in Minneapolis* (St. Paul: Minnesota Historical Society, 1966), p. 96.

47. Joseph Fulford Folsom, ed., *The Municipalities of Essex County, New Jersey, 1666–1924* (New York: Lewis Historical Publishing Co., 1925), I, 232. Newark is unusual in that it has lost more territory since 1800 than it has gained. John P. Snyder, "The Bounds of Newark: Tract, Township, and City," *New Jersey History,* LXXXVI (Summer 1968), 92–105.

48. Bigger and Kitchen, *op. cit.,* pp. 144–5.

49. The Alameda County decision, which was the first federation proposal to be put to a popular vote in the United States, lost in 9 out of 10 cities and was defeated by about 10,000 votes. Council of State Governments, *The States and the Metropolitan Problem: A Report to the Governor's Conference* (Chicago, 1956),

p. 87. See also Blake McKelvey, *Rochester: The Quest for Quality, 1890–1925* (Cambridge: Harvard University Press, 1956), p. 110.

50. *The States and the Metropolitan Problem*, pp. 72–3.

51. Quoted in Studenski, *op. cit.*, pp. 154–5. Retrenchment generally followed a huge expansion. Thus, Philadelphia cut back for a dozen years following its 1854 consolidation because most suburban governments had brought the city enormous debts and precious little cash. *Philadelphia Public Ledger*, August 11, 1853; and *Annual Message of the Mayor of Philadelphia*, January 8, 1857.

52. Among city defeats of annexation were the occasion in 1907 when Los Angeles voters rejected merger with Hyde Park, Green Meadows, Gardena, Ivanhoe, and a half-dozen other suburban communities, and another in 1926 when Detroit voted against annexing portions of Warren and Royal Oak Townships.

53. The vote, which was authorized by a constitutional amendment in 1924, would have permitted the annexation of the entire county and would have made St. Louis the largest city in the world in area.

54. A good brief account of the Pittsburgh battle is in Roy Lubove, *Twentieth-Century Pittsburgh: Government, Business and Environmental Change* (New York: Wiley, 1969), pp. 27, 97–101.

55. Quoted in Morken, *op. cit.*, p. 25.

56. Miller, *op. cit.*, p. 57; and Warner, *Streetcar Suburbs*, p. 164.

57. LeGacy, *op. cit., passim*.

58. One reason for the rapid area growth of Dallas and Houston is that Texas home rule cities may annex without the consent of residents of the territory to be annexed. American Municipal Association, *Changes in Municipal Boundaries Through Annexation, Consolidation, and Detachment*, Report No. 127 (Chicago: American Municipal Association, January 1939). In addition, many state laws do not provide for cross county annexations.

59. In a recent six-year-period, more than 35 new cities were incorporated in Los Angeles County alone. Usually the only requisite is geographical contiguity, even though the area involved may include no places of business or livelihood.

60. Betty Tableman, *Governmental Organization in Metropolitan Areas* (Ann Arbor: University of Michigan Press, 1951), p. 61.

61. The only biography of the foremost champion of New York consolidation is John Foord, *The Life and Public Services of Andrew Haswell Green* (Garden City, N.Y.: Doubleday, 1913).

62. As I have noted elsewhere, population loss at the center is a normal process in American cities and can be documented in all big cities long before 1900.

26. WHO LIVES WHERE?
Urban Housing and Discrimination

Jeanne R. Lowe

Central cities usually have to rely on what is known in the housing field as the filter process to create vacancies in standard housing for families of lower incomes.

Filter process describes the way in which the normal housing market should work. According to the theory, as new housing is built, families who can afford to pay more vacate older units which then become available to families of a somewhat lower income who are on their way up the economic ladder and who in turn move out of still less desirable quarters. The oldest and worst housing will then be taken off the market voluntarily by its owners since there is no longer a demand for it and it should no longer be profitable, as rents are reduced to the level of new tenants' pocketbooks. The filter process does work, but only to a point.

First, not enough new housing is being built, especially for moderate- and low-income families, to create the full supply upon which the filter theory is predicated and the voluntary retirement of dilapidated or obsolete housing depends.

Secondly, where vacancies exist, families too often cannot afford the rentals at legal occupancy standards. Many must pay far more than one quarter of their income for shelter. Owners, in order to accommodate the new market and still squeeze their usual annual return from properties which have probably been depreciated several times, will divide larger living units into smaller ones. They convert old single-family homes into multiple-family use, allow more people to live in an apartment than should according to the law, or lease space in structures which should be torn down. Landlords also cut costs by reducing maintenance on such buildings.

They may thus solve the immediate shelter problem of the families, and even do so legally if a city's code specifications are not too exacting or systematically enforced. Such practices, however, prolong the life of unfit housing, create newly overcrowded housing (not to overlook the schools and neighborhoods which serve them) and spread the blight and decay which comprehensive urban renewal is supposed to eliminate.

A closely related and increasingly significant reason for the failure of the

Excerpts from *Cities in a Race with Time*, by Jeanne Lowe. Copyright © 1967 by Jeanne Lowe. Reprinted by permission of Random House, Inc. and The Julian Bach Literary Agency, Inc.

filter process is that the private housing market does not work freely for the growing nonwhite portion of the urban population. Instead, it excludes this sector from a substantial part of the housing supply and then exploits their situation.

The effect of discriminatory practices by the real-estate, home-building and mortgage-lending industries was authoritatively studied and documented for the first time during the late 1950s and early 1960s by two sets of nationwide investigations—one conducted under the auspices of the Ford Foundation-sponsored Commission of Race and Housing, the other by the United States Commission on Civil Rights.* Although they found differences between regions and among some cities, and although the studies for the Commission on Race and Housing were undertaken prior to the 1960 census, the situation has remained so unchanged (the census corroborated the general findings) for the vast majority of nonwhites—who have since grown in number in cities—and it is sufficiently similar in cities across the country that the basic facts should concern anyone who is interested in the future of American cities.

The studies found that the typical nonwhite family receives less for its rental dollar than the white family, whatever its income level or social position. And since the large majority of nonwhite families are renters, the ramifications are serious. They must pay a higher proportion of family income, as much as 50 percent more, to obtain smaller, inferior accommodations† and are forced into significantly more overcrowding. Three times as many Negroes live in structurally substandard housing, in inferior neighborhoods, and overcrowding is four times more common than among white families.

Generally the quality of housing occupied by nonwhite families has improved markedly since 1950—as has that of white families. But the big gap separating the standard of accommodations occupied by the two groups has remained substantially unchanged. (A 1963 report on *Our Non-White Population and Its Housing* published by the Housing and Home Finance Agency revealed that the number of overcrowded white families decreased by 200,000 while the number of overcrowded units occupied by nonwhite families during the 1950s increased from nearly 1 million to 1,300,000, even though the total proportion decreased.)

---

* *Report of the U.S. Commission on Civil Rights 1959* and *1961 Commission on Civil Rights Report, Book 4: Housing,* Superintendent of Documents, Government Printing Office, Washington, D.C. The major studies prepared for the Commission on Race and Housing and the Commission's final report, *Residence and Race,* were published by the University of California Press, 1960.

† The lowest-income centers, who form the bulk of urban nonwhites, commonly have to pay a much larger percentage of their income for shelter than do whites of similar economic status. It is not uncommon for big-city landlords to charge and obtain a bonus for allowing nonwhites to rent their substandard accommodations.

Because Negroes can often get more for their housing dollar as home-owners than as renters, they purchase at much lower incomes than do whites. But this impulse to homeownership is exploited by realtors who capitalize on the fear they have inculcated in white property owners about minority groups' allegedly depressing effect on property values. By engaging in "blockbusting," the realtor scares white families into selling their homes at panic prices by bringing a Negro family into a street. He then exploits the pent-up demand of Negroes for decent homes in better neighborhoods by selling them houses he has acquired at deflated values at inflated prices. Markups by blockbusters as high as 112 percent were revealed in hearings conducted in 1962 by the New York City Commission on Human Relations.

But the lending institutions really determine who lives where, because they hold the key to financing home purchase. The U.S. Commission on Civil Rights found that banks operated "on the premise that only a homo-geneous neighborhood can offer an economically sound investment," and banks thus would withhold mortgages for a "first purchase" by a Negro in a white neighborhood. Once a neighborhood began to change, however, the Commission found that the banks would do "everything they can to expedite" the trend, including withholding mortgages from prospective white purchasers in those areas. Moreover, even when a Negro was fully qualified as a credit risk, lenders might charge him a higher discount on his loan or not issue one at all.

Such practices perpetuate the fear of white families that when a Negro family moves into their neighborhood, the area will inevitably become pre-dominantly nonwhite. Professor William Grigsby of the University of Penn-sylvania's Institute for Urban Studies has pointed out: "It is the pattern of market segregation which itself causes the inundation that whites observe and fear. In other words, since only a few areas are available to the expand-ing nonwhite population, when a new section 'opens up,' nonwhite demand tends to focus at this point of limited supply. In such a situation, a quick transformation from white to Negro occupancy frequently occurs."

The suburban "white noose" is another major reason the normal market process does not work. Housing is a metropolitan commodity and almost all new housing since the war has been put up in the suburbs. But scarcely any of it has been sold to nonwhites. It is held that the tract developers, who put up most new housing, fear the effect that an open-sales policy would have upon their white customers.

Suburban pressures have discouraged new interracial housing tracts. A builder who endeavors to put through such a development against the opposition of local property owners finds that town and village govern-ments can employ a host of subterfuges—large-lot zoning, the withholding of building permits, failure to install necessary water and sewer lines, even condemnation of a proposed building site for a park or other public use—without excluding him directly. Also, his usual sources of financing may dry up. At the same time, suburban realtors, like those in cities, refuse to show homes to Negro house hunters unless these are in "changed" areas.

Even new homes built privately with government mortgage guarantees or insured loans have not served the Negro market in proportion to its size. Only 1 percent of the government-insured homes constructed since World War II was purchased by nonwhites, although Negroes comprised 10 percent of the population. Generally, this 1 percent was located in segregated developments, or substandard locations to which white families did not have to resort. In addition, most suburban housing was and is priced beyond the Negro market; this is a matter to which we shall return.

For many years, the Federal Housing Administration itself contributed to these patterns of residential segregation. It actually recommended restrictive covenants until the Supreme Court outlawed them in 1948, and before 1949, its underwriting manual, which governs insuring practices, warned against "adverse influences from lower-class infiltration and inharmonious racial groups." Although the FHA officially changed its policies, during the big postwar suburban building boom the home-building industry still acted on the former basis and the federal agency did little to police them; thus the FHA allowed the suburbs to become more lily-white, and deprived the growing number of potential Negro home purchasers of the attractive terms of supposedly color-blind government insurance.

As white families left the drab older sections of cities for new and better homes in the suburbs, Negro families moved into these areas. In effect, these Negro families made possible the departure of the white families and the volume of new construction in suburbs to be sustained, although they could not benefit from it directly. The growing Negro middle class has, in fact, been denied a status symbol of major significance in the American way of life.

The metropolitan schism that has developed as a result can be seen at its extreme in the Washington, D.C., area, which has a total of 2,150,000 people. The District of Columbia itself, with a population of 801,000, is 63 percent Negro; the suburbs, with more people than the metropolitan area, is 93 percent white.

The effect of all these forces on the Negro's housing has been that the neighborhood where he may buy is usually older and lower in value, as is his home, which is thus a poorer lending risk. His down payment must be larger in proportion to what he buys, his repayment period is shorter, and interest charges are often higher. Refusal by banks to lend in some older or changing neighborhoods has frequently forced minority home purchasers to resort to loan sharks who charge outrageous terms, and to buy on insecure contract sales that do not give the owner title to a property until it is fully paid for. If he defaults one payment, he loses the house and his whole investment. Moreover, the nonwhite has less money left to spend on the higher cost of maintaining such an older property.

So lending, building, realty and even government practices have increased segregation and perpetuated the stereotypes of the Negroes as poor homeowners and neighbors who have a depressing effect on property values. They also have encouraged the deterioration of properties and neighborhoods to the detriment of entire communities, and furthered the segregated use of schools and other public facilities.

Yet the findings of a landmark study, *Property Values and Race,* undertaken for the Commission on Race and Housing refuted the time-honored myth about racial intrusion deflating property values. This ten-year study of twenty middle-aged neighborhoods in seven cities, carried out by Luigi Laurenti and published in 1960, was the first to isolate the effect on the price of homes of nonwhite entry into a formerly white neighborhood. Laurenti's authoritative work concluded that minority purchasers, far from depressing values, tended to stabilize or even to raise them.

His research has since been corroborated by other studies, the most extensive being a ten-city survey of the *Midwestern Minority Housing Market* for the Advance Mortgage Corporation. Its 1963 report stated: "Property values in neighborhoods in racial transition generally held their own or rose above the neighboring norm, thus refuting a long-held stereotype." Price declines occurred in contiguous white neighborhoods which had been "written off by one market and not yet entered by another."

Given these circumstances, and the fact that Negroes must spend more for less housing, it is hardly surprising that half of all the residents in public housing today are Negro. Yet there are far more poor white people than there are poor Negroes in cities. And here we run into the basic dilemma that has hounded city rebuilders in recent years: *who wants public housing?*

The great public-housing movement came tumbling down during the affluent 1950s with a drawn-out whimper. This was not because the need for it had disappeared. In some big cities by the end of the decade, waiting lists equaled the number of units occupied. Rather, it was because the program had become very unpopular in certain strategic quarters. Even some of its most stalwart friends, boosters and spokesmen for potential beneficiaries had deserted or were now among its outspoken critics.

Congress itself helped shrink the program from the generous six-year authorization of 810,000 units made with the Housing Act of 1949; it put low-rent housing on an uncertain annual basis during the Eisenhower administration, with from 20,000 to 45,000 units a year. When the Kennedy administration came in in 1961, public housing amounted to only 1 percent, instead of the 10 percent of new homes built each year, as Senator Taft had hoped when shaping the 1949 Act; and 100,000 units of the originally authorized units remained untouched. A certain hardening of the arteries also appeared to have taken place in the local housing authorities. They were unable to use up even their reduced authorizations from Washington.

Though from 1961 to 1965 there was an increase in the volume of public housing units contracted for, the large majority of these—90,944 out of the total 128,746—were special units for the elderly. These filled an important, previously unmet need, but the program did not confront the problem of housing the most needy: poor families with children in the big cities. Of the rest of the units, about 40 percent of the public housing starts were in cities under 50,000. Some big cities, Baltimore, Cleveland, Detroit and Boston, did not even begin public housing construction between 1962 and 1964. What had gone wrong with the great social program?

During the agonizing reappraisal which began in the late 1950s, one of the first persons to commit herself publicly was Catherine Bauer Wurster, a leading advocate of public housing during its salad days. Miss Bauer, who had been the first research director of the United States Housing Authority, blamed the large-scale community design of public housing projects for a good part of the trouble.

"We embraced too whole-heartedly functionalist and collectivist architectural theories that tended to ignore subtler esthetic values and basic social needs," she wrote. Like others, Miss Bauer was particularly critical of the "public housing skyscrapers," which put occupants into "a highly organized bee-hive of community life for which most American families have no desire and no aptitude. . . . There is no room in such schemes for individual deviation, for personal initiative and responsibility, for outdoor freedom and privacy . . . [and] small-scale business enterprise."

Architectural critic Jane Jacobs came to professional prominence at this time by opposing slum clearance itself. She contended that the disruption of neighborhood life, the removal of institutions and the replacement of dense low-rise slums with public housing super-blocks were responsible for the leaderlessness, isolation and lack of safety in low-income projects. Compared to the "safe" city street, she maintained, all those "dull" open spaces invited criminality.

Elizabeth Wood, former executive director of the Chicago Housing Authority, singled out the increasing number of "hard-core" problem families in a 1957 report to the New York Citizens' Housing and Planning Council on the problems of public housing. She wrote: "There is juvenile delinquency, prostitution and crime. The presence of problem families [is] evidenced by the deteriorated appearance of buildings and grounds and . . . excessive maintenance costs. But a more serious result of their presence is that public housing is getting a bad reputation; it is being stigmatized as a bad place to live by normal low-income families. . . ."

In 1958, Pulitzer Price-winning *New York Times* reporter Harrison Salisbury delved into New York's public housing: "I never imagined that I could find the equivalent of Moscow's newly built slums in the United States," he wrote. But in Brooklyn's mammoth Fort Greene Houses, "a massive barracks for the destitute," and other low-rent projects, he found ". . . the same shoddy shiftlessness, the broken windows, the missing light bulbs, the plaster cracking from the walls, the pilfered hardware, the cold, drafty corridors, the doors on sagging hinges, the ragged plaintive women, the playgrounds that are seas of muddy clay, planned absence of art, beauty and taste . . . human cesspools worse than those of yesterday."

How could public housing have fallen so low in less than two decades? What ever happened to those nice poor families who lived so effectively when they moved from slums into public housing projects? Tenants' listlessness, apathy and withdrawal were now a common complaint.

We have only begun to study the orientations and values attached to place of residence, environment and neighbors by working- and lower-class families. These new insights call for a reconsideration of slum clearance criteria, the design of housing for low-income families, the criteria and methods of tenant selection in public housing, and the kinds of personnel needed in projects.

Some directors are bothered because so many of today's poor are not like the old public-housing tenants. Some have even blamed urban renewal and other public improvement programs for foisting on the projects all those large, socially troubled, often apathetic and increasingly nonwhite families, who, left on their own, would probably not have applied for admission and who also scare off "normal" low-income families.

Is public housing intended to house the needy, or to create "healthy" communities? Can it do both? Two different schools of thought emerged. The first, and more pervasive, is obsessed by the poor image of public housing. This group has wanted to reconstitute projects into socially "normal," racially integrated communities with a "better cross section" of low-income families, more white families, and a minimum of problem families, the "rotten apples" that spoil a project.* They have blamed income ceilings for depriving projects of leaders; they contend that these limits rob families of the initiative to earn more money because, it is said, they will then have to pay more rent, and when their earnings reach a certain level, move out. Ceilings are also unnatural and stigmatizing, it is suggested, and they make the public-housing project, in the words of the National Federation of Settlement Houses and Neighborhood Centers, into "the modern symbol of the poor-house."

This group advocated that tenants whose incomes rise be allowed to

---

* The New York City Housing Authority in 1961 developed a list of social eligibility requirements for applicants as a way of keeping out undesirables and potential troublemakers. In this policy, eight "clear and present dangers" to other tenants are cited as making a family ineligible for admission. These include "grossly unacceptable housekeeping," and a "record of unreasonable disturbance or destruction of property." In addition, twenty-one conditions indicative of "potential problem" families are to be considered before a final decision on admission is made. These include "irregular work history," "two or more separations of husband and wife in the past five years," "out-of-wedlock children," "lack of parental control" and "retardation of any family member." Recently, pressures from civic groups and City Hall have forced a reexamination of these policies. The Housing Authority applied to the Office of Economic Opportunity for a $1,100,000 grant to pay for extra caseworkers, teachers and other personnel to work with problem families in urban renewal areas so they can qualify for public housing.

remain and pay full economic rent; they could eventually buy their project apartment or house. Smaller units in scattered sites, or rehabilitated housing are proposed as an alternative to projects. These would be preferably outside of slum-ghetto areas. Some preferred to give rent supplements or direct subsidies so the needy can live in standard, privately owned housing. The goal seems to have been well summarized by one big city planning director: make public housing "invisible."

The second, less prevalent school was exemplified by the National Capital Housing Authority. It accepted early the relocation challenge of urban renewal, and programmed all its units to facilitate the end of slums in the District. The Authority believed, as the NCHA's former director James Ring had stated, that the uprooted and disorganized families were "more acutely in need of public housing's services than other families who have taken the initiative and are eager to break away from the slums." The Washington public-housing officials tried to marshal all possible community resources to meet such tenants' immediate needs and then help them graduate to the private housing market. As far back as 1954, the annual report of the National Capital Housing Authority stated that "Public housing would not be performing its job if it retained in tenancy [over-income families] in preference to low-income families who are waiting for a chance to live in decent housing."

Yet even in Washington, by the early 1960s, it was evident that the conventional approach was not keeping pace with the pressing needs of large low-income families. If some dent were to be made in just the long list of displaced families which had been waiting for admission to public housing —some for ten and twelve years—supplementary housing resources would have to be found beyond the usual projects.

Washington, like other cities, was running into two practical obstacles. One was trying to construct large enough apartments for big low-income families within the cost limits set by the Public Housing Administration. The other was finding sites on which to build.

This immediate question of where low-rent housing is to be located raises problems that have accelerated and have been most responsible for the slowdown in recent years. In exploring the location question, one can also begin to pick out separate threads from the tangled skein, and see why new kinds of approaches had to be legislated in the Housing and Urban Development Act of 1965.

.   .   .

The Housing and Urban Development Act of 1965 presented an assortment of alternative means for housing the urban poor and, hopefully, for overcoming the many obstacles that have recently blocked public housing's traditional approach. The three major programs are all designed to avoid monster projects and sharp distinctions between public and private housing by making use of existing privately owned structures or newly built private housing for low-income families.

One new provision enables local housing authorities to either lease or purchase, and rehabilitate, private structures under somewhat shorter terms than public housing's usual forty years for new buildings, and to rent these units to low-income families under the usual formula. Another provision allows authorities to contract for the use of up to 10 percent of the apartments in private buildings on one-to-three-year renewable leases; the tenants may be selected by the owners, who are required by contract to bring buildings up to code standards. Tenant charges and rentals are on the same basis as in conventional public housing.

The most unorthodox approach is the rent supplement program, which departs entirely from the public landlord and project approach. The supplements make it possible for low-income families to live in privately owned, FHA-assisted middle-income housing built by nonprofit or limited-profit sponsors using the (d)3 program, but at full market interest rate. The Federal Housing Administration pays the difference between 25 percent of the tenants' incomes and the economic rents required in such housing. The law also authorized that the traditional projects be continued along with these new experimental programs.*

With such a variety of publicly assisted programs for both low- and middle-income families, it should be possible not only to move ahead with the task of housing the urban poor, but also to avoid the many objections raised to both public housing and urban renewal. Perhaps the new social end results, which people are coming to expect of renewal, may be realized along with physical improvements.

Among the principal objections raised are mass dislocation of the poor (often nonwhite) and destruction of communities; ghettoization by income and segregation by color. The main new social goals are planned renewal with the participation of the residents; community preservation and on-site rehousing of dislocatees; elimination of ghettos and integration of communities; economically and socially heterogeneous neighborhoods. (According to proponents of the latter view, socioeconomic distance can be bridged through residential proximity, middle-class patterns transmitted to the lower class through neighborhood interaction; ghettos, low incomes and prejudices can thus be eliminated. Talk about renewal in terms other than diversity, not merely of building types but also of racial and economic groups, has come to be regarded here as heretical and undemocratic.)

One cannot challenge the validity of these goals, taken separately. But it soon becomes obvious that realization of one goal may be detrimental or antithetical to others. Dilemmas and conflicts inevitably arise, not just

---

* Other new federal housing aids which are not part of the public housing program but will help low-income owners improve their housing include: direct grants of up to $1,500 for rehabilitation to families with incomes under $3,000 in urban renewal areas, and 100 percent loans for rehabilitated housing owned by families with somewhat higher incomes.

between physical and fiscal versus social goals, but also among the social objectives, and hard choices must be made, both by residents and by public officials. Once we have accepted this fact, certain questions arise. Whose objectives are more representative and valid? Who will benefit? If social goals become predominant, how many of the poor will get decent housing, and how soon will cities be renewed? The fact is that people of good will are not in agreement on how to proceed.

There are, for example, strong differences between the views of proponents of desegregation and ghetto dispersion through public actions, and the practices and apparent desires of many who live in so-called Negro ghettos.

At a national conference on programs for "breaking up the ghetto" held in the spring of 1966 by the National Committee Against Discrimination in Housing in cooperation with the federal Office of Economic Opportunity, the sharp disagreement expressed by some members of the audience was a shock to the sponsors. One California representative stated that it is unpopular in the Negro community to move into a white area, and that dispersion is called "political castration." A San Franciscan said of her community, Hunter's Point, "Some want to stay and some want to go. We know what we want—decent facilities. But we don't know how to get the money to get them." This viewpoint was echoed by the antipoverty program director from Los Angeles. "People in Watts aren't clamoring to get out," he said. "They want more buses, quality housing and the freedom to get out, if they want." A New Orleans representative pointed out that in his city there had always been racial dispersion, but "on a master and servant basis, not among equals. Aren't we confusing race and culture?" he asked. The dilemma several speakers raised was: do we have to strengthen the ghetto before we can disperse it?

There is deep confusion, even within civil rights ranks, about urban renewal. Title I projects that entail massive clearance and family dislocation in Negro slums have been criticized as "Negro removal." Yet integrationists condemn the newer kinds of projects which instead emphasize housing rehabilitation and improvement of Negro neighborhoods; they call this "embalming a ghetto." If one were to heed these critics, urban renewal could not win on racial grounds.

There is as yet limited experience with conservation-types of renewal in Negro communities. The Washington Park project, located in Boston's area of heaviest Negro concentration, Roxbury, was the first of this kind in that city. Social surveyors from Brandeis University were so surprised by the limited desire to move out on the part of middle-income Negro families who were faced with the alternative by renewal that they returned six months later to check on earlier findings. (Trained Negro social workers carried out all the interviews.)

"We began the study in the belief that Roxbury's Negroes would rush to embrace any opportunity to escape their relatively segregated and declining neighborhood," said the report on the Brandeis study. "Integration is in the air, and the longed-for appears at last to have become possible." But only 4 percent of the fifty families with incomes over $5,000—those financially able—actually moved away into predominantly white communities, in spite of the fact that there was plenty of housing in the $10,000 to $12,000 range for sale without discrimination in white neighborhoods with better schools in and around Boston; furthermore, a metropolitan Fair Housing Committee was active, and public agencies were interested in helping these families. Very little effort to house-hunt outside the area was even made, although a much larger percentage of the Negroes had originally expressed an interest in moving out.

A number of reasons were cited for the surprising lack of mobility: the central location of their neighborhood, near to places of work and to downtown; the good public transportation facilities; the unusually low cost of housing in Washington Park—only 12 percent of their income (moving would have required spending much more); the feelings of comfort with people of their own skin color and the desire to be near friends and institutions; the fear of being subjected to humiliation and discrimination in new homes. Virtually all the families had favorable feelings toward urban renewal. They felt confident that the Boston Redevelopment Authority's program would make their community a more satisfactory place to live. This feeling was reinforced as renewal planning advanced, as they had the opportunity to participate in decisions for bettering their environment, and as official steps were taken to improve the local schools and to get bank loans for home improvement at reasonable rates.

These factors caused the social surveyors to speculate on the dilemmas presented by "success" in renewal. The middle-income "respectable" Negro families would, it seemed, make the best pioneers for integration, yet renewal appeared to be curtailing their mobility and discouraging integration. On the other hand, the report pointed out, "the middle-income families, few though they may be, provide models of family life and bring cultural values and a degree of stability to the community." They also gave leadership to local institutions and voluntary organizations. Their outward movement would thus deprive the community of socializing agents and models, leaving Washington Park "a pocket of the poverty-stricken."

The study concluded that "another strategy is required if integration is to be accomplished": Washington Park must be made so attractive that white families will move in.

.   .   .

An impressive body of evidence casts strong doubt on the social efficacy of the balanced neighborhood. Studies of planned and unplanned neighborhoods with various economic levels and racial compositions, both in the United States and in Great Britain, show that heterogeneity of class within a community actually increases stratification. Those of higher status draw together; the less able tend to withdraw.

There is also some question whether the balanced neighborhood meets the residential needs of low-income tenants. Recent studies have begun to investigate the orientation of the lower and working classes to living space and neighborhood; such studies indicate that these differ so markedly from middle-class concepts that the balanced city neighborhood, as a means of providing equal residential satisfaction for all groups, may be, as a spokesman for a team of researchers in Boston stated, "an impossibility." (The Planning Commission's original report on the West Side renewal project noted: "The newcomer finds that other New Yorkers disapprove of his use of the outdoors as an extension of his home.") This philosophy has the earmarks of the settlement house in reverse: the poor are brought in to settle among the better-off.

.   .   .

The new kinds of programs are certainly worthwhile, but it seems that the officials are so concerned with making public housing acceptable to a larger cross section that they have failed to educate the public about unmet needs and to the fact that the program cannot house its mass market.

Public housing's biggest problem is poverty combined with the programs' financing formula. Many tenants have no place else to live, and millions of ill-housed people are too poor to get in. The program only serves a fraction of the need.

Family incomes nationally increased 17 percent between just 1960 and 1964; those of public-housing tenants advanced only 5 percent. Measured in real purchasing power, the incomes had only increased .05 percent. Median incomes were only $2,335, nearly $1,700 below the median maximum for continued occupancy, although the ceiling had been raised by $1,000 over the preceding decade. Moreover, the percentage of families found ineligible to remain on the basis of increased income declined from 22 percent in 1949 to 2 percent in 1958, and has remained there since, while the annual move-out rate has dropped.

For local public-housing authorities, the increased immobility of tenants and the relatively decreased family incomes are of serious concern. They lack the room to accommodate the growing numbers of legally eligible poor displaced by public improvements; and since they must pay projects' costs out of rent receipts, their fiscal solvency is jeopardized. But, as Secretary (then HHFA Administrator) Robert C. Weaver told Congress in 1964, "Many of those displaced by urban renewal and public housing cannot afford to pay rents sufficient even to meet the essential costs of operating and maintaining a public-housing unit. Public housing can accommodate only a limited proportion of those very poor persons. . . ." Further, the authorities are even less able to finance the supplemental health and social services required by today's public-housing tenancy or would-be tenants. And fully half the families still living in all dilapidated and deteriorated housing have very low incomes, $2,200 or less.

To continue public housing as a self-supporting operation, with the "rich" poor supplementing the rent of the really poor, seems out of step with the times and the needs of cities and people.

27. VIOLENCE IN THE CITIES
A Historical View

Richard C. Wade

Violence is no stranger to American cities. Almost from the very beginning, cities have been the scenes of sporadic violence, of rioting and disorders, and occasionally virtual rebellion against established authority. Many of these events resulted in only modest property damage and a handful of arrests. Others were larger in scale with deaths running into the scores and damages into the millions. This paper attempts to survey briefly some of these outbreaks and to analyze their origins and consequences. We confine ourselves, however, to the larger ones, and omit any discussion of individual acts of violence or the general level of crime. In addition, to keep these remarks relevant to the present crisis, we have confined our analysis to disorders in urban areas.

There has been, in fact, a good deal more violence and disorder in the American tradition than even historians have been willing to recognize. The violence on the frontier is, of course, well known, and in writing, movies, and television it has been a persistent theme in our culture. Indeed, one of America's favorite novelists, James Fenimore Cooper, transformed the slaughter and mayhem of Indians into heroic, almost patriotic, action. As the literary historian David Brion Davis has observed: "Critics who interpret violence in contemporary literature as a symptom of a sick society may be reassured to know that American writers have always been preoccupied with murder, rape, and deadly combat." To be sure, violence is not "as American as cherry pie," but it is no newcomer to the national scene.

Though serious scholarship on this dimension of the American past is shamefully thin, it is already quite clear that disorder and violence in our cities were not simply occasional aberrations, but rather a significant part of urban development and growth. From the Stamp Act riots of the pre-revolutionary age, to the assaults on immigrants and Catholics in the decades before the Civil War, to the grim confrontation of labor and manage-

Reprinted from *Urban Violence* (The University of Chicago Center for Policy Study, 1969), pp. 7–26, by permission of the author and the publisher.

ment at the end of the nineteenth century and its sporadic reappearance after World War I and during the Depression, through the long series of racial conflicts for two centuries, American cities have known the physical clash of groups, widescale breakdown of established authority, and bloody disorder.

Nor is it hard to see why this early history had more than its share of chaos. American cities in the eighteenth and nineteenth centuries were very young. They had not yet the time to develop a system of orderly government; there was no tradition of habitual consent to local authority; there was no established police system. In addition, these cities grew at a spectacular rate. In the twentieth century, we have used the term "exploding metropolis" to convey the rapid pace of urbanization. It is not often remembered that the first "urban explosion" took place more than a century ago. Indeed, between 1820 and 1860 cities grew proportionately faster than they had before or ever would again. The very speed of this urban development was unsettling and made the maintenance of internal tranquillity more difficult.

The problem was further compounded by the fact that nearly every American city was born of commerce. This meant that there was always a large transient population—seamen engaged in overseas trade, rivermen plying the inland waters, teamsters and wagonmen using the overland routes, and a constant stream of merchants and salesmen seeking customers. At any moment the number of newcomers was large and their attachments to the community slight. Hence when they hit town, there was always some liveliness. After exhausting the cities' museums and libraries, sailors and teamsters would find other things to do. In the eighteenth and nineteenth century, transients comprised a significant portion of those who engaged in rioting and civil disorders.

In addition to being young, rapidly growing, and basically commercial, American cities also had very loose social structures. Unlike the Old World, they had no traditional ruling group, class lines were constantly shifting, and new blood was persistently pumped into these urban societies. One could say that up until the last part of the nineteenth century, mercantile leaders dominated municipal government; but even that commercial leadership changed continually. Later, immigrant groups shared high offices in municipal affairs, thus underlining the shifting nature of the social structure of most cities. Within this looseness there was always a great deal of mobility, with people rising and falling in status not only from generation to generation but within a single lifetime.

This fluid social system contrasted sharply with other, older societies, yet it contained a high incidence of disorder. For it depended on the constant acceptance of new people and new groups to places of influence and importance, and their incorporation into the system on a basis of equality with others. This acceptance was only grudgingly conceded, and often only after some abrasive episodes. The American social structure thus had a large capacity to absorb revolutionary tensions and avoid convulsive upheavals. But it also bred minor social skirmishes which were not always orderly. It is significant that in the pre-Civil War South, where slavery created a more traditional social structure, there was less rioting and civil disorder than in the North (though one ought not underestimate the individual violence against the slave built into institutional bondage).

The American social structure was also unique because it was composed not only of conventional classes, but also of different ethnic, religious, and racial groups. They had at once an internal cohesion that came from a common background and a shared American experience and also a sense of sharp differences with other groups, especially with the country's older stock. These groups, the Negro excepted, were initially both part of the system and yet outside of it. The resultant friction, with the newcomers pressing for acceptance and older groups striving for continued supremacy, was a fruitful source of disorder and often violence. Since it was in the city that these groups were thrown together, became aware of their differences, and struggled for survival and advancement, it would be on the streets rather than on the countryside that the social guerrilla warfare would take place.

If the internal controls in the American social structure were loose, the external controls were weak. The cities inherited no system of police control adequate to the numbers or to the rapid increase of the urban centers. The modern police force is the creation of the twentieth century; the establishment of a genuinely professional system is historically a very recent thing. Throughout the eighteenth and nineteenth century, the force was small, untrained, poorly paid, and part of the political system. In case of any sizable disorder, it was hopelessly inadequate; and rioters sometimes routed the constabulary in the first confrontation. Josiah Quincy, for example, in Boston in the 1820s had to organize and arm the teamsters to reestablish the authority of the city in the streets. Many prudent officials simply kept out of the way until the worst was over. In New York's draft riots, to use another instance, the mayor wandered down to see what the disturbance was all about and nearly got trampled in the melee.

Moreover, since some of the rioting was political, the partisanship of the police led official force to be applied against one group, or protection to be withheld from another. And with every turnover in the mayor's office, a substantial and often a complete change occurred in the police. In Atlanta, for instance, even where there was only one party, each faction had its own men in blue ready to take over with the changes in political fortunes. In some places where the state played a role in local police appointments, the mayor might even be deprived of any control at all for the peace of the city. In New York in the 1850s there was an awkward moment when there were two police forces—the Municipals and the Metropolitans—each the instrument of opposing parties. At the point of the most massive confusion, one group tried to arrest the mayor and an armed struggle took place between the two competing forces.

The evolution toward more effective and professional forces was painfully slow. Separating the police from patronage proved difficult, the introduction of civil-service qualifications and protection came only in this century, and the development of modern professional departments came even later. To be sure, after a crisis—rioting, widescale looting, or a crime wave—there would be a demand for reform, but the enthusiasm was seldom sustained and conditions returned quickly to normal. The ultimate safety of the city thus resided with outside forces that could be brought in when local police could not handle the mob.

These general considerations account in large part for the high level of disorder and violence in American cities over the past three centuries. The larger disorders, however, often stemmed from particular problems and specific conditions and resulted in widescale bloodshed and destruction. Though these situations varied from place to place and time to time, it is perhaps useful to divide them into a few categories. Some rioting was clearly political, surrounding party struggles and often occasioned by legislation or an election. Some sprang from group conflict, especially the resistance to the rising influence of immigrant groups. Still others stemmed from labor disputes. And the largest, then as now, came out of race conflict. A few examples of each will convey some of their intensity and scale.

Politics has always been a fruitful source of disorders. Indeed, one of the most significant groups of riots surrounded the colonial break with Great Britain. In Boston, Samuel Adams and other radical leaders led the otherwise directionless brawling and gang warfare around the docks and wharfs into a political roughhouse against British policy. The Stamp Tax Riots, the Townshend Duty Riots and, of course, the Boston Massacre were all part of an organized and concerted campaign by colonial leaders. The urban middle classes initially tolerated the disorders because they too opposed certain aspects of British policy; they later pulled back when they felt that radical leadership was carrying resistance beyond their own limited objectives. Yet for nearly a decade, rioting and organized physical force was a part of the politics of the colonies.

This use of violence in politics was not as jarring to the eighteenth century as it would be today. Rioting had been a common occurrence, and not always among the underclasses. As early as 1721, Cotton Mather, one of Boston's most prominent citizens, could bewail in his diary the exploits of his "miserable, miserable, miserable son Increase. The wretch has brought himself under public infamy and trouble by bearing a part in a Night-riot, with some detestable rakes in town." Two decades later, Philadelphia witnessed widespread disorder during its "Bloody Election" in 1742. The widening of the franchise greatly reduced the resort to violence in politics for the ballot provided an alternative to rock-throwing and physical force on important public questions. Yet historically the stakes of political victory have always been high enough to induce some to employ force and mob action.

Attacks against immigrants comprise another theme in the story. Often the assault by older, more established groups was against individuals or small groups. But in other cases it would be more general. The string of riots against Catholic churches and convents in the nineteenth century, for example, represented an attack on the symbols of the rise of the new groups. In the summer of 1834, for instance, a Charlestown (Mass.) convent was sacked and burned to the ground; scuffles against the Irish occurred in various parts of nearby Boston; some Irish houses were set afire. At the outset, the episode was carefully managed; then it got out of hand as teenage toughs got into action. Nor was this an isolated incident.

Characteristic of this period too was the resistance to the incorporation of immigrants into the public life of the city. "Bloody Monday" in Louisville in 1855 will perhaps serve as an illustration. Local politicians had become worried about the increase of the immigrant (German and Irish) vote. The Know-Nothings (a party built in part on anti-immigrant attitudes) determined to keep foreign-born residents away from the polls on election day. There was only a single voting place for every ward, thus numbering only eight in the entire city. Know-Nothing followers rose at dawn and occupied the booths early in the morning. They admitted their own reliables, but physically barred their opponents. The preelection campaign had been tense and bitter with threats of force flying across party lines. By this time some on each side had armed themselves. Someone fired a shot, and the rioting commenced. When it was all through, "Quinn's Row," an Irish section, had been gutted, stores looted, and Catholic churches damaged. A newspaper which was accused of stirring up feeling only barely escaped destruction. The atrocities against the Irish were especially brutal with many being beaten and shot. Indeed, some of the wounded were thrown back into the flames of ignited buildings. Estimates of the dead range from fourteen to one hundred, though historians have generally accepted (albeit with slim evidence) twenty-two as the number killed.

Labor disputes have also often spawned widescale disorder. Indeed, at the turn of the century, Winston Churchill, already a keen student of American affairs, observed that the United States had the most violent industrial relations of any western country. Most of this rioting started with a confrontation of labor and management over the right to organize, or wages and hours, or working conditions. A large portion of these strikes found the workers, in a vulnerable if not helpless position, a fact which has led most historians to come down on the side of labor in these early disputes. Moreover, unlike the disorders we have previously discussed, these were nationwide in scope—occurring at widely scattered points. There was no question of their being directed since a union was usually involved and it had some control over local action throughout the country. Yet the violence was seldom uniform or confined to strikers. It might flare up in Chicago and Pittsburgh, while St. Louis, where the issues would be the same, might remain quiescent. Often, as in the case of the railroad strike of 1877, the damage to life and property was large. In the Homestead lockout alone, thirty-five were killed and the damage (in 1892 dollars) ran to $2,500. In the 1930s the organizing steel, auto, and rubber unions brought a recrudescence of this earlier grisly process.

The "Great Strike of 1877" conveys most of the elements of this kind of violent labor dispute. One historian of the episode observes that "frequently, law and order broke down in major rail centers across the land; what was regarded as 'domestic insurrection' and 'rebellion' took over." He calculated that "millions of dollars worth of property were destroyed, hundreds of persons were injured, and scores killed in rioting in pitched battles with law enforcement officials." The cities affected stretched across the country, including Baltimore, Pittsburgh, Philadelphia, Buffalo, Cleveland, Toledo, Columbus, Cincinnati, Louisville, Indianapolis, Chicago, St. Louis, Kansas City, Omaha, and San Francisco.

The strike began on July 16, 1877, in the midst of hard times when railroads tried to adapt to the depression by cutting wages 10 percent. The workers' resistance began in Martinsburg, West Virginia, where the militia called to the strike scene soon fraternized with the workers. President Rutherford Hayes then dispatched troops to the town and no bloodshed occurred. But in Baltimore, the situation turned ugly and spilled over into violence on July 20. It is hard to know how many genuine strikers were involved and how much of the fighting and damage was done by others. At any rate, eleven people were killed and twenty wounded and the President again dispatched troops to the troubled area. After these eruptions, the riots spread elsewhere. One historian describes the subsequent disorders as "undirected, unplanned, and unmanaged save by impromptu leaders." "Everywhere," he continued, "but especially in Baltimore, Pittsburgh, and Chicago, the striking trainmen were promptly joined by throngs of excitement seeking adolescents, by the idle, the unemployed, the merely curious and the malicious."

Pittsburgh suffered the worst. As trouble first threatened, the governor called up the local militia whose members very quickly began to fraternize with the strikers as the latter took over the trains. The governor then called for troops from Philadelphia. In the furious clash that resulted, sixteen soldiers and fifty rioters were killed. "For two days Pittsburgh was ruled by mobs," one account asserts, "which burned, looted and pillaged to their heart's content, and attacked savagely all who resisted them. Finally the riot died out; into harmlessness. The city was left in ruins." In the last stages, however, the same historian observed that "the rioting had little or no connection with the strike, and few strikers were included in the mobs." In addition to the lives lost, property destroyed included 500 freight cars, 104 locomotives, and thirty-nine buildings.

The strike reached Chicago on July 23. Men left the job and large crowds began to collect. By nightfall, the city was paralyzed. Police were dispatched to disperse the throng and in the first clash they fired into the crowd, killing seven and wounding twenty. The militia arrived and citizens groups began to arm. The superintendent of police estimated that there were 20,000 armed men in Chicago by the second day. On the 26th the United States Army arrived. At 16th Street, 350 police faced a mob of about 6,000 and after an hour's battle at least twelve died and two score or more were seriously wounded. Like most riots, the point of origin and the purpose of the strike were soon forgotten. Indeed, an astute student of the event asserts that "practically none of the rioting may be fairly ascribed to the strikers." Rather, he asserts, "the disturbances were mainly caused by roughs, idlers, unemployed persons, and the criminal element. A surprisingly large percentage of the mobs was composed of women and young boys, and these elements were at the same time the most destructive and the hardest for the police to disperse." He adds, however, that the blame was not one-sided: "It seems also that a good deal of the disturbance was precipitated by the rough tactics of the police."

The Pullman strike in Chicago almost twenty years later also contained most of the familiar elements of a riot growing out of a labor dispute. It, too, stemmed from a wage reduction in the middle of a depression. On May 11, 1894, the strike began in a quiet and orderly fashion. As the gap between the workers and the Pullman Company deepened, the American Railway Union called for a general boycott of sleeping cars. A federal court, however, issued an injunction against the boycott to insure the movement of mail. On July 4 federal troops arrived in Chicago. Until that time a labor historian observed that "there had been little violence in Chicago proper. Some acts of sabotage had occurred and there had been occasional demonstrations but the police had effectively controlled the latter."

Now the temper of the episode changed. Crowds roamed over the tracks "pushing over freight cars, setting a few of them on fire, and otherwise blocking the movement of trains. Switches were thrown, signal lights changed, and trains stoned—much of the trouble caused by half-grown boys who seemed to welcome the opportunity for excitement and deviltry." Furthermore, "a large proportion of women and children" mingled in a crowd that reached 10,000. Adding to the incendiary possibilities was an "abnormally large group of hoodlums, tramps, and semicriminals, some of whom had been attracted to Chicago by the Columbian Exposition and left stranded by the depression." "In the movement of the mobs," the same historian continues, "there was seldom any purpose or leadership. Most of the destruction was done wantonly and without premeditation."

July 6 was the day of the greatest property destruction. A reporter from the *Inter Ocean* described the scene at the height of the frenzy. "From this moving mass of shouting rioters squads of a dozen or two departed, running towards the yards with fire brands in their hands. They looked in the gloaming like specters, their lighted torches bobbing about like will-o'the-wisps. Soon from all parts of the yard flames shot up and billows of fire rolled over the cars, covering them with the red glow of destruction. The spectacle was a grand one. . . . Before the cars were fired those filled with any cargoes were looted. . . . The people were bold, shameless, and eager in their robbery. . . . It was pandemonium let loose, the fire leaping along for miles, and the men and women became drunk on their excess." By nightfall 700 cars had been destroyed. The next day clashes between the crowd and a hastily organized militia left four more dead and twenty wounded. In all, in three chaotic days, thirteen people had been killed, fifty-three seriously wounded, several hundred more hurt and incalculable property damage, not to mention money lost in wages and railroad earnings. One estimate fixes the total at $80 million.

Of all the sources of civil disorder, however, none has been more persistent than race. Whether in the North or South, whether before or after the Civil War, whether nineteenth or twentieth century, this question has been at the root of more physical violence than any other. There had been some sporadic slave uprisings before emancipation, the largest being the Nat Turner rebellion in 1831. But most which moved from plot to action occurred on the countryside rather than in the cities. Yet even the fear of a slave insurrection took its toll; in 1822, for instance, Charleston, South Carolina, officials, acting on tips and rumors, hanged thirty-seven Negroes and deported many more for an alleged plot to capture and burn the city. Seven years later, in a free state, whites invaded Cincinnati's "Little Africa" and burned and killed and ultimately drove half the colored residents from town. In the same period mobs also assaulted abolitionists, sometimes killing, otherwise sacking buildings and destroying printing presses.

Even the New York City riot against the draft in 1863 took an ugly racial twist before it had run its course. The events themselves arose out of the unpopularity of the draft and the federal government's call for more men as Lee headed into Pennsylvania. The situation was further complicated by a crisis in the police department as a result of the conflicting claims of command by a Republican mayor and a Democratic governor. The rioting broke out July 13 and the first target was the provost marshal's office. Within a short time 700 people ransacked the building and then set it afire. The crowd would not let the firemen into the area and soon the whole block lay gutted. Later the mob began to spill over into the Negro area where many blacks were attacked and some killed.

The police were helpless as the riot spread. The few clashes with the mob saw the police retreat; the crowd wandered about almost at will. Political leaders did not want to take the consequences for action against the mob, and soon it started to head toward the business district. Slowly the police reorganized, by Tuesday they began to win engagements with the rioters, and in a little while they were able to confine the action to the original area. The mobs were, however, better armed and organized and gave a good account of themselves in pitched battle. On the third day federal troops arrived and the control swung over to the authorities and quiet was restored. But in three days the casualties ran to at least seventy-four dead and many times that number wounded. The property damage was never accurately added up, but claims against the county exceeded $1,500,000 by 1865.

Emancipation freed the Negro from bondage, but it did not grant him either equality or immunity from white aggression. From the New Orleans riot of 1866, through the long list of racial disorders to the end of World War II with datelines running through Atlanta, Springfield, East St. Louis, Washington, Mobile, Beaumont, Chicago, Detroit, and Harlem, reveal something of the depth of the crisis and the vulnerability of American cities to racial disorders. These riots were on a large scale, involved many deaths, millions of dollars of property damage, and left behind deep scars which have never been fully erased. Most of these riots involved the resort to outside military help for containment; all exposed the thinness of the internal and external controls within our urban society.

In fact, the war had scarcely ended before racial violence erupted in New Orleans. The occasion of the outbreak was a Negro procession to an assembly hall where a debate over enfranchising the blacks was to take place. There was some jostling during the march and a shot fired; but it was only after the arrival at the convention that police and special troops charged the black crowd. In the ensuing struggle Negroes were finally routed, but guns, bricks, and stones were generously used. Many Negroes fell on the spot; others were pursued and killed on the streets trying to escape. Later General Sheridan reported that "at least nine-tenths of the casualties were perpetrated by the police and citizens by stabbing and smashing in the heads of many who had already been wounded or killed by policemen." Moreover, he added that it was not just a riot but "an absolute massacre by the police . . . a murder which the mayor and police . . . perpetrated without the shadow of necessity." Federal troops arrived in the afternoon, took possession of the city, and restored order. But thirty-four Negroes and four whites were already dead and over 200 injured.

Smaller places, even in the North, were also affected with racial disorder. In August 1908, for instance, a three-day riot took its toll in Springfield, Illinois. The Negro population in the capital had grown significantly in the years after the turn of the century, and some whites sensed a political and economic threat. On August 13th a white woman claimed she had been violated by a Negro. An arrest was made and the newspapers carried an inflammatory account of the episode. Crowds gathered around the jail demanding the imprisoned black, but the sheriff quickly transferred the accused and another Negro to a prison in a nearby town without letting the public know. "The crowd outside was in an ugly mood," writes an historian of the riot, "the sun had raised tempers; many of the crowd had missed their dinners, which added to their irritation; and the authorities seemed to be taking no heed of their presence. By sundown the crowd had become an ugly mob."

The first target of the rioters was a restaurant whose proprietor presumably had driven the prisoners from jail. Within a few minutes his place was a shambles. They then headed for the Negro section. Here they hit homes and businesses either owned by or catering to Negroes. White owners quickly put white handkerchiefs in their windows to show their race; their stores were left untouched. A Negro was found in his shop and was summarily lynched. Others were dragged from streetcars and beaten. On the 15th the first of 5,000 national guardsmen reached Springfield; very quickly the mob broke up and the town returned to normal. The death toll reached six (four whites and two blacks); the property damage was significant. As a result of the attack, Springfield's Negro population left the city in large numbers hoping to find better conditions elsewhere, especially in Chicago.

A decade later the depredations in East St. Louis were much larger, with the riot claiming the lives of thirty-nine Negroes and nine whites. The best student of this episode points out that the 1917 riot was not a sudden explosion but resulted from "threats to the security of whites brought on by the Negroes' gains in economic, political and social status; Negro resentment of the attempts to 'kick him back in his place'; and the weakness of the external forces of constraint—the city government, especially the police department." Tensions were raised when the Aluminum Ore Company replaced white strikers with Negro workers. In addition to these factors, race had become a political issue in the previous year when the Democrats accused Republicans of "colonizing" Negroes to swing the election in East St. Louis. The kindling seemed only to lack the match.

On May 28 came the fire. A Central Trades and Labor Union delegation formally requested the mayor to stop the immigration of Negroes to East St. Louis. As the men were leaving City Hall they heard a story that a Negro robber had accidentally shot a white man during a holdup. In a few minutes the word spread; rumor replaced fact. Now it was said the shooting was intentional; that a white woman was insulted; that two white girls were shot. By this time 3,000 people had congregated and the cry for vengeance went up. Mobs ran downtown beating every Negro in sight. Some were dragged off the streetcars, others chased down. The police refused to act except to take the injured to hospitals and to disarm Negroes. The next day the National Guard arrived to restore order.

Two days later the governor withdrew troops although tension remained high. Scattered episodes broke the peace, but no sustained violence developed. The press, however, continued to emphasize Negro crimes and a skirmish broke out between white pickets and black workers at the Aluminum Company. Then on July 1 some whites drove through the main Negro neighborhood firing into homes. The colored residents armed themselves, and when a similar car, this time carrying a plainclothesman and reporter, went down the street the blacks riddled the passing auto with gunshot.

The next day was the worst. At about 10 A.M. a Negro was shot on the main street and a new riot was underway. An historian of the event asserted that the area along Collinsville Avenue between Broadway and Illinois Avenue became a "bloody half mile" for three or four hours. "Streetcars were stopped: Negroes, without regard to age or sex, were pulled off and stoned, clubbed and kicked. . . . By the early afternoon, when several Negroes were beaten and lay bloodied in the street, mob leaders calmly shot and killed them. After victims were placed in an ambulance, there was cheering and handclapping." Others headed for the Negro section and set fire to homes on the edge of the neighborhood. By midnight the South End was in flames and black residents began to flee the city. In addition to the dead, the injured were counted in the hundreds and over 300 buildings were destroyed.

Two summers later the racial virus felled Chicago. Once again, mounting tension had accompanied the migration of blacks to the city. The numbers jumped from 44,000 in 1910 to 109,000 ten years later. Though the job market remained good, housing was tight. Black neighborhoods could expand only at the expense of white ones, and everywhere the transition areas were filled with trouble. Between July 1, 1917, and March 1921, there had been fifty-eight bombings of Negro houses. Recreational areas also witnessed continual racial conflict.

The riot itself began on Sunday, July 27, on the 29th Street Beach. There had been some stone-throwing and sporadic fighting. Then a Negro boy, who had been swimming in the Negro section, drifted into the white area and drowned. What happened is not certain, but the young blacks charged he had been hit by stones and demanded the arrest of a white. The police refused, but then arrested a Negro at a white request. When the Negroes attacked the police, the riot was on. News of the events on the beach spread to the rest of the city. Sunday's casualties were two dead and fifty wounded. On Monday, attacks were made on Negroes coming from work; in the evening cars drove through black neighborhoods with whites shooting from the windows. Negroes retaliated by sniping at any white who entered the black belt. Monday's accounting found twenty killed and hundreds wounded. Tuesday's list was shorter, a handful dead, 139 injured. Wednesday saw a further waning and a reduction in losses in life and property. Rain began to fall; the Mayor finally called in the state militia. After nearly a week a city which witnessed lawlessness and warfare, quieted down and began to assess the implications of the grisly week.

The Detroit riot of 1943 perhaps illustrates the range of racial disorders that broke out sporadically during World War II. There had been earlier conflicts in Mobile, Los Angeles, and Beaumont, Texas, and there would be some others later in the year. No doubt the war with its built-in anxieties and accelerated residential mobility accounted for the timing of these outbreaks. In Detroit, the wider problem was compounded by serious local questions. The Negro population in the city had risen sharply, with over

50,000 arriving in the fifteen months before the riot; this followed a historical increase of substantial proportions which saw black residents increase from 40,000 to 120,000 in the single decade between 1920 and 1930. These newcomers put immense pressures on the housing market, and neighborhood turnover at the edge of the ghetto bred bitterness and sometimes violence; importantly, too, recreational areas became centers of racial abrasiveness.

On June 20 the riot broke out on Belle Isle, a recreational spot used by both races, but predominantly by Negroes. Fistfighting on a modest basis soon escalated, and quickly a rising level of violence spread across the city. The Negro ghetto—ironically called Paradise Valley—saw the first wave of looting and bloodshed. The area was, as its historians have described it. "spattered with blood and littered with broken glass and ruined merchandise. The black mob had spared a few shops owned by Negroes who had chalked COLORED on their windows. But almost every store in the ghetto owned by a white had been smashed open and ransacked." Other observers noted that "crudely organized gangs of Negro hoodlums began to operate more openly. Some looters destroyed property as if they had gone berserk."

The next morning saw the violence widen. The police declared the situation out of control and the mayor asked for state troops. Even this force was ineffective, and finally the governor asked for federal help. Peace returned under the protection of 6,000 men; and the troops remained for more than a week. The dead numbered thirty-four, twenty-five Negroes and nine whites; property damage exceeded $2 million. And almost as costly was the bitterness, fear, and hate that became part of the city's legacy.

This survey covers only some of the larger and more important disorders. Others reached significant proportions but do not fall into convenient categories. For example, in the eighteenth century a protest against inoculation led to widespread rioting; mobs hit the streets to punish men who snatched bodies for medical training. In times of economic hardship, "bread riots" resulted in ransacking stores; crowds often physically drove away officials seeking to evict tenants who could not pay rent.

Two disorders perhaps best suggest the miscellaneous and unpredictable character of this process. One is so bizarre that only its bloody climax has kept it from being among the most amusing episodes of American history. It revolved around the rivalry between two prominent actors, the American Edwin Forrest, and William Macready, an Englishman. Both were appearing in "Macbeth" on the same night, May 7, 1849, in New York City. Some rowdies, mostly Irish, decided to break up the Macready performance, and when he appeared on the stage they set up such a din that he had to retire. After apologies and assurances, the English visitor agreed to try again on the 9th. This time, the police extracted the troublemakers and Macready finished the play. But a mob gathered outside after the final curtain and refused to disperse on police orders. Finally, the edgy guard fired into the crowd, killing twenty-five persons.

Another dimension is revealed in the events of March 1884, in Cincinnati. They came in the midst of what the city's best historian has dubbed "the decade of disorder." Two men were tried for the murder of a white livery man. Though one was Negro and the other German, race does not seem to be at issue. When the German was found guilty of only manslaughter, a public campaign developed to avenge the decision. A meeting at Music Hall, called by some leading citizens, attracted 10,000 people, mostly from the middle class, who were worried about a general breakdown of law and order and thought the light sentence would encourage criminals. The speakers attacked the jury and the administration of justice in the city. Afterward a crowd headed for the jail. In the first encounter with the police, casualties were light. But the next day the militia moved in and hostility climbed. Finally, a pitched battle ensued in which fifty-four died and over 200 were wounded. Thus, a meeting called to bring about law and order wound up ironically in disorder and violence.

This survey, which is only suggestive and not exhaustive, indicates that widescale violence and disorder have been man's companion in the American city from the outset. Some generalizations out of this experience might be useful in the light of the present crisis.

First, most of the rioting has usually been either limited in objective or essentially sporadic. This, of course, is not true of racial conflict, but it is characteristic of a large number of the others. In those, the event was discreet; there was no immediate violent sequel. After a labor dispute, especially if it involved union recognition, bitterness and hate persisted, but there was no annual recurrence of the violence. Attacks on immigrants seldom produced an encore, though they might have an analogue in some other city in the same month or year. In short, though there was enough disorder and mob action to create a persistent anxiety, the incidence of overt conflict was irregular enough to preclude predictions of the next "long hot summer."

Second, this sporadic quality meant that the postmortems were usually short and shallow. It was characteristic to note the large number of teenagers who got involved; to attribute the disruption to outsiders (especially anarchists and communists); to place a large responsibility on the newspapers for carrying inflammatory information and spreading unfounded rumors; to blame the local police for incompetence, for prejudice, for intervening too soon or too late, or at all. After any episode, the urge to fix blame led to all kinds of analyses. The historian of the 1877 railroad violence, for example, observes that "the riots were variously ascribed to avarice, the expulsion of the Bible from the schools, the protective tariff, the demonetization of silver, the absence of General Grant, the circulation of the *Chicago Times* and original sin." Others saw in it a labor conspiracy or a communist plot. And the *New York Times* could assert after the Chicago riot in 1919 that: "The outbreak of race riots in Chicago, following so closely on those reported from Washington, shows clearly enough that the thing is not sporadic (but has) . . . intelligent direction and management . . . (It seems probable) that the Bolshevist agitation has been extended among the Negroes."

There were a few exceptions. After the Chicago race riot, for example, an Illinois commission studied the event in some detail and also examined the deteriorating relations between the races which lay at the bottom. Others occasionally probed beneath the surface at the deeper causes of unrest. But most cities preferred to forget as soon as possible and hoped for an end to any further disorder. Indeed, even the trials that followed most riots show how rapidly popular interest faded. The number of people brought to trial was small and the number of convictions extremely small; and, most significantly, there was little clamor for sterner measures.

Third, if the analyses of the riots were shallow, the response of cities and legislatures was not very effective. After quiet was restored, there would almost certainly be a discussion of police reform. Customarily little came of it, though in Louisville the utter ineptness and obvious partisanship of the police in 1855 prompted a change from an elective to an appointive force. Legislation usually emphasized control. As early as 1721, Massachusetts responded to growing disorders with an antiriot act. And Chicago's Commercial Club made land available for Fort Sheridan after the events of 1877 in order to have troops nearby for the protection of the city. But most cities rocked back to normal as soon as the tremors died down.

Fourth, there was a general tendency to rely increasingly on outside forces for containing riots. Partly, this resulted from the fact that in labor disorders local police and even state militia fraternized with strikers and could not be counted on to discipline the workers. Partly, it was due to inadequate numbers in the face of the magnitude of the problem. Partly, too, it stemmed from the fact that sometimes the police were involved in the fighting at the outset and seemed a part of the riot. The first resort was usually to state troops; but they were often unsatisfactory, and the call for federal assistance became more frequent.

Fifth, while it is hard to assess, it seems that the bitterness engendered by riots and disorders was not necessarily irreparable. Though the immigrants suffered a good deal at the hands of nativists, it did not slow down for long the process of their incorporation into American life. Ten years after Louisville's "Bloody Monday" the city had a German mayor. The trade unions survived the assaults of the nineteenth century and a reduction of tension characterized the period between 1900 and the Depression (with the notable exception of the postwar flare-ups). And after the violence of the 1930s, labor and management learned to conduct their differences, indeed their strikes, with reduced bloodshed and violence. It is not susceptible of proof, but it seems that the fury of the defeated in these battles exacted a price on the victors that ultimately not only protected the group but won respect, however grudgingly, from the public.

At any rate the old sources of major disorders, race excepted, no longer physically agitate American society. It has been many years since violence has been a significant factor in city elections and no widespread disorders have even accompanied campaigning. Immigrant groups have now become so incorporated in American life that they are not easily visible and their election to high offices, indeed the highest, signals a muting of old hostilities. Even when people organized on a large scale against minority groups—such as the Americans' Protective Association in the 1890s or the Ku Klux Klan in the 1920s—they have seldom been able to create major riots or disorders. And though sporadic violence occasionally breaks out in a labor dispute, what is most remarkable is the continuance of the strike as a weapon of industrial relations with so little resort to force. Even the destruction of property during a conflict has ceased to be an expectation.

Sixth, race riots were almost always different from other kinds of disorders. Their roots went deeper; they broke out with increasing frequency; and their intensity mounted rather than declined. And between major disorders the incidence of small-scale violence was always high. Until recently, the Negro has largely been the object of the riot. This was true not only in Northern cities where changing residential patterns bred violence, but also in the South where this question was less pervasive. In these riots the lines were sharply drawn against the Negroes, the force was applied heavily against them, and the casualties were always highest among blacks.

Finally, in historical perspective, if racial discord be removed, the level of large-scale disorder and violence is less ominous today than it has been during much of the past. As we have seen, those problems which have produced serious eruptions in the past no longer do so. In fact, if one were to plot a graph, omitting the racial dimension, violence and disorder over a long period have been reduced. Indeed, what makes the recent rioting so alarming is that it breaks so much with this historical trend and upsets common expectations.

Yet to leave out race is to omit the most important dimension of the present crisis. For it is race that is at the heart of the present discord. Some analysts, of course, have argued that the problem is class and they emphasize the numbers caught in widening poverty, and the frustration and envy of poor people in a society of growing affluence. Yet it is important to observe that though 68 percent of the poor people in this country are white, the disorders stem almost wholly from black ghettoes. The marginal participation of a few whites in Detroit and elsewhere scarcely dilutes the racial foundations of these disorders.

In fact, a historical survey of disorders only highlights the unique character of the present problem. For the experience of the Negro in American cities has been quite different from any other group. And it is in just this difference that the crisis lies. Because the black ghetto is unlike any ghettoes that our cities have known before. Of course, other groups knew the ghetto experience too. As newcomers to the city they huddled in the downtown areas where they met unspeakably congested conditions, occupied the worst housing, got the poorest education, toiled, if fortunate enough to have a job, at the most menial tasks, endured high crime rates, and knew every facet of deprivation.

The urban slum had never been a very pleasant place, and it was tolerable only if the residents, or most of them, thought there was a way out. To American immigrants generally the ghetto was a temporary stage in their incorporation into American society. Even some of the first generation escaped, and the second and third generation moved out of the slums in very large numbers. Soon they were dispersed around the metropolitan area, in the suburbs as well as the pleasant residential city wards. Those who remained behind in the old neighborhoods did so because they chose to, not because they had to. By this process, millions of people from numberless countries, of different national and religious backgrounds made their way into the main current of American life.

It was expected that Negroes would undergo the same process when they came to the city. Thus, there was little surprise in the first generation when black newcomers did indeed find their way into the central city, the historic staging grounds for the last and poorest arrivals. But the ghetto proved to be not temporary. Instead of colored residents dispersing in the second generation, the ghetto simply expanded. Block by block it oozed out into the nearby white neighborhoods. Far from breaking up, the ghetto grew. In fact, housing became more segregated every year; and the walls around it appeared higher all the time. What had been temporary for other groups seemed permanent to Negroes.

The growth of the Negro ghetto created conditions which had not existed before and which generated the explosiveness of our present situation. In the first place, the middle-class Negroes became embittered at their exclusion from the decent white neighborhoods of the city and suburbs. These people, after all, had done what society expected of them; they got their education, training, jobs, and income. Yet even so they were deprived of that essential symbol of American success—the home in a neighborhood of their own choosing where conditions would be more pleasant and schools better for their children. For this group, now about a third of all urban Negroes, the exclusion seemed especially cruel and harsh.

As a result they comprise now a growingly alienated and embittered group. The middle-class blacks are now beginning to turn their attention to organizing among the poor in the worst parts of the ghetto. Their children make up the cadres of black militants in the colleges. And when the riots come, they tolerate the activity even though they usually do not themselves participate. In short, the fact of the ghetto forces them to identify with race, not class. When the riots break, they feel a bond with the rioters, not white society. This had not been true of the emerging middle class of any immigrant group before.

If the ghetto has new consequences for the middle class, it also creates a new situation among the poorer residents of the ghetto, especially for the young people. They feel increasingly that there is no hope for the future. For other groups growing up in the ghetto there had always been visible evidence that it was possible to escape. Many before had done it; and everyone knew it. This produced the expectation that hard work, proper behavior, some schooling, and a touch of luck would make it possible to get ahead. But the young Negro grows up in increasing despair. He asks himself—"What if I do all they say I should—stay in school, get my training, find a job, accumulate some money—I'll still be living here, still excluded from the outside world and its rewards." He asks himself, "What's the use?" Thus, the hopelessness, despair, and frustration mounts, and the temperature of the ghetto rises. Nearly all of our poverty programs are stumbling on the problem of motivation. To climb out of the slum has always required more than average incentive. Yet this is precisely what is lacking in the ghetto youth.

The present riots stem from the peculiar problems of the ghetto. By confining Negroes to the ghetto we have deprived them of the chance to enter American society on the same terms as other groups before them. And they know increasingly that this exclusion is not a function of education, training, or income. Rather, it springs from the color of their skin. This is what makes race the explosive question of our time; this is what endangers the tranquillity of our cities. In the historian's perspective, until the ghetto begins to break, until the Negro middle class can move over this demeaning barrier, until the young people can see Negroes living where their resources will carry them and hence get credible evidence of equality, the summers will remain long and hot.

SUGGESTED READINGS

The study of this nation's urban past by American historians is a relatively new endeavor. Although John Bach McMaster scattered brief descriptions of ante-bellum towns and cities throughout his multivolume *A History of the People of the United States from the Revolution to the Civil War* (1883–1913) and Edward Channing devoted a chapter to "the urban migration" between 1815 and 1848 in the fifth volume of his *History of the United States* (1921), it was not until the early 1930s that historians undertook any systematic appraisal of the role of the city in national life. Probably taking a cue from the studies of the "Chicago School" of urban sociologists —including Robert Park and Ernest Burgess—at the University of Chicago during the 1920s, Arthur M. Schlesinger, Sr., published the seminal *The Rise of the City, 1878–1898* (1933), a polemical work that presented the city as the center of most major currents of social change. In 1940 Schlesinger reiterated and expanded that theme in a significant essay, "The City in American History," *Mississippi Valley Historical Review*, XXVII (1940), 43–66, a frank attempt to counterbalance the influence of Frederick Jackson Turner's influential address "The Significance of the Frontier in American History" (1893). Although Schlesinger's essay failed to bring forth a new urban interpretation of the American past to supplant the frontier thesis, his labors did stimulate a generation of historians, including Bayrd Still, Blake McKelvey, and Bessie L. Pierce, to present single and multivolume biographies of major American cities. For detailed accounts of the historiography of American urban history see: Allen F. Davis, "The American Historian vs. the City; Parts I & II," *Social Studies*, LXI (1965), 91–6, 127–35; Charles N. Glaab, "The Historian and the American City: A Bibliographic Survey," *The Study of Urbanization*, eds. Philip M. Hauser and Leo F. Schnore (1965), pp. 53–80; Dwight W. Hoover, "The Diverging Paths of American Urban History," *American Quarterly*, XX (1968), 296–317; and Blake McKelvey, "American Urban History Today," *American Historical Review*, LVII (1952), 919–29.

Partly because of the newness of the field, and partly due to reluctance by some of its practitioners, "urban history" remains an undefined discipline. Historians have not agreed upon an answer to the question posed by Charles Glaab in his historiographic essay: "Is urban history the history of cities, the history of urbanization, or the history of anything that takes place in an urban setting?" Generally, historians have adopted the last approach, writing about political, economic, social, cultural, and intellectual activities within various cities as if the locations of the movements they describe automatically identify their subjects as "urban history." Several writers, however, have urged rigorous conceptual approaches. In his article "American Historians and the Study of Urbanization," *American Historical Review*, LXVII (1961), 49–62, Eric Lampard called for a two-pronged approach—the study of urbanization as a societal process rather than as a history of individual cities, and a comparative study of cities in a framework of human ecology, concentrating on the changing balance of population and environment mediated by community organization and technology. An even broader suggestion came from Roy Lubove in "The Urbanization Process: An Approach to Historical Research," *Journal of the American Institute of Planners*, XXXIII (1967), 33–9. Admitting the usefulness of the ecological complex theory, Lubove modified the theory by stressing the process of city building over time. This process depended heavily on technology and "related economic changes," but it also involved "decision-making, organization, [and] change mechanisms." Thus urban history hopefully could sharpen the vague relationships among personality, social organization, and environment. The emphasis on the urban impact upon personality and social organization that informs a substantial number of urban studies works derived from the classic sociological generalizations offered by Louis Wirth in "Urbanism as a Way of Life," *American Journal of Sociology*, XLIV (1938), 1–24. A more straightforward economic approach came from Eugene Smolensky and Donald Ratajczak in "The Conception of Cities," *Explorations in Entrepreneurial History*, II, 2nd ser. (1965), 90–131. They related urban growth and change to a succession of economic functions within the larger society. In effect, they provided some systematic analysis and support of the influential generalizations about the rise of the metropolitan community that were presented by economist N. S. B. Gras in *An Introduction to Economic History* (1922). More recently, Sam B. Warner, Jr., in "If All the World Were Philadelphia: A Scaffolding for Urban History, 1774–1930," *American Historical Review*, LXXIV (1968), 26–43, has tried to incorporate all of these varied approaches. Emphasizing the need for statistical analyses, over a period of time, of occupational and industrial groupings of people within the city, Warner has called for "a descriptive framework relating changes in scale to change in structure," so that historians can better concentrate on what he calls "sociotechnical categories" and the economic historians' "developmental sequences," as well as detail the city-building process.

The writing of urban history, however defined, has profited from and must continue to profit from studies of urban phenomena by sociologists, political scientists, economists, demographers, and geographers. While historians should consult cautiously the "models" and "ideal types" presented by various social scientists, they can gain useful insights from much of the social science literature. William Diamond, in his article "On the Dangers of an Urban Interpretation of History," *Historiography and Urbanization: Essays in American History in Honor of W. Stull Holt*, ed.

Eric F. Goldman (1941), pp. 67–108, summarized many of the theoretical tacks taken during the first third of the twentieth century and rightly cautioned against presenting a vague, compound definition of "city" by simply enumerating various "urban" characteristics. Useful recent summaries of social science literature include: R. T. Daland, "Political Science and the Study of Urbanism: A Bibliographical Essay," American Political Science Review, LI (1957), 491–509; a series of essays on The Study of Urbanization (1965), eds. Philip M. Hauser and Leo F. Schnore; and another work edited by Schnore, Social Science and the City: A Survey of Urban Research (1968). The ecological complex approach has received its most coherent treatment in two works—Amos H. Hawley, Human Ecology: A Theory of Community Structure (1950), and Leo F. Schnore, The Urban Scene: Human Ecology and Demography (1959). James H. Johnson's Urban Geography: An Introductory Analysis (1967) is an excellent brief summary of the theoretical literature of that discipline, and Readings in Urban Geography (1959), eds. Harold F. Mayer and Clyde F. Kohn, includes several seminal essays. The major "ideal type" construction remains the early work by sociologist Max Weber, The City, trans. Don Martindale (1958), which includes a brilliant essay by Martindale, "Prefatory Remarks; The Theory of the City," pp. 9–62. Students also should consult Oscar Handlin's provocative essay "The Modern City as a Field of Historical Study," The Historian and the City (1966), eds. Handlin and John Burchard, pp. 1–26, and other pieces in the book as well for insights into current blendings of social science and traditional historical methods.

When historians and other social scientists have attempted some definition of "urbanization," they often have been at odds over the cause-and-effect relationship between urbanization and industrialization. For discussion of this issue see: Gunnar Alexandersson, The Industrial Structure of American Cities: A Geographic Study of Urban Economy in the United States (1956); Hans Blumenfeld, "The Modern Metropolis," Cities (1965), pp. 40–57; Bert F. Hoselitz, "The City, the Factory, and Economic Growth," American Economic Review, XLV (1955), 166–84; Eric E. Lampard, "The History of Cities in the Economically Advanced Areas," Economic Development and Cultural Change, III (1958), 81–136; Allan Pred, The Spatial Dynamics of U.S. Urban-Industrial Growth, 1800–1914: Interpretive and Theoretical Essays (1966); and Julius Rubin, "Urban Growth and Regional Development," The Growth of the Seaport Cities, 1790–1825 (1967), ed. David T. Gilchrist, pp. 3–21.

Among the more informative works relating urban growth to economic development in general and to "urban imperialism" in particular are: Robert G. Albion, The Rise of the New York Port, 1815–1860 (1939); Wyatt W. Belcher, The Economic Rivalry Between St. Louis and Chicago (1947); Charles N. Glaab, Kansas City and the Railroads (1962); Carter Goodrich, Government Promotion of Canals and Railroads, 1800–1890 (1960); two major works by Edward C. Kirkland—Industry Comes of Age: Business,

Labor and Public Policy, 1860–1897 (1961), esp. chap. XII, and Men, Cities and Transportation: A Study in New England History, 1820–1900, 2 vols. (1948); James W. Livingood, The Philadelphia–Baltimore Trade Rivalry, 1780–1860 (1947); Herbert W. Rice, "Early Rivalry Among Wisconsin Cities for Railroads," Wisconsin Magazine of History, XXXV (1951), 10–15; Julius Rubin, Canal or Railroad: Imitation and Innovation in the Response to the Erie Canal in Philadelphia, Baltimore, and Boston (1961); Harry N. Scheiber, "Urban Rivalry and Internal Improvements in the Old Northwest, 1820–1860," Ohio History, LXXI (1962), 227–39; two works by George R. Taylor—"American Urban Growth Preceding the Railway Age," Journal of Economic History, XXVII (1967), 309–39, and his justly famous The Transportation Revolution, 1815–1860 (1951); and Jeffrey G. Williamson, "Ante-Bellum Urbanization in the American Northeast," Journal of Economic History, XXV (1965), 592–608.

Urban economic growth has provided a theme upon which historians have based the first modern urban biographies. The best of this characteristic (and earliest) genre of urban history include: A. Theodore Brown, The History of Kansas City, in progress, vol. I being Frontier Community: Kansas City to 1870 (1963); Edmund H. Chapman, Cleveland: Village to Metropolis (1965); Robert M. Fogelson, The Fragmented Metropolis: Los Angeles, 1850–1930 (1967); Sidney Glazer, Detroit: A Study in Urban Development (1965); several works by Constance M. Green—History of Naugatuck, Connecticut (1948), Holyoke, Massachusetts (1939), and Washington, 2 vols. (1962, 1963); Blake McKelvey, Rochester, 4 vols. (1945–1961); Rollin G. Osterweis, Three Centuries of New Haven, 1638–1939 (1953); the pioneering, model, multivolume study by Bessie L. Pierce, A History of Chicago, 3 vols. to date (1937–59); Vera Shlakman, Economic History of a Factory Town: A Study of Chicopee, Massachusetts (1935); Bayrd Still, Milwaukee, rev. ed. (1965); Sam Bass Warner, Jr., The Private City: Philadelphia in Three Periods of Its Growth (1968); and Thomas J. Wertenbaker, Norfolk, 2nd. rev. ed. (1962).

Much of the writing in American urban history (broadly defined) has concentrated on period studies and topical works, and often has focused on the experience of individual cities. The paragraphs that follow are organized along the lines of the chapters of this book, and are intended to provide suggested reading relating to the introductory essays of each section and to the selections contained within each section.

Cities in the New World, 1607–1800. Not until the mid–1960s did American historians begin to devote much attention to town and city life during the colonial period. A good amount, then, of what urban historians profess to know about colonial urban America has come from more general works on society and politics during the first two centuries of English settlement in the New World. Among that small body of writing treating towns and cities per se, the most useful and important works include: William T. Baxter, The House of Hancock: Business in Boston, 1724–1775 (1945); two

encyclopedic works by Carl Bridenbaugh, both of major importance—
Cities in the Wilderness: Urban Life in America, 1625–1742 (1938), and
Cities in Revolt: Urban Life in America, 1743–1776 (1955)—and together
with Jessica Bridenbaugh, *Rebels and Gentlemen: Philadelphia in the Age
of Franklin* (1942); John Demos, *A Little Commonwealth: Family Life in
Plymouth Colony* (1970); Anthony N. B. Garvan, *Architecture and Town
Planning in Colonial Connecticut* (1951); Philip J. Greven, Jr., *Four Genera-
tions: Population, Land, and Family in Colonial Andover, Massachusetts*
(1970); William Haller, *The Puritan Frontier: Town-Planning in New
England Colonial Development, 1630–1660* (1951); Arthur L. Jensen, *The
Maritime Commerce of Colonial Philadelphia* (1963); Benjamin W. Labaree,
Patriots and Partisans: The Merchants of Newburyport, 1764–1815 (1952);
Kenneth A. Lockridge, *A New England Town: The First Hundred Years*
(1970), and Lockridge and Alan Kreider, "The Evolution of Massachusetts
Town Government, 1640–1740," *William and Mary Quarterly*, XXIII (1966),
549–74; Sumner Chilton Powell, *Puritan Village: The Formation of a New
England Town* (1963); Darrett B. Rutman, *Winthrop's Boston: Portrait of a
Puritan Town, 1630–1649* (1965); Frederick B. Tolles, *Meetinghouse and
Counting House: The Quaker Merchants of Colonial Philadelphia, 1682–
1763* (1948); and Michael Zuckerman, *Peaceable Kingdoms: New England
Towns in the Eighteenth Century* (1969).

Historians have devoted scant attention to the role of cities in the
American Revolution and the founding of the new nation. Among the few
works in which useful information appears are: Bernard Bailyn, *The Origins
of American Politics* (1968); Oscar T. Barck, *New York City During the War
for Independence* (1931); Virginia D. Harrington, *The New York Merchant
on the Eve of the Revolution* (1935); Merrill Jensen, *The Articles of Con-
federation* (1940), *The Founding of a Nation* (1968), and *The New Nation*
(1950); Jessie Lemisch, "Jack Tar in the Streets: Merchant Seamen in the
Politics of Revolutionary America," *William and Mary Quarterly*, XXV
(1968), 371–407, and his provocative "The American Revolution Seen from
the Bottom Up," *Towards a New Past: Dissenting Essays in American
History* (1968), ed. Barton Bernstein; an important, although unread, work
by Orin G. Libby, *The Geographical Distribution of the Vote of the Thirteen
States on the Federal Constitution, 1787–8* (1894); Forrest McDonald, *We
the People: The Economic Origins of the Constitution* (1958); two articles
by Pauline Maier—"Popular Uprisings and Civil Authority in Eighteenth-
Century America," *William and Mary Quarterly*, XXVII (1970), 3–35, and
"The Charleston Mob and the Evolution of Popular Politics in Revolutionary
South Carolina, 1765–1784," *Perspectives in American History*, IV (1970),
173–96; Jackson Turner Main, *The Antifederalists* (1961), and his suggestive,
although incompletely documented, *The Social Structure of Revolutionary
America* (1965); Edmund S. Morgan's brilliant monograph *The Stamp Act
Crisis* (1953); Sidney I. Pomerantz, *New York: An American City, 1783–
1803: A Study of Urban Life* (1938); Arthur M. Schlesinger, *Prelude to*

Independence: The Newspaper War on Britain, 1764–1776 (1957), and the seminal *The Colonial Merchants and the American Revolution* (1918); Leila Sellers, *Charleston Business on the Eve of the American Revolution* (1934); Richard Walsh, *Charleston's Sons of Liberty: A Study of the Artisans, 1763–1789* (1959); Thomas J. Wertenbaker, *Father Knickerbocker Rebels: New York During the Revolution* (1948); and Hiller B. Zobel, *The Boston Massacre* (1970).

Cities in an Expanding Nation, 1780–1865. A number of the pertinent works on the subjects of the diffusion of cities and their internal patterns of growth, "boosterism" and urban imperialism, preindustrial cities and the impact of industrialization have been mentioned. Most of the literature on urban life during this period—both that which treats urban subjects directly, and more general works useful to the student of the city—falls into five general categories: (1) towns and cities in the West (2) economic activity (3) the urban work force (4) cities and the Civil War, and (5) the city-building process.

Students of urban history and of American history in general now know that national development took place on several frontiers, and that rather than "the West" of lore and legend America contained several "wests" during the years between the 1780s and the 1860s. Among the numerous works on the "old," "middle," "new," and "far" wests see: James B. Allen, *The Company Town in the American West* (1966); Floyd R. Dain, *Every House a Frontier: Detroit's Economic Progress, 1815–1825* (1956); Carl Degler, "The West as a Solution of Urban Unemployment," *New York History,* XXXVI (1955), 63–84; Robert Dykstra, *The Cattle Towns* (1968); Remi A. Nadeau, *The City Makers: The Story of Southern California's First Boom* (1965); Richard C. Overton, *Burlington West: A Colonization History of the Burlington Railroad* (1941); Bessie L. Pierce, "Changing Urban Patterns in the Mississippi Valley," *Journal of the Illinois Historical Society,* XLIII (1950), 46–57; Duane Smith, *Rocky Mountain Mining Camps: The Urban Frontier* (1967); Bayrd Still, "Patterns of Mid-Nineteenth Century Urbanization in the Middle West," *Mississippi Valley Historical Review,* XXVIII (1941), 187–206; a stimulating reinterpretation of westward expansion and a major work in urban history, Richard C. Wade's *The Urban Frontier: The Rise of Western Cities, 1790–1830* (1959); Kenneth Wheeler, *To Wear a City's Crown: The Beginnings of Urban Growth in Texas, 1836–1865* (1968); and Oscar O. Winther, "The Rise of Metropolitan Los Angeles, 1870–1910," *Huntington Library Quarterly,* X (1947), 391–405.

Aside from urban biographies and the discussions about urban rivalry noted earlier, there are few studies per se on urban manufacturing and commercial enterprise, or on the evolution of corporations during this period. Students of urban history interested in these subjects must piece together information from works such as: the informative summary and evaluation of recent literature by Stuart Bruchey, *The Roots of American Economic Growth* (1965); Roger Burlingame's suggestive book *March of the*

Iron Men: A Social History of Union Through Invention (1949); Arthur H. Cole, *The American Wool Manufacture,* 2 vols. (1926); portions of *The Age of Enterprise: A Social History of Industrial America,* rev. ed. (1961), by Thomas C. Cochran and William Miller; two first-rate examples of the quantitative "new economic history"—Albert Fishlow's *American Railroads and the Transformation of the Ante-Bellum Economy* (1965), and Robert W. Fogel's *Railroads and American Economic Growth: Essays in Econometric History* (1964); Bray Hammond, *Banks and Politics in America from the Revolution to the Civil War* (1957); Douglass C. North, *The Economic Growth of the United States, 1790–1860* (1965); and the classic account of New England textile cities by Caroline Ware, *The Early New England Cotton Manufactures* (1931).

In general, urban labor history has received scant attention from American historians. Among the useful works available see: the starting points for any work in labor history, John R. Commons, *et al., A Documentary History of American Industrial Society,* 10 vols. (1910–11), and Commons, *et al., History of Labour in the United States,* 4 vols. (1935–6); Walter Hugins, *Jacksonian Democracy and the Working Class* (1960), largely a study of New York City laboring groups; Edward Pessen, *Most Uncommon Jacksonians: The Radical Leaders of the Early Labor Movement* (1967); William A. Sullivan, *The Industrial Worker in Pennsylvania* (1955); and the still unsurpassed study of *The Industrial Worker, 1840–1860* (1924) by Norman Ware.

Similarly, there is no literature dealing with the possible roles played by cities in the complex of events leading up to the Civil War, although urban political alignments and economic interests, as well as internal class and race policies, undoubtedly were significant. The only subject that has received more than token interest is the condition of American blacks, slave and free, during the ante-bellum years. See John Hope Franklin, *The Militant South, 1800–1861* (1956); Leon Litwack, *North of Slavery: The Negro in the Free States, 1790–1860* (1961); Kenneth Stampp, *The Peculiar Institution* (1956); Robert S. Starobin, *Industrial Slavery in the Old South* (1969); and the major interpretation by Richard C. Wade in his *Slavery in the Cities: The South, 1820–1860* (1964). On questions other than slavery see: Gerald M. Capers, *Occupied City: New Orleans Under the Federals, 1862–1865* (1965); Kenneth Coleman, *Confederate Athens* (1967); Clayton James, *Antebellum Natchez* (1968); and the important article on political alignments by Charles G. Sellers, Jr., "Who Were the Southern Whigs?" *American Historical Review,* LIX (1954), 335–46.

On the city-building process, architecture, and town planning during the period see: John Coolidge, *Mill and Mansion: A Study of Architecture and Society in Lowell, Massachusetts, 1820–1865* (1942); Charles N. Glaab, "Historical Perspective on Urban Development Schemes," *Social Science and the City,* ed. Leo F. Schnore (1968), 197–219; Harold and James Kirker, *Bulfinch's Boston, 1787–1817* (1964); John W. Reps, *Town Planning in*

Frontier America (1968), and the same author's *Monumental Washington: The Planning and Development of the Capital Center* (1966); and Walter M. Whitehill's *Boston: A Topographical History* (1959).

Finally, there are several works of broad ranging interests that provide valuable insights into the social, cultural, and intellectual trends of the period. These include: Daniel J. Boorstin, *The Americans: The National Experience* (1965); Neil Harris, *The Artist in American Society: The Formative Years, 1790–1860* (1966); Leo Marx, *The Machine and the Garden* (1964); and Russell B. Nye, *The Cultural Life of the New Nation, 1776–1830* (1960).

Immigration, Migration, and Mobility, 1865–1920. On the general subject of immigration into the United States there are two invaluable collections of documents edited by Edith Abbott—*Historical Aspects of the Immigration Problem* (1926) and *Immigration: Select Documents and Case Records* (1924). Useful general introductions to the immigrant experience include: Oscar Handlin, *The Uprooted* (1951); Marcus L. Hansen, *The Atlantic Migration, 1607–1860* (1940), and a collection of penetrating essays, *The Immigrant in American History* (1940); an important statistical work by E. P. Hutchison, *Immigrants and Their Children, 1850–1950* (1956); Maldwyn A. Jones, *American Immigration* (1960); and Carl Wittke, *We Who Built America: The Saga of the Immigrant* (1939).

The largest proportion of immigrants to America during the period settled in cities—especially New York, Boston, Philadelphia, St. Louis, Chicago, Milwaukee, Baltimore, and New Orleans. Historians have devoted some attention to the immigrant experience in the cities, although far more case studies, both of individual cities and on a comparative basis, are needed. Among the better studies currently available see: the contemporary account by Jane Addams, *Twenty Years at Hull-House* (1910); Rowland T. Berthoff, *British Immigrants in Industrial America, 1790–1950* (1953); Donald B. Cole, *Immigrant City: Lawrence, Massachusetts, 1845–1921* (1963); Charlotte Erickson, *American Industry and the European Immigrant, 1860–1885* (1957); Robert Ernst, *Immigrant Life in New York City, 1825–1863* (1949); the enormously influential *Boston's Immigrants: A Study in Acculturation*, rev. ed. (1959), by Oscar Handlin; Gerd Korman, *Industrialization, Immigrants and Americanizers: The View from Milwaukee, 1866–1921* (1967); Humbert S. Nelli, *The Italians in Chicago, 1880–1930* (1970); Earl F. Niehaus, *The Irish in New Orleans, 1800–1860* (1965); Robert E. Park and Herbert A. Miller, *Old World Traits Transplanted* (1921), a classic sociological study; Moses Rischin, *The Promised City: New York's Jews, 1870–1914* (1962); Louis Wirth, *The Ghetto* (1928), a cross-cultural study of European and American (Chicago) Jewish communities; and the influential *The Zone of Emergence: Observations of the Lower Middle and Upper Working Class Communities of Boston, 1905–1914* (1914, first pub. 1962), by settlement-house workers Robert Woods and Albert J. Kennedy.

Although some of the immigrants journeying to the United States before the 1840s arrived with at least limited financial resources, most coming during the latter half of the 1800s and in the first two decades of the twentieth century debarked in the great Eastern ports nearly penniless. Their arrival swelled the ranks of the urban poor and marked the beginnings of a rapid growth in the tenement-dwelling population. On this subject see: Edith Abbott, *The Tenements of Chicago, 1908–1935* (1936); Gordon Atkins, *Health, Housing and Poverty in New York City, 1865–1898* (1947); Robert H. Bremner, *From the Depths: The Discovery of Poverty in America* (1956); *The Tenement House Problem*, 2 vols. (1903), eds. Robert W. De Forest and Lawrence Veiller; Roy Lubove, *The Progressives and the Slums: Tenement House Reform in New York City, 1890–1917* (1962); the detailed first-hand account by Jacob Riis, *How the Other Half Lives* (1890); Carroll D. Wright, *The Slums of Baltimore, Chicago, New York, and Philadelphia*, Commissioners of Labor, Special Report No. 7 (1894) as an example of numerous government reports on the subject.

Urban historians, unlike sociologists, came late to investigations of social mobility in American society. For the most part, historians, beginning in the mid–1960s, have concentrated on describing patterns of occupational, income, and status mobility within an urban context, although rarely have they made clear distinctions between "urban" and society-wide changes in social-class alignments. Among the better examples see: Stuart Blumin, "The Historical Study of Vertical Mobility," *Historical Methods Newsletter*, I (1968), 1–13; P. M. G. Harris, "The Social Origins of American Leaders: The Demographic Foundations," *Perspectives in American History*, III (1969), 159–344; Richard J. Hopkins, "Occupational and Geographic Mobility in Atlanta, 1870–1896," *Journal of Southern History*, XXXIV (1968), 200–213; Richard Jensen, "Quantitative Collective Biography: An Application to Metropolitan Elites," *Quantification in American History: Theory and Research* (1970), ed. Robert P. Swierenga; Seymour Lipset and Reinhard Bendix, *Social Mobility in Industrial Society* (1959); and several works by Stephan Thernstrom—a major study, *Poverty and Progress: Social Mobility in a Nineteenth Century City* (1964); "Urbanization, Migration, and Social Mobility in Late Nineteenth Century America," *Towards a New Past* (1967), 158–75, ed. Barton Bernstein; with Peter R. Knights, "Men in Motion: Some Data and Speculation about Urban Population Mobility in Nineteenth-Century America," *Journal of Interdisciplinary History*, I (1971); and, edited with Richard Sennett, *Nineteenth Century Cities: Essays in the New Urban History* (1969). R. Richard Wohl, "The 'Country Boy' Myth and Its Place in American Urban Culture: The Nineteenth Century Contribution," *Perspectives in American History*, III (1969), 77–156.

In recent years historians have devoted increasing attention to the migration of rural Southern and West Indian blacks during the period to the large Northern cities, and to the resultant patterns of residence, occupation, and social status. Among the plethora of works available see: a disappointing overview by Arna Bontemps and Jack Conroy, *Anyplace But Here*

(1966); Chicago Commission on Race Relations, *The Negro in Chicago* (1922); the monumental study of Chicago's black community by St. Clair Drake and Horace Cayton, *Black Metropolis,* 2 vols. (1945); W. E. B. DuBois, *The Philadelphia Negro* (1899); a statistical study by Reynolds Farley, "The Urbanization of Negroes in the United States," *Journal of Social History,* I (1968), 241–58; Harold F. Gosnell, *Negro Politicians: The Rise of Negro Politics in Chicago* (1935); Constance M. Green, *The Secret City: Race Relations in the Nation's Capital* (1967); Clyde V. Kiser, *Sea Island to City: A Study of St. Helena Islanders in Harlem and Other Urban Centers* (1932); Gilbert Osofsky, *Harlem: The Making of a Ghetto* (1966); Elliott M. Rudwick, *Race Riot at East St. Louis, July 2, 1917* (1964); Seth M. Scheiner, *Negro Mecca: A History of the Negro in New York City, 1865–1920* (1965); Robert Shogan and Thomas Craig, *The Detroit Race Riot: A Study in Violence* (1964); Allen Spear, *Black Chicago: The Making of a Negro Ghetto* (1967); Arvah E. Strickland, *History of the Chicago Urban League* (1966); and William M. Tuttle, Jr., *Race Riot: Chicago in the Red Summer of 1919* (1970).

The Recurrent Urban Crisis, 1800–1930. The provision of various municipal services has received little attention from urban historians, although attempts to secure the physical safety of cities for their inhabitants occupied much of the time of urban leaders during the nineteenth and early twentieth centuries. Among the few informative works on these subjects see: Frederick M. Bender, "Gas Light, 1816–1860," *Pennsylvania History,* XXII (1955), 359–73; John B. Blake, *Public Health in the Town of Boston, 1630–1822* (1959); Nelson M. Blake, *Water for the Cities* (1956); James H. Cassedy, *Charles V. Chapin and the Public Health Movement* (1962); John Duffy, *A History of Public Health in New York City, 1625–1866* (1968); Roger C. Lane, *Policing the City, Boston, 1822–1885* (1967); Lawrence H. Larsen, "Nineteenth-Century Street Sanitation: A Study in Filth and Frustration," *Wisconsin Magazine of History,* LII (1969), 239–47; James F. Richardson, *The New York Police: Colonial Times to 1901* (1970); George Rosen, *A History of Public Health* (1958) for both European and American materials; and Charles Rosenberg, *The Cholera Years* (1962).

Historians have yet to give proper emphasis to the changes in the technology of transportation and their implications for the physical growth, residential patterns, provisions of municipal services, and social-class structure of American cities. The limited literature contains several useful starting points: Harlan W. Gilmore, *Transportation and the Growth of Cities* (1953); a technically specialized account by George N. Hilton and John F. Due, *The Electric Interurban Railways in America* (1960); Forrest McDonald, "Street Cars and Politics in Milwaukee, 1896–1901: Parts I-II," *Wisconsin Magazine of History,* XXIX (1956), 166–70, 206–12, 253–7, 271–3; the enjoyable popular account by John A. Miller, *Fares Please!* (1941); Wilfred Owen, *Cities in the Motor Age* (1959); John B. Rae, *The American Automobile* (1965), disappointingly sparse on social implications; George

M. Smerk, "The Streetcar: Shaper of American Cities," *Traffic Quarterly,*
XXI (1967), 569–84; the important overview by George Rogers Taylor, "The
Beginnings of Mass Transportation in Urban America: Parts I-II," *Smithso-
nian Journal of History,* I (1966), 35–50, 51–4; and, the most important
book on the subject, a model of its kind, Sam Bass Warner, Jr.'s *Streetcar
Suburbs: The Process of Growth in Boston, 1870–1900* (1962).

There is a growing literature on problems of crime, intemperance, vice,
violence, and reform responses during the nineteenth and early twentieth
centuries, but only a small portion deals specifically with what we might
call "urban pathology." Social historians have yet to distinguish between
societal-wide patterns of pathology and those rooted in city life, arising
from uniquely urban circumstances. See: the fascinating popular accounts
by Herbert Asbury, *The Gangs of New York* (1927), *The Barbary Coast*
(1933), and *The French Quarter* (1936); Joseph Baylen, "A Victorian's Crusade in Chicago, 1893–94," *Journal of American History,* LI (1964), 418–34;
an invaluable overview by Allen F. Davis, *Spearheads for Reform: The Social
Settlements and the Progressive Movement, 1890–1914* (1967); Egal Feldman, "Prostitution, the Alien Woman and the Progressive Imagination,"
American Quarterly, XIX (1967), 192–206; Mark H. Haller, "Urban Crime
and Criminal Justice: The Chicago Case," *Journal of American History,*
LVII (1970), 619–35; the detailed account by Kenneth T. Jackson, *The Ku
Klux Klan in the City, 1915–1930* (1967); Michael Katz, *The Irony of Early
School Reform* (1968); Roy Lubove, *The Professional Altruist: The Emer-
gence of Social Work as a Career, 1880–1930* (1965); Raymond A. Mohl,
Poverty in New York, 1783–1825 (1971); Robert S. Pickett, *House of Refuge:
The Origins of Juvenile Reform in New York State, 1815–1857* (1969);
Leonard L. Richards, *"Gentlemen of Property and Standing": Anti-Abolition
Mobs in Jacksonian America* (1969); James H. Timberlake, *Prohibition and
the Progressive Movement, 1900–1920* (1963); and, for comparative pur-
poses, the insightful account of London by J. J. Tobias, *Crime and Industrial
Society in the Nineteenth Century* (1967).

Historians have yet to write the history of city-planning activities during
the period as an integral part of the crusades for moral and social reform
within the city. Among the few helpful works see: Stanley Buder, *Pullman:
An Experiment in Industrial Order and Community Planning, 1880–1930*
(1967); Patrick Geddes, *Cities in Evolution* (1915); Ebenezer Howard's
influential *Garden Cities of Tomorrow* (1902); Roy Lubove, *Community
Planning in the 1920's* (1964); Frederick Law Olmsted, *Public Parks and the
Enlargement of Towns* (1870); John Rep's encyclopedic overview *The Rise
of Urban America: A History of City Planning* (1965); Mel Scott, *American
City Planning Since 1890* (1969); Seymour Toll, *Zoned American* (1969) on
the social implications of the legal tool of zoning; Christopher Tunnard
and Henry H. Reed, Jr., *American Skyline* (1955); and William H. Wilson,
The City Beautiful Movement in Kansas City (1965).

Bosses, Machines, and Urban Reform. Few subjects have fascinated historians more in recent years than urban politics. Chronicling the foibles, adventures, and misadventures of city bosses and their supposedly efficient "machines" has proved nearly irresistible. We have a growing literature too on the urban reformers who sought to kill the hydra-headed beast in the name of "the people." Unfortunately, too little of the material deals with the specific functions of political organizations or leaders within the restricted confines of municipal government. We need to know more about the financial activities of the bosses, the degree to which they actually helped their constituents over time, their relationships with such urban businessmen as traction magnates and real-estate speculators, and the arena of state–city politics in which the bosses operated. Among the literature available see: Edward C. Banfield and James Q. Wilson, *City Politics* (1963); Alexander B. Callow, Jr., *The Tweed Ring* (1966); Lyle Dorsett, *The Pendergast Machine* (1968); Harold F. Gosnell, *Machine Politics: Chicago Model* (1937); Joy J. Jackson, *New Orleans in the Gilded Age: Politics and Urban Progress, 1880–1896* (1970); the provocative study by Theodore J. Lowi, *At the Pleasure of the Mayor: Patronage & Power in New York City, 1898–1958* (1964); Seymour J. Mandelbaum, *Boss Tweed's New York* (1965), an interesting though not always successful effort to wed communications theory and political history; Arthur Mann, *LaGuardia: A Fighter Against His Times, 1882–1933* (1959), and the same author's model study of a single election, *LaGuardia Comes to Power: 1933* (1965); Eric McKitrick, "The Study of Corruption," *Political Science Quarterly,* LXXII (1957), 502–14; an insightful sociological account by Robert K. Merton, "Latent Functions of the Machine," *Social Theory and Social Structure,* rev. ed. (1957), pp. 71–82; William D. Miller, *Mr. Crump of Memphis* (1965) and *Memphis During the Progressive Era, 1900–1917* (1957); Zane Miller, *Boss Cox's Cincinnati* (1968), the best study to date of an urban boss; the classic *Plunkett of Tammany Hall* (1905), ed. William Riordan; Bruce M. Stave, *The New Deal and the Last Hurrah: Pittsburgh Machine Politics* (1970); and the still valuable account of early-twentieth-century politics by Lincoln Steffens, *The Shame of the Cities* (1904).

Among the most useful works treating the reform response to urban government and misgovernment see: Richard M. Abrams, *Conservatism in a Progressive Era* (1964); John Buenker, "The Urban Political Machine and the Seventeenth Amendment," *Journal of American History,* LVI (1969), 305–22; Samuel P. Hays, "The Politics of Reform in Municipal Government in the Progressive Era," *Pacific Northwest Quarterly,* LV (1964), 157–69; Richard Hofstadter, *The Age of Reform* (1955); Melvin G. Holli, *Reform in Detroit: Hazen S. Pingree and Urban Politics* (1969); Joseph J. Huthmacher, "Urban Liberalism and the Age of Reform," *Mississippi Valley Historical Review,* XLII (1962), 231–41, and *Massachusetts People and Politics, 1919–1933* (1959); Arthur Mann, *Yankee Reformers in the Urban Age* (1954); Stanley K. Schultz, "The Morality of Politics: The Muckrakers' Vision of Democracy," *Journal of American History,* LII (1965), 527–47; Steven C.

Swett, "The Test of a Reformer: A Study of Seth Low, New York City Mayor, 1902-3," *New York Historical Society Quarterly,* XLIV (1960), 5–41; Jack Tager, *The Intellectual as Urban Reformer: Brand Whitlock and the Progressive Movement* (1968); Louise C. Wade, *Graham Taylor: Pioneer for Social Justice* (1964); James Weinstein, "Organized Business and the City Commission and Manager Movements," *Journal of Southern History,* XXVIII (1962), 167–81; and Robert H. Wiebe, *Businessmen and Reform: A Study of the Progressive Movement* (1962).

Until recently historians have devoted little attention to religious institutions and their roles in the urban social scene. Studies of some importance on the subject include: Aaron I. Abell, *The Urban Impact on American Protestantism, 1865–1900* (1943); Robert D. Cross's introductory piece to *The Church and the City, 1865–1910* (1967) and his *The Emergence of Liberal Catholicism in America* (1958); Nathan Glazer, *American Judaism* (1957); Will Herberg, *Protestant–Catholic–Jew* (1955); Charles H. Hopkins, *The Rise of the Social Gospel in American Protestantism, 1865–1915* (1940); Henry F. May, *Protestant Churches and Industrial America* (1949); and Gibson Winter, *The Suburban Captivity of the Churches* (1962).

Dilemmas of Metropolitan America. Historians and other students of the city in recent years have argued that the chief characteristic of the modern metropolis is its complexity; authors have found their tasks of interpretation complicated by the interdependence of physical growth patterns, population mobility, housing, political problems, racial and ethnic group tensions, and attempts at renewing the environment. Few have tried to comprehend the city as a whole, if indeed that is any longer possible. The works listed below, then, are given in rather arbitrary categories for the sake of convenience.

On the general subject of the physical and economic growth of the modern American city see: Hans Blumenfeld, *The Modern Metropolis* (1967); Carl Condit, *American Building* (1968) and *The Rise of the Skyscraper* (1952); Jean Gottman, *Megalopolis: The Urbanized Northeastern Seaboard of the United States* (1961); Scott Greer, *The Emerging City: Myth and Reality* (1962); Edgar M. Hoover and Raymond Vernon, *Anatomy of a Metropolis* (1959); Homer Hoyt, *One Hundred Years of Land Values in Chicago* (1933) and *The Structure and Growth of Residential Neighborhoods in American Cities* (1939); Jane Jacobs, *The Economy of Cities* (1969); Roy Lubove, *Twentieth Century Pittsburgh* (1969); two works among the many by Lewis Mumford—*The Highway and the City* (1953) and *The Urban Prospect* (1968); and demographer Leo F. Schnore's *The Urban Scene* (1959).

Useful works on the related subject of suburbanization include: Bennet M. Berger, *Working-Class Suburb* (1960); Scott Donaldson, *The Suburban Myth* (1968); the still unsurpassed account by Harlann Douglas, *The Suburban Trend* (1925); Herbert J. Gans, *The Levittowners* (1967); John Keats, *The Crack in the Picture Window* (1957); John Seeley, et al., *Crest-*

wood Heights: A Study of the Culture of Suburban Life (1956); Auguste C. Spectorsky, The Exurbanites (1955); and Robert C. Wood, Suburbia: Its People and Their Politics (1958).

There is a plentiful and growing literature on the related areas of housing, urban renewal, and city planning. Among the most helpful works are: Charles Abrams, Forbidden Neighbors: A Study of Prejudice in Housing (1955), Man's Struggle for Shelter in an Urbanizing World (1964), and The City Is the Frontier (1965); Martin Anderson's blistering attack on renewal policies, The Federal Bulldozer (1964); Paul F. Conkin, Tomorrow a New World: The New Deal Community Program (1959); Richard O. Davies, Housing Reform During the Truman Administration (1966); a fascinating legal study by Lawrence M. Friedman, Government and Slum Housing: A Century of Frustration (1968); Scott Greer, Urban Renewal and American Cities (1965); Jane Jacobs' iconoclastic The Death and Life of Great American Cities (1961); Martin Meyerson and Edward C. Banfield, Politics, Planning and the Public Interest (1955); Clarence Stein, Toward New Towns for America (1951); Urban Renewal: The Record and the Controversy (1965), ed. James Q. Wilson; and the important study of open spaces and their preservation by William H. Whyte, The Last Landscape (1968).

The social implications of urban renewal, city planning, and metropolitan growth are traced most clearly in literature that deals with ethnicity, race relations, and social conflict. Among the most useful works see: Kenneth Clark, Dark Ghetto (1966); Herbert J. Gans, The Urban Villagers (1962); Nathan Glazer and Daniel P. Moynihan, Beyond the Melting Pot (1963); Paul Jacobs, Prelude to Riot: A View of Urban America from the Bottom (1966); Oscar Lewis, La Vida (1965); Stanley Lieberson, Ethnic Patterns in American Cities (1963); Malcolm Little, The Autobiography of Malcolm X (1964); the major sociological work by Gunnar Myrdal, An American Dilemma, 2 vols. (1944); Martin Oppenheimer, The Urban Guerrilla (1969); Karl E. and Alma F. Taeuber, Negroes in Cities: Residential Segregation and Neighborhood Change (1965); and a pioneering sociological study by William F. Whyte, Street Corner Society (1943).

A growing body of literature recently has bemoaned the plight of the modern city with critics pointing to the "urban crisis," the "sick cities," the "dying cities," and employing other organismic metaphors. For views pro and con the alleged crisis and the urban environment see: the cogent, cantankerous, and controversial denial of "crisis" by Edward C. Banfield, The Unheavenly City: The Nature and Future of Our Urban Crisis (1970); Mitchell Gordon, Sick Cities (1963); Victor Gruen, The Heart of Our Cities: The Urban Crisis: Diagnosis and Cure (1964); William H. Michelson, Man and His Urban Environment: A Sociological Approach (1970); Peter Self, Cities in Flood: The Problems of Urban Growth (1957); Roger Starr's amusing critique of the prophets of doom, Urban Choices: The City and Its Critics (1967); and The States and the Urban Crisis (1970), ed. Alan K. Campbell.

There are several useful studies that treat the city as a problem in intellectual and cultural history. These include: George Dunlap, *The City in the American Novel, 1789–1900* (1934); Blanche H. Gelfant, *The American City Novel* (1954); Lewis Mumford, *The Culture of Cities* (1938); Anselm Strauss, *Images of the American City* (1961); Robert H. Walker, "The Poet and the Rise of the City," *Mississippi Valley Historical Review,* XLIV (1962), 85–99; David R. Weimer, *The City as Metaphor* (1966); and the broad, if sometimes unconvincing survey by Morton and Lucia White, *The Intellectual Versus the City* (1962).

Finally, there are several overviews of the city that should be consulted. These include: Charles N. Glaab and A. Theodore Brown, *A History of Urban America* (1967); Blake McKelvey's encyclopedic coverage of existent literature in his synthetic works *The Urbanization of America, 1860–1915* (1963) and *The Emergence of Metropolitan America, 1915–1966* (1968); the monumental work by Lewis Mumford, *The City in History* (1961); and the still valuable statistical study by Adna F. Weber, *The Growth of Cities in the Nineteenth Century* (1899).

NOTES ON CONTRIBUTORS

JOHN K. ALEXANDER grew up in Portland, Oregon, and received his M.A. and Ph.D. degrees from the University of Chicago. Now an assistant professor of history at the University of Cincinnati, he is working on a history of the poor in Philadelphia between 1760 and 1800.

LEWIS ATHERTON is a member of the history faculty of the University of Missouri and the author of *Cattle Kings* and *Main Street on the Middle Border.*

DANIEL J. BOORSTIN, currently Director of the National Museum of History and Technology of the Smithsonian Institution, was for twenty-five years a member of the history faculty of the University of Chicago. He is the author of *The Genius of American Politics* and editor of the thirty-volume Chicago History of American Civilization.

MARK H. HALLER is a native of Washington, D.C., and a graduate of Wesleyan University and the University of Wisconsin. Now associate professor of history at Temple University in Philadelphia, he is the author of *Eugenics: Hereditarian Attitudes in American Thought.*

JAMES A. HENRETTA is a member of the history faculty at Princeton University.

ROBERT HIGGS is an assistant professor of economics at the University of Washington in Seattle. He was born in Okemah, Oklahoma, and received his graduate training at The Johns Hopkins University.

MELVIN G. HOLLI, the author of *Reform in Detroit: Hazen S. Pingree and Urban Politics,* received his Ph.D. at the University of Michigan and has been teaching at the Chicago campus of the University of Illinois since 1965.

GLEN E. HOLT took his undergraduate degree at Taylor University and his M.A. and Ph.D. degrees at the University of Chicago. The holder of both Danforth and Woodrow Wilson Fellowships, he coauthored *Chicago: Growth of a Metropolis* and is now teaching at Washington University in St. Louis.

RICHARD J. HOPKINS received his B.A. degree from the University of Rochester and his Ph.D. degree from Emory University in Atlanta. He is now on the history faculty of the Ohio State University in Columbus.

KENNETH T. JACKSON is a native of Memphis and a graduate of the University of Chicago. Now an associate professor of history at Columbia University, he is the author of *The Ku Klux Klan in the City, 1915–1930* and executive secretary of The Society of American Historians.

ROGER W. LOTCHIN received his undergraduate training at Milligan University and his graduate education at the University of Chicago. He is now an assistant professor of history at the University of North Carolina at Chapel Hill.

JEANNE R. LOWE, a writer and consultant on urban affairs, is the author of *Cities in a Race with Time.*

ROY LUBOVE is professor of history at Temple University and the author of *The Progressives and the Slums* and *Twentieth Century Pittsburgh.*

ARTHUR MANN is a native of New York City and a graduate of Harvard. The author of *Yankee Reformers in the Urban Age* as well as a multivolume biography of

Mayor LaGuardia, he is now a professor of American history at the University of Chicago.

ZANE L. MILLER, who received his B.A. at Miami University and his Ph.D. at the University of Chicago, has taught at Northwestern University and since 1965 at the University of Cincinnati. He is now doing a computer analysis of a single Cincinnati ward and is also at work on a study of blacks in the urban South.

HUMBERT S. NELLI, associate professor of history at the University of Kentucky, received his M.A. degree from Columbia and his Ph.D. from the University of Chicago. He is the author of *The Italians in Chicago, 1880–1930*.

ALLAN PRED received his Ph.D. degree in geography from the University of Chicago and is now teaching at the University of California at Berkeley.

JOHN C. RAINBOLT is a native of Bedford, Indiana, and a graduate of Baldwin-Wallace College at the University of Wisconsin. He is now on the faculty of the University of Missouri at Columbia.

JAMES F. RICHARDSON was born in New York City and took his B.A. degree at Iona College and his Ph.D. degree at New York University. He is now a professor of history at the University of Akron.

MOSES RISCHIN has taught at San Francisco State College since 1964. He was born in New York City and is a graduate of Brooklyn College and Harvard.

CHARLES ROSENBERG is the author of *The Cholera Years: The United States in 1832, 1849, and 1866* and *The Trial of the Assassin Guiteau: Psychiatry and the Law in the Gilded Age*. He now teaches history at the University of Pennsylvania.

STANLEY K. SCHULTZ took his B.A. at Occidental College, his M.A. at the University of Kansas, and his Ph.D. at the University of Chicago. A native of southern California, he is now an assistant professor of history at the University of Wisconsin in Madison.

ANSELM L. STRAUSS, a professor of sociology at the University of California, San Francisco, is the author of *Images of the American City*.

WILLIAM M. TUTTLE, JR., was born in Detroit and was graduated from Dennison University and the University of Wisconsin. The author of *Race Riot*, he now teaches at the University of Kansas.

RICHARD C. WADE is the author of *The Urban Frontier; Slavery in the Cities: The South, 1820–1860;* and *Chicago: Growth of a Metropolis*.

DAVID WARD, the author of *Cities and Immigrants*, received his Ph.D. degree from the University of Wisconsin, where he now teaches geography.

SAM BASS WARNER, JR., is a professor of history at the University of Michigan. A native of Boston and a graduate of Harvard, he is the author of *Streetcar Suburbs* and *The Private City: Philadelphia in Three Periods of Its Growth*.

A NOTE ON THE TYPE

This book was set in Linotype composition. The text type face selected is Optima, a contemporary creation of Hermann Zapf in Germany. Optima merges the clarity and expressiveness of the classic form with the simplicity and efficiency of a linear sans-serif design, reflecting the early-Venetian scripts influencing Zapf's creations.

Manufactured in the United States of America. Composed by Cherry Hill Composition, Pennsauken, N.J. Printed and bound by Kingsport Press, Kingsport, Tenn.